P9-BZD-519

CONTEMPORARY ISSUES IN CURRICULUM

Edited by

ALLAN C. ORNSTEIN
Loyola University of Chicago

LINDA S. BEHAR
University of Florida

ALLYN AND BACON
Boston   London   Toronto   Sydney   Tokyo   Singapore

Series Editor: Virginia Lanigan
Production Administrator: Marjorie Payne
Editorial Assistant: Nicole DePalma
Cover Administrator: Linda Knowles
Composition Prepress Buyer: Linda Cox
Manufacturing Buyer: Louise Richardson
Editorial-Production Service: Raeia Maes
Marketing Manager: Ellen Mann

Copyright © 1995 by Allyn and Bacon
A Division of Paramount Publishing
160 Gould Street
Needham Heights, Massachusetts 02194

All rights reserved. No part of the material protected by this copyright notice may be reproduced or utilized in any form or by any means, electronic or mechanical, including photocopying, recording, or by any information storage and retrieval system, without the written permission of the copyright owner.

Credits can be found on pages 452–454, which should be considered extensions of the copyright page.

Library of Congress Cataloging-in-Publication Data

Contemporary issues in curriculum / edited by Allan C. Ornstein, Linda
    S. Behar.
        p.   cm.
    Includes bibliographical references and index.
    ISBN 0-205-15770-X
    1. Education—United States—Curricula.   2. Curriculum planning—
United States.   I. Ornstein, Allan C.   II. Behar, Linda S.
LB1570.C813   1995
375'.00973—dc20   94-7446
                                                          CIP

Printed in the United States of America

10 9 8 7 6 5 4 3 2 1   99 98 97 96 95 94

CONTENTS

PART FIVE
CURRICULUM AND SUPERVISION   279

CONTRIBUTORS

Lorin W. Anderson, University of South Carolina
Carole A. Ames, University of Illinois at Champaign-Urbana
Michael W. Apple, University of Wisconsin at Madison
David C. Berliner, Arizona State University
Benjamin S. Bloom, Emeritus, University of Chicago
Ronald S. Brandt, Association for Supervision and Curriculum Development
Jere Brophy, Michigan State University
Katherine S. Cushing, Harrison School District, Colorado
Elliot W. Eisner, Stanford University
Michael G. Fullan, University of Toronto
Henry A. Giroux, Pennsylvania State University
Allan A. Glatthorn, University of Pennsylvania
Carl D. Glickman, University of Georgia
Harold Hodgkinson, Center for Demographic Policy
Simon Hooper, University of Minnesota
M. Frances Klein, Emeritus, University of Southern California
Lawrence Kohlberg, Emeritus, Harvard University
Matthew Lipman, Montclair State College
Martin Lipton, Calabasas High School
Susan Loucks-Horsley, Regional Laboratory for Educational Improvement of the
    Northeast and Islands
Karen Seashore Louis, University of Minnesota
Todd I. Lubart, Yale University
Gail McCutcheon, Ohio State University
Matthew B. Miles, Center for Policy Research
Nel Noddings, Stanford University
Jeannie Oakes, University of California at Los Angeles
John U. Ogbu, University of California at Berkeley
Allan C. Ornstein, Loyola University of Chicago
Leonard O. Pellicer, University of South Carolina
Mary D. Phillips, University of Georgia
Diane Ravitch, Brookings Institute
Lloyd P. Rieber, University of Georgia
Donna S. Sabers, Test Consultant, Arizona State Department of Education
Thomas J. Sergiovanni, Trinity University
Lee S. Shulman, Stanford University
Robert E. Slavin, Johns Hopkins University
Dennis Sparks, National Staff Development Council
Robert J. Sternberg, Yale University
Ralph W. Tyler, Center for Advanced Study in the Behavioral Sciences
Gerald Unks, University of North Carolina
Herbert J. Walberg, University of Illinois at Chicago
Grant Wiggins, Director of Research and Development, CLASS
Eliot Wigginton, Foxfire

PREFACE

Contemporary Issues in Curriculum is a text for students studying curriculum, instruction, administration, teacher education, and educational foundations. It is written for those who are exploring the issues that have the potential to influence the implementation, planning, and evaluation of curriculum at all levels of learning. The chapters reflect the emergent trends in the field of curriculum.

The book is divided into six parts: philosophy, teaching, learning, instruction, supervision, and policy. Each part consists of six or seven chapters and is preceded by an introduction that focuses the reader's attention on the issues to be discussed and provides a brief overview of the chapters. Each chapter begins with focusing questions and ends with discussion questions. A pro-con chart that explores views for and against a controversial curricular concern and a case study appear at the end of each part. These instructional features are designed to help the reader integrate the content and issues of the book.

Most readers focus primarily on issues affecting the theoretical or practical applications of curriculum, and they present the popularly accepted views in the field. In addition, they focus on curriculum and policy as they relate to the individual, society, and groups, or else they emphasize philosophy, teaching, and trends found at various educational levels. We have tried to balance our discussion by focusing on six major areas that influence the field: philosophy, teaching, learning, instruction, supervision, and policy. We have included chapters that portray current trends and the dynamism within the field of curriculum. The chapters consist of views that reflect traditionally held beliefs and other views that might be considered more controversial in nature. Students and practitioners should have an opportunity to investigate the breadth of issues that are affecting curriculum and should be able to find such information in a single source. Readers are encouraged to examine and debate these issues, formulate their own ideas regarding the issues affecting the field of curriculum, and decide what direction the field should take.

We would like to acknowledge the many authors who granted us permission to reprint their works. We would also like to thank Debra Berringer for her assistance in the preparation of this book, as well as the following professors who reviewed the book in its formative stages: Dawna Lisa Buchanan-Berrigan, Shawnee State University; Craig Kridel, University of South Carolina; Robert Isaf, State University of New York, Cortland; and Carol Ann Pierson, University of Central Arkansas.

Thanks is also extended to Virginia Lanigan, our editor at Allyn and Bacon, who had faith in our idea and gave us the green light on nothing more than a concept and an outline. Allan Ornstein says "Hello" to his kids: Jason, Stacey, and Joel and advises them to always aim high and to his wife, Valerie. Linda Behar would like to dedicate this book to Theda Bosio, Andrea Brown, Virginia E. Goodman, Sarah J. Turner, and Jan Victor.

PART ONE

Curriculum and Philosophy

INTRODUCTION

How does philosophy influence the curriculum? To what extent does the curriculum reflect personal beliefs and societal views? How do different conceptions of curriculum affect schooling and student achievement? In what way has curriculum been a catalyst in empowering certain segments of society while disenfranchising others.

In Chapter 1, Gail McCutcheon discusses how different ways of conceiving the curriculum can assist practitioners in curriculum delivery. She explores how both teachers and students reciprocate in influencing the development of curriculum theory. Next, Allan Ornstein considers how philosophy guides the organization of the curriculum. He explores how beliefs about the purposes of education are reflected in subject matter and the process of teaching and learning.

In Chapter 3, Ronald Brandt and Ralph Tyler present a rationale for establishing educational goals. They reflect upon the sources that should be considered before articulating goals as well as the use of goals in planning learning activities and evaluation. In Chapter 4, M. Frances Klein presents an overview of the traditional models of curriculum. She argues that a narrow focus on concepts and procedures has limited curriculum delivery and student outcomes. She suggests that educators might accomplish more by considering different conceptions of curriculum.

In Chapter 5, Michael Apple points out that fundamental issues regarding what schools should teach are embedded in conflicts that are educational, political, and ideological in nature. He demonstrates how the conservative movement has marginalized the voices of many segments of the population, including curriculum scholars. Apple suggests that we need to reflect a collective voice in determining what knowledge is worth most. In the last chapter of Part One, Henry Giroux highlights how language and curriculum discourse influence teaching and outcomes. He discusses the relationship between politics, bureaucracy, and the teacher's role. He offers ways that the curriculum can be restructured to empower both teachers and students.

Curriculum Theory and Practice for the 1990s

GAIL MCCUTCHEON

FOCUSING QUESTIONS

1. *What are some of the ways in which curriculum is viewed?*
2. *How do students influence curriculum?*
3. *How does the role of conceiver of curriculum differ from executor of curriculum?*
4. *Do you prefer the role of conceiver or executor of curriculum? Why?*
5. *How does theory guide practice in the field of curriculum?*
6. *What steps do curriculum workers take in the process of developing a theory of curriculum?*

While defining the word "curriculum" does not solve the problems of deciding what we teach, how we organize, administer, plan, and supervise it, such definition does map out and delimit processes we might use in addressing and conceiving of curriculum problems.

Webster's *New Collegiate Dictionary* defines curriculum as "a course of study, as in a college; the whole body of courses offered in an educational institution or by a department thereof."

This definition is not too far removed from how many people probably think of curriculum—as a document outlining what is to be taught. In this sense it is the intended, formal, policy-level curriculum. Schools and school systems typically have curriculum guides, graded courses of study listing the content to be covered or adopted, and mandated-for-use textbooks.

ANOTHER VIEW OF CURRICULUM

Curriculum can also be thought of as what students have an opportunity to learn under the auspices of schools. Here, the formally intended,

policy-level curriculum is one part of what students can learn when teachers use the curriculum guide. Another part of the intended curriculum may be teacher-created in cases where teachers perceive students' needs and interests are not being met through the formal, policy-level curriculum.

Here, for instance, a teacher might develop a unit about teenage suicide, tornadoes, or earthquakes because of recent problems in close proximity to the school that have heightened students' fears. A teacher might also notice an interest among students in a particular kind of animal, a particular country, piece of literature, or medium in art, and decide to create a unit. A teacher might notice that while students meet the minimum objectives of the formal curriculum, they are not learning higher level thinking skills.

STUDENTS INFLUENCE CURRICULUM

Students can also influence the intended curriculum more directly. For example, two middle level boys brought their microscopes to class during a health unit about diseases, and the teacher arranged for small groups of students to examine slides. This modified the curriculum in that classroom, for it gave students the opportunity to learn things that neither the teacher nor the formal, policy-level curriculum had originally intended.

It is important to note that when teachers formulate such units alone or with students, they are *conceivers* of the curriculum, not merely *executors*.[1] In cases where teachers add units, they might justify the addition as related to an objective in the formal curriculum. At times, the teacher creates a unit of the curriculum, sometimes alone and sometimes as a reaction to or in concert with students.

The intended (or overt) curriculum, then, can be seen as being composed of two parts: the formal curriculum, and teacher-created (sometimes student-influenced) curricula. It is important to recognize that in the case of the formal curriculum, the teacher is generally its executor, although also reconceiving it to meet students' needs. However, when designing units that fall within the formal curriculum, perhaps to present them better, the teacher is partly a conceiver and partly an executor.

In the case of teacher-created curricula, teachers are conceivers. This role calls on a great deal of professional expertise to develop goals, create and sequence lessons, and determine appropriate evaluation strategies. Simultaneously, this role encourages professional development as teachers gain practical wisdom about what to do in certain situations.

In addition to what we intend to teach, students have an opportunity to learn things we do not intend to teach. This is often called the "hidden" curriculum, and it has two characteristics: it is not intended, and it is transmitted through normal, everyday occurrences in schools.

In both cases—the intended and the hidden curriculum—teachers, supervisors, researchers, and administrators have important duties to perform: observing what students actually have an opportunity to learn; reflecting upon it; and making changes as warranted. Further, both the intended and hidden curricula change as society and its demands on schools change. The hidden curriculum changes because as people we are part of society as well as being educators, and we learn societal norms and change ourselves somewhat as we live our everyday lives. The intended curriculum changes as textbooks change, and as we learn of educational reform efforts and other innovations in our culture that bear attention in schools.

THEORY IN EDUCATION

Theories in education are integrated clusters, bundles, or sets of interpretations, analyses, and understandings about educational phenomena. They are about the actions we take as we teach, do research, develop, supervise, and administer educational programs.

Theories have an empirical dimension. That is, they are based on our observations and other data about the real world. They also have a strong ethical dimension, for curriculum work is inherently and unavoidably a moral enterprise.

Many important decisions we make have ethical dimensions: What should we teach? How should we treat students, parents, teachers, and administrators? Is it more important to teach science, art, and social studies, or to teach language arts and mathematics, given the press of time? Should we order art materials or repair the gutters?

Should we use computer graded testing in mathematics? Which general programs for computers should we purchase? Dare we teach about AIDS? Dare we *not?* Can a zooming increase in teenage pregnancy be treated in the health curriculum? Should we ban some books from the library collections? Should we group students for instruction? If so, how? What might they learn that we don't intend from such a practice?

In order to address such matters, we must conceive of moral bases on which to make these decisions and try to forecast the potential ramifications of them for individuals and society. Further, curriculum decisions have a moral dimension in that we are morally obligated to act and therefore to make wise decisions. That is, when we notice the need for a new unit, a revised sequence or organization for the curriculum, as educators we are morally obligated to take such action.

These theories in education, then, are not esoteric, objective laws, but rather are ruminations that serve as practical guides to the decisions we make and actions we take. These ruminations are based on our interpretations of what has worked well in the past, out of which we form bundles of the interpretations—theories— through which we conceive of what might work well in future actions.

Hence, as we plan lessons and other actions to teach, do research, develop, supervise, and administer the curriculum, we take these theories into account and through them we envision future courses of action. We do this in our everyday lives as well as in our workplaces, as we read recipes and envision their merit in terms of what our families enjoy eating, preparation time, cost, and the like.

Some people can also read musical scores and mentally hear them as part of deciding whether to purchase or play them; read knitting and sewing patterns and envision what materials to use to best effect and whether they would be worn if made; or read home improvement plans and consider whether the change would be used, doable, and affordable.

John Dewey could have been discussing this when he wrote of deliberation:

> We begin with a summary assertion that deliberation is a dramatic rehearsal (in imagination) of various competing possible lines of action . . . Deliberation is an experiment in finding out what the various lines of possible action are really like. It is an experiment in making various combinations of selected elements of habits and impulses, to see what the resultant action would be like if it were entered upon. But the trial is in imagination, not in overt fact. . . . An act overtly tried out is irrevocable, its consequences cannot be blotted

out. An act tried out in imagination is not final or fatal. It is retrievable.[2]

Further, it should not surprise us that we educators are not the only practitioners who learn from our work experience, develop theories of action, and apply that wisdom to future courses of action. In doing research about "practical intelligence" in business, Streufert and Streufert[3] found expert business executives to differ from less successful peers in that they made planning decisions by taking into account their past and prospective plans.

They further seemed to "model run" rather than "model fit," to use decision terminology. That is to say, they mentally tried out their model before all data were available rather than awaiting data and retrospectively fitting a model to them.

In studying dairy workers, Scribner[4] found that what separates experts from nonexperts seems to be specific knowledge gained on the job that permitted them to make rapid assessments of possibilities through a visual gestalt rather than a more mechanical or technical manner.

It appears that people in general (not just those of us who treat curriculum problems) apply wisdom gained in work and in everyday experience to solving practical job problems. Perhaps this is the basis for the adage, "Experience is the best teacher."

In practice, theories have a reciprocal relationship with the actions we take. Each informs the other as we form theories from the actions we've taken, and actions reflective of theories we formulate. Hence, the, relationship between theory and practice is one of integration. Indeed, it could be said that our actions are our theories in that they represent our theories and frequently constitute further small experiments about our theories. Perhaps this theory/action integration is the basis for the maxim, "actions speak louder than words."

Because people, schools, and communities vary, these theories have another characteristic. In addition to being moral and integrally bound to practices, theories are also ideographic—site specific—although some aspects of one educator's theory may overlap someone else's.

Like theory, educators' practice is also ideographic and morally committed, for it flows out of and is bound to the theory we hold, in that our practice and theory inform one another.

For example, one principal reflects on teachers' theories of action in giving advice about how to study them:

> I think you can tell a lot about a teacher's theory merely by looking at the classroom, even when no one is there. One of my Spanish teachers, for instance, really works hard about the relationship between language and culture, and in his room are lots of enormous, colorful posters and other pictures from Spain and Central America. The other one has vocabulary words posted around the room. So you can even start just by looking at physical evidence, although I agree that looking at actions and talking with teachers about them is a more powerful way. The physical evidence, though, gives one something to go on at least as a starter.

It may well be true that the physical evidence in a classroom might reveal something about a teacher's theory of action, but a word of caution is necessary here in that teachers use materials differently.

It is easy to envision two teachers with the same literature books in their rooms. One teacher might assign readings sequentially through the book, with several short written assignments focusing on particular readings. The other teacher might use the same text but have students examine what the stories have to say about our culture. Thus, the same physical evidence in two classrooms does not necessarily mean the teachers hold the same theories of action.

As we act, we observe what transpires and develop a repertoire of practices based on our observations of whether a practice we try is effective and conditions in which it is effective. If it is effective, we remember it and add it to our repertoire. The practice may be, for example, a new way of asking questions, a new way of encouraging teachers to try innovative practices on their own, a new way of teaching grammar, a new mini-unit to enrich the curriculum, a new way of leading a curriculum development project. a new way of encouraging teachers to use new materials, a new way of treating discipline problems, and so forth.

Over the years, educators build a wide repertoire of practices that have worked well. One danger here is the danger of complacency and the loss of experimentation with new practices to add to this repertoire. This is dangerous because society constantly changes and additions are made to society's store of knowledge, so we constantly have to change the curriculum.

Hence, while we can develop a rich repertoire of practices, we must be constantly aware of whether the practice is still beneficial, and we must be prepared to modify it when conditions change. A unit developed last year may need substantial revision this year because of changes in how the curriculum is organized, the nature of students in this class, or a new emphasis in the formal curriculum of the school. As educators, we work within a system—a configuration of relationships—in addition to working as individual professional agents.

HOW EDUCATORS DEVELOP THEORIES

Educators do not acquire theories; they develop them through a series of small, specific experiences that constitute investigations into whether a particular practice works.

These action studies follow a process discussed in detail elsewhere:[5]

1. An educator encounters a new idea (such as an idea to have people work in pairs) and pays attention to that idea if it seems potentially beneficial or important. He or she "model runs," in decision terminology.
2. The educator senses that the idea might be beneficial and examines it to consider its plausibility and the likelihood of its success

in terms of her or his existing theory, past experience with similar ideas, present school policies and conditions.

3. If the idea passes this conceptual test, the educator tests it empirically by trying it in practice and observing its consequences.

4. After reflection on the empirical test, the educator interprets it in light of his or her existing theory and may revise that existing theory by augmenting it with what was learned from the test of the new idea.

In this manner, an educator's theory changes and becomes more elaborate as his or her repertoire of practice grows. This process may account for some differences between novice and expert teachers.

When we begin our practice, we begin to draw on many sources to inform our practice, such as reading professional books and articles; participating in committees; looking through curriculum materials; attending workshops, inservice, and graduate courses; talking with other educators, parents, and students; and perhaps observing in other schools.

Educators do not act on all this information. Some is filtered out because it does not accord with beliefs about matters such as how people learn, what is important to learn, motivation, and so forth. Many of our beliefs about such matters are the result of our experience as students, jobholders, and observers of life before we become educators.

Other ideas simply do not work in our own situations, so we discard them, sometimes before using them. Perhaps they take more time than is available, they call for use of unavailable materials, or they do not fit with the people in our sphere of action.

Neither theory nor practice in curriculum is a set of technical rules to be followed like a cookbook, for each case is ideographic—site specific and context-bound—with decisions more appropriate for the particular case that may not be universally generalizable. While we possess theories

of action, it is important to recognize that we developed them in a particular setting, and components of them are not explicitly taught to us but are fundamental to our success.

For this reason, large aspects of our theories of action may remain in the realm of tacit knowledge. We may know the theory, but not know that we know it, and be unable to articulate it.[6]

However, implicit in individuals' actions are unstated "rules" of those actions, such as:

— We must treat other people's ideas with respect
— Students learn best by being actively involved in learning
— Each person should be successful in at least one thing as a student, teacher, curriculum developer, supervisor, or administrator, and attention should be called to that success to encourage other successes
— High, but reasonable, expectations are important for supporting achievement
— Equity of access to the curriculum is important because of our society
— Friendly badgering of students in a supportive environment will lead to success
— Risk taking is important
— Fairness is important
— And so forth.

By observing each other and reflecting on our own practice, we can come to recognize some of these tacit dimensions of our theory of action and call them into question if needed.

One way we might encourage and support the development of theories of action and practices is to devote inservice time to developing small units, lessons, materials, and ideas in a collegial, resource-rich environment in which plans and ideas could be shared, critiqued, and elaborated upon. Further, schools could create files of such units, ideas, and their authors on which others could draw.

Additionally, in writing directions to teachers about materials, serious thought should be given to how we might write them in ways that would invite teachers to ponder the materials, reshape them if needed, and use them, rather than merely directing teachers in what to say and do. This direction-giving is counterproductive to supporting and developing professionalism.

Forming these theories of action is probably the most professional aspect of our practice as teachers, administrators, and supervisors as we develop, implement, and evaluate the intended and hidden curriculum. Rather than adopting strategies that assume others to be mindless robots, it would behoove us to conceive of processes that facilitate this development of a repertoire of successful practices and theories of action.

As Duckworth points out:[7]

> The assumption seems to be that teachers are a kind of civil servant, to be "trained" by those who know better, to carry out the job as they are directed to do, to be assessed managerially, to be understood through third-party studies. In conceiving of teachers as civil servants, with no professional understanding worth paying attention to, we miss the enormous potential power of their knowledge. Even more serious: in considering them as civil servants, we fail to develop their knowledge and understanding still further . . . To the extent that they are conceived of as civil servants, to carry out orders from above, teachers are deprived of the occasion to bring to bear on their work the whole of their intelligence, understanding, and judgment. To that extent, the students are deprived of those qualities, and the educational enterprise is impoverished.

CONCLUSION

People develop theories of action out of their practical intelligence and wisdom gained from their job experiences. The picture painted here, then, is one of inquisitive, morally committed people eager to do their work in a professional manner; that is, to do it in the very best way they can.

While not all teachers, administrators, textbook authors, supervisors, and other curriculum workers possess these traits, it seems clear that many do, and this poses several issues for our consideration. The issues will be raised in hopes that we can begin to act to address some of these matters in a timely manner and in ways that seem sensible to the context in which we practice, document how we address them, and share what transpires.

One important issue related to this conceptualization of curriculum theory and practice concerns how we might facilitate the development of practical wisdom about curriculum work and of theories of action. Since some of this wisdom is in the realm of tacit knowledge, how might we come to recognize what we know?

Further, what can we do to help novices develop practical intelligence and theories of action? How can experienced educators continue to examine their theories of action and other practical intelligence critically? How can we maintain a sense of new experimentation, that our theory of action has not been set in cement, rendering it unmalleable? Further, how can we develop and write curriculum materials that facilitate teachers' applying their theories of action to them in a professional manner rather than materials calling for "use as directed"?

Finally, it could be argued that believing in a view of curriculum theory as discussed in this article will lead only to chaos because everyone will be "doing her or his own thing." This is not necessarily the case.

For one thing, the conceptualization presented here incorporates a policy-level curriculum into it. However, it is clear that new ways of thinking about systemwide curriculum organization are needed in order to take advantage of the solid evidence that teachers think. Rather than formulating methods for making educators bow to all administrative edicts, it seems worth our efforts to conceive of ways to take advantage of this thinking. Teacher ingenuity and practical intelligence are likely to be better nurtured than fettered and lead to more professional practice.

This, I believe, is the biggest and most exciting challenge facing us in the 1990s and beyond.

ENDNOTES

1. See W. J. Smyth, *A Rationale for Teachers' Critical Pedagogy: A Handbook* (Victoria, Australia: Deakin University Press, 1987).
2. John Dewey, *Human Nature and Conduct* (Rahway, N.J.: Henry Holt and Co., 1922).
3. S. Streufert and S. C. Streufert, *Behavior in the Complex Environment* (Washington, D.C.: Winston, 1978).
4. S. Scribner, "Studying Working Intelligence." In *Everyday Cognition: Its Development in Social Context,* edited by B. Rogoff and J. Lave (Cambridge, Mass.: Harvard University Press, 1984).
5. D. Sanders and G. McCutcheon, "The Development of Practical Theories of Teaching," *Journal of Curriculum and Supervision,* Fall 1986.
6. R. F. Sternberg and R. K. Wagner, *Practical Intelligence* (Cambridge, Mass.: Cambridge University Press, 1986).
7. E. Duckworth, "What Teachers Know: The Best Knowledge Base," *Harvard Educational Review, 54:1,* pp. 15–19.

DISCUSSION QUESTIONS

1. What are the ways in which curriculum theory has helped you in (a) teaching, (b) organizing, (c) administering, (d) planning, and/or (e) supervising curriculum?
2. Using your school or institution as a model, what are the ways in which a theory of curriculum could be used as a tool to guide practice?
3. How have students influenced curriculum delivery in your classroom or school?
4. How has the intended and hidden curriculum influenced your roles about the curriculum? Which curriculum is more important to you, the intended or the hidden? Why?
5. There has been much controversy about ways in which to incorporate teachers' practical experience into curriculum theorizing. In what ways might teachers' practical experiences be used to develop a theory of curriculum?

Philosophy as a Basis for Curriculum Decisions

ALLAN C. ORNSTEIN

FOCUSING QUESTIONS

1. *How does philosophy guide the organization and implementation of curriculum?*
2. *What are the sources of knowledge that shape a person's philosophy of curriculum?*
3. *What are the sources of knowledge that shape your philosophical view of curriculum?*
4. *How do the aims, means, and ends of education differ?*
5. *What is the major philosophical issue that must be determined before we can define a philosophy of curriculum?*
6. *What are the four major educational philosophies that have influenced curriculum in the United States?*
7. *What is your philosophy of curriculum?*

Philosophic issues always have and still do impact on schools and society. Contemporary society and its schools are changing fundamentally and rapidly, much more so than in the past. There is a special urgency that dictates continuous appraisal and reappraisal of the role of schools, and calls for a philosophy of education. Without philosophy, educators are directionless in the whats and hows of organizing and implementing what we are trying to achieve. In short, our philosophy of education influences, and to a large extent determines, our educational decisions, choices, and alternatives.

PHILOSOPHY AND CURRICULUM

Philosophy provides educators, especially curriculum specialists, with a framework for organizing schools and classrooms. It helps them answer what are the school's purpose, what subjects are of value, how students learn, and what

methods and materials to use. Philosophy provides them with a framework for broad issues and tasks, such as determining the goals of education, subject content and its organization, the process of teaching and learning, and, in general, what experiences and activities to stress in schools and classrooms. It also provides educators with a basis for making such decisions as what workbooks, textbooks, or other cognitive and non-cognitive activities to utilize and how to utilize them, what homework to assign and how much of it, how to test students and how to use the test results, and what courses or subject matter to emphasize.

The importance of philosophy in determining curriculum decisions is expressed well by the classic statement of Thomas Hopkins (1941); "Philosophy has entered into every important decision that has ever been made about curriculum and teaching in the past and will continue to be the basis of every important decision in the future . . . There is rarely a moment in a school day when a teacher is not confronted with occasions where philosophy is a vital part of action." Hopkin's statement reminds us of how important philosophy is to all aspects of curriculum decisions, whether it operates overtly or covertly. Indeed, almost all elements of curriculum are based on philosophy. As John Goodlad (1979) points out, philosophy is the beginning point in curriculum decision making and is the basis for all subsequent decisions regarding curriculum. Philosophy becomes the criterion for determining the aims, means, and ends of curriculum. The aims are statements of value, based on philosophical beliefs; the means represent processes and methods, which reflect philosophical choices; and the ends connote the facts, concepts, and principles of the knowledge or behavior learned—what is felt to be important to learning.

Smith, Stanley, and Shores (1957) also put great emphasis on the role of philosophy in developing curriculum, asserting it is essential when formulating and justifying educational purposes, selecting and organizing knowledge, formulating basic procedures and activities, and dealing with verbal traps (what we see versus what is read). Curriculum theorists, they point out, often fail to recognize both how important philosophy is to developing curriculum and how it influences aspects of curriculum.

Philosophy and the Curriculum Specialist

The philosophy of curriculum specialists reflects their life experiences, common sense, social and economic background, education, and general beliefs about people. An individual's philosophy evolves and continues to evolve as long as there is personal growth, development, and learning from experience. Philosophy is a description, explanation, and evaluation of the world as seen from personal perspective, or through what some social scientists call "social lenses."

Curriculum specialists can turn to many sources of knowledge, but no matter how many sources upon which they may draw or how many authorities to whom they listen, their decisions are shaped by all the experiences that have affected them and the social groups with which they identify. These decisions are based on values, attitudes, and beliefs, that they have developed, involving their knowledge and interpretation of causes, events, and their consequences. Philosophy determines principles for guiding action.

No one can be totally objective in a cultural or social setting, but curriculum specialists can broaden their base of knowledge and experiences by trying to understand other people's sense of values, and to analyze problems from various perspectives. They can also try to modify their own critical analyses and points of view by learning from their experiences and those of others. Curriculum specialists who are unwilling to modify their points of view, or compromise philosophical positions when school officials or their colleagues espouse another philosophy, are at risk of causing conflict and disrupting the school. Ronald Doll (1986) puts it this way: "Conflict among curriculum planners occurs when persons . . . hold positions along a continuum of [different] beliefs and . . . persuasions." The conflict may become so intense that "curriculum study grinds to a halt." Most of the time, the differences can be reconciled "temporarily in deference to the demands of a temporary, immediate task." However, Doll further explains that "teachers and administrators who are clearly divided in philosophy can seldom work together in close proximity for long periods of time."

The more mature and understanding, and the less personally threatened and ego-involved individuals are, the more capable they are of reexamining or modifying their philosophy, or at least of being willing to appreciate other points of view. It is important for curriculum specialists to regard their attitudes and beliefs as tentative—as subject to reexamination whenever facts or trends challenge them. Equally dangerous for curricula specialists is the opposite—indecision or lack of any philosophy, which can be reflected in attempts to avoid commitment to sets of values. A measure of positive conviction is essential to prudent action. Having a personal philosophy that is tentative or subject to modification does not lead to lack of conviction or disorganized behavior. Curriculum specialists can arrive at their conclusions on the best evidence available, and they then can change when better evidence surfaces.

Philosophy as a Curriculum Source

The function of philosophy can be conceived as either the base for the starting point in curriculum development, or an interdependent function of other functions in curriculum development. John Dewey (1916) represents the first school of thought, by contending that "philosophy may . . . be defined as the general theory of education," and that "the business of philosophy is to provide [the framework] for the aims and methods" of schools. For Dewey, philosophy provides a generalized meaning to our lives and a way of thinking, "an explicit formulation of the . . . mental and moral attitudes in respect to the difficulties of contemporary social life." Philosophy is not only a starting point for schools, it is also crucial for all curriculum activities. For as Dewey adds, "Education is the laboratory in which philosophic distinctions become concrete and are tested."

Highly influenced by Dewey, Ralph Tyler's (1949) framework of curriculum includes philosophy as only one of five criteria commonly used for selecting educational purposes. The relationship between philosophy and the other criteria—studies of learners, studies of contemporary life, suggestions from subject specialists, and the psychology of learning—is the basis for determining the school's purposes. Although philosophy is not the starting point in Tyler's curriculum, but rather interacts on an equal basis with the other criteria, it does seem to place more importance on philosophy for developing educational purposes. Tyler (1949) writes, "The educational and social philosophy to which the school is committed can serve as the first screen for developing the social program." He concludes that "philosophy attempts to define the nature of the good life and a good society," and that the

"educational philosophies in a democratic society are likely to emphasize strongly democratic values in schools."

There can be no serious discussion about philosophy until we embrace the question of what is education. When we agree on what is education, we can ask what is the school's purpose. We can then pursue philosophy, aims, and goals of curriculum. According to Goodlad (1979), the school's first responsibility is to the social order, what he calls the "nation-state," but in our society the sense of individual growth and potential is paramount. This duality—society vs. the individual—has been a major philosophical issue in western society for centuries and was a very important issue in Dewey's works. As Dewey (1916) claimed, we not only wish "to make [good] citizens and workers" but also we ultimately want "to make human beings who will live life to the fullest."

The compromise of the duality between national allegiance and individual fulfillment is a noble aim that should guide all curriculum specialists—from the means to the ends. When many individuals grow and prosper, then society flourishes. The original question set forth by Goodlad can be answered: Education is growth and the focal point for the individual and as well as society; it is a never ending process of life, and the more refined the guiding philosophy the better the quality of the educational process.

Major Educational Philosophies: In considering the influence on philosophic thought on curriculum, several classification schemes are possible; therefore, no superiority is claimed for the categories used in the tables. The cluster of ideas are organized here as those that often evolve openly or unwittingly during curriculum planning.

Four major educational philosophies have influenced curriculum in the United States: Perennialism, Essentialism, Progressivism, and Reconstructionism. Table 2.1 provides an overview of these education philosophies, and how they affect curriculum, instruction, and teaching. Teachers and administrators should compare the

TABLE 2.1 Overview of Educational Philosophies

	Philosophical Base	Instructional Objective	Knowledge	Role of Teacher	Curriculum Focus	Related Curriculum Trends
Perennialism	Realism	To educate the rational person; to cultivate the intellect	Focus on past and permanent studies; mastery of facts and timeless knowledge	Teacher helps students think rationally; based on Socratic method and oral exposition; explicit teaching of traditional values	Classical subjects; literary analysis; constant curriculum	Great books; Paideia proposal
Essentialism	Idealism, Realism	To promote the intellectual growth of the individual; to educate the competent person	Essential skills and academic subjects; mastery of concepts and principles of subject matter	Teacher is authority in his or her field; explicit teaching of traditional values	Essential skills (three Rs) and essential subjects (English, arithmetic, science, history, and foreign language)	Back to basics; excellence in education
Progressivism	Pragmatism	To promote democratic, social living	Knowledge lends to growth and development; a living-learning process; focus on active and interesting learning	Teacher is a guide for problem solving and scientific inquiry	Based on students' interests; involves the application of human problems and affairs; interdisciplinary subject matter; activities and projects	Relevant curriculum; humanistic education; alternative and free schooling
Reconstructionism	Pragmaticism	To improve and reconstruct society; education for change and social reform	Skills and subjects needed to identify and ameliorate problems of society; learning is active and concerned with contemporary and future society	Teacher serves as an agent of change and reform; acts as a project director and research leader, helps students become aware of problems confronting humankind	Emphasis on social sciences and social research methods; examination of social, economic and political problems; focus on present and future trends as well as rational and international issues	Equality of education; cultural pluralism; international education; futurism

Source: Allan C. Ornstein and Francis P. Hunkins, *Curriculum: Foundations, Principles, and Theory,* 2nd ed. (Needham Heights, MA: Allyn and Bacon, 1993), p. 62.

content of the categories with their own philosophical "lens" in terms of how they view curriculum, and how other views of curriculum and related instructional and teaching issues may disagree.

Another way of interpreting philosophy and its effect on curriculum is to analyze philosophy in terms of polarity. The danger of this method is to simplify it in terms of a dichotomy, not to recognize that there are overlaps and shifts. Table 2.2 illustrates philosophy in terms of traditional and contemporary categories. The traditional philosophy, as shown, tends to overlap with Perennialism and Essentialism. Contemporary philosophy tends to coincide with Progressivism and Reconstructionism.

Table 2.2 shows that traditional philosophy focuses on the past, emphasizes fixed and absolute values, and glorifies our cultural heritage. Contemporary philosophy emphasizes the present and future, and views events as changeable and relative; for the latter, nothing can be preserved forever, for despite any attempt, change is inevitable. The traditionalists wish to train the mind, emphasize subject matter, and fill the learner with knowledge and information. Those who ascribe to contemporary philosophies are more concerned with problem solving and emphasize student interests and needs. Whereas subject matter is considered important for its own sake, according to traditionalists, certain subjects are more important than others. For contemporary educators, subject matter is considered a medium for teaching skills and attitudes, and most subjects have similar value. According to the traditionalists, the teacher is an authority in subject matter, who dominates the lesson with explanations and lectures; as for the contemporary proponent, the teacher is a guide for learning, as well as an agent for change; students and teachers often are engaged in dialogue.

In terms of social issues and society, the traditionalist views education as a means of providing direction, control, and restraint, while their counterparts focus on individual expression and freedom from authority. Citizenship is linked to cognitive development for the traditional educator, and it is linked to moral and social development for the contemporary educator. Knowledge and the disciplines prepare students for freedom, according to the traditional view, but it is direct experience in democratic living and political/social action which prepares students for freedom, according to the contemporary ideal. Traditionalists believe in excellence and contemporary educators favor equality. The traditional view of education maintains that group values come first, where cooperative and conforming behaviors are important for the good of society. Contemporary educators assert that what is good for the individual should come first, and they believe in the individual modifying and perhaps reconstructing society.

The Curriculum Specialist at Work

Philosophy gives meaning to our decisions and actions. In the absence of a philosophy, educators are vulnerable to externally imposed prescriptions, to fads and frills, to authoritarian schemes, and to other "-isms." Dewey (1916) was so convinced of the importance of philosophy that he viewed it as the all-encompassing aspect of the educational process—as necessary for "forming fundamental dispositions, intellectual and emotional, toward nature and fellow man." If this conclusion is accepted, it becomes evident that many aspects of a curriculum, if not most of the educational processes in school, are developed from a philosophy. Even if it is believed that Dewey's point is an overstatement, the pervasiveness of philosophy in determining views of reality, the values and knowledge that are worthwhile, and the decisions to be made about education and curriculum should still be recognized.

Very few schools adopt a single philosophy; in practice, most schools combine various philosophies. Moreover, the author's position is that no single philosophy, old or new, should serve as

TABLE 2.2 Overview of Traditional and Contemporary Philosophies

Philosophical Consideration	Traditional Philosophy	Contemporary Philosophy
Educational philosophy	Perennialism, Essentialism	Progressivism, Reconstructionism
Direction in time	Superiority of past; education for preserving past	Education is growth; reconstruction of present experiences; changing society; concern for future and shaping it
Values	Fixed, absolute, objective and/or universal	Changeable, subjective, and/or relative
Educational process	Education is viewed as instruction; mind is discipline and filled with knowledge	Education is viewed as creative self-learning; active process in which learner reconstructs knowledge
Intellectual emphasis	To train or discipline the mind; emphasis on subject matter	To engage in problem-solving activities and social activities; emphasis on student interest and needs
Worth of subject matter	Subject matter for its own importance; certain subjects are better than others for training the mind	Subject matter is a medium for teaching skills, attitudes and intellectual processes; all subjects have similar value for problem-solving activities
Curriculum content	Curriculum is composed of three Rs, as well as liberal studies or essential academic subjects	Curriculum is composed of three Rs, as well as skills and concepts in arts, sciences, and vocational studies
Learning	Emphasis on cognitive learning; learning is acquiring knowledge and/or competency in disciplines	Emphasis on whole child; learning is giving meaning to experiences and/or active involvement in reform
Grouping	Homogeneous grouping and teaching of students by ability	Heterogeneous grouping and integration of students by ability (as well as race, sex and class)
Teacher	Teacher is an authority on subject matter, teacher plans activities, teacher supplies knowledge to student; teacher talks, dominates lesson. Socratic method	Teacher is a guide for inquiry and change agent; teacher and students plan activities; students learn on their own independent of the teacher; teacher-student dialogue, student initiates much of the discussion and activities
Social roles	Education involves direction, control, and restraint; group (family, community, church, nation, etc.) always comes first	Education involves individual expression and imposition from authority; individual comes first
Citizenship	Cognitive development leads to good citizenship	Moral and social development leads to good citizenship
Freedom and democracy	Acceptance of one's fate, conformity and compliance with authority; knowledge and discipline prepares students for freedom	Emphasis on creativeness, noncomformity and self-actualization; direct experiences in democratic living and political/social action prepares students for freedom
Excellence vs Equality	Excellence in education; education as far as human potential permits; academic rewards and jobs based on merit	Equality of education; education which permits more than one chance and more than an equal change to disadvantaged groups; education and employment sectors consider unequal abilities of individuals and put some restraints on achieving individuals so that different outcomes and group scores, if any, are reduced
Society	Emphasis on group values; acceptance of norms of and roles in society; cooperative and conforming behavior; importance of society; individual restricted by custom and tradition of society	Emphasis on individual growth and development; belief in individual with ability to modify, even reconstruct the social environment; independent and self-realizing, fully functioning behavior, importance of person; full opportunity to develop one's own potential.

the exclusive guide for making decisions about schools or about the curriculum. All philosophical groups want the same things of education— that is, they wish to improve the educational process, to enhance the achievement of the learner, to produce better and more productive citizens, and to improve society. Because of their different views of reality, values, and knowledge, however, they find it difficult to agree on how to achieve these ends.

What needs to be done, as curricularists, is to search for the middle ground, a highly elusive and abstract concept, where there is no extreme emphasis on subject matter or student, cognitive development or sociopsychological development, excellence or equality. What we need is a prudent school philosophy, one that is politically and economically feasible, that serves the needs of students and society. Implicit in this view of education is that too much emphasis on any one philosophy may do harm and cause conflict. How much one philosophy is emphasized, under the guise of reform (or for whatever reason), is critical because no one society can give itself over to extreme "-isms" or political views and still remain a democracy. The kind of society which evolves is in part reflected in the education system, which is influenced by the philosophy that is eventually defined and developed.

CONCLUSION

In the final analysis, curriculum specialists must understand that they are continuously faced with curriculum decisions, and that philosophy is important in determining these decisions. Unfortunately, few school people test their notions of curriculum against their school's statement of

philosophy. According to Brandt and Tyler (1983), it is not uncommon to find teachers and administrators developing elaborate lists of behavioral objectives with little or no consideration to the overall philosophy of the school. Curriculum workers need to provide assistance in developing and designing school practices that coincide with the philosophy of the school and community. Teaching, learning, and curriculum are all interwoven in school practices and should reflect a school's and a community's philosophy.

REFERENCES

Brandt, R. S. and Tyler, R. W. (1983). "Goals and Objectives," in F. W. English, ed., *Fundamental Curriculum Decisions,* Alexandria, VA: Association for Supervision and Curriculum Development.
Dewey, J. (1916). *Democracy and Education.* New York, N.Y.: Macmillan, p. 383–384.
Doll, R. C. (1986). *Curriculum Improvement: Decision-making and Process,* 6th ed. Boston, MA: Allyn and Bacon, p. 30.
Goodlad, J. I. (1984). *A Place Called School.* New York, N.Y.: McGraw-Hill.
Goodlad, J. I. (1979a). *Curriculum Inquiry.* New York, N.Y.: McGraw-Hill.
Goodlad, J. I. (1979b). *What Schools Are For.* Bloomington, IN: Phi Delta Kappa Educational Foundation.
Hopkins, L. T. (1941). *Interaction: The Democratic Process.* Boston, MA: D. C. Heath, p. 198–200.
Smith, B. O., Stanley, W. O., and Shores, J. H. (1957). *Fundamentals of Curriculum Development,* rev. ed. New York, N.Y.: Worldbook.
Tyler, R. W. (1949). *Basic Principles of Curriculum and Instruction.* Chicago, IL: University of Chicago Press, p. 33–34.

DISCUSSION QUESTIONS

1. Which philosophical approach reflects your beliefs about (a) the school's purpose, (b) what subjects are of value, (c) how students learn, and (d) the process of teaching and learning?

2. What curriculum focus would the perennialists and essentialists recommend for our increasingly diverse school age population?

3. What curriculum would the progressivists and reconstructionists select for a multicultural student population?

4. Should curriculum workers adopt a single philosophy to guide their practices? Why? Why not?

5. Which philosophy is most relevant to contemporary education? Why?

3

Goals and Objectives

RONALD S. BRANDT
RALPH W. TYLER

FOCUSING QUESTIONS

1. *Why is it important to establish goals for student learning?*
2. *How do goals and objectives differ?*
3. *What are three types of goals?*
4. *What are the factors that should be considered when developing educational goals?*
5. *What is the relationship between goals and learning activities?*
6. *In what ways are curriculum goals integral to the process of evaluation?*
7. *What types of goals should be addressed by schools?*

Whether planning for one classroom or many, curriculum developers must have a clear idea of what they expect students to learn. Establishing goals is an important and necessary step because there are many desirable things students could learn—more than schools have time to teach them—so schools should spend valuable instructional time only on high priority learnings.

Another reason for clarifying goals is that schools must be able to resist pressures from various sources. Some of the things schools are asked to teach are untrue, would hinder students' development, or would help make them narrow, bigoted persons. Some would focus students' learning so narrowly it would reduce, rather than increase, their life options.

FORMS OF GOALS AND OBJECTIVES

Statements of intent appear in different forms, and words such as goals, objectives, aims, ends, outcomes, and purposes are often used interchangeably. Some people find it useful to think of goals as long-term aims to be achieved eventually and objectives as specific learning students are to acquire as a result of current instruction.

Planners in the Portland, Oregon, area schools say these distinctions are not clear enough to meet organizational planning requirements. They use "goal" to mean any desired outcome of a program, regardless of its specificity, and "objective" only in connection with *program change objectives,* which are defined as statements of intent to change program elements in specified ways. Doherty and Peters (1981) say this distinction avoids confusion and is consistent with the philosophy of "management by objectives."

They refer to three types of goals: instructional, support, and management. Educational goals are defined as learnings to be acquired; support goals as services to be rendered; and management goals as functions of management, such as planning, operating, and evaluating. Such a goal structure permits evaluation to focus on measures of learning acquired (educational outcomes), measures of quantity and quality of service delivery (support outcomes), and measures of quality and effectiveness of management functions (management outcomes).

The Tri-County Goal Development Project, which has published 14 volumes containing over 25,000 goal statements,[1] is concerned only with *educational goals*. For these collections, the following distinctions are made within the general category of "goals":

> *System level goals* (set for the school district by the board of education)
> *Program level goals* (set by curriculum personnel in each subject field)
> *Course level goals* (set by groups of teachers for each subject or unit of instruction)
> *Instructional level goals* (set by individual teachers for daily planning)

Examples of this outcome hierarchy are shown in Figure 3.1.

What distinguishes this system of terminology from others is its recognition that a learning outcome has the same essential character at all levels of planning (hence the appropriateness of a single term, goal, to describe it); and that the level of generality used to represent learning varies with the planning requirements at each level of school organization. The degree of generality chosen for planning at each level is, of course, a matter of judgment; there is no "correct" level but only a sense of appropriateness to purpose.

Teachers, curriculum specialists, and university consultants who write and review course goals use the following guidelines (Doherty and Peters, 1980, pp. 26–27):

1. Is the stated educational outcome potentially significant?
2. Does the goal begin with "The student knows . . ." if it is a knowledge goal and "The student is able to . . ." if it is a process goal?
3. Is the goal stated in language that is sufficiently clear, concise, and appropriate? (Can it be stated in simpler language and/or fewer words?)
4. Can learning experiences be thought of that would lead to the goal's achievement?
5. Do curricular options exist for the goal's achievement? (Methodology should not be a part of the learning outcome statement.)
6. Does the goal clearly contribute to the attainment of one or more of the program goals in its subject area?
7. Can the goal be identified with the approximate level of student development?
8. Can criteria for evaluating the goal be identified?

Curriculum developers need to decide the types and definitions of goals most useful to them

System Goal:	The student knows and is able to apply basic scientific and technological processes.
Program Goal:	The student is able to use the conventional language, instruments, and operations of science.
Course Goal:	The student is able to classify organisms according to their conventional taxonomic categories.
Instructional Goal:	The student is able to correctly classify cuttings from the following trees as needleleaf, hemlock, pine, spruce, fir, larch, cypress, redwood, and cedar.

FIGURE 3.1 Examples of Goals at Each Level of Planning

and to users of their materials. Some authors advise avoiding vagueness by using highly specific language.[2] Mager (1962) and other writers insist that words denoting observable behaviors, such as "construct" and "identify" should be used in place of words like "understand" and "appreciate." Others reject this approach, claiming that behavioral objectives "are in no way adequate for conceptualizing most of our most cherished educational aspirations" (Eisner, 1979, p. 101). Unfortunately this dispute has developed into a debate about behavioral objectives rather than dialogue over the kinds of behavior appropriate for a humane and civilized person.

The debate is partly semantic and partly conceptual. To some persons the word "behavior" carries the meaning of an observable act, like the movement of the fingers in typing. To them, behavioral objectives refer only to overt behavior. Others use the term "behavior" to emphasize the active nature of the learner. They want to emphasize that learners are not passive receptacles but living, reasoning persons. In this sense behavior refers to all kinds of human reactions.

For example, a detailed set of "behavioral goals" was prepared by French and associates (1957). Organized under the major headings of "self-realization," "face-to-face relationships," and "membership in large organizations," *Behavioral Goals of General Education in High School* includes aims such as "Shows growing ability to appreciate and apply good standards of performance and artistic principles." These are expanded by illustrative behaviors such as "Appreciates good workmanship and design in commercial products."

The other aspect of the debate over behavioral objectives arises from focusing on limited kinds of learning, such as training factory workers to perform specific tasks. The term "conditioning" is commonly used for the learning of behaviors initiated by clear stimuli and calling for automatic, fixed responses. Most driving behavior, for example, consists of conditioned responses to traffic lights, to the approach of other cars and pedestrians, and to the sensations a driver receives from the car's movements. Conditioning is a necessary and important type of learning.

In some situations, though, an automatic response is inappropriate. A more complex model of learning compatible with development of responsible persons in a changing society conceives of the learner as actively seeking meaning. This implies understanding and conscious pursuit of one's goals. The rewards of such learning include the satisfaction of coping with problems successfully.

Planning curriculum for self-directed learning requires goals that are not directly observable: ways of thinking, understanding of concepts and principles, broadening and deepening of interests, changing of attitudes, developing satisfying emotional responses to aesthetic experiences, and the like.

Even these goals, however, should use terms with clearly defined meanings. Saying that a student should "understand the concept of freedom" is far too broad and ambiguous, both because the meaning of the term "concept" is not sufficiently agreed on among educators, and because concept words such as "freedom" have too great a range of possible informational loadings to ensure similar interpretation from teacher to teacher. If used at all, such a statement would be at the program level, and would require increasingly specific elaboration at the course and lesson plan levels.

Some educators find it useful to refer to a particular type of goal as a *competency*. Used in the early 1970s in connection with Oregon's effort to relate high school instruction to daily life (Oregon State Board, 1972), the term "minimum competency" has become identified with state and district testing programs designed to ensure that students have a minimum level of basic skills before being promoted or graduated. Spady (1978) and other advocates of performance-based education point out that competency involves more than "capacities" such as the ability to read and calculate; it should refer to *application* of school-learned skills in situations outside of school.

One definition of competency is the ability to perform a set of related tasks with a high degree of skill. The concept is especially useful in vocational education, where a particular competency can be broken down through task analysis into its component skills so that teachers and curriculum planners have both a broad statement of expected performance and an array of skills specific enough to be taught and measured (Chalupsky and others, 1981).

CONSIDERATIONS IN CHOOSING GOALS

Educational goals should reflect three important factors: the nature of organized knowledge, the nature of society, and the nature of learners (Tyler, 1949). An obvious source is the nature of organized fields of study. Schools teach music, chemistry, and algebra because these fields have been developed through centuries of painstaking inquiry. Each academic discipline has its own concepts, principles, and processes. It would be unthinkable to neglect passing on to future generations this priceless heritage and these tools for continued learning.

Another factor affecting school goals is the nature of society. For example, the goals of education in the United States are quite different from those in the Soviet Union. In the United States we stress individuality, competition, creativity, and freedom to choose government officials. Soviet schools teach loyalty to the state and subordination of one's individuality to the welfare of the collective. One result is that most American schools offer a great many electives, while the curriculum in Soviet schools consists mostly of required subjects. For example, all students in the U.S.S.R. must study advanced mathematics and science to serve their technologically advanced nation (Wirszup, 1981).

U.S. schools have assumed, explicitly or implicitly, many goals related to the nature of society. For example, schools offer drug education, sex education, driver education, and other programs because of concerns about the values and behavior of youth and adults. Schools teach vis-

ual literacy because of the influence of television, consumer education because our economic system offers so many choices, and energy education because of the shortage of natural resources.

A goal statement by Ehrenberg and Ehrenberg (1978) specifically recognizes the expectations of society. Their model for curriculum development begins with a statement of "ends sought": "It is intended that as a result of participating in the K–12 educational program students will consistently and effectively take *intelligent, ethical action:* (1) to accomplish the tasks society legitimately expects of all its members, and (2) to establish and pursue worthwhile goals of their own choosing."

The curriculum development process outlined by the Ehrenbergs involves preparing a complete rationale for the ends-sought statement and then defining, for example, areas of societal expectations. The work of the curriculum developer consists of defining a framework of "criterion tasks," all derived either from expectations of society or necessary to pursue individual goals. These tasks, at various levels of pupil development, become the focus of day-to-day instruction. In this way, all curriculum is directly related to school system goals.

A third consideration in choosing goals, sometimes overlooked, is the nature of learners. For example, because Lawrence Kohlberg (1980) has found that children pass through a series of stages in their moral development, he believes schools should adopt the goal of raising students' levels of moral reasoning. Sternberg (1981) and other "information processing" psychologists believe that intelligence is, partly at least, a set of strategies and skills that can be learned. Their research suggests, according to Sternberg, that schools can and should set a goal of improving students' intellectual performance.

Recognizing that students often have little interest in knowledge for its own sake or in adult applications of that knowledge, some educators believe goals should not only be based on what we know about students, but should come from students themselves. Many alternative schools emphasize this source of goals more than conventional schools typically do (Raywid, 1981).

While knowledge, society, and learners are all legitimate considerations, the three are sometimes in conflict. For example, many of the products of the curriculum reform movement of the 1960s had goals based almost exclusively on the nature of knowledge. The emphasis of curriculum developers was on the "structure of the disciplines" (Bruner, 1960). Goals of some curriculums failed to fully reflect the nature of society and students, so teachers either refused to use them or gave up after trying them for a year or two (Stake and Easley, 1978).

In the 1970s educators and the general public reacted against this discipline-centered emphasis by stressing practical activities drawn from daily life. Schools were urged to teach students how to balance a checkbook, how to choose economical purchases, how to complete a job application, and how to read a traffic ticket. Career education enthusiasts, not content with the reasonable idea that education should help prepare students for satisfying careers, claimed that *all* education should be career-related in some way.

Conflicts of this sort between the academic and the practical are persistent and unavoidable, but curriculum developers err if they emphasize only one source of goals and ignore the others. If noneducators are preoccupied with only one factor, educational leaders have a responsibility to stress the importance of the others and to insist on balance.

SCOPE OF THE SCHOOL'S RESPONSIBILITY

There have been many attempts to define the general aims of schools and school programs, including the well-known Cardinal Principles listed by a national commission in 1918. The seven goals in that report—health, fundamental processes, worthy home membership, vocation, civic education, worthy use of leisure, and ethical character—encompass nearly every aspect of human existence, and most goal statements written since that time have been equally comprehensive.

Some authors contend that schools are mistaken to assume such broad aims. Martin (1980) argued that intellectual development and citizenship are the only goals for which schools should have primary responsibility and that other institutions should be mainly responsible for such goals as worthy home membership. He proposed that schools undertake a new role of coordinating educational efforts of all community agencies.

Paul (1982) reported that in three different communities large numbers of teachers, students, and parents agreed on a limited set of goals confined mostly to basic skills. Paul contended that schools often confuse the issue when involving citizens in setting goals because they ask what students should learn rather than what schools should teach. Goal surveys conducted by her organization showed, she said, that adults want young people to develop many qualities for which they do not expect schools to be responsible.

Undeniably, the aims and activities of U.S. schools are multiple and diverse. They not only teach toothbrushing, crafts, religion, care of animals, advertising, cooking, automobile repair, philosophy, hunting, and chess; they also provide health and food services to children, conduct parent education classes, and offer a variety of programs for the elderly. Periodic review of these obligations is clearly in order. However, in trying to delimit their mission schools must not minimize concern for qualities that, though hard to define and develop, distinguish educated persons from the less educated.

A carefully refined statement of goals of schooling in the United States was developed by Goodlad (1979) and his colleagues in connection with their Study of Schooling. Deliberately derived from an analysis of hundreds of goal statements adopted by school districts and state departments of education so as to reflect accurately the currently declared aims of American education, the list comprises 65 goals in 12 categories, including "intellectual development," "self-concept," and "moral and ethical character."

An equally broad set of goals is used in Pennsylvania's Educational Quality Assessment, which includes questions intended to measure such elusive aims as "understanding others" and "self-esteem." School districts must give the tests at least once every five years as part of a plan to make schools accountable for the 12 state-adopted goals (Seiverling, 1980). An adaptation of the Pennsylvania goals was used by the ASCD Committee on Research and Theory (1980) in connection with their plan for *Measuring and Attaining the Goals of Education.*

In many cases schools contribute modestly or not at all to helping students become loving parents and considerate neighbors. In other cases, school experiences may have lasting effects on values, attitudes, and behavior. We believe school goals should include such aims as "interpersonal relations" and "autonomy," as well as "intellectual development" and "basic skills" (Goodlad, 1979), although the goal statement should specifically recognize that most goals are not the exclusive domain of schools but are a shared responsibility with other institutions.

ESTABLISHING LOCAL GOALS

It is usually helpful to begin identification of goals by listing all the promising possibilities from various sources. Consider contemporary *society.* What things could one's students learn that would help them meet current demands and take advantage of future opportunities? General data about modern society may be found in studies of economic, political, and social conditions. Data directly relevant to the lives of one's students will usually require local studies, which can be made by older students, parents, and other local people.

Consider the *background of the students:* their previous experiences, things they have already learned, their interests and needs; that is, the gaps between desired ways of thinking, feeling, and acting and their present ways. This information should be specific to one's own students, although generalized studies of the development of children and youth in our culture will suggest what to look for.

Consider the potential of the various *subject fields.* What things could one's students learn

about their world and themselves from the sciences, history, literature, and so on? What can mathematics provide as a resource for their lives? Visual arts? Music? Each new generation is likely to find new possibilities in these growing fields of knowledge and human expression.

In the effort to identify possible goals don't be unduly concerned about the form in which you state these "things to be learned." For example, you may find a possibility in "learn new ways of expressing emotions through various experiences provided in literature," and another in "understanding how animal ecologies are disturbed and the consequences of the disturbance." These are in different forms and at different levels of generality, but at this stage the purpose is only to consider carefully all the promising possibilities. Later on, those selected as most important and appropriate for one's students can be refined and restated in common form so as to guide curriculum developers in designing learning experiences. At that point, it will probably be helpful to standardize terms and definitions. At early stages, however, curriculum developers should use terminology familiar and understandable to teachers, principals, parents, and citizens rather than insisting on distinctions that others may have difficulty remembering and using.

The comprehensive list of possible outcomes should be carefully scrutinized to sift out those that appear to be of minor importance or in conflict with the school's educational philosophy. The list should also be examined in the light of the apparent prospects for one's students being able to learn these things in school. For example, we know that things once learned are usually forgotten unless there are continuing opportunities to use them. So one criterion for retaining a goal is that students will have opportunities in and out of school to think, feel, and act as expected. We also know that learning of habits requires continuous practice with few errors, so work and study habits should be selected as goals only if they are to be emphasized consistently in school work.

This procedure for identifying what students are to be helped to learn is designed to prevent a common weakness in curriculum development: selection of goals that are obsolete or irrelevant, inappropriate for students' current level of development, not in keeping with sound scholarship, not in harmony with America's democratic philosophy, or for which the school cannot provide the necessary learning conditions.

A common practice when planning curriculum is to refer to published taxonomies (Bloom and others, 1956; Krathwohl and others, 1964). Taxonomies can be useful for their original purpose—classifying goals already formulated—but they do not resolve the issue of the relevance of any particular goal to contemporary society or to one's own students. The Bloom and Krathwohl taxonomies are organized in terms of what the authors conceive to be higher or lower levels, but higher ones are not always more important or even necessary. In typewriting, for example, so-called "higher mental processes" interfere with the speed and accuracy of typing.

A similar caution applies to uncritically taking goals from curriculum materials of other school systems. The fact that educators in Scarsdale or some other district chose certain goals is not in itself evidence that they are appropriate for your students.

Development of general goals for a school system should be a lengthy process with opportunities for students, parents, and others to participate. This can be done, for example, by sponsoring "town meetings," publishing draft statements of goals in local newspapers with an invitation to respond, and by holding and publicizing hearings on goals sponsored by the board of education.

A factor that complicates the matter is that some sources of goals are simply not subject to a majority vote. Knowledge—whether about physics, poetry, or welding—is the province of specialists. Educators sometimes know more about the nature of children and the learning process than many other adults in the community. Nevertheless, in a democracy there is no higher authority than the people, so the people must be involved in deciding what public schools are to teach.

Most general goals, because they are so broad and because they deal with major categories of human experience, are acceptable to most people. Few will quarrel with a goal such as "Know about human beings, their environments and their achievements, past and present." The problem in developing a general goal statement is usually not to decide which goals are proper and which are not, but to select among many possibilities those which are most important, are at the proper level of generality, and are at least partially the responsibility of schools.

While general goals are not usually controversial, more specific ones can be. For example, parents might not quarrel with "Understand and follow practices associated with good health," but some would reject "Describe two effective and two ineffective methods of birth control." Thus, parents and other citizens should be involved in formulating course and program goals as well as general system goals.

USING GOALS TO PLAN LEARNING ACTIVITIES

To some extent, well-stated goals imply the kinds of learning activities that would be appropriate for achieving them. For example, if an instructional goal is "Solve word problems requiring estimation involving use of simple fractions such as $\frac{1}{2}$, $\frac{1}{4}$, $\frac{2}{3}$," students would have to practice estimating solutions to practical problems as well as learning to calculate using fractions. In many instances, however, knowing the goal does not automatically help an educator know how to teach it. For example, to enable students to "understand and appreciate significant human achievements," one teacher might have students read about outstanding scientists of the 19th century, supplement the readings with several lectures, and give a multiple choice examination. Another teacher might decide to divide students into groups and have each group prepare a presentation to the class about a great scientist using demonstrations, dramatic skits, and so on. Forging the link between goals and other steps in curriculum development requires professional knowledge, experience, and imagination.

A factor that distorts what might appear to be a straightforward relationship between goals and activities is that every instructional activity has multiple goals. The goal-setting process is sometimes seen as a one-to-one relationship between various levels of goals and levels of school activity. For example, the mission of a local school system might be to "Offer all students equitable opportunities for a basic education plus some opportunities to develop individual talents and interests." "Basic education" would be defined to include "Communicate effectively by reading, writing, speaking, observing, and listening." A middle school in that district might have a goal such as "Read and understand nonfiction at a level of the average article in *Reader's Digest*," or more specifically, "Students will be able to distinguish between expressions of fact and opinion in writing."

While similar chains of related goals are basic to sound curriculum planning, developers should never assume that such simplicity fully represents the reality of schools. When a teacher is engaged in teaching reading he or she must also be conscious of and teach toward other goals: thinking ability, knowledge of human achievements, relationships with others, positive self-concept, and so on.

Not only must teachers address several officially adopted "outside" goals all at once; they must cope with "inside" goals as well. Although Goodlad (1979) uses declared goals to remind educators and the public what schools are said to be for, he cautions that the ends-means model doesn't do justice to the educational process and offers, as an alternative, an ecological perspective. Insisting that school activities should "be viewed for their intrinsic value, quite apart from their linkage or lack of linkage to stated ends" (p. 76), he points out that in addition to "goals that have been set outside of the system for the system" there are also goals inside the system— "students' goals, teachers' goals, principals' goals, and so on—and . . . these goals are not necessarily compatible" (p. 77).

The message to curriculum developers is that although "outside" goals and objectives are fundamental to educational planning, the relationship between purposes and practices is more complex than it may seem.

USING GOALS IN CURRICULUM EVALUATION

Some writers argue that specific objectives are essential in order to design suitable evaluation plans and write valid test items. The work of the National Assessment of Educational Progress shows, however, that even evaluators may not require objectives written in highly technical language.[3] National Assessment objectives do not contain stipulations of conditions or performance standards; in fact they are expected to meet just two criteria: clarity and importance. The educators, citizens, and subject matter experts who review the objectives are asked, "Do you understand what this objective means? How important is it that students learn this in school?" Objectives are often considered clear and important even though they are stated briefly and simply. When the objectives have been identified, National Assessment staff members or consultants develop exercises develop exercises designed to be operational definitions of the intended outcomes. Conditions, standards of performance, and so on are specified for the exercises, not for the objectives.

Setting goals is difficult because it requires assembling and weighing all the factors to be considered in selecting the relatively few but important goals that can be attained with the limited time and resources available to schools. The demands and opportunities of society, the needs of students, the resources of scholarship, the values of democracy, and the conditions needed for effective learning must all be considered.

A common error is the failure to distinguish purposes appropriate for the school from those attainable largely through experiences in the home and community. The school can reinforce the family in helping children develop punctuality, dependability, self-discipline, and other important habits. The school can be and usually is a community in which children and adults respect each other, treat each other fairly, and cooperate. But the primary task for which public schools were established is to enlarge students' vision and experience by helping them learn to draw upon the resources of scholarship, thus overcoming the limitations of direct experience and the narrow confines of a local environment. Students can learn to use sources of knowledge that are more accurate and reliable than folklore and superstition. They can participate vicariously through literature and the arts with peoples whose lives are both similar and different from those they have known. The school is the only institution whose primary purpose is enabling students to explore these scholarly fields and to learn to use them as resources in their own lives. Great emphasis should be given to goals of this sort.

Goals are frequently not stated at the appropriate degree of generality-specificity for each level of educational responsibility. Goals promulgated by state education authorities should not be too specific because of the wide variation in conditions among districts in the state. State goals should furnish general guidance for the kinds and areas of learning for which schools are responsible in that state. The school district should furnish more detailed guidance by identifying goals that fall between the general aims listed by the state and those appropriate to the local school. School goals should be adapted to the background of students and the needs and resources of the neighborhood, especially the educational role the parents can assume. The goals of each teacher should be designed to attain the goals of the school. The test of whether a goal is stated at the appropriate degree of generality-specificity is its clarity and helpfulness in guiding the educational activities necessary at that level of responsibility.

CONCLUSION

When states list specific skills as goals and develop statewide testing programs to measure them, they may overlook a significant part of what schools should teach: understanding, analysis, and problem solving. If students are taught only to follow prescribed rules, they will be un-

able to deal with varied situations. Another common limitation of such lists is their neglect of affective components, such as finding satisfaction in reading and developing the habit of reading to learn.

The form and wording of goals and objectives should be appropriate for the way they are to be used. For clarity, we have generally used the term "goal" for all statements of intended learning outcomes regardless of their degree of specificity, but we recognize that no one formula is best for all situations. The criterion for judging goals and objectives is their usefulness in communicating educational purposes and their helpfulness to teachers in planning educational activities.

ENDNOTES

1. Available from Commercial-Educational Distributing Service, P.O. Box 4791, Portland, OR 97208.
2. Collections of "measurable objectives" may be purchased from Instructional Objectives Exchange, Box 24095-M, Los Angeles, CA 90024-0095.
3. National Assessment has developed objectives for a number of subject areas, including art, citizenship, career and occupational development, literature, mathematics, music, reading, science, social studies, and writing. Because they have been carefully written and thoroughly reviewed, the objectives and accompanying exercises are a helpful resource for local curriculum developers, although they are designed only for assessment, not for curriculum planning.

REFERENCES

ASCD Committee on Research and Theory, Wilbur B. Brookover, Chairman. *Measuring and Attaining the Goals of Education.* Alexandria, Va.: Association for Supervision and Curriculum Development, 1980.

Bloom, Benjamin S., ed. *Taxonomy of Educational Objectives: The Classification of Educational Goals. Handbook 1: Cognitive Domain.* New York: David McKay Co., Inc., 1956.

Bruner, Jerome. *The Process of Education.* Cambridge: Belknap Press, 1960.

Chalupsky, Albert B.; Phillips-Jones, Linda; and Danoff, Malcolm N. "Competency Measurement in Vocational Education: A Review of the State of the Art." Prepared by American Institute for Research. Washington, D.C.: Office of Vocational and Adult Education, U.S. Department of Education, 1981.

Commission on the Reorganization of Secondary Education, U.S. Office of Education. *Cardinal Principles of Secondary Education.* Washington, D.C.: Government Printing Office, 1918.

Doherty, Victor W., and Peters, Linda B. "Introduction to K–12 Course Goals for Educational Planning and Evaluation." 3rd ed. Portland, Oregon: Commercial-Educational Distributing Services, 1980.

Doherty, Victor W., and Peters, Linda B. "Goals and Objectives in Educational Planning and Evaluation." *Educational Leadership* 38 (May 1981): 606.

Ehrenberg, Sydelle D., and Ehrenberg, Lyle, M. *A Strategy for Curriculum Design—The ICI Model.* Miami, Florida: Institute for Curriculum and Instruction, 1978.

Eisner, Eliot W. *The Educational Imagination.* New York: Macmillan Publishing Co., Inc., 1979.

French, Will. *Behavioral Goals of General Education in High School.* New York: Russell Sage Foundation, 1957.

Goodlad, John I. *What Schools Are For?* Bloomington, Indiana: Phi Delta Kappa, 1979.

Kohlberg, Lawrence. "Moral Education: A Response to Thomas Sobol." *Educational Leadership* 38 (October 1980): 19–23.

Krathwohl, David R., and others. *Taxonomy of Educational Objectives: The Classification of Educational Goals, Handbook II: Affective Domain.* New York: David McKay Company, Inc., 1964.

Lindvall, C. M., ed. *Defining Educational Objectives.* Pittsburgh: University of Pittsburgh Press, 1964.

Mager, R. F. *Preparing Instructional Objectives.* Palo Alto: Fearon Publishers, 1962.

Martin, John Henry. "Reconsidering the Goals of High School Education." *Educational Leadership* 37 (January 1980): 278–285.

Mathematics Objectives, Second Assessment. Denver: National Assessment of Educational Programs, 1978.

Oregon State Board of Education. "Minimum State Requirements Standards for Graduation from High School." Salem, Oregon, 1972.

Paul, Regina. "Are You Out On a Limb?" *Educational Leadership* 39 (January 1982): 260–264.

Raywid, Mary Anne. "The First Decade of Public School Alternatives." *Phi Delta Kappan* 62 (April 1981): 551–554.

Saylor, J. Galen; Alexander, William M.; and Lewis, Arthur J. *Curriculum Planning for Better Teaching and Learning.* 4th ed. New York: Holt, Rinehart and Winston, 1981.

Seiverling, Richard F., ed. *Educational Quality Assessment: Getting Out The EQA Results.* Harrisburg, Pa.: Pennsylvania Department of Education, 1980.

Spady, William G. "The Concept and Implications of Competency-Based Education." *Educational Leadership* 36 (October 1978): 16–22.

Stake, R. E., and Easley, J. A., Jr. *Case Studies in Science Education.* 2 vols. Washington, D.C.: U.S. Government Printing Office, 1978.

Sternberg, Robert J. "Intelligence as Thinking and Learning Skills." *Educational Leadership* 39 (October 1981): 18–20.

Tyler, Ralph W. *Basic Principles of Curriculum and Instruction.* 1974 ed. Chicago: University of Chicago Press, 1949.

Ward, Barbara. "The National Assessment Approach to Objectives and Exercise Development." Report No. 12-IP-55. Denver, Colo.: Education Commission of the States, September 1980.

Wirszup, Izaak. "The Soviet Challenge." *Educational Leadership* 38 (February 1981): 358–360.

DISCUSSION QUESTIONS

1. What should the goals of contemporary education be?

2. Should the goals of education be the same for all students?

3. What is the best method for defining goals, by behavioral objectives or by competencies?

4. Who should assume responsibility for determining educational goals, the federal government, the state board of education, local school districts, building principals, or the faculty at each school? Why?

5. What is the best criterion for judging goals and objectives?

Alternative Curriculum Conceptions and Designs

M. FRANCES KLEIN

FOCUSING QUESTIONS

1. *What is the measured curriculum?*
2. *In what ways do alternative curriculum conceptions and designs influence curriculum delivery and evaluation?*
3. *What common ideas do technological, cognitive processes, and academic rationalism embrace?*
4. *How do social reconstructionism and self-actualization differ?*
5. *How do the means-end, naturalistic observation, educational connoisseurship, and case study forms of evaluation differ?*
6. *Which type of curriculum conception and design do you prefer? Why?*

The field of curriculum is not without its critics. Schwab (1978) has called the study of curriculum moribund and Jackson (1981) has even questioned the existence of curriculum as a field of study. Most curriculum scholars, however, are more confident about the existence of the curriculum field since they have spent their careers in an effort to conceptualize it and study those practices which are called curriculum. Although some scholars may debate whether curriculum studies exist and if so, how to conceptualize them, few practitioners would question the existence or importance of curriculum. Curriculum is the substance of schooling—the primary reason why people attend school.

Many educational resources go to direct and support the curriculum. Countless committee meetings are held to develop it; teachers are hired, trained, and supervised in order to implement it; administrators are exhorted to provide curriculum leadership as their primary role; materials are purchased or created; learning resource centers are built to support the curriculum; and educational researchers seek bases for improving it.

In the comparatively short time since its generally recognized "birth" with the publication of Bobbitt's book, *The Curriculum* (1918), the growth of the field has been slow and difficult. Curriculum scholars have debated significant ideas and proposed changes, but have not always addressed themselves to what difference their ideas make to the practitioner. Little wonder, then, that the practice of curriculum continues along a single strand of development with few alternative ideas considered.

Tyler's syllabus, *Basic Principles of Curriculum and Instruction* (1950), was selected by the leadership group, Professors of Curriculum, as one of two publications which has had the most influence over the field of curriculum (Shane, 1981).[1] In the Tyler syllabus, concepts and procedures are spelled out as a way to view curriculum and they have been applied in diverse situations all over the world in curriculum development efforts. Some curriculum scholars owe their careers to their refinements and modifications of the Tyler rationale.

Tyler identified three data sources which must be used in curriculum development: society, student, and subject matter. These three data sources have historically stimulated alternative conceptions of curriculum and the development of different curriculum designs. Scholars have long recognized the importance of the three data sources, but too often missed Tyler's message—that the use of one of the data sources alone is inadequate in developing curricula. A comprehensive curriculum must use all three.

Current curriculum practice and research focus almost exclusively on just one of these data sources, subject matter. Curricula have been developed using what Eisner and Vallance (1974) call the technological conception. Referred to here as the measured curriculum, it has emerged into dominance over all other alternative conceptions and designs.

THE MEASURED CURRICULUM

The measured curriculum is familiar to all educators. Behavioral objectives, time on task, sequential learning, positive reinforcement, direct instruction, achievement testing, mastery in skills and content, and teacher accountability are essential concepts used in practice and research. The measured curriculum should neither be condemned nor used exclusively to direct curriculum practice and research. It must be recognized for its strengths and limitations. It is compatible with some of the major educational outcomes valued by society—a store of knowledge about the world, command of the basic processes of communication, and exposure to new content areas. But this conception and design of curriculum cannot accomplish everything students are expected to learn.

Most curriculum scholars have long advocated the use of different designs for a school's curriculum; subject-centered, societal-centered, and individual-centered designs are the most commonly discussed. Unless alternatives to the technological, subject-matter-based curriculum (i.e., the measured curriculum) are used, some of the time-honored and persistently stated educational outcomes will not be accomplished.

OTHER CONCEPTIONS

Eisner and Vallance (1974) identified four other conceptions of curriculum in addition to the technological process: cognitive processes, self-actualization, social reconstruction, and academic rationalism. These four conceptions propose something the technological process does not—desired outcomes and a focus on the substance of curriculum. Two of the conceptions of curriculum, cognitive processes and academic rationalism, are often planned and implemented through the use of the technological process and a subject matter design. The other two, self-actualization and social reconstruction, require different curriculum designs and different concepts and procedures from the measured curriculum for planning and implementation.

Cognitive Processes and Academic Rationalism

Most similar to and compatible with the concepts and procedures of the measured curriculum are academic rationalism and cognitive processes. Academic rationalism advocates that the curriculum be based on the storehouse of knowledge which has enabled humankind to advance civilization. This storehouse is defined as organized subject matter in the form of the academic disciplines. The subject-centered curriculum design and the efficient technological process of curriculum building are compatible with this conception. It has been used well in the past and continues to have strong and prestigious advocates—Adler in *The Paideia Proposal* (1982), for example. Classroom practices and research are familiar to all when they are based on this conception. It is a form of the measured curriculum.

Cognitive processes as a conception of curriculum is less tied to specific content than is academic rationalism. Cognitive processes are thought to be "content-free" in the sense that they are generalizable from one subject area to another. The concept emphasizes the ability to think, reason, and engage in problem-solving activities. The specific content used is somewhat less important than the processes to be learned. This conception, too, has its strong proponents—Bruner (1961) and Bloom (1956), for example. Many curricula include this conception of outcomes as a major part of their intent and substance.

Curriculum development in both of these conceptions occurs in a similar way. The technological approach of the Tyler rationale (1950) is commonly used as a basis for planning and implementing curricula. The subject-centered design also is commonly employed, using concepts such as behavioral objectives, sequential organization of content, time on task, appropriate practice, and achievement tests. However, teachers using the cognitive processes conception might operate more from the information processing models of teaching as conceptualized by Joyce and Weil (1980), while academic rationalists might more often employ behavioristic models.

Social Reconstruction and Self-Actualization

The last two conceptions of curriculum, social reconstruction and self-actualization, are quite different and require different approaches to their development. The concepts from the measured curriculum are not automatically transferable to research and practice based on these conceptions.

Social reconstructionists look to society as a basis for the substance of curriculum. In their view, the problems and dilemmas of society are what ought to be studied by students with the intent of creating a more just, equitable, and humane society. Students must be involved in studying how obstacles can be overcome so that a more ideal society can be created. This becomes the content of the curriculum. Students are not to learn about them simply through a subject-centered design, however. The traditional textbook coverage in sociology or political science is not what these curriculum advocates favor. They want the students out in the community, using original sources, interviewing people, formulating solutions, testing hypotheses, and solving real problems—not just reading about them.

This design is societal centered rather than subject centered. The disciplines are used only as they relate to the problems being studied. Science is not studied as science nor history as history, but both subjects may be essential to understanding and developing possible resolutions to a local pollution problem. If so, students are expected to draw upon both disciplines. Through this conception and design of curriculum, students learn how to learn. They attack real problems, become meaningfully involved as citizens of the society, and begin to critically examine and help mold a better society.

Traditional concepts and processes from the measured curriculum are not applicable in practice for social reconstruction. No defined body of content can be spelled out in behavioral objectives. Time on task cannot be tracked easily since schooling is extended beyond the classroom. Time may even be "wasted" in tracking down important resources. Efficiency is not inherent to this design. Achievement also takes on a different definition, relating not to a body of prescribed content or skills but rather to how effectively the problem was studied and potentially resolved.

Testing as a form of evaluation is not applicable since each student or group of students may have studied different problems, used different resources, and posed different solutions. Other forms of evaluation emphasizing process more than content must be used. Students must be more involved in the planning, implementation, and evaluation of such a curriculum. In a social reconstructionist approach, curriculum development is not conducted prior to classroom interaction as in the measured curriculum. The curriculum must be developed jointly with the students.

The planning and implementation of a social reconstructionist's curriculum using a societal-based design would be distinctively different from other conceptions and designs. Rather than using behavioral objectives, practice would be guided by goals or general objectives such as those proposed by Zahorik (1976) or by problem-solving objectives as suggested by Eisner (1979). The use of general objectives such as learning how to study a problem or studying about discrimination, or of problem-solving objectives such as investigating the control of pollutants within the community or how the school could be a more democratic institution, allow for greater diversity in what is learned by students. All students are not expected to have the same experience or learn the same content. General objectives or problem-solving objectives open up the parameters for teaching and learning.

Classroom activities and evaluation procedures in social reconstruction would be developed through the use of criteria as proposed by Raths (1971) instead of according to the concepts of appropriate practice and achievement tests. Rather than activities which primarily provide appropriate practice for the behavior and content of the objectives, activities would be planned which permit students to make informed choices and reflect on their consequences; take risks of success or failure; and share the development, implementation, and evaluation of a plan. Evaluation procedures would focus on the provision of such activities and what is learned through them, not on the mastery of content or skills.

Teacher accountability would shift from a focus on how well students learn content to such considerations as processes used, community involvement achieved, and the diversity of relevant resources available to and used by the students. Learning in this design would not be sequential or like a stairstep as in the measured curriculum, but more like Eisner's (1979) spider-web model of learning. Teachers would draw most often from

the social interaction family of teacher models as conceptualized by Joyce and Weil (1980).

Curriculum as self-actualization is even further removed from the traditional curriculum practices and research of the measured curriculum. In this conception, students become the curriculum developers, selecting for study what they are interested in, intrigued by, and curious about. The curriculum is not preplanned by adults, but evolves as a student or a group of students and their teacher explore something of interest. Growth is viewed as the process of becoming a self-actualizing person, not learning a body of content, a set of cognitive processes, or studying the problems of society. Content is important to the extent that it is relevant and meaningful to the individual student, not as it is defined by someone else. The design becomes individual centered with the role of the student rather than that of the teacher being dominant.

In this conception and design, traditional concepts guiding practice are incompatible. Objectives are too directing; time on task becomes unmanageable as students pursue different ideas, at different paces, and in different ways; achievement testing is impossible when students learn different things; and appropriate practice becomes idiosyncratically defined based on students' own interests. The classroom becomes an enriched, stimulating environment to challenge and appeal to students, an active, noisy place where students interact with each other as needed, and an extension of a learning resource laboratory with diverse and plentiful materials. Students and teachers become co-learners embarked on a study plan of their own making.

For this conception of curriculum as self-actualization, new concepts and procedures must be developed and legitimatized. Eisner's (1979) concept of expressive outcomes seems uniquely fitted to this conception and design, and educational criticism and connoisseurship are better suited as a mode of evaluation (Eisner, 1979). The personal family of teaching models would be most representative of how teachers and students would interact (Joyce & Weil, 1980).

Macdonald, Wolfson, and Zaret (1973) propose learning organized around a continuous cycle of exploring, integrating, and transcending. They also identify self-evaluation as an important aspect of this conception. Accountability according to them should be social accountability. Is the school exemplifying the values which the society desires to foster within young people? Other compatible concepts will need to be developed through an exploration of this design in practice, an opportunity curriculum workers do not frequently have. From such a curriculum students learn to develop their unique talents and interests, to value learning as a process, to become even more creative, curious, and imaginative, and to become more integrated, humane, caring human beings.

NEEDED CHANGES IN
CURRICULUM RESEARCH

The procedures and concepts used in research help determine what is "seen" in the curriculum. When researchers structure interviews, questionnaires, and observation around behavioral objectives, time on task, appropriate practice, and achievement testing, those are the concepts which are documented. Rather than rely exclusively on those concepts used in the practices of the measured curriculum (upon which much of the current research on curriculum is based), alternative approaches to curriculum research must be applied for different conceptions and designs.

More naturalistic observations in classrooms for the self-actualization conception and individual-based design are needed. New approaches to determining individual perceptions of growth and relating those to classroom practices would be one way to proceed. Eisner's (1979) concepts of educational connoisseurship and criticism seem to have considerable compatibility and already offer an alternative approach to traditional curriculum research. Case studies of classrooms using the social reconstruction conception and societal-centered design may be needed as research documentation.

However the research methodologies and constructs are developed and used in relation to the alternative approaches to curriculum, they must honor and be compatible with the unique expected outcomes of each and the different concepts upon which practice is based. To do otherwise is to destroy the potential any alternative in curriculum conception and design has to enhance the growth of students. This undoubtedly will require the use of ideas other than our traditional research concepts such as validity, reliability, objectivity, and generalizability.

Research methodology and the type of research study conducted must accommodate the alternative shifts in curriculum conceptions and designs which are developed to guide practice. Researchers must learn to operationalize new concepts, to ask different questions, to view curriculum from different conceptions. The new research concepts and procedures must be compatible with the practices and reflective of the differing educational outcomes each design will encourage.

CONCLUSION

For the purposes of this article, the placement of basic concepts and procedures has been perhaps too narrow and somewhat rigid in order to make the case for using alternative concepts and processes for different conceptions and designs. It may well be that several concepts have applicability in more than one conception and design. Only as they are given rigorous study in research and practice will this become clear, however.

The extent to which schooling can accommodate these designs—and newer ones being developed—is a matter for debate and experimentation. However, much more can be accomplished with alternative conceptions and designs than is even thought about now. Curriculum does not have to be *either* one conception *or* another. With the use of varying conceptions and designs in each classroom, schools might well become much more attractive, challenging, and relevant places for students. And schooling as a process may become more responsive to the needs and desires of both the individual student and society.

The field of study called curriculum is alive, but not as healthy as it might be. Its health could be enhanced by enriching the diet currently restricted to the measured curriculum with more diverse nutrients from the storehouse of alternative conceptions and designs. This enrichment is a fundamental task to which future curriculum workers must address themselves.

ENDNOTE

1. The other most influential book was Dewey's *Democracy and Education* (1916).

REFERENCES

Adler, M. J. (1982). *The Paideia proposal. An educational manifesto.* New York: Macmillan.

Bloom, B. S. (Ed.). (1956). *Taxonomy of educational objectives: Cognitive domain.* New York: Longmans, Green.

Bobbitt, F. (1918). *The curriculum.* Boston, MA: Houghton Mifflin.

Bruner, J. (1961). *The process of education.* Cambridge, MA: Harvard University Press.

Dewey, J. (1916). *Democracy and education.* New York: Macmillan.

Eisner, E. W. (1979). *The educational imagination.* New York: Macmillan.

Eisner, E. W., & Vallance, E. (1974). *Conflicting conceptions of curriculum.* Berkeley, CA: McCutchan.

Jackson, P. W. (1981). Curriculum and its discontents. In H. A. Giroux, A. N. Penna, & W. F. Pinar (Eds.), *Curriculum and instruction: Alternatives in education* (pp. 367–381). Berkeley, CA: McCutchan.

Joyce, B., & Weil, M. (1980). *Models of teaching.* Englewood Cliffs, NJ: Prentice-Hall

Macdonald, J. B., Wolfson, B. J., & Zaret, E. (1973). *Reschooling society; A conceptual model.* Washington, DC: Association for Supervision and Curriculum Development.

Raths, J. D. (April, 1971). Teaching without specific objectives. *Educational Leadership, 28,* 714–720.

Schwab, J. (1978). The practical: A language for curriculum. In I. Westbury & N. J. Wilkof (Eds.), *Science, curriculum and liberal education* (pp. 287–321). Chicago, IL: University of Chicago Press.

Shane, H. G. (1981, January). Significant writings that have influenced the curriculum: 1906–81. Phi Delta Kappan, 62 (5), 311–314.

Tyler, R. W. (1950). *Basic principles of curriculum and instruction.* Chicago, IL: University of Chicago Press.

Zahorik, J. A. (1976, April). The virtue of vagueness in instructional objectives. Elementary School Journal, 76, 411–419.

DISCUSSION QUESTIONS

1. Which type of curriculum conception is most relevant to contemporary education? Which is the most irrelevant?

2. Which method of evaluation is most relevant to contemporary education?

3. Suppose you are the curriculum director and can determine the curriculum for your school. Which type of curriculum conception and method of evaluation would guide your selection? Would you use a single approach to curriculum design and evaluation?

4. What is the relationship between types of curriculum conceptions and educational philosophies?

5. How might schools become more relevant and challenging places for students?

Is There a Curriculum Voice to Reclaim?

MICHAEL W. APPLE

FOCUSING QUESTIONS

1. *In what ways does current curriculum delivery reflect a conservative societal movement?*
2. *Why have curriculum workers not had a voice in conceptions of curriculum at the school level?*
3. *In what ways have developments in the field of curriculum tended to marginalize the delivery of education?*
4. *How has the textbook industry influenced curriculum implementation?*
5. *What are the advantages and disadvantages of a technocratic belief system in relationship to conceptions of curriculum?*

Herbert Spencer was not wrong when he reminded educators that one of the fundamental questions we should ask about schooling is, "What knowledge is of most worth?" The question is a deceptively simple one, however, since the conflicts over what should be taught have been sharp and deep. The issue is not only an educational one, but also an inherently ideological and political one. Whether we recognize it or not, curriculum and more general educational issues in the U.S. have always been caught up in the history of class, race, gender, and religious relations.[1]

A better way of phrasing the question—a way that highlights the profoundly political nature of educational debate—is, "*Whose* knowledge is of most worth?"[2] That this question is not simply academic is strikingly clear from the fact that calls for censorship and controversies over the values that the schools teach (or don't teach) have made the curriculum a political football in school districts throughout the country.

The public debate on education and on all social issues has shifted profoundly to the right in the past decade. The effects of this shift can be seen in a number of trends now gaining momentum nationally: proposals for voucher plans and tax credits to make school systems more like the thoroughly idealized free market economy; the movement in state legislatures and state departments of education to "raise standards" and to mandate teacher and student "competencies," thereby increasing the centralization of control of teaching and curricula; the often-effective assault on the school curriculum for its supposed biases against the family and free enterprise, for its "secular humanism," for its lack of patriotism, and for its failure to teach the content, values, and character traits that have made the "western tradition" what it is; and the consistent pressure to make the needs of business and industry the primary concerns of the education system.[3]

The rightist and neoconservative movements have entered education as the social democratic goal of expanding equality of opportunity has lost much of its political potency and appeal. The prevailing concerns today—panic over falling standards and rising rates of illiteracy, the fear of violence in the schools, and the perceived destruction of family and religious values—have allowed culturally and economically dominant groups to move the arguments about education into their own arena by emphasizing standardization, productivity, and a romanticized past when all children sat still with their hands folded and learned a common curriculum. Parents are justifiably concerned about their children's future in an economy that is increasingly conditioned by lower wages, the threat of unemployment, and cultural and economic insecurity—and the neoconservative and rightist positions address these fears.[4]

One of the conservative movement's major successes has been to marginalize a number of voices in education. The voices of the economically disadvantaged, of many women, of people of color, and of many other groups are hard to hear over the din of the attacks on schools for inefficiency, lack of connection to the economy, and failure to teach "real knowledge." One group of people who have supposedly been silenced are the curriculum scholars. For them, the "wrong people" have captured the debate about what should be taught in schools. Individuals such as E. D. Hirsch—whose *Cultural Literacy* owed much of its popularity to the propensity of many educators and others to play an intellectual version of Trivial Pursuit—now provide answers to Spencer's question.[5]

I agree in part with the judgment that the "wrong people" may have too much power in the debate about the curriculum, but the situation is considerably more complicated than this scenario of "good" versus "bad" would have it. And the problem certainly will not be solved by simply giving back to curriculum scholars the determining voice they once supposedly had.

What some people define as a crisis of loss of voice, others of course see as progress. In the view of former Secretary of Education William Bennett, for example, we are not involved in a deepening crisis but are emerging from one in which "we neglected and denied much of the best in American education." In the process "we simply stopped doing the right things [and] allowed an assault on intellectual and moral standards." This assault has supposedly led schools to fall away from "the principles of our tradition."[6] Moreover, it has been led by liberal intellectuals, not by "the people."

In Bennett's view, "the people" have now risen up. "The 1980s gave birth to a grass-roots movement for educational reform that has generated a renewed commitment to excellence, character, and fundamentals." Because of this, we have "reason for optimism." Why?

> [Because] the national debate on education is now focused on truly important matters: mastering the basics—math, history, science, and English; insisting on high standards and expectations; ensuring discipline in the classroom; conveying a grasp of our moral and political principles; and nurturing the character of our young.[7]

Part of the solution for Bennett and others is to take authority *away* from many of those professional educators who have supposedly had it. This attitude bespeaks a profound mistrust of teachers, administrators, and curriculum scholars. They are decidedly not part of the solution; they are part of the problem.

As all these developments have been taking place, most people in the field of curriculum have largely stood by, watching from the sidelines as if this were a fascinating game that had to do with politics but not with education. Others bemoaned their fate but fled to the relative calm of increasingly technical and procedural matters, thereby confirming the artificial separation between "how to" curriculum questions and those involving the real relations of culture and power in the world.

This situation is not a new phenomenon by any means. Curriculum workers have witnessed a slow but very significant change in the way their work has been defined over the past decades. Professional discourse about the curriculum has shifted from a focus on *what* we should teach to a focus on *how* the curriculum should be organized, built, and evaluated. The difficult and—as any examination of the reality of schooling would show—contentious ethical and political questions of content, of whose knowledge is of most worth, have been pushed into the background in our attempt to define technical methods that will "solve" all our problems. For years, professional debate about the curriculum has been over procedures, not over what counts as legitimate knowledge.

Although the process did not start in the late 1950s and early 1960s, it was certainly exacerbated during those years, which saw a resurgence of the discipline-centered curriculum. Government, industry, and academe formed an alliance that attempted to shift the curriculum radically in the direction of "real knowledge," that knowledge housed in the discipline-based departments at major universities. Since most teachers and curriculum workers were perceived to be incapable of dealing with such "real knowledge," it became clear that—to be effective—this alliance had to select the knowledge and organize it in particular ways. The National Defense Education Act, the massive curriculum development efforts that produced so much teacher-proof material, and the boxes upon boxes of standardized kits that still line the walls of many schools and classrooms bear witness to these attempts.

There are few better examples of the de-skilling of a field than this. If curricula are *purchased* (and remember that 80% of the cost of most of these new curriculum materials was repaid by the federal government) and if all curricula come ready-made, largely teacher-proof, and already linked to pretests and posttests, why would teachers need the skills to deliberate about the curriculum?[8] Of what use are those increasingly isolated curriculum scholars, unattached to "real disciplines" and housed primarily in schools of education, when what counts as legitimate knowledge is already largely predetermined by its disciplinary matrix?

At this point we need to remember a simple but telling fact. Most teachers, especially at the elementary level, are *women*. By disempowering them, by using governmental intervention to put curriculum deliberation, debate, and control into the hands of academics in the disciplines, we undercut the skills of curriculum design and teaching for which women teachers had long struggled in an attempt to gain respect.[9] The issue of the relative power of teachers bears directly on the question of who has really made decisions about curriculum in the past.

Yet it was not only teachers who lost power during the period of the discipline-based curriculum movement. A good deal of the scholarly literature in curriculum at this time was devoted to the declining power of curriculum "experts" in determining what should be taught.[10] Power was seen to have shifted from those people who were closely attached to a long tradition of curriculum debate to those who—like Jerome Bruner and his coterie of discipline-based experts—may have had interesting things to say about what should be taught in schools but whose primary affiliations were to their academic disciplines, not to teachers and schools. And while many curriculum scholars raised serious objections to what they believed to be an unwise move to a subject-based and perhaps elitist curriculum, they were by and large ignored outside of the limited professional audiences for whom they wrote.

The parallels between then and now are more than a little interesting. Powerful groups and alliances in the larger society, in government, and in the academy had more to do with determining curricular debate than those individuals whose special purchase on educational reality was supposed to be expertise in curriculum.

This problem was exacerbated by the propensities of the curriculum field itself—by the increasing dominance of procedural models of curriculum deliberation and design. The model that became, in essence, the paradigm of the field was articulated by Ralph Tyler in *Basic Principles of Curriculum and Instruction.*[11] Even with its avowed purpose of synthesizing nearly all that had gone before, it was largely a behaviorally oriented, procedural model. It was of almost no help whatsoever in determining the difficult issues of whose knowledge should be taught and *who* should decide. It focused instead on the methodological steps one should go through in selecting, organizing, and evaluating the curriculum.[12] One of the ultimate effects of Tyler's model, though perhaps not intentional, was the elimination of political and cultural conflict from the center of curriculum debate.[13] Today, in confrontations with resurgent conservative movements that have thoroughly politicized the curriculum and the entire schooling experience, the curriculum field finds that it has lost any substantive ways of justifying why *x* should be taught rather than *y*.[14]

While it may be too harsh an assessment, it seems that curriculum specialists have become increasingly irrelevant. They are often transformed into "experts for hire"—people who know the procedures for writing documents based on what other people have decided is important for students to know, who have expertise in quantitative or qualitative evaluation, in methods of goal-setting and assessment, and in techniques of writing behavioral objectives. What they are decidedly not experts in is the immensely more difficult and contentious issue of what specifically we should teach. And because of the ahistorical nature of the field and the increasingly technical and specialized quality of graduate education, the knowledge of the different traditions for dealing with that issue is dwindling. Many people are simply unequipped to deal with the issue of what a society's "collective memory" should be.[15]

This state of affairs has its democratic side, to be sure. By not centralizing curriculum decisions in the hands of a few experts, we are trying to insure that more power will reside at a local level. This is a meritorious goal. Yet, as we know,

the notion of local control is often a fiction, since, like it or not, we do have a national curriculum. Today, however, that curriculum is determined not by academics and the government but by the market for *textbooks.* And this market in turn is shaped by what is seen as important in the Sun Belt states that have textbook adoption policies. Curriculum scholars have very limited influence at this level. By ignoring the actual processes that establish the most important elements of the curriculum—what I have called "the culture and commerce of the textbooks"[16]—they have little to say about the political, economic, and ideological conditions that make the curriculum look the way it does.

Instead of focusing on the social realities that underlie the curriculum and on the way in which the curriculum has once again become an arena where different groups fight for their distinct social agendas, we look back nostalgically to a time when teachers, administrators, parents, business leaders, government officials, and others all sat up and paid attention to our "words of wisdom." In many ways, this picture of the past is just as romanticized as the one the conservatives paint of a time when we all shared the same values and had perfect schools, families, and communities.

I want to focus on this mythic past a bit more since I believe it is very much a part of the problem we face. We need to be very cautious about assuming that there once was a golden age in which curriculum scholars had an immense amount of independent power over the content of the curriculum. As I have stressed here and elsewhere, controversies over the content and form of the curriculum are most often informed by larger conflicts between and within groups that have or wish to have power.[17]

If we took an honest look at the historical record, we would see that the school curriculum has always been created by the conflicts and compromises that are themselves products of wider social movements and pressures that extend well beyond the school. More often than not, curriculum people have been carried along by these movements. Rather than being leaders, they have quite often been followers. Indeed, it is difficult to find more than a few instances in the last 30 years in which scholars *specifically within the curriculum field* have had any appreciable impact on debates over the content of the curriculum.

If curriculum scholars have not been primarily responsible for shaping the curriculum, what are some of the major forces that have? As I have argued in detail in *Teachers and Texts,* among the least talked about but most significant factors are the gendered nature of teaching and the dominance of the standardized textbook.

For example, it is not simply an accident that the curriculum of the elementary school has been tightly controlled and subject to continued rationalization. Women's paid work in a number of fields has historically been dealt with in the same way. Yet the fact that elementary teaching has largely been women's paid work also means that women teachers have been activists. Indeed, the prominence of the standardized textbook was the result not only of rationalizing influences imposed from above or of the lure of a lucrative market for textbook publishers, but also of collective pressure from elementary teachers to change the awful conditions in which many of them worked. Overcrowded classrooms and the difficulties of planning for multi-age groups and for teaching a variety of subjects led teachers to argue for textbooks to help them.[18] The result was a curriculum increasingly dominated by standardized—and finally, grade-specific—texts. This meant that the authors and publishers of textbooks had a significant amount of power in determining the form and content of the curriculum.

Thus the fact that the textbook became the *major* organizing element of the curriculum had little to do with curriculum scholars but was the complicated result of social policies and attitudes regarding gender, the politics of rationalization and bureaucratization in the schools and the teachers' responses to it, and the economics of profit and loss in the field of publishing. To look for the determining impact of a few specialized curriculum scholars in this situation is to look for what never was.

Among the other "external" forces that shaped curriculum was the rise of what has been called a "technocratic" belief system—both in education and in the larger society—which seemed to assume that if something moved, it should be measured. Of great importance as well was the steady growth of federal and state intervention in the shaping of curriculum policy, which was stimulated by cold war ideologies and the pressures of international economic competition.[19] As the conservative restoration gained power during the 1980s, this intervention became even more visible.

Of course, much more could be said about the influence of state intervention or economic crises on the national reform reports, on who has the power to speak and to be listened to on educational matters, and on where the money goes. We should consider, as well, how a conservative government has masterfully used the media to control the public debate on education. On a more positive note, we should also devote attention to the story of how African-Americans, women, Hispanics, and others have brought about major shifts in curricular content and authority. And we could focus on many other areas.

Yet my point is a simple one. Almost none of these developments can be traced to the efforts—no matter how well-intentioned—of curriculum scholars. The nostalgic gaze into a golden age is largely a misreading of the historical record. It is a flight from acknowledging where power often lies and an even more dangerous flight from seeing the real depth of the problem.

Oddly, however, the feeling that curriculum scholars have lost their voice in the debate over the curriculum might be the first step in the right direction. Perhaps that feeling means that curriculum scholars do recognize the objective conditions that surround not only their own lives but the lives of so many talented and committed educators. The process of determining the curriculum for the classroom and for teacher education is increasingly politicized and increasingly subject to legislative mandates, mandates from state departments of education, and so on. Test-driven curricula, hyperrationalized and bureaucratized school experiences and planning models, atomized and reductive curricula—all of these *are* realities. There *has* been a de-skilling of teachers and of curriculum workers, a separation of conception from execution as planning is removed from the local level, and a severe intensification of educators' work as more and more has to be done in less and less time.[20] Power over curricula is being centralized and taken out of the hands of front-line educators, and this process is occurring at a much faster rate than are the experiments with school-based governance models.

Why should this surprise us? Tendencies toward de-skilling jobs and disempowering workers, toward the elimination of reflection and thoughtfulness from work, and toward technically oriented and amoral centralized management are unfortunately part and parcel of our society. Many millions of people in the United States have already experienced a loss of power and control in their own daily lives.[21] Why should we assume that this won't happen to people involved in curriculum and education in general? The real issue is not what is happening, but why it has taken us so long to realize that we, like most other educators, do not stand above the centralizing and disempowering impulses and the political and economic forces that affect so many other individuals in this society. Perhaps the way that people in the field of curriculum are themselves educated—to believe that education is unconnected to economic, political, and ideological conflicts and that we can solve our problems by looking only within the school—is part of the reason for our reluctance to acknowledge these problems.

CONCLUSION

What can we do about this state of affairs? It should be obvious that I am not optimistic that curriculum scholars can make their solitary voices heard above those of the conservatives and neoconservatives, the centralizers, and the bureaucrats who now hold center stage. I am not arguing that curriculum scholars are powerless puppets controlled by large-scale social forces beyond their control. But I am suggesting that we

be realistic. If social, political, and economic forces and movements have played such a large role in determining the shape and content of the curriculum in the past, then individual action by curriculum scholars will not be enough. We can and must join forces with other groups that stand in need of the knowledge of curricular debates and traditions and that wish to make schools more progressive in intent and outcome.

Numerous groups throughout the country are fighting to build a curriculum that reflects the knowledge and beliefs of all of us and not just those of one political and cultural group. Among them are the teachers in the Rethinking Schools group in Milwaukee, those involved in Substance in Chicago, and those involved in Chalkdust in New York City. Community-based advocacy groups, such as the Southern Coalition for Educational Equity, which has done important work in New Orleans; Chicago Schoolwatch; Parents United for Full Public School Funding in Washington, D.C.; the Citizens Education Center in Seattle; and People United for Better Schools in Newark are engaged in defending and building on many of the gains made over the past two decades in democratizing curriculum and teaching.[22] Curriculum scholars can join with these groups, contribute something of value to them, and—perhaps just as important—learn from them. Only by forming coalitions to restore a democratic vision in education will we be able to restore the voice of curriculum scholars to the public debates over whose knowledge should be taught. If we continue to stand above the fray, perhaps we don't deserve to have our voice restored.

The Right has done a good job of showing that decisions about the curriculum, about whose knowledge is to be made "official," are *inherently* matters of political and cultural power. And unless we learn to live in the real world and to find a *collective* voice that speaks for the long progressive educational tradition that lives in so many of us, the knowledge taught our children will reflect the fact that power is not shared equally. The sidelines may be comfortable places to sit. But sitting there will give us little influence on the lives of real children and teachers.

ENDNOTES

1. See, for example, William Reese, *Power and the Promise of School Reform* (New York: Routledge & Kegan Paul, 1986).
2. For further discussion of this point, see Michael W. Apple, *Ideology and Curriculum,* 2nd ed. (New York: Routledge, 1990).
3. Michael W. Apple, *Teachers and Texts* (New York: Routledge & Kegan Paul, 1986).
4. This is treated in considerably more detail in Michael W. Apple, "Redefining Equality," *Teachers College Record,* Winter 1988, pp. 167–84.
5. For interesting criticisms of Hirsch's proposals for "cultural literacy," see Herbert M. Kliebard, "Cultural Literacy or the Curate's Egg," *Journal of Curriculum Studies,* vol. 21, 1989, pp. 61–70; and Stanley Aronowitz and Henry Giroux, "Schooling, Culture, and Literacy in an Age of Broken Dreams," *Harvard Educational Review,* May 1988, pp. 172–94.
6. William J. Bennett, *Our Children and Our Country* (New York: Simon & Schuster, 1988), pp. 9–10.
7. Ibid., p. 10.
8. Michael W. Apple, *Education and Power* (New York: Routledge & Kegan Paul, 1985), Ch. 5.
9. Apple, *Teachers and Texts,* Ch. 3.
10. See, for example, some of the reflections on the previous decade of curriculum work in Elliot W. Eisner, ed., *Confronting Curriculum Reform* (Boston: Little, Brown, 1971); A. Harry Passow, ed., *Curriculum Crossroads* (New York: Teachers College Press, 1962); and Glenys Unruh and Robert Leeper, eds., *Influences in Curriculum Change* (Washington, D.C.: Association for Supervision and Curriculum Development, 1968).
11. Ralph Tyler, *Basic Principles of Curriculum and Instruction* (Chicago: University of Chicago Press, 1949).
12. Herbert M. Kliebard, "The Tyler Rationale," *School Review,* February 1970, pp. 259–72.
13. Apple, *Ideology and Curriculum.* Ch. 6.
14. Michael W. Apple, "Curriculum in the Year 2000: Tensions and Possibilities," *Phi Delta Kappan,* January 1983, pp. 321–26.
15. See Herbert M. Kliebard, *The Struggle for the American Curriculum* (New York: Routledge & Kegan Paul, 1986); and Kenneth Teitelbaum, "Contestation and Curriculum: The Efforts of American Socialists, 1900–1920," in Landon E. Beyer and Michael W. Apple, eds., *The Curriculum: Problems, Politics, and Possibilities* (Albany: State University of New York Press, 1988), pp. 32–55.
16. Apple, *Teachers and Texts,* Ch. 4; and Michael W. Apple, "Regulating the Text: The Socio/Historical Roots of State Control," *Educational Policy,* vol. 3, 1989, pp. 107–24.
17. See Apple, *Ideology and Curriculum, Education and Power,* and *Teachers and Texts.*
18. Apple, *Teachers and Texts,* Ch. 3.
19. See Apple, *Ideology and Curriculum;* and Aronowitz and Giroux, op. cit.
20. Apple, *Teachers and Texts,* Ch. 2; and idem, *Education and Power,* Ch. 5.
21. Marcus Raskin, *The Common Good* (New York: Routledge & Kegan Paul, 1986).
22. Ann Bastian et al., *Choosing Equality: The Case for Democratic Schooling* (Philadelphia: Temple University Press, 1986).

DISCUSSION QUESTIONS

1. How has training in professional educational programs contributed to the politics of rationalization and bureaucratization of schools?
2. How could graduate programs be conceived to ensure that curriculum specialists are trained to meet the challenges facing contemporary educators?
3. What role should curricular scholars play in current curricular debates?
4. What role should curricular scholars assume in determining the ethical and political questions concerning what content should be taught?
5. What must curriculum scholars do to make schools more progressive?

Teachers, Public Life, and Curriculum Reform

HENRY A. GIROUX

FOCUSING QUESTIONS

1. How does curriculum discourse influence teaching?
2. What role does the language of curriculum play in influencing student outcomes?
3. How are curriculum and politics related?
4. In what ways does the curriculum reflect dominant social views?
5. How does politics influence the role of the teacher?
6. Why are the notions of accountability and practicality superordinate to concerns related to equity, equality, community, and social justice?

REASSERTING THE PRIMACY OF THE POLITICAL IN CURRICULUM THEORY

The connection between curriculum and teaching is structured by a series of issues that are not always present in the language of the current educational reform movement. This is evident, for instance, in the way mainstream educational reformers often ignore the problematic relationship between curriculum as a socially constructed narrative, on the one hand, and the interface of teaching and politics on the other. Mainstream curriculum reformers often view curriculum as an objective text that merely has to be imparted to students.[1]

In opposition to this view, I want to argue that the language used by administrators, teachers, students, and others involved in either constructing, implementing, or receiving the classroom curriculum actively produces particular social identities, "imagined communities," specific competencies, and distinctive ways of life. Moreover, the language of curriculum like other discourses does not merely reflect a pregiven reality; on the contrary, it selectively offers depictions of the larger world through representations that people struggle over to name what counts as knowledge, what counts as communities of learning, what social relationships matter, and what visions of the future can be represented as legitimate (Aronowitz & Giroux, 1993).

Of course, if curriculum is seen as a terrain of struggle, one that is shot through with ethical considerations, it becomes reasonable to assume that talk about teaching and curriculum should not be removed from considerations of history, power, and politics. After all, the language of curriculum is both historical and contingent. Theories of curriculum have emerged from past struggles and are often heavily weighted in favor of those who have power, authority, and institutional legitimation.

Curriculum is also political in that state governments, locally elected schools boards, and powerful business and publishing interests exercise enormous influence over teaching practices and curriculum policies (Apple & Christian-

Smith, 1991). Moreover, the culture of the school is often representative of those features of the dominant culture that it affirms, sustains, selects, and legitimizes. Thus, the distinction between high and low status academic subjects, the organization of knowledge into disciplines, and the allocation of knowledge and symbolic rewards to different groups indicates how politics work to influence the curriculum.

Within dominant versions of curriculum and teaching, there is little room theoretically to understand the dynamics of power as it works in the schools, particularly around the mechanisms of tracking, racial and gender discrimination, testing, and other mechanisms of exclusion (Oaks, 1985). Mainstream educational reformers such as William Bennett, Chester Finn, and Dianne Ravitch exhibit little understanding of schooling as a site that actively produces different histories, social groups, and student identities who exist under profound conditions of inequality. This is true, in part, because many dominant versions of curriculum and teaching legitimate themselves through unproblematized claims to objectivity and an obsession with empiricist forms of accountability. But, more importantly, many mainstream theorists of curriculum refuse to link schooling to the complex political, economic, and cultural relations that structure it as a borderland of movement and translation rather than as a fixed and unitary site.

When inserted into this matrix of power, difference, and social justice, schools cannot be abstracted from the larger society in which histories mix, languages and identities intermingle, values clash, and different groups struggle over how they are represented and how they might represent themselves. Questions of representation, justice, and power are central to any critical theory of curriculum. This is especially true in a society in which African Americans, women, and other people of color are vastly underrepresented in both schools and other dominant cultural institutions. Of course, the, issue of representation as I am using it here suggests that meaning is always

political, actively involved in producing diverse social positions and inextricably implicated in relations of power.

Educators generally exhibit a deep suspicion of politics, and this is not unwarranted when politics is reduced to a form of dogmatism. And, yet, it is impossible for teachers to become agents in the classroom without a broader understanding of politics and the emancipatory possibilities that it provides for thinking about and shaping their own practices. Recognizing the politics of one's location as an educator should not imply that one's pedagogical practice is inflexible, fixed, or intolerant. To insist that teachers recognize the political nature of their own work can be understood as part of a broader critical effort to make them self-reflective of the interests and assumptions that shape their classroom practices. Roger Simon (1992) captures this sentiment by arguing that by inserting the political back into the discourse of teaching, educators can "initiate rather than close off the problem of responsibility" (p. 16) for those classroom practices generated by their claim to knowledge and authority.

In what follows, I want to offer an alternative language for defining the purpose and meaning of teacher work. While I have talked about teachers as intellectuals in another context, I want to extend this analysis by analyzing what implications exist for redefining teachers as public intellectuals.[2] In part, I want to explore this position by drawing upon my own training as a teacher and some of the problems I had to face when actually working in the public schools. I will conclude by highlighting some of the defining principles that might structure the content and context of what it means for teachers to assume the role of a public intellectual.

TRADITION AND THE PEDAGOGY OF RISK

> Let me begin by saying that we are living through a very dangerous time. . . . We are in a revolutionary situation, no matter how unpopular that word has become in this country. The society in which

we live is desperately menaced, not by [the cold war] but from within. So any citizen of this country who figures himself as responsible—and particularly those of you who deal with the minds and hearts of young people—must be prepared to "go for broke." Or to put it another way, you must understand that in the attempt to correct so many generations of bad faith and cruelty, when it is operating not only in the classroom but in society, you will meet the most fantastic, the most brutal, and the most determined resistance. There is no point in pretending that this won't happen. . . . [And yet] The obligation of anyone who thinks of him or herself as responsible is to examine society and try to change it and to fight it—at no matter what risk. This is the only hope society has. This is the only way societies change (Baldwin, 1988, p. 3).

I read the words of the famed African-American novelist James Baldwin less as a prescription for cynicism and powerlessness than I do as an expression of hope. Baldwin's words are moving because he confers a sense of moral and political responsibility upon teachers by presupposing that they are critical agents who can move between theory and practice in order to take risks, to refine their visions, and to make a difference for both their students and the world in which they live. In order to take up Baldwin's challenge for teachers to "go for broke," to act in the classroom and in the world with courage and dignity, it is important for educators to recognize that the current challenge facing public schools is one of the most serious that any generation of existing and prospective teachers has ever had to face. Politically, the United States has lived through twelve years of reforms in which teachers have been invited to de-skill themselves, to become technicians, or, in more ideological terms, to accept their role as "clerks of the empire." We live at a time when state legislators and federal officials are increasingly calling for the testing of teachers and the implementation of standardized curriculum; at the same time, legislators and government officials are ignoring the most important people in the reform effort, the teachers. Within this grim

scenario, the voices of teachers have been largely absent from the debate about education. It gets worse.

Economically, the working conditions of teachers, especially those in the urban districts with a low tax base, have badly deteriorated. The story is a familiar one: overcrowded classrooms, inadequate resources, low salaries, and a rise in teacher-directed violence. In part, this is due to the increased financial cutbacks to the public sector by the federal government, the middle-class tax revolt of the 1970s that has put a ceiling on the ability of cities and states to raise revenue for public services, and the refusal by wide segments of the society to believe that public schooling is essential to the health of a democratic society. Compounding these problems is a dominant vision of schooling defined largely through the logic of corporate values and the imperatives of the marketplace. Schools are being treated as if their only purpose is to train future workers, and teachers are being viewed as corporate foot soldiers whose role is to provide students with the skills necessary for the business world. In short, part of the crisis of teaching is the result of a vision of schooling that subordinates issues of equity, community, and social justice to pragmatic considerations that enshrine the marketplace and accountability schemes that standardize the social relations of schooling. The political and ideological climate does not look favorable for teachers at the moment. But it does offer prospective and existing teachers the challenge to engage in dialogue and debate on important issues such as the nature and purpose of teacher preparation, the meaning of educational leadership, and the dominant forms of classroom teaching.

I think that if existing and future teachers are willing to go for broke, they will need to re-imagine teaching as part of a project of critique and possibility. But there is more at stake here than simply a change in who controls the conditions under which teachers work. Although this is important, what is also needed is a new language, a new way of naming, ordering, and representing how power works in schools. It is precisely through a more critical language that teachers might be able to recognize the power of their own agency to raise and act upon such questions as: What range of purposes should schools serve? What knowledge is of most worth? What does it mean for teachers and students to know something? What direction should teachers and students choose? What notions of authority should structure teaching and learning? These questions are important because they force educators to engage in a process of self-critique while simultaneously they highlight the central role that teachers might play in any viable attempt to reform the public schools.

My own journey into teaching was largely shaped by undergraduate education training and my first year of student teaching. While the content and context of these experiences shaped my initial understanding of myself as a teacher, they did not prepare me for the specific tasks and problems that I had to confront in my first job. In what follows, I want to speak from my own experiences to illuminate the shortcomings of the educational theories that both shaped my perceptions of teaching and the classroom practices I was expected to implement.

LEARNING TO BE A TECHNICIAN

During the time that I studied to be a teacher, for the most part, I learned how to master classroom methods, read Bloom's taxonomy, and became adept at administering tests, but I was never asked to question how testing might be used as a sorting device to track and marginalize certain groups. Like many prospective teachers of my generation, I was taught how to master a body of knowledge defined within separate academic disciplines, but I never learned to question what the hierarchical organization of knowledge meant and how it conferred authority and power. For example, I was never taught to raise questions about what knowledge was worth knowing and why, why schools legitimated some forms of knowledge and ignored others, why English was more important

than art, and why it was considered unworthy to take a course in which one worked with one's hands. I never engaged in a classroom discussion about whose interests were served through the teaching and legitimacy of particular forms of school knowledge, or how knowledge served to silence and disempower particular social groups. Moreover, I was not given the opportunity to reflect upon the authoritarian principles that actually structure classroom life and how these could be understood by analyzing social, political, and economic conditions outside of schools. If a student slept in the morning at his or her desk, I was taught to approach the issue as a problem of discipline and management. I was not taught to recognize the social conditions that may have caused such behavior. That is, to the possibility that the student might have a drug-related problem or might be hungry, sick, or simply exhausted because of the conditions in his or her home life. I learned quickly to separate out the problems of society from the problems of schooling and hence became illiterate in understanding the complexity of the relationship between schools and the larger social order.

My initial teaching assignment was in a school in which the teacher turnover rate exceeded 85% each year. The first day I walked into that school I was met by some students hanging out in the lobby. They greeted me with stares born of territorial rights and suspicion and one of them jokingly asked me: "Hey man, your new, what's your name?" I remember thinking they had violated some sort of rule regarding teacher-student relationships by addressing me in that way. Questions of identity, culture, and racism had not been factored into my understanding of teaching and schooling. I had no idea that the questions that would be raised for me that year had less to do with the sterile language of methods I had learned as an undergraduate than they did with my becoming culturally and politically literate about the context-specific histories and experiences that revealed the places from which my students came and how they viewed themselves and others. I had no idea of how important it was to create a meaningful and safe classroom so that I could connect my teaching to their own languages, cultures, and life experiences. I soon found out that giving students some sense of power and ownership over their own educational experience has more to do with developing a language that was risk taking and self-critical for me and meaningful, practical, and transformative for them. During that first year, I also learned something about the ways in which many school administrators are educated.

LEADERSHIP WITHOUT VISION

During that first year, I rented movies from the American Friends Service Committee, ignored the officially designated curriculum textbooks, and eventually put my own books and magazine articles on reserve in the school library for my students to read. Hoping to give my students some control over the conditions in which they could produce knowledge, I encouraged them to produce their own texts through the use of school video equipment, cameras, and daily journals. Within a very short time, I came in conflict with the school principal. He was a mix between General Patton and the Encino Man. At six foot three, weighing in at 250 pounds, his presence seemed a bit overwhelming and intimidating. The first time he called me into his office, I learned something about how he was educated. He told me that students should be quiet in classrooms, teachers should stick to giving lectures and writing on the board, and that I was never to ask a student a question that he or she could not answer. He further suggested that rather than developing my own materials in class I should use the curricula packages made available through the good wishes of local businesses and companies. While clearly he was a reflection, if not a parody, of the worst kind of teacher training, he adamantly believed that strict management controls, rigid systems of accountability, and lock-step discipline were at the heart of educational leadership. Hence, I found myself in a secular version of hell. This was a school in which teaching became reduced to the sterile logic of flow charts. Moreover, it

was a school in which power was wielded largely by white, male administrators who further reinforced the isolation and despair of most of the teachers. I engaged in forms of guerrilla warfare with this administration. But in order to survive I had to enlist the help of a few other teachers and some members of the community. At the end of the school year, I was encouraged not to come back. Fortunately, I had another teaching job back east and ended up in a much better school.

In retrospect, this dominant view of educational leadership had a resurgence during the Reagan and Bush eras. Its overall effect has been to limit a teacher's control over the development and planning of curriculum, to reinforce the bureaucratic organization of the school, and to remove teachers from the process of judging and implementing classroom instruction. This is evident in the growing call for national testing, national curriculum standards, and the concerted attack on multicultural curricula. The ideology that guides this model and its view of pedagogy is that the behavior of teachers needs to be controlled and made consistent and predictable across different schools and student populations. The effect is not only to remove teachers from the process of deliberation and reflection, but also to routinize the nature of learning and classroom pedagogy. In this approach, it is assumed that all students can learn from the same standardized materials, instructional techniques, and modes of evaluation. That students come from different histories, experiences, and cultures is strategically ignored within this approach. The notion that pedagogy should be attentive to specific contexts is ignored.

TEACHERS AS PUBLIC INTELLECTUALS

I want to challenge these views my arguing that one way to rethink and restructure the nature of a teacher's work is to view teachers as public intellectuals. The unease expressed about the identity and role of teachers as public intellectuals has a long tradition in the United States and has become the focus of a number of recent debates. On one level, there are conservatives who argue that teachers who address public issues from the perspective of a committed position are simply part of what they call the politically correct movement. Thus, there is a deep suspicion of any attempt to open up for educators the possibility of addressing pressing social issues and connecting them to their teaching. Moreover, within the broad parameters of this view, schools are seen as apolitical institutions whose primary purpose is to both prepare students for the work place and to reproduce the alleged common values that define the "American" way of life.[3] At the same time, many liberals have argued that while teachers should address public issues they should do so from the perspective of a particular teaching methodology. This is evident from Gerald Graff's (1992) call for educators to teach the conflicts. In this view, the struggle over representations replaces how a politics of meaning might help students identify, engage, and transform relations of power that generate the material conditions of racism, sexism, poverty, and other oppressive conditions. Moreover, some radical feminists have argued that the call for teachers to be public intellectuals promotes leadership models that are largely patriarchal and overly rational in the forms of authority that they secure. While there may be an element of truth in all of these positions, they all display enormous theoretical shortcomings. Conservatives often refuse to problematize their own version of what is legitimate intellectual knowledge and how it works to secure particular forms of authority by simply labeling as "politically correct" those individuals, groups, or views that challenge the basic tenets of the status quo. Liberals, on the other hand, inhabit a terrain that is conflicted, wavering between rejecting a principled standpoint from which to teach and staunchly arguing for a pedagogy that is academically rigorous and fair. Caught between a discourse of fairness and the appeal to use provocative teaching methods, liberals have no language for clarifying the moral visions that structure their views of the relationship between knowledge and authority and the practices that it promotes. Moreover, increasingly they have come to believe that teaching from a particular standpoint is tantamount to imposing an ideological position upon students. This has led in some cases to a form of McCarthyism in which critical educators are summarily dismissed as being guilty of ideological indoctrination. While the feminist critique is the most interesting, it underplays the possibility for using authority in ways that allow teachers to be more self-critical while simultaneously providing conditions in which students can recognize the possibility for democratic agency in both themselves and others. Operating out of a language of dichotomies, some feminist education critics essentialize the positions of their opponents and in doing so present a dehistoricized and reductionistic view of critical pedagogy. Most importantly, all of these positions share in the failure to address the possibility for teachers to become a force for democratization both within and outside of schools.

As public intellectuals, teachers must bring to bear in their classrooms and other pedagogical sites the courage, analytical tools, moral vision, time, and dedication that are necessary to return schools to their primary task and that are to be places of critical education in the service of creating a public sphere of citizens who are able to exercise power over their own lives and especially over the conditions of knowledge acquisition. Central to any such reform effort is the recognition that democracy is not a set of formal rules of participation, but the lived experience of empowerment for the vast majority. Moreover, the call for schools as democratic public spheres should not be limited to the call for equal access to schools, equal opportunity, or other arguments defined in terms of the principles of equality. Equality is a crucial aspect of school democratization, but teachers should not limit their demands to the call for equality. Instead, the rallying cry of teachers should be organized around the practice of empowerment for the vast majority of students in this country who need to be educated in the spirit of a critical democracy.[4]

This suggests another dimension in defining the role of public intellectuals. Such intellectuals must combine their role as educators and citizens. This implies they must connect the practice of classroom teaching to the operation of power in the larger society. At the same time, they must be attentive to those broader social forces that influence the workings of schooling and pedagogy. What is at issue here is a commitment on the part of teachers as public intellectuals to extend the principles of social justice to all spheres of economic, political, and cultural life. Within this discourse, the experiences that constitute the production of knowledge, identities, and social values in the schools are inextricably linked to the quality of moral and political life of the wider society. Hence, the reform of schooling must be seen as a part of a wider revitalization of public life.

This should not suggest that as public intellectuals, teachers represent a vanguard group dedicated to simply reproducing another master narrative. In fact, as public intellectuals it is important for them to link their role as critical agents to their ability to be critical of their own politics while constantly engaging in dialogue with other educators, community people, various cultural workers, and students. As public intellectuals, teachers need to be aware of the limits of their own positions, make their pedagogies context specific, challenge the current organization of knowledge into fixed disciplines, and work in solidarity with others to gain some control over their working conditions. At the very least, this suggests that teachers will have to struggle on many different fronts in order to transform those conditions of work and learning that exist in the schools. This means not only working with community people, teachers, students, and parents to open up progressive spaces within classrooms but also forming alliances with other cultural workers in order to debate and shape educational policy at the local, state, and federal levels of government.

As public intellectuals, teachers need to provide those conditions for students in which they can learn that knowledge and power can be emancipatory, that their histories and experiences matter, and that what they say and do can play a part in the wider struggle to change the world around them. More specifically, teachers need to argue for forms of pedagogy that close the gap between the school and the real world. The curriculum needs to be organized around knowledge that relates to communities, cultures, and traditions in a way that give students a sense of history, identity, and place. This suggests pedagogical approaches that do more than make learning context specific, it also points to the need to expand the range of cultural texts that inform what counts as knowledge. As public intellectuals, teachers need to understand and use those electronically-mediated knowledge forms that constitute the terrain of popular culture. This is the world of media texts-videos, films, music, and other mechanisms of popular culture that exist outside of the technology of print and the book. Put another way, the content of the curriculum needs to affirm and critically enrich the meaning, language, and knowledge that students actually use to negotiate and inform their lives.

While it is central for teachers to expand the relevance of the curriculum to include the richness and diversity of the students they actually teach, they also need to correspondingly decenter the curriculum. That is, students should be actively involved with issues of governance, "including setting learning goals, selecting courses, and having their own, autonomous organizations, including a free press" (Aronowitz, forthcoming). Not only does the distribution of power among teachers, students, and administrators provide the conditions for students to become agents in their learning process, it also provides the basis for collective learning, civic action, and ethical responsibility. Moreover, such agency emerges as a lived experience rather than as the mastery of an academic subject.

In addition, as public intellectuals, teachers need to make the issue of cultural difference a defining principal of curriculum development and research. In an age of shifting demographics, large scale immigration, and multiracial communities, teachers must make a firm commitment to cultural difference as central to the relationship of schooling and citizenship (Giroux, 1992). In the first instance, this means dismantling and deconstructing the legacy of nativism and racial chauvinism that has defined the rhetoric of school reform for the last decade. The Reagan and Bush era witnessed a full fledged attack on the rights of minorities, civil rights legislation, affirmative action, and the legitimation of curriculum reforms pandering to Eurocentric interests. Teachers can affirm their commitment to democratic public life and cultural democracy by struggling in and outside of their classrooms in solidarity with others to reverse these policies in order to make schools more attentive to the cultural resources that students bring to the public schools. At one level, this means working to develop legislation that protects the civil rights of all groups. Equally important is the need for teachers to take the lead in encouraging programs that open school curricula to the narratives of cultural difference, without falling into the trap of merely romanticizing the experience of Otherness. At stake here is the development of an educational policy that asserts public education as part of a broader ethical and political discourse, one that both challenges and transforms those curricula reforms of the last decade that are profoundly racist in context and content. This suggests at least changing the terms of the debate on the relationship between schooling and national identity, moving away from an assimilationist ethic and the profoundly Eurocentric fantasies of a common culture to one that links national identity to diverse traditions and histories.

CONCLUSION

In short, as public intellectuals, teachers need to address the imperatives of citizenship. In part, this means addressing how schools can create the conditions for students to be social agents willing to struggle for expanding the critical public cultures that make a democracy viable. Conse-

quently, any notion of pedagogy must be seen as a form of cultural politics, that is, a politics that highlights the role of education, as it takes place in a variety of public sites, to open up rather than close down the possibilities for keeping justice and hope alive at a time of shrinking possibilities.

ENDNOTES

1. This is particularly true with respect to those mainstream reformers arguing for national standards and testing. In this discourse, students are always on the receiving end of the learning experience. It is as if the histories, experiences, and communities that shape their identities and sense of place are irrelevant to what is taught and how it is taught. See, for example, Hirsch (1987), Finn, Jr., and Ravitch (1987). For an alternative to this position, see Apple (1993), Giroux (1988b), and Giroux (1993). For an examination of schools that view teachers as more than clerks and technicians, see Wood (1993).
2. I have taken up this issue more extensively in Giroux (1988) and Aronowitz and Giroux (1993).
3. For a trenchant analysis of the political correctness movement, see Aronowitz (1993), especially Chapter 1. See also Frank (1993).
4. I take this issue up in Giroux (1988).

REFERENCES

Apple, M. (1993). *Official Knowledge* (New York: Routledge, 1993).
Apple, M., and L. K. Christian-Smith, eds. (1992). *The Politics of the Textbook* (New York: Routledge).
Aronowitz, S. (1993). *Roll Over Beethoven: The Return of Cultural Strife* (Hanover: Wesleyan University Press, 1993).
Aronowitz, S. (forthcoming). "A Different Perspective on Educational Inequality." *The Review of Education/Pedagogy/Cultural Studies.*
Aronowitz, S., and H. A. Giroux (1993). *Education Still Under Siege* (Westport, Conn.: Bergin and Garvey Press).
Baldwin, J. (1988) . "A Talk to Teachers." In Rick Simonson and Scott Waler, eds. *Multicultural Literacy: Opening the American Mind* (Saint Paul, Minn.: Graywolf Press, 1988), pp. 3–12.
Finn, Jr. C., and D. Ravitch (1987). *What Our 17-Year-Olds Know* (New York: Harper and Row).

Frank, J. (1993). "In the Waiting Room: Canons, Communities, 'Political Correctness'." In Mark Edmunson, ed. *Wild Orchids: Messages from American Universities* (New York: Penguin).

Giroux, H. (1988a). *Teachers as Intellectuals* (Westport, Conn: Bergin and Garvey Press).

Giroux, H. (1988b). *Schooling and the Struggle for Public Life* (Minneapolis: University of Minnesota Press).

Giroux, H. (1992). *Border Crossings* (New York: Routledge).

Giroux, H. (1993). *Living Dangerously: The Politics of Multiculturalism* (New York: Peter Lang).

Graff, G. (1992). "Teaching the Conflicts." In Darryl J. Gless and Barbara Hernstein Smith, eds. *The Politics of Liberal Education* (Durham: Duke University Press), pp. 57–73.

Hirsch, E. D. (1987). *Cultural Literacy* (Boston: Houghton Mifflin).

Oaks, J. (1985). *Keeping Track: How Schools Structure Inequality* (New Haven: Yale University Press).

Simon, R. (1992). *Teaching Against the Grain* (Westport, Conn.: Bergin and Garvey Press).

West, C. (1990). "The New Politics of Difference," *October,* 53: 93–109.

Wood, G. (1993). *Schools That Work.* (New York: Penguin Books).

DISCUSSION QUESTIONS

1. How do bureaucratic organization structures influence the teacher's role?
2. What kinds of organizational changes would be needed to create schools that were authentic democratic institutions?
3. In what ways will the curriculum need to be restructured in order to empower students? Teachers?
4. How can pedagogy influence cultural politics?
5. As public intellectuals, what do teachers need to provide?

PRO-CON CHART 1

Should the schools introduce a values-centered curriculum for all students?

PRO	CON
1. There are certain basic core values that educators involved in curriculum development should be able to agree upon.	1. Values are not objective or neutral. Therefore educators involved in curriculum development cannot easily agree upon them.
2. The classroom is a place in which students can define what values are and share a diversity of viewpoints.	2. Engaging students in discussion will lead to peer pressure and indoctrination.
3. Students should be able to explore their values in a classroom setting.	3. Unstated teacher attitudes may impinge upon students' ability to identify their own preferences.
4. Valuing is part of citizenship education and therefore schools have a responsibility to teach valuing.	4. Values is not part of civic education. Moreover, values education is the responsibility of the home, not the school.
5. Students need to learn to express themselves forthrightly and to make choices without fear and condemnation.	5. There is no assurance that the teacher can model values or choosing, much less provide appropriate instructional activities that will promote these behaviors.

CASE STUDY 1

A Clash Concerning the Arts Curriculum

Andrea Brown had recently been hired as the assistant principal in charge of curriculum at the Newberry Elementary School. Brown, an advocate for arts education, had a humanistic orientation to curriculum. The principal, Al Sigel, had a essentialist view of the curriculum. Adhering to a back to basics focus, Sigel felt that math, science, and computer education should be emphasized and that arts courses were frivolous.

The state code and the school's educational manuals indicated that all students were required to receive 40 minutes of music, art, and dance per week. Without discussing his intentions with Brown or eliciting faculty reactions, Sigel distributed a memo to the staff at the first faculty meeting of the school year indicating that music, art, and dance courses were to be eliminated from the academic schedule as specific courses and that teachers should integrate these subjects into social studies and English. This extra class time was to be equally distributed to provide additional math, science, and computer education classes.

Upon learning about this decision, several parents approached Brown and asked that she assist them in getting the arts classes placed back into the schedule. Brown felt an ethical and educational obligation to address the parents' concern. While cognizant of the legal implications, she also believed the arts are an essential curriculum component. She pondered how she might approach this situation.

Assume that you are the assistant principal. Consider the circumstances described in the case. How would you propose to handle the parents' concerns?

Consider also the implications of taking one of the following actions in response to the parents' request:

1. Confront the principal and cite the state and school mandated requirements concerning course time allocations?

2. Resign from the position and state that she and Sigel had irresolvable differences regarding their philosophical orientation to curriculum?

3. Take these curriculum-related concerns to the district superintendent in charge of instruction?

4. Present an inservice workshop to the teaching staff about the intrinsic and utilitarian values of an arts education?

5. Lead a coalition of concerned parents and ask for a meeting with the principal?

PART TWO

Curriculum and Teaching

INTRODUCTION

What are the trends in teaching that influence student outcomes and teachers' selection of instructional approaches? What method is most appropriate for a diverse population of learners? In Chapter 7, Herbert Walberg considers the advantages and disadvantages of different teaching techniques. He explores how information from psychology has influenced curriculum development. Next, Jere Brophy discusses how research on school effects and teacher effects have influenced teaching and learning. He examines the strategies that characterize good subject matter teaching and that lead to successful student outcomes.

In Chapter 9, Allan Ornstein describes the confusion concerning the referents that should be measured in teacher effectiveness research. He explores the limitations of product oriented research and recommends that we emphasize both process and product teacher research. He suggests that research on teaching should focus on learners, not teachers and be revised to fit varied teaching contexts. In Chapter 10, Elliot Eisner criticizes formalized methods and bureaucratized procedures for stifling spontaneity and the potential of unanticipated discoveries. He advocates for an approach to teaching that permits teachers to use their intuition. This perspective would consider the teacher's ability to respond to the nuances that arise in teacher-student interaction, an everyday occurrence.

In Chapter 11, Lee Shulman argues that the results of teacher effectiveness research should not constitute the sole basis for defining the knowledge base of teaching. He suggests that teaching involves understanding, reasoning, transformation, and reflection. Shulman presents a six-step model that supports his conception of pedagogy and he portrays the processes involved in pedagogical reasoning and action.

In the final chapter of Part Two, Katherine Cushing, Donna Sabers, and David Berliner explore the factors that influence the perceptions of teachers at different stages in their professional development. The authors point out how expert, advanced beginners, and novices differ in ways that they view classroom processes and the teacher's role.

Productive Teachers: Assessing the Knowledge Base

HERBERT J. WALBERG

FOCUSING QUESTIONS

1. *What are the components of teaching that emphasize what teachers do?*
2. *What does the behavioral model emphasize concerning cues, engagement, correctives, and reinforcement?*
3. *How do explicit teaching and comprehension teaching differ?*
4. *What is open education?*
5. *How does programmed instruction, mastery learning, adaptive, and computer-assisted instruction differ in terms of planning and instructional components?*
6. *How do the aims of accelerated programs, ability grouping, whole-group instruction, and cooperative learning programs differ?*
7. *What approaches and goals are emphasized by microteaching and inservice education?*

Some teaching techniques have remarkable effects on learning, while others confer only trivial advantages or even hinder the learning process. Over the past decade, there has been an explosion of research activity centering on the question of what constitutes effective teaching. Ten years ago, several psychologists observed signs of a "quiet revolution" in educational research. Five years later, nearly 3,000 studies of effective teaching techniques existed. By 1987 an Australian/U.S. team was able to assess 134 reviews of 7,827 field studies and several large-scale U.S. and international surveys of learning.[1]

In this article I will give an overview of the findings to date on elementary and secondary school students and will evaluate the more recent and definitive reviews of research on teaching and instruction. Surveying the vast literature on the effects of various instructional methods allows us to consider the advantages and disadvantages of different techniques—including some effective ones that are no longer popular.

I will begin by considering the effects of the psychological elements of teaching, and I will discuss methods and patterns of teaching that a single teacher can accomplish without unusual arrangements or equipment. Then I will turn to systems of instruction that require special planning, student grouping, and materials. Next I will describe effects that are unique to particular methods of teaching reading, writing, science, and mathematics. Finally, I will discuss special students and techniques for dealing with them and the effects of particular types of training on teachers. It is important to bear in mind that, when we try to apply in our own classrooms the methods we have read about, we may attain results that are half—or twice—as good as the average estimates reported below. Our success will depend not only on careful implementation but also on our purposes. The best saw swung as a hammer does little good.

PSYCHOLOGICAL ELEMENTS

A little history will help us to understand the evolution of psychological research on teaching. Even though educators require balance, psychologists have often emphasized thought, feeling, or behavior at the expense of the other two components of the psyche. Today, thinking or cognition is sovereign in psychology, but half a century ago behaviorists insisted on specific operational definitions (and they continue to do so). In particular, Yale psychologists John Dollard and Neal Miller, stimulated by E. L. Thorndike and B. F. Skinner, wrote about cues, responses, and positive reinforcement, especially in psychotherapy. Later Miller and Dollard isolated three components of teaching—cues, engagement, and reinforcement—that are similar to the elements of input, process, and output in physiology.[2] Their influential work led researchers to consider what teachers *do* instead of focusing on their age, experience, certification, college degrees, or other factors not directly connected to what their students learn.[3]

The behavioral model emphasized 1) the quality of the instructional cues impinging on the learner, 2) the learner's active engagement, and 3) the reinforcements or rewards that encourage continuing effort over time. Benjamin Bloom recognized, however, that in cycles of cues and effort learners may fail the first time or even repeatedly. Thus they may practice incorrect behavior, and so they cannot be reinforced. Therefore, he emphasized feedback to correct errors and frequent testing to check progress. Inspired by John Carroll's model of school learning, Bloom also emphasized engaged learning time and stressed that some learners require much more time than others.[4]

The effects of cues, engagement, reinforcement, and corrective feedback on student learning are enormous.[5] The research demonstrating these effects has been unusually rigorous and well-controlled. Even though the research was conducted in school classes, the investigators helped to insure precise timing and deployment of the elements and relied on short-term studies, which usually lasted less than a month. Similar effects are difficult to sustain for long time periods.

Cues

As operationalized, cues show students what is to be learned and explain how to learn it. Their quality depends on the clarity, salience, and meaningfulness of explanations and directions provided by the teacher, the instructional materials, or both. Ideally, as the learners gain confidence, the salience and number of cues can be reduced.

Engagement

The extent to which students actively and persistently participate in learning until appropriate responses are firmly entrenched in their repertoires is known as engagement. Such participation can be indexed by the extent to which the teacher engages students in overt or covert activity. A high degree of engagement is indicated by an absence of irrelevant behavior and by concentration on tasks, enthusiastic contributions to group discussion, and lengthy study.

Corrective Feedback

Corrective feedback remedies errors in oral or written responses. Ideally, students should waste little time on incorrect responses, and teachers should detect difficulties rapidly and then remedy them by reteaching or using alternative methods. When necessary, teachers should also provide students with additional time for practice.

Reinforcement

The immense effort elicited by athletics, games, and other cooperative and competitive activities illustrates the power of immediate and direct reinforcement and shows that some endeavors are intrinsically rewarding. By comparison, classroom reinforcement may seem crass or jejune. The usual classroom reinforcers are acknowledgment of correctness and social approval, typically expressed by praise or a smile. More unusual reinforcers include providing contingent activity—for example, initiating a music lesson or other enjoyable activity as a reward for 90% correctness on a math test. Other reinforcers are tokens or check marks that are accumulated for discrete accomplishments and that can be exchanged for tangible reinforcers such as cookies, trinkets, or toys.

In special education programs, students have been reinforced not only for academic achievement but also for minutes spent on reading, for attempts to learn, and for the accuracy with which they perform tasks. Margo Mastropieri and Thomas Scruggs have shown that results can be impressive when the environment can be rigorously controlled and when teachers can accurately gear reinforcement to performance, as in programs for unruly or emotionally disturbed students. Improved behavior and achievement, however, may fail to extend past the period of reinforcement or beyond the special environment.[6]

Educators ordinarily confine reinforcement to marks, grades, and awards because they must assume that students work for such intangible, long-term goals as pleasing parents, furthering their education, achieving success in later life, and the intrinsic satisfaction of learning itself. Even so, when corrective feedback and reinforcement are clear, rapid, and appropriate, they can powerfully affect learning by efficiently signaling students what to do next. In ordinary classrooms, then, the chief value of reinforcement is informational rather than motivational.

METHODS OF TEACHING

The psychological elements just discussed undergird many teaching methods and the design of most instructional media. Techniques to improve the affective or informational content of cues, engagement, correctives, and reinforcement have shown a wide range of effects.

Cues

Advance organizers are brief overviews that relate new concepts or terms to previous learning. They are effective if they connect new learning and old. Those delivered by the teacher or graphically illustrated in texts work best.

Adjunct questions alert students to key questions that should be answered—particularly in texts. They work best when questions are repeated on posttests, and they work moderately well when posttest questions are similar or related to the adjuncts. As we might expect, however, adjunct questions divert attention from incidental material that might otherwise be learned.

Goal setting suggests specific objectives, guidelines, methods, or standards for learning that can be spelled out explicitly. Like the use of adjunct questions, goal setting sacrifices incidental for intended learning.

Learning hierarchies assume that instruction can be made more efficient if the facts, skills, or ideas that logically or psychologically precede others are presented first. Teaching and instructional media sequenced in this way appear to be slightly more effective. However, learners may adapt themselves to apparently ill-sequenced material, and it may even be advantageous to learn to do so, since human life, as Franz Kafka showed, may depart from logic.

Pretests are benchmarks for determining how much students learn under various methods of teaching. Psychologists have found, however, that pretests can have positive cuing effects if they show students what will be emphasized in instruction and on posttests.

Several principles follow from surveying the effects of these methods. To concentrate learning on essential points and to save time (as would be appropriate in training), remove elaborations and extraneous oral and written prose. To focus learners on selected questions or to teach them to find answers in elaborated prose, use adjunct questions and goal setting. To encourage the acquisition of as much undifferentiated material as possible, as in college lecture courses, assign big blocks of text and test students on randomly selected points.

Although the means of producing certain results may seem clear, reaching a consensus on educational purposes may be difficult. Clarity at the start saves time and helps learners to see things the teacher's way, but it limits individual autonomy and deep personal insights. Zen masters ask novices about the sound of one hand clapping and wait a decade or two for an answer. Hiroshi Azuma and Robert Hess find that Japanese mothers use more indirection and vagueness in teaching their young children than do assertive American mothers, and I have observed Japanese science teachers asking questions and leaving them long unresolved. Do the Japanese cultivate initiative and perseverance by these methods?

Engagement

High expectations transmit teachers' standards of learning and performance. They may function both as cues and as incentives for students to put extended effort and perseverance into learning.

Frequent tests increase learning by stimulating greater effort and providing intermittent feedback. However, the effects of tests on performance are larger for quizzes than for final examinations.

Questioning also appears to work by promoting engagement and may encourage deeper thinking—as in Plato's accounts of Socrates. Questioning has bigger effects in science than in other subjects. Mary Budd Rowe and Kenneth Tobin have shown that *wait time*—allowing students several seconds to reflect rather than the usual .9 of a second—leads to longer and better answers.

Correctives and Reinforcement

Corrective feedback remedies errors by reteaching, either with the same or with a different method. This practice has moderate effects that are somewhat higher in science—perhaps because learning science often involves more conceptualizing while learning other subjects may allow more memorizing.

Homework by itself constructively extends engaged learning time. Correctives and reinforcement in the form of grades and comments on homework raise its effects dramatically.

Praise has a small positive effect. For young or disturbed children, praise may lack the power of the tangible reinforcers used in psychological experiments. For students who are able to see ahead, grades and personal standards may be more powerful reinforcers than momentary encouragement. Moreover, praise may be under- or oversupplied; it may appear demeaning or sardonic; and it may pale in comparison with the disincentives to academic achievement afforded by youth culture in the form of cars, clothing, dating, and athletics.

None of this is to say that encouragement, incentives, and good classroom morale should be abandoned; honey may indeed be better than vinegar. Yet, as cognitive psychologists point out, the main classroom value of reinforcement may lie in its capacity to inform the student about progress rather than in its power to reward.

PATTERNS OF TEACHING

As explained above, methods of teaching enact or combine more fundamental psychological elements. By further extension, *patterns* of teaching integrate elements and methods of teaching. The process of determining these more inclusive formulations was another step in the evolution of psychological research on education. Behavioral research evolved in the 1950s from psychological laboratories to short-term, controlled classroom experiments on one element at a time. In the 1970s educational researchers tried to find patterns of effective practices from observations of ordinary teaching.

Thus behaviorists traded educational realism for theoretical parsimony and scientific rigor;

later psychologists preferred realism until their insights could be experimentally confirmed. Fortunately, the results of both approaches appear to converge. Moreover, it seems possible to incorporate the work of cognitive psychologists of the 1980s into an enlarged understanding of teaching.

Explicit Teaching

Explicit teaching can be viewed as traditional or conventional whole-group teaching done well. Since most teaching has changed little in the last three-quarters of a century and may not change substantially in the near future,[7] it is worth knowing how to make the usual practice most productive. Since it has evolved from ordinary practice, explicit teaching seems natural to carry out and does not disrupt conventional institutions and expectations. Furthermore, it can incorporate many previously discussed elements and methods.

Systematic research was initiated in the early 1960s by N. L. Gage, Donald Medley, and others who employed "process-product" investigations of the association between what teachers do and how much their students learn. Jere Brophy, Carolyn Evertson, Thomas Good, and Jane Stallings later contributed substantially to this effort. Walter Doyle, Penelope Peterson, and Lee Shulman put the results into a psychological context. Barak Rosenshine has periodically reviewed the research, and Gage and Margaret Needels recently measured the results and pointed out their implications.

The various contributors to the knowledge base do not completely agree about the essential components of explicit teaching, and they refer to it by different names, such as process-product, direct, active, and effective teaching. The researchers weigh their own results heavily, but Rosenshine, a long-standing and comprehensive reviewer, has taken an eagle's-eye view of the results.[8]

In his early reviews of the correlational studies, Rosenshine discussed the traits of effective teachers, including clarity, task orientation, enthusiasm, and flexibility, as well as their tendency to structure their presentations and occasionally to use student ideas. From later observational and control-group research, Rosenshine identified six phased functions of explicit teaching: 1) daily review, checking of homework, and reteaching if necessary; 2) rapid presentation of new content and skills in small steps; 3) guided student practice with close monitoring by teachers; 4) corrective feedback and instructional reinforcement; 5) independent practice in seatwork and homework, with a success rate of more than 90%; and 6) weekly and monthly review.

Comprehension Teaching

The heirs of Aristotle and of the Anglo-American tradition of Bacon, Locke, Thorndike, and Skinner objected to philosophical "armchair" opinions; mid-century behaviorists, particularly John Watson, constructively insisted on hard empirical data about learning. But they also saw the child's mind as a blank tablet and seemed to encourage active teaching and passive acquisition of isolated facts. Reacting to such atomism and to William James' "bucket" metaphor, cognitive psychologists in the early 1980s revived research on student-centered learning and "higher mental processes," in the tradition of Plato, Socrates, Kant, Rousseau, Dewey, Freud, and Piaget. In American hands, however, this European tradition has sometimes led to vacuity and permissiveness, as in the extremes of the "progressive education" movement of the 1930s.

Oddly, the Russian psychologist Lev Vygotsky hit on an influential compromise: emphasizing the two-way nature of teaching, he identified a "zone of proximal development," which extends from what learners can do independently to the maximum that they can do with the teacher's help.[9] Accordingly, teachers should set up "scaffolding" for building knowledge and then remove it when it becomes unnecessary. In mathematics, for example, the teacher can give prompts and examples, foster independent use, and then withdraw support. This approach is similar to the "prompting" and "fading" of the behavioral cues, and it seems commonsensical. It has revived interest in granting some autonomy to students.

During the 1980s cognitive research on teaching sought ways to encourage self-monitoring, self-teaching, or "metacognition" to foster independence. Skills were seen as important, but the learner's monitoring and management of them had priority, as though the explicit teaching functions of planning, allocating time, and reviewing were partly transferred to the learner.

For example, David Pearson outlined three phases: 1) modeling, in which the teacher exhibits the desired behavior; 2) guided practice, in which students perform with help from the teacher; and 3) application, in which students perform independently of the teacher—steps that correspond to explicit teaching functions. Anne Marie Pallincsar and Anne Brown described a program of "reciprocal teaching" that fosters comprehension by having students take turns in leading dialogues on pertinent features of a text. By assuming the kind of planning and executive control ordinarily exercised by teachers, students learn planning, structuring, and self-management. Perhaps that is why tutors learn from teaching and why we say that to learn something well, one should teach it.

Comprehension teaching encourages students to measure their progress toward explicit goals. If necessary, they can reallocate their time to different activities. In this way, self-awareness, personal control, and positive self-evaluation can be increased.[10]

LEARNER AUTONOMY IN SCIENCE

The National Science Foundation sponsored many studies of student inquiry and autonomy that showed that giving students opportunities to manipulate science materials, to contract with teachers about what to learn, to inquire on their own, and to engage in activity-based curricula all had substantial positive effects. Group- and self-direction, however, had smaller positive effects, and pass/fail and self-grading had small negative effects. Methods of providing greater learner autonomy may also work well in subjects other than science, as in the more radical approach that I discuss next.

OPEN EDUCATION

In the late 1960s, open educators expanded autonomy in the primary grades by enabling students to join teachers in planning educational purposes, means, and evaluation. In contrast to teacher- and textbook-centered education, open education gave students a voice in deciding what to learn— even to the point of writing their own texts to share with one another. Open educators tried to foster cooperation, critical thinking, constructive attitudes, and self-directed lifelong learning. They revived the spirit of the New England town meeting, Thoreau's self-reliance, Emerson's transcendentalism, and Dewey's progressivism. Their ideas also resonate with the "client-centered" psychotherapy of Carl Rogers, which emphasizes the "unconditional worth" of the person.

Rose Giaconia and Larry Hedges' synthesis of 153 studies showed that open education had worthwhile effects on creativity, independence, cooperation, attitudes toward teachers and schools, mental ability, psychological adjustment, and curiosity. Students in open programs had less motivation for grade grubbing, but they differed little from other students in actual achievement, self-concept, and anxiety.

However, Giaconia and Hodges also found that the open programs that were more effective in producing the positive outcomes with regard to attitudes, creativity, and self-concept sacrificed some academic achievement on standardized tests. These programs emphasized the role of the child in learning and the use of individualized instruction, manipulative materials, and diagnostic rather than norm-referenced evaluation. However, they did not include three other components thought by some to be essential to open programs: multi-age grouping, open space, and team teaching.

Giaconia and Hedges speculated that children in the most extreme open programs may do somewhat less well on conventional achievement tests because they have little experience with them. At any rate, it appears that open classrooms enhance several nonstandard outcomes without detracting from academic achievement unless they are radically extreme.[11]

INSTRUCTIONAL SYSTEMS

All the techniques discussed thus far can be planned and executed by a single teacher. They may entail some extra effort, encouragement, or training, but they do not call for unusual preparation or materials. In contrast, instructional systems require special arrangements and planning, and they often combine several components of instruction. Moreover, they tend to emphasize the adaptation of instruction to individual students rather than the adaptation of students to a fixed pattern of teaching. A little history will aid our understanding of current instructional systems.

Programmed Instruction

Developed in the 1950s, programmed instruction presents a series of "frames," each one of which conveys an item of information and requires a student response. *Linear programs* present a graduated series of frames that require such small increments in knowledge that learning steps may be nearly errorless and may be continuously reinforced by progression to the next frame. Able students proceed quickly under these conditions. *Branched programs* direct students back for reteaching when necessary, to the side for correctives, and ahead when they already know parts of the material. The ideas of continuous progress and branching influenced later developers, who tried to optimize learning by individualization, mastery learning, and adaptive instruction.

Individualization adapts instruction to individual needs by applying variations in speed or branching and by using booklets, worksheets, coaching, and the like. Perhaps because they have been vaguely defined and poorly operationalized, individualized programs have had small effects.

Other systems (discussed below) appear more effective for adapting instruction to the needs of individual learners.

Mastery Learning

Combining the psychological elements of instruction with suitable amounts of time, mastery learning employs formative tests to allocate time and to guide reinforcement and corrective feedback. In the most definitive synthesis of research on mastery learning, James Kulik and Chen-Lin Kulik reported substantial positive effects. Mastery programs that yielded larger effects established a criterion of 95% to 100% mastery and required repeated testing to mastery before allowing students to proceed to additional units (which yielded gigantic effects of one standard deviation). Mastery learning yielded larger effects with less-able students and reduced the difference between their performance and that of abler groups.

The success of mastery learning is attributable to several factors. The Kuliks, for example, found that when control groups were provided feedback from quizzes, the mastery groups' advantage was smaller. As Bloom pointed out, mastery learning takes additional time; the Kuliks found that mastery learning required a median of 16% (and up to 97%) more time than conventional instruction. The seven studies that provided equal time for mastery and control groups showed only a small advantage for mastery learning on standardized tests. However, the advantage was moderate on experimenter-made, criterion-referenced tests for nine equal-time studies. These results illustrate the separate contributions to mastery learning of cuing, feedback, and time.

Mastery learning yielded larger effects in studies of less than a month's duration than in those lasting more than four months. Retention probably declines sharply no matter what the educational method, but the decline can be more confidently noted with regard to mastery learning since it has been more extensively studied than other methods.

Bloom and his students have reported larger effects than has Robert Slavin, who reviewed their work. Thomas Guskey and S. L. Gates, for example, reported an average effect size of .78 estimated from 38 studies of elementary and secondary students. In response to Slavin, Lorin Anderson and Robert Burns pointed out two reasons for larger effects in some studies, especially those under Bloom's supervision. Bloom has been more interested in what is possible than in what is likely; he has sought to find the limits of learning. His students, moreover, have conducted tightly controlled experiments over time periods of less than a semester or less than a year.[12]

Adaptive Instruction

Developed by Margaret Wang and others, adaptive instruction combines elements of mastery learning, cooperative learning, open education, tutoring, computer-assisted instruction, and comprehension teaching into a complex system whose aim is to tailor instruction to the needs of individuals and small groups. Managerial functions—including such activities as planning, allocating time, delegating tasks to aides and students, and quality control—are carried out by a master teacher. Adaptive instruction is a comprehensive program for the whole school day rather than a single method that requires simple integration into one subject or into a single teacher's repertoire. Its effects on achievement are substantial, but its broader effects are probably underestimated, since adaptive instruction aims at diverse ends—including student autonomy, intrinsic motivation, and teacher and student choice—which are poorly reflected by the usual outcome measures.

COMPUTER-ASSISTED INSTRUCTION

Ours is an electronic age, and computers have already had a substantial impact on learning. With the costs of hardware declining and with software becoming increasingly sophisticated,

we may hope for still greater effects as computers are better integrated into school programs.

Computers show the greatest advantage for handicapped students—probably because they are more adaptive to their special needs than teachers might be. Computers may also be more patient, discreet, nonjudgmental, or even encouraging about progress. Perhaps for the same reasons, computers generally have bigger effects in elementary schools than in high schools or colleges.

Another explanation for the disparate results is also plausible. Elementary schools provide less tracking and fewer differentiated courses for homogeneous groups. Computers may be better adapted to larger within-class differences among elementary students because they allow them to proceed at their own pace without engaging in invidious comparisons.

Simulations and games, with or without computer implementation, require active, specific responses from learners and may strike a balance between vicarious book learning and the dynamic, complicated, and competitive "real world." The interactiveness, speed, intensity, movement, color, and sound of computers add interest and information to academic learning. Unless geared to educational purposes, however, computer games can also waste time.

STUDENT GROUPING

Teaching students what they already know and teaching them what they are yet incapable of learning are equally wasteful practices and may even be harmful to motivation. For this reason, traditional whole-class teaching of heterogeneous groups can present serious difficulties—a problem that is often unacknowledged in our egalitarian age. Outside of universities, however, most educators recognize that it is difficult to teach arithmetic and trigonometry at the same time. (Even some English professors might balk at teaching phonics and deconstructionism simultaneously.) If we want to teach students as much as possible rather than to make them all alike, we need to consider how they are grouped and try to help the full range of students.

Acceleration

Accelerated programs identify talented youth (often in mathematics and science) and group them together or with older students. Such programs provide counseling, encouragement, contact with accomplished adults, grade skipping, summer school, and the compression of the standard curriculum into fewer years. The effects are huge in elementary schools, substantial in junior high schools, and moderate in senior high schools. The smaller effects at more advanced levels may be attributable to the smaller advantage of acceleration over the tracking and differentiated course selection practiced in high schools.

The effects of acceleration on educational attitudes, vocational plans, participation in school activities, popularity, psychological adjustment, and character ratings have been mixed and often insignificant. These outcomes may not be systematically affected in either direction.

Ability Grouping

Students are placed in ability groups according to achievement, intelligence test scores, personal insights, and subjective opinions. In high school, ability grouping leaves deficient and average students unaffected, but it has beneficial effects on talented students and on attitudes toward the subject matter. In elementary school, the grouping of students with similar reading achievement but from different grades yields substantial effects. Within-class grouping in mathematics yields worthwhile effects, but generalized ability grouping does not.

Tutoring

Because it gears instruction to individual or small-group needs, tutoring is highly beneficial to both tutors and tutees. It yields particularly large effects in mathematics—perhaps because of the subject's well-defined scope and organization.

In whole-group instruction, teachers may ordinarily focus on average or deficient students to insure that they master the lessons. When talented students are freed from repetition and slow progression, they can proceed quickly. Grouping may work best when students are accurately grouped according to their specific subject-matter needs rather than according to I.Q., demeanor, or other irrelevant characteristics.

Well-defined subject matter and student grouping may be among the chief reasons why Japanese students lead the world in academic achievement: the curriculum is explicit, rigorous, and nationally uniform. In primary schools, weaker students, with maternal help, study harder and longer to keep up with these explicit requirements. Subject-matter tests are administered to screen students for "lower" and "upper" secondary schools and for universities of various gradations of rigor and prestige. Each such screening determines occupational, marital, and other adult prospects; long-term adult rewards thus reinforce educational effort.[13]

SOCIAL ENVIRONMENT

Cooperative learning programs delegate some control of the pacing and methods of learning to groups of between two and six students, who work together and sometimes compete with other groups within classes. Such programs are successful for several reasons. They provide relief from the excessive teacher/student interaction of whole-group teaching, they free time for the interactive engagement of students, and they present opportunities for targeted cues, engagement, correctives, and reinforcement. As in comprehension teaching, the acts of tutoring and teaching may encourage students to think for themselves about the organization of subject matter and the productive allocation of time.

Many correlational studies suggest that *classroom morale* is associated with achievement gains, with greater interest in subject matter, and with the worthy outcome of voluntary participation in nonrequired subject-related activities. Morale is assessed by asking students to agree or disagree with such statements as "Most of the students know one another well" and "The class members know the purpose of the lessons."

Students who perceive the atmosphere as friendly, satisfying, focused on goals, and challenging and who feel that the classroom has the required materials tend to learn more. Those who perceive the atmosphere as fostering student cliques, disorganization, apathy, favoritism, and friction learn less. The research on morale, though plausible, lacks the specificity and causal confidence of the controlled experiments on directly alterable methods.

READING EFFECTS

Comprehension teaching, because it may extend to several subjects in elementary school, has already been discussed as a pattern of teaching. Several other methods have substantial effects on reading achievement.

Adaptive speed training involves principles that are similar to those of comprehension training. Students learn to vary their pace and the depth of their reflection according to the difficulty of the material and their reading purposes.

Reading methods vary widely, but their largest effects seem to occur when teachers are systematically trained, almost irrespective of particularities of method. Phonics or "word-attack" approaches, however, have a moderate advantage over guessing and "whole-word" approaches in the teaching of beginning reading—perhaps because early misconceptions are avoided. Phonics may also reduce the need for excessive reteaching and correctives.

Pictures in the text can be very helpful, although they add to the cost of a book and occupy space that could otherwise be used for prose. In order of their effectiveness, several types of pictures can be distinguished. Transformative pictures recode information into concrete and memorable form, relate information in a well-organized context, and provide links for systematic retrieval. Interpretive pictures, like advance organizers, make the text comprehensible by relating abstract terms to concrete ones and by connecting the unfamiliar and difficult to previously acquired knowledge. Organizational pictures, including maps and diagrams, show the coherence of objects or events in space and time. Representational pictures are photos or other concrete representations of what is discussed in the text. Decorative pictures present (possibly irrelevant or conflicting) information that is incidental to intended learning (although decoration may add interest if not information).

Pictures can provide vivid imagery and metaphors that facilitate memory, show what is important to learn, and intensify the effects of prose. Pictures may sometimes allow students to bypass the text, but memorable, well-written prose may obviate pictures.[14]

WRITING EFFECTS

Sixty well-designed studies of methods of teaching writing compared 72 experimental groups with control groups. The methods below are presented in the order of their effectiveness.

The inquiry method requires students to find and state specific details that convey personal experience vividly, to examine sets of data to develop and support explanatory generalizations, or to analyze situations that present ethical problems and arguments.

Scales are criteria or specific questions that students can apply to their own and others' writing to improve it.

Sentence combining shows students how to build complex sentences from simpler ones.

Models are presentations of good pieces of writing to serve as exemplars for students.

Free writing allows students to write about whatever occurs to them.

Grammar and mechanics include sentence parsing and the analysis of parts of speech.

SCIENCE EFFECTS

Introduced in response to the launch of Sputnik I, the "new" science curricula, sponsored by the National Science Foundation, yielded substantial effects on learning. They efficiently added value by producing superior learning on tests of their intended outcomes and on tests of general subject-matter goals. The new curricula also yielded effects ranging from small to substantial on such often-unmeasured outcomes as creativity, problem solving, scientific attitudes and skills, logical thinking, and achievement in nonscience subject matter.

Perhaps these advantages are attributable to the combined efforts of teachers, psychologists, and scientists, who collaborated to insure that the curricula would be based on modern content and would foster effective teaching practices. The scientists may have been able to generate enthusiasm for teaching scientific methods, for laboratory work, and for other reforms.

The new science curricula worked well in improving achievement and other outcomes. Ironically, they are often forgotten today, despite the fact that, by international standards, U.S. students score poorly in mathematics and science.

Inquiry teaching. Often practiced in Japan, this method requires students to formulate hypotheses, reason about their credibility, and design experiments to test their validity. Inquiry teaching yields substantial effects, particularly on the understanding of scientific processes.

Audio-tutorials. These are tape-recorded instructions for using laboratory equipment, manipulatives, and readings for topical lessons or whole courses. This simple approach yields somewhat better results than conventional instruction, allows independent learning, and has the further advantage of individual pacing—allowing students to pursue special topics or to take courses on their own.

Original source papers. This method derives from the Great Books approach of the late Robert Maynard Hutchins, former president of the University of Chicago, and his colleague Mortimer Adler. They saw more value in reading Plato or Newton than in resorting to predigested textbook accounts. The use of original sources in teaching trades breadth for depth in the belief that it is better to know a few ideas of transcending importance than to learn many unconnected bits of soon-forgotten information. Advocates of this approach have shown that such knowledge can be acquired by studying and discussing original scientific papers of historical or scientific significance.

Other methods of teaching science have effects that are near zero—that is, close to the effects of traditional methods of teaching. They include team teaching, departmentalized elementary programs, and media-based instruction. The equal results for media methods, however, suggest that choices can be based on cost and convenience. Since television programs and films can be broadcast, they can provide equally effective education in different and widespread locations (even in different parts of the world by satellite). Moreover, students today can interact "on-line" with teachers and fellow students who are far away.

There are some successful precedents for the use of media-based instruction. For a decade, the Chicago community colleges provided dozens of mainly one-way television courses to hundreds of thousands of students, who did most of their studying at home but participated in discussion and testing sessions at several sites in the metropolitan area. The best lecturers, media specialists, and test constructors could be employed, and tapes of the courses could be rebroadcast repeatedly.

In several Third World countries that are gaining in achievement and school enrollments, ministries of education make efficient and successful use of such low-cost, effective "distance education" for remote elementary and secondary schools.

The Oklahoma and Minnesota state departments of education apparently lead the nation in providing small high schools in rural areas with specialized television teachers and interactive courses in advanced science, mathematics, foreign language, and other subjects.

MATHEMATICS EFFECTS

In the heyday of its Education Directorate, the National Science Foundation sponsored considerable research not only on science but also on mathematics. Some worthwhile effects were found.

Manipulative Materials

The use of Cuisenaire rods, balance beams, counting sticks, and measuring scales allows students to engage directly in learning instead of passively following abstract presentations by the teacher. Students can handle the materials, see the relation of abstract ideas and concrete embodiments, and check hypothesized answers by quick empirical testing without having to wait for quiz results or feedback from the teacher. This method apparently results in enormous effects.

Problem Solving

In mathematics teaching, a focus on problem solving yields worthwhile effects. Such an approach requires comprehension of terms and their application to varied examples. It may motivate students by showing them the application of mathematical ideas to "real-world" questions.

New Math

The so-called new math produced beneficial results, although it was not as successful as the new science curricula. Both reforms probably gained their learning advantages partly by testing what they taught.

SPECIAL POPULATIONS AND TECHNIQUES

We can also gain insights from programs that lie outside the usual scope of elementary and secondary classrooms.

Early Intervention

Programs of early intervention include educational, psychological, and therapeutic components for handicapped, at-risk, and disadvantaged children from the ages of one month to $5\frac{1}{2}$ years. Studies of these programs found that the large, immediate effects of these programs declined rapidly and disappeared after three years.

Preschool Programs

Preschool programs also showed initial learning effects that were not sustained. It appears that young children can learn more than is normally assumed, but, like other learners, they can also forget. The key to sustained gains may be sustained programs and effective families—not one-shot approaches.

Programs for the Handicapped

Students classified as mentally retarded, emotionally disturbed, or learning disabled have been subjects in research that has several important implications. When they serve as tutors of one another and of younger students, handicapped students can learn well—a finding similar to those in comprehension-monitoring and tutoring studies of nonhandicapped children. Moreover, handicapped students are often spuriously classified, and we may underestimate their capacities.

Mainstreaming

Studies show that mildly to moderately handicapped students can prosper in regular classes and thereby avoid the invidious "labeling" that is often based on misclassification.

Psycholinguistic Training

Providing psycholinguistic training to special-needs students yields positive effects. This approach consists of testing and remedying specific deficits in language skills.

Patient Education

Educating patients about diseases and treatments can affect mortality, morbidity, and lengths of illness and hospitalization. In studies of the acquisition of knowledge regarding drug usage for hypertension, diabetes, and other chronic conditions, one-to-one and group counseling (with or without instructional material) produced greater effects than providing instruction through labels on bottles or package inserts for patients.

Labels, special containers, memory aids, and behavior modification were successful in minimizing later errors in drug usage. The most efficacious educational principles were: specification of intentions; relevance to the needs of the learner; provision of personal answers to questions; reinforcement and feedback on progress; facilitation of correct dosage, e.g., the use of unit-dose containers; and instructional and treatment regimens suited to personal convenience, e.g., prescribing drugs for administration at mealtimes.

Inservice Training of Physicians

Such training shows large effects on doctors' knowledge and on their classroom or laboratory performance but only moderate effects on the outcomes of treating actual patients. Knowledge and performance, even in practical training, may help, but they hardly guarantee successful application in practice. Can an accomplished mathematician handle the intricacies of federal income tax?

Panaceas and Shortcuts

At the request of the U.S. Army, the National Academy of Sciences evaluated exotic techniques for enhancing learning and performance that are described in popular psychology (and presumably are being exploited in California and the USSR).[15] However, little or no evidence was found for the efficacy of learning during sleep; for mental practice of motor skills; for "integration" of left and right hemispheres of the brain; for parapsychological techniques; for biofeedback; for extrasensory perception, mental telepathy, and "mind over matter" exercises; or for "neurolinguistic programming," in which instructors identify the students' modes of learning and mimic the students' behaviors as they teach.

The Greeks found no royal road to geometry; even kings, if they desired mastery, had to sweat over Euclid's elements. Perhaps brain research will eventually yield a magic elixir or a panacea, but for proof of its existence educators should insist on hard data in refereed scientific journals.

EFFECTS ON TEACHERS

Programs to help teachers in their work have had substantial effects—notwithstanding complaints about typical inservice training sessions. Do physicians complain about the medical care they get?

Microteaching

Developed at Stanford University in the 1960s, microteaching is a behavioral approach for preservice and inservice training that has substantial effects. It employs the explanation and modeling of selected teaching techniques; televised practice with small groups of students; discussion, correctives, and reinforcement while watching playback; and recycling through subsequent practice and playback sessions with new groups of students.

Inservice Education

Inservice training for teachers also proves to have substantial effects. Somewhat like the case of inservice training of physicians, the biggest effects are on the teacher's knowledge, but effects on classroom behavior and student achievement are also notable.

For inservice training, authoritative planning and execution seem to work best; informal coaching by itself seems ineffective. Allowing the instructor to be responsible for the design and teaching of the sessions works better than relying on presentations by teachers and group discussions. The best techniques are observation and classroom practices, video/audio feedback, and practice. The most effective training combines lectures, modeling, practice, and coaching. The size of the training group, ranging from one to more than 60, makes no detectable difference.

Some apparent effects may be attributable to the selectivity of the program rather than to its superior efficacy. For example, federal-, state-, and university-sponsored programs appear more effective than locally initiated programs. Competitive selection of participants and the granting of college credit apparently work better as incentives than extra pay, renewal of certification, or no incentives. Independent study seems to have larger effects than workshops, courses, minicourses, and institutes.

CONCLUSION

Psychological research provides first-order estimates of the effects of instructional means on educational ends under various conditions. But some instructional practices may be costly—not in terms of dollars but in terms of new or complicated arrangements that may be difficult for some teachers and districts to adopt. Thus estimates of effects are only one basis for decision making. We need to consider the productivity or value of effects in relation to total costs, including the time and energies of educators and students.

Knowledge from the field of psychology alone is not sufficient to prescribe practices, since different means bring about different ends. Educators must decide whether the learning effort is to be directed by teachers, by students, or by the curriculum. They must choose among a range of facts and concepts, breadth and depth, short- and long-term ends, academic knowledge and knowledge that has direct application in the real world, equal opportunity and equal results. They must decide which aspect of Plato's triumvirate of thinking, feeling, and acting will take precedence. Once these choices are made, educators can turn to the researchers' estimates of effects as one basis for determining the most productive practices.

ENDNOTES

1. Herbert J. Walberg, Diane Schiller, and Geneva D. Haertel, "The Quiet Revolution in Educational Research," *Phi Delta Kappan,* November 1979, pp. 179–83; Herbert J. Walbert, "Improving the Productivity of America's Schools," *Educational Leadership,* vol. 41, 1984, pp. 19–27; and Barry J. Fraser, Herbert J. Walberg, Wayne W. Welch, and John A. Hattie, "Syntheses of Educational Productivity Research," *International Journal of Educational Research,* vol. 11, 1987, pp. 73–145.

2. Neal Miller and John Dollard, *Social Learning and Imitation* (New Haven, Conn.: Yale University Press, 1941); and John Dollard and Neal Miller, *Personality and Psychotherapy* (New York: McGraw-Hill, 1950).

3. Eric A. Hanushek, "Throwing Money at Schools," *Journal of Policy Analysis and Management,* vol. 1, 1981, pp. 19–41; and Herbert J. Walberg and William F. Fowler, "Expenditure and Size Efficiencies of Public School Districts," *Educational Researcher,* vol. 16, 1987, pp. 515–26.

4. Benjamin S. Bloom, *Human Characteristics and School Learning* (New York: McGraw-Hill, 1976); and John B. Carroll, "A Model of School Learning," *Teachers College Record,* vol. 64, 1963, pp. 723–33.

5. The effects are expressed as differences between experimental and control groups in units of standard deviations. For further details and references, see my chapter in Merlin C. Wittrock, ed., *Handbook of Research on Teaching* (New York: Macmillan, 1986), and the research monograph by Fraser, myself, and others cited above. For a time I will send a table of effects and number of studies, as well as a graphic display, to readers who send a self-addressed, stamped envelope (two first-class stamps) to me at the University of Illinois, College of Education, P. O. Box 4348, Chicago, IL 60680.

6. Margo A. Mastropieri and Thomas E. Scruggs, *Effective Instruction for Special Education* (Boston: Little, Brown, 1987).

7. John Hoetker and William P. Ahlbrand, "The Persistence of the Recitation," *American Educational Research Journal,* vol. 6, 1969, pp. 145–67.

8. For a full account of most views, see Penelope L. Peterson and Herbert J. Walberg, eds., *Research on Teaching* (Berkeley, Calif.: McCutchan, 1979); and Wittrock, op. cit.

9. Lev Vygotsky, *Mind in Society* (Cambridge, Mass.: Harvard University Press, 1978).

10. Anne Marie Pallincsar and Anne Brown, "Reciprocal Teaching of Comprehension-Fostering and Comprehension-Monitoring Activities," *Cognition and Instruction,* vol. 1, 1984, pp. 117–76; David Pearson, "Reading Comprehension Instruction: Six Necessary Steps," *Reading Teacher,* vol. 38, 1985, pp. 724–38; and Paul R. Pintrich et al., "Instructional Psychology," *Annual Review of Psychology,* vol. 37, 1986, pp. 611–51.

11. Rose M. Giaconia and Larry V. Hedges, "Identifying Features on Effective Open Education," *Review of Educational Research,* vol. 52, 1982, pp. 579–602.

12. James A. Kulik and Chen-Lin Kulik, "Mystery Testing and Student Learning," *Journal of Educational Technology Systems,* vol. 15, 1986, pp. 325–45; Lorin W. Anderson and Robert B. Burns, "Values, Evidence, and Mastery Learning," *Review of Educational Research,* vol. 57, 1988, pp. 215–23; Thomas R. Guskey and S. L. Gates, "Synthesis of Research on the Effects of Mastery Learning in Elementary and Secondary Classrooms," *Educational Leadership,* May 1986, pp. 73–80; and Robert E. Slavin, "Mastery Learning Reconsidered," *Review of Educational Research,* vol. 57, 1988, pp. 175–213.

13. Herbert J. Walberg, "What Can We Learn from Japanese Education?," *The World and I,* March 1988, pp. 661–65.

14. Joel R. Levin, Gary J. Anglin, and Russell N. Carney, "On Empirically Validating Functions of Pictures in Prose," in D. M. Willows and H. A. Houghton, eds., *Illustrations, Graphs, and Diagrams* (New York: Springer-Verlag, forthcoming).

15. Daniel Druckman and John A. Swets, eds., *Enhancing Human Performance* (Washington, D.C.: National Academy Press, 1988).

DISCUSSION QUESTIONS

1. How can teachers use improve cues, engagement, correctives, and reinforcement to facilitate student achievement?

2. How do explicit teaching and comprehension teaching differ in terms of methods and elements?

3. Consider the advantages and disadvantages of open education. Is open education appropriate for all educational settings and students? Why? Why not?

4. How can knowledge from the field of psychology be used to guide curriculum development?

5. In what ways have programs and techniques developed for special populations influenced elementary and secondary curriculum development?

Probing the Subtleties of Subject-Matter Teaching

JERE BROPHY

FOCUSING QUESTIONS

1. *How do school effects and teacher effects research differ?*
2. *What were the contributions and limitations of the process-outcome research of the 1970s?*
3. *What are the critical dimensions that underline research on teaching?*
4. *What does students' behavior influence in the construction of meaning?*
5. *How can teachers facilitate students in their efforts to understand new material?*
6. *What components are indigenous to good subject matter teaching?*

Research on teaching, if interpreted appropriately, is a significant resource to teachers; it both validates good practice and suggests directions for improvement. All too often, however, reviews of the research assume an "out with the old, in with the new" stance, which fosters swings between extremes. Practitioners are left confused and prone to believe that research is not helpful. This summary of the research conducted during the last 25 years attempts not only to highlight the changing implications of research but also to emphasize how the research has built on what was learned before.

PROCESS-OUTCOME RESEARCH

Especially relevant findings come from studies designed to identify relationships between classroom processes (what the teacher and students do in the classroom) and student outcomes (changes in students' knowledge, skills, values, or dispositions that represent progress toward instructional goals). Two forms of *process-outcome research* that became prominent in the

1970s were school effects research and teacher effects research.

School effects research (reviewed in Good and Brophy 1986) identified characteristics in schools that elicit good achievement gains from their students: (1) strong academic leadership that produces consensus on goal priorities and commitment to instructional excellence; (2) a safe, orderly school climate; (3) positive teacher attitudes toward students and expectations regarding their abilities to master the curriculum; (4) an emphasis on instruction in the curriculum (not just on filling time or on nonacademic activities); (5) careful monitoring of progress toward goals through student testing and staff evaluation programs; (6) strong parent involvement programs; and (7) consistent emphasis on the importance of academic achievement, including praise and public recognition for students' accomplishments.

Teacher effects research (reviewed in Brophy and Good 1986) identified teacher behaviors and patterns of teacher-student interaction associated with student achievement gains. This research firmly established three major conclusions:

1. *Teachers make a difference.* Some teachers reliably elicit greater gains than others, because of differences in how they teach.

2. *Differences in achievement gains occur in part because of differences in exposure to academic content and opportunity to learn.* Teachers who elicit greater gains: (a) place more emphasis on developing mastery of the curriculum, in establishing expectations for students, and defining their own roles; (b) allocate most of the available time for activities designed to foster such mastery; and (c) are effective organizers and managers who make their classrooms efficient learning environments, minimize the time spent getting organized or making transitions, and maximize student engagement in ongoing academic activities.

3. *Teachers who elicit greater achievement gains do not merely maximize "time on task"; in addition, they spend a great deal of time actively instructing their students.* Their classrooms feature more time spent in interactive lessons, featuring much teacher-student discourse and less time spent in independent seatwork. Rather than depend solely on curriculum materials as content sources, these teachers interpret and elaborate the content for students, stimulate them to react to it through questions, and circulate during seatwork times to monitor progress and provide assistance. They are active instructors, not just materials managers and evaluators, although most of their instruction occurs during interactive discourse with students rather than during extended lecture-presentations.

The process-outcome research of the 1970s was important, not only for contributing the findings summarized above but also for providing education with a knowledge base capable of moving the field beyond testimonials and unsupported claims toward scientific statements based on credible data. However, this research was limited in several respects. First, it focused on important but very basic aspects of teaching. These aspects differentiate the least effective teachers from other teachers, but they do not include the more subtle points that distinguish the most outstanding teachers.

Second, most of this research relied on standardized tests as the outcome measure, which meant that it focused on mastery of relatively isolated knowledge items and skill components without assessing the degree to which students had developed understanding of networks of subject-matter content or the ability to use this information in authentic application situations.

RESEARCH ON TEACHING FOR UNDERSTANDING AND USE OF KNOWLEDGE

During the 1980s, research emerged that emphasized teaching subject matter for understanding and use of knowledge. This research focuses on particular curriculum units or even individual lessons, taking into account the teacher's instructional goals and assessing student learning accordingly. The researchers find out what the teacher is trying to accomplish, record detailed information about classroom processes as they unfold, and then assess learning using measures keyed to the instructional goals. Often these include detailed interviews or portfolio assessments, not just conventional short-answer tests.

Current research focuses on attempts to teach both the individual elements in a network of related content and the connections among them, to the point that students can explain the information in their own words and can use it appropriately in and out of school. Teachers accomplish this by explaining concepts and principles with clarity and precision and by modeling the strategic application of skills via "think aloud" demonstrations. These demonstrations make overt for students the usually covert strategic thinking that guides the use of the skills for problem solving.

CONSTRUCTION OF MEANING

Current research, while building on findings indicating the vital role teachers play in stimulating student learning, also focuses on the role of the student. It recognizes that students do not merely passively receive or copy input from teachers, but instead actively mediate it by trying to make sense of it and to relate it to what they already know (or think they know) about the topic. Thus, students develop new knowledge through a process of *active construction.* In order to get beyond rote memorization to achieve true understanding, they need to develop and integrate a network of associations linking new input to preexisting knowledge and beliefs anchored in concrete experience. Thus, teaching involves inducing *conceptual change* in students, not infusing knowledge into a vacuum. Students' preexisting beliefs about a topic, when accurate, facilitate learning and provide a natural starting place for teaching. Students' misconceptions, however, must be corrected so that they do not distort the new learning.

To the extent that new learning is complex, the construction of meaning required to develop clear understanding of it will take time and will be facilitated by the interactive *discourse* that occurs during lessons and activities. Clear explanations and modeling from the teacher are important, but so are opportunities to answer questions about the content, discuss or debate its meanings and implications, or apply it in authentic problem-solving or decision-making contexts. These activities allow students to process the content actively and "make it their own" by paraphrasing it into their own words, exploring its relationships to other knowledge and to past experience, appreciating the insights it provides, or identifying its implications for personal decision making or action. Increasingly, research is pointing to thoughtful discussion, and not just teacher lecturing or student recitation, as characteristic of the discourse involved in teaching for understanding.

Researchers have also begun to stress the complementary changes in teacher and student roles that should occur as learning progresses. Early in the process, the teacher assumes most of the responsibility for structuring and managing learning activities and provides students with a great deal of information, explanation, modeling, and cueing. As students develop expertise, however, they can begin regulating their own learning by asking questions and by working on increasingly complex applications with increasing degrees of autonomy. The teacher still provides task simplification, coaching, and other "scaffolding" needed to assist students with challenges that they are not yet ready to handle on their own. Gradually, this assistance is reduced in response to gradual increases in student readiness to engage in self-regulated learning.

PRINCIPLES OF GOOD SUBJECT MATTER TEACHING

Although research on teaching school subjects for understanding and higher-order applications is still in its infancy, it already has produced successful experimental programs in most subjects. Even more encouraging, analyses of these programs have identified principles and practices that are common to most if not all of them (Anderson 1989, Brophy 1989, Prawat 1989). These common elements are:

1. The curriculum is designed to equip students with knowledge, skills, values, and dispositions useful both inside and outside of school.

2. Instructional goals underscore developing student expertise within an application context and with emphasis on conceptual understanding and self-regulated use of skills.

3. The curriculum balances breadth with depth by addressing limited content but developing this content sufficiently to foster understanding.

4. The content is organized around a limited set of powerful ideas (key understandings and principles).

5. The teacher's role is not just to present information but also to scaffold and respond to students' learning.

6. The students' role is not just to absorb or copy but to actively make sense and construct meaning.

7. Activities and assignments feature authentic tasks that call for problem solving or critical thinking, not just memory or reproduction.

8. Higher-order thinking skills are not taught as a separate skills curriculum. Instead, they are developed in the process of teaching subject-matter knowledge within application contexts that call for students to relate what they are learning to their lives outside of school by thinking critically or creatively about it or by using it to solve problems or make decisions.

9. The teacher creates a social environment in the classroom that could be described as a learning community where dialogue promotes understanding.

IN-DEPTH STUDY OF FEWER TOPICS

Embedded in this approach to teaching is the notion of "complete" lessons carried through to include higher-order applications of content. The breadth of content addressed, thus, is limited to allow for more in-depth teaching of the content. Unfortunately, typical state and district curriculum guidelines feature long lists of items and subskills to be "covered," and typical curriculum packages supplied by educational publishers respond to these guidelines by emphasizing breadth over depth of coverage. Teachers who want to teach for understanding and higher-order applications of subject-matter will have to both: (1) limit what they teach by focusing on the most important content and omitting or skimming over the rest, and (2) structure what they do teach around important ideas, elaborating it considerably beyond what is in the text.

Besides presenting information and modeling skill applications, such teachers will need to structure a great deal of thoughtful discourse by using questions to stimulate students to process and reflect on the content, recognize relationships among and implications of its key ideas, think critically about it, and use it in problem-solving or decision-making applications. Such discourse downplays rapid-fire questioning and short answers and instead features sustained examination of a small number of related topics. Students are invited to develop explanations, make predic-

tions, debate alternative approaches to problems, or otherwise consider the content's implications or applications. Some of the questions admit to a range of possible correct answers, and some invite discussion or debate (for example, concerning the relative merits of alternative suggestions for solving problems). In addition to asking questions and providing feedback, the teacher encourages students to explain or elaborate on their answers or to comment on classmates' answers. The teacher also capitalizes on "teachable moments" offered by students' comments or questions (by elaborating on the original instruction, correcting misconceptions, or calling attention to implications that have not been appreciated yet).

HOLISTIC SKILLS INSTRUCTION

Teaching for understanding and use of knowledge also involves holistic skills instruction, not the practice of skills in isolation. For example, most practice of writing skills is embedded within activities calling for authentic writing. Also, skills are taught as strategies adapted to particular purposes and situations, with emphasis on modeling the cognitive and metacognitive components involved and explaining the necessary conditional knowledge (of when and why the skills would be used). Thus, students receive instruction in when and how to apply skills, not just opportunities to use them.

Activities, assignments, and evaluation methods incorporate a much greater range of tasks than the familiar workbooks and curriculum-embedded tests that focus on recognition and recall of facts, definitions, and fragmented skills. Curriculum strands or units are planned to accomplish gradual transfer of responsibility for managing learning activities from the teacher to the students, in response to their growing expertise on the topic. Plans for lessons and activities are guided by overall curriculum goals (phrased in terms of student capabilities to be developed), and evaluation efforts concentrate on assessing the progress made.

Reading

Reading is taught as a sense-making process of extracting meaning from texts that are read for information or enjoyment, not just for practice. Important skills such as decoding, blending, and noting main ideas are taught and practiced, but primarily within the context of reading for meaning. Activities and assignments feature more reading of extended texts and less time spent with skills worksheets. Students often work cooperatively in pairs or small groups, reading to one another or discussing their answers to questions about the implications of the text. Rather than being restricted to the artificial stories written for basal readers, students often read literature written to provide information or pleasure (Anderson et al. 1985, Dole et al. 1991).

Writing

Writing is taught as a way for students to organize and communicate their thinking to particular audiences for particular purposes, using skills taught as strategies for accomplishing these goals. Most skills practice is embedded within writing activities that call for composition and communication of meaningful content. Composition activities emphasize authentic writing intended to be read for meaning and response. Thus, composition becomes an exercise in communication and personal craftsmanship. Students develop and revise outlines, develop successive drafts for meaning, and then polish their writing. The emphasis is on the cognitive and metacognitive aspects of composing, not just on mechanics and editing (Englert and Raphael 1989, Rosaen 1990, Scardamalia and Bereiter 1986).

Mathematics

Mathematics instruction focuses on developing students' abilities to explore, conjecture, reason logically, and use a variety of mathematical models to solve nonroutine problems. Instead of working through a postulated linear hierarchy from isolated and low-level skills to integrated and higher-level skills, and only then attempting application, students are taught within an application context right from the beginning through an emphasis on authentic problem solving. They spend less time working individually on computation skills sheets and more time participating in teacher-led discourse concerning the meanings of the mathematical concepts and operations under study (Carpenter et al. 1989; National Council of Teachers of Mathematics 1989, 1991; Steffe and Wood 1990).

Science

In science, students learn to understand, appreciate, and apply connected sets of powerful ideas that they can use to describe, explain, make predictions about, or gain control over real-world systems or events. Instruction connects with students' experience-based knowledge and beliefs, building on accurate current knowledge but also producing conceptual change by confronting and correcting misconceptions. The teacher models and coaches the students' scientific reasoning through scaffolded tasks and dialogues that engage them in thinking about scientific issues. The students are encouraged to make predictions or develop explanations, then subject them to empirical tests or argue the merits of proposed alternatives (Anderson and Roth 1989, Neale et al. 1990).

Social studies

In social studies, students are challenged to engage in higher-order thinking by interpreting, analyzing, or manipulating information in response to questions or problems that cannot be resolved through routine application of previously learned knowledge. Students focus on networks of connected content structured around powerful ideas rather than on long lists of disconnected facts, and they consider the implications of what they are learning for social and civic decision making. The teacher encourages students to formulate and communicate ideas about the topic, but also presses them to clarify or justify their assertions rather than merely accepting and reinforcing them indiscriminately (Brophy 1990, Newmann 1990).

CONCLUSION

The type of teaching described here is not yet typical of what happens in most schools. For it to become more common, several things must occur. First, researchers need to articulate these principles more clearly. Second, states and districts must adjust their curriculum guidelines, and publishers must modify their textbooks and teachers' manuals. Finally, professional organizations of teachers and teacher educators must build on the beginnings that they have made in endorsing the goals of teaching subjects for understanding, appreciation, and life application by creating and disseminating position statements, instructional guidelines, videotaped examples, and other resources for preservice and inservice teachers. Clearly, the kind of instruction described here demands more from both teachers and students than traditional reading-recitation-seatwork teaching does. However, it also rewards their efforts with more satisfying and authentic accomplishments.

ENDNOTE

Author's note: This work is sponsored in part by the Center for the Learning and Teaching of Elementary Subjects, Institute for Research on Teaching, Michigan State University. The Center for Learning and Teaching of Elementary Subjects is funded primarily by the Office of Educational Research and Improvement, U.S. Department of Education. The opinions expressed here do not necessarily reflect the position, policy, or endorsement of the Office or Department (Cooperative Agreement No. G0087C0226).

REFERENCES

Anderson, L. (1989). "Implementing Instructional Programs to Promote Meaningful, Self-Regulated Learning." In *Advances in Research on Teaching,* Vol. 1, edited by J. Brophy, pp. 311–343. Greenwich, Conn.: JAI.

Anderson, C., and K. Roth. (1989). "Teaching for Meaningful and Self-Regulated Learning of Science." In *Advances in Research on Teaching,* Vol. 1, edited by J. Brophy, pp. 265–309. Greenwich, Conn.: JAI.

Anderson, R., E. Hiebert, J. Scott, and I. Wilkinson. (1985). *Becoming a Nation of Readers: A Report of the Commission on Reading.* Washington, D.C.: National Institute of Education.

Brophy, J., ed. (1989). *Advances in Research on Teaching,* Vol. 1. Greenwich, Conn.: JAI.

Brophy, J. (1990). "Teaching Social Studies for Understanding and Higher-Order Applications." *Elementary School Journal* 90: 351–417.

Brophy, J., and T. Good. (1986). "Teacher Behavior and Student Achievement." In *Handbook of Research on Teaching,* 3rd. ed., edited by M. Wittrock, pp. 328–375. New York: Macmillan.

Carpenter, T., E. Fennema, P. Peterson, C. Chiang, and M. Loef. (1989). "Using Knowledge of Children's Mathematics Thinking in Classroom Teaching: An Experimental Study." *American Educational Research Journal* 26: 499–532.

Dole, J., G. Duffy, L. Roehler, and P. D. Pearson. (1991). "Moving From the Old to the New: Research on Reading Comprehension Instruction." *Review of Educational Research* 61: 239–264.

Englert, C., and T. Raphael. (1989). "Developing Successful Writers Through Cognitive Strategy Instruction." In *Advances in Research on Teaching,* Vol. 1, edited by J. Brophy, pp. 105–151. Greenwich, Conn.: JAI.

Good, T., and J. Brophy. (1986). "School Effects." In *Handbook of Research on Teaching,* 3rd ed., edited by M. Wittrock, pp. 570–602. New York: Macmillan.

National Council of Teachers of Mathematics. (1989). *Curriculum and Evaluation Standards for School Mathematics.* Reston, Va.: NCTM.

National Council of Teachers of Mathematics. (1991). *Professional Standards for Teaching Mathematics.* Reston, Va.: NCTM.

Neale, D., D. Smith, and V. Johnson. (1990). "Implementing Conceptual Change Teaching in Primary Science." *Elementary School Journal* 91: 109–131.

Newmann, F. (1990). "Qualities of Thoughtful Social Studies Classes: An Empirical Profile." *Journal of Curriculum Studies* 22: 253–275.

Prawat, R. (1989). "Promoting Access to Knowledge, Strategy, and Disposition in Students: A Research Synthesis." *Review of Educational Research* 59: 1–41.

Rosaen, C. (1990). "Improving Writing Opportunities in Elementary Classrooms." *Elementary School Journal* 90: 419–434.

Scardamalia, M., and C. Bereiter. (1986). "Written Composition." In *Handbook of Research on Teaching,* 3rd ed., edited by M. Wittrock, pp. 778–803. New York: Macmillan.

Steffe, L., and T. Wood, eds. (1990). *Transforming Children's Mathematics Education: International Perspectives.* Hillsdale, N.J.: Erlbaum.

DISCUSSION QUESTIONS

1. What types of instructional strategies promote successful student learning?

2. Should depth or breadth of coverage be a central focus in classroom teaching? Why? Why not?

3. How are depth and breadth of coverage related to higher order applications?

4. What kinds of learning activities promote the development of higher order thinking skills?

5. How will district level curriculum guides need to be modified to incorporate holistic instruction in content area subjects?

Research for Improving Teaching[1]

ALLAN C. ORNSTEIN

FOCUSING QUESTIONS

1. *What factors have restricted teacher effectiveness research?*
2. *In what ways is theory advantageous and disadvantageous to the practice of teaching?*
3. *How do the art and science of teaching differ?*
4. *Do you prefer a scientific or artistic approach to education? Why?*
5. *What aspects of teaching are not evaluated in the product oriented teaching model?*
6. *Why should research on teacher styles be incorporated into the study of teacher effectiveness?*

It is not an exaggeration to say that the literature on teaching is a morass of ill-defined and changing concepts. Investigators have examined teacher personality, traits, behaviors, attitudes, values, abilities, competencies, and many other characteristics. A host of measuring instruments have been employed: personality tests, attitudinal scales, observation instruments, rating scales, checklists, bipolar descriptors, and close-ended and open-ended written statements. The results of teaching have been studied in terms of student achievement, adjustment, attitudes, socioeconomic status, and creativity. Despite all this activity and thousands of studies conducted in the last fifty years, common denominators and agreed-on generalizations are hard to come by; hence, few facts concerning teacher effectiveness have been established (Borich, 1986; Ornstein, 1986a, 1990).

Confusion over terms, measurement problems, and the complexity of the teaching act are major reasons for the negligible results in judging teacher effectiveness. The studies themselves are often confirmations of common sense (a "demo-cratic" teacher is an effective teacher) or contradictory ("direct" behaviors are effective; "indirect" behaviors are effective), or the contexts within which the studies take place have little bearing on classroom settings, subject, or grade level of the individual teacher.

Because we are unable to agree on or precisely define what a good teacher is, we can use almost any definition, so long as it makes sense or seems logical. Despite the elusive and complex nature of teaching, research on teaching should continue with the hope we can better understand it. This chapter, then, is concerned with the understanding of teacher effectiveness—and with some of the theoretical issues related to defining effective teaching.

THEORY VERSUS THE PRACTICE OF TEACHING

The test of a good theory is whether it can guide practice. In reverse, good practice is based on theory. By practice, we mean the methods, strategies, and skills that apply to the working world, when a person is on the job and actively involved in his or her profession. These theoretical procedures are teachable and can be applied in different situations. When applied, they should result in the practitioner (the teacher) being considered "successful" or "effective" (Ornstein, 1987). By theory, we mean knowledge gained by research and experience that is generalizable and whereby potential users (teachers) can make informed estimates of the probable effects and effectiveness of practices (Bolin, 1988; Wise et al., 1985). Without theory, we cannot assess whether a particular method or strategy will suit the purpose or effect we are trying to achieve. Also, without theory, we operate haphazardly, intuitively, and instinctively. This is not always bad, but it is often difficult to put confidence in our judgments while teaching because of its swift and complex nature. The nature of teaching, therefore, makes it difficult to repeat and interpret what we are doing when we teach.

Regardless of our theories, those who work with or prepare teachers in one way or another have to deal with practice—that is, with what works. Good theories are workable for practitioners, make sense, can be applied to the real world of classrooms and schools, and are generalizable to the greatest number of real situations. Theories that are not workable and generalizable are not good theories and cannot be translated into practice. Theories about teaching may not provide specific answers or quick solutions to vexing problems. Theories must be adjusted to the situation, given the fact that people (teachers and students) differ—they are not nuts and bolts on an assembly line or tiny transistors in a computer, which can be shaped precisely to specifications. Thus, we commonly hear teachers saying, "That's all good theory, but it doesn't work in practice."

In defense of teachers, most teaching experts have difficulty fusing theory and practice. Perhaps we have trouble connecting theory and practice because the methods of inquiry lend themselves more to theoretical discussions and less to practical matters. Also, while discovering good theory is recognized as a worthwhile endeavor, a repertoire of good practice is often misconstrued by theoreticians as a "cookbook" or as "do's and don'ts" that are second-rate or unimportant. Despite the claims of some theoreticians, we seem unable to make the leap from theory to practice, from the textbook and college course to the classroom and school. Good theory in teaching often gets lost as practitioners try to apply what they have learned in college to the classroom setting in a search for practical solutions to common, everyday problems.

The problem of translating theory into practice is further aggravated by researchers and professors, many of whom are more concerned with the teacher "knowing that" than with the teacher "knowing how." This distinction "refers to the difference between being able to state factual propositions [theory] and being able to perform skills or operations [practice]" (Gage 1978, p. 44). The one kind of knowledge does not necessarily follow from the other; this is the reason why teaching texts and courses can stress either theory or practice. According to Gage, "much of the teacher education program is given over to providing teachers with a great deal of knowledge that certain things are true, in the subject [and grade levels] to be taught" (p. 44). This kind of knowledge is acquired by most prospective teachers at the expense of theory that could help them understand the basic principles and phenomena underlying their work.

The problem is further compounded by practitioners, including teachers, supervisors, and administrators, who feel that practical considerations are more worthwhile than theory; most teachers and supervisors view theory as impractical and "how-to" approaches as helpful. Thus, while many theoreticians ignore the practitioners, at the same time many practitioners ignore the theoreticians. Moreover, many theoretical discussions of teaching are divorced from practical application in the classroom, and many practical discussions of teaching rarely consider theoretical relationships.

Practice involves selecting strategies and methods that apply to specific situations. Theory involves principles and propositions that can be generalized to many situations. The problem is that every situation is unique. This becomes especially evident when practitioners try to apply the theory they learn from the professional literature. Adopting the right method for the appropriate situation is not an easy task and involves a good deal of common sense and experience, which no one can learn from a theoretical discussion. No matter how good our theories may be, they are not always predictable or generalizable from one situation to another.

THE SCIENCE VERSUS THE ART OF TEACHING

Another problem with preparing teachers is that we cannot agree on whether teaching is a science or an art. Some readers may say that this is a hopeless dichotomy, similar to that of theory versus practice, because the real world rarely consists of neat packages or either/or situations. Gage (1978) uses this distinction between teaching as a science and as an art to describe the elements of predictability in teaching and what constitutes "good" teaching. A science of teaching is attainable, he contends, because it "implies that good teaching will some day be attainable by closely following vigorous laws that yield high predictability and control." Teaching is more than a science, he observes, because it also involves "artistic judgment about the best ways to teach" (p. 17). When teaching leaves the laboratory or textbook and goes face to face with students, "the opportunity for artistry expands enormously." No science can prescribe successfully all the twists and turns as teaching unfolds, or as teachers respond with "judgment, sudden insight, sensitivity, and agility to promote learning" (p. 15). These are expressions of art that depart from the rules and principles of science.

Is such a limited scientific basis of teaching even worthwhile to consider? Yes, but the practitioner must learn as a teacher to draw not only from his or her professional knowledge (which is grounded in scientific principles), but also from a set of personal experiences and resources that are uniquely defined and exhibited by the teacher's own personality and "gut" reaction to classroom events that unfold (which form the basis for the art of teaching). For Jackson (1990), the hunches, judgments, and insights of the teacher, as he or she responds spontaneously to events in the classroom, are as important as, and perhaps even more important than, the science of teaching.

To some extent, the act of teaching must be considered intuitive and interactive, not prescriptive or predictable. According to Eisner (1983), teaching is based primarily on feelings and artistry, not scientific rules. In an age of science and technology, there is a special need to consider teaching as an "art and craft." Eisner condemns the scientific movement in psychology, especially behaviorism, and the scientific movement in education, especially in school management, as reducing the teaching act to trivial specifications. He regards teaching as a "poetic metaphor," more suited to satisfying the soul than informing the head, more concerned with the whole than with a set of discrete skills or stimuli. Our role as teachers, he claims, should not be that of a "puppeteer," an "engineer," or a manager; rather, it is "to orchestrate the dialogue [as the conductor of a symphony] moving from one side of the room to the other" (p. 8). The idea is to perceive patterns in motion, to improvise within the classroom, and to avoid mechanical or prescribed rules.

Rubin (1985) has a similar view of teaching—that effectiveness and artistry go hand in hand. The interplay of students and teacher is crucial and cannot be predetermined with carefully devised strategies. Confronted with everyday problems that cannot be easily predicted, the teacher must rely on intuition and on "insight acquired through long experience" (p. 61). Rubin refers to such terms as "with-it-ness," "instructional judgments," "quick cognitive leaps," and "informal guesses" to explain the difference between the effective teacher and the ineffective teacher. Recognizing limits to rationality, he claims that for the artistic teacher a "feel for what is right often is more productive than prolonged analysis" (p. 69). In the final analysis, Rubin compares the teacher's pedagogy with the "artist's colors, poet's words, sculptor's clay, and musician's notes" (p. 60)—in all of which a certain amount of artistic judgment is needed to get the right mix, medium, or blend.

Dawe (1984a, 1984b) is most extreme in his analysis of teaching solely as an art, providing romantic accounts and tales of successful teaching and teaching strategies, described in language that could hardly be taken for social science research. He considers the act of teaching akin to drama, and feels that those who wish to teach should audition in a teaching studio before teachers trained as performing artists. Good teaching is likened to good theater, and a good teacher is likened to a good actor.

Blending Science and Art

The more we consider teaching as an art, packed with emotions, feelings, and excitement, the more difficult it is to derive rules or generalizations. If teaching is more of an art than a science, then principles and practices cannot be easily codified or developed in the classroom or easily learned by others. Hence, there is little reason to offer to teachers methods courses in education. If, however, teaching is more of a science, or at least partly a science, then pedagogy is predictable to that extent; it can be observed and measured with some accuracy, and the research can be applied to the practice of teaching (as a physician applies scientific knowledge to the practice of medicine) and also learned in a university or on the job (Bolster, 1983; Ornstein, 1985, 1990).

But a word of caution is needed. The more we rely on artistic interpretations or on old stories and accounts about teachers, the more we fall victim to fantasy, wit, and romantic rhetoric, and the more we depend on hearsay and conjecture rather than on social science or objective data in evaluating teacher competency. On the other hand, the more we rely on the scientific interpretations of teaching, the more we overlook those commonsense and spontaneous processes of teaching, and the sounds, smells, and visual flavor of the classroom. The more scientific we are in our approach to teaching, the more we ignore what we cannot accommodate to our empirical assumptions or principles. What sometimes occurs, according to Eisner (1993), is that the educationally significant but difficult to measure or observe is replaced by what is insignificant but comparatively easy to measure or observe.

It is necessary to blend artistic impressions and relevant stories about teaching, because good teaching involves emotions and feelings, with the objectivity of observations and measurements and the precision of language. There is nothing wrong with considering good teaching to be art, but we must also consider it to lend itself to a prescriptive science or practice. If it does not, then there is little assurance that prospective teachers can be trained to be teachers—told what to do, how to instruct students, how to manage students, and so forth—and educators will be extremely vulnerable to public criticism and to people outside the profession telling them how and what to teach.

TEACHER–STUDENT VARIABLES

The kind of teacher effectiveness studies that make up the mainstream of educational research considers relationships between variables. We can have *predictive* relationships and *causal* relationships. For example, Flanders (1965) in his classic study shows that students who are taught by an "indirect" teacher learn more and exhibit more constructive behaviors than do those who are taught by a "direct" teacher. The results of that study have been cited in thousands of studies on teaching, including some fifteen times in the most recent edition of the *Handbook of Research on Teaching,* edited by Wittrock (1986).

However, such a predictive relationship may not really reflect a causal relationship or a cause-effect relationship. It is possible that students who are nonachievers or unruly cause teachers to exhibit direct behaviors and that students who are achievers and well mannered permit teachers to exhibit indirect behaviors. We can raise this point with about 90 percent of the research on teacher effectiveness, since the results are overwhelmingly correlational. Furthermore, many teacher behaviors and methods that seem to have a positive effect in one situation may be ineffective and inappropriate in another. Different teacher behaviors and methods have different effects on different students, in different grades, subjects, classrooms, and schools. For example, does the "warm" teacher have the same effect on first graders and twelfth graders? In mathematics, history, and physical education? With low-income and middle-income students, with low achievers and high achievers, with boys and girls, and so on? Moreover, it is difficult to isolate the teacher effects from the effects of other agents such as parents, peer group, television, and other teachers (Ornstein, 1986b, 1989). Failure to control for these variables and their interaction effects leads to inappropriate research findings and to nonrelevant and misleading data for the teacher. But once we start to analyze the various relationships among the variables, we come to numerous interactions and still other new and untested interactions, which in turn can be analyzed. This process is endless; we enter a hall of mirrors that extends to infinity.

Not only do process variables (different behaviors and/or methods) mean different things to different researchers, but also similar behaviors or methods are sometimes considered effective in one study and ineffective in another study. These are constructs that interact with numerous presage and context variables, and they entail such a diversity of specifics that they defy precise definitions and exact quantification. Moreover, if we break them down into precise, agreed-on, quantifiable constructs and variables, the number would vastly increase to the point of trivia and the importance of each would be reduced to the specific study. How far we extend our analysis depends on our purpose and knowledge; nonetheless, the existing relationships are not linear or clear, but rather multiple and sketchy.

Process Versus Product

Most of the research from the turn of the century to the early 1970s focused on process variables in terms of their relationships to presage or context variables. The idea was to focus on teacher behaviors or methods and to use such measures as ratings, classroom observations, and personality tests to obtain information on what the teacher was doing in the classroom. A basic assumption of many investigators during this period was that assessment of teacher behavior sufficed for describing teaching and learning. The focus was on what the teacher was doing, with little consideration given to the resulting behavior or performance of the students. Although one can make a good case for focusing on teachers, more emphasis should have been given to student outcomes.

Only recently has the research moved from the processes to the products of teaching. Emphasis on the products of teaching makes the behavior of the teacher, or what the teacher is doing, of secondary importance to student outcomes or results, and these are usually measured through standardized tests of achievement. Process variables are still considered part of the research; but, they are often used as part of a process-product paradigm whereby certain teacher behaviors or methods are determined to be "effective" in contributing to student achievement (which is usually based on reading or mathematics tests).

TEACHER EFFECTIVENESS RESEARCH

The current research on teacher effectiveness delineates a host of easily measured businesslike, structured, and tasklike behaviors (i.e., Doyle, 1985, 1986; Evertson, 1993; Good and Brophy, 1990; Rosenshine, 1987, 1992). But these models fail to consider that teachers differ, and that many successful teachers do not exhibit such direct behaviors.

The new and popular teacher effectiveness models lock us into a narrow mold that misses many nuances of teaching. Many of these prescriptions (sometimes called principles) themselves are old ideas bottled under new labels such as "with-it-ness," "smoothness," "clarity," "alertness," "pacing," "momentum," "overlapping," and "student accountability." These terms are rooted in Kounin's (1970) research on classroom management, and in some cases it is not clear that the current crop of researchers on teacher effectiveness gives Kounin his full credit. This explains in part the current emphasis on routines, rules, and control—in short, on teaching behaviors and methods that enhance classroom management. Furthermore, much of the new research deals with low achievers and at-risk students—another reason why many of its recommended teacher behaviors and methods coincide with managerial and structured techniques. Indeed, the new research tends to confirm that effective teachers are good classroom managers, which is something most teachers already know and knew even before Kounin established his "principles" of classroom management.

In our efforts to identify good teaching, the teacher effectiveness research is often published as if its findings are new or ground breaking. But the findings are nothing more than behaviors and methods that good teachers have been using for many years. What these product-oriented researchers have done is to summarize what we have known for a long time but have often passed on as "tips for teachers" or "practical suggestions." (And we were once criticized by researchers as being recipe oriented.) These researchers confirm the basic behaviors and methods of experienced teachers; however, they give beginning teachers a better yardstick or starting point to understand effective teaching than did previous researchers, and they give credibility to the teachers' practices by correlating their behaviors (processes) with student achievement (products).

The Purposes of Teacher Effectiveness Research

The fundamental question in the conduct and appreciation of research into teacher effectiveness is whether or not teachers influence student outcomes and, if so, to what extent. The need to establish the relative contribution of the teacher to student learning is particularly important for three reasons:

1. *It provides teacher educators a rationale for their job.* Teacher educators must screen and prepare future teachers, as well as provide in-service

education for experienced teachers. If teachers have little or no impact on student outcomes, then there is no reason to guard the gates with credentials or to make such a fuss about teacher education. If teachers have minimal or no impact on students, then there is little or no reason to provide pedagogical knowledge in order to enhance professional competence.

2. *It provides a rationale for the recent reforms regarding teacher evaluation, teacher accountability, teacher performance, and teacher competence.* If teachers have little effect on student outcomes, or if replicable findings of teacher effectiveness cannot be found, then all these new reform policies are at best theoretical exercises and at worst politicize the evaluation of teachers. If such data are lacking, then various methods for effective teaching have been sold unproven, and sound teacher evaluation policies cannot be formulated. Moreover, assessing teachers or making judgments about their competence cannot be supported; making inferences from observations or rating scales to support personnel decisions are invalid; and labels such as "incompetent," "competent," or "master" teacher are premature. The absence of teacher influence on student performance suggests that remediation, probation, or performance-related programs cannot be statistically or legally supported, and it is difficult for supervisors and administrators to give constructive evaluation and feedback to teachers.

3. *It provides support for the ideas that teacher differences exist and that teachers make a difference.* Since the 1980s, the prominent view is that teachers affect student outcomes. This new research assumes that the process (teacher behaviors and/or methods) can be controlled, modified, or taught, and that teacher-student interactions can be analyzed and predicted; it also assumes that what teachers do in the classroom does affect students and that narrowly defined teacher behaviors or methods affect student performance. (Ornstein, 1990).

4. *It provides a professional knowledge base for teacher educators and teacher training institutions.* If this knowledge base continues to develop and is appropriately used, it can help provide information to use when making decisions about appropriate teaching techniques—even who should teach. This information base allows us to act confidently on a theoretical basis, whereby we establish certain principles or methods of teaching. Whether these theoretical generations apply to the real world of teaching, that is, the practice of teaching, is not clear. It is assumed that much of the teacher effectiveness research can be integrated into what teachers already know or think they know about teaching, and it is also assumed that the behaviors that are codified and measured lead to desired learning outcomes.

In general, the new research on teacher effectiveness opposes a wealth of large-scale research considered conventional wisdom in the 1960s and 1970s, which held that teacher effects were secondary or irrelevant and that each student's IQ, family, home life, peer group, and social class were crucial in determining his or her achievement (Coleman, 1966; Husén, 1967; Jencks, 1972; Moynihan, 1965; Thorndike, 1973). This research attributed only a small fraction of the independent variation in student achievement to school variables (about 15 to 20 percent, depending on the research study), and only a small part to teachers. Their analysis points the finger of responsibility for achievement to students, not teachers; thus we should remember their findings and discuss publicly the influence of family structure and parental responsibility on student outcomes.

Caution and Criticism

There is some danger in the new research. The conclusions overwhelmingly portray the effective teacher as task-oriented, organized, and structured—nothing more than Ryans's (1960) Pattern Y or businesslike teacher and Flanders's (1965) direct teacher (who was considered ineffective). These teacher effectiveness models tend to overlook the friendly, warm, and democratic teacher;

the creative teacher who is stimulating and imaginative; the dramatic teacher who bubbles with energy and enthusiasm; the philosophical teacher who encourages students to play with ideas and concepts; and the problem-solving teacher who requires that students think out the answers. In their desire to identify and prescribe measurable and quantifiable behaviors, the new researchers overlook the emotional, qualitative, and interpretive descriptions of classrooms, and the joys of teaching. Most of the new research has been conducted at the elementary grade levels, where one would expect more social, psychological, and humanistic factors to be observed, recorded, and recommended as effective.

The new teacher effectiveness models fail to consider that a good deal of effective teaching may not directly correlate with student performance measured by achievement tests. For Greene (1986, 1993), good teaching and learning involve such intangibles as values, experiences, insights, and appreciation—the "stuff" that cannot be easily observed or measured. Teaching and learning is an "existential" encounter, a philosophical process involving creative ideas and inquiries that cannot be easily quantified. We might add that much of teaching involves caring, nurturing, and valuing behaviors—attributes not easily assessed by evaluation instruments.

Much of teaching also deals with hunches and intuitive judgments that teachers make as classroom events and interactions evolve; the teachers' behaviors or responses are not preplanned, and they cannot easily be categorized or made to fit into measurable units that correspond with the classroom context. Indeed, teaching is a holistic enterprise and trying to slice, isolate, or categorize it into some set of recommendations or hierarchy of principles and methods may not be realistic. It may be the best we can offer as researchers continue the struggle to define good teaching, but it is merely an abstraction from a host of classroom events that rarely considers prior teacher-student experiences and the thinking and feelings that interact with behaviors to influence learning.

What is not measurable goes unnoticed in a process-product teaching model. By breaking down the teaching act into behaviors, competencies, or criteria that can be defined operationally and quantified, educators overlook the hard-to-measure aspects of teaching, the personal and humanistic aspects of teaching. To say that excellence in teaching requires measurable behaviors and outcomes is to miss a substantial part of teaching—what some educators refer to as artistry, drama, tone, and flavor. It can be argued, too, that teacher behaviors that correlate with measurable outcomes often lead to rote learning, drill, and automatic responses.

In their attempts to observe and measure what teachers do and to detail whether students improve their performance (usually on reading or mathematics tests), these models ignore the learners' imaginations, fantasies, and aesthetic thoughts, including their dreams, hopes, and aspirations, and how teachers influence these hard-to-define but very important aspects of students' lives. The chief variable in this current research is knowledge of facts, as evidenced by scores on achievement tests (Ornstein, 1989, 1990).

The fact is that the research on teaching tends to neglect the "subject knowledge" of the teacher—how it relates to student understanding, how it is taught and how it is integrated with "pedagogical knowledge"—the genetic principles and methods of teaching. Teacher effectiveness research also neglects learning experiences that deal with metacognition, critical thinking, and learning how to learn, as well as more global learning outcomes such as cultural sensitivity, spiritual outlook, and philosophy. It correlates with specific knowledge—the content of Walt Whitman's poems and the outcomes of Hiroshima—but not how students feel about these subjects, or how it has affected their own learning or outlook on life. In the same view, teacher behavior research seems to miss moral and ethical outcomes, as well as social, personal, and self-actualizing processes related to life—the affective domain of learning and the psychology of being human.

Quantifiable Research Methods

The traditional world of measuring teacher behavior assumes that educational research is a matter of identifying and adding more variables and providing sophisticated analysis to a one-way, or input-output, explanation of human behavior. The intent is to discover a number of "right" input variables that will define human behavior as output in educational settings (Cziko, 1992). But this basic model and its assumptions, which drives group-based statistics, miss the mark for fully explaining purposeful behavior.

Regardless of the statistical procedures used—correlation tests, t-tests, analysis of variances, and multiple regression, among others—proponents are convinced that human behavior can be explained by causality, where an independent variable (usually some condition or treatment effect) causes or affects the dependent variable (an outcome). This is a quick and snappy method of exhibiting "expertise," especially when mixed with professional or research jargon. Well, life is not that simple, especially when it comes to teaching and learning. Outcomes in life, as well as life in classrooms, depend on a host of complex interactions that cannot be fully explained by isolating or breaking down abstractions of human behavior into discrete categories or statistical units, at least not without interpreting the data within the context of what is happening. All these quantifiable (independent-dependent variables) procedures merely provide the researcher with frequency of outcomes; they assume a one-way cause-effect explanation—similar to classical behaviorist psychology—but are inadequate for fully explaining the complex aspect of teaching and learning.

Many of us who are satisfied in analyzing the world of psychology or education in term of quantifiable outcomes believe that if research or evaluation problems exist it is because the methods need to be improved. When critics mention that causality is sometimes unknown, or blurred by other factors not accounted for, the most common reaction is to ignore or criticize the information.

Even worse, once we try to analyze the various relationships among variables, we come to numerous interactions and still other new and untested interactions. The process is endless, especially in the teaching-learning equation, and we enter into a hall of mirrors that extends into infinity. How far we carry our analysis depends on our knowledge and purposes; nonetheless, the relationships are not linear or clear, but rather multiple and sketchy.

The traditional, quantifiable model of research on teaching is hard to criticize, because it represents mainstream thinking and is derived from predictable behavior. To discuss human behavior with fuzzy phenenoma or hard-to-define processes or products is to leave oneself open to professional ridicule, especially in a well governed by "technocratic" researchers and Skinnerian logic.

THE HUMAN FACTOR IN TEACHING

Good teachers know, although they may not be able to prove it, that good teaching is really about caring and sharing; the capacity to accept, understand, and appreciate students on their terms and through their world; making students feel good about themselves; having positive attitudes and setting realistic achievement goals; and getting all fired up with enthusiasm and a cheerful presence.

These are basically fuzzy qualities that the scientific theories and paradigms of effective teaching tend to overlook. Indeed teachers who place high priority on humanistic and effective practices, and on the personal and social development of their students, are not really interested in devoting much time to the empirical or behavioral literature, or in teaching small pieces of information that can be measured and correlated with their own teaching behaviors.

Teachers who are confident about themselves are not overly concerned about their evaluation ratings, or even what the research has to say about their teacher behaviors. How does the profession reconcile the fact that so many competent teachers consider teacher research as "irrelevant and counterintuitive" to their own practice of teaching? Why do we often hear the complaint— "That's all good theory, but it does not work in practice."

Teaching is a people industry, and people (especially young people) perform best in places in which they feel wanted and respected. To be sure, it is possible for a teacher to "disengage" or "disinvite" students by belittling them, ignoring them, undercutting them, comparing them to other siblings or students, or even "yessing" them (failing to hold them accountable for the right answer), and still perform high on other discrete competencies or behaviors associated with the teacher as a technician: "The teacher came to class on time." "The teacher's objectives were clearly stated." "The teacher checked homework on a regular basis." "The teacher's expectations were clearly stated." "The teacher graded quizzes on a timely basis." Such a checklist or behaviorist approach is common today, as we search for a research-based model of what is a "good" or "effective" teacher. This mentality can make us technically right but never really describe good teaching; it coincides with the bureaucratic process, where rules, regulations, and memos prevail. But it misses the essence of classroom teaching, where feelings, attitudes, and imagination are crucial and should take precedence over tiny, measurable pieces of information that border on silliness and trivia. Of course, some of the research that characterizes good teaching is reasonable and warranted, but most of this "wisdom" is old hat, and what experienced teachers already know.

The focus of teacher research should be on the learner, not on the teacher; on the feelings and attitudes of the students, not on knowledge and information (since feelings and attitudes will eventually determine what knowledge and information are sought after and acquired); and on long-term objectives or specific tasks. But if teachers spend more time on the learner, on his or her feelings and attitudes, and on the social or personal growth and development of their students, they may be penalized when cognitive outcomes (little pieces of information) are correlated with their teaching behaviors.

Students need to be encouraged and nurtured by their teachers, especially when they are young. They are too dependent on approval from significant adults—first their parents, then their teachers. Because of this, parents and teachers need to help young children and adolescents establish a source of self-esteem within themselves by focusing on their strengths, supporting them, and by discouraging negative self-talk while helping them to take control of their lives and living by their own values.

People (including young people) with high self-esteem achieve at high levels, and the more one achieves, the better one feels about oneself. The opposite is also true. Students who fail to master the subject matter get down on themselves and eventually give up. Students with low self-esteem give up quickly. In short, student self-esteem and achievement are related, as are student self-esteem and self-reliance (Ames, 1990; Corno, 1993). Put in different words, if we can nurture the students' self-esteem, almost everything else should fall into place, including achievement scores and academic outcomes. If we can get the students' feelings and emotions on track, cognition will follow. Cognition cannot be successful if teachers fail to guide students who have serious social or personal problems.

This builds a strong argument for creating success experiences for students to help them feel good about themselves. The long-term benefits are obvious. The more students learn to like themselves, the more they will achieve, and the more they achieve, the more they will like themselves. But that takes time, that is nurturing learners for future benefits. However, these benefits do not show up on a classroom or standardized test within a semester or school year; it doesn't help the teacher who is being evaluated by a content-driven or test-driven school administrator. It certainly does not benefit the teacher who is being evaluated for how many times he or she attended departmental meetings, whether the shades in the classroom were even, or whether the instructional objectives were clearly stated.

The current research on teaching is primarily concerned with the present—with processes and products that are measured in one term (or year) and by a standardized test of cognitive outcomes (not affective outcomes). Thus, one might conclude that the new teacher effectiveness research misses the humanistic mark. Students need to engage in growth-enhancing experiences and we need to recognize that the most effective teachers endow their students with a "you can do it" attitude, with good feelings about themselves, which are indirectly and eventually related to cognitive achievement. While every teacher needs to demand high academic standards and teach the content, there needs to be understanding that the content interacts with the process. If the process can be cultivated in a humanistic way, then the outcomes of the content should be improved.

Beyond Effective Teaching

The current research on teacher effectiveness needs to be revised to fit varied teaching contexts. Teachers must be permitted to incorporate specific teacher behaviors and methods according to their personality, philosophy, and goals—to pick and choose from a wide range of research and theory and to discard other teacher behaviors and methods that conflict with their style, without being considered ineffective. It also needs to include, according to Prawat (1992), what students do outside of school because the time spent outside of school surpasses the time spent in classrooms. Out-of-school variables are certainly more important than school variables, but that brings us back to Coleman, Jencks, and Moynihan and the family and peer group—which many educators would rather not discuss; moreover, it is the research that the current model on teacher effectiveness wishes to refute.

It is obvious that certain behaviors contribute to good teaching. The trouble is, there is little agreement on exactly what behaviors or methods are most important. There will be some teachers who gain theoretical knowledge of "what works," but will be unable to put the ideas into practice. Some teachers will act effortlessly in the classroom and others will consider teaching a chore. All this suggests that teaching cannot be described in terms of a checklist or a precise model. It also suggests that teaching is a holistic activity that deals with people (not tiny behaviors or competencies) and how they (teachers and students) develop and behave in a variety of classroom and school settings.

While the research on teacher effectiveness provides a vocabulary and system for improving our insight into good teaching, there is a danger that it may lead to some of us becoming too rigid in our view of teaching. Following only research on teaching effectiveness can lead to too much emphasis on specific behaviors that can be easily measured or prescribed in advance, at the expense of ignoring humanistic behaviors and hard-to-measure behaviors.

Most teacher evaluation instruments tend to deemphasize the human side of teaching, because it is difficult to measure. In an attempt to be scientific, to predict and control behavior, and to assess group patterns, we sometimes lose sight of effective behaviors and individual preferences. Although some educators have moved to a search for humanistic factors that influence teaching, we continue to mainly define most teacher behaviors in terms of behaviorist and cognitive factors.

Similarly, most teacher evaluation instruments still do not address the question of how to change teacher behavior. The developers of evaluation instruments assume that once they have discovered what ought to be done, teachers will naturally do what is expected. If our purpose is to change or improve the practices of teachers, then it is necessary to come to grips with teachers' beliefs and attitudes and with their concepts of "good" and "effective."

In providing feedback and evaluation for teachers many factors need to be considered so that advice or information does not fall in deaf ears. Teachers appreciate feedback processes whereby they can improve their teaching, so long as the processes are honest and fair and are professionally planned and administered; so long as teachers are permitted to make mistakes; and so long as more than one model of effectiveness is

considered so that they can adopt recommended behaviors and methods that fit their personality and philosophy of teaching.

The current research on teacher effectiveness needs to be revised to include varied teaching styles. Teachers must be permitted to incorporate specific teacher behaviors and methods according to their own unique personality, philosophy, and goals; to pick and choose from a wide range of research and theory; and to discard those teacher behaviors that conflict with their own style, without fear of being considered ineffective. A good many school districts, even state departments of education, have developed evaluation instruments and salary plans based exclusively on these prescriptive and product-oriented behaviors. Even worse, teachers who do not exhibit these behaviors are often penalized or labeled as "marginal" or "incompetent" (Holdzkom, 1987; Milner, 1991; Ornstein, 1988a, 1988b). There is an increased danger that many more school districts and states will continue to jump on this bandwagon and make decisions based on these models without recognizing or giving credibility to other teacher effectiveness research.

CONCLUSION

Few, if any, activities are as crucial in schooling as teaching; and, as elusive and complex as teaching may be, research toward understanding it must continue. The problem, however, is that most of the research on teaching is not read by the most important group—teachers, who can and should benefit by knowing, understanding, and integrating the concepts and principles of the research on teaching.

It is obvious that certain behaviors contribute to good teaching. The trouble is that there is little agreement on exactly what behaviors or methods are most important. Some teachers will learn most of the rules about good teaching, yet be unsuccessful. Other teachers will break the rules of "good" teaching, yet be profoundly successful. Some teachers will gain theoretical knowledge of "what works," but be unable to put the ideas into practice. And yet other teachers will act effortlessly in the classroom, while others will consider teaching a chore. All this suggests that teaching is more art than science and practice is more important than theory.

While the research on teacher effectiveness provides a vocabulary and system for improving our insight into good teaching, there is a danger that it may lead to some of us becoming too rigid in our view of teaching. Following only the research on teaching can lead to too much emphasis on specific behaviors that cannot be easily measured or prescribed in advance.

Most teacher evaluation processes do not address the question of how to change teacher behavior. The developers of evaluation instruments assume that once they have discovered what ought to be done, teachers will naturally do what is expected. If our purpose is to change or improve the practices of teachers, then it is necessary to come to grips with teachers' beliefs and attitudes and with their concepts of "good" or "effective."

In providing feedback and evaluation to teachers, many factors need to be considered so that the advice or information does not fall on deaf ears. Teachers appreciate feedback processes whereby they can improve their teaching, if the processes are honest and fair and are professionally planned and administered; if teachers are permitted to make mistakes; and if more than one model of effectiveness is considered so that teachers can adopt recommended behaviors and methods that fit their own personality and philosophy of teaching.

ENDNOTES

1. This article is based on three of the author's works: "Teacher Effectiveness Research: Theoretical Considerations," in H. C. Waxman and H. J. Walberg, eds., *Effective Teaching: Current Research.* Berkeley: McCutchan Press, 1991, pp. 63–80; "How to Recognize Good Teaching," *American School Board Journal,* 180 (1993), pp. 24–29; and "The Human Dimension of Teaching," *Educational Forum,* in print (1995).

REFERENCES

Ames, Carol. "Motivation: What Teachers Need to Know." *Teachers College Record* 91 (1990): 409–421.

Bolin, Frances G. "Helping Student Teachers Think about Teaching." *Journal of Teacher Education* 39 (1988): 48–55.

Bolster, Arthur S. "Toward a More Effective Model of Research on Teaching." *Harvard Educational Review* 53 (1983): 294–398.

Borich, G. D. "Paradigms of Teacher Effectiveness Research." *Education and Urban Society* 18 (1986): 143–167.

Brophy, Jere E. "Classroom Management Techniques." *Education and Urban Society* 18 (1986): 182–194.

Brophy, Jere E. "Educating Teachers about Managing Classrooms and Students." *Teaching and Teacher Education* 4 (1988): 1–18.

Coleman, James S. *Equality of Educational Opportunity.* Washington, D.C.: U.S. Government Printing Office, 1966.

Corno, Lyn. "Modern Conceptions of Volition and Educational Research." *Educational Researcher* 22 (1993): 14–22.

Cziko, Gary A. "Purposeful Behavior as the Control of Perception." *Educational Researcher* 21 (1992): 10–18.

Dawe, Harry A. "Teaching: A Performing Art." *Phi Delta Kappan* 65 (1984a): 548–552.

Dawe, Harry A. "Teaching: Social Science or Performing Art?" *Harvard Educational Review* 54 (1984b): 111–114.

Doyle, Walter E. "Effective Teaching and the Concept of Master Teacher." *Elementary School Journal* 86 (1985): 27–34.

Doyle, Walter E. "Classroom Organization and Management." In *Handbook of Research on Teaching,* 3d ed. Edited by Merlin C. Wittrock. New York: Macmillan, 1986.

Eisner, Elliot W. "The Art and Craft of Teaching." *Educational Leadership* 40 (1983): 4–13.

Eisner, Elliot W. *The Educational Imagination,* 3rd ed. New York: Macmillan, 1993.

Evertson, Carolyn M. "Do Teachers Make a Difference?" *Education and Urban Society* 18 (1986): 195–210.

Evertson, Carolyn M., et al. *Classroom Management for Secondary Teachers,* 3rd ed. Englewood Cliffs, N.J.: Prentice-Hall, 1993.

Flanders, Ned. *Teacher Influence, Pupil Attitudes and Achievement.* Washington, D.C.: U.S. Government Printing Office, 1965.

Gage, N. L. *The Scientific Basis of the Art of Teaching.* New York: Teachers College Press, 1978.

Good, Thomas L., and Jere E. Brophy. *Looking in Classrooms,* 5th ed. New York: HarperCollins, 1990.

Greene, Maxine. "Philosophy and Teaching." In *Handbook of Research on Teaching,* 3rd ed. Edited by Merlin C. Wittrock. New York: Macmillan. 1986.

Greene, Maxine. "The Passions of Pluralism." *Educational Researcher,* 22 (1993): 13–18.

Holdzkom, David. "Appraising Teacher Performance in North Carolina." *Educational Leadership* 44 (1987): 40–44.

Husen, Torsten. *International Study of Achievement in Mathematics: A Comparison of Twelve Countries.* New York: Wiley, 1967.

Jencks, Christopher, et al. *Inequality: A Reassessment of the Effect of Family and Schooling in America.* New York: Basic Books, 1972.

Kounin, Jacob. *Discipline and Group Management in Classrooms.* New York: Holt, Rinehart, 1970.

Milner, Joseph O. "Working Together For Better Evaluation," *Phi Delta Kappan* 72 (1991): 788–789.

Moynihan, D. P. *The Negro Family: The Case for National Action.* Washington, D.C.: U.S. Government Printing Office, 1965.

Ornstein, Allan C. "Research on Teaching: Issues and Trends." *Journal of Teacher Education* 36 (1985): 27–31.

Ornstein, Allan C. "Research on Teacher Behavior: Trends and Policies." *High School Journal* 69 (1986a): 399–402.

Ornstein, Allan C. "Teacher Effectiveness: Current Research and Issues." *Educational and Urban Society* 18 (1986b): 168–175.

Ornstein, Allan C. "Theory and Practice of Curriculum." *Kappa Delta Pi Record* 24 (1987): 15–17.

Ornstein, Allan C. "The Changing Status of the Teaching Profession." *Urban Education* 23 (1988a): 261–279.

Ornstein, Allan C. "The Evolving Accountability Movement." *Peabody Journal of Education* 65 (1988b): 12–20.

Ornstein, Allan C. "Theoretical Issues Related To Teaching." *Education and Urban Society* 22 (1989): 95–104.

Ornstein, Allan C. "A Look at Teacher Effectiveness Research." *NASSP Bulletin* 74 (1990): 78–88.

Prawat, Richard S. "From Individual Differences to Learning Communities." *Educational Leadership* 49 (1992): 9–13.

Rosenshine, Barak V. "Explicit Teaching and Teacher Training." *Journal of Teacher Education* 38 (1987): 34–36.

Rosenshine, Barak V., and Carla Meister. "The Use of Scaffolds for Higher-Level Cognitive Strategies." *Educational Leadership* 49 (1992): 26–33.

Rubin, Louis J. *Artistry in Teaching.* New York: Random House, 1985.

Ryans, David G. *Characteristics of Teachers.* Washington, D.C.: America Council on Education, 1960.

Thorndike, Robert L. *Reading Comprehension Education in Fifteen Countries.* New York: Wiley, 1973.

Wise, Arthur, Darling-Hammond, Linda, McLaughlin, Milbrey, and Berstein, Harriet. "Teacher Evaluation: A Study of Effective Practices." *Elementary School Journal* 86 (1985): 61–121.

Wittrock, Merlin C., ed. *Handbook of Research on Teaching,* 3d ed. New York: Macmillan, 1986.

DISCUSSION QUESTIONS

1. How do presage, context, process, and product variables differ?

2. What are some of the limitations of current teacher effectiveness research?

3. Why should researchers study teacher effectiveness?

4. What is the fallacy associated with attempting to correlate teacher effectiveness behaviors and student achievement?

5. Should graduate students in education be required to demonstrate an understanding of the literature on teacher effectiveness research? Why? Why not?

The Art and Craft of Teaching

ELLIOT W. EISNER

FOCUSING QUESTIONS

1. *What are the pros and cons of a science of education and a science of curriculum?*
2. *How has the history of psychology and business influenced teaching and curriculum?*
3. *Why is it important for curriculum workers to be reflective practitioners?*
4. *In what ways is teaching both an art and a science?*
5. *How do the art and craft of teaching differ?*
6. *Why is aesthetics an integral aspect of teaching?*

My aim in this essay is to recover on a theoretical level what I believe practitioners—teachers and school administrators—have never relinquished in the private, quiet moments of their professional lives. I wish to help re-establish, to legitimatize, to publicly acknowledge the art and craft of teaching. To write about the art and craft of teaching in a period in which we are sending a space shuttle through the heavens, when we are able to place man on the moon and, as Frank Buck used to say, "to bring 'em back alive" is seemingly to hearken back to a bygone era. We pride ourselves, and we should, on the achievements of science and the technology science has made possible.

Indeed, to write about the craft of teaching today is likely to evoke images of the elderly working painstakingly on a handcrafted item in a tiny cottage located in a small village sitting next to the delicate but limited glow of a flickering fire. Our images of science and technology are much sleeker, and these images have penetrated contemporary education. In education we talk about diagnosis and prescription, of entry and exit skills, of the use of token economies, and of feedback loops for inputs that fail to meet specifications when they become output. Such talk reminds me of the story of a conversation between the senior officer of a large corporation and a new business school graduate:

> "Sir, I think that by bringing up a small model to simulate aggregate income-expenditure alternatives over various time frames, by integrating those results with appropriate ZBB reviews to assess minimum core expenditure levels, and then by relating to managers in an MBO framework, we can get this administration moving again," said the young colleague with eagerness and authority.
>
> The senior man gazed out the window, pondered the words so redolent with modern techniques, then spoke:
>
> "Shut up," he explained.[1]

Why is it the art and craft of teaching—and of school administration—should seem so quaint? Why is it that the art of teaching should be regarded as a poetic metaphor, but like poetry, more suited to satisfy the soul than to inform the head? Why is it that one so seldom hears of workshops or conferences devoted to the art and craft of teaching? And what would re-emergence of such concepts mean for the improvement of teaching and for educational administrators? To find out we must first look back in time.

When one examines the intellectual history of American education, particularly as it emerged during the 19th century, one finds that a distinctive form of professional preparation developed with the creation of the first state normal school in 1839.[2] By the end of the 1870s, 80 such schools had been established and by 1900 there were over 150.[3] When schools are established for training practitioners, it's nice to have something to teach them. During the same period in Europe and later in America the field of psychology was itself being formalized, and the work of Wilhelm Wundt in Germany, Francis Galton in England, and G. Stanley Hall and William James in the United States provided much of the substance on which to build a profession of education.[4] Hall, the first person to receive a Ph.D. in psychology from Harvard University in 1878,[5] was the father of the child study movement[6] and editor of the influential *Pedagogical Seminary*.[7] James, whose *Talks to Teachers*[8] remains a classic, was himself influenced by Wundt and later was to train the giant of American psychology, the man to whom B. F. Skinner once wrote: "I seem to identify your point of view with the modern psychological view taken as a whole. It has always been obvious that I was merely carrying on your puzzle box experiments. . . ."[9] That man was Edward L. Thorndike.

Thorndike was a great psychologist. He did about everything. He studied children's drawings, he studied handwriting, he studied aptitude and motivation, he wrote yards of books and articles, but what he did most was study learning. It was Thorndike who developed the idea of the S-R bond and who coined the term "Connectionism"[10]: Learning, he argued, was the result of

connections in the cortex, connections strengthened by reinforcements provided to responses to particular stimuli. To the extent to which each stimulus was unique, the responses to be learned were also unique. Rationality was a concept fit for philosophy of mind, but not for a scientific psychology of learning.

As for the transfer of learning, Thorndike believed it was quite limited: One was able to transfer what one had learned only insofar as the elements in one situation were identical with those in the next. It was, as he called it, a theory of identical elements.[11] Memory drums, rat mazes, positive and negative reinforcement, frequency, recency, and intensity were the metaphors with which he worked. Thorndike's task was to develop a science of learning so that brick by brick a science of education could be built. For those seeking a respectable basis for teacher training and school administration, such a view was understandably attractive.

When the first issue of the *Journal of Educational Psychology* was published in 1910, it was Edward L. Thorndike who had the lead article. He wrote:

> A complete science of psychology would tell every fact about everyone's intellect and character and behavior, would tell the cause of every change in human nature, would tell the result which every educational force—every act of every person that changed any other or the agent himself—would have. It would aid us to use human beings for the world's welfare with the same surety of the result that we now have when we use falling bodies or chemical elements. In proportion we get such a science we shall become masters of heat and light. Progress toward such a science is being made.[12]

What we see here is a noble ambition, an expression of faith in the power of scientific inquiry to shape, indeed to determine the future, and thus to enable humankind to create a better, more predictable world. Science is, after all, associated with progress. To have a science of education is to have know-how, to understand not only what works, but why. A scientific technology of teaching would reduce noise in the system, make the system more systematic, more efficient, and hence give taxpayers the products they wanted schools to produce.

Science became the faith: scientific technology, the good works that the faith made possible.

It is hard to underestimate Thorndike's legacy. His ideas, his research, but even more his faith in science, helped set the tone for educational research for the next 70 years. To understand that tone is to understand why it is that the art and craft of teaching were and are regarded as relics having only marginal relevance to the study and practice of education.

But even as influential as Thorndike was, he was not alone in shaping assumptions on which current conceptions of teaching and education rest. During the same period the concept of scientific management, developed by Francis Taylor and applied to the problems of making industrial plants more efficient, also entered the educational scene.[13]

School administrators embraced scientific management as a way to reduce their vulnerability to public criticism and to make schools more efficient. In this approach management of education was hyper-rationalized. Teachers were regarded as workers to be supervised by specialists who made sure that goals were being attained, that teachers were performing as prescribed, and that the public who paid for the schools were getting their money's worth.

The guiding metaphor was industrial and the scope for personal ingenuity on the teacher's part was accordingly diminished.[14] The task was to get teachers to follow the one best method, a method that scientific management of education would prescribe. Thorndike's ideas, working in conceptual tandem with Taylor's, set a tone for American education that is still with us.

There are several characteristics of scientifically oriented ideology in education that deserve more than a casual mention. I say ideology because any perspective one embraces comes replete with values and assumptions about what is valid and trustworthy, what methods are legitimate, what counts as evidence, and hence helps determine the ends that are worth pursuing. If an aim cannot be accommodated within the dominant ideology, it is dropped from view; it is not considered meaningful.[15]

One assumption used in the effort to build a science of educational practice is that education cannot in principle become a discipline in its own right. It is rather "an area of study" and the most promising way to study that area is through the social science disciplines. The ramifications of this view were then and are today substantial. Consider only one—its impact on theory.

Since the concepts and categories that constitute theory in the social sciences were originally designed for noneducationally specific phenomena—rat maze learning, socialization in prisons, churches, and the home, for example—what such categories and theories illuminate is largely what education has in common with other phenomena rather than what is unique or special about schools, classrooms, teaching, or curriculum. The theoretical windows through which we peer circumscribe that portion of the landscape we shall see.

A second widely accepted assumption is that what we can learn through research about learning will be less ambiguous if the units treated are segmented and small. The operating belief is that once these small units are brought under control, variables can be isolated, effective educational treatments identified and then, finally, aggregated in order to build a technology of educational practice. First you learn how to introduce a lesson, then how to pose questions to students, then how to demonstrate a principle, then how to bring a lesson to closure, and when these and several other dozen—dare I say hundreds?—of teaching skills are learned, the ability to teach skillfully will have been achieved.[16]

Because long periods of experimental treatment time tend to lead to confounding—that is, long experimental periods increase the probability that uncontrolled variability will contaminate the treatment making the results difficult to explain—experiments in classrooms tend to be "cleaner" if they are brief.[17] The result is that much educational experimentation takes the form of commando raids designed to get in and out of classrooms in as little time as possible or consists of very short microexperiments that compare the effects of bits and pieces. The modal amount of experimental treatment time in experimental studies reported in the *American Education Research Journal* in 1977–78 was about 45 minutes. Studies are undertaken that are designed to determine if giving an example first and then an explanation, or an explanation first and then an example make any difference. The tacit assumption is that such knowledge, although discrete, is cumulative and independent of context. The variations that are possible in such approaches are, of course, endless. Like tadpoles they come forth filling the pages of learned journals.

Third, because the believability, of conclusions can be no greater than the reliability of the instruments used, instruments used to measure classroom practice and student learning need to be very reliable indeed. What this has meant all too often is that what is educationally significant but difficult to measure or observe is replaced with what is insignificant but comparatively easy to measure or observe.

Hence, we have a spate of studies that use the majestic to treat the trivial and others whose results are so qualified in character, for example, "The results hold for classrooms when the children are of low socioeconomic status if grouped homogeneously by reading score and taught by a male teacher who participated in at least five sessions of inservice education," that their practical utility is next to nil.

Fourth, and finally—although this critique could be extended further—is the assumption, and the primary one as far as I am concerned, that (1) a prescriptive educational science will make prediction and control of human behavior possible, and (2) such achievements are educationally desirable: the more prediction and control, the better. Prediction and control are of course virtues in the space program. The last place we want

surprises is on the launching pad or on the moon. The best thing that can be said for such operations is that they were uneventful. But are such aspirations quintessential in education? Do we want—even if we could achieve it—to be able to predict and control all or even most of what a student will think, feel, or be? Is E. L. Thorndike's aspiration an appropriate one for education? Is Francis Taylor's model of scientific management what students need today? By this time you might have guessed that I have my doubts.

The critique I have provided concerning the aspiration to develop a science of education and the assumptions and consequences of that approach should not lead you to believe that I see no place for scientific study in education or that I believe that scientific metaphors should be replaced with artistic ones. This is not the case. What I do not believe holds promise in education is a prescriptive view of science. I do not believe that with greater specificity or by reducing the whole to its most essential parts we can produce the kind of prescriptions that have made the space shuttle, radar, or laser beam possible. The aspiration to create a prescriptive science of educational practice is, I believe, hopeless.

What I think scientific inquiry can provide in education are rules of thumb, not rules.[18] Rules of thumb are schematics that make interpretation and judgment more acute. Scientific inquiry can provide frames of reference that can sophisticate our perceptions, not mechanisms that will control the behavior of students, teachers, or administrators. In short, if a distinction can be made between the *prescriptive* and the *interpretive,* between rules and schematics, between algorithms and heuristics, in the human situation I opt for interpretation, schematics, and heuristics, rather than prescriptions, rules, and algorithms.

To assert these views is not to provide for holding them. Let me provide a few. First, those of us who work with human beings work with people who do not, despite Thorndike's view, simply respond to stimuli. Human beings *construe* situations, they make sense of classrooms, they anticipate the world in which they live. What constitutes a stimulus depends not simply on what is injected in the classroom but what students take from it. And what various students take from the classroom and what they make of what they take differs. It differs because of their prior experience, their capabilities, their friends, their predispositions, and their relationship with the teacher. Because the perspectives they bring are multiple, no teacher can depend on a script or a prestructured sequence for guarantees about effective teaching. Indeed, the more opportunities a teacher provides to students to idiosyncratically construe and express what they have gotten out of a lesson, the less the teacher controls what they are likely to learn: the students teach each other.

Second, what students learn from educational encounters increases the differences among them.[19] Students with high levels of interest and aptitudes for particular subjects are likely to go farther and faster. Their satisfactions are likely to be greater than their opposite. Students who are ingenious arrive at answers that are often unpredictable. Where in all of this is the power of a prescribed method of instruction? Unlike automobiles rolling down an assembly line where an additive model works fairly well, (interaction effects are small), the children a classroom teacher deals with are unique configurations that change over time. Unlike electrons or billiard balls, students have ambitions and purposes and refuse to be treated as lumps of clay or sheets of steel passively awaiting the impact of a scientifically based teaching technology that provides little or no scope in its assumptions for what the students make of all of this. Our roles as teachers are closer to those of negotiators than to puppeteers or engineers. And even when we succeed in shaping our students' surfaces, unless we touch their souls we will be locked out of their inner lives. Much of contemporary education in both the public school and the university seldom gets more than skin deep.

Third, the idea that the skills of teaching can be treated as discrete elements and then aggregated to form a whole reflects a fundamental mis-

conception of what it means to be skilled in teaching. What skilled teaching requires is the ability to recognize dynamic patterns, to grasp their meaning, and the ingenuity to invent ways to respond to them. It requires the ability to both lose oneself in the act and at the same time maintain a subsidiary awareness of what one is doing. Simply possessing a set of discrete skills ensures nothing.

The importance of perceiving patterns in motion while at the same time being able to monitor oneself should not come as a surprise to anyone who has reflected on what being in a social situation requires. Humans have a built-in need to seek structures of signification. They find it necessary to make sense of the world. They learn to improvise within a changing field, whether in the classroom, the board room, or the principal's office. The mechanical application of prescribed routines is the surest way I know of to get into trouble.

But what of the art and craft of teaching? Thus far I have discussed our intellectual heritage in education, but have said little that is explicit about the art and craft of teaching. The time has come to address these concepts.

Given what I have already said about the kind of science appropriate for education, it should be clear that the space is very large between the ideas that science can provide and the kinds of decisions and actions a teacher must take. Classrooms and students are particular in character. Theory is general. What the teacher must be able to do is see the connection—if there is one—between the principle and the case. But even where such a connection exists, the fit is never perfect.

An imaginative leap is always required. But if we have no rules to follow, then how shall we take this leap? How shall we decide how to act? How do we fill the space between the theoretical frameworks and scientific findings we get from educational research and the concrete realities that we face on the job.

I suggest that it is in this space—the interstices between framework and action—that the art and craft of teaching is most crucial. We face a class, we raise a question, we get little or no response. Theoretical frameworks and the findings of research studies provide only limited help. What we do is to look for clues. We try to read the muted and enigmatic messages in our students' faces, in their posture, in their comportment. We look for a light at one end of the room and then at the other. Our sensibilities come into play as we try to construe the meaning of the particular situation we face.

And what do we face? Do we call on a particular student to get the ball rolling? Do we recast the question? Do we keep on talking and hope for the best? Our educational imagination begins to operate and we consider options. Theory helps, but as a guide not a prescription. It helps us consider options and once selected, we listen for messages given in the tone and pace of our students' conversations and questions. But even these options are options considered in the preactive, rather than in the interactive phase of teaching.

Teaching is typically too dynamic for the teacher to stop in order to formulate hypotheses or to run through a series of theories to form a productive eclectic relationship among them as the basis for deciding on a course of action. Students are not inclined to wait—and teachers know this. Teaching action is more immediate than reflective—unless we have a problem that we cannot solve—and even then reflection is likely to occur outside of the class. The teacher reads the qualitative cues of the situation as it unfolds and thinks on her feet, in many cases like a stand-up comedian. Reflection is not absent, theory is not irrelevant, even research conclusions might be considered, but they provide guidance, not direction. They are more in the background than the forefront of the action.

What we do as teachers is to orchestrate the dialogue moving from one side of the room to the other. We need to give the piccolos a chance—indeed to encourage them to sing more confidently—but we also need to provide space for the brass. And as for the violins, they always seem to have a major part to play. How is it going? What does the melody sound like? Is the music full enough? Do we need to stretch the orchestra further? When shall we pause and recapitulate the introductory theme? The clock is reaching ten and we have not yet crescendoed? How can we bring it to closure when we can't predict when a stunning question or an astute observation will bring forth a new melodic line and off we go again? Such are the pleasures and trials of teaching and when it goes well, there is nothing more that we would rather do.

Is such a story apocryphal? Clearly teachers are not orchestra conductors. Yet teachers orchestrate. The analogue rings true. Is artistry involved? Clearly it is. But where does it occur and of what does it consist? Let me suggest that it occurs first of all in those places—and they are legion—in the conduct of teaching when rules fail.

When rules cannot be used to decode meaning and when prescriptions cannot be used to control practice, the teacher must rely on art and craft. To function as an artist or a craftsperson one must be able to read the ineffable yet expressive messages of classroom life. It requires a level of what I have called in previous writings "educational connoisseurship"—the ability to appreciate what one has encountered.[20]

But appreciation, even by an educational connoisseur, is not enough. A teacher—like a school administrator—must act. And it is here that another characteristic of the art and craft of teaching comes into play: The ability to draw on the educational imagination. Like an artist, a teacher must be able to invent moves that will advance the situation from one place in a student's intellectual biography to another. What to do? What kind of question to raise? Do I keep on talking? Do I raise another question? Or do I do something that I never did before? Do I create a new move in another way? Do I let myself fly and thus take the risk of failing? It is here in this pedagogical space that the distinction found in the tide of this essay can be explained—"The Art and Craft of Teaching."

What is it that distinguishes the art of teaching from the craft of teaching? It is precisely the willingness and ability to create new forms of teaching—new teaching moves—moves that were not a part of one's existing repertoire.[21] The craftsperson in the classroom has the repertoire, is skilled in its use, and manages the performance quite well indeed. But the craftsperson creates essentially nothing new as a performer. This person's mark is known by the skill with which he or she uses known routines.

The artist in the classroom invents new ones in the process. Such modes of performance are not plentiful, and they require ingenuity and all of the skill that the person possesses. The artist is rarer than the craftsperson. Is the notion of the artist in the classroom really obsolete?

What can we say thus far about what the art and craft of teaching means? First, it means that we recognize that no science of teaching exists, or can exist, that will be so prescriptive as to make teaching routine. The best we can hope for—and it is substantial—is to have better tools from science with which teachers can use their heads.

Second, because the classroom, when not hog-tied or mechanically regimented, is a dynamic enterprise, teachers must be able to read the dynamic structures of signification that occur in such settings. Such reading requires attention to pattern and expressive nuance created by the students and the teacher's own activities.

Third, appreciation is not enough. The teacher must be able to call on or invent a set of moves that create an educationally productive tempo within a class. When we say of some lesson, "It went flat," we mean it both visually and aurally: It had no life, it didn't take hold. What is needed is either, or both, a better reading of the class by the teacher or a more imaginative set of teaching acts.

Fourth, it means that we acknowledge that artistry in teaching represents the apotheosis of educational performance and rather than try to diminish or replace it with rule-governed prescriptions, we ought to offer it a seat of honor. Artistry in teaching is always likely to be rare but it is even rarer when one works in an educational climate that is so concerned about academic achievement that it often stifles intellectual risk-taking on the part of both students and teachers.

This leads me to the final points I wish to address in my examination of the art and craft of teaching. One of those points deals with what it is that we have come to expect from art and craft: the provision of a very special kind of experience we sometimes call aesthetic. Just what does the aesthetic have to do with teaching and education? What is its import? Is it the frosting that makes the cake palatable or is it the marrow of education?

By art in education I am not talking about the visual arts, or music, or dance, but rather about the fact that activities motivated by the aesthetic satisfactions they provide—those that are intrinsic—are among the few that have any durability.[22] Extrinsic rewards for teachers are always likely to be small compared to those secured by people working in other fields. Despite longer vacation periods and sabbaticals, professional opportunities and satisfactions for teachers are limited largely to the lives they lead in their classrooms. Few people regard teachers as receiving handsome salaries—and they are right. The perks related to sabbaticals and vacation periods are distant and short-lived.

When one finds in schools a climate that makes it possible to take pride in one's craft, when one has the permission to pursue what one's educational imagination adumbrates, when one receives from students the kind of glow that says you have touched my life, satisfactions flow that exceed whatever it is that sabbaticals and vacations can provide. The aesthetic in teaching is the experience secured from being able to put your own signature on your own work—to look at it and say it was good. It comes from the contagion of excited students discovering the power of a new idea, the satisfaction of a new skill, or the dilemma of an intellectual paradox that once discovered creates. It means being swept up in the task of making something beautiful—and teachers do make their own spaces and places. They provide, perhaps more than they realize, much of the score their students will experience.

Such moments of aesthetic experience will not of course be constant. We could not, I am convinced, endure it if they were. Only a few scattered throughout the week are enough to keep us going. But without them teaching will be draining rather than nourishing and the likelihood of keeping in teaching those who need and value intellectual stimulation and challenge is very small. The aesthetic moments of teaching are among the deepest and most gratifying aspects of educational life.

But such moments in teaching are not the children of mechanical routine, the offspring of prescriptive rules for teaching, the progeny of rigid lesson plans that stifle spontaneity and discourage exploring the adventitious. Formalized method, bureaucratized procedures, and pressure to get students to perform at any price are their eviscerating conditions. Teachers need the psychological space and the permission to maintain a sense of excitement and discovery for themselves as teachers so that such excitement can be shared with their students.

Does the unabashedly romantic image of teaching I have portrayed have any implications for what we ought to be doing in the schools or is it simply an unrealistic conception of what it means to teach? A conception that will be amply corrected by a Betty Crocker view of teaching or by a teacher-proof curriculum?

I believe the image of the teacher as craftsperson and artist is an ideal toward which we should strive. I believe that our intellectual roots have mistakenly regarded such images as suspect. I believe that many of the solutions being proposed to cure what people believe to be educational ills, solutions such as minimum competency testing, state mandated evaluation procedures, and other legislative panaceas, to be fundamentally misguided. They were born of suspicion and tend to motivate by the stick. Human growth and development, whether for teachers or for students, need richer soil in which to flourish. How might such conditions be provided and what

might they be? First teachers need to be de-isolated in schools. Hardly anyone knows how or even what their colleagues are doing.

What is the logic in assuming that teachers can be trained once and for all in preservice university programs and then assigned to classrooms for the bulk of their careers with nothing more than brief excursions for inservice education that are usually provided by university professors who themselves have not taught in an elementary or secondary school classroom for a decade or two? The school needs to become a professional community with space enough for teachers to grow as professionals. They have much to offer each other, but these contributions are not easily made when teachers are isolated.

It is well past the time that schools create the organizational structure in which teachers and administrators can reflect on their activities as a regular part of their jobs, not simply within the scope of an inservice education program. Staff development needs to be a continuing part of what it means to be a teacher. The overstaffing of one teacher for every ten would be a step in the right direction. Joint planning could help contribute to it. And a school community that would not judge the quality of its educational program by SAT scores or enrollment in AP courses would also help. Is our educational imagination so impoverished that the only thing we can think of doing for the most able college-bound students is to give them what they will get in college a semester or two later?

We also need administrators who are at least as interested in teaching and curriculum as in organizational maintenance and public relations. We need principals who think of themselves *both* as teachers of teachers and as their teachers' staff. We need school superintendents who can help close the breach between administration and faculty and who remember from whence they came. But how can a principal be an instructional leader when he believes that he knows little about teaching or curriculum?

While it's true that legal mandates, problems between teachers and administrators, increasingly vocal community concern with the quality of schooling need attention and appropriate professional skills, it is the instructional program and the skill with which it is mediated for which all of the former issues are to be instrumental. Without attention to the instructional program and to the quality of teaching provided, successful arbitration and positive relationships with the community will amount to little from an educational point of view.

At a time when programs in educational administration are focusing on "policy studies" and the "politics of education," it would be ironic if administrators learned how to survive but forgot what survival was for. Our beneficiaries are the students—and without teachers skilled in the craft of teaching, and a curriculum worth teaching, schooling is likely to be educationally vapid.

We need, too, an attitude in schools that expects that experimentation in educational practices is a normal part of doing educational business. Where are the equivalents of Varian's, Xerox's, and IBM's think tanks in our schools? Where are our educational studios? Must we always be in a responsive posture or can we too dream dreams and pursue them?

CONCLUSION

I said at the beginning of this essay that I was intent on re-establishing the legitimacy of the art and craft of teaching. The image I portrayed at the outset was that of a single individual working painstakingly on something about which he or she cared a great deal. Craftspersons and artists tend to care a great deal about what they do, they get a great deal of satisfaction from the journey as well as from the destination, they take pride in their work, and they are among the first to appreciate quality. Is such an image really inappropriate today? I hope not. I hope such an image always has a place in our schools. And somehow, just somehow, I think that in the private, quiet moments of our professional lives, we do too.

ENDNOTES

1. I am indebted to Ray Bachetti for this tale. Its source is a case study paper that he wrote for Education 279X, Managing in Higher Education, School of Education, Stanford University.

2. Elwood P. Cubberley, *Public Education in the United States* (Boston: Houghton Mifflin Company, 1934), p. 380.

3. Ibid., p. 384.

4. Lawrence Cremin, *The Transformation of the School* (New York: Alfred Knopf, 1961).

5. Ibid., p. 101

6. Ibid, pp. 100–103.

7. Hall was not only the first editor of *Pedagogical Seminary,* he was its founder. He served as editor from its inception in 1881 to 1924.

8. William James, *Talks to Teachers on Psychology* (New York: H. Holt & Co., 1901).

9. Geraldine Joncich, *The Sane Positivist: The Biography of Edward L. Thorndike* (Middletown, Conn.: Wesleyan University Press, 1968).

10. Ibid., p. 336.

11. Edward L. Thorndike and Robert S. Woodworth, "The Influences of Special Training on General Ability," *Psychological Abstracts* 7 (March 1900).

12. Edward L. Thorndike, "The Contribution of Psychology to Education," *Journal of Educational Psychology* 1 (1910): 618.

13. For a brilliant discussion of this period see, Raymond Callahan, *Education and the Cult of Efficiency* (Chicago: The University of Chicago Press, 1962).

14. Ibid.

15. Alfred Jules Ayer, *Language, Truth and Logic* (New York: Dover, no date).

16. The concept of micro-teaching as the practice of discrete teaching skills is related to this view of the skills of teaching.

17. The average amount of experimental treatment time for experimental studies reported in the *American Educational Research Journal* in 1977–78 is approximately 45 minutes per subject.

18. The distinction I wish to underscore is between sciences like anthropology, archeology, and psychoanalysis that aim at explication and those like physics that not only explain but lead to prediction and control.

19. Because aptitudes for learning different skills and concepts differ among human beings, the effective

school will tend to increase individual differences among students rather than diminish them.

20. Elliot W. Eisner, *The Educational Imagination: On the Design and Evaluation of School Programs* (New York: The Macmillan Company, 1979).

21. This view of art is based on the work of R. G. Collingwood. See his *Principles of Art* (New York: Oxford University Press, 1958).

22. Mark Lepper, ed., *The Hidden Cost of Reward* (Hillsdale, N.J.: Erlbaum Associates, 1978).

DISCUSSION QUESTIONS

1. What curricular changes will be needed to encourage teachers to function as craft persons and artists?

2. How can preservice university training programs help shape the development of artist-teachers?

3. How might the organizational structure of a school be altered to help teachers pursue continuing professional development?

4. What role should principals and superintendents assume in developing artist-teachers?

5. What does the metaphor of teacher as orchestra conductor suggest about teaching?

Knowledge and Teaching: Foundations of the New Reform

LEE S. SHULMAN

FOCUSING QUESTIONS

1. *Why is a codified compendium of knowledge and skills insufficient for articulating a knowledge base of teaching?*
2. *What sources should comprise teaching the knowledge base according to the author?*
3. *What is pedagogical content knowledge?*
4. *Which role should the liberal arts college, school and departments of education assume in training teachers for the twenty-first century?*
5. *What is the purpose of transformation and reflection in the process of pedagogical reasoning and action?*
6. *What should be the goal of teacher education?*

Lee S. Shulman builds his foundation for teaching reform on an idea of teaching that emphasizes comprehension and reasoning, transformation and reflection. "This emphasis is justified," he writes, "by the resoluteness with which research and policy have so blatantly ignored those aspects of teaching in the past." To articulate and justify this conception, Shulman responds to four questions: What are the sources of the knowledge base for teaching? In what terms can these sources be conceptualized? What are the processes of pedagogical reasoning and action? and What are the implications for teaching policy and educational reform? The answers—informed by philosophy, psychology, and a growing body of casework based on young and experienced practitioners—go far beyond current reform assumptions and initiatives. The outcome for educational practitioners, scholars, and policymakers is a major redirection in how teaching is to be understood and teachers are to be trained and evaluated.

This article was selected for the November 1986 special issue on "Teachers, Teaching, and Teacher Education," but appears here because of the exigencies of publishing.

PROLOGUE: A PORTRAIT OF EXPERTISE

Richly developed portrayals of expertise in teaching are rare. While many characterizations of effective teachers exist, most of these dwell on the teacher's management of the classroom. We find few descriptions or analyses of teachers that give careful attention not only to the management of students in classrooms, but also to the management of *ideas* within classroom discourse. Both kinds of emphasis will be needed if our portrayals of good practice are to serve as sufficient guides to the design of better education. Let us examine one brief account.

A twenty-five-year veteran English teacher, Nancy, was the subject of a continuing study of experienced teachers that we had been conducting. The class was nearing the end of the second week of a unit on *Moby Dick*. The observer had been well impressed with the depth of Nancy's understanding of that novel and her skill as a pedagogue, as she documented how Nancy helped a group of California high school juniors grasp the many faces of that masterpiece. Nancy was a highly active teacher, whose classroom style employed substantial interaction with her students, both through recitations and more open-ended discussion. She was like a symphony conductor, posing questions, probing for alternative views, drawing out the shy while tempering the boisterous. Not much happened in the classroom that did not pass through Nancy, whose pacing and ordering, structuring and expanding, controlled the rhythm of classroom life.

Nancy characterized her treatment of literature in terms of a general theoretical model that she employed.

Basically, I break reading skills into four levels:

Level 1 is simply translation. . . . It is understanding the literal meaning, denotative, and frequently for students that means getting a dictionary.

Level 2 is connotative meaning and again you are still looking at the words. . . . What does that mean, what does that tell us about the character? . . . We looked at *The Scarlet Letter.* Hawthorne described a rose bush in the first chapter. Literal level is: What is a rose bush? More important, what does a rose bush suggest, what is it that comes to mind, what did you picture?

Level 3 is the level of interpretation. . . . It is the implication of Levels 1 and 2. If the author is using a symbol, what does that say about his view of life? In *Moby Dick,* the example I used in class was the boots. The boots would be the literal level. What does it mean when he gets under the bed? And the students would say, he is trying to hide something. Level 3 would be what does Melville say about human nature? What is the implication of this? What does this tell us about this character?

Level 4 is what I call application and evaluation and I try, as I teach literature, to get the students to Level 4, and that is where they

take the literature and see how it has meaning for their own lives. Where would we see that event occur in our own society? How would people that we know be behaving if they are doing what these characters are doing? How is this piece of literature similar to our common experiences as human beings? . . . So my view of reading is basically to take them from the literal on the page to making it mean something in their lives. In teaching literature I am always working in and out of those levels. (Gudmundsdottir, in preparation)

Nancy employed this conceptual framework in her teaching, using it to guide her own sequencing of material and formulation of questions. She taught the framework explicitly to her students over the semester, helping them employ it like a scaffolding to organize their own study of the texts, to monitor their own thinking. Although as a teacher she maintained tight control of the classroom discourse, her teaching goals were to liberate her students' minds through literacy, eventually to use great works of literature to illuminate their own lives. Whichever work she was teaching, she understood how to organize it, frame it for teaching, divide it appropriately for assignments and activities. She seemed to possess a mental index for these books she had taught so often—*The Red Badge of Courage, Moby Dick, The Scarlet Letter, The Adventures of Huckleberry Finn*—with key episodes organized in her mind for different pedagogical purposes, different levels of difficulty, different kinds of pupils, different themes or emphases. Her combination of subject-matter understanding and pedagogical skill was quite dazzling.

When the observer arrived at the classroom one morning, she found Nancy sitting at her desk as usual. But her morning greeting elicited no response from Nancy other than a grimace and motion toward the pad of paper on her desktop. "I have laryngitis this morning and will not be able to speak aloud," said the note. What's more, she appeared to be fighting the flu, for she had little energy. For a teacher who managed her classroom through the power of her voice and her manner, this was certainly a disabling condition. Or was it?

Using a combination of handwritten notes and whispers, she divided the class into small groups by rows, a tactic she had used twice before during this unit. Each group was given a different character who has a prominent role in the first chapters of the novel, and each group was expected to answer a series of questions about that character. Ample time was used at the end of the period for representatives of each group to report to the whole class. Once again the class had run smoothly, and the subject matter had been treated with care. But the style had changed radically, an utterly different teaching technology was employed, and still the students were engaged, and learning appeared to occur.

Subsequently, we were to see many more examples of Nancy's flexible style, adapted to the characteristics of learners, the complexities of subject matter, and her own physical condition. When learners experienced serious problems with a particular text, she self-consciously stayed at the lower levels of the reading ladder, helping the students with denotative and connotative meanings, while emphasizing literary interpretations somewhat less. When teaching *Huck Finn,* a novel she saw as less difficult than *Moby Dick,* her style changed once again. She gave much more autonomy to the students and did not directly run the classroom as much.

> For *Huck Finn,* she abandoned the stage early on and let the students teach each other. She had the students working independently in eight multi-ability groups, each group tracing one of eight themes: hypocrisy; luck and superstition; greed and materialism; romantic ideas and fantasy; religion and the Bible; social class and customs; family, racism, and prejudice; freedom and conscience. There were only two reading checks at the beginning and only two rounds of reporting. Once the groups were underway, Nancy took a seat at the back of the class and only interacted with students when she was called upon, and during group presentations. (Gudmundsdottir, in preparation)

Thus Nancy's pattern of instruction, her style of teaching, is not uniform or predictable in some simple sense. She flexibly responds to the difficulty and character of the subject matter, the capacities of the students (which can change even over the span of a single course), and her educational purposes. She can not only conduct her

orchestra from the podium, she can sit back and watch it play with virtuosity by itself.

What does Nancy believe, understand, and know how to do that permits her to teach as she does? Can other teachers be prepared to teach with such skill? The hope that teaching like Nancy's can become typical instead of unusual motivates much of the effort in the newly proposed reforms of teaching.

THE NEW REFORMS

During the past year the U.S. public and its professional educators have been presented with several reports on how to improve teaching as both an activity and a profession. One of the recurring themes of these reports has been the professionalization of teaching—the elevation of teaching to a more respected, more responsible, more rewarding and better rewarded occupation. The claim that teaching deserves professional status, however, is based on a more fundamental premise: that the standards by which the education and performance of teachers must be judged can be raised and more clearly articulated. The advocates of professional reform base their arguments on the belief that there exists a "knowledge base for teaching"—a codified or codifiable aggregation of knowledge, skill, understanding, and technology, of ethics and disposition, of collective responsibility—as well as a means for representing and communicating it. The reports of the Holmes Group (1986) and the Carnegie Task Force (1986) rest on this belief and, furthermore, claim that the knowledge base is growing. They argue that it should frame teacher education and directly inform teaching practice.

The rhetoric regarding the knowledge base, however, rarely specifies the character of such knowledge. It does not say what teachers should know, do, understand, or profess that will render teaching more than a form of individual labor, let alone be considered among the learned professions.

In this paper, I present an argument regarding the content, character, and sources for a knowledge base of teaching that suggests an answer to the question of the intellectual, practical, and normative basis for the professionalization of teaching. The questions that focus the argument are: What are the sources of the knowledge base for teaching? In what terms can these sources be conceptualized? What are the implications for teaching policy and educational reform?[1]

In addressing these questions I am following in the footsteps of many eminent scholars, including Dewey (1904), Scheffler (1965), Green (1971), Fenstermacher (1978), Smith (1980), and Schwab (1983), among others. Their discussions of what qualities and understandings, skills and abilities, and what traits and sensibilities render someone a competent teacher have continued to echo in the conference rooms of educators for generations. My approach has been conditioned, as well, by two current projects: a study of how new teachers learn to teach and an attempt to develop a national board for teaching.

First, for the past three years, my colleagues and I have been watching knowledge of pedagogy and content grow in the minds of young men and women. They have generously permitted us to observe and follow their eventful journeys from being teacher education students to becoming neophyte teachers. In this research, we are taking advantage of the kinds of insights Piaget provided from his investigations of knowledge growth. He discovered that he could learn a great deal about knowledge and its development from careful observation of the very young—those who were just beginning to develop and organize their intelligence. We are following this lead by studying those just learning to teach. Their development from students to teachers, from a state of expertise as learners through a novitiate as teachers exposes and highlights the complex bodies of knowledge and skill needed to function effectively as a teacher. The result is that error, success, and refinement—in a word, teacher-knowledge growth—are seen in high profile and in slow motion. The neophyte's stumble becomes the scholar's window.

Concurrently, we have found and explored cases of veteran teachers such as Nancy (Baxter,

in preparation; Gudmundsdottir, in preparation; Hashweh, 1985) to compare with those of the novices. What these studies show is that the knowledge, understanding, and skill we see displayed haltingly, and occasionally masterfully, among beginners are often demonstrated with ease by the expert. But, as we have wrestled with our cases, we have repeatedly asked what teachers knew (or failed to know) that permitted them to teach in a particular manner.

Second, for much of the past year, I have engaged in quite a different project on the role of knowledge in teaching. In conjunction with the recent Carnegie initiative for the reform of the teaching profession, my colleagues and I have been studying ways to design a national board assessment for teaching, parallel in several ways to the National Board of Medical Examiners (Shulman & Sykes, 1986; Sykes, 1986). This challenge renders the questions about the definition and operationalization of knowledge in teaching as far more than academic exercises. If teachers are to be certified on the basis of well-grounded judgments and standards, then those standards on which a national board relies must be legitimized by three factors: they must be closely tied to the findings of scholarship in the academic disciplines that form the curriculum (such as English, physics, and history) as well as those that serve as foundations for the process of education (such as psychology, sociology, or philosophy); they must possess intuitive credibility (or "face validity") in the opinions of the professional community in whose interests they have been designed; and they must relate to the appropriate normative conceptions of teaching and teacher education.

The new reform proposals carry assumptions about the knowledge base for teaching: when advocates of reform suggest that requirements for the education of teachers should be augmented and periods of training lengthened, they assume there must be something substantial to be learned. When they recommend that standards be raised and a system of examinations introduced, they assume there must exist a body of knowledge and skill to examine. Our research and that of others (for example, Berliner, 1986; Leinhardt & Greeno, 1986) have identified the sources and suggested outlines of that knowledge base. Watching veterans such as Nancy teach the same material that poses difficulties for novice teachers helped focus our attention on what kinds of knowledge and skill were needed to teach demanding materials well. By focusing on the teaching of particular topics—*Huck Finn,* quadratic equations, the Indian subcontinent, photosynthesis—we learned how particular kinds of content knowledge and pedagogical strategies necessarily interacted in the minds of teachers.

What follows is a discussion of the sources and outlines of the required knowledge base for teaching. I divide this discussion into two distinct analyses. First, after providing an overview of one framework for a knowledge base for teaching, I examine the *sources* of that knowledge base, that is, the domains of scholarship and experience from which teachers may draw their understanding. Second, I explore the processes of pedagogical reasoning and action within which such teacher knowledge is used.

THE KNOWLEDGE BASE

Begin a discussion on the knowledge base of teaching, and several related questions immediately arise: What knowledge base? Is enough known about teaching to support a knowledge base? Isn't teaching little more than personal style, artful communication, knowing some subject matter, and applying the results of recent research on teaching effectiveness? Only the last of these, the findings of research on effective teaching, is typically deemed a legitimate part of a knowledge base.

The actions of both policymakers and teacher educators in the past have been consistent with the formulation that teaching requires basic skills, content knowledge, and general pedagogical skills. Assessments of teachers in most states consist of some combination of basic-skills tests,

an examination of competence in subject matter, and observations in the classroom to ensure that certain kinds of general teaching behavior are present. In this manner, I would argue, teaching is trivialized, its complexities ignored, and its demands diminished. Teachers themselves have difficulty in articulating what they know and how they know it.

Nevertheless, the policy community at present continues to hold that the skills needed for teaching are those identified in the empirical research on teaching effectiveness. This research, summarized by Brophy and Good (1986), Gage (1986), and Rosenshine and Stevens (1986), was conducted within the psychological research tradition. It assumes that complex forms of situation-specific human performance can be understood in terms of the workings of underlying generic processes. In a study of teaching context, the research, therefore, seeks to identify those general forms of teaching behavior that correlate with student performance on standardized tests, whether in descriptive or experimental studies. The investigators who conduct the research realize that important simplifications must be made, but they believe that these are necessary steps for conducting scientific studies. Critical features of teaching, such as the subject matter being taught, the classroom context, the physical and psychological characteristics of the students, or the accomplishment of purposes not readily assessed on standardized tests, are typically ignored in the quest for general principles of effective teaching.

When policymakers have sought "research-based" definitions of good teaching to serve as the basis for teacher tests or systems of classroom observation, the lists of teacher behaviors that had been identified as effective in the empirical research were translated into the desirable competencies for classroom teachers. They became items on tests or on classroom-observation scales. They were accorded legitimacy because they had been "confirmed by research." While the researchers understood the findings to be simplified and incomplete, the policy community accepted them as sufficient for the definitions of standards.

For example, some research had indicated that students achieved more when teachers explicitly informed them of the lesson's objective. This seems like a perfectly reasonable finding. When translated into policy, however, classroom-observation competency-rating scales asked whether the teacher had written the objective on the blackboard and/or directly told the student the objectives at the beginning of class. If the teacher had not, he or she was marked off for failing to demonstrate a desired competency. No effort was made to discover whether the withholding of an objective might have been consistent with the form of the lesson being organized or delivered.

Moreover, those who hold with bifurcating content and teaching processes have once again introduced into policy what had been merely an act of scholarly convenience and simplification in the research. Teaching processes were observed and evaluated without reference to the adequacy or accuracy of the ideas transmitted. In many cases, observers were not expected to have content expertise in the areas being observed, because it did not matter for the rating of teacher performance. Thus, what may have been an acceptable strategy for research became an unacceptable policy for teacher evaluation.

In this paper I argue that the results of research on effective teaching, while valuable, are not the sole source of evidence on which to base a definition of the knowledge base of teaching. Those sources should be understood to be far richer and more extensive. Indeed, properly understood, the actual and potential sources for a knowledge base are so plentiful that our question should not be, Is there really much one needs to know in order to teach? Rather, it should express our wonder at how the extensive knowledge of teaching can be learned at all during the brief period allotted to teacher preparation. Much of the rest of this paper provides the details of the argument that there exists an elaborate knowledge base for teaching.

A View of Teaching

I begin with the formulation that the capacity to teach centers around the following commonplaces of teaching, paraphrased from Fenstermacher (1986). A teacher knows something not understood by others, presumably the students. The teacher can transform understanding, performance skills, or desired attitudes or values into pedagogical representations and actions. These are ways of talking, showing, enacting, or otherwise representing ideas so that the unknowing can come to know, those without understanding can comprehend and discern, and the unskilled can become adept. Thus, teaching necessarily begins with a teacher's understanding of what is to be learned and how it is to be taught. It proceeds through a series of activities during which the students are provided specific instruction and opportunities for learning,[2] though the learning itself ultimately remains the responsibility of the students. Teaching ends with new comprehension by both the teacher and the student.[3] Although this is certainly a core conception of teaching, it is also an incomplete conception. Teaching must properly be understood to be more than the enhancement of understanding; but if it is not even that, then questions regarding performance of its other functions remain moot. The next step is to outline the categories of knowledge that underlie the teacher understanding needed to promote comprehension among students.

Categories of the Knowledge Base

If teacher knowledge were to be organized into a handbook, an encyclopedia, or some other format for arraying knowledge, what would the category headings look like?[4] At minimum, they would include:

—content knowledge;
—general pedagogical knowledge, with special reference to those broad principles and strategies of classroom management and organization that appear to transcend subject matter;

—curriculum knowledge, with particular grasp of the materials and programs that serve as "tools of the trade" for teachers;

—pedagogical content knowledge, that special amalgam of content and pedagogy that is uniquely the province of teachers, their own special form of professional understanding;

—knowledge of learners and their characteristics;

—knowledge of educational contexts, ranging from the workings of the group or classroom, the governance and financing of school districts, to the character of communities and cultures; and

—knowledge of educational ends, purposes, and values, and their philosophical and historical grounds.

Among those categories, pedagogical content knowledge is of special interest because it identifies the distinctive bodies of knowledge for teaching. It represents the blending of content and pedagogy into an understanding of how particular topics, problems, or issues are organized, represented, and adapted to the diverse interests and abilities of learners, and presented for instruction. Pedagogical content knowledge is the category most likely to distinguish the understanding of the content specialist from that of the pedagogue. While far more can be said regarding the categories of a knowledge base for teaching, elucidation of them is not a central purpose of this paper.

Enumerating the Sources

There are at least four major sources for the teaching knowledge base: (1) scholarship in content disciplines, (2) the materials and settings of the institutionalized educational process (for example, curricula, textbooks, school organizations and finance, and the structure of the teaching profession), (3) research on schooling, social organizations, human learning, teaching and development, and the other social and cultural phenomena that affect what teachers can do, and (4) the wisdom of practice itself. Let me elaborate on each of these.

Scholarship in content disciplines. The first source of the knowledge base is content knowledge—the knowledge, understanding, skill, and disposition that are to be learned by school children. This knowledge rests on two foundations: the accumulated literature and studies in the content areas, and the historical and philosophical scholarship on the nature of knowledge in those fields of study. For example, the teacher of English should know English and American prose and poetry, written and spoken language use and comprehension, and grammar. In addition, he or she should be familiar with the critical literature that applies to particular novels or epics that are under discussion in class. Moreover, the teacher should understand alternative theories of interpretation and criticism, and how these might relate to issues of curriculum and of teaching.

Teaching is, essentially, a learned profession. A teacher is a member of a scholarly community. He or she must understand the structures of subject matter, the principles of conceptual organization, and the principles of inquiry that help answer two kinds of questions in each field: What are the important ideas and skills in this domain? and How are new ideas added and deficient ones dropped by those who produce knowledge in this area? That is, what are the rules and procedures of good scholarship or inquiry? These questions parallel what Schwab (1964) has characterized as knowledge of substantive and syntactic structures, respectively. This view of the sources of content knowledge necessarily implies that the teacher must have not only depth of understanding with respect to the particular subjects taught, but also a broad liberal education that serves as a framework for old learning and as a facilitator for new understanding. The teacher has special responsibilities in relation to content knowledge, serving as the primary source of student understanding of subject matter. The manner in which that understanding is communicated conveys to students what is essential about a subject and what is peripheral. In the face of student diversity, the teacher must have a flexible and multifaceted comprehension, adequate to impart alternative explanations of the same concepts or principles. The teacher also communicates, whether consciously or not, ideas about the ways in which "truth" is determined in a field and a set of attitudes and values that markedly influence student understanding. This responsibility places special demands on the teacher's own depth of understanding of the structures of the subject matter, as well as on the teacher's attitudes toward and enthusiasms for what is being taught and learned. These many aspects of content knowledge, therefore, are properly understood as a central feature of the knowledge base of teaching.

Educational materials and structures. To advance the aims of organized schooling, materials and structures for teaching and learning are created. These include: curricula with their scopes and sequences; tests and testing materials; institutions with their hierarchies, their explicit and implicit systems of rules and roles; professional teachers' organizations with their functions of negotiation, social change, and mutual protection; government agencies from the district through the state and federal levels; and general mechanisms of governance and finance. Because teachers necessarily function within a matrix created by these elements, using and being used by them, it stands to reason that the principles, policies, and facts of their functioning comprise a major source for the knowledge base. There is no need to claim that a specific literature undergirds this source, although there is certainly abundant research literature in most of these domains. But if a teacher has to "know the territory" of teaching, then it is the landscape of such materials, institutions, organizations, and mechanisms with which he or she must be familiar. These comprise both the tools of the trade and the contextual conditions that will either facilitate or inhibit teaching efforts.

Formal educational scholarship. A third source is the important and growing body of scholarly literature devoted to understanding the processes of schooling, teaching, and learning. This literature includes the findings and methods of empirical research in the areas of teaching, learning, and human development, as well as the normative, philosophical, and ethical foundations of education.

The normative and theoretical aspects of teaching's scholarly knowledge are perhaps most important. Unfortunately, educational policymakers and staff developers tend to treat only the findings of empirical research on teaching and learning as relevant portions of the scholarly knowledge base. But these research findings, while important and worthy of careful study, represent only one facet of the contribution of scholarship. Perhaps the most enduring and powerful scholarly influences on teachers are those that enrich their images of the possible: their visions of what constitutes good education, or what a well-educated youngster might look like if provided with appropriate opportunities and stimulation.

The writings of Plato, Dewey, Neill, and Skinner all communicate their conceptions of what a good educational system should be. In addition, many works written primarily to disseminate empirical research findings also serve as important sources of these concepts. I count among these such works as Bloom's (1976) on mastery learning and Rosenthal and Jacobson's (1968) on teacher expectations. Quite independent of whether the empirical claims of those books can be supported, their impact on teachers' conceptions of the possible and desirable ends of education is undeniable. Thus, the philosophical, critical, and empirical literature which can inform the goals, visions, and dreams of teachers is a major portion of the scholarly knowledge base of teaching.

A more frequently cited kind of scholarly knowledge grows out of the empirical study of teaching effectiveness. This research has been summarized recently by Gage (1978, 1986), Shulman (1986a), Brophy and Good (1986), and Rosenshine and Stevens (1986). The essential goal of this program of research has been to identify those teacher behaviors and strategies most likely to lead to achievement gains among students. Because the search has focused on generic relationships—teacher behaviors associated with student academic gains irrespective of subject matter or grade level—the findings have been much more closely connected with the management of classrooms than with the subtleties of content pedagogy. That is, the effective-teaching principles deal with making classrooms places where pupils can attend to instructional tasks, orient themselves toward learning with a minimum of disruption and distraction, and receive a fair and adequate opportunity to learn. Moreover, the educational purposes for which these research results are most relevant are the teaching of skills. Rosenshine (1986) has observed that effective teaching research has much less to offer to the teaching of understanding, especially of complex written material; thus, the research applies more to teaching a skill like multiplication than to teaching critical interpretations of, say, the *Federalist Papers*.

There are a growing number of such generic principles of effective teaching, and they have already found their way into examinations such as the National Teachers Examination and into state-level assessments of teaching performance during the first teaching year. Their weakness, that they essentially ignore the content-specific character of most teaching, is also their strength. Discovering, explicating, and codifying general teaching principles simplify the otherwise outrageously complex activity of teaching. The great danger occurs, however, when a general teaching principle is distorted into prescription, when maxim becomes mandate. Those states that have taken working principles of teaching, based solely on empirical studies of generic teaching

effectiveness, and have rendered them as hard, independent criteria for judging a teacher's worth, are engaged in a political process likely to injure the teaching profession rather than improve it.

The results of research on learning and development also fall within the area of empirical research findings. This research differs from research on teaching by the unit of investigation. Studies of teaching typically take place in conventional classrooms. Learning and development are ordinarily studied in individuals. Hence, teaching studies give accounts of how teachers cope with the inescapable character of schools as places where groups of students work and learn in concert. By comparison, learning and development studies produce principles of individual thought or behavior that must often be generalized to groups with caution if they are to be useful for schoolteaching.

The research in these domains can be both generic and content-specific. For example, cognitive psychological research contributes to the development of understanding of how the mind works to store, process, and retrieve information. Such general understanding can certainly be a source of knowledge for teachers, just as the work of Piaget, Maslow, Erikson, or Bloom has been and continues to be. We also find work on specific subject matter and student developmental levels that is enormously useful; for example, we learn about student misconceptions in the learning of arithmetic by elementary school youngsters (Erlwanger, 1975) or difficulties in grasping principles of physics by university and secondary school students (for example, Clement, 1982). Both these sorts of research contribute to a knowledge base for teaching.

Wisdom of practice. The final source of the knowledge base is the least codified of all. It is the wisdom of practice itself, the maxims that guide (or provide reflective rationalization for) the practices of able teachers. One of the more important tasks for the research community is to work with practitioners to develop codified representations of the practical pedagogical wisdom of able teachers. As indicated above, much of the conception of teaching embodied in this paper is derived from collecting, examining, and beginning to codify the emerging wisdom of practice among both inexperienced and experienced teachers.

The portrait of Nancy with which this paper began is only one of the many descriptions and analyses of excellent teaching we have been collecting over the past few years. As we organize and interpret such data, we attempt to infer principles of good practice that can serve as useful guidelines for efforts of educational reform. We attempt to keep the accounts highly contextualized, especially with respect to the content-specificity of the pedagogical strategies employed. In this manner we contribute to the documentation of good practice as a significant source for teaching standards. We also attempt to lay a foundation for a scholarly literature that records the details and rationales for specific pedagogical practice.

One of the frustrations of teaching as an occupation and profession is its extensive individual and collective amnesia, the consistency with which the best creations of its practitioners are lost to both contemporary and future peers. Unlike fields such as architecture (which preserves its creations in both plans and edifices), law (which builds a case literature of opinions and interpretations), medicine (with its records and case studies), and even unlike chess, bridge, or ballet (with their traditions of preserving both memorable games and choreographed performances through inventive forms of notation and recording), teaching is conducted without an audience of peers. It is devoid of a history of practice.

Without such a system of notation and memory, the next steps of analysis, interpretation, and codification of principles of practice are hard to pursue. We have concluded from our research with teachers at all levels of experience that the potentially codifiable knowledge that can be gleaned from the wisdom of practice is extensive. Practitioners simply know a great deal that they have never even tried to articulate. A major portion of the research agenda for the next decade will be to collect, collate, and interpret the practical knowledge of teachers for the purpose of establishing a case literature and codifying its principles, precedents, and parables (Shulman, 1986b). A significant portion of the research agenda associated with the Carnegie program to develop new assessments for teachers involves the conducting of "wisdom-of-practice" studies. These studies record and organize the reasoning and actions of gifted teachers into cases to establish standards of practice for particular areas of teaching.[5]

A knowledge base for teaching is not fixed and final. Although teaching is among the world's oldest professions, educational research, especially the systematic study of teaching, is a relatively new enterprise. We may be able to offer a compelling argument for the broad outlines and categories of the knowledge base for teaching. It will, however, become abundantly clear that much, if not most, of the proposed knowledge base remains to be discovered, invented, and refined. As more is learned about teaching, we will come to recognize new categories of performance and understanding that are characteristic of good teachers, and will have to reconsider and redefine other domains. Our current "blueprint" for the knowledge base of teaching has many cells or categories with only the most rudimentary placeholders, much like the chemist's periodic table of a century ago. As we proceed, we will know that something can be known in principle about a particular aspect of teaching, but we will not yet know what that principle or practice entails. At base, however, we believe that scholars and expert teachers are able to define, describe, and reproduce good teaching.

THE PROCESSES OF PEDAGOGICAL REASONING AND ACTION

The conception of teaching I shall discuss has emerged from a number of sources, both philosophical and empirical. A key source has been the several dozen teachers whom we have been studying in our research during the past three years. Through interviews, observations, structured tasks, and examination of materials, we have attempted to understand how they commute from the status of learner to that of teacher,[6] from being able to comprehend subject matter for themselves, to becoming able to elucidate subject matter in new ways, reorganize and partition it, clothe it in activities and emotions, in metaphors and exercises, and in examples and demonstrations, so that it can be grasped by students.

As we have come to view teaching, it begins with an act of reason, continues with a process of reasoning, culminates in performances of imparting, eliciting, involving, or enticing, and is then thought about some more until the process can begin again. In the discussion of teaching that follows, we will emphasize teaching as comprehension and reasoning, as transformation and reflection. This emphasis is justified by the resoluteness with which research and policy have so blatantly ignored those aspects of teaching in the past.

Fenstermacher (1978, 1986) provides a useful framework for analysis. The goal of teacher education, he argues, is not to indoctrinate or train teachers to behave in prescribed ways, but to educate teachers to reason soundly about their teaching as well as to perform skillfully. Sound reasoning requires both a process of thinking about what they are doing and an adequate base of facts, principles, and experiences from which to reason. Teachers must learn to use their knowledge base to provide the grounds for choices and actions. Therefore, teacher education must work with the beliefs that guide teacher actions, with the principles and evidence that underlie the choices teachers make. Such reasons (called "premises of the practical argument" in the analysis of Green, 1971, on which Fenstermacher bases his argument) can be predominantly arbitrary or idiosyncratic ("It sure seemed like the right idea at the time!" "I don't know much about teaching, but I know what I like."), or they can

rest on ethical, empirical, theoretical, or practical principles that have substantial support among members of the professional community of teachers. Fenstermacher argues that good teaching not only is effective behaviorally, but must rest on a foundation of adequately grounded premises.

When we examine the quality of teaching, the idea of influencing the grounds or reasons for teachers' decisions places the emphasis precisely where it belongs: on the features of pedagogical reasoning that lead to or can be invoked to explain pedagogical actions. We must be cautious, however, lest we place undue emphasis upon the ways teachers reason to achieve particular ends, at the expense of attention to the grounds they present for selecting the ends themselves. Teaching is both effective and normative; it is concerned with both means and ends. Processes of reasoning underlie both. The knowledge base must therefore deal with the purposes of education as well as the methods and strategies of educating.

This image of teaching involves the exchange of ideas. The idea is grasped, probed, and comprehended by a teacher, who then must turn it about in his or her mind, seeing many sides of it. Then the idea is shaped or tailored until it can in turn be grasped by students. This grasping, however, is not a passive act. Just as the teacher's comprehension requires a vigorous interaction with the ideas, so students will be expected to encounter ideas actively as well. Indeed, our exemplary teachers present ideas in order to provoke the constructive processes of their students and not to incur student dependence on teachers or to stimulate the flatteries of imitation.[7]

Comprehension alone is not sufficient. The usefulness of such knowledge lies in its value for judgment and action. Thus, in response to my aphorism, "those who can, do; those who understand, teach" (Shulman, 1986b, p. 14), Petrie (1986) correctly observed that I had not gone far enough. Understanding, he argued, must be linked to judgment and action, to the proper uses of understanding in the forging of wise pedagogical decisions.

Aspects of Pedagogical Reasoning

I begin with the assumption that most teaching is initiated by some form of "text": a textbook, a syllabus, or an actual piece of material the teacher or student wishes to have understood. The text may be a vehicle for the accomplishment of other educational purposes, but some sort of teaching material is almost always involved. The following conception of pedagogical reasoning and action is taken from the point of view of the teacher, who is presented with the challenge of taking what he or she already understands and making it ready for effective instruction. The model of pedagogical reasoning and action is summarized in Table 11.1.

Given a text, educational purposes, and/or a set of ideas, pedagogical reasoning and action involve a cycle through the activities of comprehension, transformation, instruction, evaluation, and reflection.[8] The starting point and terminus for the process is an act of comprehension.

Comprehension.   To teach is first to understand. We ask that the teacher comprehend critically a set of ideas to be taught.[9] We expect teachers to understand what they teach and, when possible, to understand it in several ways. They should understand how a given idea relates to other ideas within the same subject area and to ideas in other subjects as well.

TABLE 11.1   A Model of Pedagogical Reasoning and Action

Comprehension
Of purposes, subject matter structures, ideas within and outside the discipline

Transformation
Preparation: critical interpretation and analysis of texts, structuring and segmenting, development of a
   curricular repertoire, and clarification of purposes
Representation: use of a representational repertoire which includes analogies, metaphors, examples,
   demonstrations, explanations, and so forth
Selection: choice from among an instructional repertoire which includes modes of teaching, organizing,
   managing, and arranging
Adaptation and Tailoring to Student Characteristics: consideration of conceptions, preconceptions,
   misconceptions, and difficulties, language, culture, and motivations, social class, gender, age, ability,
   aptitude, interests, self concepts, and attention

Instruction
Management, presentations, interactions, group work, discipline, humor, questioning, and other aspects
   of active teaching, discovery or inquiry instruction, and the observable forms of classroom teaching

Evaluation
Checking for student understanding during interactive teaching
Testing student understanding at the end of lessons or units
Evaluating one's own performance, and adjusting for experiences

Reflection
Reviewing, reconstructing, reenacting and critically analyzing one's own and the class's performance,
   and grounding explanations in evidence

New Comprehensions
Of purposes, subject matter, students, teaching, and self
Consolidation of new understandings, and learnings from experience

Comprehension of purposes is also central here. We engage in teaching to achieve educational purposes, to accomplish ends having to do with student literacy, student freedom to use and enjoy, student responsibility to care and care for, to believe and respect, to inquire and discover, to develop understandings, skills, and values needed to function in a free and just society. As teachers, we also strive to balance our goals of fostering individual excellence with more general ends involving equality of opportunity and equity among students of different backgrounds and cultures. Although most teaching begins with some sort of text, and the learning of that text can be a worthy end in itself, we should not lose sight of the fact that the text is often a vehicle for achieving other educational purposes. The goals of education transcend the comprehension of particular texts, but may be unachievable without it.

Saying that a teacher must first comprehend both content and purposes, however, does not particularly distinguish a teacher from non-teaching peers. We expect a math major to understand mathematics or a history specialist to comprehend history. But the key to distinguishing the knowledge base of teaching lies at the intersection of content and pedagogy, in the capacity of a teacher to transform the content knowledge he or she possesses into forms that are pedagogically powerful and yet adaptive to the variations in ability and background presented by the students. We now turn to a discussion of transformation and its components.

Transformation.   Comprehended ideas must be transformed in some manner if they are to be taught. To reason one's way through an act of teaching is to think one's way from the subject matter as understood by the teacher into the minds and motivations of learners. Transformations, therefore, require some combination or ordering of the following processes, each of which employs a kind of repertoire: (1) preparation (of the given text materials) including the process of critical interpretation, (2) representation of the ideas in the form of new analogies, metaphors,

and so forth, (3) instructional selections from among an array of teaching methods and models, and (4) adaptation of these representations to the general characteristics of the children to be taught, as well as (5) tailoring the adaptations to the specific youngsters in the classroom. These forms of transformation, these aspects of the process wherein one moves from personal comprehension to preparing for the comprehension of others, are the essence of the act of pedagogical reasoning, of teaching as thinking, and of planning—whether explicitly or implicitly—the performance of teaching.

Preparation involves examining and critically interpreting the materials of instruction in terms of the teacher's own understanding of the subject matter (Ben-Peretz, 1975). That is, one scrutinizes the teaching material in light of one's own comprehension and asks whether it is "fit to be taught." This process of preparation will usually include (1) detecting and correcting errors of omission and commission in the text, and (2) the crucial processes of structuring and segmenting the material into forms better adapted to the teacher's understanding and, in prospect, more suitable for teaching. One also scrutinizes educational purposes or goals. We find examples of this preparation process in a number of our studies. Preparation certainly draws upon the availability of a curricular repertoire, a grasp of the full array of extant instructional materials, programs, and conceptions.

Representation involves thinking through the key ideas in the text or lesson and identifying the alternative ways of representing them to students. What analogies, metaphors, examples, demonstrations, simulations, and the like can help to build a bridge between the teacher's comprehension and that desired for the students? Multiple forms of representation are desirable. We speak of the importance of a representational repertoire in this activity.[10]

Instructional selections occur when the teacher must move from the reformulation of content through representations to the embodiment of representations in instructional forms or methods.

Here the teacher draws upon an instructional repertoire of approaches or strategies of teaching. This repertoire can be quite rich, including not only the more conventional alternatives such as lecture, demonstration, recitation, or seatwork, but also a variety of forms of cooperative learning, reciprocal teaching, Socratic dialogue, discovery learning, project methods, and learning outside the classroom setting.

Adaptation is the process of fitting the represented material to the characteristics of the students. What are the relevant aspects of student ability, gender, language, culture, motivations, or prior knowledge and skills that will affect their responses to different forms of representation and presentation? What student conceptions, misconceptions, expectations, motives, difficulties, or strategies might influence the ways in which they approach, interpret, understand, or misunderstand the material? Related to adaptation is tailoring, which refers to the fitting of the material to the specific students in one's classrooms rather than to students in general. When a teacher thinks through the teaching of something, the activity is a bit like the manufacture of a suit of clothing. Adaptation is like preparing a suit of a particular style, color, and size that can be hung on a rack. Once it is prepared for purchase by a particular customer, however, it must be tailored to fit perfectly.

Moreover, the activity of teaching is rarely engaged with a single student at a time. This is a process for which the special term "tutoring" is needed. When we speak of teaching under typical school circumstances, we describe an activity which brings instruction to groups of at least fifteen—or more typically, twenty-five to thirty-five—students. Thus, the tailoring of instruction entails fitting representations not only to particular students, but also to a group of a particular size, disposition, receptivity, and interpersonal "chemistry."

All these processes of transformation result in a plan, or set of strategies, to present a lesson, unit, or course. Up to this point, of course, it is all a rehearsal for the performances of teaching which have not yet occurred. Pedagogical reasoning is as much a part of teaching as is the actual performance itself. Reasoning does not end when instruction begins. The activities of comprehension, transformation, evaluation, and reflection continue to occur during active teaching. Teaching itself becomes a stimulus for thoughtfulness as well as for action. We therefore turn next to the performance that consummates all this reasoning in the act of instruction.

Instruction. This activity involves the observable performance of the variety of teaching acts. It includes many of the most crucial aspects of pedagogy: organizing and managing the classroom; presenting clear explanations and vivid descriptions; assigning and checking work; and interacting effectively with students through questions and probes, answers and reactions, and praise and criticism. It thus includes management, explanation, discussion, and all the observable features of effective direct and heuristic instruction already well-documented in the research literature on effective teaching.

We have compelling reasons to believe that there are powerful relationships between the comprehension of a new teacher and the styles of teaching employed. An example, based on the research of Grossman (1985), will illustrate this point.

> Colleen had completed a master's degree in English before entering a teacher education program. She expressed confidence in her command of the subject matter and began her internship with energy and enthusiasm. Her view of literature and its teaching was highly interpretive and interactive. She saw fine literature as layered communication, capable of many diverse readings and interpretations. Moreover, she felt that these various readings should be provided by her students through their own careful reading of the texts.
>
> Colleen was so committed to helping students learn to read texts carefully, a habit of mind not often found among the young or old, that she constructed one assignment in which each student was asked to bring to school the lyrics of a favorite rock song. (She may have realized that some of these song lyrics were of questionable taste,

but preferred to maximize motivation rather than discretion in this particular unit.) She then asked them to rewrite each line of the song, using synonyms or paraphrases to replace every original word. For many, it was the first time they had looked at any piece of text with such care.

When teaching a piece of literature, Colleen performed in a highly interactive manner, drawing out student ideas about a phrase or line, accepting multiple competing interpretations as long as the student could offer a defense of the construction by reference to the text itself. Student participation was active and hearty in these sessions. Based on these observations, one would have characterized Colleen's teaching style with descriptors such as student-centered, discussion-based, occasionally Socratic, or otherwise highly interactive.

Several weeks later, however, we observed Colleen teaching a unit on grammar. Although she had completed two university degrees in English, Colleen had received almost no preparation in prescriptive grammar. However, since a typical high school English class includes some grammar in addition to the literature and writing, it was impossible to avoid teaching the subject. She expressed some anxiety about it during a pre-observational interview.

Colleen looked like a different teacher during that lesson. Her interactive style evaporated. In its place was a highly didactic, teacher-directed, swiftly paced combination of lecture and tightly-controlled recitation: Socrates replaced by DISTAR. I sometimes refer to such teaching as the Admiral Farragut style, "Damn the questions, full speed ahead." Students were not given opportunities to raise questions or offer alternative views. After the session, she confessed to the observer that she had actively avoided making eye contact with one particular student in the front row because that youngster always had good questions or ideas and in this particular lesson Colleen really didn't want to encourage either, because she wasn't sure of the answers. She was uncertain about the content and adapted her instructional style to allay her anxiety.[11]

Colleen's case illustrates the ways in which teaching behavior is bound up with comprehension and transformation of understanding. The flexible and interactive teaching techniques that she uses are simply not available to her when she does not understand the topic to be taught. Having examined the processes of pedagogical reasoning and performance that are prospective and enactive in nature, we now move to those that are retrospective.

Evaluation.   This process includes the on-line checking for understanding and misunderstanding that a teacher must employ while teaching interactively, as well as the more formal testing and evaluation that teachers do to provide feedback and grades. Clearly, checking for such understanding requires all the forms of teacher comprehension and transformation described above. To understand what a pupil understands will require a deep grasp of both the material to be taught and the processes of learning. This understanding must be specific to particular school subjects and to individual topics within the subject. This represents another way in which what we call pedagogical content knowledge is used. Evaluation is also directed at one's own teaching and at the lessons and materials employed in those activities. In that sense it leads directly to reflection.

Reflection.   This is what a teacher does when he or she looks back at the teaching and learning that has occurred, and reconstructs, reenacts, and/or recaptures the events, the emotions, and the accomplishments. It is that set of processes through which a professional learns from experience. It can be done alone or in concert, with the help of recording devices or solely through memory. Here again, it is likely that reflection is not merely a disposition (as in, "she's such a reflective person!") or a set of strategies, but also the use of particular kinds of analytic knowledge brought to bear on one's work (Richert, in preparation). Central to this process will be a review of the teaching in comparison to the ends that were sought.

New comprehension.   Thus we arrive at the new beginning, the expectation that through acts of teaching that are "reasoned" and "reasonable" the teacher achieves new comprehension, both of the purposes and of the subjects to be taught, and also of the students and of the processes of pedagogy themselves. There is a good deal of transient experiential learning among teachers, characterized by the "aha" of a moment that is never consolidated and made part of a new understanding or a reconstituted repertoire (Brodkey, 1986). New comprehension does not automatically occur, even after evaluation and reflection. Specific strategies for documentation, analysis, and discussion are needed.

Although the processes in this model are presented in sequence, they are not meant to represent a set of fixed stages, phases, or steps. Many of the processes can occur in different order. Some may not occur at all during some acts of teaching. Some may be truncated, others elaborated. In elementary teaching, for example, some processes may occur that are ignored or given short shrift in this model. But a teacher should demonstrate the capacity to engage in these processes when called upon, and teacher education should provide students with the understandings and performance abilities they will need to reason their ways through and to enact a complete act of pedagogy, as represented here.

KNOWLEDGE, TEACHING POLICY, AND EDUCATIONAL REFORM

The investigations, deliberations, and debates regarding what teachers should know and know how to do have never been more active. Reform efforts are underway: they range from raising standards for admission into teacher education programs, to establishing state and national examinations for teachers; from insisting that teacher preparation require at least five years of higher education (because there is so much to learn), to organizing elaborate programs of new-teacher induction and mentoring (because the most important learning and socialization can occur only in the workplace).

Most of the current reforms rest on the call for greater professionalization in teaching, with higher standards for entry, greater emphasis on the scholarly bases for practice, more rigorous programs of theoretical and practical preparation, better strategies for certification and licensure, and changes in the workplace that permit greater autonomy and teacher leadership. In large measure, they call for teaching to follow the model of other professions that define their knowledge bases in systematic terms, require extended periods of preparation, socialize neophytes into practice with extended periods of internship or residency, and employ demanding national and state certification procedures.

Implicit in all these reforms are conceptions of teacher competence. Standards for teacher education and assessment are necessarily predicated on images of teaching and its demands. The conception of the knowledge base of teaching presented in this paper differs in significant ways from many of those currently existing in the policy community. The emphasis on the integral relationships between teaching and the scholarly domains of the liberal arts makes clear that teacher education is the responsibility of the entire university, not the schools or departments of education alone. Moreover, teachers cannot be adequately assessed by observing their teaching performance without reference to the content being taught.

The conception of pedagogical reasoning places emphasis upon the intellectual basis for teaching performance rather than on behavior alone. If this conception is to be taken seriously, both the organization and content of teacher education programs and the definition of the scholarly foundations of education will require revision. Teacher education programs would no longer be able to confine their activity to the content-free domains of pedagogy and supervision. An emphasis on pedagogical content knowledge would permeate the teacher preparation curriculum. A national board examination for teachers would focus upon the teacher's ability to reason about teaching and to teach specific topics, and to base his or her actions on premises that can bear the scrutiny of the professional community.

We have an obligation to raise standards in the interests of improvement and reform, but we must avoid the creation of rigid orthodoxies. We must achieve standards without standardization. We must be careful that the knowledge-base approach does not produce an overly technical image of teaching, a scientific enterprise that has lost its soul. The serious problems in medicine and other health professions arise when doctors treat the disease rather than the person, or when the professional or personal needs of the practitioner are permitted to take precedence over the responsibilities to those being served.

CONCLUSION

Needed change cannot occur without risk. The currently incomplete and trivial definitions of teaching held by the policy community comprise a far greater danger to good education than does a more serious attempt to formulate the knowledge base. Nancy represents a model of pedagogical excellence that should become the basis for the new reforms. A proper understanding of the knowledge base of teaching, the sources for that knowledge, and the complexities of the pedagogical process will make the emergence of such teachers more likely.

ENDNOTES

Preparation of this paper was made possible, in part, by grants to Stanford University from the Spencer Foundation for the project, Knowledge Growth in a Profession, and from the Carnegie Corporation of New York for research on the development of new modes of assessment for teachers, Lee S. Shulman, principal investigator. Suzanne Wilson, Pamela Grossman, and Judy Shulman provided criticism and counsel when it was most needed. A longer version of this paper will be available from the Carnegie Forum on Education and the Economy. The views expressed are the author's and are not necessarily shared by these organizations or individuals.
1. Most of the empirical work on which this essay rests has been conducted with secondary-school teachers, both new and experienced. While I firmly believe that much of the emphasis to be found here on the centrality of content knowledge in pedagogy holds reasonably well for the elementary level as well, I am reluctant to make that claim too boldly. Work currently underway at the elementary level, both by Leinhardt (1983) and her colleagues (for example, Leinhardt & Greeno, 1985; Leinhardt & Smith, 1986) and by our own research group, may help clarify this matter.

2. There are several aspects of this formulation that are unfortunate, if only for the impression they may leave. The rhetoric of the analysis, for example, is not meant to suggest that education is reduced to knowledge transmission, the conveying of information from an active teacher to a passive learner, and that this information is viewed as product rather than process. My conception of teaching is not limited to direct instruction. Indeed, my affinity for discovery learning and inquiry teaching is both enthusiastic and ancient (for example, Shulman & Keislar, 1966). Yet even in those most student-centered forms of education, where much of the initiative is in the hands of the students, there is little room for teacher ignorance. Indeed, we have reason to believe that teacher comprehension is even more critical for the inquiry-oriented classroom than for its more didactic alternative.

Central to my concept of teaching are the objectives of students learning how to understand and solve problems, learning to think critically and creatively as well as learning facts, principles, and rules of procedure. Finally, I understand that the learning of subject matter is often not an end in itself, but rather a vehicle employed in the service of other goals. Nevertheless, at least at the secondary level, subject matter is a nearly universal vehicle for instruction, whatever the ultimate goal.

3. This formulation is drawn from the teacher's perspective and, hence, may be viewed by some readers as overly teacher-centered. I do not mean to diminish the centrality of student learning for the process of education, nor the priority that must be given to student learning over teacher comprehension. But our analyses of effective teaching must recognize that outcomes *for teachers* as well as pupils must be considered in any adequate treatment of educational outcomes.

4. I have attempted this list in other publications, though, admittedly, not with great cross-article consistency (for example, Shulman, 1986b; Shulman & Sykes, 1986; Wilson, Shulman & Richert, in press).

5. It might he argued that the sources of skilled performances are typically tacit, and unavailable to the practitioner. But teaching requires a special kind of expertise or artistry, for which explaining and showing are the central features. Tacit knowledge among teachers is of limited value if the teachers are held responsible for explaining what they do and why they do it, to their students, their communities, and their peers.

6. The metaphor of commuting is not used idly. The journey between learner and teacher is not one-way. In the best teachers, as well as in the more marginal, new learning is constantly required for teaching.

7. The direction and sequence of instruction can be quite different as well. Students can literally initiate the process, proceeding by discovering, inventing, or inquiring, to prepare their own representations and transformations. Then it is the role of the teacher to respond actively and creatively to those student initiatives. In each case the teacher needs to possess both the comprehension and the capacities for transformation. In the student-initiated case, the flexibility to respond, judge, nurture, and provoke student creativity will depend on the teacher's own capacities for sympathetic transformation and interpretation.

8. Under some conditions, teaching may begin with "given a group of students." It is likely that at the early elementary grades, or in special education classes or other settings where children have been brought together for particular reasons, the starting point for reasoning about instruction may well be at the characteristics of the group itself. There are probably some days when a teacher necessarily uses the youngsters as a starting point.

9. Other views of teaching will also begin with comprehension, but of something other than the ideas or text to be taught and learned. They may focus on comprehension of a particular set of values, of the characteristics, needs, interests, or propensities of a particular individual or group of learners. But some sort of comprehension (or self-conscious confusion, wonder, or ignorance) will always initiate teaching.

10. The centrality of representation to our conception of pedagogical reasoning is important for relating our model of teaching to more general approaches to the study of human thinking and problem solving. Cognitive psychologists (for example, Gardner, 1986; Marton, 1986; Norman, 1980) argue that processes of internal representation are key elements in any cognitive psychology. "To my mind, the major accomplishment of cognitive science has been the clear demonstration of the validity of positing a level of mental representation: a set of constructs that can be invoked for the explanation of cognitive phenomena, ranging from visual perception to story comprehension" (Gardner, 1986, p. 383). Such a linkage between models of pedagogy and models of more general cognitive functioning can serve as an important impetus for the needed study of teacher thinking.

11. In no way do I wish to imply that effective lectures are out of place in a high school classroom. On the contrary, good lecturing is an indispensable teaching technique. In this case I am more interested in the relationship between knowledge and teaching. It might be suggested that this teaching style is more suited to grammar than to literature because there is little to discuss or interpret in a grammar lesson. I do not agree, but will not pursue the matter here. In Colleen's case, the rationale for a linear lecture was not grounded in such an argument, but quite clearly in her concern for limiting the range of possible deviations from the path she had designed.

REFERENCES

Baxter, J. (in preparation). *Teacher explanations in computer programming: A study of knowledge transformation.* Unpublished doctoral dissertation in progress, Stanford University.

Ben-Peretz, M. (1975). The concept of curriculum potential. *Curriculum Theory Network, 5,* 151–159.

Berliner, D. (1986). In pursuit of the expert pedagogue. *Educational Researcher, 15*(7) 5–13.

Bloom, B. S. (1976). *Human characteristics and school learning.* New York: McGraw-Hill.

Brodkey, J. J. (1986). *Learning while teaching: Self-assessment in the classroom.* Unpublished doctoral dissertation, Stanford University.

Brophy, J. J., & Good, T. (1986). Teacher behavior and student achievement. In M. C. Wittrock (Ed.), *Handbook of research on teaching* (3rd ed., pp. 328–375). New York: Macmillan.

Carnegie Task Force on Teaching as a Profession. (1986). *A nation prepared: Teachers for the 21st Century.* Washington, DC: Carnegie Forum on Education and the Economy.

Clement, J. (1982). Students' preconceptions in introductory mechanics. *American Journal of Physics, 50,* 67–71.

Dewey, J. (1904). The relation of theory to practice in education. In C. A. McMurry (Ed.), *The relation of theory to practice in the education of teachers* (Third Yearbook of the National Society for the Scientific Study of Education, Part I). Bloomington, IL: Public School Publishing.

Erlwanger, S. H. (1975). Case studies of children's conceptions of mathematics, Part I. *Journal of Children's Mathematical Behavior, 1,* 157–283.

Fenstermacher, G. (1978). A philosophical consideration of recent research on teacher effectiveness. In L. S. Shulman (Ed.), *Review of research in education* (Vol. 6, pp. 157–185). Itasca, IL: Peacock.

Fenstermacher, G. (1986). Philosophy of research on teaching: Three aspects. In M. C. Wittrock (Ed.), *Handbook of research on teaching* (3rd ed., pp. 37–49). New York: Macmillan.

Gage, N. L. (1978). *The scientific basis of the art of teaching.* New York: Teachers College Press.

Gage, N. L. (1986). *Hard gains in the soft sciences: The case of pedagogy.* Bloomington, IN: Phi Delta Kappa.

Gardner, H. (1986). *The mind's new science: A history of cognitive revolution.* New York: Basic Books.

Green, T. F. (1971). *The activities of teaching.* New York: McGraw-Hill.

Grossman, P. (1985). *A passion for language: From text to teaching* (Knowledge Growth in Teaching Publications Series). Stanford: Stanford University, School of Education.

Gudmundsdottir, S. (in preparation). *Knowledge use among experienced teachers: Four case studies of high school teaching.* Unpublished doctoral dissertation in progress, Stanford University.

Hashweh, M. Z. (1985). *An exploratory study of teacher knowledge and teaching: The effects of science teachers' knowledge of subject-matter and their conceptions of learning on their teaching.* Unpublished doctoral dissertation, Stanford University.

The Holmes Group (1986). *Tomorrow's teachers: A report of the Holmes Group.* East Lansing, MI: Author.

Leinhardt, G. (1983). Novice and expert knowledge of individual student's achievement. *Educational Psychologist, 18,* 165–179.

Leinhardt, G., & Greeno, J. G. (1986). The cognitive skill of teaching. *Journal of Educational Psychology, 78,* 75–95.

Leinhardt, G., & Smith, D. A. (1985). Expertise in mathematics instruction: Subject matter knowl-

edge. *Journal of Educational Psychology, 77,* 247–271.

Marton, F. (1986). *Towards a pedagogy of content.* Unpublished manuscript, University of Gothenburg, Sweden.

Norman, D. A. (1980). What goes on in the mind of the learner? In W. J. McKeachie (Ed.), *New directions for teaching and learning: Learning, cognition, and college teaching* (Vol. 2). San Francisco: Jossey-Bass.

Petrie, H. (1986, May). *The liberal arts and sciences in the teacher education curriculum.* Paper presented at the Conference on Excellence in Teacher Preparation through the Liberal Arts, Muhlenberg College, Allentown, PA.

Richert, A. (in preparation). *Reflex to reflection: Facilitating reflection in novice teachers.* Unpublished doctoral dissertation in progress, Stanford University.

Rosenshine, B. (1986, April). *Unsolved issues in teaching content: A critique of a lesson on Federalist Paper No. 10.* Paper presented at the meeting of the American Educational Research Association, San Francisco, CA.

Rosenshine, B., & Stevens, R. S. (1986). Teaching functions. In M. C. Wittrock (Ed.) *Handbook of research on teaching* (3rd ed., pp. 376–391). New York: Macmillan.

Rosenthal, R., & Jacobson, L. (1968). *Pygmalion in the classroom.* New York: Holt, Rinehart & Winston.

Scheffler, I. (1965). *Conditions of knowledge: An introduction to epistemology and education.* Chicago: University of Chicago Press.

Schwab, J. J. (1964). The structure of the disciplines: Meanings and significances. In G. W. Ford & L. Pugno (Eds.), *The structure of knowledge and the curriculum.* Chicago: Rand McNally.

Schwab, J. J. (1983). The practical four: Something for curriculum professors to do. *Curriculum Inquiry, 13,* 239–265.

Shulman, L. S. (1986a). Paradigms and research programs for the study of teaching. In M. C. Wittrock (Ed.), *Handbook of research on teaching* (3rd ed., pp. 3–36). New York: Macmillan.

Shulman, L. S. (1986b). Those who understand: Knowledge growth in teaching. *Educational Researcher, 15*(2), 4–14.

Shulman, L. S., & Keislar, E. R. (Eds.). (1966). *Learning by discovery: A critical appraisal.* Chicago: Rand McNally.

Shulman, L. S., & Sykes, G. (1986, March). *A national board for teaching?: In search of a bold standard* (Paper commissioned for the Task Force on Teaching as a Profession, Carnegie Forum on Education and the Economy).

Smith, B. O. (1980). *A design for a school of pedagogy.* Washington, DC: U.S. Department of Education.

Sykes, G. (1986). *The social consequences of standard-setting in the professions* (Paper commissioned for the Task Force on Teaching as a Profession, Carnegie Forum on Education and the Economy).

Wilson, S. M., Shulman, L. S., & Richert, A. (in press). "150 different ways" of knowing: Representations of knowledge in teaching. In J. Calderhead (Ed.), *Exploring teacher thinking.* Sussex, Eng.: Holt, Rinehart & Winston.

DISCUSSION QUESTIONS

1. Why is research on teacher effectiveness on its own an insufficient source for defining the knowledge base of teaching?

2. In what ways are (a) content area scholarship, (b) educational materials and structures, (c) formal educational scholarship, and (d) wisdom of practice integral components of the teacher knowledge base?

3. Which domains should comprise the conception of teacher competence?

4. What do you think teachers should know and be able to do as a result of their training?

5. Should teacher education require national board examinations for certification? Why? Why not?

Investigations of Expertise in Teaching

KATHERINE S. CUSHING
DONNA S. SABERS
DAVID C. BERLINER

FOCUSING QUESTIONS

1. **What factors distinguish expert and novice teachers?**
2. **What elements influence the ways in which experts, advanced beginners, and novices view classrooms?**
3. **How do experts, advanced beginners, and novices define instruction?**
4. **How do experts, advanced beginners, and novices differ in their perception of the teacher's role?**
5. **In what ways do experts, advanced beginners, and novices interpret "typicality" within classrooms?**

What makes an expert teacher an expert? The authors conducted studies aimed at unraveling the nature of expertise in teaching. Following the general model of expertise in many fields, they studied expert teachers, advanced beginners, and novices. This article contains their findings, conclusions, and recommendations for developing and nurturing expertise in all teachers.

In this year of the 25th Summer Olympiad we are intrigued by the performances of experts. We hold our collective breath as one-by-one each competitor takes to the track, court, or arena. Who will win the Gold, the Silver, the Bronze? Will the Unified Team from the former Soviet Union and the German Unified Team perform as well as they did in the XV Olympic Winter Games? It is not so much the medal count that intrigues us, but the instinctiveness with which the athletes perform. We know this level of skill comes from years or practice, but these Olympic athletes make it look so easy and graceful.

Like Olympians, the performances of expert teachers also intrigue us. Expert teachers make classroom management and instruction look easy. Yet we know that teaching is a complex task, and that good teaching requires a teacher to do many things at the same time. Griffin has described the ideal teacher as: "well-organized, alert to classroom events, concerned about classroom groups as well as about individuals, and skillful in the management of a complex social system. . . . The teacher [is able to] diagnose cognitive and social behaviors of students . . . monitor the understanding of the students . . . monitor learning as well as . . . behavior. . . . The ideal teacher is in command of subject matter and [of] delivering that subject matter so that effective, efficient, and long-term learning takes place."[1] This description of the ideal teacher only serves to draw our attention to the many performance demands on classroom teachers. Some researchers have suggested that elementary teachers have many hundreds of distinct interactions with individual students each day;[2] a teacher's ability to manage these interactions, maintain order, and maintain the instruction flow is testimony to their level of expertise.

In a series of studies conducted at the University of Arizona and Arizona State University we have attempted to unravel the nature of expertise in teaching. In our efforts to add to the knowledge base about pedagogical expertise we asked: What is it that makes an expert teacher an expert? We were particularly interested in whether expert teachers resemble experts in other fields. Further, we believed that if we found differences in the perceptions, understanding, and problem-solving skills of expert and beginning teachers such findings would have implications for teacher training and certification as well as for discussions about master teacher and career ladder plans.

Three studies, each part of a larger research project, assessed expert-novice differences in processing and using information about students, in perceiving and processing static visual classroom information, and in perceiving and processing dynamic and simultaneous events within a classroom.

The data presented here follow the general model of the development of expertise across many fields proposed by Dreyfus and Dreyfus.[3] They describe five stages: in the novice stage (stage one) behavior is relatively inflexible as context-free rules are followed; the advanced beginner (stage two) begins to meld on-the-job experience with book learning; however, they are still not very flexible in behavior. At the third stage, that of competent performer, behavior becomes more flexible, whereas the proficient performer (stage four) recognizes patterns and inter-relationships and has a holistic understanding of the processes involved. Experts (stage five) have the same integrated, holistic view and also respond effortlessly, fluidly, and appropriately to the demands of the situations with which they are confronted. This heuristic way of thinking about pedagogical expertise, and the policy implications of such a model, have been described in detail by Berliner.[4]

For these studies we compared the perceptions and performances of three groups of participants. Experts were junior or senior high school teachers of science or mathematics, identified as outstanding teachers by their supervisors and by members of the research team. Advanced Beginners were those who had completed student teaching or who were in their first year of classroom teaching and who were viewed by supervisory personnel as having the potential to develop into an "excellent" teacher. A third group of participants was designated as Novices. These were individuals employed by business and industry who expressed an interest in classroom teaching but who had no formal teacher training or experience in public school teaching. These individuals had expertise in fields such as computer technology, chemistry, and physics. They indicated an interest in teaching, and we believe they represent those individuals who might enter the teaching profession through an alternative certification route. Details regarding the identification and selection of these individuals is described elsewhere;[5] however, it is important to note that by our criteria they represented the best in each category.

FINDINGS FROM THREE INVESTIGATIONS OF EXPERTISE

Because we were particularly interested in differences in how experts, advanced beginners, and novices see and understand classroom events, we designed three research studies to assess these differences. In the Student Information Task[6] participants were presented with a simulation in which they were asked to "take over" a science or mathematics class six weeks into the school year. After reviewing classroom materials and information about individual students and student performance, participants were asked to plan the first two days of instruction, and then to explain their lesson plans and answer questions about students, instruction, and classroom management.

In the Slide Task[7] participants were asked to view and interpret static information: slides of classroom instruction. This included both a one-second viewing of particular slides, and the viewing of a sequence of 50 slides depicting a classroom lesson. While viewing the sequence of slides, participants had control of the pace of the slide presentation, and were asked to stop and comment on slides that caught their attention.

In the Simultaneity Task[8] participants were asked to simultaneously view three video monitors of classroom instruction and then to answer both general and specific questions about what they saw. During a second viewing participants were asked to "talk aloud" about what they were viewing and to indicate which monitor they were referring to by touching a designated computer key.

For each task, propositions suggested interesting contrasts among groups. Patterns of differences across tasks were also discernable. This article presents findings in the form of propositions that appear consistent in these three tasks. Each proposition is followed by an explanation and excerpts from individual protocols which instantiate these findings.

PROPOSITION ONE: EXPERTS, ADVANCED BEGINNERS, AND NOVICES DIFFER IN THEIR PERCEPTIONS AND UNDERSTANDING OF CLASSROOM EVENTS

Perhaps because of their classroom experience, experts viewed the visual materials presented to them differently than did either advanced beginners or novices. In all three tasks, experts acted in one of two very different ways: either they made hypotheses to explain or interpret the information presented, or they were very cautious and refrained from interpreting the information presented to them. On the other hand, advanced beginners and novices provided literal and often valid descriptions of the information presented, seeming to appreciate and accept as valid the information provided to them. Lacking in the protocols of the advanced beginners and novices was interpretation of the meaning of this information for instructional purposes.

For example, on the Student Information Task experts were much less interested than either advanced beginners or novices in remembering specific "facts" about students, but instead indicated that they would like to develop their own, very personal feeling for the students. In describing this preference experts stated:

> Expert 6: I didn't read the [student information] cards. I never do, unless there's a comment about a physical impairment such as hearing or sight or something I get from the nurse. I never want to place a judgment on the student before they start. I find I have a higher success rate if I don't. . . . My expectations going in are the same for everybody. So if I bias that by any knowledge other than the fact that I presume they can succeed, then I feel that I might not give them a fair chance going into the class.

> Expert 8: I think it's good reference material [information left by the previous teacher], but I sure wouldn't put a whole lot of stock in it.

Novices, however, paid serious attention to the comments left by the previous teacher on the student information cards and used that information for categorizing students. For example, novices reported:

> Novice 1: I sorted the bad kids from the good kids from some of the ones that were just good-natured, if they liked to work, that type of thing.

> Novice 4: I went through her student cards and also went through test scores and tried to divide the students into three groups, one group which I thought might be disruptive, one which I thought would not be disruptive and that wouldn't need intense watching, and the third group I really

didn't know because the back of the card was blank.

Thus, novices appeared to consider the teacher's comments on the student information cards as accurately reflecting the students in the classroom. As such, they believed that information was relevant when planning instruction. Perhaps due to inexperience or a lack of confidence in their own instructional skills, novices heeded all the material presented them and appeared unable to filter and judge the relevancy of different information.

This interpretative-descriptive distinction in the responses among group members was also apparent in the Slide Task where participants viewed static information of classroom scenes. The following typical comments were provided by experts after a one second viewing of a classroom slide:

Expert 1: It's a hands-on activity of some type. Group work with a male and female of maybe late junior high school age.

Expert 8: A group of students maybe doing small group discussion or a project as seats were not in rows.

Expert responses indicate that what is important to "see" during this brief viewing is what is happening instructionally for students in the classroom. Advanced beginners and novices, on the other hand, provided literal, and quite accurate, descriptions of the slides:

Advanced Beginner 3: A room full of students sitting at tables.

Advanced Beginner 4: Two students at the chalkboard working.

Novice 3: A fellow and girl in the foreground standing. She had her hand near her face—other activity in the background.

Novice 4: Whole classroom—teacher standing up front, windows behind him. Chalkboard to left of room.

Such limited information, while accurate, emphasizes the different meanings group members bring to classroom observations. Only the experts provided an instructional interpretation of what was observed.

Findings from the Slide Task were confirmed in the Simultaneity Task where participants were asked to view and respond to dynamic rather than static information. In this task, experts were better able to monitor all three screens and to respond to the audio cues, whereas advanced beginners experienced difficulty, and novices reported it was "almost impossible" to watch all three video monitors at once. Further, the responses of the experts indicated they were, once again, interpreting and making sense of the classroom events they were viewing. Examples from protocols follow:

Expert 2: In the center monitor, I hear a buzzer and nobody is getting up, so I assume that's some sort of a warning bell that . . . indicates a certain length of time till the end of the period.

Expert 3: On the left-hand monitor, when the bell rings it appears that students know exactly what they're supposed to do without any prior instruction. They get right to work.

Expert 4: Again viewing the middle monitor, I think there is an indication here of the type of structure of the classroom. It's pretty loose, the kids come in and go out without checking with the teacher.

On the other hand, advanced beginners and novices generally focused on the middle monitor and, for the most part, described what they observed happening in a step-by-step, almost radio announcer-type fashion:

Advanced Beginner 2: Middle monitor, the boy in red, was talking to someone else, while the teacher was talking.

Advanced Beginner 3: In the middle monitor, the teacher's reminding the students that it's very important to label all their work, or they will receive no credit.

In all three tasks, experts were better able than either advanced beginners or novices to make sense of and interpret classroom phenomena, whether presented as archival and anecdotal information, static visual information, or dynamic, simultaneous information. The experts focused on events that had instructional implications. In contrast, advanced beginners and novices, not knowing what was important instructionally, provided descriptions of what they saw, but did not provide interpretations. This interpretative-descriptive difference has important implications for classroom management and instruction. If we extrapolate from these studies, we would expect the expert teachers to better understand and make sense of what was happening in the classroom than beginning teachers. Expert teachers would attend to different information, whether presented through the visual or auditory mode, and would be better able to monitor instructional activities and management issues.

PROPOSITION TWO: EXPERTS, ADVANCED BEGINNERS, AND NOVICES DIFFER IN THE ROLE THEY ASSUME IN CLASSROOM INSTRUCTION.

In all three tasks, participants were asked to attend to, focus on, or comment about anything they believed important for classroom management or instruction. We have already noted differences among group members in how they perceive and understand classroom events—now we find differences among group members in how they define instruction and the role of the teacher. Experts' comments focused on the role of the teacher as instructor and monitor of student learning; they made evaluative comments or suggestions on ways in which instruction might be modified or improved to ensure student learning. While advanced beginners and novices were generally as aware of "off-task" student behaviors as experts, the comments of advanced beginners and novices generally focused on issues of management or control, rather than on issues of instructional methodology or content.

In the Student Information Task experts thought differently about preparing to take over a class than did either advanced beginners or novices. Experts talked about how to get the classroom going, and about how to determine where the students were in terms of understanding the course content. Experts emphasized the importance of breaking the old ties and "starting over"; they stressed that this was a new beginning. Experts' protocols documented routines for beginning a new class and finding out just what it is that students already know. For example, when asked about instructional activities for the first day experts responded:

> Expert 5: Well, Day One, I just wanted to meet the kids and find out who they were. I would lay down what my rules are, what my grading would be, and my policies. Then I would question them to find out what chapters they had covered in this book. And then what I wanted to do was verbally review with them and ask questions to find out the techniques they've been taught . . .
>
> Expert 7: The first day I had in mind that I'm going into a brand new class, they possibly don't know me at all. I would quickly go over what I would expect for rules and expectations, raising their hand before talking, courtesy to teacher and students. . . . I'd give them some rules to follow to get us started.

Both advanced beginners and novices were willing to begin wherever the previous teacher had left off, and although they might spend some time introducing themselves, it was with the idea of continuing, not starting over.

> Advanced Beginner 1: I would first introduce myself. . . . I might have them introduce themselves. Then I would ask them what their prior teacher expected from them and how she ran the class and what they liked or disliked.

Novice 2: I guess my biggest problem with the lesson plan was to figure out where they are now and where they were going.

Thus we see that experts choose to make the classroom their own, often changing the instructional techniques and focus of the previous teacher. Advanced beginners and novices, on the other hand, were planning to follow in the previous teacher's footsteps.

This notion of the teacher's role in monitoring instruction emerged clearly in the Slide Task when participants were asked to talk about and make sense of the sequence of classroom slides. Although experts, advanced beginners, and novices all commented about "on-task" and "off-task" behaviors, experts talked, to a much greater degree, about their role (as teacher) of "monitoring" the laboratory experiments, calculations, and laboratory write-ups. For example, about the science slides experts commented: Expert 1: [Slide 61] I would remind people that if they have long hair . . . it can be a real hazard and it needs to be tied back or somehow held back.

Expert 1: [Slide 9] [I would] monitor situations where you've got water up on high (boiling water above a Bunsen burner) . . . [these are] not real stable situations that you could get burns on.

Expert 1: [Slide 21] [I would] probably go around and just monitor making sure that they're reading the right kinds of observations. Just make some visual checks on their data that they're recording . . . [maybe] give them a little guidance.

Throughout the rest of the slides this expert continually offered suggestions about what he would do to ensure student learning was "on track" and to alleviate management concerns before they became issues needing attention. This expert's comments were not atypical—examples from protocols of other experts who participated in this study document consistent monitoring of the class activity and student behavior to ensure optimal learning.

Only one advanced beginner discussed the instructional role of monitoring, and none of the novices commented on this instructional activity. Instead, members of both groups made more comments related to behavioral management and control. For example, from the science lesson protocol:

Novice 2: [Slide 20] The one girl isn't paying attention while the other is adding something to her test tube.

Novice 2: [Slide 24] We've got a lot of movement, conversing back and forth between groups. That's potentially a problem.

Novice 3: [Slide 11] Something is going on in the background. I don't know what they are doing.

Novice 3: [Slide 34] Now they're horsing around in the back.

And from the mathematics protocols:

Advanced Beginner 4: [Slide 13] This is where the young fellow . . . was out of his seat. A potential problem.

Advanced Beginner 5: [Slide 9] This is the type of picture you like to see . . . all the students are doing work . . .

Thus, advanced beginners and novices again described what they saw and expressed concerns about behavior, but appeared less likely to focus on the role of the teacher in either classroom management or instruction. Experts, on the other hand, appeared comfortable with the role of assessing classroom events in terms of the teacher's role in instructional activities, and they seemed less worried about management issues.

In the Simultaneity Task, experts, advanced beginners, and novices differed in their interpretations of what instructional strategies were used by the teacher. While all agreed that lecture was the primary instructional methodology, experts provided details, explanations, and interpretations of the instruction, whereas advanced beginners and novices tended to focus on the materials the teacher used rather than the actual instruction, as if the materials, themselves, were the instruction. Examples from representative protocols follow:

> Expert 4: The teacher wanted to have, I think, a lot of classroom interaction. . . . I think the technique that she used was very low-key, perhaps a process type approach to teaching science, rather than a very structured approach.
>
> Expert 5: It was generally a "stand-up-in-front" type lecture over the material. It wasn't a guided practice or anything. It wasn't keyed toward questions and answers of what they were looking at.
>
> Expert 6: This was a teacher centered-class! The teacher had the information to present. The students were there to listen and to assimilate. There wasn't any evidence of any inquiry or any hands-on activities.

Excerpts from the advanced beginner and novice protocols revealed different concerns:

> Advanced Beginner 1: It looks . . . well, mostly lecture. . . . Some use of media. She used the overhead a little bit.
>
> Advanced Beginner 4: She did lecture near the beginning with the overhead projector. She was using some audio-visual things.
>
> Novice 1: She gave them a diagram and then she explained it with an overhead projector.
>
> Novice 2: There was an attempt by the teacher to, you know, lecture with some questioning of the students.

From this data, it seems that advanced beginners and novices view instruction as the presentation or use of materials with which one teaches a lesson: methodology (lecture) and materials used (overhead projector) became "instruction" for these participants. On the other hand, experts attempted to understand and interpret the instructional activity they observed and were not particularly interested in the materials the classroom teacher used. To experts, instruction was an interactive process, and they appeared concerned about student participation and the effect of that interactive process (or lack of it) on student learning.

Again, if we extrapolate from this data we would expect the expert teachers to define their role differently than beginning teachers. Experts would perceive themselves as "teachers,"—as instructors of content. Their focus would be on the interactive nature of learning, and on monitoring to ensure that learning occurs. We would expect beginning teachers to be less comfortable with this interactive role and instead focus on classroom management and on the instructional materials or activities needed to present a lesson. Furthermore, we might expect the expert and beginning teachers to begin the school year differently, to interact differently with students, and to focus on different issues.

PROPOSITION THREE: EXPERTS, ADVANCED BEGINNERS, AND NOVICES DIFFER IN THEIR NOTION OF "TYPICALITY" WITHIN THE CLASSROOM ENVIRONMENT.

Throughout these studies experts responded to the information presented them, whether visual or auditory, whether as a single event or as multiple events, based on a notion of typicality. Experts talked about typical students, typical classrooms, typical student behavior. In this sense, they were already familiar with management and instructional issues in ways that advanced beginners and novices could never be because they lack the rich experiential base of the experts.

This notion of typicality was apparent in the Student Information Task where experts paid little attention to the student information cards presented to them. After deciding that this new class of students was somehow "typical" of classes in general, the experts seemed to have a clear sense of what kinds of students they would be teaching—most likely this was a result of their numerous years of teaching experience. This finding was not unexpected, for it replicates work done by Calderhead. In his study comparing experienced, student, and novice teachers, Calderhead noted that experienced teachers had acquired a large amount of information about students and, in a sense, "they seemed to 'know' their students before they met them."[9] Advanced beginners and novices did not show that same kind of well developed schemata for students.

In the Slide Task, expert protocols revealed sensitivity to unusual situations that attracted their attention. Experts focused on these atypical situations until they could explain them. When a situation was assessed as "typical," the need for additional processing was reduced. These concerns about "typicality" were rare in the protocols of either advanced beginners or novices.

In the Simultaneity Task, the notion of "typicality" emerged as experts discussed the demands of the task. Experts commented that the task of viewing three monitors, touching a computer key, and talking aloud simultaneously was a fair representation of what they were required to do all day long as classroom teachers. Advanced beginners and novices, on the other hand, found the task difficult and often overwhelming. One novice acknowledged an awareness that he "probably ought" to be able to perform the task better, but found it simply too difficult to do all that was requested of him at once!

Again, based on these studies we might expect beginning and expert teachers to have a different understanding of events within a classroom. Beginning teachers would not always know what to expect, or what was "normal" student behavior, and might respond in ways that increase the confusion or lead to management problems within a classroom. Expert teachers, on the other hand, appear able to identify a wide range of events as typical. Thus, they almost automatically know how to respond or handle those events.

CONCLUSION

We began this paper by comparing the performance of Olympic competitors and expert teachers. We suggested that, as a result of practice, Olympic athletes make their performances look easy and graceful. But it is not just practice. As with teaching expertise, it is much, much more. Expert teachers don't just practice the same techniques over and over again. They stop, reflect on what they are doing, and try different methods. They attend workshops and collaborate with colleagues—always searching for a better way to perfect their craft.

What is it that makes an expert teacher an expert? We believe we have some plausible answers to that question.

Like experts in other fields, expert teachers perceive and understand information in their area of expertise differently from novices. Thus, expert teachers see and make sense of classroom events differently than do beginning teachers. This appears to be the case regardless of how information about those events is presented to the experts. Perhaps because they see and understand classroom events differently they also plan for and deliver instruction differently. Planning differences were evident in the Student Information Task, and more recent studies have documented behavioral and affective differences among expert, advanced beginner, and novice teachers.[10]

Because of these differences it makes little sense to expect the same performances from beginning teachers as we do from experienced and expert teachers. It seems that the first year or two will most likely be spent trying to figure out what is important about students and instruction and management in a classroom. If there are many variables to attend to (students come and go, several different content preparations, the most difficult students to teach) those first few years are likely to be even more difficult. Providing support and help for beginning teachers makes sense. Help could come in many forms: observations of expert performances, mentor experiences, or seminar-discussion-type groups to name but a few. The help offered, however, should not be overwhelming. Learning to teach is difficult enough so that additional requirements for learning during the first year on the job should be minimal.

Our data suggest that qualitative differences of considerable importance exist among expert teachers, beginning teachers with some training, and those who want to be teachers through the alternative certification route. One example of the importance of these findings concerns alternative certification. However well-meaning these individuals are, and however good they may ultimately become, we believe that when they enter teaching they are fundamentally unenlightened about classrooms. What shall we do about that? As another example, our data suggests that evaluative instruments are unfair if they do not recognize differences between expert and novice teachers. What may be appropriate evaluative criteria for the novice may not be appropriate for the expert.

These data also lead us to conclude that teacher education programs must re-think the nature of their graduates. Teacher education programs do not graduate competent teachers, merely beginners. Thus, the colleges may need to have an educational program that follows up its graduates over the first few years. Perhaps colleges should provide only provisional degrees, certifying only that their graduates are ready for an apprenticeship. Permanent degrees might be issued after three or so years. Our data lead us to believe, also, that the pool of experts, as in chess and other fields, is likely to be small. While such individuals need to be honored and ways must be found to have them stay in classroom teaching, the primary goal of preservice and inservice education in America may be the development and the maintenance of competence. This is a level of performance that virtually all who enter teaching should reach in a few years. The building up of competence, however, and the subsequent growth to a level regarded as expert, does require time. There seem to be few shortcuts since experience

is the necessary, though not sufficient, condition for this kind of growth. Episodic and strategic knowledge must be built up and reflected upon, and this cannot occur in a few months or years. This has implications for the tenure laws in states. We would think that five years, rather than three, would be a better point at which to make these important judgments.

Learning the ways one grows from novice to expert in pedagogy is not easy, either for the practitioner or the researcher. But for both of them, the rewards for studying the process are likely to be quite high.

ENDNOTES

1. Gary A. Griffin, "Clinical Teacher Education," *Reality and Reform in Clinical Teacher Education,* eds. J. V. Hoffman and S. A. Edwards (New York: Random House, 1986), 1–24.

2. P. V. Gump, *The Classroom Behavior Setting: Its Nature and Relation to Student Behavior,* final report prepared by the U.S. Office of Education, Bureau of Research (Washington, D.C., 1967) (ED 015 515); P. W. Jackson, Life in Classrooms (New York: Holt, Rinehart, & Winston, 1968).

3. Hubert L. Dreyfus and Stuart E. Dreyfus, *Mind Over Machine* (New York: Free Press, 1986); see also Patricia Benner, From Novice to Expert (Reading, MA: Addison-Wesley, 1984).

4. David C. Berliner, "Implications of Studies of Expertise in Pedagogy for Teacher Education and Evaluation," *New Directions for Teacher Assessment: Proceedings of the 1988 ETS Invitational Conference* (Princeton, NJ: Educational Testing Service, 1989).

5. Donna S. Sabers, Katherine S. Cushing, and David C. Berliner, "Differences Among Teachers in a Task Characterized by Simultaneity, Multidimensionality, and Immediacy," *American Educational Research Journal,* 28 (Spring, 1991): 63–88.

6. Kathy Carter, Donna Sabers, Katherine Cushing, Stefinee Pinnegar, and David C. Berliner. "Processing and Using Information About Students: A Study of Expert, Novice, and Postulant Teachers," *Teaching and Teacher Education* 3 (1987): 147–157.

7. Kathy Carter, Katherine Cushing, Donna Sabers, Pamela Stein, and David Berliner, "Expert-Novice Differences in Perceiving and Processing Visual

Classroom Information," *Journal of Teacher Education* 39 (May–June, 1988); 25–31.

8. Sabers, Cushing, and Berliner, p. 63–88.

9. James Calderhead, "Research into Teachers' and Student Teachers' Cognitions: Exploring the Nature of Classroom Practice" (Paper presented at the annual meeting of the American Educational Research Association, Montreal, 1983).

10. Donna Sabers, Katherine Cushing, and David C. Berliner, "Students' Evaluations of Teachers Who Dif-

fer in Experience and Expertise. (Paper presented at the annual meeting of the American Educational Research Association, New Orleans, 1988); and Pamela Stein and David C. Berliner, "Expert, Novice and Postulant Teachers' Thoughts During Teaching" (Paper presented at the annual meeting of the American Educational Research Association, New Orleans, 1988).

DISCUSSION QUESTIONS

1. How might the Dreyfus and Dreyfus model of expertise development be used to guide teacher training?

2. What should the role of reflection in teacher training be?

3. Should colleges provide only provisional degrees for teachers? Why? Why not?

4. What changes might be implemented in teacher training programs to facilitate teachers' professional growth during their first few years in the field?

5. How do experts, advanced beginners, and novices perceive the teacher's role?

PRO-CON CHART 2

Should teachers be held accountable for their teaching?

PRO	CON
1. Teaching should be guided by clear objectives and outcomes.	1. Many factors influence teaching and learning that have little to do with measurable objectives and outcomes.
2. Students have a right to receive a quality education, whereby professionals are held accountable for their behavior.	2. Educational accountability is a cooperative responsibility of students, teachers, parents, and taxpayers.
3. Accountability will encourage teachers to uphold high standards for instruction.	3. Teachers can provide instruction but they cannot force students to learn.
4. Feedback from accountability evaluation measures will provide teachers with information about their instructional strengths and weaknesses.	4. Mandating accountability will demoralize teachers and reduce their professional status.
5. Accountability will provide standards that are derived through consensual agreement and will offer objective assessment.	5. There will always be disagreement on who is accountable, for what, and by whom.

CASE STUDY 2

School District Proposes Evaluations by Students

Kamhi County School District in West Suburb had proposed to vote on implementing a change to their current teacher evaluation procedures. The proposed change would permit junior high students to participate in the evaluation process of their teachers, beginning in the spring. As a way of gathering feedback, all thirty principals were asked to complete an anonymous three-part survey. In Parts One and Two, the principals were asked to cite the advantages and disadvantages of this proposed change. In Part Three, they were asked to provide a plan that outlined how they would implement this approach in their building site if it were enacted.

While reading the survey responses, Marilyn Lauter, assistant superintendent for instruction, noticed two items, unsigned letters from both a student and a teacher, that caught her attention. The student argued that because students are consumers of teachers' services, they should have a right to have their voices heard. The teacher's letter expressed complete opposition to the proposed change, citing that students lacked the maturity to provide feedback. The teacher's letter also stated that such a change would advocate the philosophy and teaching styles of certain administrators, thereby limiting the teacher's voice. Furthermore, the letter stated that if the district voted to enact this change as policy, the teachers would probably strike. Lauter was feeling very uncomfortable with both letters, but also knew that more discussion was needed before any policy change should be taken to a vote.

Discuss the issues raised by the student and the teacher and consider the following questions:

1. Should junior high students be involved in the evaluation of their teachers? Why? Why not?

2. If you were the assistant superintendent for instruction, how would you handle this situation?

3. What other approaches might have been used to elicit feedback from the teachers, parents, and students concerning the proposed policy change to the teacher evaluation process?

4. In what ways might students' evaluations of teachers affect their instruction or your own instruction?

5. What evidence does research provide about the ability of junior high students to evaluate teachers?

6. How might teachers and parents in your school district react to this proposed policy change in teacher evaluation procedures?

PART THREE

Curriculum and Learning

INTRODUCTION

What is the relationship between learning and curriculum? What role does motivation play in student achievement? To what extent is higher order thinking, creativity, and moral education emphasized in curriculum delivery? How has cooperative learning and the use of standards influenced student outcomes?

In Chapter 13, Carole Ames explains the relationship between motivational concepts and student learning. She points out how teachers, classrooms, and family context influence student motivation. She describes how teachers can plan instruction that enhances student motivation. In the next chapter, Matthew Lipman distinguishes between critical and ordinary thinking. He suggests that an emphasis on critical thinking will promote intellectual responsibility and describes the processes that encourage critical thinking.

In Chapter 15, Robert Sternberg and Todd Lubart discuss the factors that characterize creative thinking. The authors explore the type of instruction that fosters creative thinking. They suggest that students should be given more responsibility for selecting the type of problems that they investigate rather than relying on teacher-constructed problems. In Chapter 16, Lawrence Kolhberg describes how moral education promotes the aims of education. He compares the cognitive-developmental approach with other approaches to moral education and discusses the school's role in moral and civic education.

In Chapter 17, Robert Slavin describes how cooperative learning results in improved academic achievement. He highlights how cooperative learning techniques enhance the quality of interpersonal relationships. In the final chapter of Part Three, Grant Wiggins argues that schools need to establish high and consistent standards for all students. He suggests that the use of criteria-based standards will promote intellectual discipline and empower students.

Motivation: What Teachers Need to Know

CAROLE A. AMES

FOCUSING QUESTIONS

1. *Why should teachers be concerned with the concept of motivation?*
2. *How does working for extrinsic versus intrinsic rewards influence student learning?*
3. *Why is the quantitative view of motivation that focuses on intensity, duration, and direction of behavior insufficient in helping teachers understand how motivation influences student learning? Do you agree or disagree?*
4. *How are self-efficacy and attribution related to the concept of motivation?*
5. *What factors influence whether students adopt mastery or performance goals?*

Motivation, one of the foremost problems in education, is often inadequately addressed in typical foundational (educational psychology) courses. In this chapter, Ames clarifies the complex construct of motivation as it relates to learning and offers a revamped curriculum that applies motivation theory and research to practice. She recommends instruction in how motivation constructs relate to each other, to developmental changes, to individual and culturally related differences, and to the classroom context.

There are three things to remember about education. The first one is motivation. The second one is motivation. The third one is motivation.

—Terrell H. Bell

What is it about the academic motivation of students that teachers should know? Certainly, knowledge of motivation concepts, principles,

and theories should be basic elements in a foundations course in educational psychology, but this is not really what educational psychology should be about. Teachers need to know how this conceptual knowledge relates to the classroom and to their instructional role in the classroom. Teachers also need to know how to rely on this knowledge when dealing with issues that involve motivational concerns and when making instructional decisions.

For example, consider a not very unusual problem facing a teacher about homework. How can a teacher set homework policy so that students complete the homework and still maintain their interest in the material? Teacher A's policy states that all homework must be turned in daily, that all homework will be graded daily with letter or percentage grades, and that homework counts for 30 percent of the quarter grade. Teacher B's policy states that students are to spend no more than thirty minutes per night on homework, that homework will be graded satisfactory or unsatisfactory, that students can redo and correct their work, and that homework counts for 10 percent of the quarter grade. We may think the stringency of Teacher A's policy might be more effective, but research on motivation would suggest that Teacher B's policy is more likely to fulfill both objectives. At the classroom level, teachers are often faced with a child who continually avoids challenge. At the beginning level, teachers must come together and decide how to structure a reading program so that students will read more but also enjoy reading more. These are simple examples of everyday problems and decisions that involve motivation questions.

Student motivation has, for some time, been described as one of the foremost problems in education.[1] It is certainly one of the problems most commonly cited by teachers. Motivation is important because it contributes to achievement, but it is also important itself as an outcome.

Motivation is not synonymous with achievement, and student motivation cannot necessarily be inferred by looking at achievement test scores. Immediate achievement and test performance are determined by a variety of factors and may even be assured through a variety of ways, and some practices that serve to increase immediate achievement may actually have the effect of diminishing students' interest in learning as well as their long-term involvement in learning. When we talk about motivation as an outcome, we are concerned with students' "motivation to learn."[2] If we place a value on developing a motivation to learn in students, we are concerned with whether students initiate learning activities and maintain an involvement in learning as well as a commitment to the process of learning. Effective schools and effective teachers are those who develop goals, beliefs, and attitudes in students that will sustain a long-term involvement and that will contribute to quality involvement in learning.

If we evaluate our schools and classrooms strictly by how much students achieve, we can easily lose sight of these other educational goals and values. We not only want students to achieve, we want them to value the process of learning and the improvement of their skills, we want them to willingly put forth the necessary effort to develop and apply their skills and knowledge, and we want them to develop a long-term commitment to learning.[3] It is in this sense that motivation is an outcome of education. Students who elect to take advanced science classes because they want to learn more and not just because they think they can do well is an example of this outcome.

It is therefore a first priority to help teachers develop an understanding of why motivation is important. This, indeed, may be a challenge when educational psychology textbooks typically allot only one chapter to motivation, and this chapter usually provides little more than an overview of theories and concepts. Moreover, topics that are intricately related to motivation, such as classroom management, individual differences, testing and evaluation, grouping, and family, are often treated in separate chapters with little or no linkage to motivational concepts and without discussion of motivational processes. Educational psychology is about application; it is not enough to highlight theories or review basic constructs and dot these presentations with a few examples.

Motivation has often been characterized within what has been called a quantitative view of motivation,[4] in which motivation has been described as the *intensity* of behavior, the *direction* of behavior, and the *duration* of behavior.[5] The question for classroom teachers is how to get students to do what you want them to do and to do it consistently over time. This focus, however, does not help us in thinking about how to develop and nurture a motivation to learn in students.

Rather than the duration of behavior (or what has been called engaged time), we need to think about the quality of task engagement. Students need to develop motivational thought patterns that contribute to self-regulated learning. Observing students' time on task does not tell us about what they are attending to, how they are processing information, how they are reacting to their performance, and how they are interpreting feedback. What is critical is the quality of engaged time, not the duration of engaged time.

Rather than the direction of behavior, we need to think about students' goals or reasons for learning. Two students may choose to work on a science project or complete a math worksheet, but they may pursue quite different goals in doing so. A student who works for extrinsic rewards such as grades is likely to engage in very different thought processes and behaviors compared with the student who wants to learn something new about the subject matter or improve a skill. Students' reasons for learning have important consequences for how they approach and engage in learning.

Motivation is also not a matter of increasing the intensity of behavior. The task facing teachers is not one of maximizing or even optimizing the level of motivation; to suggest so perpetuates a view that motivation is a state of arousal or energy. What is assumed is that by increasing or optimizing this state, performance will be enhanced. What we often find, however, is that students can be equally motivated but for very different reasons. Often, it is not that the child is not motivated, but that the child is not motivated to do what *we* want him to do. Rather than focus on differentiating high, low, and optimally motivated students, we instead need to define adaptive and maladaptive or positive and negative motivation patterns and to understand how and why these patterns develop over time.

MOTIVATION CONSTRUCTS

To teach quantitative concepts such as duration, intensity, and direction is not going to help teachers understand how or why students develop adaptive, positive, or effective thought patterns. At a very general level, these thought patterns include goals, beliefs, and attitudes that are involved in how students approach learning situations, engage in the process of learning, and respond to learning experiences. Some examples are self-worth or self-concept of ability, attributions, self-regulated learning, and achievement goals. We need to pay more attention to how teachers can become more successful in socializ-

ing these adaptive motivation patterns in students. To set the stage for some later points, let me briefly describe just a few of these constructs.

Self-Worth

Students' self-worth is intricately tied to their self-concept of ability in school settings.[6] This self-concept of ability or self-efficacy has significant consequences for student achievement behavior. Self-efficacy is an expectation or belief that one is capable of performing a specific task, organizing and carrying out required behaviors in a situation.[7] Efficacy is not self-concept of ability in a general sense; it is task- or situation-specific. One's self-worth is implicated when the task is important and when one's ability is threatened. Clearly, in the classroom, all tasks can be made important through the use of external rewards and certain evaluation procedures. Indeed, it is very difficult to look in a classroom and determine what is or is not important to different children. As a consequence, self-efficacy is often a critical factor predicting children's task choices, willingness to try and persist on difficult tasks, and even actual performance in many classrooms.

At first glance, it may appear that increasing student's self-efficacy is merely a matter of increasing children's confidence that they can do well. This is not necessarily the case. Consider an example where a teacher tells all her students that everyone's story is going to become part of the class newspaper. Although all the children can expect success in getting their stories "published," a child may still harbor intense doubts about whether he or she can write a story. The child's self-confidence of ability to write the story has not been changed. Children's self-efficacy does respond positively when they learn to act short-term, realistic goals and are shown how to make progress toward these goals. It is not a matter of convincing them they can do well or even guaranteeing it; it is giving them the strategies to do so.

Children's understanding about their ability is responsive to developmental changes as well as situational influences, and this also has important implications for practice. Young children tend to have an optimistic view of their ability, high expectations for success, and a sort of resilience after failure.[8] Moreover, young children tend to equate effort with ability. To them, hard workers are smart and smart children work hard. As children progress through school, their perceptions of their ability decrease and tend to reflect the teacher's evaluation of their ability. Older children's self-evaluations are more responsive to failure or negative feedback, meaning that they are more likely to adjust their expectations downward after failing. Older children also develop a more differentiated view of effort and ability. While effort can increase the chance for success, ability sets the boundaries of what one's effort can achieve. Effort now becomes the "double-edged sword."[9] Trying hard and failing threatens one's self-concept of ability.

What does this mean to teachers? First, for young children, praising their effort may actually convey to them a sense of confidence in their ability. Because ability and effort are not well differentiated, praise for children's efforts can enhance their self-confidence. However, this does not work with older children. To them, effort and ability are not the same, and they are more concerned with being perceived as able. It is at this point that teachers' and students' preferences diverge. While teachers may value effort and hard work, students prefer to maximize their chances for success and at the same time minimize their effort expenditure. Ability is important in most classrooms; when students' self-concept of ability is threatened, they display failure-avoidance motivation.[10] They engage in failure-avoiding tactics such as not trying, procrastinating, false effort, and even the denial of effort. Why would they do this when these behaviors most assuredly will increase the likelihood of failure? What these behaviors accomplish is reducing the negative implications of failure. From the students' point of view, failure without effort does not negatively reflect on their ability. What they have achieved is "failure with honor."[11]

Attributions and Related Metacognitive Beliefs

The consequences of students' attributions for success and failure for their subsequent achievement behavior have been well described in the research literature. Attributions are related to expectations about the likelihood of success, to judgments about one's own ability, to emotional reactions of pride or hopelessness, and to a willingness to engage in effort-driven cognitions as in self-regulated learning. Over time, children who believe that failure is caused by a lack of ability are likely to exhibit a sense of helplessness. Low expectations, negative affect, and ineffective strategies characterize these children. Children with this dysfunctional attribution pattern are less likely to develop or enact those metacognitive skills that will enable them to tackle a wide range of classroom tasks. By contrast, children who perceive a relationship between their own effort and success are likely to respond to failure or problem situations with a sense of hopefulness and engage in strategic task behavior.[12]

Related to attributional beliefs is students' use of learning strategies and other self-regulated thought processes. These are effort-driven processes, and in that sense, they are motivational. They include, for example, organizing and planning, goal-setting, self-monitoring, and self-instruction. These strategies have been called generic or general learning strategies in that they can be applied across situations and across domains. Of course, students have to have knowledge of the strategies and an awareness of their appropriateness to the situation, but beyond knowledge and awareness is the volitional (motivational) question of whether students will apply the strategies. Whether students choose to engage in such strategic thinking is largely dependent on whether they are willing to apply the necessary effort and whether they believe effort will lead to success. Thus, there are two issues concerning students' strategy use. The first issue concerns whether students have and can apply the necessary skills or strategies. The second issue is motivational: whether students believe that effort is linked to success and that the outcome is worth the effort, and whether they are willing to expend the effort.[13]

Achievement Goals

Related to attributions are students' reasons for learning and their achievement-related goals.[14] The issue here is *why* students engage in learning and choose to engage in academic tasks rather than whether they choose to do so. For example, students may choose to participate in specific activities to gain external rewards, to develop their skills and ability, or to demonstrate that they are smart by outperforming others or by trying to achieve success with minimal effort.

Students who are interested in learning new things and developing their skills and ability have been described as mastery-oriented. These students are willing to expend the necessary effort to learn something new and confront challenging tasks. It is this mastery-goal orientation that is more likely to produce independent learning and sustained involvement in achievement activities. These students are motivated to learn.

Students who instead perceive that normative performance is important and want to demonstrate that they have ability or to protect their ability when threatened are labeled performance-oriented. Such students tend to think more about their ability than about "how to do the task." Their strategies, such as memorizing facts or reading or studying only what they think will be on a test, tend to serve their performance only over the short term.

Whether students adopt mastery or performance goals is, in part, dependent on their classroom experiences, essentially their perceptions of how the teacher structures the classroom.[15] Many children enter school with mastery or learning goals but many become socialized into a performance-goal orientation.[16] When we consider the preponderance of public evaluation practices,

normative comparisons, extrinsic rewards, ability grouping, and emphasis on production, speed, and perfection, it is no wonder that children find it difficult to maintain a learning or mastery orientation.

ENHANCING MOTIVATION

In most of our foundational courses, we stop once we have covered the basic theories or motivational constructs. We cannot assume, however, that teachers are prepared to translate these ideas into classroom practice. This is a major problem for foundations courses. We give too little attention to how motivation concepts interface with the instructional program, too little attention to how the social context of the classroom can undermine or facilitate the development of students' motivation to learn, and too little attention to how motivation principles relate to each other. What we do is cover the basics, highlight a few principles, maybe even review a case study or two, and then hope that the teacher's intuition has somehow been enlightened and that the teacher will be able to apply this knowledge. Many textbooks, when it comes to dealing with applications, rely on conventional wisdom. There are several major texts that present a problem (e.g., how to deal with a child who exhibits poor motivation) and then present teachers' solutions. These solutions are not linked to any conceptual framework. There is even an implicit endorsement of these ideas and solutions as credible, viable, and conceptually sound because the source is practicing teachers. Unfortunately, it is often the case that this is not so. The problem is that many strategies for enhancing student-motivation involve the use of principles that are counter-intuitive. Let me illustrate this point with examples that are related to the motivation constructs described in the preceding section.

1. If children lack confidence in their ability to succeed, we might infer that these low-confident children should receive a heavy dose of success experience. The considerable literature on learned helplessness and attribution retraining, however, has shown that success alone does not alleviate a helplessness syndrome.[17] In contrast to what we might surmise, providing or ensuring successful outcomes or feedback does not necessarily bolster children's confidence in their abilities. Such a prescription ignores the role of cognitive motivational factors in determining how children interpret their classroom experiences. For many children success is not sufficient to create or maintain a belief that they have the ability to reverse failure. Children who are convinced that they lack the necessary ability to do school tasks do not take responsibility for success and even underestimate their performance when they do well. Thus, it is not a matter of persuading them they can do well or even guaranteeing it; instead, practice should involve giving them short-term goals and strategies for making progress toward the goals.[18] Once students understand how to reach a goal and focus on strategies, rather than outcomes, they are more likely to "own" the outcome.

2. Related to an emphasis on success is the prescription "try to find *something* positive to say about a child's work." Reinforcing children's work even if it involves some small aspect of the total effort should be a step in the direction of giving the child more confidence. Unfortunately, for the very children who most need positive feedback, the "something positive" is often something unimportant and irrelevant to the task requirements. For example, if the task is to write a book report in a certain format, commenting positively on the child's neat handwriting is not likely to have the intended effect.

On the one hand, the generous use of praise would seem to be an obvious and salient way of encouraging children who generally perform poorly, but as Brophy has shown, the way praise is often used in elementary school classrooms can undermine the achievement behavior of these children.[19] The praise children receive is often on irrelevant aspects of a task; in these instances,

children discount the praise. Praise on easy tasks or praise that is noncontingent on children's effort or performance quality can be interpreted by children as evidence that they lack ability; it can, therefore, have unintended negative effects on children's self-confidence.

The effects of praise must also be considered from a developmental perspective. Praise can be interpreted quite differently by younger and older children. Praising young children's effort conveys to them a positive expectation that they can do the work and can enhance their perceptions of their competence. Because older children have differentiated concepts of ability and effort, praising their effort may actually be interpreted by them as low expectations for their ability. It is therefore important to understand how developmental changes in cognition mediate the effects of well-intended behaviors. The application of basic psychological principles requires more than just a casual understanding of how cognition gives meaning to actions and classroom events.

3. One of the seeming paradoxes of research on student learning concerns the effects of rewards and incentives on student motivation. We have been taught that, if we want to increase the probability of a behavior, the most efficient method is to apply reinforcement principles. In fact, it seems that we have been indoctrinated into this way of thinking so well that these extrinsic reinforcements are often overused. Recent research by Boggiano and her colleagues certainly supports this assertion.[20] They presented a number of scenarios that described children involved in both high- and low-interest activities to adults, college students, and parents and asked them to judge how well certain strategies would maintain or increase the child's interest over time. For example, they described one ten-year-old child as one "who really enjoys reading and particularly likes to read books to learn about new things." Another ten-year-old was described as a child who "does not enjoy reading and chooses the easiest books to read when asked to write a book report." What is particularly striking is that regardless of the

child's interest level, extrinsic rewards (such as adding 50 percent extra to the child's allowance) were preferred over other strategies as a way of maintaining or increasing the child's interest. Reward was preferred to reasoning, punishment, and even noninterference. Moreover, Boggiano et al. found that adults consistently preferred large rewards over small rewards, which they interpreted as reflecting a belief that interest level would vary with the size of the reward.

Certainly programs involving extrinsic rewards tend to be pervasive in our schools as a mechanism for increasing achievement behavior. In many schools and classrooms, extrinsic incentives are seen as necessary to get children to spend time on various tasks and lessons. Over twenty years ago, Jackson suggested that many of children's schooling experiences involve a hidden curriculum of controls and social constraints.[21] As students progress through school, they become more and more extrinsically controlled.

What are the consequences of using extrinsic incentives to try to shape children's achievement behaviors, to get them to complete their work, to increase the quality of work, and to get them to spend more time on particular tasks? The evidence from considerable research converges in identifying the "hidden cost" of using extrinsic rewards to motivate children.[22] This is not to say that incentives cannot be effective in some situations and for some children. The fundamental problem is that when we look into classrooms, we see the same incentive system being used for all the children in the classroom.

I am not suggesting that we need to inculcate the idea that incentives are ineffective or motivationally detrimental. The use of extrinsic incentives can have multiple effects on children's motivation; predicting the specific effects requires an analysis of a number of component processes. For instance, it is important to consider the relationship of extrinsic incentives to other motivation variables. In certain instances, rewards may have the effect of increasing self-efficacy, which can positively influence students' motivation or willingness to learn. The relation of extrinsic rewards to individual differences is of critical importance. In the classroom, extrinsic incentives are often intended to motivate the least attentive students or those who typically perform poorly; however, the rewards are typically applied to the entire classroom or even the entire school population, as in many reading incentive programs. The hidden costs become most apparent when they are applied to these larger groups where individual differences in interest, performance, and ability are ignored.

4. From the work on intrinsic motivation comes the recommendation to give children choices and thus a sense of personal control in the classroom.[23] Choice of tasks or activities is viewed as fostering belief in personal control and increasing interest and involvement in learning. This is easy enough to endorse and gives us a nice, simple application of intrinsic motivation theory to the classroom. A problem arises when we consider the context or structure of many classrooms. When normative evaluation and public comparisons are expected, students' choices reflect an avoidance of challenge and a preference for tasks that ensure success. In other words, a choice is not an equal choice in some contexts. When evaluation is pending on one's final product, choices are not based on interest; they more likely reflect a protection of one's ability and concern for one's level of performance. In this case, motivation theory cannot be applied without considering the context of the classroom.

5. On the basis of attribution theory, we might infer that it is a good idea to try to persuade students that they are not working hard enough or that they need to work harder on occasions of failure or poor performance. The implication is that students must perceive that outcome varies with effort expenditure and that increased effort will result in more positive outcomes.

The first consideration here is that the admonishment to try harder is to no avail to the student who believes he or she is already trying hard. This is a very likely scenario for young children, who believe they always try hard because it is not smart not to try. Telling these children that they did not work hard enough may actually decrease their sense of efficacy.

Second, problems arise when we put too much emphasis on effort. We do not want to impress on students that sustained maximal effort is what leads to success. Students may feel very satisfied when they have worked very hard and achieved success, but this is usually accompanied by the feeling that "I don't want to work that hard again." Conveying the expectation that a maximized effort is necessary may spark a child's investment once in a while, but over time students are more likely to become discouraged. In classrooms where the goal is to demonstrate one's ability over the long term, continuously maximizing one's effort is not desirable.

Finally, in most classrooms, students do not perceive the classroom hierarchy as effort-determined. As Nicholls suggests, students at the bottom of the hierarchy are not there because they are not effortful;[24] convincing students that this is, in fact, the case has little credence. If we want teachers to apply attribution theory to classroom practice, they need to know that whether they convey to students that effort is important depends on how they structure tasks, evaluate students, and give recognition and rewards.

These examples illustrate the complex nature of classroom learning and motivation. One of the major problems in our training of teachers is that we do not adequately address how motivation theory, constructs, and principles relate to practice: How can teachers develop in students a motivation to learn? As the preceding five examples illustrate, we currently rely on the wisdom of experience or derive applications without regard to the complexities involved. We need to consider how motivation constructs relate to each other, to developmental changes, to individual and culturally related differences, and to the context or structure of the classroom itself when we apply motivation theory and research to practice.

CONTEXT OF MOTIVATION

Finally, if we want teachers to apply these constructs in order to develop these motivational patterns in students, it is important to recognize that motivation occurs within a context—the school, the classroom, and the family. We spend a great deal of time discussing individual differences in motivation, treating motivation as a trait, but not enough time attending to how the organization and structure of the classroom shapes and socializes adaptive and maladaptive motivation patterns. Moreover, developing a positive motivational orientation in students is necessarily a matter of dealing with diversity among students in the classroom.[25] Teachers need to know ways of dealing with this diversity, and these methods ought to involve a comprehensive look at the classroom.

Thus, the teacher must first be guided by goals that assign primary importance to developing in students a motivation to learn. Second, we need a framework for identifying those aspects or structures of the classroom that are manipulable. These structures must represent the classroom organization and must relate to instructional planning. Then we need to identify strategies that will serve to enhance the motivation of all students. These strategies or applications must be grounded in theory and research and evaluated in relation to developmental factors and in relation to other motivation constructs, as well as individual differences. Many educational psychology textbooks describe one or two ideas for application but do not provide a comprehensive view of classroom organization.

When we look at the classroom, there are six areas of organization that are manipulable and that involve motivational concerns; task, authority, recognition, grouping, evaluation, and time. These structures have been described in considerable detail by Epstein.[26] There is considerable research that relates to each area, and there are many motivational strategies that can be extracted from the research; the point is to apply appropriate strategies in all of these areas frequently and consistently. Preservice teachers often learn a great deal about only one area, and practicing teachers often focus on one or two areas but do little in the others. As a consequence, motivation becomes restricted to one area of the classroom. Often that area is reward or recognition (providing rewards and incentives), and even in that area inappropriate strategies are used.

CONCLUSION

This framework offers a starting point for extracting motivational strategies and applications from research and theory, and for relating them to all areas of classroom organization and instructional planning. This is important because motivation enhancement cannot be reserved for Friday afternoons, or be viewed as something to be used during free time or extra time or as superfluous to academic activities. Nor can motivational concerns surface only when a student does not do well. Motivation as an outcome is important to all students in the classroom all the time. This view gives student motivation a central place as an educational outcome, important in its own right. The emphasis is on identifying strategies that will foster a mastery-goal orientation in students and that relate to all aspects of classroom learning and organization. It requires a comprehensive approach to looking at how motivation theory and research interface with classroom learning.

ENDNOTES

1. See Lawrence A. Cremin, *The Transformation of the School* (New York: Random House, 1961).

2. See Carole Ames and Jennifer Archer, "Achievement Goals and Learning Strategies," *Journal of Educational Psychology* 80 (1989): 260–67; Jere Brophy, "Conceptualizing Student Motivation," *Educational Psychologist* 18 (1983): 200–15; Elaine S. Elliott and Carol S. Dweck. "Goals; An Approach to Motivation and Achievement," *Journal of Personality and Social Psychology* 54 (1988): 5–12; Martin L. Maehr, "Meaning and Motivation: Toward a Theory of Personal Investment," in *Research on Motivation in Education, Vol. 1: Student Motivation,* ed. Russell Ames and Carole Ames (Orlando: Academic Press, 1984), pp. 115–44; and John Nicholls, "Quality and Equality in Intellectual Development," *American Psychologist* 34 (1979): 1071–84.

3. Brophy, "Conceptualizing Student Motivation," pp. 200–15.

4. Carole Ames and Russell Ames, "Systems of Student and Teacher Motivation: Toward a Qualitative Definition," *Journal of Educational Psychology* 76 (1984): 535–56.

5. For example, Nathan Gage and David C. Berliner, *Educational Psychology* (Boston: Houghton-Mifflin, 1984).

6. See Martin Covington and Richard Beery, *Self-Worth and School Learning* (New York: Holt, Rinehart & Winston, 1976); and Martin Covington, "The Motive for Self-Worth," in *Research on Motivation in Education, Vol. 1.* pp. 77–113.

7. Dale Schunk, "Self-efficacy and Cognitive Skill Learning," in *Research on Motivation in Education, Vol. 3: Goals and Cognitions,* ed. Carole Ames and Russell Ames (San Diego: Academic Press, 1989), pp. 13–44.

8. Deborah Stipek, "The Development of Achievement Motivation," in *Research on Motivation in Education, Vol. 1,* pp. 145–74.

9. Martin Covington and Carol Omelich, "Effort: The Double-Edged Sword in School Achievement," *Journal of Educational Psychology* 71 (1979): 169–82.

10. Covington and Beery, *Self-Worth and School Learning.*

11. Ibid.

12. Ames and Archer, "Achievement Goals," pp. 260–67; and Carole Diener and Carol Dweck, "An Analysis of Learned Helplessness: Continuous Changes in Performance, Strategy, and Achievement Cognitions following Failure," *Journal of Personality and Social Psychology* 36 (1978): 451–62.

13. Ames and Archer, "Achievement Goals," p. 260.

14. Ibid.; Elliott and Dweck, "Goals," pp. 5–12; Nicholls, "Quality and Equality," pp. 1071–84; and Maehr, "Meaning and Motivation," pp. 115–44.

15. Covington and Beery, *Self-Worth and School Learning;* Ames and Archer, "Achievement Goals," pp. 260–67; and Ames and Ames, "Systems of Student and Teacher Motivation," pp. 535–56.

16. John Nicholls, *The Competitive Ethos and Democratic Education* (Cambridge: Harvard University Press, 1989).

17. Carole Dweck, "Motivation," in *Handbook of Psychology and Education,* ed. R. Glaser and A. Lesgold (Hillsdale, N.J.: Erlbaum, 1985).

18. Schunk, "Self-efficacy and Cognitive Skill Learning."

19. Jere Brophy, "Teacher-Praise: A Functional Analysis," *Review of Educational Research* 51 (1981): 5–32.

20. Ann Boggiano et al., "Use of Manimal-Operant Principle to Motivate Children's Intrinsic Interest," *Journal of Personality and Social Psychology* 53 (1987): 866–79.

21. Philip W. Jackson, *Life in Classrooms* (New York: Holt, Rinehart & Winston, 1968); see also Mark Lepper and Melinda Hodell, "Intrinsic Motivation in the Classroom," in *Research on Motivation in Education, Vol. 3,* pp. 73–105.

22. Mark Lepper, "Extrinsic Reward and Intrinsic Motivation: Implications for the Classroom," in *Teacher and Student Perceptions: Implications for Learning,* ed. J. Levine and M. Wang (Hillsdale, N.J.: Erlbaum, 1983a), pp. 281–317; and idem, "Social Control Processes and the Internalization of Social Values: An Attributional Perspective," in *Developmental Social Cognition: A Sociocultural Perspective,* ed. E. Tory Higgins et al. (New York: Cambridge University Press, 1983), pp. 294–330.

23. See Richard deCharms, *Enhancing Motivation: Change in the Classroom* (New York: Irvington, 1976); Edward Deci and Richard Ryan, *Intrinsic Motivation and Self-determination in Human Behavior* (New York: Plenum, 1985); and Richard Ryan, James Connell, and Edward Deci, "A Motivational Analysis of Self-determination and Self-regulation in Education," in *Research on Motivation in Education, Vol. 2: The Classroom Milieu,* ed. Carole Ames and Russell Ames (Orlando: Academic Press, 1985), pp. 13–51.

24. Nicholls, *The Competitive Ethos and Democratic Education.*

25. Joyce Epstein, "Effective Schools or Effective Students: Dealing with Diversity," in *Policies for America's Public Schools: Teachers, Equity, Indicators,* ed. Ron Haskins and Duncan MacRae (Norwood, N.J.: Ablex, 1988).

26. Ibid.; and idem, "Family Structures and Student Motivation: A Developmental Perspective," in *Research on Motivation in Education, Vol. 3,* pp. 259–95.

DISCUSSION QUESTIONS

1. How does a teacher's understanding of motivation influence his or her instruction?

2. In what ways does classroom and family context influence student motivation?

3. How does motivation influence student outcomes?

4. How can teachers plan instruction that enhances the students' motivation in relationship to motivational concerns such as task, authority, grouping, and evaluation?

5. What are the effects of rewards and incentives on student learning?

14

Critical Thinking—What Can It Be?

MATTHEW LIPMAN

FOCUSING QUESTIONS

1. *What are the characteristics of critical thinking?*
2. *In what ways does critical thinking differ from ordinary thinking?*
3. *How does critical thinking assist students in becoming self-regulated learners?*
4. *What kind of curriculum needs to be implemented to encourage the development of critical thinking students?*
5. *How does the critical thinking model differ from (a) explicit instruction, (b) generative model of teaching, (c) cooperative learning methods, and (d) mastery model of learning?*

If we are to foster and strengthen critical thinking in schools and colleges, we need a clear conception of what it is and what it can be. We need to know its defining features, its characteristic outcomes, and the underlying conditions that make it possible.

THE OUTCOMES OF CRITICAL THINKING ARE JUDGMENTS

Let's begin with outcomes. If we consult current definitions of critical thinking, we cannot help being struck by the fact that the authors stress the *outcomes* of such thinking but generally fail to note its essential characteristics. What is more, they specify outcomes that are limited to *solutions* and *decisions*. Thus, one writer defines critical thinking as "the mental processes, strategies, and representations people use to solve problems, make decisions, and learn new concepts."[1] Another conceives of critical thinking as "reasonable reflective thinking that is focused on deciding what to believe and do."[2]

These definitions provide insufficient enlightenment because the outcomes (solutions, decisions, concept-acquisition) are too narrow, and the defining characteristics (reasonable, reflective) are too vague. For example, if critical thinking is *thinking that results in decisions,* then selecting a doctor by picking a name at random out of a phone book would count as critical thinking. *We must broaden the outcomes, identify the defining characteristics, and then show the connection between them.*

Our contemporary conception of education as inquiry combines two aims—the transmission of knowledge and the cultivation of wisdom. But what is wisdom? Consulting a few dictionaries will yield such phrases as "intelligent judgment," "excellent judgment," or "judgment tempered by experience." But what is judgment?[3] Here again, recourse to dictionaries suggests that judgment is "the forming of opinions, estimates, or conclusions." It therefore includes such things as solving problems, making decisions, and learning new concepts; but it is more inclusive and more general.

The line of inquiry we are taking shows wisdom to be the characteristic outcome of good judgment and good judgment to be the characteristic of critical thinking. Perhaps the point where we are now, where we want to know how ordinary judgment and good judgment differ, is a good place to consider some illustrations.

Wherever knowledge and experience are not merely possessed but *applied to practice,* we see clear instances of judgment. Architects, lawyers, and doctors are professionals whose work constantly involves the making of judgments. It is true of any of us when we are in moral situations: we have to make moral judgments. It is true of teachers and farmers and theoretical physicists as well: all must make judgments in the practice of their occupations and in the conduct of their lives. There are practical, productive, and theoretical judgments, as Aristotle would have put it. Insofar as we make such judgments well, we can be said to behave wisely.

It should be kept in mind that good professionals make good judgments about their own practice as well as about the subject-matter of their practice. A good doctor not only makes good diagnoses of patients and prescribes well for them, but also makes good judgments about the field of medicine and his or her ability to practice it. Good judgment takes everything into account, including itself.

A judgment, then, is a determination—of thinking, of speech, of action, or of creation. A gesture, such as the wave of a hand, can be a judgment; a metaphor, like "John is a worm," is a judgment; an equation, like $E=mc^2$, is a judgment. They are judgments because, in part, they have been reached in certain ways, relying on certain instruments or procedures in the process. They are likely to be *good* judgments if they are the products of *skillfully* performed acts guided by or facilitated by appropriate instruments and procedures. If we now look at the process of critical thinking and identify its essential characteristics, we can better understand its relationship to judgment. I will argue that critical thinking is *skillful, responsible thinking that facilitates good judgment because it (1) relies upon criteria,*[4] *(2) is self-correcting, and (3) is sensitive to context.*

CRITICAL THINKING RELIES ON CRITERIA

We suspect an association between the terms *critical* and *criteria* because they have a common ancestry. We are also aware of a relationship between criteria and judgments, for the very meaning of *criterion* is "a rule or principle utilized in the making of judgments." A criterion is an instrument for judging as an ax is an instrument for chopping. It seems reasonable to conclude, therefore, that there is some sort of logical connection between "critical thinking" and "criteria" and "judgment." The connection, of course, is to be found in the fact that judgment is a skill, critical thinking is skillful thinking, and skills cannot be defined without criteria by means of which allegedly skillful performances can be evaluated. So critical thinking is thinking that both employs criteria and that can be assessed by appeal to criteria.

The fact that critical thinking relies upon criteria suggests that it is well-founded, structured, and reinforced thinking, as opposed to "uncritical" thinking, which is amorphous, haphazard, and unstructured. Critical thinking seems to be defensible and convincing. How does this happen?

Whenever we make a claim or utter an opinion, we are vulnerable unless we can back it up with *reasons.* What is the connection between reasons and criteria? Criteria *are* reasons: they are one kind of reason, but it is a particularly *reliable* kind. When we have to sort things out descriptively or evaluationally—and these are two very important tasks—we have to use the most reliable reasons we can find, and these are classificatory and evaluational criteria. Criteria may or may not have a high level of acceptance and respect in the community of inquiry. The competent use of such respected criteria is a way of establishing the objectivity of our prescriptive, descriptive, and evaluative judgments. Thus, architects will judge a building by employing such criteria as *utility, safety,* and *beauty;* and presumably, critical thinkers rely upon such time-tested criteria as *validity, evidential warrant,* and *consistency.* Any area of practice—architectural, cognitive, and the like—should be able to cite the criteria by which that practice is guided.

The intellectual domiciles we inhabit are often of flimsy construction; we can strengthen them by learning to reason more logically. But this will help little if their foundations are soft and spongy. We need to rest our claims and opinions—all of our thinking—upon footings as firm as bedrock. One way of putting our thinking upon a solid foundation is to rely upon sound criteria.

Here then, is a brief list of the sorts of things we invoke or appeal to and that therefore represent specific kinds of criteria:

- standards;
- laws, by-laws, rules, regulations;
- precepts, requirements, specifications;
- conventions, norms, regularities;
- principles, assumptions, presuppositions, definitions;
- ideals, goals, objectives;
- tests, credentials, experimental findings;
- methods, procedures, policies.

All of these instruments are part of the apparatus of rationality. Isolated in categories in a taxonomy, as they are here, they appear inert and sterile. But when they are at work in the process of inquiry, they function dynamically—and critically.

As noted, by means of logic we can validly extend our thinking; by means of reasons such as criteria we can justify and defend it. The improvement of student thinking—from ordinary thinking to good thinking—depends heavily upon students' ability to identify and site good reasons for their opinions (see Fig. 14.1). Students can be brought to realize that, for a reason to be called good, it must be *relevant* to the opinion in question and *stronger* (in the sense of being more readily accepted, or assumed to be the case) than the opinion in question.

Critical thinking is a sort of *cognitive accountability.*[5] When we openly state the criteria we employ—for example, in assigning grades to students—we encourage students to do likewise. By demonstrating models of *intellectual responsibility,* we invite students to assume responsibility for their own thinking and, in a larger sense, for their own education.

When we have to select among criteria, we must of course rely on other criteria to do so. Some criteria serve this purpose better than others and can therefore be said to operate as *meta-criteria.* For example, when I pointed out earlier that criteria are especially reliable reasons and that good reasons are those that reveal strength and

Ordinary Thinking . . . . Critical Thinking/Reasoning
Guessing . . . . Estimating
Preferring . . . . Evaluating
Grouping . . . . Classifying
Believing . . . . Assuming
Inferring . . . . Inferring logically
Associating concepts . . . . Grasping principles
Noting relationships . . . . Noting relationships among other relationships
Supposing . . . . Hypothesizing
Offering opinions without reasons . . . . Offering opinions with reasons
Making judgments without criteria . . . . Making judgments with criteria

FIGURE 14.1   Comparing Ordinary Thinking to Good Thinking

relevance, I was saying that *reliability, strength,* and *relevance* are important meta-criteria. *Coherence* and *consistency* are others.

Some criteria have a high level of generality and are often presupposed, explicitly or implicitly, whenever critical thinking takes place. Thus the notion of knowledge presupposes the criterion of *truth,* and so wherever scientific knowledge is claimed, the concomitant claim being made is that it is true. In this sense, philosophical domains such as epistemology, ethics, and aesthetics do not dictate the criteria relevant to them; rather, the criteria define the domains. Epistemology consists of judgments to which truth and falsity are the relevant criteria; ethics compromises judgments to which right and wrong are relevant; and aesthetics contains judgments to which beautiful and not-beautiful are relevant. *Truth, right, wrong, just, good, beautiful*—all of these are such vast scope that we should probably consider them *mega-criteria.* And they in turn are instances of the great galactic criterion of *meaning.*

One of the primary functions of criteria is to provide a basis for comparisons. When a comparison is made and no basis or criterion is given (for example, "Tokyo is better than New York"), confusion results. On the other hand, if several competing criteria might be applicable (as when someone says, "Tokyo is larger than New York" but does not specify whether in size or in population), the situation can be equally confusing. Just as opinions should generally be backed up with reasons, comparisons should generally be accompanied by criteria.

Sometimes criteria are introduced "informally" and extemporaneously, as when someone remarks that Tuesday's weather was good compared with Monday's, while Wednesday's weather was bad compared with Monday's. In this case, Monday's weather is being used as an informal criterion. Even figurative language can be understood as involving the use of informal criteria. Thus, an open simile such as "The school was like an army camp" suggests the regimentation of an army camp as an informal criterion against which to measure the orderliness of the school.

On the other hand, when criteria are considered by an authority or by general consent to be a basis of comparison, we might speak of them as "formal" criteria. When we compare the quantities of liquid in two tanks in terms of gallons, we are employing the unit of the gallon on the say-so of the Bureau of Weights and Measures. The gallon measure at the Bureau is the institutionalized paradigm case to which our gallon measure is comparable.

So things are compared by means of more or less formal criteria. But there is also the distinction between comparing things with one another and comparing them with an ideal standard, a distinction Plato addresses in *The Statesman.*[6] For example, in grading test papers, we may compare a student's performance with the performances of other students in the class (using "the curve" as a criterion); or we may compare it with the standard of an error-free performance.[7]

Standards and *criteria* are terms often used interchangeably in ordinary discourse. Standards, however, represent a vast subclass of criteria. It is vast because the concept of *standard* can be understood in many different ways. There is the interpretation cited in the preceding paragraph, where we are talking about a standard of perfection. There are, in contrast standards as *minimal* levels of performance, as in the oft-heard cry, "We must not lower our standards!" There is a sense in which standards are conventions of conduct: "When in Rome, do as the Romans do." There is also the sense in which standards are the units of measurement defined authoritatively by a bureau of standards.

There is of course, a certain arbitrariness about even the most reliable standards, such as units of measurement, in that we are free to define them as we like. We could, if we liked, define a yard as containing fewer inches than it presently does. But the fact is that, once defined, we prefer such units to be unchanging: they are so much more reliable that way.

Perhaps we can sum up the relationship between criteria and standards by saying that criteria specify general requirements, while standards represent the degree to which these requirements need be satisfied in particular instances. Criteria—and particularly standards among them—are among the most valuable instruments of rational procedure. Teaching students to use them is essential to the teaching of critical thinking (see Fig. 14.2).

CRITICAL THINKING IS SELF-CORRECTING

The most characteristic feature of inquiry is that it aims to discover its own weaknesses and rectify what is at fault in its own procedures. Inquiry, then, is *self-correcting.*[8]

Much of our thinking unrolls impressionistically, from association to association, with little concern for either truth or validity, and with even less concern for the possibility that it might be erroneous. Among the many things we may reflect upon is our own thinking, yet we can do so in a way that is still quite uncritical. And so, "meta-cognition," or thinking about thinking, need not be equivalent to critical thinking.

One of the most important advantages of converting the classroom into a community of inquiry (in addition to the improvement of moral climate) is that the members of the community not only become conscious of their own thinking but begin looking for and correcting each other's methods and procedures. Consequently, insofar as each participant can internalize the methodology of the community as a whole, each participant is able to become self-correcting in his or her own thinking.

CRITICAL THINKING IS SENSITIVE TO CONTEXT

Just as critical thinking is sensitive to uniformities and regularities that are genetic and intercontextual, it is sensitive to situational characteristics that are holistic or context-specific. Thinking that is sensitive to context takes into account:

(a) *exceptional or irregular circumstances and conditions*—for example, a line of investigation ordinarily considered *ad hominem* and there-

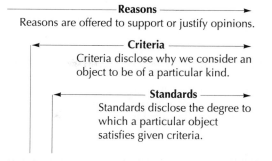

FIGURE 14.2 Relationship of Standards to Criteria to Reasons

fore fallacious might be found permissible in a trial;

(b) *special limitations, contingencies, or constraints*—for example, the rejection of certain Euclidean theorems, such as that parallel lines never meet, in non-Euclidean geometries;

(c) *overall configurations*—for instance, a remark taken out of context may seem to be flagrantly in error but in the light of the discourse taken as a whole appears valid and proper, or vice versa;

(d) *the possibility that evidence is atypical*—for example, a case of overgeneralizing about national voter preferences based on a tiny regional sample of ethnically and occupationally homogeneous individuals.

(e) *the possibility that some meanings do not translate from one context or domain to another*—there are terms and expressions for which there are no precise equivalents in other languages and whose meanings are therefore wholly context-specific.

With regard to *thinking with criteria* and *sensitivity to context,* a suitable illustration might be an exercise involving the application of a particular criterion to a set of fictional situations. Suppose the criterion in question is *fairness* (which is itself a way of construing the still broader criterion of justice). One form that fairness assumes is *taking turns.* Figure 14.3 is an exercise taken from *Wondering at the World,*[9] the instructional

Taking Turns

To the teacher: There are times when people engage in sharing. For example, they go to a movie and share the pleasure of looking at the movie together. Or they can share a piece of cake by each taking half.

In other cases, however, simultaneous sharing is not so easily accomplished. If two people ride a horse, someone has to ride in front. They can take turns riding in front, but they can't both ride in front at the same time. Children understand this very well. They recognize that certain procedures must be followed in certain ways.

For example, ask your students to discuss the number of ways they "take turns" in the classroom during the ordinary day. They take turns washing the blackboard, going to the bathroom, going to the cloakroom, and passing out the papers. On the playground, they take turns at bat, they take turns lining up for basketball, and they take turns at the high bar.

Ask your students what they think the connection is between "taking turns" and "being fair." The resulting discussion should throw light on the fact that sometimes being fair involves the way children are to be treated simultaneously, while at other times it involves the way they are to be treated sequentially. For example, if it is one child's birthday and there is going to be a party with cupcakes, there should be at least one cupcake for every child. This is being fair simultaneously. Later, if you want to play "Pin the Tail on the Donkey," children should sequentially take turns in order to be fair. (The prospect of everyone *simultaneously* being blindfolded and searching about with a pin boggles the mind.)

Exercise: When is it appropriate to take turns?

	Appropriate	Not Appropriate	?
1. Pam: "Louise, let's take turns riding your bike. I'll ride it Mondays, Wednesdays, and Fridays, and you ride it Tuesdays, Thursdays, and Saturdays."	☐	☐	☐
2. Gary: "Burt, let's take turns taking Louise to the movies. I'll take her the first and third Saturday of every month, and you take her the second and fourth Saturday."	☐	☐	☐
3. Jack: "Louise, let's take turns doing the dishes. You wash and I'll dry."	☐	☐	☐
4. Chris: "Okay, Louise, let's take turns with the TV. You choose a half-hour program, then I'll choose one."	☐	☐	☐
5. Melissa: "Louise, what do you say we take turns doing our homework? Tonight I'll do yours and mine, and tomorrow you can do mine and yours."	☐	☐	☐
6. Hank: "Louise, I hate to see you struggle to school each day, carrying those heavy books! Let me carry yours and mine today, and you can carry yours and mine tomorrow."	☐	☐	☐

FIGURE 14.3 "Taking Turns" Exercise

Reprinted from Matthew Lipman and Ann Margaret Sharp. *Wondering at the World.* Lanham, Md.: University Press of America and IAPC, co-publishers, 1986.

manual accompanying *Kio and Gus,*[10] a Philosophy for Children program for children 9 to 10 years of age.

In performing this exercise, students apply the criterion of *turn-taking* (i.e., *fair play* or *justice*) to six situations requiring sensitivity to context. Classroom discussion should distinguish between those situations in which the procedure of turn-taking is appropriate and those in which it is dubious. Using exercises like these in a community of inquiry sets the stage for critical thinking in the classroom. It is not the only way to accomplish this, but it is one way.

THE PROMISE OF INTELLECTUAL EMPOWERMENT

What, then, is the relevance of critical thinking to the enhancement of elementary school, secondary school, and college education? Part of the answer lies in the gradual shift that is occurring in the focus of education—the shift from *learning* to *thinking.* We want students to think for themselves and not merely to learn what other people have thought.

But another part of the answer lies in the fact that we want students who can do more than merely think: it is equally important that they exercise good judgment. It is good judgment that characterizes the sound interpretation of written text; the well-balanced, coherent composition; the lucid comprehension of what one hears; and the persuasive argument. It is good judgment that enables one to weigh and grasp what a statement or passage states, assumes, implies, or suggests. And this good judgment cannot be operative unless it rests upon proficient reasoning skills that can assure competency in inference, as well as upon proficient inquiry, concept-formation, and translation skills. Students who are *not* taught to use criteria in a way that is both sensitive to context and self-corrective are *not* being taught to think critically. If teaching critical thinking can improve education, it will be because it increases the quantity and quality of meaning that students derive from what they read and perceive and that they express in what they write and say.

CONCLUSION

Last, a word about the employment of criteria in critical thinking that facilitates good judgment. Critical thinking, as we know, is skillful thinking, and skills are proficient performances that satisfy relevant criteria. When we think critically, we are required to orchestrate a vast variety of cognitive skills, grouped in families such as reasoning skills, concept-formation skills, inquiry skills, and translation skills. Without these skills, we would be unable to draw meaning from written text or from conversation, nor could we impart meaning to a conversation or to what we write.

We all know that an otherwise splendid musical performance can be ruined if so much as a single instrumentalist performs below acceptable standards. Likewise, the mobilization and perfection of the cognitive skills that make up critical thinking cannot omit any of these skills without jeopardizing the process as a whole. We cannot be content, then, to give students practice in a handful of cognitive skills while neglecting all the others necessary for the competency in inquiry, in language, and in thought that is the hallmark of proficient critical thinkers. Instead of selecting and polishing a few skills that we think will do the trick, we must begin with the raw subject matter of communication and inquiry—with reading, listening, speaking, writing, and reasoning—and we must cultivate all the skills that the mastery in such processes entails. It is only when we do this that we realize that the philosophical disciplines alone provide both the skills and the criteria that are presently lacking in the curriculum.

ENDNOTES

1. Robert Sternberg, "Critical Thinking: Its Nature, Measurement, and Improvement" in *Essays on the Intellect,* ed. Frances R. Link (Alexandria, Va.: Association for Supervision and Curriculum Development, 1985), p. 46.
2. Robert H. Ennis, "A Taxonomy of Critical Thinking Dispositions and Abilities" in *Teaching Thinking Skills: Theory and Practice,* ed. Joan Boykoff Baron and Robert J. Sternberg (New York: W. H. Freeman and Co., 1987), p. 10.

3. For a penetrating discussion of judgment, see Justus Buchler, *Toward a General Theory of Human Judgment* (New York: Columbia University Press, 1951).

4. Useful discussions of the nature of criteria are to be found in Michael Anthony Slote, "The Theory of Important Criteria," *The Journal of Philosophy* LXIII, 8 (April 1966): 221–224; and Michael Scriven, "The Logic of Criteria," *The Journal of Philosophy* 56 (October 1959): 857–868; and Stanley Cavell, *The Claim of Reason* (Oxford: The Clarendon Press, 1979), pp. 3–36.

5. I see no inconsistency between urging "cognitive accountability" and urging the development of intellectual autonomy among students. There are times when we cannot let other people do our thinking for us; we must think for ourselves. And we must learn to think for ourselves by thinking for ourselves; no one can instruct us in how to do it, although a community of inquiry makes it relatively easy. The point is that students must be encouraged to become reasonable for their own good (i.e., as a step toward their own autonomy) and not just for our good (i.e., because the growing rationalization of the society requires it).

6. The Stranger remarks to young Socrates, "We must posit two types and two standards of greatness and smallness . . . The standard of relative comparison will remain, but we must acknowledge a second standard, which is a standard of comparison with the due measure." *Statesman* (283e) in *Plato: The Collected Dialogues,* ed. Edith Hamilton and Huntington Cairns (Princeton: Princeton University Press, 1969), p. 1051.

7. For a contemporary interchange regarding comparison of things with one another vs. comparison of things with an ideal, see Gilbert Ryle, "Perceiving" in *Dilemmas* (London: Cambridge University Press, 1966), pp. 93–102; and D. W. Hamlyn, *The Theory of Knowledge* (London: Doubleday and Company and Macmillan, 1970), pp. 16–21.

8. Charles Peirce, in "Ideals of Conduct," *Collected Papers of Charles Sanders Peirce,* ed. by Charles Hartshorne and Paul Weiss (Cambridge, Mass.: Harvard University Press, 1931–35) discusses the connection between self-correcting inquiry, self-criticism, and self-control.

9. Matthew Lipman and Ann Margaret Sharp, *Wondering at the World* (Lanham, Md.: University Press of America and IAPC, co-publishers, 1986), pp. 226–299.

10. Matthew Lipman, *Kio and Gus* (Upper Montclair, N.J.: IAPC, 1982).

DISCUSSION QUESTIONS

1. How does critical thinking promote intellectual responsibility?

2. How do standards, criteria, and reasons differ?

3. How is good judgment related to critical thinking?

4. How can critical thinking be promoted in classroom instruction?

5. What modifications would you make to specific subject area content such as the art, science, reading, math, social studies, or science curriculum to help students become critical thinkers?

Creating Creative Minds

ROBERT J. STERNBERG
TODD I. LUBART

FOCUSING QUESTIONS

1. *How are intelligence and creativity related?*
2. *What is the relationship between knowledge and creativity?*
3. *How are intellectual styles related to creativity?*
4. *What are the advantages and disadvantages for giving students the responsibility for selecting problems they would like to solve?*
5. *What distinguishes creative thinking and ordinary thinking?*
6. *How can the use of ill-structured problems help students to think insightfully?*
7. *How do the norms of a school's environment influence the development of creativity?*

Creativity is not simply inborn. On the contrary, schooling can create creative minds—though it often doesn't. To create creativity, we need to understand the resources on which it draws and to determine how we can help children develop these resources. In particular, we need to know how we can invest in our children's futures by helping them invest in their own creative endeavors.

We propose an "investment theory of creativity."[1] The basic notion underlying our theory is that, when making any kind of investment, including creative investment, people should "buy low and sell high." In other words, the greatest creative contributions can generally be made in areas or with ideas that at a given time are undervalued. Perhaps people in general have not yet realized the importance of certain ideas, and hence there is a potential for making significant advances. The more in favor an idea is, the less potential there is for it to appreciate in value, because the idea is already valued.

A theory of creativity needs to account for how people can generate or recognize undervalued ideas. It also needs to specify who will actually pursue these undervalued ideas rather than join the crowd and make contributions that, while of some value, are unlikely to turn around our existing ways of thinking. Such a theory will enable us and our children to invest in a creative future.[2] As is sometimes said, nothing is as practical as a good theory.

We hold that developing creativity in children—and in adults—involves teaching them to use six resources: intelligence, knowledge, intellectual style, personality, motivation, and environmental context. Consider each of these resources in turn.

INTELLIGENCE

Two main aspects of intelligence are relevant to creativity. These aspects, based on the triarchic theory of human intelligence, are the ability to define and redefine problems and the ability to think insightfully.[3]

Problem Definition and Redefinition

Major creative innovations often involve seeing an old problem in a new way. For example, Albert Einstein redefined the field of physics by proposing the theory of relativity; Jean Piaget redefined the field of cognitive development by conceiving of the child as a scientist; Pablo Picasso redefined the field of art through his cubist perspective on the world.

In order to *re*define a problem, a student has to have the option of defining a problem in the first place. Only rarely do schools give students this luxury. Tests typically pose the problems that students are to solve. And if a student's way of seeing a problem is different from that of the test constructor, the student is simply marked wrong. Similarly, teachers typically structure their classes so that they, not the students, set the problems to be solved. Of course, textbooks work the same way. Even when papers or projects are assigned, teachers often specify the topics. Some teachers, who view themselves as more flexible, allow students to define problems for themselves. These same teachers may then proceed to mark students down when students' definitions of problems do not correspond to their own.

In the "thinking-skills movement," we frequently hear of the need for schools to emphasize more heavily the teaching of problem-solving skills. Educators are then pleased when students do not merely memorize facts but rather use the facts to solve problems. Certainly, there is much to be said for a problem-solving approach to education. But we need to recognize that creative individuals are often most renowned not for solving problems, but for posing them. It is not so much that they have found the "right" answers (often there are none); rather, they have asked the right questions—they recognized significant and substantial problems and chose to address them. One only has to open almost any professional journal to find articles that are the fruit of good problem solving on bad—or at least fairly inconsequential—problems.

If we are to turn schooling around and emphasize creative definition and redefinition of problems, we need to give our students some of the control we teachers typically maintain. Students need to take more responsibility for the problems they choose to solve, and we need to

take less. The students will make mistakes and attempt to solve inconsequential or even wrongly posed problems. But they learn from their mistakes, and, if we do not give them the opportunity to make mistakes, they will have no mistakes to learn from. Instead of almost always giving children the problems, we more often need to let them find the problems that they are to solve. We need to help them develop their skills in defining and redefining problems, not just in solving them.

Insight Skills

Insight skills are involved when people perceive a high-quality solution to an ill-structured problem to which the solution is not obvious. Being truly creative involves "buying low"—that is, picking up on an idea that is out of favor. But just picking up on any idea that is out of favor is not sufficient. Insight is involved in spotting the *good* ideas. We have proposed a theory of insight whereby insights are of three kinds.[4]

The first kind of insight involves seeing things in a stream of inputs that most people would not see. In other words, in the midst of a stream of mostly irrelevant information, an individual is able to zero in on particularly relevant information for his or her purposes. For example, the insightful reader observes clues to an author's meaning that others may miss. An insightful writer is often one whose observations about human behavior, as revealed through writing, go beyond those of the rest of us.

The second kind of insight involves seeing how to combine disparate pieces of information whose connection is nonobvious and usually elusive. For example, proving mathematical theorems requires seeing how to fit together various axioms and theorems into a coherent proof. Interpreting data from a scientific experiment often involves making sense of seemingly disparate pieces of information.

The third kind of insight involves seeing the nonobvious relevance of old information to a new problem. Creative analogies and metaphors are representative of this kind of insight. For example, the student of history comes to see how understanding events of long ago can help us understand certain events in the present. A scientist might recall a problem from the past that was solved by using a certain methodology and apply this methodology to a current scientific problem.

Problems requiring insightful solution are almost always ill-structured; that is, there are no readily available paths to solution. Rather, much of the difficulty in solving the problem is figuring out what the steps toward solution might be. For example, when James Watson and Francis Crick sought to find the structure of DNA, the nature of the problem was clear. The way in which to solve it was not clear at all.

Problems presented in schools, however, are usually well-structured; that is, there is a clear path—or several paths—to a prompt and expedient solution. In standardized tests, for example, there is always a path that guarantees a "correct" solution. The examinee's problem is, in large part, to find that guaranteed path. Similarly, textbook problems are often posed so that there can be an answer key for the teacher that gives the "correct" answers. Problems such as these are unlikely to require insightful thinking. One ends up trying to "psych out" the thought processes of the person who formulated the problem, rather than to generate one's own insightful thought processes.

While not exclusively limited to ill-structured problems, creative innovations tend to address such problems—not the well-structured ones that we typically use in school settings. If we want students to think insightfully, we need to give them opportunities to do so by increasing our use of ill-structured problems that allow insightful thinking. Project work is excellent in this regard, for it requires students not only to solve problems but also to structure the problems for themselves.

KNOWLEDGE

In order to make a creative contribution to a field of knowledge, one must, of course, have knowledge of that field. Without such knowledge, one risks rediscovering what is already known. Without knowledge of the field, it is also difficult for an individual to assess the problems in the field and to judge which are important. Indeed, during the past decade or so, an important emphasis in psychology has been on the importance of knowledge to expertise.

Schools can scarcely be faulted for making insufficient efforts to impart knowledge. Indeed, that seems to be their main function. Yet we have two reservations about the extent to which the knowledge they impart is likely to lead to creativity.

First, there is a difference between knowledge and usable knowledge. Knowledge can be learned in a way that renders it inert. Knowledge may be stored in the brain, but an individual may nonetheless be unable to use it. For example, almost every college undergraduate who majors in psychology takes a course in statistics as a part of that major. Yet very few undergraduates who have taken statistics are able to use what they have learned in the design and analysis of scientific experiments. (At the secondary level, many physics and chemistry students are unable to use basic algebra when they need to apply it.) Undergraduates in psychology do fine as long as they are given highly structured problems in which it is obvious which statistical technique applies. But they have trouble when they have to figure out which technique to apply and when to apply it. The context in which they acquired their knowledge is so different from the context in which they must use it that their knowledge is simply unavailable.

Our experience with knowledge learned in statistics courses is, we believe, the rule rather than the exception. Students do not generally learn knowledge in a way that renders it useful to them. To the contrary, they are likely to forget much of what they learn soon after they are tested on it. We have all had the experience of studying for an exam and then quickly forgetting what we studied. The information was learned in such a way as to make it useful in the context of a structured exam; once the exam is finished, so is that use of the knowledge.

Our second reservation about the knowledge that schools typically impart is that students are not taught in a way that makes clear to them why the information they are learning is important. Students do much better in learning if they believe that they can use what they learn. Foreign language provides a good example. People who need to use a foreign language learn it. Those who don't need it rarely retain much of it. Unless we show students why what they are learning should matter to them, we cannot expect them to retain what they are taught. Unfortunately, we often don't really know ourselves how students might use what we are teaching them. And if we don't know, how can we expect them to?

We also need to be concerned about the tradeoff that can develop between knowledge and flexibility. We have suggested that increased expertise in terms of knowledge in a given domain often comes at the expense of flexibility in that domain.[5] We can become so automatic about the way we do certain things that we lose sight of the possibility of other ways. We can become entrenched and have trouble going beyond our very comfortable perspective on things. Because creativity requires one to view things flexibly, there is a danger that, with increasing knowledge, one will lose creativity by losing the ability to think flexibly about the domain in which one works. We need to recognize that sometimes students see things that we do not see—that they may have insights we have not had (and that initially we may not even recognize as insights). Teachers who have been doing the same thing year after year can become so self-satisfied and happy with the way they do things that they are closed to new ways of doing these things. They are unwilling to "buy low"—to try an idea that is different from those they have favored in the past.

On the one hand, we do not wish to underemphasize the importance of knowledge to creativity. On the other hand, we cannot overemphasize the importance of usable knowledge that does not undermine flexibility. Often we need to adopt the maintenance of flexibility as a goal to be achieved self-consciously. We might go to inservice training sessions, read new kinds of books, learn about a new domain of knowledge, seek to learn from our students, or whatever. If we want students to be creative, we have to model creativity for them, and we won't be able to do that if we seek to turn students' minds into safe-deposit boxes in which to store our assorted and often undigested bits of knowledge.

INTELLECTUAL STYLES

Intellectual styles are the ways in which people choose to use or exploit their intelligence as well as their knowledge. Thus intellectual styles concern not abilities, but how these abilities and the knowledge acquired through them are used in day-to-day interactions with the environment.

Elsewhere one of the authors has presented details of a theory of intellectual styles based on a notion of "mental self-government."[6] Hence we need not cover the theory in detail here. The basic idea is that people need to govern themselves mentally and that styles provide them with ways to do so. The ways in which people govern themselves are internal mirrors of the kinds of government we see in the external world.

Creative people are likely to be those with a legislative proclivity. A legislative individual is someone who enjoys formulating problems and creating new systems of rules and new ways of seeing things. Such a person is in contrast to an individual with an executive style: someone who likes implementing the systems, rules, and tasks of others. Both differ from an individual with a judicial style: someone who enjoys evaluating people, things, and rules. Thus the creative person not only has the ability to see things in new ways but likes to do so. The creative person is also likely to have a global—not just a local—perspective on problems. Seeing the forest despite all the trees is the mark of creative endeavor.

PERSONALITY

Creative people seem to share certain personality attributes. Although one can probably be creative in the short term without these attributes, long-term creativity requires most of them. The attributes are tolerance of ambiguity, willingness to surmount obstacles and persevere, willingness to grow, willingness to take risks, and courage of one's convictions.

Tolerance for ambiguity. In most creative endeavors, there is a period of time during which an individual is groping—trying to figure out what the pieces of the puzzle are, how to put them together, how to relate them to what is already known. During this period, an individual is likely to feel some anxiety—possibly even alarm—because the pieces are not forming themselves into a creative solution to the problem being confronted. Creative individuals need to be able to tolerate such ambiguity and to wait for the pieces to fall into place.

In many schools, most of the assignments students are given are due the next day or within a very short period of time. In such circumstances students cannot develop a tolerance for ambiguity, because they cannot spare the time to allow a situation to be ambiguous. If an assignment is due in a day or two, ambiguities need to be resolved quickly. A good way to help students develop a tolerance for ambiguity is to give them more long-term assignments and encourage them to start thinking about the assignments early on so that they can mull over whatever problems they face. Moreover, students need to realize that a period of ambiguity is the rule, not the exception, in creative work and that they should welcome this period as a chance to hatch their ideas, rather than dread it as a time when their ideas are not fully formed.

Willingness to Surmount Obstacles and Persevere

Almost every major creative thinker has surmounted obstacles at one time or another, and the willingness not to be derailed is a crucial element of success. Confronting obstacles is almost a certainty in creative endeavor because most such endeavors threaten some kind of established and entrenched interest. Unless one can learn to face adversity and conquer it, one is unlikely to make a creative contribution to one's field.

We need to learn to think of obstacles and the need to surmount them as part of the game, rather than as outside it. We should not think of obstacles as something only we have, but as something that everyone has. What makes creative people special is not that they have obstacles but how they face them.

Schools can be fairly good proving grounds for learning to surmount obstacles, because we face so many of them while we are in school (whether as students or as teachers). But students sometimes leave school with the feeling that society is more likely to get in the way of creativity than to support it. Sometimes they are right, of course. And ultimately, they may have to fight for their ideas, as creative people have done before them. However, training to overcome resistance to new ideas shouldn't be the main contribution of the schools to students' creativity.

Willingness to Grow

When a person has a creative idea and is able to have others accept it, that person may be highly rewarded for the idea. It then becomes difficult to move on to still other ideas. The rewards for staying with the first idea are often great, and it feels comfortable to stick with that idea. At the same time, the person who has had a creative idea often acquires a deep-seated fear that his or her next idea won't be as good as the first one. Indeed, the phenomenon of "statistical" regression toward the mean would suggest that subsequent ideas actually will not be as good—that they will regress toward the mean. This is the same phenomenon that operates when the "rookie of the year" in baseball doesn't play as well in his second year as in his first or when a restaurant that seems outstanding when we first eat there isn't quite as good the second time. In short, there is a fair amount of pressure to stay with what one has and knows. But creativity exhibited over prolonged periods of time requires one to move beyond that first creative idea and even to see problems with what at one time may have seemed a superb idea. While schools often encourage the growth of a student's knowledge, such growth will by no means lead automatically to creativity, in part because schools do not encourage students to take risks with their newly acquired knowledge and abilities.

Willingness to Take Risks

A general principle of investment is that, on the average, greater return entails greater risk. For the most part, schools are environments that are not conducive to risk taking. On the contrary, students are as often as not punished for taking risks. Taking a course in a new area or in an area of weakness is likely to lead to a low grade, which in turn may dim a student's future prospects. Risking an unusual response on an exam or an idiosyncratic approach in a paper is a step likely to be taken only with great trepidation, because of the fear that a low or failing grade on a specific assignment may ruin one's chances for a good grade in the course. Moreover, there is usually some safe response that is at least good enough to earn the grade for which one is aiming.

In addition, many teachers are not themselves risk-takers. Teaching is not a profession that is likely to attract the biggest risk-takers, and hence many teachers may feel threatened by students who take large risks, especially if the teacher perceives those risks to be at his or her expense. Unfortunately, students' unwillingness to take risks derives from their socialization in the schools, which are environments that encourage conformity to societal norms. The result is often stereotyped thinking.

Courage of One's Convictions and Belief in Oneself

There are times in the lives of almost all creative people when they begin to doubt their ideas—and

themselves. Their work may not be achieving the recognition it once achieved, or they may not have succeeded in getting recognition in the first place. At these times, it is difficult to maintain a belief in one's ideas or in oneself. It is natural for people to go through peaks and valleys in their creative output, and there are times when creative people worry that their most recent good idea will end up being their final good idea. At such times, one needs to draw upon deep-seated personal resources and to believe in oneself, even when others do not.

Schools do teach some students to believe in themselves: namely, those who consistently receive high grades. But the skills one needs to earn high grades are often quite different from those one needs to be creative. Thus those who go out and set their own course may receive little encouragement, whereas those who play the game and get good grades may develop a confidence in themselves that, though justified, is not necessarily related to their past or potential creative contributions. Those who most need to believe in themselves may be given every reason not to.

MOTIVATION

There is now good evidence to suggest that motivation plays an important part in creative endeavors. Two kinds of motivation are particularly important: intrinsic motivation and the motivation to excel. Both kinds of motivation lead to a focus on tasks rather than on the external rewards that performance of these tasks might generate.

Intrinsic Motivation

Teresa Amabile has conducted and reviewed a number of studies suggesting the importance of intrinsic motivation to creativity.[7] People are much more likely to respond creatively to a task that they enjoy doing for its own sake, rather than a task that they carry out exclusively or even primarily for such extrinsic motivators as grades. Indeed, research suggests that extrinsic rewards undermine intrinsic motivation.[8]

There is little doubt as to the way in which most schools motivate students today: namely, through grades. Grades are the ultimate criterion of one's success in school, and, if one's grades are not good, love of one's work is unlikely to be viewed as much compensation. Therefore, many students chart a path in school that is just sufficient to get them an A. (If they put too much effort into a single course, they risk jeopardizing their performance in the other courses they are taking.) Students who once may have performed well for love of an intellectual challenge may come to perform well only to get their next A. Whatever intrinsic motivation children may have had at the start is likely to be drummed out of them by a system that rewards extrinsically, not intrinsically.

Motivation to Excel

Robert White identified as an important source of motivation a desire to achieve competence in one or more of a person's endeavors.[9] In order to be creative in a field, one generally will need to be motivated not only to be competent, but also to excel. The best "investors" are almost always those who put in the work necessary to realize their goals. Success does not just come to them—they work for it.

Schools vary in the extent to which they encourage students to excel. Some schools seem to want nothing more than for all their students to be at some average or "golden mean." Many schools, however, encourage excellence. Unfortunately, it is rare in our experience for the kind of excellence that is encouraged to be *creative* excellence. It may be excellence in grades, which generally does not require great creativity to attain; it may be excellence in sports or in extracurricular activities. There is nothing wrong with excellence of these kinds. Indeed, they are undoubtedly important in today's world. But seeking such excellences does not foster creativity—and may even interfere with it. When a student is simultaneously taking five or six courses, there is not much opportunity to spend the time or

to expend the effort needed to be creative in any of them.

ENVIRONMENTAL CONTEXT

Creativity cannot be viewed outside an environmental context. What would be viewed as creative in one context might be viewed as trivial in another. The role of context is relevant to the creative enterprise in at least three different ways: in sparking creative ideas, in encouraging follow-up of these ideas, and in rewarding the ideas and their fruits.

Sparking Creative Ideas

Some environments provide the bases for lots of creative sparks, whereas other environments may provide the basis for none at all. Do schools provide environments for sparking creative ideas? Obviously, the answer to this question is necessarily subjective. Given the discussion above, we would have difficulty saying that they do. Schools provide environments that encourage learning about and dealing with existing concepts rather than inventing new ones. There is a lot of emphasis on memorization and some emphasis on analysis, but there is little emphasis on creative synthesis. Indeed, it is difficult for us to remember more than a handful of tests we ever took in school that encouraged creative thinking. On the contrary, the tests students typically take reward them for spitting back what they have learned—or, at best, analyzing it in a fairly noncreative way.

Encouraging Follow-up of Creative Ideas

Suppose a student has a genuinely creative idea and would like to pursue it within the school setting. Is there any vehicle for such follow-up? Occasionally, students will be allowed to pursue projects that encourage them to develop their creative thinking. But again, spending a great deal of time on such projects puts them at risk in their other courses and in their academic work. It is quite rare that any allowance is made whereby students can be excused from normal requirements in order to pursue a special interest of their own.

Evaluating and Rewarding Creative Ideas

Most teachers would adamantly maintain that, when grading papers, they reward creativity. But, if the experience of other teachers is similar to that of the teachers with whom we have worked, they don't find a great deal of creativity to reward. And we sometimes worry whether they would recognize creativity in student work were they to meet it. Please note that we do not except ourselves from this charge. We have failed more than once to see the value of a student's idea when we first encountered it, only to see that value later on—after the student had decided to pursue some other idea, partly at our urging. Teachers genuinely believe that they reward creativity. But the rewards are few and far between.

Look at any school report card, and assess the skills that the report card values. You will probably not find creativity anywhere on the list. One of us actually analyzed the report cards given to children in several elementary schools. A number of skills were assessed. However, not a single one of the report cards assessed creativity in any field whatsoever. The creative child might indeed be valued by the teacher, but it would not show up in the pattern of check marks on the report card.

TEACHING FOR CREATIVITY

How can we help develop students' creativity in the classroom? Consider an example. A few weeks ago, one of us had the opportunity to teach a class of 9- and 10-year-olds in a New York City school. The children ranged fairly widely in abilities and came from various socioeconomic backgrounds. The guest teacher was asked to demonstrate how to "teach for thinking" and decided to do so in the context of teaching about psychology. However, he wanted to impart not merely a set of decontextualized "facts" about the field, but rather the way psychologists think when they develop ideas for creative scientific theory and research.

He didn't tell the students what problem they were going to solve or even offer them suggestions. Rather, he asked each of them to share with the class some aspect of human behavior—their own, their parents', their friends'—that intrigued them and that they would like to understand better. In other words, the students were asked to *define problems* rather than have the teacher do it for them. At first, no one said anything. The children may never have been asked to formulate problems for themselves. But the teacher waited. And then he waited some more (so as not to teach them that, if only they said nothing, he would panic and start to answer his own questions).

Eventually, one student spoke up, and then another, and then another. The ice broken, the children couldn't wait to contribute. Rather than adopting the executive and largely passive style to which they were accustomed, they were adopting a *legislative style* whereby they enjoyed and actively participated in the opportunity to create new ideas. And create ideas they did. Why do parents make children dress up on special occasions? Why do parents sometimes have unreasonable expectations for their children? Why do some siblings fight a lot while others don't? How do we choose our friends?

Because these problems were the children's own problems and not the teacher's, the children were *intrinsically motivated* to seek answers. And they came up with some very perceptive answers indeed. We discussed their ideas and considered criteria for deciding which potential experiment to pursue as a group. The criteria, like the ideas, were the students' own, not the teacher's. And the students considered such factors as *taking risks* in doing experiments, *surmounting obstacles to doing an experiment,* and so on.

The children entered the class with almost no formal knowledge about psychology. But they left it with at least a rudimentary *procedural knowledge* of how psychologists formulate research. The teacher didn't give them the knowledge; they created it for themselves, in an environment that *sparked* and then *rewarded* creative ideas. To be sure, not all of the ideas were creative or even particularly good. But the students were encouraged to give it their best shot, and that's what they did.

The class didn't have time in one 75-minute period to complete the full design of an experiment. However, it did have time to demonstrate that even children can do the kind of creative work that we often reserve until graduate school. We can teach for creativity at any level, in any field. And if we want to improve our children and our nation, this is exactly what we need to do.

Does teaching for creativity actually work? We believe that it does. Moreover, the effectiveness of such teaching has been demonstrated.[10] After five weeks of insight training involving insight problems in language arts, mathematics, science, and social studies, students in grades 4 through 6 displayed significant and substantial improvements (from a pretest to a posttest) over an untrained control group on insight skills and general intelligence. In addition, the training transferred to insight problems of kinds not covered in the course, and, a year later, the gains were maintained. These children had improved their creative skills with only a relatively small investment of instructional time.

Those who invest are taught that most obvious of strategies: buy low and sell high. Yet few people manage to do so. They don't know when a given security is really low or when it is really high. We believe that those who work in the schools do not have much better success in fostering creativity. We often don't recognize creativity when we see it. And although most of us believe that we encourage it, our analysis suggests that schools are probably as likely to work against the development of creativity as in its favor. The conventional wisdom is likely correct: schools probably do at least as much to undermine creativity as to support it.

It is important to realize that our theory of creativity is a "confluence" theory: the elements of creativity work together interactively, not alone. The implication for schooling is that addressing just one—or even a few—of the resources we have discussed is not sufficient to induce creative thinking. For example, a school might teach "divergent thinking," encouraging students to see multiple solutions to problems. But children will not suddenly become creative in the absence of an environment that tolerates ambiguity, encourages risk taking, fosters task-focused motivation, and supports the other aspects of creativity that we have discussed.

It is also important to realize that obtaining transfer of training from one domain to another is at least as hard with creative thinking as with critical thinking. If you use trivial problems in your classroom (e.g., "What are unusual uses of a paper clip?"), you are likely to get transfer only to trivial problems outside the classroom. We are not enthusiastic about many so-called tests of creativity, nor about many training programs, because the problems they use are trivial. We would encourage the use of serious problems in a variety of disciplines in order to maximize the transfer of training. Better to ask students to think of unusual ways to solve world problems—or school problems, for that matter—than to ask them to think of unusual ways to use a paper clip!

CONCLUSION

Perhaps the greatest block to the enhancement of creativity is a view of the "ideal student" that does not particularly feature creativity. Paul Torrance used an "Ideal Child Checklist," composed of characteristics that had been found empirically to differentiate highly creative people from less creative people.[11] A total of 264 teachers in the state of New York ranked the items in terms of desirability. The teachers' rankings showed only a moderate relation with the rankings of 10 experts on creativity. The teachers supported more strongly than the experts such attributes as popularity, social skills, and acceptance of authority. The teachers disapproved of asking questions, being a good guesser, thinking independently, and risk taking. A replication of this study in Tennessee showed only a weak relation between the views of teachers and those of experts on creativity.[12] Clearly, to engender creativity, first we must value it!

Schools could change. They could let students define problems, rather than almost always doing it for them. They could put more emphasis on ill-structured rather than well-structured problems. They could encourage a legislative rather than (or in addition to) an executive style, by providing assignments that encourage students to see things in new ways. They could teach knowledge for use, rather than for exams; they could emphasize flexibility in using knowledge, rather than mere recall. They could encourage risk taking and other personality attributes associated with creativity, and they could put more emphasis on motivating children intrinsically rather than through grades. Finally, they could reward creativity in all its forms, rather than ignore or even punish it.

But for schools to do these things, it would take a rather fundamental re*valuation* of what schooling is about. We, at least, would like to see that process start now. Rather than put obstacles in their paths, let's do all that we can to *value* and encourage the creativity of students in our schools.

ENDNOTES

1. Robert J. Sternberg, "A Three-Facet Model of Creativity," in idem, ed., *The Nature of Creativity* (New York: Cambridge University Press, 1988), pp. 125–47; and Robert J. Sternberg and Todd I. Lubart, "An Investment Theory of Creativity and Its Development," *Human Development,* vol. 34, 1991, pp. 1–31.
2. Herbert J. Walberg, "Creativity and Talent as Learning," in Sternberg, *The Nature of Creativity,* pp. 340–61.

3. Robert J. Sternberg, *Beyond IQ: A Triarchic Theory of Human Intelligence* (New York: Cambridge University Press, 1985); and idem, *The Triarchic Mind: A New Theory of Human Intelligence* (New York: Viking, 1988).
4. Janet E. Davidson and Robert J. Sternberg, "The Role of Insight in Intellectual Giftedness," *Gifted Child Quarterly,* vol. 28, 1984, pp. 58–64; and Robert J. Sternberg and Janet E. Davidson, "The Mind of the Puzzler," *Psychology Today,* June 1982, pp. 37–44.
5. Robert J. Sternberg and Peter A. Frensch, "A Balance-Level Theory of Intelligent Thinking," *Zeitschrift für Pädagogische Psychologie,* vol. 3, 1989, pp. 79–96.
6. Robert J. Sternberg, "Mental Self-Government: A Theory of Intellectual Styles and Their Development," *Human Development,* vol. 31, 1988, pp. 197–224; and idem, "Thinking Styles: Keys to Understanding Student Performance," *Phi Delta Kappan,* January 1990, pp. 366–71.
7. Teresa M. Amabile, *The Social Psychology of Creativity* (New York: Springer-Verlag, 1983).
8. Mark Lepper, David Greene, and Richard Nisbett, "Undermining Children's Intrinsic Interest with Extrinsic Rewards: A Test of the 'Overjustification' Hypothesis," *Journal of Personality and Social Psychology,* vol. 28, 1973, pp. 129–37.
9. Robert White, "Motivation Reconsidered: The Concept of Competence," *Psychological Review,* vol. 66, 1959, pp. 297–323.
10. Davidson and Sternberg, op. cit.
11. E. Paul Torrance, *Role of Evaluation in Creative Thinking* (Minneapolis: Bureau of Educational Research, University of Minnesota, 1964).
12. Bill Kaltsounis, "Middle Tennessee Teachers' Perceptions of Ideal Pupil," *Perceptual and Motor Skills,* vol. 44, 1977, pp. 803–6.

DISCUSSION QUESTIONS

1. How can curriculum workers plan instruction that encourages students to use legislative intellectual styles?

2. In what ways will the curriculum need to be structured to promote creative thinking?

3. What kinds of changes at the school level might be necessary to foster creative thinking?

4. What instructional approaches are most likely to promote creative thinking?

5. What personality attributes do creative people seem to share?

16

The Cognitive-Developmental Approach to Moral Education

LAWRENCE KOHLBERG

FOCUSING QUESTIONS

1. *How does moral education promote the aims of education?*
2. *What are the levels of moral development?*
3. *How do moral judgment, content of moral judgment, and moral action differ?*
4. *How do conventional rules and principles influence moral choice?*
5. *How do indoctrination and values clarification differ as approaches to moral education?*
6. *What is the cognitive developmental approach to moral education?*

In this article, I present an overview of the cognitive-developmental approach to moral education and its research foundations, compare it with other approaches, and report the experimental work my colleagues and I are doing to apply the approach.

MORAL STAGES

The cognitive-developmental approach was fully stated for the first time by John Dewey. The approach is called *cognitive* because it recognizes that moral education, like intellectual education, has its basis in stimulating the *active thinking* of the child about moral issues and decisions. It is called developmental because it sees the aims of moral education as movement through moral stages. According to Dewey:

> The aim of education is growth or *development,* both intellectual and moral. Ethical and psychological principles can aid the school in the *greatest of all the constructions—the building of a free and powerful character.* Only knowledge

of the *order and connection of the stages in psychological development can insure this.* Education is the work of *supplying the conditions* which will enable the psychological functions to mature in the freest and fullest manner.[1]

Dewey postulated three levels of moral development: (1) the *pre-moral* or *preconventional* level "of behavior motivated by biological and social impulses with results for morals," (2) the *conventional* level of behavior "in which the individual accepts with little critical reflection the standards of his group," and (3) the *autonomous* level of behavior in which "conduct is guided by the individual thinking and judging for himself whether a purpose is good, and does not accept the standard of his group without reflection."[2]

Dewey's thinking about moral stages was theoretical. Building upon his prior studies of cognitive stages, Jean Piaget made the first effort to define stages of moral reasoning in children through actual interviews and through observations of children (in games with rules).[3] Using this interview material, Piaget defined the premoral, the conventional, and the autonomous levels as follows: (1) the *premoral stage,* where there was no sense of obligation to rules; (2) the *heteronomous stage,* where the right was literal obedience to rules and an equation of obligation with submission to power and punishment (roughly ages four to eight); and (3) the *autonomous stage,* where the purpose and consequences of following rules are considered and obligation is based on reciprocity and exchange (roughly ages eight to twelve).[4]

In 1955 I started to redefine and validate (through longitudinal and cross-cultural study) the Dewey-Piaget levels and stages. The resulting stages are presented in Table 16.1.

We claim to have validated the stages defined in Table 1. The notion that stages can be *validated* by longitudinal study implies that stages have definite empirical characteristics.[5] The concept of stages (as used by Piaget and myself) implies the following characteristics:

1. Stages are "structured wholes," or organized systems of thought. Individuals are *consistent* in level of moral judgment.
2. Stages form an *invariant sequence.* Under all conditions except extreme trauma, movement is always forward, never backward. Individuals never skip stages; movement is always to the next stage up.
3. Stages are "hierarchical integrations." Thinking at a higher stage includes or comprehends within it lower-stage thinking. There is a tendency to function at or prefer the highest stage available.

Each of these characteristics has been demonstrated for moral stages. Stages are defined by responses to a set of verbal moral dilemmas classified according to an elaborate scoring scheme. Validating studies include:

1. A twenty-year study of fifty Chicago-area boys, middle- and working-class. Initially interviewed at ages ten to sixteen, they have been reinterviewed at three-year intervals thereafter.

2. A small, six-year longitudinal study of Turkish village and city boys of the same age.
3. A variety of other cross-sectional studies in Canada, Britain, Israel, Taiwan, Yucatan, Honduras, and India.

With regard to the structured whole or consistency criterion, we have found that more than 50 percent of an individual's thinking is always at one stage, with the remainder at the next adjacent stage (which he is leaving or which he is moving into).

With regard to invariant sequence, our longitudinal results have been presented in the *American Journal of Orthopsychiatry* (see endnote 12), and indicate that on every retest individuals were either at the same stage as three years earlier or had moved up. This was true in Turkey as well as in the United States.

With regard to the hierarchical integration criterion, it has been demonstrated that adolescents exposed to written statements at each of the six stages comprehend or correctly put in their own words all statements at or below their own stage but fail to comprehend any statements more than one stage above their own.[6] Some individuals comprehend the next stage above their own; some do not. Adolescents prefer (or rank as best) the highest stage they can comprehend.

To understand moral stages it is important to clarify their relations to stage of logic or intelligence, on the one hand, and to moral behavior on the other. Maturity of moral judgment is not highly correlated with IQ or verbal intelligence (correlations are only in the 30s, accounting for 10 percent of the variance). Cognitive development, in the stage sense, however, is more important for moral development than such correlations suggest. Piaget has found that after the child learns to speak there are three major stages of reasoning: the intuitive, the concrete operational, and the formal operational. At around age seven, the child enters the stage of concrete logical thought: He can make logical inferences, classify, and handle quantitative relations about concrete things. In adolescence individuals usually enter

TABLE 16.1   Definition of Moral Stages

I. Preconventional level

At this level, the child is responsive to cultural rules and labels of good and bad, right or wrong, but interprets these labels either in terms of the physical or the hedonistic consequences of action (punishment, reward, exchange of favors) or in terms of the physical power of those who enunciate the rules and labels. The level is divided into the following two stages:

Stage 1: *The punishment-and-obedience orientation.* The physical consequences of action determine its goodness or badness, regardless of the human meaning or value of these consequences. Avoidance of punishment and unquestioning deference to power are valued in their own right, not in terms of respect for an underlying moral order supported by punishment and authority (the latter being Stage 4).

Stage 2: *The instrumental-relativist orientation.* Right action consists of that which instrumentally satisfies one's own needs and occasionally the needs of others. Human relations are viewed in terms like those of the marketplace. Elements of fairness, of reciprocity, and of equal sharing are present, but they are always interpreted in a physical, pragmatic way. Reciprocity is a matter of "You scratch my back and I'll scratch yours," not of loyalty, gratitude, or justice.

II. Conventional level

At this level, maintaining the expectations of the individual's family, group, or nation is perceived as valuable in its own right, regardless of immediate and obvious consequences. The attitude is not only one of *conformity* to personal expectations and social order, but of loyalty to it, of actively *maintaining,* supporting, and justifying the order, and of identifying with the persons or group involved in it. At this level, there are the following two stages:

Stage 3: *The interpersonal concordance or "good boy-nice girl" orientation.* Good behavior is that which pleases or helps others and is approved by them. There is much conformity to stereotypical images of what is majority or "natural" behavior. Behavior is frequently judged by intention—"he means well" becomes important for the first time. One earns approval by being "nice."

Stage 4: *The "law and order" orientation.* There is orientation toward authority, fixed rules, and the maintenance of the social order. Right behavior consists of doing one's duty, showing respect for authority, and maintaining the given social order for its own sake.

III. Postconventional level

At this level, there is a clear effort to define moral values and principles that have validity and application apart from the authority of the groups or persons holding these principles and apart from the individual's own identification with these groups. This level also has two stages:

Stage 5: *The social-contract, legalistic orientation,* generally with utilitarian overtones. Right action tends to be defined in terms of general individual rights and standards which have been critically examined and agreed upon by the whole society. There is a clear awareness of the relativism of personal values and opinions and a corresponding emphasis upon procedural rules for reaching consensus. Aside from what is constitutionally and democratically agreed upon, the right is a matter of personal "values" and "opinion." The result is an emphasis upon the "legal point of view," but with an emphasis upon the possibility of changing law in terms of rational considerations of social utility (rather than freezing it in terms of Stage 4 "law and order"). Outside the legal realm, free agreement and contract is the binding element of obligation. This is the "official" morality of the American government and constitution.

Stage 6: *The universal-ethical-principle orientation.* Right is defined by the decision of conscience in accord with self-chosen *ethical principles* appealing to logical comprehensiveness, universality, and consistency. These principles are abstract and ethical (the Golden Rule, the categorical imperative); they are not concrete moral rules like the Ten Commandments. At heart, these are universal principles of *justice,* of the *reciprocity* and *equality* of human *rights,* and of respect for the dignity of human beings as *individual persons* ("From Is to Ought," pp. 164, 165).

the stage of formal operations. At this stage they can reason abstractly, i.e., consider all possibilities, form hypotheses, deduce implications from hypotheses, and test them against reality.[7]

Since moral reasoning clearly is reasoning, advanced moral reasoning depends upon advanced logical reasoning; a person's logical stage puts a certain ceiling on the moral stage he can attain. A person whose logical stage is only concrete operational is limited to the preconventional moral stages (Stages 1 and 2). A person whose logical stage is only partially formal operational is limited to the conventional moral stages (Stages 3 and 4). While logical development is necessary for moral development and sets limits to it, most individuals are higher in logical stage than they are in moral stage. As an example, over 50 percent of late adolescents and adults are capable of full formal reasoning, but only 10 percent of these adults (all formal operational) display principled (Stages 5 and 6) moral reasoning.

The moral stages are *structures of moral judgment* or *moral reasoning. Structures* of moral judgment must be distinguished from the *content* of moral judgment. As an example, we cite responses to a dilemma used in our various studies to identify moral stage. The dilemma raises the issue of stealing a drug to save a dying woman. The inventor of the drug is selling it for ten times what it costs him to make it. The woman's husband cannot raise the money, and the seller refuses to lower the price or wait for payment. What should the husband do?

The choice endorsed by a subject (steal, don't steal) is called the *content* of his moral judgment in the situation. His reasoning about the choice defines the structure of his moral judgment. This reasoning centers on the following ten universal moral values or issues of concern to persons in these moral dilemmas:

1. Punishment
2. Property
3. Roles and concerns of affection
4. Roles and concerns of authority
5. Law
6. Life
7. Liberty
8. Distributive justice
9. Truth
10. Sex

A moral choice involves choosing between two (or more) of these values as they *conflict* in concrete situations of choice.

The stage or structure of a person's moral judgment defines: (1) *what* he finds valuable in each of these moral issues (life, law), i.e., how he defines the value, and (2) *why* he finds it valuable, i.e., the reasons he gives for valuing it. As an example, at Stage 1 life is valued in terms of the power or possessions of the person involved; at Stage 2, for its usefulness in satisfying the needs of the individual in question or others; at Stage 3, in terms of the individual's relations with others and their valuation of him; at Stage 4, in terms of social or religious law. Only at Stages 5 and 6 is each life seen as inherently worthwhile, aside from other considerations.

MORAL JUDGMENT VS. MORAL ACTION

Having clarified the nature of stages of moral *judgment,* we must consider the relation of moral judgment to moral *action.* If logical reasoning is a necessary but not sufficient condition for mature moral judgment, mature moral judgment is a necessary but not sufficient condition for mature moral action. One cannot follow moral principles if one does not understand (or believe in) moral principles. However, one can reason in terms of principles and not live up to these principles. As an example, Richard Krebs and I found that only 15 percent of students showing some principled thinking cheated as compared to 55 percent of conventional subjects and 70 percent of preconventional subjects.[8] Nevertheless, 15 percent of the principled subjects did cheat, suggesting that factors additional to moral judgment are necessary for principled moral reasoning to be translated into "moral action." Partly, these factors include the situation and its pressures. Partly, what happens depends upon the individual's motives and emotions. Partly, what the individual does depends upon a general sense of will, purpose, or "ego strength." As an example of the role of will or ego strength in moral behavior, we may cite the study by Krebs: Slightly more than half of his conventional subjects cheated. These subjects were also divided by a measure of attention/will. Only 26 percent of the "strong-willed" conventional subjects cheated; however, 74 percent of the "weak-willed" subjects cheated.

If maturity of moral reasoning is only one factor in moral behavior, why does the cognitive-developmental approach to moral education focus so heavily upon moral reasoning? For the following reasons:

1. Moral judgment, while only one factor in moral behavior, is the single most important or influential factor yet discovered in moral behavior.

2. While other factors influence moral behavior, moral judgment is the only distinctively *moral* factor in moral behavior. To illustrate, we noted that the Krebs study indicated that "strong-willed" conventional stage subjects resisted cheating more than "weak-willed" subjects. For those at a preconventional level of moral reasoning, however, "will" had an opposite effect. "Strong-willed" Stages 1 and 2 subjects cheated more, not less, than "weak-willed" subjects, i.e., they had the "courage of their (amoral) convictions" that it was worthwhile to cheat. "Will," then, is an important factor in moral behavior, but it is not distinctively moral; it becomes moral only when informed by mature moral judgment.

3. Moral judgment change is long-range or irreversible; a higher stage is never lost. Moral behavior as such is largely situational and reversible or "losable" in new situations.

AIMS OF MORAL AND CIVIC EDUCATION

Moral psychology describes what moral development is, as studied empirically. Moral education must also consider moral philosophy, which strives to tell us what moral development ideally *ought to be.* Psychology finds an invariant sequence of moral stages; moral philosophy must be invoked to answer whether a later stage is a better stage. The "stage" of senescence and death follows the "stage" of adulthood, but that does not mean that senescence and death are better. Our claim that the latest or principled stages of moral reasoning are morally better stages, then, must rest on considerations of moral philosophy.

The tradition of moral philosophy to which we appeal is the liberal or rational tradition, in particular the "formalistic" or "deontological" tradition running from Immanuel Kant to John Rawls.[9] Central to this tradition is the claim that an adequate morality is *principled,* i.e., that it makes judgments in terms of *universal* principles applicable to all mankind. *Principles* are to be distinguished from *rules.* Conventional morality is grounded on rules, primarily "thou shalt nots" such as are represented by the Ten Commandments, prescriptions of kinds of actions. Principles are, rather, universal guides to making a moral decision. An example is Kant's "categorical imperative," formulated in two ways. The first is the maxim of respect for human personality "Act always toward the other as an end, not as a means." The second is the maxim of universalization, "Choose only as you would be willing to have everyone choose in your situation." Principles like that of Kant's state the formal conditions of a moral choice or action. In the dilemma in which a woman is dying because a druggist refuses to release his drug for less than the stated price, the druggist is not acting morally, though he is not violating the ordinary moral rules (he is not actually stealing or murdering). But he is violating principles: He is treating the woman simply as a means to his ends of profit, and he is not choosing as he would wish anyone to choose (if the druggist were in the dying woman's place, he would not want a druggist to choose as he is choosing). Under most circumstances, choice in terms of conventional moral rules and choice in terms of principles coincide. Ordinarily, principles dictate not stealing (avoiding stealing is implied by acting in terms of a regard for others as ends and in terms of what one would want everyone to do). In a situation where stealing is the only means to save a life, however, principles contradict the ordinary rules and would dictate stealing. Unlike rules which are supported by social authority, principles are freely chosen by the individual because of their intrinsic moral validity.[10]

The conception that a moral choice is a choice made in terms of moral principles is related to the claim of liberal moral philosophy that moral principles are ultimately principles of justice. In essence, moral conflicts are conflicts between the claims of persons, and principles for resolving these claims are principles of justice, "for giving each his due." Central to justice are the demands of *liberty, equality,* and *reciprocity.* At every moral stage, there is a concern for justice. The most damning statement a school child can make about a teacher is that "he's not fair." At each higher stage, however, the conception of justice is reorganized. At Stage 1, justice is punishing the bad in terms of "an eye for an eye and a tooth for a tooth." At Stage 2, it is exchanging favors and goods in an equal manner. At Stages 3 and 4, it is treating people as they desire in terms of the conventional rules. At Stage 5, it is recognized that all rules and laws flow from justice, from a social contract between the governors and the governed designed to protect the equal rights of all. At Stage 6, personally chosen moral principles are also principles of justice, the principles any member of a society would choose for that society if he did not know what his position was to be in the society and in which he might be the least advantaged.[11] Principles chosen from this point of view are, first, the maximum liberty compatible with the like liberty of others and, second, no inequalities of goods and respect which are not to the benefit of all, including the least advantaged.

As an example of stage progression in the orientation to justice, we may take judgments about capital punishment.[12] Capital punishment is only firmly rejected at the two principled stages, when the notion of justice as vengeance or retribution is abandoned. At the sixth stage, capital punishment is not condoned even if it may have

some useful deterrent effect in promoting law and order. This is because it is not a punishment we would choose for a society if we assumed we had as much chance of being born into the position of a criminal or murderer as being born into the position of a law abider.

Why are decisions based on universal principles of justice better decisions? Because they are decisions on which all moral men could agree. When decisions are based on conventional moral rules, men will disagree, since they adhere to conflicting systems of rules dependent on culture and social position. Throughout history men have killed one another in the name of conflicting moral rules and values, most recently in Vietnam and the Middle East. Truly moral or just resolutions of conflicts require principles which are, or can be, universalizable.

Alternative Approaches

We have given a philosophic rationale for stage advance as the aim of moral education. Given this rationale, the developmental approach to moral education can avoid the problems inherent in the other two major approaches to moral education. The first alternative approach is that of indoctrinative moral education, the preaching and imposition of the rules and values of the teacher and his culture on the child. In America, when this indoctrinative approach has been developed in a systematic manner, it has usually been termed "character education."

Moral values, in the character education approach, are preached or taught in terms of what may be called the "bag of virtues." In the classic studies of character by Hugh Hartshorne and Mark May, the virtues chosen were honesty, service, and self-control.[13] It is easy to get superficial consensus on such a bag of virtues—until one examines in detail the list of virtues involved and the details of their definition. Is the Hartshorne and May bag more adequate than the Boy Scout bag (a Scout should be honest, loyal, reverent, clean, brave, etc.)? When one turns to the details of defining each virtue, one finds equal uncertainty or difficulty in reaching consensus. Does honesty mean one should not steal to save a life? Does it mean that a student should not help another student with his homework?

Character education and other forms of indoctrinative moral education have aimed at teaching universal values (it is assumed that honesty or service is a desirable trait for all men in all societies), but the detailed definitions used are relative; they are defined by the opinions of the teacher and the conventional culture and rest on the authority of the teacher for their justification. In this sense character education is close to the unreflective valuings by teachers which constitute the hidden curriculum of the school.[14] Because of the current unpopularity of indoctrinative approaches to moral education, a family of approaches called "values clarification" has become appealing to teachers. Values clarification takes the first step implied by a rational approach to moral education: the eliciting of the child's own judgment or opinion about issues or situations in which values conflict, rather than imposing the teacher's opinion on him. Values clarification, however, does not attempt to go further than eliciting awareness of values; it is assumed that becoming more self-aware about one's values is an end in itself. Fundamentally, the definition of the end of values education as self-awareness derives from a belief in ethical relativity held by many value-clarifiers. As stated by Peter Engel, "One must contrast value clarification and value inculcation. Value clarification implies the principle that in the consideration of values there is no single correct answer." Within these premises of "no correct answer," children are to discuss moral dilemmas in such a way as to, reveal different values and discuss their value differences with each other. The teacher is to stress that "our values are different," not that one value is more adequate than others. If this program is systematically followed, students will themselves become relativists, believing there is no "right" moral answer. For instance, a student caught cheating might argue that he did nothing wrong, since his own hierarchy of values, which

may be different from that of the teacher, made it right for him to cheat.

Like values clarification, the cognitive-developmental approach to moral education stresses open or Socratic peer discussion of value dilemmas. Such discussion, however, has an aim: stimulation of movement to the next stage of moral reasoning. Like values clarification, the developmental approach opposes indoctrination. Stimulation of movement to the next stage of reasoning is not indoctrinative, for the following reasons:

1. Change is in the way of reasoning rather than in the particular beliefs involved.
2. Students in a class are at different stages; the aim is to aid movement of each to the next stage, not convergence on a common pattern.
3. The teacher's own opinion is neither stressed nor invoked as authoritative. It enters in only as one of many opinions, hopefully one of those at a next higher stage.
4. The notion that some judgments are more adequate than others is communicated. Fundamentally, however, this means that the student is encouraged to articulate a position which seems most adequate to him and to judge the adequacy of the reasoning of others.

In addition to having more definite aims than values clarification, the moral development approach restricts value education to that which is moral or, more specifically, to justice. This is for two reasons. First, it is not clear that the whole realm of personal, political, and religious values is a realm which is nonrelative, i.e., in which there are universals and a direction of development. Second, it is not clear that the public school has a right or mandate to develop values in general.[15] In our view, value education in the public schools should be restricted to that which the school has the right and mandate to develop: an awareness of justice, or of the rights of others in our Constitutional system. While the Bill of Rights prohibits the teaching of religious beliefs, or of specific value systems, it does not prohibit the teaching of the awareness of rights and principles of justice fundamental to the Constitution itself.

When moral education is recognized as centered in justice and differentiated from value education or affective education, it becomes apparent that moral and civic education are much the same thing. This equation, taken for granted by the classic philosophers of education from Plato and Aristotle to Dewey, is basic to our claim that a concern for moral education is central to the educational objectives of social studies.

The term *civic education* is used to refer to social studies as more than the study of the facts and concepts of social science, history, and civics. It is education for the analytic understanding, value principles, and motivation necessary for a citizen in a democracy if democracy is to be an effective process. It is political education. Civic or political education means the stimulation of development of more advanced patterns of reasoning about political and social decisions and their implementation directly derivative of broader patterns of moral reasoning. Our studies show that reasoning and decision making about political decisions are directly derivative of broader patterns of moral reasoning and decision making. We have interviewed high school and college students about concrete political situations involving laws to govern open housing, civil disobedience for peace in Vietnam, free press rights to publish what might disturb national order, and distribution of income through taxation. We find that reasoning on these political decisions can be classified according to moral stage and that an individual's stage on political dilemmas is at the same level as on nonpolitical moral dilemmas (euthanasia, violating authority to maintain trust in a family, stealing a drug to save one's dying wife). Turning from reasoning to action, similar findings are obtained. In 1963 a study was made of those who sat in at the University of California, Berkeley, administration building and those who did not in the Free Speech Movement crisis. Of those at Stage 6, 80 percent sat in, believing that principles of free speech were being compromised, and that all efforts to

compromise and negotiate with the administration had failed. In contrast, only 15 percent of the conventional (Stage 3 or Stage 4) subjects sat in. (Stage 5 subjects were in between.)[16]

From a psychological side, then, political development is part of moral development. The same is true from the philosophic side. In the *Republic*, Plato sees political education as part of a broader education for moral justice and finds a rationale for such education in terms of universal philosophic principles rather than the demands of a particular society. More recently, Dewey claims the same.

In historical perspective, America was the first nation whose government was publicly founded on postconventional principles of justice, rather than upon the authority central to conventional moral reasoning. At the time of our founding, postconventional or principled moral and political reasoning was the possession of the minority, as it still is. Today, as in the time of our founding, the majority of our adults are at the conventional level, particularly the "law and order" (fourth) moral stage. (Every few years the Gallup Poll circulates the Bill of Rights unidentified, and every year it is turned down.) The Founding Fathers intuitively understood this without benefit of our elaborate social science research; they constructed a document designing a government which would maintain principles of justice and the rights of man even though principled men were not the men in power. The machinery included checks and balances, the independent judiciary, and freedom of the press. Most recently, this machinery found its use at Watergate. The tragedy of Richard Nixon, as Harry Truman said long ago, was that he never understood the Constitution (a Stage 5 document), but the Constitution understood Richard Nixon.[17]

Watergate, then, is not some sign of moral decay of the nation, but rather of the fact that understanding and action in support of justice principles are still the possession of a minority of our society. Insofar as there is moral decay, it represents the weakening of conventional morality in the face of social and value conflict today. This can lead the less fortunate adolescent to fixation at the preconventional level, the more fortunate to movement to principles. We find a larger proportion of youths at the principled level today than was the case in their fathers' day, but also a larger proportion at the preconventional level.

Given this state, moral and civic education in the schools becomes a more urgent task. In the high school today, one often hears both preconventional adolescents and those beginning to move beyond convention sounding the same note of disaffection for the school. While our political institutions are in principle Stage 5 (i.e., vehicles for maintaining universal rights through the democratic process), our schools have traditionally been Stage 4 institutions of convention and authority. Today more than ever, democratic schools systematically engaged in civic education are required.

Our approach to moral and civic education relates the study of law and government to the actual creation of a democratic school in which moral dilemmas are discussed and resolved in a manner which will stimulate moral development.

Planned Moral Education

For many years, moral development was held by psychologists to be primarily a result of family upbringing and family conditions. In particular, conditions of affection and authority in the home were believed to be critical, some balance of warmth and firmness being optimal for moral development. This view arises if morality is conceived as an internalization of the arbitrary rules of parents and culture, since such acceptance must be based on affection and respect for parents as authorities rather than on the rational nature of the rules involved.

Studies of family correlates of moral stage development do not support this internalization view of the conditions for moral development. Instead, they suggest that the conditions for moral development in homes and schools are similar and that the conditions are consistent with cognitive-developmental theory. In the cognitive-developmental view, morality is a natural product of a universal human tendency toward empathy or role taking, toward putting oneself in the shoes of other conscious beings. It is also a product of a universal human concern for justice, for reciprocity or equality in the relation of one person to another. As an example, when my son was four, he became a morally principled vegetarian and refused to eat meat, resisting all parental persuasion to increase his protein intake. His reason was, "It's bad to kill animals." His moral commitment to vegetarianism was not taught or acquired from parental authority; it was the result of the universal tendency of the young self to project its consciousness and values into other living things, other selves. My son's vegetarianism also involved a sense of justice, revealed when I read him a book about Eskimos in which a real hunting expedition was described. His response was to say, "Daddy there is one kind of meat I would eat—Eskimo meat. It's all right to eat Eskimos because they eat animals." This natural sense of justice or reciprocity was Stage 1—an eye for an eye, a tooth for a tooth. My son's sense of the value of life was also Stage 1 and involved no differentiation between human personality and physical life. His morality, though Stage 1, was, however, natural and internal. Moral development past Stage 1, then, is not an internalization but the reconstruction of role taking and conceptions of justice toward greater adequacy. These reconstructions occur in order to achieve a better match between the child's own moral structures and the structures of the social and moral situations he confronts. We divide these conditions of match into two kinds: those dealing with moral discussions and communication and those dealing with the total moral environment or atmosphere in which the child lives.

In terms of moral discussion, the important conditions appear to be:

1. Exposure to the next higher stage of reasoning

2. Exposure to situations posing problems and contradictions for the child's current moral structure, leading to dissatisfaction with his current level
3. An atmosphere of interchange and dialogue combining the first two conditions, in which conflicting moral views are compared in an open manner.

Studies of families in India and America suggest that morally advanced children have parents at higher stages. Parents expose children to the next higher stage, raising moral issues and engaging in open dialogue or interchange about such issues.[18]

Drawing on this notion of the discussion conditions stimulating advance, Moshe Blatt conducted classroom discussions of conflict-laden hypothetical moral dilemmas with four classes of junior high and high school students for a semester.[19] In each of these classes, students were to be found at three stages. Since the children were not all responding at the same stage, the arguments they used with each other were at different levels. In the course of these discussions among the students, the teacher first supported and clarified those arguments that were one stage above the lowest stage among the children; for example, the teacher supported Stage 3 rather than Stage 2. When it seemed that these arguments were understood by the students, the teacher then challenged that stage, using new situations, and clarified the arguments one stage above the previous one: Stage 4 rather than Stage 3. At the end of the semester, all the students were retested; they showed significant upward change when compared to the controls, and they maintained the change one year later. In the experimental classrooms, from one-fourth to one-half of the students moved up a stage, while there was essentially no change during the course of the experiment in the control group.

Given the Blatt studies showing that moral discussion could raise moral stage, we undertook the next step: to see if teachers could conduct moral discussions in the course of teaching high school social studies with the same results. This step we took in cooperation with Edwin Fenton, who introduced moral dilemmas in his ninth- and eleventh-grade social studies texts. Twenty-four teachers in the Boston and Pittsburgh areas were given some instruction in conducting moral discussions around the dilemmas in the text. About half of the teachers stimulated significant developmental change in their classrooms—upward stage movement of one-quarter to one-half a stage. In control classes using the text but no moral dilemma discussions, the same teachers failed to stimulate any moral change in the students. Moral discussion, then, can be a usable and effective part of the curriculum at any grade level. Working with filmstrip dilemmas produced in cooperation with Guidance Association, second-grade teachers conducted moral discussions yielding a similar amount of moral stage movement.

Moral discussion and curriculum, however, constitute only one portion of the conditions stimulating moral growth. When we turn to analyzing the broader life environment, we turn to a consideration of the *moral atmosphere* of the home, the school, and the broader society. The first basic dimension of social atmosphere is the role-taking opportunities it provides, the extent to which it encourages the child to take the point of view of others. Role taking is related to the amount of social interaction and social communication in which the child engages, as well as to his sense of efficacy in influencing attitudes of others. The second dimension of social atmosphere, more strictly moral, is the level of justice of the environment or institution. The justice structure of an institution refers to the perceived rules or principles for distributing rewards, punishments, responsibilities, and privileges among institutional members. This structure may exist or be perceived at any of our moral stages. As an example, a study of a traditional prison revealed that inmates perceived it as Stage 1, regardless of their own level.[20] Obedience to arbitrary command by power figures and punishment for disobedience were seen as the governing justice norms of the prison. A behavior-modification prison using point rewards for conformity was perceived as a Stage 2 system of instrumental exchange. Inmates at Stage 3 or 4 perceived this institution as more fair than the traditional prison, but not as fair in their own terms.

These and other studies suggest that a higher level of institutional justice is a condition for individual development of a higher sense of justice. Working on these premises, Joseph Hickey, Peter Scharf, and I worked with guards and inmates in a women's prison to create a more just community.[21] A social contract was set up in which guards and inmates each had a vote of one and in which rules were made and conflicts resolved through discussions of fairness and a democratic vote in a community meeting. The program has been operating four years and has stimulated moral stage advance in inmates, though it is still too early to draw conclusions as to its overall long-range effectiveness for rehabilitiation.

One year ago, Fenton, Ralph Mosher, and I received a grant from the Danforth Foundation (with additional support from the Kennedy Foundation) to make moral education a living matter in two high schools in the Boston area (Cambridge and Brookline) and two in Pittsburgh. The plan had two components. The first was training counselors and social studies and English teachers in conducting moral discussions and making moral discussion an integral part of the curriculum. The second was establishing a just community school within a public high school.

We have stated the theory of the just community high school, postulating that discussing real-life moral situations and actions as issues of fairness and as matters for democratic decision would stimulate advance in both moral reasoning and moral action. A participatory democracy provides more extensive opportunities for role taking and a higher level of perceived institutional justice than does any other social arrangement. Most alternative schools strive to establish a democratic governance, but none we have observed has achieved a vital or viable participatory democ-

racy. Our theory suggested reasons why we might succeed where others failed. First, we felt that democracy had to be a central commitment of a school, rather than a humanitarian frill. Democracy as moral education provides that commitment. Second, democracy in alternative schools often fails because it bores the students. Students prefer to let teachers make decisions about staff, courses, and schedules, rather than to attend lengthy, complicated meetings. Our theory said that the issues a democracy should focus on are issues of morality and fairness. Real issues concerning drugs, stealing, disruptions, and grading are never boring if handled as issues of fairness. Third, our theory told us that if large democratic community meetings were preceded by small-group moral discussion, higher-stage thinking by students would win out in later decisions, avoiding the disasters of mob rule.[22]

Currently, we can report that the school based on our theory makes democracy work or function where other schools have failed. It is too early to make any claims for its effectiveness in causing moral development, however.

Our Cambridge just community school within the public high school was started after a small summer planning session of volunteer teachers, students, and parents. At the time the school opened in the fall, only a commitment to democracy and a skeleton program of English and social studies had been decided on. The school started with six teachers from the regular school and sixty students, twenty from academic professional homes and twenty from working-class homes. The other twenty were dropouts and troublemakers or petty delinquents in terms of previous record. The usual mistakes and usual chaos of a beginning alternative school ensued. Within a few weeks, however, a successful democratic community process had been established. Rules were made around pressing issues: disturbances, drugs, hooking. A student discipline committee or jury was formed. The resulting rules and enforcement have been relatively effective and reasonable. We do not see reasonable rules as ends in themselves, however, but as vehicles for moral discussion and an emerging sense of community. This sense of community and a resulting morale are perhaps the most immediate signs of success. This sense of community seems to lead to behavior change of a positive sort. An example is a fifteen-year-old student who started as one of the greatest combinations of humor, aggression, light-fingeredness, and hyperactivity I have ever known. From being the principal disturber of all community meetings, he has become an excellent community meeting participant and occasional chairman. He is still more ready to enforce rules for others than to observe them himself, yet his commitment to the school has led to a steady decrease in exotic behavior. In addition, he has become more involved in classes and projects and has begun to listen and ask questions in order to pursue a line of interest.

CONCLUSION

We attribute such behavior change not only to peer pressure and moral discussion but to the sense of community which has emerged from the democratic process in which angry conflicts are resolved through fairness and community decision. This sense of community is reflected in statements of the students to us that there are no cliques—that the blacks and the whites, the professors' sons and the project students, are friends. These statements are supported by observation. Such a sense of community is needed where students in a given classroom range in reading level from fifth-grade to college.

Fenton, Mosher, the Cambridge and Brookline teachers, and I are now planning a four-year curriculum in English and social studies centering on moral discussion, on role taking and communication, and on relating the government, laws, and justice system of the school to that of the American society and other world societies. This will integrate an intellectual curriculum for a higher level of understanding of society with the experiential components of school democracy and moral decision.

There is very little new in this—or in anything else we are doing. Dewey wanted democratic experimental schools for moral and intellectual development seventy years ago. Perhaps Dewey's time has come.

ENDNOTES

1. John Dewey, "What Psychology Can Do for the Teacher," in Reginald Archambault, ed., *John Dewey on Education: Selected Writings* (New York: Random House, 1964).
2. These levels correspond roughly to our three major levels: the preconventional, the conventional, and the principled. Similar levels were propounded by William McDougall, Leonard Hobhouse, and James Mark Baldwin.
3. Jean Piaget, *The Moral Judgment of the Child,* 2nd ed. (Glencoe, Ill: Free Press, 1948).
4. Piaget's stages correspond to our first three stages: Stage 0 (premoral), Stage 1 (heteronomous), and Stage 2 (instrumental reciprocity).
5. Lawrence Kohlberg, "Moral Stages and Moralization: The Cognitive-Developmental Approach," in Thomas Lickona, ed., *Man, Morality, and Society* (New York: Holt, Rinehart and Winston, in press).
6. James Rest, Elliott Turiel, and Lawrence Kohlberg, "Relations Between Level of Moral Judgment and Preference and Comprehension of the Moral Judgment of Others," *Journal of Personality,* vol. 37, 1969, pp. 225–52, and James Rest, "Comprehension, Preference, and Spontaneous Usage in Moral Judgment," in Lawrence Kohlberg, ed., *Recent Research in Moral Development* (New York: Holt, Rinehart and Winston, in preparation).
7. Many adolescents and adults only partially attain the stage of formal operations. They do consider all the actual relations of one thing to another at the same time, but they do not consider all possibilities and form abstract hypotheses. A few do not advance this far, remaining "concrete operational."
8. Richard Krebs and Lawrence Kohlberg, "Moral Judgment and Ego Controls as Determinants of Resistance to Cheating," in Lawrence Kohlberg, ed., *Recent Research.*
9. John Rawls, *A Theory of Justice* (Cambridge, Mass.: Harvard University Press, 1971).
10. Not all freely chosen values or rules are principles, however. Hitler chose the "rule," "exterminate the enemies of the Aryan race," but such a rule is not a universalizable principle.
11. Rawls, *A Theory of Justice.*

12. Lawrence Kohlberg and Donald Elfenbein, "Development of Moral Reasoning and Attitudes Toward Capital Punishment," *American Journal of Orthopsychiatry,* Summer, 1975.

13. Hugh Hartshorne and Mark May, *Studies in the Nature of Character: Studies in Deceit,* vol. 1; *Studies in Service and Self-Control,* vol. 2; *Studies in Organization of Character,* vol. 3 (New York: Macmillan, 1928–30).

14. As an example of the "hidden curriculum," we may cite a second-grade classroom. My son came home from this classroom one day saying he did not want to be "one of the bad boys." Asked "Who are the bad boys?" he replied, "The ones who don't put their books back and get yelled at."

15. Restriction of deliberate value education to the moral may be clarified by our example of the second-grade teacher who made tidying up of books a matter of moral indoctrination. Tidiness is a value, but it is not a moral value. Cheating is a moral issue, intrinsically one of fairness. It involves issues of violation of trust and taking advantage. Failing to tidy the room may under certain conditions be an issue of fairness, when it puts an undue burden on others. If it is handled by the teacher as a matter of cooperation among the group in this sense, it is a legitimate focus of deliberate moral education. If it is not, it simply represents the arbitrary imposition of the teacher's values on the child.

16. The differential action of the principled subjects was determined by two things. First, they were more likely to judge it right to violate authority by sitting in. But second, they were also in general more consistent in engaging in political action according to their judgment. Ninety percent of all Stage 6 subjects thought it right to sit in, and all 90 percent lived up to this belief.

Among the Stage 4 subjects, 45% thought it right to sit in, but only 33% lived up to this belief by acting.

17. No public or private word or deed of Nixon ever rose above Stage 4, the "law and order" stage. His last comments in the White House were of wonderment that the Republican Congress could turn on him after so many Stage 2 exchanges of favors in getting them elected.

18. Bindu Parilch, "A Cross-Cultural Study of Parent-child Moral Judgment," unpublished doctoral dissertation, Harvard University, 1975.

19. Moshe Blatt and Lawrence Kohlberg, "Effects of Classroom Discussions upon Children's Level of Moral Judgment," in Lawrence Kohlberg, ed., *Recent Research.*

20. Lawrence Kohlberg, Peter Scharf, and Joseph Hickey, "The Justice Structure of the Prison: A Theory and an Intervention," *The Prison Journal,* Autumn-Winter, 1972.

21. Lawrence Kohlberg, Kelsey Kauffman, Peter Scharf, and Joseph Hickey, *The Just Community Approach to Corrections: A Manual, Part I* (Cambridge, Mass.: Education Research Foundation, 1973).

22. An example of the need for small-group discussion comes from an alternative school community meeting called because a pair of the students had stolen the school's video-recorder. The resulting majority decision was that the school should buy back the recorder from the culprits through a fence. The teachers could not accept this decision and returned to a more authoritative approach. I believe if the moral reasoning of students urging this solution had been confronted by students at a higher stage, a different decision would have emerged.

DISCUSSION QUESTIONS

1. Should moral and civic education be the responsibility of the schools? Why? Why not?

2. What type of curriculum design lends itself to promoting the aims of moral education?

3. How do the family and norms of school cultures influence children's moral development?

4. What is the role of the social atmosphere in moral education?

5. Should values be infused into the curriculum or explicitly taught? Why? Why not?

Synthesis of Research on Cooperative Learning

ROBERT E. SLAVIN

FOCUSING QUESTIONS

1. *What are the concepts that underlie the cooperative learning methods?*
2. *What ideas are common to all student learning teams?*
3. *How do STAD and TGT differ from TAI and CIRC cooperative learning methods?*
4. *How might cooperative learning methods be used to facilitate mainstreaming?*
5. *What type of curriculum design is most appropriate for cooperative learning methods?*
6. *How do cooperative learning methods promote the aims of education?*

There was once a time when it was taken for granted that a quiet class was a learning class, when principals walked down the hall expecting to be able to hear a pin drop. Today, however, many schools are using programs that foster the hum of voices in classrooms. These programs, called *cooperative learning,* encourage students to discuss, debate, disagree, and ultimately to teach one another.

Cooperative learning has been suggested as the solution for an astonishing array of educational problems: it is often cited as a means of emphasizing thinking skills and increasing higher-order learning; as an alternative to ability grouping, remediation, or special education; as a means of improving race relations and acceptance of mainstreamed students; and as a way to prepare students for an increasingly collaborative work force. How many of these claims are justified? What effects do the various cooperative learning methods have on student achievement and other outcomes? Which forms of cooperative

learning are most effective, and what components must be in place for cooperative learning to work?

To answer these questions, I've synthesized in this article the findings of studies of cooperative learning in elementary and secondary schools that have compared cooperative learning to traditionally taught control groups studying the same objectives over a period of at least four weeks (and up to a full school year or more). Here I present a brief summary of the effects of cooperative learning on achievement and noncognitive outcomes; for a more extensive review, see *Cooperative Learning: Theory, Research, and Practice* (Slavin 1990).

COOPERATIVE LEARNING METHODS

There are many quite different forms of cooperative learning, but all of them involve having students work in small groups or teams to help one another learn academic material. Cooperative

> ## Highlights of Research on Cooperative Learning
>
> In cooperative learning, students work in small groups to help one another master academic material. There are many quite different forms of cooperative learning, and the effectiveness of cooperative learning (particularly for achievement outcomes) depends on the particular approach used.
>
> - For enhancing student achievement, the most successful approaches have incorporated two key elements: group goals and individual accountability. That is, groups are rewarded based on the individual learning of all group members.
> - When group goals and individual accountability are used, achievement effects of cooperative learning are consistently positive; 37 of 44 experimental/control comparisons of at least four weeks' duration have found significantly positive effects, and none have favored traditional methods.
> - Achievement effects of cooperative learning have been found to about the same degree at all grade levels (2–12), in all major subjects, and in urban, rural, and suburban schools. Effects are equally positive for high, average, and low achievers.
> - Positive effects of cooperative learning have been consistently found on such diverse outcomes as self-esteem, intergroup relations, acceptance of academically handicapped students, attitudes toward school, and ability to work cooperatively.
>
> —Robert E. Slavin

learning usually supplements the teacher's instruction by giving students an opportunity to discuss information or practice skills originally presented by the teacher; sometimes cooperative methods require students to find or discover information on their own. Cooperative learning has been used—and investigated—in every imaginable subject in grades 2–12, and is increasingly used in college.

Small-scale laboratory research on cooperation dates back to the 1920s (see Deutsch 1949; Slavin 1977a); research on specific applications of cooperative learning to the classroom began in the early 1970s. At that time, four research groups, one in Israel and three in the U.S., began independently to develop and study cooperative learning methods in classroom settings.

Now researchers all over the world are studying practical applications of cooperative learning principles, and many cooperative learning methods have been evaluated in one or more experi-

mental/control comparisons. The best evaluated of the cooperative models are described below (adapted from Slavin 1990). These include four Student Team Learning variations, Jigsaw, Learning Together, and Group Investigation.

Student Team Learning

Student Team Learning (STL) techniques were developed and researched at Johns Hopkins University. More than half of all experimental studies of practical cooperative learning methods involve STL methods.

All cooperative learning methods share the idea that students work together to learn and are responsible for one another's learning as well as their own. STL methods, in addition to this idea, emphasize the use of team goals and team success, which can only be achieved if all members of the team learn the objectives being taught. That is, in Student Team Learning the students' tasks are not to *do* something as a team but to *learn* something as a team.

Three concepts are central to all Student Team Learning methods: *team rewards, individual accountability,* and *equal opportunities for success.* Using STL techniques, teams earn certificates or other team rewards if they achieve above a designated criterion. The teams are not in competition to earn scarce rewards; all (or none) of the teams may achieve the criterion in a given week. *Individual accountability* means that the team's success depends on the individual learning of all team members. This focuses the activity of the team members on explaining concepts to one another and making sure that everyone on the team is ready for a quiz or other assessment that they will take without teammate help. *Equal opportunities for success* means that students contribute to their teams by improving over their own past performances. This ensures that high, average, and low achievers are equally challenged to do their best and that the contributions of all team members will be valued.

The findings of these experimental studies (summarized in this section) indicate that team rewards and individual accountability are essential elements for producing basic skills achievement (Slavin 1983a, 1983b, 1990). It is not enough to simply tell students to work together. They must have a reason to take one another's achievement seriously. Further, if students are rewarded for doing better than they have in the past, they will be more motivated to achieve than if they are rewarded based on their performance in comparison to others, because rewards for improvement make success neither too difficult nor too easy for students to achieve (Slavin 1980).

Four principal Student Team Learning methods have been extensively developed and researched. Two are general cooperative learning methods adaptable to most subjects and grade levels: Student Teams-Achievement Divisions (STAD) and Teams-Games-Tournament (TGT). The remaining two are comprehensive curriculums designed for use in particular subjects at particular grade levels: Team Assisted Individualization (TAI) for mathematics in grades 3–6 and Cooperative Integrated Reading and Composition (CIRC) for reading and writing instruction in grades 3– 5.

Student Team-Achievement Divisions (STAD). In STAD (Slavin 1978, 1986), students are assigned to four-member learning teams mixed in performance level, sex, and ethnicity. The teacher presents a lesson, and then students work within their teams to make sure that all team members have mastered the lesson. Finally, all students take individual quizzes on the material, at which time they may *not* help one another.

Students' quiz scores are compared to their own past averages, and points are awarded based on the degree to which students can meet or exceed their own earlier performances. These points are then summed to form team scores, and teams that meet certain criteria earn certificates or other rewards. The whole cycle of activities, from teacher presentation to team practice to quiz, usually takes three to five class periods.

STAD has been used in a wide variety of subjects, from mathematics to language arts and social studies. It has been used from grade 2 through college. STAD is most appropriate for teaching well-defined objectives with single right answers, such as mathematical computations and applications, language usage and mechanics, geography and map skills, and science facts and concepts.

Teams-Games-Tournament (TGT). Teams-Games-Tournament (DeVries and Slavin 1978; Slavin 1986) was the first of the Johns Hopkins cooperative learning methods. It uses the same teacher presentations and teamwork as in STAD, but replaces the quizzes with weekly tournaments. In these, students compete with members of other teams to contribute points to their team scores. Students compete at three-person "tournament tables" against others with similar past records in mathematics. A "bumping" procedure changes table assignments to keep the competition fair. The winner at each tournament table brings the same number of points to his or her team, regardless of which table it is; this means that low achievers (competing with other low achievers) and high achievers (competing with other high achievers) have equal opportunities for success. As in STAD, high-performing teams earn certificates or other forms of team rewards. TGT is appropriate for the same types of objectives as STAD.

Team Assisted Individualization (TAI).

Team Assisted Individualization (TAI; Slavin et al. 1986) shares with STAD and TGT the use of four-member mixed ability learning teams and certificates for high-performing teams. But where STAD and TGT use a single pace of instruction for the class, TAI combines cooperative learning with individualized instruction. Also, where STAD and TGT apply to most subjects and grade levels, TAI is specifically designed to teach mathematics to students in grades 3–6 (or older students not ready for a full algebra course).

In TAI, students enter an individualized sequence according to a placement test and then proceed at their own rates. In general, team members work on different units. Teammates check each others' work against answer sheets and help one another with any problems. Final unit tests are taken without teammate help and are scored by student monitors. Each week, teachers total the number of units completed by all team members and give certificates or other team rewards to teams that exceed a criterion score based on the number of final tests passed, with extra points for perfect papers and completed homework.

Because students take responsibility for checking each others' work and managing the flow of materials, the teacher can spend most of the class time presenting lessons to small groups of students drawn from the various teams who are working at the same point in the mathematics sequence. For example, the teacher might call up a decimals group, present a lesson, and then send the students back to their teams to work on problems. Then the teacher might call the fractions group, and so on.

Cooperative Integrated Reading and Composition (CIRC).

The newest of the Student Team Learning methods is a comprehensive program for teaching reading and writing in the upper elementary grades called Cooperative Integrated Reading and Composition (CIRC) (Stevens et al. 1987). In CIRC, teachers use basal or literature-based readers and reading groups, much as in traditional reading programs. However, all students are assigned to teams composed of two pairs from two different reading groups. For example, a team might have two "Bluebirds" and two "Redbirds." While the teacher is working with one reading group, the paired students in the other groups are working on a series of cognitively engaging activities, including reading to one another, making predictions about how narrative stories will come out, summarizing stories to one another, writing responses to stories, and practicing spelling, decoding, and vocabulary. If the reading class is not divided into homogeneous reading groups, all students in the teams work with one another. Students work as a total team to master "main idea" and other comprehension skills. During language arts periods, students engage in writing drafts, revising and editing one another's work, and preparing for "publication" of team books.

In most CIRC activities, students follow a sequence of teacher instruction, team practice, team pre-assessments, and quizzes. That is, students do not take the quiz until their teammates have determined that they are ready. Certificates are given to teams based on the average performance of all team members on all reading and writing activities.

Other Cooperative Learning Methods

Jigsaw.

Jigsaw was originally designed by Elliot Aronson and his colleagues (1978). In Aronson's Jigsaw method, students are assigned to six-member teams to work on academic material that has been broken down into sections. For example, a biography might be divided into early life, first accomplishments, major setbacks, later life, and impact on history. Each team member reads his or her section. Next, members of different teams who have studied the same sections meet in "expert groups" to discuss their sections. Then the students return to their teams and take turns teaching their teammates about their sections. Since the only way students can learn sections other than their own is to listen carefully to their teammates, they are motivated to support and show interest in one another's work.

Slavin (1986) developed a modification of Jigsaw at Johns Hopkins University and then incorporated it in the Student Team Learning program. In this method, called Jigsaw II, students work in four- or five-member teams as in TGT and STAD. Instead of each student's being assigned a particular section of text, all students read a common narrative, such as a book chapter, a short story, or a biography. However, each student receives a topic (such as "climate" in a unit on France) on which to become an expert. Students with the same topics meet in expert groups to discuss them, after which they return to their teams to teach what they have learned to their teammates. Then students take individual quizzes, which result in team scores based on the improvement score system of STAD. Teams that meet preset standards earn certificates. Jigsaw is primarily used in social studies and other subjects where learning from text is important.

Learning Together. David Johnson and Roger Johnson at the University of Minnesota developed the Learning Together models of cooperative learning (Johnson and Johnson 1987). The methods they have researched involve students working on assignment sheets in four- or five-member heterogeneous groups. The groups hand in a single sheet and receive praise and rewards based on the group product. Their methods emphasize team-building activities before students

begin working together and regular discussions within groups about how well they are working together.

Group Investigation. Group Investigation, developed by Shlomo Sharan and Yael Sharan at the University of Tel-Aviv, is a general classroom organization plan in which students work in small groups using cooperative inquiry, group discussion, and cooperative planning and projects (Sharan and Sharan 1976). In this method, students form their own two- to six-member groups. After choosing subtopics from a unit being studied by the entire class, the groups further break their subtopics into individual tasks and carry out the activities necessary to prepare group reports. Each group then makes a presentation or display to communicate its findings to the entire class.

RESEARCH ON COOPERATIVE LEARNING

Cooperative learning methods are among the most extensively evaluated alternatives to traditional instruction in use today. Outcome evaluations include:

— academic achievement,
— intergroup relations,
— mainstreaming,
— self-esteem,
— others.

Academic Achievement. More than 70 high-quality studies have evaluated various cooperative learning methods over periods of at least four weeks in regular elementary and secondary schools; 67 of these have measured effects on student achievement (see Slavin 1990). All these studies compared the effects of cooperative learning to those of traditionally taught control groups on measures of the same objectives pursued in all classes. Teachers and classes were either randomly assigned to cooperative or control conditions or matched on pretest achievement level and other factors.

Overall, of 67 studies of the achievement effects of cooperative learning, 41 (61 percent) found significantly greater achievement in cooperative than in control classes. Twenty-five (37 percent) found no differences, and in only one study did the control group outperform the experimental group. However, the effects of cooperative learning vary considerably according to the particular methods used. As noted earlier, two elements must be present if cooperative learning is to be effective: *group goals* and *individual accountability* (Slavin 1983a, 1983b, 1990). That is, groups must be working to achieve some goal or to earn rewards or recognition, and the success of the group must depend on the individual learning of every group member.

In studies of methods such as STAD, TGT, TAI, and CIRC, effects on achievement have been consistently positive; 37 out of 44 such studies (84 percent) found significant positive achievement effects. In contrast, only 4 of 23 studies (17 percent) lacking group goals and individual accountability found positive effects on student achievement. Two of these positive effects were found in studies of Group Investigation in Israel (Sharan et al. 1984; Sharan and Shachar 1988). In Group Investigation, students in each group are responsible for one unique part of the group's overall task, ensuring individual accountability. Then the group's overall performance is evaluated. Even though there are no specific group rewards, the group evaluation probably serves the same purpose.

Why are group goals and individual accountability so important? To understand this, consider the alternatives. In some forms of cooperative learning, students work together to complete a single worksheet or to solve one problem together. In such methods, there is little reason for more able students to take time to explain what is going on to their less able groupmates or to ask their opinions. When the group task is to *do* something, rather than to *learn* something, the participation of less able students may be seen as interference rather than help. It may be easier in this circumstance for students to give each other answers than to explain concepts or skills to one another.

In contrast, when the group's task is to ensure that every group member *learns* something, it is in the interests of every group member to spend time explaining concepts to his or her groupmates. Studies of students' behaviors within cooperative groups have consistently found that the students who gain most from cooperative work are those who give and receive elaborated explanations (Webb 1985). In contrast, Webb found that giving and receiving answers without explanations were *negatively* related to achievement gain. What group goals and individual accountability do is to motivate students to give explanations and to take one another's learning seriously, instead of simply giving answers.

Cooperative learning methods generally work equally well for all types of students. While occasional studies find particular advantages of high or low achievers, boys or girls, and so on, the great majority find equal benefits for all types of students. Sometimes teachers or parents worry that cooperative learning will hold back high achievers. The research provides absolutely no support for this claim; high achievers gain from cooperative learning (relative to high achievers in traditional classes) just as much as do low and average achievers (see Slavin, this issue, p. 63).

Research on the achievement effects of cooperative learning has more often taken place in grades 3–9 than 10–12. Studies at the senior high school level are about as positive as those at earlier grade levels, but there is a need for more research at that level. Cooperative learning methods have been equally successful in urban, rural, and suburban schools and with students of different ethnic groups (although a few studies have found particularly positive effects for black students; see Slavin and Oickle 1981).

Among the cooperative learning methods, the Student Team Learning programs have been most extensively researched and most often found instructionally effective. Of 14 studies of STAD and closely related methods, 11 found significantly higher achievement for this method than for traditional instruction, and two found no differences. For example, Slavin and Karweit (1984) evaluated STAD over an entire school year in inner-city Philadelphia 9th grade mathematics classes. Student performance on a standardized mathematics test increased significantly more than in either a mastery learning group or a control group using the same materials. Substantial differences favoring STAD have been found in such diverse subjects as social studies (e.g., Allen and Van Sickle 1984), language arts (Slavin and Karweit 1981), reading comprehension (Stevens, Slavin, Farnish, and Madden 1988), mathematics (Sherman and Thomas 1986), and science (Okebukola 1985). Nine of 11 studies of TGT found similar results (DeVries and Slavin 1978).

The largest effects of Student Team Learning methods have been found in studies of TAI. Five of six studies found substantially greater learning of mathematics computations in TAI than in control classes, while one study found no differences (see Slavin 1985b). Experimental control differences were still substantial (though smaller) a year after the students were in TAI (Slavin and Karweit 1985). In mathematics concepts and applications, one of three studies (Slavin et al. 1984) found significantly greater gains in TAI than control methods, while two found no significant differences (Slavin and Karweit 1985).

In comparison with traditional control groups, three experimental studies of CIRC have found substantial positive effects on scores from standardized tests of reading comprehension, reading vocabulary, language expression, language mechanics, and spelling (Madden et al. 1986, Stevens et al. 1987, Stevens et al. 1990). Significantly greater achievement on writing samples was also found favoring the CIRC students in the two studies which assessed writing.

Other than STL methods, the most consistently successful model for increasing student achievement is Group Investigation (Sharan and Sharan 1976). One study of this method (Sharan et al. 1984) found that it increased the learning of English as a foreign language, while Sharan and Shachar (1988) found positive effects of Group Investigation on the learning of history and geography. A third study of only three weeks' duration (Sharan et al. 1980) also found positive effects on social studies achievement, particularly on higher-level concepts. The Learning Together methods (Johnson and Johnson 1987) have been found instructionally effective when they include the assignment of group grades based on the average of group members' individual quiz scores (e.g., Humphreys et al. 1982, Yager et al. 1985). Studies of the original Jigsaw method have not generally supported this approach (e.g., Moskowitz et al. 1983); but studies of Jigsaw II, which uses group goals and individual accountability, have shown positive effects (Mattingly and VanSickle 1990, Ziegler 1981).

Intergroup Relations. In the laboratory research on cooperation, one of the earliest and strongest findings was that people who cooperate learn to like one another (Slavin 1977b). Not surprisingly, the cooperative learning classroom studies have found quite consistently that students express greater liking for their classmates in general as a result of participating in a cooperative learning method (see Slavin 1983a, 1990). This is important in itself and even more important when the students have different ethnic backgrounds. After all, there is substantial evidence that, left alone, ethnic separateness in schools does not naturally diminish over time (Gerard and Miller 1975).

Social scientists have long advocated interethnic cooperation as a means of ensuring positive intergroup relations in desegregated settings. Contact Theory (Allport 1954), which is in the U.S. the dominant theory of intergroup relations, predicted that positive intergroup relations would arise from school desegregation if and only if students participated in cooperative, equal-status interaction sanctioned by the school. Research on cooperative learning methods has borne out the predictions of Contact Theory. These techniques emphasize cooperative, equal-status interaction between students of different ethnic backgrounds sanctioned by the school (Slavin 1985a).

In most of the research on intergroup relations, students were asked to list their best friends at the beginning of the study and again at the end. The number of friendship choices students made outside their own ethnic groups was the measure of intergroup relations.

Positive effects on intergroup relations have been found for STAD, TGT, TAI, Jigsaw, Learning Together, and Group Investigation models (Slavin 1985b). Two of these studies, one on STAD (Slavin 1979) and one on Jigsaw II (Ziegler 1981), included follow-ups of intergroup friendships several months after the end of the studies. Both found that students who had been in cooperative learning classes still named significantly more friends outside their own ethnic groups than did students who had been in control classes. Two studies of Group Investigation (Sharan et al. 1984, Sharan and Shachar 1988) found that students' improved attitudes and behaviors toward classmates of different ethnic backgrounds extended to classmates who had never been in the same groups, and a study of TAI (Oishi 1983) found positive effects of this method on cross-ethnic interactions outside as well as in class. The U.S. studies of cooperative learning and intergroup relations involved black, white, and (in a few cases) Mexican-American students. A study of Jigsaw II by Ziegler (1981) took place in Toronto, where the major ethnic groups were Anglo-Canadians and children of recent European immigrants. The Sharan (Sharan et al. 1984, Sharan and Shachar 1988) studies of Group Investigation took place in Israel and involved friendships between Jews of both European and Middle Eastern backgrounds.

Mainstreaming.   Although ethnicity is a major barrier to friendship, it is not so large as the one between physically or mentally handicapped children and their normal-progress peers. Mainstreaming, an unprecedented opportunity for handicapped children to take their place in the school and society, has created enormous practical problems for classroom teachers, and it often leads to social rejection of the handicapped children. Because cooperative learning methods have been successful in improving relationships across the ethnicity barrier—which somewhat resembles the barrier between mainstreamed and normal-progress students—these methods have also been applied to increase the acceptance of the mainstreamed student.

The research on cooperative learning and mainstreaming has focused on the academically handicapped child. In one study, STAD was used to attempt to integrate students performing two years or more below the level of their peers into the social structure of the classroom. The use of STAD significantly reduced the degree to which the normal-progress students rejected their mainstreamed classmates and increased the academic achievement and self-esteem of all students, mainstreamed as well as normal-progress (Madden and Slavin 1983). Similar effects have been found for TAI (Slavin et al. 1984), and other research using cooperative teams has also shown significant improvements in relationships between mainstreamed academically handicapped students and their normal-progress peers (Ballard et al. 1977, Cooper et al. 1980).

In addition, one study in a self-contained school for emotionally disturbed adolescents found that the use of TGT increased positive interactions and friendships among students (Slavin 1977a). Five months after the study ended, these positive interactions were still found more often in the former TGT classes than in the control classes. In a study in a similar setting, Janke (1978) found that the emotionally disturbed students were more on-task, were better behaved, and had better attendance in TGT classes than in control classes.

Self-Esteem.   One of the most important aspects of a child's personality is his or her self esteem. Several researchers working on cooperative learning techniques have found that these methods do increase students' self-esteem. These improvements in self-esteem have been found for TGT and STAD (Slavin 1990), for Jigsaw (Blaney et al. 1977), and for the three methods combined (Slavin and Karweit 1981). Improvements in student self-concepts have also been found for TAI (Slavin et al. 1984).

Other Outcomes. In addition to effects on achievement, positive intergroup relations, greater acceptance of mainstreamed students, and self-esteem, effects of cooperative learning have been found on a variety of other important educational outcomes. These include liking school, development of peer norms in favor of doing well academically, feelings of individual control over the student's own fate in school, and cooperativeness and altruism (see Slavin 1983a, 1990). TGT (DeVries and Slavin 1978) and STAD (Slavin 1978, Janke 1978) have been found to have positive effects on students' time-on-task. One study found that lower socioeconomic status students at risk of becoming delinquent who worked in cooperative groups in 6th grade had better attendance, fewer contacts with the police, and higher behavioral ratings by teachers in grades 7–11 than did control students (Hartley 1976). Another study implemented forms of cooperative learning beginning in kindergarten and continuing through the 4th grade (Solomon et al. 1990). This study found that the students who had been taught cooperatively were significantly higher than control students on measures of supportive, friendly, and prosocial behavior; were better at resolving conflicts; and expressed more support for democratic values.

CONCLUSION

Returning to the questions at the beginning of this article, we now see the usefulness of cooperative learning strategies for improving such diverse outcomes as student achievement at a variety of grade levels and in many subjects, intergroup relations, relationships between mainstreamed and normal-progress students, and student self-esteem. Further, their widespread and growing use demonstrates that cooperative learning methods are practical and attractive to teachers. The history of the development, evaluation, and dissemination of cooperative learning is an outstanding example of the use of educational research to create programs that have improved the educational experience of thousands of students and will continue to affect thousands more.

ENDNOTE

Author's note. This article was written under funding from the Office of Educational Research and Improvement, U.S. Department of Education (Grant No. OERI-R-117-R90002). However, any opinions expressed are mine and do not represent OERI positions or policy.

REFERENCES

Allen, W. H., and R. L. Van Sickle. (1984). "Learning Teams and Low Achievers." *Social Education:* 60–64.

Allport, G. (1954). *The Nature of Prejudice.* Cambridge, Mass.: Addison-Wesley.

Aronson, E., N. Blaney, C. Stephan, J. Sikes, and M. Snapp. (1978). *The Jigsaw Classroom.* Beverly Hills, Calif: Sage.

Ballard, M., L. Corman, J. Gottlieb, and M. Kauffman. (1977). "Improving the Social Status of Mainstreamed Retarded Children." *Journal of Educational Psychology* 69: 605–611.

Blaney, N. T., S. Stephan, D. Rosenfeld, E. Aronson, and J. Sikes. (1977). "Interdependence in the Classroom: A Field Study." *Journal of Educational Psychology* 69: 121–128.

Cooper, L., D. W. Johnson, R. Johnson, and F. Wilderson. (1980). "Effects of Cooperative, Competitive, and Individualistic Experiences on Interpersonal Attraction Among Heterogeneous Peers." *Journal of Social Psychology* 111: 243–252.

Deutsch, M. (1949). "A Theory of Cooperation and Competition." *Human Relations* 2: 129–152.

DeVries, D. L., and R. E. Slavin. (1978). "Teams-Games-Tournament (TGT): Review of Ten Classroom Experiments." *Journal of Research and Development in Education* 12: 28–38.

Gerard, H. B., and N. Miller. (1975). *School Desegregation: A Long-Range Study.* New York: Plenum.

Hartley, W. (1976). *Prevention Outcomes of Small Group Education with School Children: An Epidemiologic Follow-Up of the Kansas City School Behavior Project.* Kansas City: University of Kansas Medical Center.

Humphreys, B., R. Johnson, and D. W. Johnson. (1982). "Effects of Cooperative, Competitive, and Individualistic Learning on Students' Achievement in Science Class." *Journal of Research in Science Teaching* 19: 351–356.

Janke, R. (April 1978). "The Teams-Games-Tournament (TGT) Method and the Behavioral Adjustment and Academic Achievement of Emotionally Impaired Adolescents." Paper presented at the annual convention of the American Educational Research Association, Toronto.

Johnson, D. W., and R. T. Johnson. (1987). *Learning Together and Alone.* 2nd ed. Englewood Cliffs, N.J.: Prentice-Hall.

Madden, N. A., and R. E. Slavin. (1983). "Cooperative Learning and Social Acceptance of Mainstreamed Academically Handicapped Students." *Journal of Special Education* 17: 171–182.

Madden, N. A., R. J. Stevens, and R. E. Slavin. (1986). *A Comprehensive Cooperative Learning Approach to Elementary Reading and Writing: Effects on Student Achievement.* Report No. 2. Baltimore, Md.: Center for Research on Elementary and Middle Schools, Johns Hopkins University.

Mattingly, R. M., and R. L. VanSickle. (1990). *Jigsaw II in Secondary Social Studies: An Experiment.* Athens, Ga.: University of Georgia.

Moskowitz, J. M., J. H. Malvin, G. A. Schaeffer, and E. Schaps. (1983). "Evaluation of a Cooperative Learning Strategy." *American Educational Research Journal* 20: 687–696.

Oishi, S. (1983). "Effects of Team-Assisted Individualization in Mathematics on Cross-Race Interactions of Elementary School Children." Doctoral diss., University of Maryland.

Okebukola, P. A. (1985). "The Relative Effectiveness of Cooperative and Competitive Interaction Techniques in Strengthening Students' Performance in Science Classes." *Science Education* 69: 501–509.

Sharan, S., and C. Shachar. (1988). *Language and Learning in the Cooperative Classroom.* New York: Springer.

Sharan, S., and Y. Sharan. (1976). *Small-group Teaching.* Englewood Cliffs, N.J.: Educational Technology Publications.

Sharan, S., R. Hertz-Lazarowitz, and Z. Ackerman. (1980). "Academic Achievement of Elementary School Children in Small-group vs. Whole Class Instruction." *Journal of Experimental Education* 48: 125–129.

Sharan, S., P. Kussell, R. Hertz-Lazarowitz, Y. Bejarano, S. Raviv, and Y. Sharan. (1984). *Cooperative Learning in the Classroom: Research in Desegregated Schools.* Hillsdale, N.J.: Erlbaum.

Sherman, L. W., and M. Thomas. (1986). "Mathematics Achievement in Cooperative Versus Individualistic Goal-structured High School Classrooms." *Journal of Educational Research* 79: 169–172.

Slavin, R. E. (1977a). "A Student Team Approach to Teaching Adolescents with Special Emotional and Behavioral Needs." *Psychology in The Schools* 14: 77–84.

Slavin, R. E. (1977b). "Classroom Reward Structure: An Analytical and Practical Review." *Review of Educational Research* 47: 633–650.

Slavin, R. E. (1978). "Student Teams and Achievement Divisions." *Journal of Research and Development in Education* 12: 39–49.

Slavin, R. E. (1979). "Effects of Biracial Learning Teams on Cross-Racial Friendships." *Journal of Educational Psychology* 71: 381–387.

Slavin, R. E. (1983a). *Cooperative Learning.* New York: Longman.

Slavin, R. E. (1983b). "When Does Cooperative Learning Increase Student Achievement?" *Psychological Bulletin* 94: 429–445.

Slavin, R. E. (March 1985a). "Cooperative Learning: Applying Contact Theory in Desegregated Schools." *Journal of Social Issues* 41: 45–62.

Slavin, R. E. (1985b). "Team Assisted Individualization: A Cooperative Learning Solution for Adaptive Instruction in Mathematics." In *Adapting Instruction to Individual Differences,* edited by M. Wang and H. Walberg. Berkeley, Calif.: McCutchan.

Slavin, R. E. (1986). *Using Student Team Learning.* 3rd ed. Baltimore, Md.: Center for Research on Elementary and Middle Schools, Johns Hopkins University.

Slavin, R. E. (1990). *Cooperative Learning: Theory, Research, and Practice.* Englewood Cliffs, N.J.: Prentice-Hall.

Slavin, R. E. (February 1991). "Are Cooperative Learning and 'Untracking' Harmful to the Gifted?" *Educational Leadership* 48: 63–74.

Slavin, R. E., and N. Karweit. (1981). "Cognitive and Affective Outcomes of an Intensive Student Team Learning Experience." *Journal of Experimental Education* 50: 29–35.

Slavin, R. E., and N. Karweit. (1984). "Mastery Learning and Student Teams: A Factorial Experiment in Urban General Mathematics Classes." *American Educational Research Journal* 21: 725–736.

Slavin, R. E., and N. L. Karweit. (1985). "Effects of Whole-Class, Ability Grouped, and Individualized Instruction on Mathematics Achievement." *American Educational Research Journal* 22: 351–367.

Slavin, R. E., M. Leavey, and N. A. Madden. (1984). "Combining Cooperative Learning and Individualized Instruction: Effects on Student Mathematics Achievement Attitudes and Behaviors." *Elementary School Journal* 84: 409–422.

Slavin, R. E., M. B. Leavey, and N. A. Madden. (1986). *Team Accelerated Instruction-Mathematics.* Watertown, Mass.: Mastery Education Corporation.

Slavin, R. E., N. A. Madden, and M. B. Leavey. (1984). "Effects of Team Assisted Individualization on the Mathematics Achievement of Academically Handicapped and Nonhandicapped Students." *Journal of Educational Psychology* 76: 813–819.

Slavin, R. E., and E. Oickle. (1981). "Effects of Cooperative Learning Teams on Student Achievement and Race Relations: Treatment x Race Interactions." *Sociology of Education* 54: 174–180.

Solomon, D., M. Watson, E. Schaps, V. Battistich, and J. Solomon. (1990). "Cooperative Learning as Part of a Comprehensive Classroom Program Designed to Promote Prosocial Development." In *Current Research on Cooperative Learning,* edited by S. Sharan, New York: Praeger.

Stevens, R. J., N. A. Madden, R. E. Slavin, and A. M. Farnish. (1987). "Cooperative Integrated Reading and Composition: Two Field Experiments." *Reading Research Quarterly* 22: 433–454.

Stevens, R. J., R. E. Slavin, and A. M. Farnish. (April 1990). "A Cooperative Learning Approach to Elementary Reading and Writing Instruction: Long-Term Effects." Paper presented at the annual convention of the American Educational Research Association, Boston.

Stevens, R. J., R. E. Slavin, A. M. Farnish, and N. A. Madden. (April 1988). "The Effects of Cooperative Learning and Direct Instruction in Reading Comprehension Strategies on Main Idea Identification." Paper presented at the annual convention of the American Educational Research Association, New Orleans.

Webb, N. (1985), "Student Interaction and Learning in Small Groups: A Research Summary." In *Learning to Cooperate, Cooperating to Learn,* edited by R. Slavin, S. Sharan, S. Kagan, R. Hertz-Lazarowitz, C. Webb, and R. Schmuck. New York: Plenum.

Yager, S., D. W. Johnson, and R. T. Johnson. (1985). "Oral Discussion, Group-to-Individual Transfer, and Achievement in Cooperative Learning Groups." *Journal of Educational Psychology* 77: 60–66.

Ziegler, S. (1981). "The Effectiveness of Cooperative Learning Teams for Increasing Cross-Ethnic Friendship: Additional Evidence." *Human Organization* 40: 264–268.

DISCUSSION QUESTIONS

1. What are the pros and cons of the cooperative learning strategies?

2. Which approaches have been most successful in enhancing student achievement?

3. How does the cooperative learning model differ from conventional teaching methods, generative teaching, and explicit instruction?

4. Should cooperative learning models be used with special needs students?

5. What are the advantages and disadvantages of implementing the cooperative learning models during the process of mainstreaming?

18

Standards, Not Standardization: Evoking Quality Student Work

GRANT WIGGINS

FOCUSING QUESTIONS

1. *What distinguishes standards from standardization?*
2. *What are authentic standards?*
3. *What are the implicit strengths and weaknesses of using standards as a method of assessment?*
4. *What factors should teachers and administrators think about when formulating consistent criteria for grading?*
5. *How can standards be used to empower students?*

What would you picture if I asked you to imagine a person of high intellectual standards? Surely not someone who merely earned good grades or scored well on tests. The term *standards* implies a passion for excellence and habitual attention to quality. A school has standards when it has high and consistent expectations of *all* learners in *all* courses. High standards, whether in people or institutions, are revealed through reliability, integrity, self-discipline, passion, and craftsmanship.

Alas, it is thus not too strong to say that many schools exhibit no standards. Imagine, for example, going to a diving meet where the judges alter their standards from dive to dive based on each diver's background, "track," or effort. Further imagine that they do not agree as to what constitutes a well-executed dive nor about the difficulty of the dive—and feel no obligation to agree. This would be intolerable at any high school diving meet in America; in classrooms everywhere it is business as usual.

The solution is not to mandate a few paper-and-pencil "items" on diving that can be "objec-tively" scored. Standards have nothing to do with standardized proxy tests and arbitrary cutoff scores. Standards are educative, *specific* examples of excellence on the tasks we value: the four-minute mile is a usable standard as well as a genuine one; so is the ability to read and effectively cite articles in the *New York Times*. Standards are upheld by the daily, local demand for quality and consistency at the tasks we deem important; standards are met by rigorous evaluation of *necessarily varied* student products and performances against those standards.

The only way to improve schools, therefore, is to ensure that faculties judge local work using authentic standards and measures. We need concrete benchmarks for judging student work at essential tasks, and we need to feel duty-bound by the results if they are unsatisfactory. That means meeting *self-imposed targets* relating to the quality of work expected from *all* students, not just those in advanced classes. And it means doing away with the current extremes of private, eccentric teacher grading, on the one hand; and secure, standardized tests composed of simplistic items on the other: in both cases we prevent students and teachers from understanding intellectual excellence and raising their own standards.

WHAT IS A "STANDARD"?

There are different meanings to the word *standard,* and we would do well to clarify them. When used in the singular to describe human accomplishment, a "standard" is an exemplary performance serving as a benchmark. The music of Yo-Yo Ma and Wynton Marsalis each sets a standard for other musicians; the fiction of Tom Wolfe and Mark Twain each sets a standard for American writers. These standards are educative and enticing: they provide not only models for young musicians or writers but a set of implicit criteria against which to measure their own achievement. Progress involves successive approximations in the direction of the exemplary.

But there is no single model of excellence; there are always a variety of exemplars to emulate. Excellence is not a mere uniform correctness but the ability to unite personal style with mastery of a subject in a product or performance of one's design. There is thus no possible generic test of whether student work is "up to standard." Rather, the "test" of excellence amounts to applying a set of *criteria* that we infer from various idiosyncratic excellent performances, in the judging of *diverse* forms of local student work.

Here we see where American education has gone so wrong: we have uniformity in testing, but no exemplars; we have standardization of *input*—the items on the test—but no standards for judging the quality of all student *output*—performance on authentic tasks. We have cutoff scores, but no way of ensuring that scores correspond to qualitative distinctions in real-world performance—authentic standards. By over-relying on these audits of performance, our students are just as the Resnicks declared: the most tested but the least examined in the world.[1] Or we devise standards that offer only vague statement of value or intent, providing neither exemplars of them nor insight into how the standard might be met.[2]

The greatest harm of these proxy tests and standards is their reliance on secrecy. People improve—that is, raise their own standards—by judging all their work against the exemplary performances that set the standard and by valuing the performances in question. But if test validity depends upon secure tests with seemingly arbitrary standards, how will students and teachers improve their performance?

Nor are we likely to meet a standard if it isn't used to judge our work when we are young. Giving grades only according to age-related norms prevents students from knowing where they stand in terms of genuine excellence. Why don't districts publish the best teacher assessments and student products at all grades? How can a 3rd grade teacher of reading demand excellence without knowing what 6th grade students are routinely expected to produce in our best schools? Why don't middle school social studies teachers routinely use the questions and rubrics on Advanced Placement history essays for practice—just as the basketball or music coach uses genuine exemplars to improve the performance and raise the sights of student performers?

It makes no sense, therefore, to talk of different standards and expectations for different groups of students. A standard offers an objective ideal, serving as a worthy and tangible goal for everyone—even if, at this point in time, for whatever reason, some cannot (yet!) reach it. Watch kids play basketball, Nintendo, or the keyboard. They are making measurable progress toward meeting the high standard set by the best performers before them. Our task in assessment is to similarly provide students with a record of the longitudinal progress they make in emulating a standard. (We can still give age-cohort letter grades in addition, so that useful comparisons might be made if that seems desirable; and we might set targets whereby students who are far from meeting standards would have some guideposts along the way to judge the quality of their progress.)

Eight decades ago, Thorndike called for evaluation that would compare student work to standards instead of to each other's work.[3] We are no closer to it, but the British have developed such a scoring system for their new national assessment.[4] Student work would be judged on a 10-point scale built from a standard of exit-level excellence and used *over the course of the student's career.* Thus, elementary students are expected to produce good work (in the sense of norms for one's age-group), but the best work would likely receive a 3 or 4 out of 10. No stigma to low scores here: the point is to give students a realistic sense of where they are in terms of where they ultimately need to be. A smaller-scale effort is under way in Upper Arlington, Ohio, where language arts teachers are scoring all work across the K-3 grades using the same rubrics and locally devised reading tests that use real books deemed worthy by the faculties of those schools.

I remain mystified by the view that such a system would be debilitating to the less able, thus increasing the drop-out rate. If such a view were true, no novice would persevere at any challenging task—where initial failure is *unavoidable.* We persist with music, debate, soccer, or computer games because we perceive value in the challenge. We see models of those before us who prove it can be done well, and there is a record of our slow but tangible progress toward a standard we can be proud of.

Standards are thus not abstract aims, wishful thinking, or the effect of arcane psychometric tricks. They are *specific* and guiding pictures of worthy goals. Real standards enable all performers to understand their *daily* work in terms of specific exemplars for the work in progress, and thus how to monitor and raise their standards.[5] We are losing the standards battle because faculties assume that the only tests that matter are the secure ones over which they have no control and about which they know far too little to adjust *their* standards. Without high-quality local assessment, by which faculties gain control over the setting and upholding of standards, site-based management of schools may turn out to be an empty promise or a cruel hoax.

STANDARDS AS INTELLECTUAL VIRTUES

If a *standard* is an exemplar, the plural form, *standards,* means something quite different. When we speak of persons or institutions with standards—especially when modified by the word *high*—we mean they live by a set of mature, coherent, and consistently applied values evident in all their actions. Ultimately, mastery of a subject and autonomy as a thinker are completely dependent on such virtues: our work will be "up to standard" only if we work to high standards in all we do. Higher standards are not stiffer test-result quotas but a more vigorous commitment to intellectual values upheld consistently and daily in the face of entropy, fatalism, and the occasional desire on everyone's part to not give a damn.

A harmful consequence of multiple-choice tests, therefore, comes from their exclusive concern with mere right answers. High standards are only to be found in completed tasks, products, and performances that *require* such intellectual virtues as craftsmanship, self-criticism, and persistence; when complex tasks are done consistently well, we easily and validly infer that the worker has high standards. By requiring only a circling of an already formed answer to a simplistic question, our tests cannot reveal anything about student intellectual virtues or vices. And worse, such tests may be abetting the very vices we deplore: students learn to quickly go through each test item without lingering too long on any one, and they learn that being right matters a great deal more than whether one can justify a result.

Unless we recapture this view of standards as intellectual virtues, we will fail to see the harm of linking standards to cutoff scores on sets of test items, given to students once a year on a rigid schedule. We now wrongly chastise the merely slow, thus confusing learning speeds with standards. Is a 5th grader reading at a 3rd grade level necessarily working in a substandard way? Our state and national testing assumes so. But what of the bright 5th grader who writes at the 7th grade level, yet who regularly produces substandard work in class—absence of precision, style, thoroughness, and so forth? Our tests overvalue their right answers and underexamine the quality of work they can produce—*given* the material they have mastered to this point in time.

Virtues are habits, reinforced or undermined by what is valued daily at the local level. If we are serious about raising standards, therefore, we need to look where few would-be reformers have the patience to look: in the grading policies, criteria, and standards used in judging (and thus reinforcing) student performance. Here is where we find *de facto* standards, irrespective of professed values: are grades and comments routinely sending the message that diligence, craft, insight, and "voice" matter? Or do teacher evaluations routinely focus only on the mistakes easiest to count (such as spelling, computation, or correctable errors of fact) or on "student attitude"—neither of which have much to do with work that meets high standards? Are there shared teacher exemplars and criteria for assessing student performance? Are teachers consistent in their grading—as individuals and across teachers? Clearly not, on all counts.

Large-scale performance assessment is no better. On even the best state writing tests, the prompts are woefully generic and devoid of links to curriculum, to high-quality tasks. The anchor papers used in statewide writing assessments may be the best of the batch, but not necessarily the highest quality. By comparing only 8th grade work to itself and by using rubrics that rely heavily on general, comparative language (*excellent, good,* and *poor* show up frequently in the scoring descriptors), we end up with merely a fancy norm-referenced test.

To develop scoring criteria linked to real exemplars, "testers have to get out of their offices . . . and into the field where they actually analyze performance into its components."[6] The foreign language proficiency guidelines of the American Council on the Teaching of Foreign Languages show what such a system would entail. There, the scores reflect significant and specific strengths and weaknesses about the speaker's performance.

The guidelines go so far as to identify typical errors for each stage of language performance. For example, the mistake of responding to the question *Quel sport preferez-vous?* with the answer *Vous preferez le sport tennis* is noted as "an error characteristic of speakers" at the mid-novice level, where "utterances are marked and often flawed by repetition of an interlocutor's words . . . "[7] These are the kinds of standards that need to be developed in all subjects.[8]

STANDARDS AS CONSISTENCY AND QUALITY CONTROL

To speak of exemplars and intellectual virtues is still to think of standards in terms of the individual student. But if we are to obtain better quality from schools, we are going to have to challenge the current low expectations for all students in a course, age-cohort, and entire school population.

A quality school is not judged by the work of its best students or its average performance. An exemplary school is one in which the gap between its best and its worst student performances is approaching zero or at least far narrower than the norm. In quality organizations there is a team ethos: our performance is only as good as our weakest members—a far cry from schools, where tracking often institutionalizes low expectations and exaggerates differences.

Standard-setting in schools thus begins with specific targets and public plans to reduce performance differences by school subgroups—track, socioeconomic status, gender, courses, and departments—to near zero, over a set period of time. Otherwise we remain imprisoned in the low (and sometimes racist) expectations that doom schools to mediocrity and students in lower tracks to an alienated intellectual life.

It is also essential to ensure that all students are judged at the same standards of performance, regardless of tracking or special needs, if we are to have any handle on a school's overall performance. Again, such standards are concrete: one superintendent argued that since we profess that "all children can learn," it makes sense to expect

100 percent of the students in her New York district to pass the Regents Exams in every course. This was greeted with howls of protest by the high school faculty, who pronounced it impossible. She then turned it right around: What, then, was the faculty willing to set as a specific target percentage for next year? After some discussion the faculty set themselves the goal of a passing rate some 11 percent higher for the year than preceding years—and proceeded to meet the target. South Carolina did the same when it quadrupled the number of students taking Advanced Placement courses and tests and successfully sought to keep the state passing rate constant.

Our grading system actually encourages teachers and administrators to avoid such considerations. That is not a slur: I am talking about the absence of specific policies for judging and adjusting school and teacher performance by the performance of cohorts of students. Few teachers and administrators are compelled now to answer the questions: What are you willing to guarantee? What exit-level results for the cohort will you regard as "up to standard"? Effective reform begins with such self-obligating standards. But if we lack tests with face validity or standards for judging exit-level performance (as almost all schools do), we will be unable to pose, never mind act on, the questions. If we want to see greater consistency in student performance, we have to begin by meeting a more basic, prior standard: consistency of grading by teachers. We need to begin from the commonsense view of standards that grades should represent a stable set of shared exemplars. School performance would improve overnight if superintendents and school boards said something like: "We do not feel it is our place to tell you how to assess student work, but we expect different teachers to agree on grading policies and to agree on the grade for a given piece of work within a tolerable standard. Please devise such a policy and uphold it." It would follow that districts should devise standards for the *tolerable variance in the grading of student work across teachers, departments, schools, and districts where the same papers are scored by different teachers*. In fact, to gain public credibility for local assessing, faculties must periodically seek and publish audits of their own grading practices.

STANDARDS AND QUALITY

To meet standards is not merely to comply with imposed quotas. It is to produce work that one can be proud of; it is to produce quality.

We do not judge Xerox, the Boston Symphony, the Cincinnati Reds, or Dom Perignon vineyards on the basis of indirect, easy to test, and common indicators. Nor would the workers in those places likely produce quality if some generic, secure test served as the only measure of their success in meeting a standard. Demanding *and getting* quality, whether from students or adult workers, means framing standards in terms of the work that we undertake and value. And it means framing expectations about that work which make quality a necessity, not an option. Consider:

— the English teacher who instructs peer-editors to mark the place in a student paper where they lost interest in it or found it slapdash and to hand it back for revision at that point;
— the professor who demands that all math homework be turned in with another student having signed off on it, where one earns the grade for one's work *and* the grade for the work that each person (willingly!) countersigned;
— the social studies teacher of 6th graders who demands a book report that is "perfect" in execution. We might quibble with what *perfect* means here, but the kids understand. They drop business-as-usual, blasé, behavior. They scurry and scramble for help—from each other and other adults. They double-check spelling and facts. They make the prose interesting. And students who typically turn in substandard work find to their delight that they can produce excellent work.

Until we send the message, from day one in each classroom, that quality matters and that work will be rejected unless and until it is up to standard, then students will know we do not require excellence. Why don't we routinely require poorly done work to be resubmitted in acceptable form? Why don't standards for passing grades require the student to have produced at least *some* quality products (thus undoing the harm to quality caused by computing only averages that do not reveal shoddy, inconsistent work)? Though many of the Mastery Learning and Outcome-Based Education programs have been plagued by poor-quality assessment tasks and exemplars, the guiding ideas remain sound and need to be emulated: by requiring students to work until standards are met, we teach students and teachers that work is not done until it is done right. Too many students learn now that work is satisfactory if they merely followed the directions and turned something in.

The key to any quality control is to avoid substandard work *before* it happens, before the final "test." The aim is to adjust our practices *before* it is too late to avoid substandard performance: this is true for teachers as well as students. When we operate in a school system with authentic standards, we do not wait for year-end results on external audit-tests, nor grade work in a vacuum. We routinely alter syllabi, teaching methods, schedules, and policies as necessary to *ensure* that students end up meeting the standard.

Since quality is a function of being dissatisfied with our work to the point of revising it until it is excellent, it is absurd to use only tests that cannot be known in advance or retaken because their validity is compromised, whether they be externally or internally designed tests. Quality emerges only when we are held to higher and higher standards on essential "tests" of performance. How else will students learn that we are serious about the virtues such as persistence and craftsmanship that we claim to value unless important tasks keep recurring?

Assessment that effectively improves performance is ultimately inseparable from accurate self-assessment, therefore impossible, if the only standards come from secure, one-shot tests. Us-

ing explicit benchmarks and criteria, we should routinely assess the student's self-assessments in the upper grades if we want to ensure that they are capable of independently producing quality work.

Intellectual excellence is not about conformity or uniformity of views but of conformity of all kinds of work to high standards. Think of the ultimate educational test: the graduate thesis and orals. We expect high-quality written and oral performance on what must always be a unique challenge. Other countries use local and diverse assessment for accountability at the school level.[9] In German *gymnasia* each teacher designs his or her own oral and written exams for the *Abitur* and has the exam approved by a regional board; in England, candidates for the secondary certificate (GCSE) submit individualized portfolios for scoring according to standard criteria. Similarly, on the Advanced Placement art portfolio exam in this country, the student submits a variety of work to be judged according to fixed criteria.

OUTPUT, NOT INPUT

The standards question is ultimately twofold: What are the essential tasks worth mastering? And how good is good *enough* at those tasks? The former question concerns the quality of the *input*—the work we give to students to do. The second question concerns *output*—what are the criteria student work must meet, and how demanding should the standard be?

But many people assume that a good answer to the first question will solve the problem of the second question. A better curriculum and better tests will surely help raise standards.[10] But while necessary, such improvements are not sufficient to obtain excellent student performance. Putting Yugo assembly-line workers in a Mercedes plant will not necessarily yield quality cars. Some of our alternative schools, for example, involve students in authentic and engaging tasks; but because work is not compared to exemplars and the criteria used in assessing may involve no more than the student's good-faith effort, the results are often not of high quality.

The view that only high-quality curriculums can yield high-quality work is more than myopic. It is pernicious because it leads to the truly undemocratic and dysfunctional view that students taking low-level courses cannot be held to high standards. In the lower tracks we rarely give students quality work to do, and we rarely expect quality products in return. Why is this so? Isn't it more sensible to say that the point of tracking (as in band or athletics) is to maximize our expectations of students and *increase* the quality of their work, that using easier versions of *worthy* tasks should make it *more* likely that student work should exhibit style, craftsmanship, thoroughness, "voice," and so on? Pride in one's work depends on such traits being expected by all forms of assessment.[11]

College admissions offices are no help. They perpetually send the message that the quality of student performance equates with the quality of work assigned—that is, course title or track. Thus, a *B* in a course called Physics or European History is considered a better performance than an *A* in Consumer Math or Home Economics. Local grading only completes the vicious circle: since grades are not given according to set standards and criteria, the transcript is unreliable, and colleges have to increasingly rely on test scores and hard-sounding courses.

To reverse the trend we need to realize that high test scores follow from excellent local assessment and uniform standards. We thus need standards for both input and output. For, if we are going to raise performance levels of all students (especially those in the lowest tracks), we will need to ensure that they are routinely given quality work to do. Thus, we need standards for the design of *all* local assignments and assessments—what I would call a Student Bill of Intellectual Rights. For me, the first right is for all students to have equal access to high-quality intellectual tasks, but faculties should be the ones to develop the standards they are willing to publicly uphold and be judged by if reform is to take place.

EXIT-LEVEL STANDARDS

Schools would meet a higher, more apt standard if officials took seriously the idea that *de facto* high standards are set by the quality colleges and jobs we wish students to enter. A comment by a Dow Chemical quality control executive shows how far we have to go in terms of linking our standards to the wider world's:

> Specifications should define what it takes to satisfy the customer.... Quality is the customer's perception of excellence. Quality is what the customer says he needs, not what *our* tests indicate is satisfactory.[12]

This is old news in most vocational programs, athletic departments, and in many art, music, and debate classes. but it is unfortunately a novelty in the traditional academic subjects. Let's get beyond myth, anecdote, and intramural guessing about standards, then. How good is good enough—as determined by the actual expectations of the best schools our students now enter? Survey your graduates and their teachers; collect the tests routinely given at the nation's best colleges and what it takes to earn *A*'s and *B*'s on them; examine the current records of your former students; get from the faculty and employers of your alumni samples of assigned tasks, criteria for grading, and an assessment of how your graduates stack up against others from similar schools.

Two high schools in Colorado have made a modest start in redressing this problem by requiring an essay for graduation. All faculty, trained by the English department, grade the student papers. The essay prompt and the criteria and scoring standards used in the assessment are borrowed from the local university's freshman placement exam and scored in terms of those standards. The average score last year in one school was a 4.2 on a 9-point scale—showing, by the way, that local control of standards is not necessarily a conflict of interest: when asked to publicly set and uphold standards, the faculty is quite demanding.

Once such high standards were set, younger students could obtain practical insight about exit-level standards by having to regularly submit some work to be judged against such standards. With each piece of work judged "blind" (so that neither the author's name nor year is known), younger students—and their teachers—would know where they stand because they would receive grades as if they were seniors.

CONCLUSION

Standard-setting and -upholding is a paradoxical affair. The work must be local, but it must be done in terms of exemplars that come from a national benchmarking process. Tests, and the criteria by which results on them are judged, must themselves be standard-setting and standard-revealing.[13] We will need standards for local standards, therefore, if we are to retain the promise of local control of schools while remaining mindful of the historical weaknesses of local assessment.

Developing local quality control will challenge deep-seated habits and beliefs, however. Impatient policy-makers will clamor for the efficient external leverage provided by multiple-choice tests that allow for easy (if misleading) comparability. And naive teachers will continue to think that their groundless and unreliable grading habits are adequate to uphold, never mind raise, genuine standards. Let us somehow find the vision and confidence to resist both views, and salvage the promise of local control of schools by helping them develop commitment to uniform quality. Let us have standards and measures that empower their users: through exemplars and criteria that give insight into the performances and virtues most valued by the wider society and through the requirement of quality, whatever local form it might take.

ENDNOTES

1. See Resnick and Resnick (1985).
2. As much as I think the National Council of Teachers of Mathematics' Standards in mathematics are wonderful, they are really not Standards at all. They are more like Principles or Worthy Objectives.
3. See Thomdike (1913), p. 262.
4. See Department of Education and Science and the Welsh Office, (1989), and the publications now available for each subject area in which the 10 levels of performance are specified. See also the recently developed *Literacy Profiles Handbook* (1990) from the Victoria, Australia, schools, for a similar set of criteria and standards in language arts.
5. See Gilbert (1978).
6. See McClelland, (1973), pp. 7–8. This is an essential but little-known earlier paper on assessment reform. McClelland offers a series of important principles upon which test reform might be built.
7. From the *ACTFL Provisional Proficiency Guidelines* (1982).
8. Note that most of the British scales mentioned above and the proposed scales in New York and other states do not solve this problem. The rubrics use vague, general language that invariably leans too heavily on relative comparisons—a "5" is "less thorough" than a "6" paper, for example. There is thus no criterion-referenced standard at work. Look at state writing assessment rubrics used for different grade-levels: they are almost indistinguishable, showing that the "standard" is relative to the anchor papers they choose, not embedded in the language of the rubric.
9. Invariably the use of tests designed primarily for easy comparability stems from the tester's desire to quickly rank and sort for gate-keeping reasons, not educational reasons—and from having the one-sided power to do so. See the report of the National Commission on Testing and Public Policy (1990).
10. See Resnick and Resnick (1985), for example.
11. Higher standards are inexorably linked to better incentives for students, in my view. Space doesn't allow me to develop these ideas here; on offering better extrinsic incentives, see Wiggins (1988); on the intrinsic incentives found in more engaging and thought-provoking curriculums, see Wiggins (1989b).
12. Peters (1987), pp. 101–102. This does *not* imply that the schools are fodder for business! It implies that every level of schooling must judge the quality of its

work by the success of students at the succeeding levels of education and in adulthood.

13. See Wiggins (1989a) and (1989b).

REFERENCES

American Council on the Teaching of Foreign Languages. (1982). *ACTFL Provisional Proficiency Guidelines.* Hastings-on Hudson. N.Y.: ACTFL Materials Center.

Department of Education and Science and the Welsh Office (U.K.). (1989). *National Curriculum: Task Group on Assessment and Testing: A Report.* London: Department of Education and Science, England and Wales.

Gilbert, T. (1978). *Human Competence: Engineering Worthy Performance.* New York: McGraw-Hill.

McClelland, D. (1973). "Testing for Competence Rather than for 'Intelligence.'" *American Psychologist* 28: 1–14.

National Commission on Testing and Public Policy. (1990). *From Gatekeeper to Gateway: Transforming Testing in America.* Chestnut Hill, Mass.: NCTPP, Boston College.

Peters, T. (1987). *Thriving on Chaos: Handbook for a Management Revolution.* New York: Harper & Row.

Resnick, D. P., and L. B. Resnick. (1985). "Standards, Curriculum, and Performance: A Historical and Comparative Perspective." *Educational Researcher* 14, 4: 5–21.

Thorndike, E. (1913). *Educational Psychology, Volume 1.* New York: Teacher's College Press.

Wiggins, G. (Winter 1998). "Rational Numbers: Scoring and Grading That Helps Rather Than Hurts Learning." *American Educator* 12, 4.

Wiggins, G. (May 1989a). "A True Test: Toward More Authentic and Equitable Assessment." *Phi Delta Kappan* 70, 9.

Wiggins, G. (April 1989b). "Teaching to the (Authentic) Test." *Educational Leadership* 46, 7: 41–47.

DISCUSSION QUESTIONS

1. In what way is the establishment of specific policies for student outcomes an integral component of effective reform?

2. What is the relationship between maximizing expectations for the quality of students' work and meeting standards?

3. What type of curriculum designs are most likely to encourage the use of authentic standards?

4. Should school curriculum be modified to accommodate the use of authentic standards? Why? Why not?

5. Suppose you are the principal of a school that has decided to create a set of standards to judge the quality of students' work. How would you facilitate the implementation of this proposal change?

PRO-CON CHART 3

Should special education students be grouped (mainstreamed) into regular education classes?

PRO	CON
1. Schools should be organized so that all students achieve their maximum potential.	1. Serving the special education population diminishes resources from students who are most likely to benefit from public schooling.
2. Schools should implement curriculum that is student-centered and responsive to the students learning needs.	2. Schools should not have to provide alternative curriculum designed for a small group of special needs students within a regular classroom setting.
3. Students need to work side by side with peers who have different learning needs.	3. Legislating teachers to fulfill the role of parent, home, and counselor for special education students is unrealistic and unproductive.
4. Teachers must develop a broad-based repertoire of instructional strategies so that they can teach students with different needs and abilities in the same classroom.	4. Students who cannot conform to classroom structure and attend to learning tasks will not benefit from regular education instruction.
5. Mainstreaming can improve the social acceptance of special education students.	5. Most educators have not been adequately prepared to work with special education students.

CASE STUDY 3

Parents Seek to Dismantle the Tracking System

Benjamin High School had a long history of placing students in fixed and homogeneous curriculum tracks. Observation by both the administration and teachers led them to conclude that several undesirable consequences were occurring. The faculty noted that within the school there seemed to be a competitive atmosphere, racial and social isolation, and a community of under and unachieving students who exhibited lower self-esteem. More importantly, achievement test scores demonstrated that tracking by ability groups did not result in significant gains in student test scores.

A group of parents threatened to sue the district stating that it was their contention that some students were not receiving a quality education. The parent group claimed that the school was in direct violation of federal law by not providing equal access to educational opportunity to all students.

To advert the possibility of litigation, the Benjamin staff voted to implement a revised plan and promised the parent group that they would rectify the inequities that resulted from curriculum segregation. The staff explained that they planned to teach honors and regular students in the same classrooms. The parent group accepted the staff's proposed action as a promise of good faith and withdrew the suit. Now Benjamin's administration and faculty were faced with the more difficult issue of how to structure the curriculum to teach students of different ability levels in the same class.

Consider the implications of such a plan and discuss the following:

1. What are the advantages and disadvantages of teaching honors and regular students in the same classrooms?

2. Which curriculum model would be most effective for teaching a heterogeneous group of students?

3. How might teachers use grouping for instruction without substantially increasing the amount of planning and preparation they already do?

4. Is ability group teaching an appropriate instructional approach? Why? Why not?

5. What kind of teaching strategies are most appropriate for the teaching model proposed in this case study?

6. What type of learning styles should be used to foster the development of critical thinking skills for students of different ability levels?

7. Should a discipline-based, separate-subject, multidisciplinary, integrative, or problem-centered curriculum model be used? Why? Why not?

PART FOUR

Curriculum and Instruction

INTRODUCTION

In what ways are curriculum and instruction related? How does time on task, allocated, and engaged time influence students' outcomes? Which instructional strategies are most effective for learners? How are technological and electronic achievements impacting instruction?

In the first chapter of Part Four, Chapter 19, Allan Ornstein considers the relationships between academic time and instruction. He points out how allocated time affects student achievement and suggests some ways that teachers can maximize use of instructional time. Next, Benjamin Bloom describes the advantages and disadvantages of conventional instruction, mastery learning, and tutoring. He explains how context variables including home environment, school learning, and teachers' differential interaction with students are related to outcomes.

In Chapter 21, Jeannie Oakes and Martin Lipton present an overview of the issues encountered in projects focused on detracking schools. They analyze the factors that have impeded or supported such efforts and conclude that the process of tracking is more crucial than the strategies employed to implement it. In Chapter 22, Lorin Anderson and Leonard Pellicer describe the intended goals and actual outcomes associated with compensatory and remedial education. They point out the how teacher staffing, organizational structure, and administrative leadership support or impede the efforts of Chapter One programs.

Eliot Wigginton suggests, in Chapter 23, that the school curriculum should include the study of cultures. He demonstrates how the Foxfire method, by immersing students in contextually relevant environments, promotes democracy and authentic learning. In the next chapter, Simon Hooper and Lloyd Rieber follow with a discussion on educational technology and the ways in which it is influencing classroom instruction. The authors present a model that characterizes the adoption of technology in education. Hooper and Rieber describe the role of contemporary educational technology and suggest several teaching strategies to guide effective teaching.

In Chapter 25, Allan Ornstein outlines those contemporary technical advancements and social developments that have the potential to influence curriculum content and delivery. He points out that while curriculum should reflect the needs of the changing society, achieving a balance between integrating new knowledge and preserving the time-tested enduring aspects of former curricula is important.

Academic Time Considerations for Curriculum Leaders

ALLAN C. ORNSTEIN

FOCUSING QUESTIONS

1. *What is the relationship between academic time and instruction?*
2. *Which content areas should receive greater proportions of allocated time?*
3. *How does allocated time influence student achievement?*
4. *What is the difference between academic time and academic engaged time?*
5. *What are some ways in which teachers can better utilize instructional time?*
6. *How can teachers help students maximize their use of engaged time?*

Increasing time in school without changing other aspects of academic time will not result in increased achievement.[1] Nonetheless, if instructional quality is kept constant, then extra instructional quantity should have positive effects on student academic outcomes. In other words, if students have more time to learn specific skills or tasks, then they should learn more than students who have less time.

Using five hours and eight minutes of instruction a day as a yardstick (as is average in U.S. public schools), increasing the school day by 40 minutes to provide one extra academic subject, or additional time for existing academic subject matter, will result in what translates to 1 1/2 extra years of schooling over 12 years.

ACADEMIC ALLOCATED TIME

Allocated time—directly related to the curriculum—is the amount of time the school assigns for various subjects. Some educators classify allocated time as the percent of the school day (or school year) allotted to academic and nonacademic instruction; about 60 to 80 percent of the school day is allotted to academic content.[2]

More than half the states set their own recommendations, although some have established requirements for allocating time in curriculum content at the elementary grade levels. The school districts usually modify the recommendations and/or requirements upward, especially in math and English (which includes reading) because of recent statewide testing programs and public reporting of results in math and reading.

Modifications of allocated time at the school level also reflect the philosophy of the community, school board, district superintendent, and school principal. For example, a progressive educator would allocate more time for socialization than an essentialist one who would probably put more emphasis on the three Rs and subtract time from art, music, and physical education.

Although state policies vary widely, as illustrated in Table 19.1, English (reading) receives the most allocated time in the early grades and

TABLE 19.1   Allocated Time by Subject and Grade Level

SUBJECT	GRADE	ILLINOIS (MINIMUM RECOMMENDATIONS)	MICHIGAN (MINIMUM RECOMMENDATIONS)	TEXAS (MINIMUM REQUIREMENTS)
Math	3	50	15	60
	6	49	15	60
	8	47	15	45
Science	3	26	9	20
	6	39	9	45
	8	44	15	45
English	3	142	40	120
	6	107	32	90
	8	87	15	45
Social Studies	3	45	4	20
	6	42	9	45
	8	44	15	45

Source: Based on telephone conversation with curriculum specialists in the respective state departments of education, January 5, 1989. Updated May 24, 1993.

less in the higher grades. Math receives the second most attention and remains relatively constant across grade levels; science and social studies increase in allocated time to the point that they are at par with other subjects by grade 8.

If standardized testing included science and social studies, then there would most likely be more allocated time for these subjects in grades 3 and 6. The states that do not establish allocated time allotments (such as California, Florida, and New York) focus on instructional objectives and test for performance in subject areas.

At the secondary school level, allocated time is better defined and influenced by the students' program: academic, technical, vocational, etc. Corresponding with the reform movement of the 1980s, along with increased academic productivity and stiffer academic course requirements for graduation, the curriculum has been upgraded, with more emphasis on such core subjects as English, social studies, math, and science.

Table 19.2 shows that there was a marked increase in required coursework for public high school graduation in all major academic subjects,

especially in math and science, between 1981–82 and 1987–88.

Graduation requirements in English and social studies for public schools are now only slightly below the recommendations of the National Commission's report, *A Nation at Risk.* They are still substantially below the recommended levels in math, science, and especially foreign language.

Almost no school districts required computer science in 1981–82, but 22 percent had such requirements by 1987–88, and this should increase in the 1990s. Only 2 percent required foreign language study for graduation in 1981–82; the number rose to 11 percent by 1987–88.[3]

Table 19.3 provides supplementary data on the percent of high school students having completed one year and three years of coursework in 1980 and 1987 in four major subject areas. Dramatic increases are shown for 1987, reflecting the national reform movement and concurrent demands for upgrading academic requirements.

The percent of subjects for which high school seniors completed more than three years

TABLE 19.2 Average Years of Coursework Required for Public High School Graduation

SCHOOL YEAR	SUBJECT AREA				
	Mathematics	Science	English	Foreign Languages	Social Studies
1981–82	1.6	1.5	3.6	(a)	2.6
1984–85	1.9	1.8	3.8	.1	2.8
1987–88[b]	2.3	2.0	3.9	.2	2.9
Recommendations of National Commission on Excellence in Education[c]	3.0	3.0	4.0	2.0[d]	3.0

a. Less than 0.05 years.

b. Expectations as of fall 1985 about requirements for seniors graduating in 1988.

c. Another half year of coursework was recommended in computer science. Almost no school districts had requirements in this area in 1981–82. That situation changed by 1984–85, when the average for all school districts was 0.1 years of coursework required for graduation in computer science; the expected average for 1987–88 is 0.2 years.

d. The Commission's recommendations about foreign languages applied only to the college-bound, not to all students. The figures for actual requirements represent requirements for all graduates.

Source: U.S. Department of Education, Center for Education Statistics, "Public High School Graduation Requirements," *OERI Bulletin,* 1986; and unpublished tabulations.

Source: The Condition of Education 1987 (Washington, D.C.: U.S. Government Printing Office, 1987), Table 1.37b, p. 84.

of coursework in 1987: English, 87 percent; mathematics, 36 percent; science, 23 percent; and history (or social studies), 12 percent.

Considering that we live in a highly technocratic and scientific society, one in which knowledge has great impact on our standard of living, and in a world in which the push of a button can have enormous impact on our lives, the small enrollments in science and mathematics have serious implications for the future of our country.

A similar concern was voiced nearly 30 years ago, when our standard of living was increasing more rapidly and when we were more influential as a superpower. Then, James Conant stressed that students needed to enroll in more courses in science, mathematics, and foreign languages.[4] The seeds of the Sputnik era have resurfaced in the 1980s under the theme of excellence in education, and there is the same feeling of urgency.

Our failure to heed Conant's warning may be viewed as one reason for our decline as the leading political and economic giant of the world and for the general decline of our manufacturing capability and standard of living.

As a point of comparison, consider that Japanese students are required to take 23 percent of their total junior high school curricula in science and mathematics. In high school, they are required to take 1.25 science courses per year and 1.5 math courses per year (including calculus and statistics). Because 94 percent of the Japanese

TABLE 19.3   Years of Coursework Completed by High School Seniors, 1980 and 1987

	ONE YEAR OR LESS		MORE THAN THREE YEARS	
	1980	*1987*	*1980*	*1987*
English	2.1%	0.4%	26.0%	87.1%
Mathematics	23.5%	5.0%	8.5%	36.0%
Science	35.0%	11.5%	6.1%	23.3%
History	12.2%	23.4%	9.7%	12.4%

Source: The Condition of Education, 1983 (Washington, D.C.: U.S. Government Printing Office, 1984), Table 1–11, p. 34; High School Transcript Study Percentage of Graduates Earning Various Number of Credits (Carnegie Units), Preliminary Data for Educational Research and Improvement, Table 2, p. 42.

attend high school, their requirement produces a more scientifically literate public than ours.[5]

In addition, Japanese students outperform American students in science and mathematics on the International Association for the Evaluation of Educational Achievement (IEA) study. In fact, according to recent comparisons of student achievement in math and science, Americans score slightly below the mean among 14 industrial nations, and more than 15 percent below Japanese student scores in both subject areas.[6]

ACADEMIC INSTRUCTIONAL TIME

Academic instructional time refers to the actual amount of time the teacher spends in the various curriculum areas and is sometimes referred to as "academic learning time" or "content covered." This time rarely exceeds the school's allocated time, and when it does, it connotes that the teacher is spending more time on a particular subject or aspect of a subject than is expected by the school or curriculum guidelines.

Whereas academic allocated time refers to maximum opportunity time, academic instructional time connotes what really happens in the classroom—how much time the teacher actually spends on specific content.

Recently, Ornstein analyzed the academic coverage devoted to teaching language arts. In general, the ranges for each content area are wide.

One teacher devotes 124 minutes each year to creative writing while another spends 967 minutes. One teacher spends 261 minutes each year on grammar and another 1,486 minutes. One spends 71 minutes on spelling, another spends 216 minutes. We can make a safe bet about which students will perform better as a whole in certain content areas and related tests.

Even in junior high and senior high schools, where departmentalization forces time allocating for each subject, teachers must still decide how much actual time to spend on lesson units or topics. How much time should be spent on subjects such as creative writing that achievement tests don't usually evaluate?

Two cautionary observations should be noted. First, we should not necessarily conclude that "more is always better." Quality is crucial, and we must remember that a diminishing point is reached when "more" of the same thing becomes boring. On the other hand, teachers must allocate sufficient, and sometimes extra time, so their students can learn the required subject matter.

Second, teachers vary in the way they efficiently use time—or avoid wasting time. A good portion of classroom time, what we sometimes think is devoted to instruction, is often wasted on clerical and housekeeping activities, managerial problems, and students working on homework during class time. Much time in secondary schools is spent on nonacademic subjects, transition time between classes, announcements, and procedural and maintenance tasks.

Two high school administrators estimate that the amount of time wasted on nonacademic activities during the school year, plus teacher and student absences, amounts to a loss of nearly 60 to 90 days or one-third to half the school year. The biggest time waster is estimated to be the changing and beginning of classes. An estimated 75 hours or 15 days is lost here each year.[7]

To increase academic learning time, teachers should have a system of rules and procedures that facilitate clerical and housekeeping tasks and deal with disruptions and disciplinary problems. Similarly, the schools need to implement policies that improve absenteeism and lateness.

ACADEMIC ENGAGED TIME

Academic engaged time is the time a student spends attending to academic tasks or content. For some educators, it also means performing with a high success rate (80 percent or more).[8] Although actual instructional time, or content covered, is a more important variable because it is closer to the products being measured, it is easier to obtain data on academically engaged time because of precision in measuring time. Moreover, different teachers use different texts, materials, and methods to cover the same content, and they focus on different aspects or issues related to content. Since researchers have not developed a science for coding content in such situations they often turn to academic engaged time as a proxy for content covered.[9]

Recently, Susan Stodolsky studied 20 mathematics classes and 19 social studies classes in 11 Chicago city and suburban school districts. She identified 15 instructional formats or activities—ways in which teachers chose to instruct. Mathematics teachers emphasized skill development in terms of content and used 47 percent of their instructional time for seatwork (mostly uniform seatwork) and another 31 percent on recitation. Students spent 6 percent of their time checking or reviewing their work. Other instructional activi-

ties occurred infrequently.[10] These instructional formats in mathematics are shown in Table 19.4, along with the instructional formats for social studies.

Social studies classes were more varied in terms of content and instruction. The content drew from many disciplines such as history, economics, government, sociology, etc. and encouraged not only recall of information (dates, names, or events), but also concepts, problem solving, and research skills.

Stodolsky found a much greater amount of time spent on group work (11 percent), student reports (7 percent), and audiovisual materials (7 percent) than in mathematics (0.1, 0, 0 respectively). Although students in both subjects spent a similar amount of time on recitation, they spent no time on individualized seatwork in social studies.

In general, the source for new knowledge, and learning how to learn in math was the teachers. These teachers were expected to present new materials and explain how to do problems. In contrast, social studies students were expected to learn on their own by reading the text and other materials. They were supposed to develop research skills by gathering and using information from many sources, whereas math students were expected to first learn the fundamentals and then become problem solvers.

In the final analysis, both the quantity and quality of academic engaged time (as well as actual instructional time) are considered to be important in improving the outcomes of student learning, although quantity is easier to agree upon and measure.

Students of teachers who provide more academic engaged time (as well as actual instructional time) learn more than students of teachers who provide relatively less time. In a review of more than 20 different studies, the correlations between student achievement in reading and mathematics and learning time is between .40 and .60.[11]

Since academic time, both instructional and engaged, seems to be a scarcer commodity than most of us probably realized, what we might fo-

TABLE 19.4 Distribution of Instructional Activities in Mathematics and Social Studies

Format	MATHEMATICS			SOCIAL STUDIES		
	N	*% Segments*	*% Time*	*N*	*% Segments*	*% Time*
Uniform seatwork	144	26.9	29.8	69	12.7	21.8
Individualized seatwork	59	11.0	13.7	—	—	—
Diverse seatwork	14	2.6	3.8	26	4.8	6.1
Recitation	155	28.9	30.9	96	17.6	28.1
Group work	1	.2	0.1	183	33.6	10.7
Contest, game	44	8.2	6.2	8	1.5	1.5
Checking work	42	7.8	5.9	12	2.2	2.4
Giving instructions/ task preparation	33	6.2	1.7	58	10.9	5.4
Student reports	—	—	—	20	3.7	6.9
Discussion	2	0.4	0.4	19	3.5	3.1
Test	18	3.4	5.1	10	1.8	3.9
Lecture/Demonstration	15	2.8	1.9	12	2.2	2.5
Film/Audiovisual	—	—	—	24	4.4	6.8
Tutorial	8	1.5	0.2	—	—	—
Stocks	—	—	—	8	1.5	0.8
Totals	535	100.0	100.0	545	100.0	100.0

Source: Susan Stodolsky, "How Content Changes Teaching," *University of Chicago Education News,* Annual ed., 1989, p. 9.

cus on in the future is how teachers can better utilize their time when they are actually teaching (instructional time) and how students can better utilize their time when on task (engaged time).

Another factor to consider is homework time. When students are alone and without the support or feedback from their teachers, they can misuse time because of lack of motivation or frustration related to the difficulty of the assignment.

ENDNOTES

1. Gene V. Glass, "What Works: Politics and Research." *Educational Researcher,* April 1987, pp. 5–11; Nancy Karweit, "Should We Lengthen the School Term?" *Educational Researcher,* June 1985, pp. 9–15.
2. Nancy Karweit, "Time on Task: The Second Time Around," *NASSP Bulletin,* February 1988, pp. 31–39.
3. Allan C. Ornstein, "The Evolving Accountability Movement," *Peabody Journal of Education,* Spring 1988, pp. 12–20.
4. James B. Conant, *The American High School Today* (New York: McGraw-Hill, 1959).
5. Allan C. Ornstein, "Sources of Change and the Curriculum," *High School Journal,* April–May 1988, pp. 192–199; Kay M. Troost, "What Accounts for Japan's Success in Science Education?" *Educational Leadership,* December/January 1984, pp. 26–29.
6. *Digest of Education Statistics 1988* (Washington, D.C.: U.S. Government Printing Office, 1988). Tables 289–290, pp. 342–343.
7. Robert Lowe and Robert Gervais, "Increasing Instructional Time in Today's Classroom." *NASSP Bulletin,* February 1988, pp. 19–22.
8. James H. Block, Helen E. Efthim, and Robert B. Burns, *Building Effective Mastery Learning Schools* (New York: Longman, 1989); Benjamin S. Bloom, *Human Characteristics and School Learning* (New York: McGraw-Hill, 1976).
9. Allan C. Ornstein, "Emphasis on Student Outcomes Focuses Attention on Quality of Instruction," *NASSP* Bulletin, January 1987, pp. 88–95. Barak Rosenshine. "Content, Time, and Direct Instruction," in *Research on Teaching: Concepts, Findings,*

and Implications, edited by P. L. Peterson and H. J. Walberg (Berkeley, Calif.: McCutchan, 1979), pp. 28–56.

10. Susan Stodolsky, *The Subject Matters* (Chicago: University of Chicago Press, 1988).

11. Bloom, *Human Characteristics and School Learning;* Charles W. Fisher, et al., "Teacher Behaviors, Academic Learning Time and Student Achievement," in *Time to Learn,* edited by C. Denham and A. Lieberman (Washington, D.C.: National Institute of Education, 1980), pp. 27–45.

DISCUSSION QUESTIONS

1. What is your district's curriculum philosophy as it is reflected in academic time allocations?
2. What is the relationship between allocated time and the aims of education?
3. What factors should be considered in determining minimum standards for allocated time?
4. Who are the key players in establishing allocated time requirements?
5. How are allocated time requirements for particular subjects across grade levels determined?

The Search for Methods of Instruction

BENJAMIN S. BLOOM

FOCUSING QUESTIONS

1. *What is the difference between conventional instruction, mastery learning, and tutoring?*
2. *How does mastery learning influence student achievement?*
3. *What are the advantages and disadvantages of the mastery learning model and tutoring?*
4. *In what ways are home environment processes and a student's school learning related?*
5. *How does tutoring influence student achievement?*

Two University of Chicago doctoral students in education, Anania (1982, 1983) and Burke (1984), completed dissertations in which they compared student learning under the following three conditions of instruction:

1. *Conventional.* Students learn the subject matter in a class with about 30 students per teacher. Tests are given periodically for marking the students.

2. *Mastery Learning.* Students learn the subject matter in a class with about 30 students per teacher. The instruction is the same as in the conventional class (usually with the same teacher). Formative tests (the same tests used with the conventional group) are given for feedback followed by corrective procedures and parallel formative tests to determine the extent to which the students have mastered the subject matter.

3. *Tutoring.* Students learn the subject matter with a good tutor for each student (or for two or three students simultaneously). This tutoring instruction is followed periodically by formative tests, feedback-corrective procedures, and paral-

lel formative tests as in the mastery learning classes. It should be pointed out that the need for corrective work under tutoring is very small.

The students were randomly assigned the three learning conditions, and their initial aptitude tests scores, previous achievement in the subject, and initial attitudes and interests in the subject were similar. The amount of time for instruction was the same in all three groups except for the corrective work in the mastery learning and tutoring groups. Burke (1984) and Anania (1982, 1983) replicated the study with four different samples of students at grades four, five, and eight and with two different subject matters, Probability and Cartography. In each sub-study, the instructional treatment was limited to 11 periods of instruction over a 3-week block of time.

Most striking were the differences in final achievement measures under the three conditions. Using the standard deviation (sigma) of the control (conventional) class, it was typically found that the average student under tutoring was about two standard deviations above the average of the control class (the average tutored student was above 98% of the students in the control class).[1] The average student under mastery learning was about one standard deviation above the average of the control class (the average mastery learning student was above 84% of the students in the control class).

The variation of the students' achievement also changed under these learning conditions such that about 90% of the tutored students and 70% of the mastery learning students attained the level of summative achievement reached by only the highest 20% of the students under conventional instructional conditions. (See Figure 20.1.)

There were corresponding changes in students' time on task in the classroom (65% under conventional instruction, 75% under Mastery Learning, and 90+% under tutoring) and students' attitudes and interests (least positive under conventional instruction and most positive under tutoring). There were great reductions in the relations between prior measures (aptitude or achievement) and the summative achievement measures. Typically, the aptitude-achievement correlations changed from +.60 under conventional to +.35 under mastery learning and +.25 under tutoring. It is recognized that the correlations for the mastery learning and tutoring groups were so low because of the restricted range of scores under these learning conditions. However, the most striking of the findings is that under the best learning conditions we can devise (tutoring), the average student is 2 sigma above the average control student taught under conventional group methods of instruction.

The tutoring process demonstrates that *most* of the students do have the potential to reach this high level of learning. I believe an important task of research and instruction is to seek ways of accomplishing this under more practical and realistic conditions than the one-to-one tutoring, which is too costly for most societies to bear on a large scale. This is the "2 sigma" problem. Can researchers and teachers devise teaching-learning conditions that will enable the majority of students under *group instruction* to attain levels of

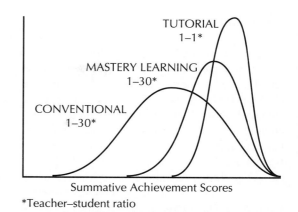

Summative Achievement Scores

*Teacher–student ratio

FIGURE 20.1   Achievement Distribution for Students Under Conventional, Mastery Learning, and Tutorial Instruction.

achievement that can at present be reached only under good tutoring conditions?

It has taken almost a decade and a half to develop the Mastery Learning (ML) strategy to a point where large numbers of teachers at every level of instruction and in many countries can use the feedback-corrective procedures to get the 1 sigma effect (the average ML student is above 84% of the students under conventional instruction—even with the same teacher teaching both the ML and the conventional classes). If the research on the 2 sigma problem yields *practical methods* (methods that the average teacher or school faculty can learn in a brief period of time and use with little more cost or time than conventional instruction), it would be an educational contribution of the greatest magnitude. It would change popular notions about human potential and would have significant effects on what the schools can and should do with the educational years each society requires of its young people.

This paper is a brief presentation of the work on solutions to the 2 sigma problem. It is hoped that it will interest both educational researchers and teachers in further research and application of these ideas.

THE SEARCH

In a number of articles, my graduate students and I have attempted to contrast alterable educational variables with more stable or static variables (Bloom, 1980). In our treatment of this topic, we summarized the literature on such alterable variables as the *quality of teaching,* the *use of time* by teachers and students, *cognitive* and *affective* entry characteristics of students, *formative testing, rate of learning,* and the *home environment.* In each case, we contrasted these alterable variables with the more *stable* variables (e.g., personal characteristics of teachers, intelligence measures, achievement tests for grading purposes, socioeconomic status of the family, etc.) and indicated some of the ways in which the alterable variables influence learning and the processes by which these variables have been altered.

But not all alterable variables are likely to have equal effects on learning. Our research summaries were intended to emphasize the alterable variables that have had the strongest effects on school learning. Within the last 3 years, this search has been aided by the rapid growth of the meta-analysis literature. In this literature, each writer has summarized the research literature on a particular set of alterable variables to indicate the effect size between control and experimental groups of students. They have standardized the results in terms of the *difference* between the experimental and control groups divided by the standard deviation of the control group.[2]

In each study, the reviewer also analyzed the effect size under different conditions, level of school, sex of student, school subject, size of sample, and so on. Such reviews are very useful in selecting alterable variables that are most likely to contribute significantly to the 2 sigma solution.

Table 20.1 is adapted from a summary of effect sizes of key variables by Walberg (1984) who, with other co-authors, has contributed greatly to this literature. In Table 20.1 he has listed the selected variables in order of magnitude of effect size. (We have added other variables and

indicated the equivalent percentile for each effect size.) Thus, in the first entry, *tutorial instruction,* we have indicated the effect size (2 sigma) and indicated that under tutorial instruction, the average student is above 98% of the students under the control teaching conditions. A list of effect size studies appears in the Appendix at the end of this article.

In our own attempts to solve the 2 sigma problem we assume that two or three alterable variables must be used that *together* contribute more to the learning than any one of them alone. Because of more than 15 years of experience with ML at different levels of education and in different countries, we have come to rely on ML as one of the possible variables to be combined with selected other variables. ML (the feedback corrective process) under good conditions yields approximately a 1 sigma effect size. We have systematically tried other variables which, in combination with ML, might approach the 2 sigma effect size. So far, we have *not* found any two variable combination that has exceeded the 2 sigma effect. Thus, some of our present research reaches the 2 sigma effect but does not go beyond it.

We have classified the variables in Table 20.1 in terms of the direct object of the change process: (a) the learner; (b) the instructional material; (c) the home environment or peer group; and (d) the teacher and the teaching process.

We have speculated that two variables involving different objects of the change process may, in some instances, be additive, whereas two variables involving the same object of the change process are less likely to be additive (unless they occur at different times in the teaching-learning process). Our research is intended to determine when these rules are true and when they are not. Several of the studies done so far suggest that they may be true. Thus the ML process (which affects the learner most directly), when combined with changes in the teaching process (which affects the teacher most directly), yield additive results. (See Tenenbaum, p. 13 of this article and Mevarech, p. 14 of this article). Although we do

TABLE 20.1 Effect of Selected Alterable Variables on Student Achievement
(See Appendix)

		EFFECT SIZE	PERCENTILE EQUIVALENT
D[a]	Tutorial instruction	2.00	98
D	Reinforcement	1.20	
A	Feedback-corrective (ML)	1.00	84
D	Cues and explanations	1.00	
(A)D	Student classroom participation	1.00	
A	Student time on task	1.00[b]	
A	Improved reading/study skills	1.00	
C	Cooperative learning	.80	79
D	Homework (graded)	.80	
D	Classroom morale	.60	73
A	Initial cognitive prerequisites	.60	
C	Home environment intervention	.50[b]	69
D	Peer and cross-age remedial tutoring	.40	66
D	Homework (assigned)	.30	62
D	Higher order questions	.30	
(D)B	New science & math curricula	.30[b]	
D	Teacher expectancy	.30	
C	Peer group influence	.20	58
B	Advance organizers	.20	
	Socio-economic status (for contrast)	.25	60

Note. This table was adapted from Walberg (1984) by Bloom.
[a]*Object of change process*—A-Learner; B-Instructional Material; C-Home environment or peer group; D-Teacher.
[b]Averaged or estimated from correlational data or from several effect sizes.

not believe these two rules are more than *suggestive* at present, future research on this problem will undoubtedly yield a stronger set of generalizations about how the effects of separable variables may be best combined.

In our work so far we have restricted the search to two or three variables, each of which is likely to have a .5 sigma effect or greater. We suspect that the research, as well as the applications to school situations, would get too complex if more than three alterable variables are used. In any case, our work has begun with variables in the top half of Table 20.1. Perhaps as the research moves on, it will be necessary to include some of the variables in the lower part of Table 20.1.

In our research with two variables, we have made use of a 2 × 2 randomized design with ML

and one other variable. So far we have not done research with three variables. Where possible, we try to replicate the study with at least two subject fields, two levels of schooling, or some combination of subject fields and levels of schooling. We hope that others will take up this 2 sigma search and that some guidelines for the research can be set up to make the combined results more useful and to reduce the time and costs for experimental and demonstration studies.

IMPROVING STUDENT PROCESSING OF CONVENTIONAL INSTRUCTION

In this section of the paper we are concerned with ways in which students can learn more effectively without basically changing the teaching. If students develop good study habits, devote more time to the learning, improve their reading skills, and so on, they will be better able to learn from a particular teacher and course—even though neither the course nor the teacher has undergone a change process.

For example, the ML feedback-corrective approach is addressed primarily to providing students with the cognitive and affective prerequisites for each new learning task. As we have noted before, when the ML procedures are done systematically and well, the school achievement of the average student under ML is approximately 1 sigma (84 percentile) above the average student in the control class, even when both classes are taught by the *same teacher* with much the same instruction and instructional material. As we view the ML process, we regard it as a method of improving the students' learning from the same teaching over a series of learning tasks.

The major changes under the ML process are that more of the students have the cognitive prerequisites for each new learning task, they become more positive about their ability to learn the subject, and they put in more active learning time than do the control students. As we observe the students' learning and the test results in the ML and the conventional class, we note the improvements in the student learning under ML and the lack of such improvement in conventional classes.

One of our University of Chicago doctoral students, Leyton (1983), suggested that one approach to the 2 Sigma problem would be to use ML during the advanced course in a sequence, but in addition attempt to *enhance the students' initial cognitive entry prerequisites* at the beginning of the course. Working with high school teachers in Algebra 2 and French 2, they developed an initial test of the prerequisites for each of these courses. The procedure in developing the initial test was to take the final examination in the prior course (Algebra 1 or French 1) and have a committee of four to six teachers in the subject independently check each test item that they believed measured an idea or skill that was a necessary prerequisite for the next course in the subject. There was very high agreement on most of the selected items, and discussion among the teachers led to consensus about some of the remaining items.

Two of the classes were helped to review and relearn the specific prerequisites they lacked. This was not done for the students in the other two classes—they spent the time on a more general and informal review of the content taught in the previous course (Algebra 1 or French 1). The method of enhancing the prerequisites was much like the ML feedback-corrective process where the teacher retaught the items that the majority of students had missed, small groups of students helped each other over items that had been missed, and the students reviewed items they were not sure about by referring to the designated pages in the instructional material. The corrective process took about 3 to 4 hours during the first week of the course. After the students completed the corrective process, they were given a parallel test. As a result of the corrective process, most of the students reached the mastery standard (80%) on the parallel test given at the end of the first week of the course. In a few cases, students who didn't reach this standard were given further help.

More important was the improved performance of the enhanced classes over the other two classes on the first *formative* test in the advanced course (French 2 or Algebra 2). The two enhanced classes, which had been helped on the initial prerequisites, were approximately .7 sigma higher than the other two classes on the first formative test given at the end of a 2-week period of learning in the advanced course.

When one of the enhanced classes was also provided with ML feedback-corrective procedures over a series of learning tasks, the final results after a 10- to 12-week period of instruction was that this experimental group was approximately 1.6 sigma above the control group on the summative examination. (The average student in the ML plus enhanced initial prerequisites was above 95% of the control students on this examination.) There were also attitudinal and other affective differences in students related to these achievement differences. These included positive academic self-concept, greater interest in the subject, and greater desire to learn more in the subject field.

In Leyton's (1983) study, he found that the average effect of initial enhancement of prerequisites alone is about .6 sigma (see differences between conventional and conventional plus enhanced prerequisites and between ML and ML plus enhanced prerequisites in Figure 20.2). That is, we have two processes—*ML* and *initial enhancement of cognitive prerequisites*—that have

sizeable but separate effects. When they are combined, their separate effects tend to be additive. We believe these two variables are additive because they occur at different times. The enhancement of the initial prerequisites is completed during the first week of the new course, while the ML feedback-corrective process takes place every 2 or 3 weeks during the course, after the initial enhancement.

This solution to the 2 sigma problem is likely to be applicable to sequential courses in most school subjects. (In the United States, over two-thirds of the academic courses in elementary-

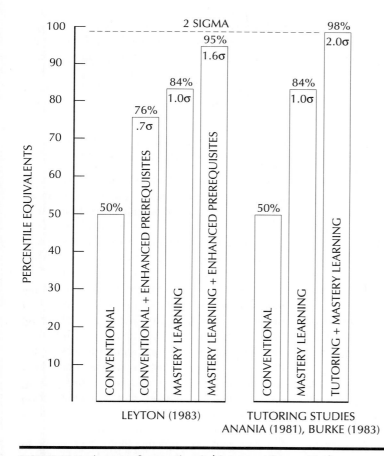

FIGURE 20.2 Average Summative Achievement Scores Under Different Learning Conditions. Comparison of Tutoring Studies, Mastery Learning, and Enhanced Prerequisites.

secondary schools are sequential courses.) This solution, of course, applies most clearly to the second courses in a sequence. It probably will not work as well with the third, fourth, or later courses in a sequence if there has been no earlier use of initial enhancement of prerequisites or ML procedures. We hope these ideas will be further explored in the United States as well as in other countries. We believe this solution is relevant at all levels of education, including elementary-secondary, college, and even the graduate and professional school level.

We also regard this approach as widely applicable within a country because the prerequisites for a particular sequential subject or course are likely to be very similar even though different textbooks and teachers may be involved. Thus, a well made test of the initial prerequisites for a particular sequential course—Arithmetic 2, French 2, Reading 2, and so on—may with only minor changes apply to other versions of the same course within a particular country. Also, the procedures that work well in enhancing these prerequisites in one school should work equally well in other schools. Further research is needed to establish the sequential courses in which this approach is most effective.

Finally, the time cost of the initial enhancement procedures is limited to the class hours of the course during the first week of the sequential course, while the time or other costs of the ML procedures have usually been very small. We hope that this approach to the 2 sigma problem will be found to be a widely applicable as well as economical solution available to most teachers who wish to improve student learning, student academic self-concept, and student attitudes and interest in the learning.

Our graduate students have written papers on several other approaches for improving student processing of conventional instruction:

1. Help students develop a student support system in which groups of two or three students study together, help each other when they encounter difficulties in the course, help each other

review in advance of taking tests, and review their learning periodically. A student support system that provides support, encouragement and even help when needed can do much to raise the level of learning of the participants. There is evidence that these and other cooperative learning efforts are almost as effective as ML procedures. (Cooperative Learning—Effect size .80 (79 percentile) Slavin, 1980.)

2. There is evidence that students who take special programs to improve their reading and/or their study and learning methods tend to learn more effectively. Ideally, such special programs should be available at the beginning of each new school level, that is, junior high school, high school, and so on. One would hope that the special programs would be closely related to the academic courses the student is currently taking. (Improved reading/study skills—Effect size 1.00 (84 percentile) (Pflaum, Walberg, Karegianes, & Rasher, 1980).

IMPROVE INSTRUCTIONAL MATERIALS AND EDUCATIONAL TECHNOLOGY

The textbook in the United States, as well as in most advanced countries in the world, is an almost universal part of school instruction. There has been much work on the improvement of the textbooks for reading and, to some extent, arithmetic, mathematics, and science subjects. Most of these are in relation to special curricular improvements, which include improvements in the sequential nature of the topics, the attempt to find important ideas or schema that help to interrelate the different parts of the subject, and improvements in the illustrations and exercises in the books. However, as far as we can find, these improvements have not had very significant effects on student achievement unless the teachers were provided with much inservice education for the new curriculum or the new textbook.

My graduate students and I have been intrigued by the possibility that the organization of a particular section (or chapter) of the textbook might be better integrated or the parts of the section more closely related to each other. Preorganizers or advanced organizers (Ausubel, 1960), have been moderately effective when provided in the textbook or provided by the teacher at the beginning of the new unit of the course. These may be provided in the form of objectives, some ideas about what will be learned in the unit, or a brief discussion of the relation between what has already been learned and what will be learned in the unit. Such advanced organizers (Luiten, Ames, & Ackerson, 1980) appear to have an average effect size on achievement of about .2 sigma. (Incidentally, such advance organizers have about a .4 sigma effect on retention of the learning.) Although this effect is rather consistent, by itself it is not enough to contribute significantly to the 2 sigma effect. It is likely that a *combination* of advance organizers at the beginning of a new topic, further organizational aids during the chapter or unit, as well as appropriate questions, summaries, or other organizational aids at the end of the unit, may have a substantial effect on the student's learning of that chapter.

In Process

One of our students, Carlos Avalos, is working on a study of the effect of *organizational aids* in the instructional material combined with the *initial enhancement of cognitive prerequisites* and the ML *feedback-corrective* procedures. Avalos is planning a research design that will enable him to determine the separate effects of each of the three processes, the effect of any two of the processes, and the combined effect of all three processes. At the least, it is anticipated that the combination of any two of the processes will be greater than the effects of any one of the same processes. It is hoped that the effect of any two will be above 1.3 sigma (90 percentile). If this is found, it will provide several new solutions to the 2 sigma problem—some of which can be done with very little cost or effort by the teachers or the school system.

Avalos expects the results noted above because the organizational aids can be built into new textbooks and can be used by the students with a minimum of emphasis by the teachers. The initial enhancement of the prerequisites is completed before the students begin the study of the new course subject matter, whereas the ML feedback-corrective procedures take place every 2 or 3 weeks during the course. We believe that each of these processes is somewhat independent of the other processes.

Other suggestions for the improvement of instructional materials and educational technology include the following:

1. Some of our students have used computer learning courses, such as the Plato system, which appear to work very well for highly motivated students. We believe that it should be possible to determine whether particular computer courses enable sizeable proportions of students to attain the 2 sigma achievement effect. The effectiveness of the computer courses can be determined in terms of the time required, completion rates, student performance on achievement tests, and student retention of the learned material. It is hoped that the more effective computer courses will also have positive effects on such affective characteristics as academic self-concept, interest in the subject, and desire to learn further with computer learning methods.

2. Although the average effect size for new science and math curricula in the United States is only .3 sigma, some of the new curricula (or textbooks) in these and other subjects may be much more effective than others. We propose a careful search of the new curricula and textbooks to determine which ones are more effective and to determine what characteristics make them more effective than the others.

HOME ENVIRONMENT AND THE PEER GROUP

In this section, we are primarily concerned with the out-of-school support that the student receives from the home or the peer group. We are interested in the ways in which the student's achievement, academic aspirations and goals, and progress in learning are influenced by these types of support. We know that the home environment does have great influence on the pupil's school learning and that this influence is especially effective at the elementary school level or earlier. The peer group's influence is likely to be strongest (both positively or negatively) at the secondary school level.

Home Environment Processes

There have been a large number of studies of the home environment processes that affect the students' school learning. These studies involve interviews and observations directed at determining the relevant interactions between parents and their children. The studies find correlations of +.70 to +.80[3] between an index of the home environment processes and the children's school achievement. Some of the home environment processes that appear to have high relationships with school achievement include the following:

1. Work habits of the family—the degree of routine in the home management, the emphasis on regularity in the use of space and time, and the priority given to schoolwork over other more pleasurable activities.

2. Academic guidance and support—the availability and quality of the help and encouragement parents give the child for his or her schoolwork and the conditions they provide to support the child's schoolwork.

3. Stimulation in the home—the opportunity provided by the home to explore ideas, events, and the larger environment.

4. Language development—opportunities in the home for the development of correct and effective language usage.

5. Academic aspirations and expectations—the parents' aspirations for the child, the standards they set for the child's school achievement, and their interests in and knowledge of the child's school experiences.

These studies of the home environment processes began with the work of Dave (1963) and Wolf (1964, 1966), and since then have been replicated in other studies done in the United States and other countries (Marjoribanks, 1974; Kalinowski & Sloane, 1981).

These previous studies of the relationship between the home and the children's school achievement suggest a strong effect of the home environment on the school learning of the children, but they do not provide evidence on the extent to which the home environment can be *altered* and the effect of such alteration on changes in the children's school achievement.

A recent study done in Thailand by Janhom (1983) involved a control group and three experimental groups of parents (and their children). In this study, the most effective treatment of the parents was for the group of parents to meet with a parent educator for about 2 hours twice a month for 6 months. In these meetings, the parents discussed ways in which they could support their children's learning in the school. There was usually an initial presentation made by the parent educator on one of the home environment processes and then the parents discussed what they did as well as what they hoped to do to support their children's school learning.

Another experimental approach included visits to each home separately by a parent educator twice a month for 6 months. A third experimental approach was that newsletters about the same topics were sent to the home twice a month for 6 months.

The parents of all four groups were observed and interviewed at the beginning and end of the 6-month period using the Dave (1963) interview and observational methods. Although the three experimental approaches show significantly greater changes in the parents' home environment index than the control group, the most effective method was the series of meetings between groups of parents and the parent educator. The changes in the home environment of this group were highly significant when compared with the changes in the other three groups of parents.

The fourth grade children of all these parents were given a national standardized test on reading and mother tongue as well as arithmetic at the beginning and end of the 6-month period. It was found that the children of the meeting group of parents had changed by 1 sigma in achievement, as contrasted with the change in the control group of children. In comparison, the parent educators' visit to each of the homes every other week had only a .5 sigma effect on the children's school achievement.

Other methods of changing the home environment have been reported by Dolan (1980), Bronfenbrenner (1974), and Kalinowski and Sloane (1981). Again, the most effective approaches to changing the home environment processes result in changes in the children's school achievement. (Home Environment—Effect size .50 (69 percentile), Iverson & Walberg, 1982.)

The methods of changing the home environments are relatively costly in terms of parent educators meeting with groups of parents over a series of semi-monthly meetings, but the payoff of this approach is likely to be very great. If parents continue to encourage and support each of their children to learn well in school throughout the elemetary school years, this should greatly help the children during the years they will attend schools and colleges.

Although such research has not been done as yet, we hope that others will explore an approach to the 2 sigma problem of providing effective parent education combined with the mastery learning method. Because parent support takes place in the home and ML takes place in the school, we expect that these two effects will be additive. The result should be close to a 2 sigma improvement in student learning.

Ideally, if both methods began with first or second grade children, one might hope that the combination would result in consistently good learning, at least through the elementary school years, with less and less need for effort expended by the parents or by the use of ML procedures in the school.

Peer Group

During the adolescent years, it is likely that the peer group will have considerable influence on the student's activities, behavior, attitudes, and academic expectations. The peer group(s) to which the individual "belongs" also has some effect on the student's high school achievement level as well as further academic aspirations. These effects appear to be greatest in urban settings. Although it is difficult to influence the student's choice of friends and peer groups, the availability in the school of a variety of extracurricular activities and clubs (e.g., athletics, music, science, mathematics, social, etc.) should enable students to be more selective in their peer choices within the school setting. (Peer Group Influence—Effect size .20 (58 percentile) (Ide, Haertel, Parkerson, & Walberg, 1981).

IMPROVEMENT OF TEACHING

When we compare student learning under conventional instruction and tutoring we note that approximately 20% of the students under conventional instruction do about as well as the tutored students. (See Figure 20.1). That is, tutoring probably would not enable these top students to do any better than they already do under conventional instruction. In contrast, about 80% of the students do relatively poorly under conventional instruction as compared with what they might do under tutoring. We have pondered these facts and believe that this in part results from the unequal treatment of students within most classrooms.

Observations of teacher interaction with students in the classroom reveal that teachers frequently direct their teaching and explanations to some students and ignore others. They give much positive reinforcement and encouragement to some students but not to others, and they encourage active participation in the classroom from some students and discourage it from others. The studies find that typically teachers give students in the top third of the class the greatest attention and students in the bottom third of the class receive the least attention and support. These differences in the interaction between teachers and students provide some students with much greater opportunity and encouragement for learning than is provided for other students in the same classroom (Brophy & Good, 1970.)

It is very different in a one-to-one tutoring situation where there is a constant feedback and corrective process between the tutor and the tutee. If the explanation is not understood by the tutee, the tutor soon becomes aware of it and explains it further. There is much reinforcement and encouragement in the tutoring situation, and the tutee must be actively participating in the learning if the tutoring process is to continue. In contrast, there is less feedback from each student in the group situation to the teacher—and frequently the teacher gets most of the feedback on the clarity of his or her explanations, the effect of the reinforcements, and the degree of active involvement in the learning from a *small* number of high achieving students in the typical class of 30 students.

Teachers are frequently unaware of the fact that they are providing more favorable conditions of learning for some students than they are for other students. Generally, they are under the impression that all students in their classes are given equality of opportunity for learning. One basic assumption of our work on teaching is the belief that when teachers are helped to secure a more accurate picture of their own teaching methods and styles of interaction with their students, they will increasingly be able to provide more favorable learning conditions for more of their students, rather than just for the top fraction of the class.

In some of our research on the 2 sigma problem, we have viewed the task of teaching as providing for more equal treatment of students. We have been trying to give teachers feedback on their differential treatment of students. We attempt to provide teachers with a mirror of what they are now doing and have them develop techniques for equalizing their interactions with the students. These include such techniques as: (a) attempt to find something positive and encouraging

in each student's response, (b) find ways of involving more of the students in active engagement in the learning process, (c) secure feedback from a small random sample of students to determine when they comprehend the explanations and illustrations, and (d) find ways of supplying additional clarification and illustrations as needed. The major emphasis in this work was *not* to change the teachers' *methods* of instruction, but to have the teacher become more aware of the ways in which he or she could more directly teach to a cross section of the students at each class section.

The first of our studies on improving instruction was done by Nordin (1979, 1980), who found ways of improving the cues and explanations for students as well as increasing the active participation of students.

He found it helpful to meet frequently with the teachers to explain these ideas as well as to observe the teachers and help them determine when they still needed to improve these qualities of the instruction. He also had independent observers noting the frequency with which the experimental teachers were using these ideas well or poorly. Similarly, he had students note the frequency with which they were actively participating in the learning and any problems they had with understanding the ideas or explanations.

In this research he compared student learning under conventional instruction and under enhanced cues (explanations) and participation conditions. During the experiment, observers noted that the student participation and the explanations and directions were positive in about 57% of the observations in the control class as compared with about 67% in the enhanced cue + participation classes. Students in the control classes noted that the cues and participation were positive for them about 50% of the time as compared with about 80% of the time for the students in the enhanced cue + participation classes.

In terms of final achievement, the average student in the enhanced cue and participation group was 1.5 sigma higher than the average student in the control classes. (The average student in the enhanced group was above 93% of the students in the control classes.) (See Figure 20.3.) Nordin (1979, 1980) also made use of the ML procedures in other classes and found that they worked even better than the enhanced cue + participation procedures. Unfortunately, he did not use the ML in combination with the enhanced cue + participation methods.

In any case, Nordin (1979, 1980) did demonstrate that teachers could be taught ways to be more responsive to most of the students in the class, secure increased participation of the stu-

dents, and insure that most of the students understood the explanations and illustrations that the teacher provided. The observers noted that the students in the enhanced participation and cue classes were actively engaged in learning (time on task) about 75% of the classroom time, whereas the control students were actively learning only about 57% of the time.

In a later study, Tenenbaum (1982) compared control groups, ML groups, and Enhanced Cues, Participation, and Reinforcement in combination with ML (CPR + ML). Tenenbaum studied

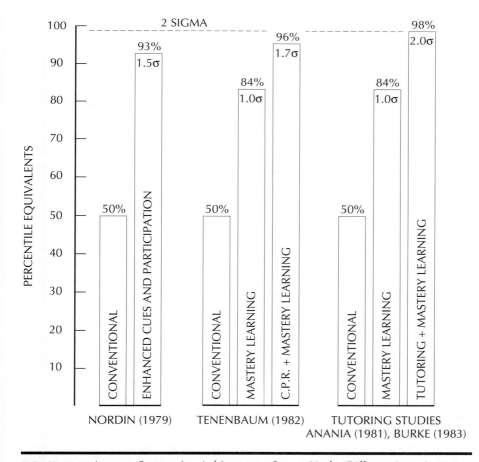

FIGURE 20.3 Average Summative Achievement Scores Under Different Learning Conditions. Comparison of Tutoring Studies, Mastery Learning, and Enhanced Instructional Methods.

these three methods of teaching with randomly assigned students in two different courses—sixth grade science and ninth grade algebra.

Tenenbaum also used student observation of their own classroom processes on cues, participation, and reinforcement. He found that under the CPR + ML, students responded positively about their own participation about 87% of the time as contrasted with 68% in the control classes.

The results of this study demonstrated large differences between the three methods of instruction with the final achievement scores of the CPR + ML group about 1.7 sigmas above the control students (the average student in this group was above 96% of the students in the control group.) The average student in the ML groups was the usual 1 sigma above the control students. (See Figure 20.3).

We believe that this research makes it clear that teachers in both the Nordin and Tenenbaum studies could (at least temporarily) change their teaching methods to provide more equal treatment of the students in their classes. When this more equal treatment is provided and supplemented with the ML feedback and corrective procedures, the average student approaches the level of learning found under tutoring methods of instruction.

We believe there are a variety of methods of giving feedback to teachers on the extent to which they are providing equality of interaction with their students. The tactic of providing a "mirror" to the teacher of the ways in which he or she is providing cues and explanations, appropriate reinforcement, and securing overt as well as covert participation of the students in the learning, seems to us to be an excellent approach. This may be in the form of an observer's notes on what the teacher and students did, student observations of their own interactions with the teaching (preferably anonymous, but coded as to whether the students are in the top third, middle third, or the bottom third of the class in achievement), such as their understanding of the cues and explanations, the extent of their overt & covert participation, and the amount of reinforcement they are getting.

Perhaps a video-tape or audio tape recording of the class could serve the same purpose if the teacher is given brief training on ways of summarizing the classroom interaction between the teacher and the students in the class.

It is our hope that when teachers are helped to secure a more accurate picture of their own teaching methods and styles of interaction with their students, they will be better able to provide favorable learning conditions for most of their students.

IMPROVEMENT OF TEACHING OF THE HIGHER MENTAL PROCESSES

Although there is much of rote learning in schools through the world, in some of the national curriculum centers in different countries (e.g., Israel, Malaysia, South Korea) I find great emphasis on problem-solving, application of principles, analytical skills, and creativity. Such higher mental processes are emphasized because these centers believe that they enable the student to relate his or her learning to the many problems he or she encounters in day-to-day living. These abilities are also stressed because they are retained and used long after the individual has forgotten the detailed specifics of the subject matter taught in the schools. These abilities are regarded as one set of essential characteristics needed to continue learning and to cope with a rapidly changing world. Some curriculum centers believe that these higher mental processes are important because they make learning exciting and constantly new and playful.

In these countries, subjects are taught as methods of inquiry into the nature of science, mathematics, the arts, and the social studies. The subjects are taught as much for the ways of thinking they represent as for their traditional content. Much of this learning makes use of observations, reflections on these observations, experimentation with phenomena, and the use of first hand data and daily experiences, as well as the use of primary printed sources. All of this is reflected in the materials of instruction, the learning and teaching processes used, and the questions and problems used in the quizzes and formative testing, as well as on the final summative examinations.

In sharp contrast with some of these other countries, teachers in the United States typically make use of textbooks that rarely pose real problems. These textbooks emphasize specific content to be remembered and give students little opportunity to discover underlying concepts and principles and even less opportunity to attack real problems in the environments in which they live. The teacher-made tests (and standardized tests) are largely tests of remembered information. After the sale of over one million copies of the *Taxonomy of Educational Objectives—Cognitive Domain* (Bloom, Engelhart, Furst, Hill, & Krathwohl, 1956) and over a quarter of a century of use of this domain in preservice and in-service teacher training, it is estimated that over 90% of test questions that U.S. public school students are *now* expected to answer deal with little more than information. Our instructional material, our classroom teaching methods, and our testing methods rarely rise above the lowest category of the Taxonomy-knowledge.

In the tutoring studies reported at the beginning of this paper, it was found that the tutored students' Higher Mental Process (HMP) achievement was 2.0 sigma above the control students. (See Figure 20.4.) (The average tutored student was above 98% of the control students on the HMP part of the summative examination.) It should be noted that in these studies higher mental processes as well as lower mental process questions were included in the formative tests used in the feedback-corrective processes for both the ML and tutored groups. Again, the point is that students can learn the higher mental processes if they become more central in the teaching-learning process.

Several studies have been made in which the researcher was seeking to improve the higher mental processes.

We have already referred to the Tenenbaum (1982) study, which emphasized changing teacher-student interaction. In this study, the Cue-Participation-Reinforcement + Mastery Learning student group was 1.7 sigma higher than the control students on the higher mental process part of the summative examination. (The average CPR + ML student was above 96% of the control students on the higher mental processes.) (See Figure 20.4.)

Another study done by Levin (1979) was directed to improving the higher mental processes by emphasizing the mastery of the lower mental processes and providing learning experiences in which the students applied principles in a variety of different problem situations. On the summative examinations, the students were very high on the knowledge of principles and facts and in their ability to apply the principles in new problem situations. These experimental students were compared with a control group that was only taught the principles (but not their application). On the higher mental processes, the experimental group was 2 sigma above the control students (the average experimental student was above 98% of the control students) in the ability to apply the principles to new problem situations.

A third study by Mevarech (1980) was directed at improving the higher mental processes by emphasizing heuristic problem solving and including higher and lower mental process questions in the formative testing and in the feedback-corrective processes. On the higher mental process part of the summative tests, the group using the heuristic methods + ML (HMP Teaching + ML) was 1.3 sigma above the control group (L.M.P. Teaching) taught primarily by learning algorithms—a set of rules and procedures for solving particular math problems (the average student in this experimental group was above 90% of the control students).

In all of these studies, attempts to improve higher mental processes included group instruction emphasizing higher mental processes and feedback-corrective processes, which also emphasized higher mental processes. In addition, the tutoring studies included an instructional emphasis on both higher and lower mental processes, as

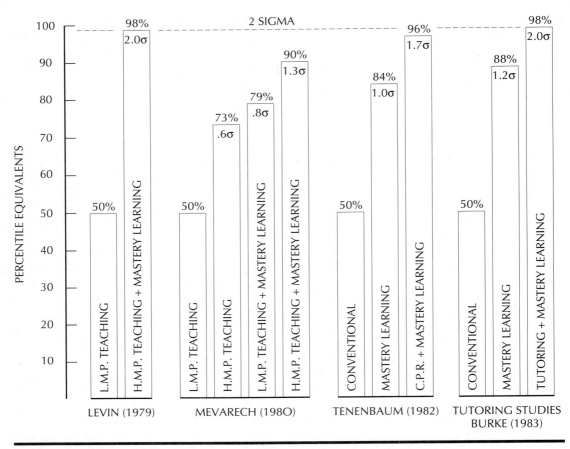

FIGURE 20.4 Average Higher Mental Process Achievement Scores Under Different Learning Conditions. Comparison of Tutoring Studies, Mastery Learning, and Higher Mental Process Instructional Methods.

well as the feedback-corrective processes, which included both higher and lower mental processes. It was evident in all of these studies that in the formative feedback and corrective processes the students needed and received more corrective help on the higher mental processes questions and problems than they did on the lower mental process questions.

CONCLUSION

The Anania (1982, 1983) and Burke (1984) studies comparing student learning under one-to-one

tutoring, ML, and conventional group instruction began in 1980. As the results of these separate studies at different grade levels and in different school subjects began to emerge, we were astonished at the consistency of the findings as well as the great differences in student cognitive achievement, attitudes, and academic self-concept under tutoring as compared with the group methods of instruction.

During the past 4 years, the graduate students in my seminars at the University of Chicago and Northwestern University considered various approaches to the search for group methods of instruction that might be as effective as one-to-one tutoring. This paper reports on the research studies these students have completed, the studies that are still in process, and some of the other ideas we explored in these seminars.

Although all of us at first thought it was an impossible task, we did agree that if we succeeded in finding *one* solution, there would soon be a great many solutions. In this paper, I report on six solutions to the 2 sigma problem. In spite of the difficulties, our graduate students found the problem to be very intriguing because the goal was so clear and specific—*find methods of group instruction as effective as one-to-one tutoring.*

Early in the work, it became evident that more than group instruction in the school had to be considered. We also needed to find ways of improving the students' learning processes, the curriculum and instructional materials, as well as the home environmental support of the students' school learning. This paper is only a preliminary report on what has been accomplished to date, but it should be evident that much can now be done to improve student learning in the schools. However, the search is far from complete. We look for additional solutions to the 2 sigma problem to be reported in the next few years. I hope some of the readers of this article will also find this problem challenging.

APPENDIX: EFFECT SIZE REFERENCES

Tutorial Instruction*
Anania, J. (1982). The effects of quality of instruction on the cognitive and affective learning of students (Doctoral dissertation, University of Chicago, 1981). *Dissertation Abstracts International, 42,* 4269A.

Burke, A. J. (1984). Students' potential for learning contrasted under tutorial and group approaches to instruction (Doctoral dissertation, University of Chicago, 1983). *Dissertation Abstracts International, 44,* 2025A.

*Not effect size studies

Reinforcement
Lysakowski, R. S., & Walberg, H. J. (1981). Classroom reinforcement: A quantitative synthesis. *Journal of Educational Research, 75,* 69–77.

Feedback-Corrective, Cues & Explanations, and Student Classroom Participation
Lysakowski, R. S., & Walberg, H. J. (1982). Instructional effects of cues, participation, and corrective feedback: A quantitative synthesis. *American Educational Research Journal, 19,* 559–578.

Student Time on Task (in the classroom)
Frederick, W. C., & Walberg, H. J. (1980). Learning as a function of time. *Journal of Educational Research, 73,* 183–194.

Improved Reading/Study Skills
Pflaum, S. W., Walberg, H. J., Karegianes, M. L., & Rasher, S. (1980). Reading instruction: A quantitative synthesis. *Educational Researcher, 9,* 12–18.

Cooperative Learning
Slavin, R. E. (1980). Cooperative learning. *Review of Educational Research, 50,* 315–342.

Home Work (graded) and Home Work (assigned)
Paschal, R., Weinstein, T., & Walberg, H. J. (in press). Effects of homework: A quantitative synthesis. *Journal of Educational Research.*

Classroom Morale
Haertel, G. D., Walberg, H. J., & Haertel, E. H. (1981). Social-psychological environments and learning: A quantitative synthesis. *British Educational Research Journal, 7,* 27–36.

Initial Cognitive Prerequisites*
Leyton, F. S. (1983). The extent to which group instruction supplemented by mastery of the initial cognitive prerequisites approximates the learning effectiveness of one-to-one tutorial instruction (Doctoral dissertation, University of Chicago, 1983). *Dissertation Abstracts International, 44,* 974A.

Home Environment Intervention (parental educational program)
Iverson, B. K., & Walberg, H. J. (1982). Home environment and learning: A quantitative synthesis. *Journal of Experimental Education, 50,* 144–151.

Peer & Cross-Age Remedial Tutoring

Cohen, P. A., Kulik, J. A., & Kulik, C. C. (1982). Educational outcomes of tutoring: A meta-analysis of findings. *American Educational Research Journal 19,* 237–248.

Higher Order Questions

Redfield, D. L., & Rousseau, E. W. (1981). Meta-analysis of experimental research on teacher questioning behavior. *Review of Educational Research, 51,* 235–245.

New Science & Math Curricula and Teacher Expectancy

Walberg, H. J. (1984). Improving the productivity of America's schools. *Educational Leadership, 41,* 8, 19–27.

Peer Group Influence

Ide, J., Haertel, G. D., Parkerson, J. A., & Walberg, H. J. (1981). Peer-group influences on learning: A quantitative synthesis. *Journal of Educational Psychology, 73,* 472–484.

Advance Organizers

Luiten, J., Ames, W., & Ackerson, G. (1980). A meta-analysis of the effects of advance organizers on learning and retention. *American Educational Research Journal, 17,* 211–218.

ENDNOTES

1. In giving the percentile equivalent we make use of the normal curve distribution. The control class distributions were approximately normal, although the mastery learning and tutoring groups were highly skewed.

2. $\dfrac{\text{Mean experimental} - \text{Mean control}}{\text{standard deviation of the control}} =$

$$\frac{\text{Mex} - \text{Mc}}{\text{sigma of control}} = \textit{effect size.}$$

3. When questionnaires rather than interviews and observations have been used, the correlations are somewhat lower, with the average being between +.45 and +.55.

REFERENCES

Anania, J. (1982). The effects of quality of instruction on the cognitive and affective learning of students. (Doctoral dissertation, University of Chicago, 1981). *Dissertation Abstracts International, 42,* 4269A.

Anania, J. (1983). "The influence of instructional conditions on student learning and achievement." *Evaluation in Education: An International Review Series, 7,* 1, 1–92.

Ausubel, D. (1960). The use of advanced organizers in the learning and retention of meaningful verbal material. *Journal of Educational Psychology, 51,* 267–272.

Bloom, B. S. (1980). The new direction in educational research: alterable variables. *Phi Delta Kappan, 61,* 6, 382–385.

Bloom, B. S., Engelhart, M. D., Furst, E. J., Hill, W. H., & Krathwohl, D. R. (1956). *Taxonomy of Educational Objectives: Handbook I, Cognitive Domain.* New York: Longman.

Bronfenbrenner, U. (1974). Is Early Intervention Effective? In H. J. Leichter, (Ed.), *The Family as Educator.* New York: Teachers College Press.

Brophy, J. E., & Good, T. L. (1970). Teachers' communication of differential expectations for children's classroom performance: Some behavioral data. *Journal of Educational Psychology, 61,* 365–374.

Burke, A. J. (1984). Students' potential for learning contrasted under tutorial and group approaches to instruction. (Doctoral dissertation, University of Chicago, 1983). *Dissertation Abstracts International, 44,* 2025A.

Dave, R. H. (1963). The identification and measurement of environment process variables that are related to educational achievement. (Unpublished doctoral dissertation, University of Chicago).

Dolan, L. J. (1980). The affective correlates of home concern and support, instructional quality, and achievement. (Unpublished doctoral dissertation, University of Chicago).

Ide, J., Haertel, G. D., Parkerson, J. A., & Walberg, H. J. (1981). Peer group influences on leaning: A quantitive synthesis. *Journal of Educational Psychology, 73,* 472–484.

Iverson, B. K., & Walberg, H. J. (1982). Home environment and learning: A quantitative synthesis. *Journal of Experimental Education, 50,* 144–151.

Janhom S. (1983) Educating parents to educate their children. (Unpublished doctoral dissertation, University of Chicago).

Kalinowski, A., & Sloane, K. (1981). The home environment and school achievement. *Studies in Educational Evaluation, 7,* 85–96.

Levin, T. (1979). Instruction which enables students to develop higher mental processes. *Evaluation in Education: An International Review Series, 3,* 3, 173–220.

Leyton, F. S. (1983). The extent to which group instruction supplemented by mastery of the initial cognitive prerequisites approximates the learning effectiveness of one-to-one tutorial methods. (Doctoral dissertation, University of Chicago, 1983). *Dissertation Abstracts International, 44,* 974A.

Luiten, J., Ames, W., & Ackerson, G. (1980). A meta-analysis of the effects of advance organizers on learning and retention. *American Educational Research Journal, 17,* 211–218.

Marjoribanks, K. (1974). *Environments for Learning.* London: National Foundation for Educational Research.

Mevarech, Z. R. (1980). The role of teaching-learning strategies and feedback-corrective procedures in developing higher cognitive achievement. (Unpublished doctoral dissertation, University of Chicago).

Nordin, A. B. (1979). The effects of different qualities of instruction on selected cognitive, affective, and time variables. (Unpublished doctoral dissertation, University of Chicago).

Nordin, A. B. (1980). Improving learning: An experiment in rural primary schools in Malaysia. *Evaluation in Education: An International Review Series, 4,* 2, 143–263.

Pflaum, S. W., Walberg, H. J., Karegianes, M. L., & Rasher, S. (1980). Reading instruction: A quantitative synthesis. *Educational Researcher, 9,* 12–18.

Slavin, R. E. (1980). Cooperative Learning. *Review of Educational Research, 50,* 315–342.

Tenenbaum, G. (1982). A method of group instruction which is as effective as one-to-one tutorial instruction. (Doctoral dissertation, University of Chicago, 1982). *Dissertation Abstracts International, 43,* 1822A.

Walberg, H. J. (1984). Improving the productivity of America's schools. *Educational Leadership, 41,* 8, 19–27.

Wolf, R. M. (1964). The identification and measurement of home environmental process variables that are related to intelligence. (Upublished doctoral dissertation, University of Chicago).

Wolf, R. M. (1966). The Measurement of Environments. In A. Anastasi (Ed.), *Testing Problems in Perspective.* Washington D.C.: American Council on Education.

DISCUSSION QUESTIONS

1. Is the mastery learning approach appropriate for all students?

2. How does a teacher's differential interaction with students influence student achievement?

3. How are conditions of learning integrally related to student outcomes?

4. What type of staff development initiatives might be undertaken to provide teachers with an accurate perception of the quality of learning conditions that they provide for their students?

5. How effective are conventional instruction, mastery learning, and tutoring?

Detracking Schools: Early Lessons from the Field

JEANNIE OAKES
MARTIN LIPTON

FOCUSING QUESTIONS

1. *What are the characteristics that underlie detracking?*
2. *How is tracking related to beliefs about the capacity of humans?*
3. *How do different conceptions of intelligence support the practice of detracking?*
4. *What role do social norms and cultural values play in the debate on tracking?*
5. *How might conceptions of teaching be altered to support detracking?*

During the past decade, research on tracking and ability-grouped class assignments has provided striking evidence that these practices have a negative impact on most children's school opportunities and outcomes. Moreover, the negative consequences of these practices disproportionately affect low-income, African-American, and Latino children.[1]

Increasingly, this research evidence is triggering responses from reform-minded policy makers and educators. The National Governors' Association has recommended detracking as part of its strategy for meeting the national education goals; the Carnegie Corporation endorses detracking in *Turning Points,* its report on reforms for the middle grades; and the College Board's report, *Access to Knowledge: An Agenda for Our Nation's Schools,* identifies tracking as a barrier in many students' paths to college. After vigorous discussion, the National Education Association resolved to eliminate tracking as it is now practiced. Across the country, local educators and policy makers are questioning their own local practices, and many are moving toward alternatives.

While there has yet to be a comprehensive study of detracking,[2] the stories we've been told by those engaged in detracking projects, our informal observations in schools, and accounts reported in the media and by other analysts provide rich information about attempts to detrack. These individual anecdotes and analyses are of great interest to educators and policy makers who are contemplating detracking. But far more useful is the general lesson that can be drawn from them. This lesson is that a *culture of detracking* is more important than the specific alternative or implementation strategy chosen. While the particulars of detracking vary considerably from school to school, there appear to be commonalities in the cultures of schools that detrack successfully. These commonalities don't always take the same form, and they don't follow any particular sequence. But in some form, at some time, the following characteristics become part of the culture of "detracked" schools:

- recognition that tracking is supported by powerful norms that must be acknowledged and addressed as alternatives are created;
- willingness to broaden the reform agenda, so that changes in the tracking structure become part of a comprehensive set of changes in school practice;

- engagement in a process of inquiry and experimentation that is idiosyncratic, opportunistic, democratic, and politically sensitive;
- alterations in teachers' roles and responsibilities, including changes in the ways adults in the school work together; and
- persistence over the long haul that is sustained by risk-taking leaders who are clearly focused on scholarship and democratic values.

CONFRONTING POWERFUL NORMS

Schools that choose to undertake detracking may try jumping to agreement on new policies and practices. However, easy agreement usually proves elusive, and successful schools move away rather quickly from an exclusively practical focus. Instead, they pay considerable attention to the philosophies, values, and beliefs that underlie their tracking practices and that make agreement about alternatives so difficult. We suspect that this happens because it becomes apparent that tracking makes perfectly good sense, given prevailing school norms, and that most of the proposed alternatives do not.

For example, tracking structures are firmly grounded in widespread and historically rooted beliefs about human capacity and about individual and group differences. Tracking is also supported by outmoded conceptions that intelligence is global (i.e., a single entity that can be measured and reported as an I.Q. score), that it is fixed quite early (either before birth or soon thereafter), and that learning is the accumulation of a sequence of knowledge and skills.

If the *capacity to learn* is understood as unalterable and the range in capacity among schoolchildren is perceived to be great, then tracking must appear sensible. In this view, schools accommodate differences by separating students according to their measured ability and by adapting curriculum and instruction accordingly. The fact that learning capacity seems to be unevenly distributed among groups—with disadvantaged members of minority groups exhibiting less capacity to learn—appears to be beyond the control

of the school. Thus schools typically conclude that the disproportionate assignment of low-income and minority students to low-track classes is an appropriate, if regrettable, response.

Alternatives to tracking begin to make sense when schools seriously entertain other conceptions of intelligence and learning: when detracking is not merely a response to an abstract sense of fairness but is also a practical way to act on new knowledge about intelligence and learning. A number of educators have told us that their views have been dramatically altered by the work of Howard Gardner and of Robert Sternberg, both of whom argue compellingly that intelligence is multifaceted and developmental and that learning is a complex process of constructing meaning. Serious consideration of their work has enabled these educators to invest new meanings in such popular notions as "all children can learn," rather than simply to mouth them as meaningless, if well-intentioned, slogans. And when they no longer interpret such statements to mean that all children can achieve their very different "potentials," educators can let go of the belief that children of "like potentials" must be grouped together.

These shifting conceptions of intelligence and learning have enabled a number of schools to support detracking by setting up heterogeneous classrooms in which instruction challenges the sense-making abilities of all capable (if different) children and in which differences become assets rather than liabilities. For example, Susan Benjamin of Highland Park (Illinois) High School described the values underlying untracked classrooms at her school. "In the English Department," Benjamin wrote in the March 1990 *English Journal,* "the basic philosophy is that diversity within the classroom enriches the learning environment."[3]

But powerful beliefs about the purposes of schooling also support tracking. For example, most Americans believe that schools should transmit the essential knowledge and values of the culture to all students as well as prepare a highly productive work force. While the first part of this belief argues for common schooling experiences, the second often provides a rationale for tracked schools with differentiated curricula that prepare students for different types of jobs. When schools explicitly acknowledge these seemingly contradictory purposes, they are likely to find that *all* students benefit from the diversity of learning experiences previously reserved either for college-bound or work-force-bound students.

Detracking, then, seems to involve a critical and unsettling rethinking of fundamental educational norms. This rethinking asks people to challenge their entrenched views of such matters as human capacities, individual and group differences, the purposes of schooling, and the ever-present tensions between the norms of competitive individualism and the more democratic norms of support and community. As Paula Hatfield of the J. A. Leonard Middle School in Old Town, Maine, observed, "Simply eliminating tracking will not cure all of the ills of schooling and society. However, it may set off a powerful synergistic reaction requiring other institutional changes, changes in how teachers teach, how students relate to each other, and how the school hierarchy operates. Most important, it may liberate students' and teachers' beliefs about who should and could achieve."[4]

CHANGE IS COMPREHENSIVE

Proposals for detracking often trigger the expectation that schools will simply mix their classes and then teach all children in the same way, at the same time. Of course, that has happened in some schools, and the "reform" has nearly always been frustrating, counterproductive, and short-lived. However, altered conceptions of students' learning capacity notwithstanding, most schools do not gloss over the fact that children are different and that they need opportunities to learn differently in heterogeneous schools and classrooms.

This realization almost inevitably leads to a much broader set of changes in school structures and practices. Most educators find that they must confront simultaneously the complex and often muddy interactions of the many dimensions of schooling: curriculum, teaching practices, the social organization of the classroom, responses to children's special needs, assessment, and much more. The following discussion illustrates how this can happen.[5]

Reconstructed Curriculum

Most schools undergoing detracking redesign their curriculum around rich and complex ideas and steer away from a highly sequenced curriculum that focuses on discrete topics and skills. Educators at these schools don't assume that all children in heterogeneous classes will eventually know the same things (nor should they, given the many differences among them), but they proceed on the assumption that all children can understand—and should be engaged in—the core ideas of the curriculum. Educators report that a rich, concept-based curriculum enables them to:

- frame learning tasks as complex problems,
- provide contexts that give meaning to facts,
- take informal knowledge seriously,
- allow for multiple right answers,
- promote socially constructed knowledge,
- require long-term projects.

A curriculum so designed appears to be much more accommodating of differences in students' prior knowledge and skills. More practically, it permits educators to generate lessons that make it less likely that some students will be left behind or that others will be bored because the lessons have been watered down.

We find examples of such curricular shifts in a number of schools that are detracking. For example, when the San Diego City Schools and the Denver Public Schools jettisoned their remedial classes in middle schools and high schools, the curriculum shifted from an emphasis on skills to an emphasis on contextual learning and problem solving. When Fox Lane High School in Bedford, New York, detracked its ninth grade, teachers formed interdisciplinary teams and organized the curriculum around such themes as the Cold War or the Middle East. They've also scheduled periods of flexible "team time" into the day, when students can work together on academic projects, use the library/media center resources, and meet with teachers for extra help.

At Pioneer Valley Regional School in Northfield, Massachusetts, the English Department chair reports that traditional approaches to curriculum and instruction needed to be revamped when classes became heterogeneous. He describes how neither teaching as he always had nor watering down the curriculum worked with mixed groups of students. Consequently, the English Department decided to develop a new curriculum around themes. "The first year it bombed," he acknowledges. "We did not know what to do. We had always been the center of the class, made the decisions, told the kids how to look at material and judge its quality. The secret was to create a situation where everyone learned together, and no one dominated."[6]

Expanded Instructional Repertoire

It should come as no surprise that traditional, teacher-and-textbook-dominated instruction becomes inadequate when teachers design lessons intended to engage diverse groups of students in rich, complex ideas. Most educators look for alternative instructional strategies that depend less on students' similarities in prior achievement and that more easily accommodate multiple approaches to learning.

That's why so many schools engaged in detracking turn to cooperative learning. Many educators have observed the positive effects on achievement when diverse groups of children work together on well-structured cooperative tasks, with even the strongest students making considerable intellectual gains.[7] Many are aware, too, of evidence that the status hierarchy related to levels of ability can also break down when teachers help students acquire the social skills for working together productively.[8] However, most detracking schools realize that cooperative groups alone can't provide the entire social, psy-

chological, or intellectual context children require and that the effectiveness of cooperative learning can be limited if it is the only change in heterogeneous classrooms. Other strategies, such as long-term individual projects and classroom tasks that require active learning, are also well-suited to heterogeneous classrooms.

New Provisions for Special Needs

One of the most logistically difficult and politically volatile aspects of tracking reform is whether and how heterogeneous schools and classrooms serve students with special needs—including those identified as having learning difficulties and those identified as intellectually gifted. Schools that are detracking successfully make sure that the special needs of these children are addressed—even when they are members of heterogeneous classes.

Most parents of and advocates for learning-disabled students are eager to have them included in heterogeneous classrooms—as long as teachers are sensitive to their needs and have access to specialized help. And most of them find detracking with appropriate assistance a constructive response to the stigma and reduced opportunities that often accompany special education placements. For example, some schools schedule students' time with special education or Chapter 1 resource teachers after school; others team regular and special education teachers so that specialized help can be incorporated into the regular classroom. In some schools, students who are having difficulty keeping up in heterogeneous academic classes are enrolled in a support or booster class (taken in place of an elective) where they receive additional instruction; in others, peer- or cross-age tutoring programs offer after-school help. Some schools make reading assignments available on cassette tapes so that less accomplished readers can participate fully in academic coursework. Most schools find that once they accept the idea of providing extra help without tracking—once the norms change—devising specific strategies is quite easy.

It is a far more difficult political problem to integrate students who've had access to gifted and talented programs or honors classes, partly because of the high status that accompanies these placements. Educators and parents are aware that these students have been advantaged educationally by these special programs, and, even if those advantages have been gained at the expense of other students, no one is eager to see any students wind up with less than they had before. Thus schools must develop heterogeneous classes that don't compromise the educational opportunities of gifted and talented students.

Many elementary and middle schools have taken the position that well-designed heterogeneous classes (built on the types of curriculum and instructional changes mentioned above) can meet the needs of most intellectually gifted students. But many schools also provide special activities for high achievers either within the regular classroom or after school. Most schools report success with this approach—but only after considerable time and work with parents.

Senior highs—particularly in districts where students have been tracked throughout elementary and middle school—have been less successful in detracking, especially in such highly sequenced subjects as mathematics. By the time students are in high school, the achievement and motivation gaps between the highest and lowest achievers have grown quite wide, and many teachers cannot envision a high-quality curriculum that could accommodate the range of student abilities, especially in mathematics and science. English and social studies teachers often seem less daunted, but even they find that their efforts to combine honors or gifted programs with regular classes—even regular college-preparatory classes—generate enormous resistance from parents.

In some districts, parents have used their political clout to halt any detracking efforts, and in others they have threatened to withdraw their children and enroll them in private schools. For both substantive and political reasons, many high schools choose to leave their honors and gifted programs in place, particularly for 11th- and 12th-graders. However, some schools have adopted more of an "open admissions" policy, recruiting students with varying abilities into honors and advanced placement classes, rather than enforcing strict entry criteria.

Alternative assessment and grading practices. Traditional assessment strategies often have a profoundly negative impact in heterogeneous classes. When teachers routinely compare students with their peers and make those comparisons public (whether in as benign a way as posting charts with stars for every book read or in as crass a way as announcing test scores aloud), the status hierarchy of "ability" that detracking seeks to eliminate simply resurfaces within heterogeneous classes. In addition, public comparisons of students' performance lead many children to underrate their capacity for learning, and even very young students may come to believe that success or failure in school is beyond their control and so exert less effort and accomplish less.[9] This consequence—worrisome in any classroom—is particularly troubling in mixed-ability groups.

Not surprisingly, then, schools developing alternatives to tracking often look for new assessment strategies. Many eagerly await the refinement of technologies of portfolio assessments and structured observations of students engaged in tasks and experiments. Others are forging ahead and creating their own. For example, John Blaydes, principal of McGaugh Elementary School in Los Alamitos, California, engaged his staff in a process of obtaining more authentic assessments of children in detracked classes by having teachers try alternative types of testing, observe experiments, and collect portfolio samples. By these private and more personalized strategies, Blaydes and his teachers hope to develop the belief that hard work pays off and to prevent assessment from becoming the raw material for judgments about who is smart and who isn't.

Senior high schools face a tougher challenge as they confront normative grading practices held firmly in place by long-established traditions and by the admissions requirements of colleges and universities. In states in which grades are weighted according to the track level of academic classes, detracking threatens to deflate the grade-point averages of students who would ordinarily be in the highest tracks. For example, in California, guidance counselors are routinely told that students not taking honors classes are at a distinct disadvantage when they seek admission to the University of California.

Politically acceptable alternatives seem beyond the reach of most schools, in spite of many sensible proposals and some successful beginnings. Some schools, such as Parkway South High School in Manchester, Missouri, offer heterogeneous classes wherein students can choose to meet the standards for either an honors grade (additional research or advanced reading) or a regular grade. Others have made special arrangements with college admissions offices to allow alternative assessment information to supplement students' transcripts.

These few examples illustrate the point that successful detracking inevitably triggers many other changes. The reason is fairly clear: each current school structure and practice is consistent with and serves to hold others in place; changing any one—like tracking—invariably upsets the balance of the rest.

NURTURING INQUIRY

Attention to new norms, curriculum, instruction, assessment, and special needs constitute the "what" of detracking. We have also been able to observe some consistent patterns in the "how," the process of detracking.

Schools that have found some measure of success have proceeded in ways that are strategic, idiosyncratic, timely, and politically sensitive. In most places, educators, policy makers, and parents engage in difficult but fascinating inquiry into their own schools. They experiment with small-scale alternatives of their own design— moving and changing where they can, when they can, and with those who are eager to go along.

This process is politically savvy in schools where not everyone favors detracking. But even in the unlikely event that everyone did favor detracking, schools could not simply replace tracking with a "correct" off-the-shelf alternative. This fact reflects an important lesson from the history of school improvement: one school's successful alternative or restructured practice can become another school's slick, packaged, and soon-to-be-abandoned flash in the pan.

An essential element of the process of detracking seems to be opening up a dialogue about tracking—both within and outside the school. Many districts and schools have convened task forces of interested members of the school community, including those vocal on both sides of the issue. Such task forces often read research on tracking, assess local practices, and explore alternatives. Schools often correct data about their own grouping structures and course placements and analyze these by race, socioeconomic background, language, gender, and special education status. Such data can form the basis for the discussion of such questions as, What are our school's grouping goals, and are they currently being met? What is the procedure for placing students in ability groups? Are there ample opportunities for interaction among students from different ability groups? What successful practices are employed within high-ability classes that can be replicated schoolwide?

For example, in 1984 the San Diego City Schools undertook a five-year study of their grouping practices and of the effects of tracking on educational opportunities. The data stimulated vigorous debate about the nature of the problem and ways to confront it. As in most school systems, the process was often uncomfortable, but it has led to a set of slow, incremental steps toward detracking.[10]

In Ann Arbor, Michigan, a 62-member task force that included parents, community representatives, teachers, and administrators spent two years reviewing the literature on tracking, collecting data about local practices, developing a board policy on ability grouping and tracking, and making recommendations for modifying existing practices. The participatory process educated decision makers, encouraged the thoughtful use of information, emphasized the importance of teacher judgment and reflection, and laid the groundwork for pilot projects and experiments. The policy that resulted from the efforts of the task force set guidelines and expectations for further decision making and created a five-year plan for detracking that wisely avoided rules, regulations, or specific prescriptions for change. The joint leadership provided by the superintendent, the board, and the task force helped establish communication, encouraged persistence when things got rough, and institutionalized the sharing of responsibility.[11]

In the Crete-Monee Central Unified School District in Crete, Illinois, progress toward alternatives occurred when teachers and administrators piloted alternatives to tracking and generated guidelines for new policies.[12] The following "insights" emerged:

- a proportion of teachers will maintain a "residual suspicion" of heterogeneous grouping;
- the curriculum is not set up to accommodate heterogeneous grouping;
- teachers must expand their perception of useful instructional strategies;
- unintended or covert tracking must be identified and anticipated;
- flexible skill-adjusted grouping and other potentially beneficial grouping practices "should be acknowledged and efforts taken to curtail any negative effects"; and
- teachers must receive appropriate training and preparation.

These aren't earth-shattering realizations. In some form or another they can be found in most research on educational change. Perhaps the only true surprise is that this knowledge was developed on site, "reinvented" by people who actually had to make use of the insights.

And it is important that productive inquiry and experimentation go beyond understanding the technology of tracking. As Ann Arbor's par-

ticipatory process aptly demonstrates, successful efforts to create alternatives to tracking require careful attention to the prevailing norms and politics of the school and of the larger community.

"It takes a long time." "Attitudes have to change, and that's not easy." "People feel threatened all over the place." We have yet to encounter an attempt to detrack a school or district that didn't generate comments such as these. "It's not a painless process," says Everett Masters, principal of Pioneer Valley Regional School in Northfield, Massachusetts, in referring to his school's eight-year effort to move toward heterogeneous classes.

Yet Pioneer Valley School seems to have brought together the essential ingredients for genuine school change, including persistence over time and attention to the beliefs, politics, and technologies that seem to make for successful heterogeneous grouping. An ad hoc committee at Pioneer Valley drew attention to the problems generated by tracking. With the support of the chair of the school committee, workshops for teachers were held, and courses on new teaching styles and strategies were taught by university faculty members. In the fall of 1990 the school sponsored its second conference on "Derailing the Tracked School" and shared its successes with other schools—even as it continues to struggle with its own thorny problems of heterogeneity.

The primary lesson to be drawn from these experiences is that, if whole institutions can be said to learn new things, then schools must *make sense* of their own experiences and learn new ways through their own inquiry and investigation. To some degree, each detracking school reinvents the wheel.

CHANGES FOR TEACHERS

Perhaps most important, these promising moves toward detracking suggest that school systems must avoid dividing the tasks of inquiry and experimentation according to conventional notions of "who's good at what." Usually, inquiry into new policies and practices is thought to be the purview of the principal or the superintendent. These leaders are expected to read, discuss, and investigate research findings; to attend symposia on new topics; and so on. Conversely, teachers are expected to gain the technical competence to try out new teaching strategies—with little attention to theory and research.

Much is lost by this division of effort, and we doubt that detracking can succeed if the division persists. Where changes are occurring, site and district administrators take the time to become immersed in new practices and to become familiar with the new roles teachers will be asked to assume. When they do, administrators sense firsthand the full range of schoolwide changes that are needed to support new classroom practices, they can better explain and defend new practices to their communities, and they can more completely assess the effectiveness of those practices. Teachers, on the other hand, must be able to make sense out of the new practices and structures—not simply implement them. If teachers' roles are reduced to simply following new sets of teaching protocols or simply learning new classroom scripts, they are unlikely to be effective—if indeed they adopt the new practices at all.

The comprehensive changes that detracking requires almost always trigger significant changes in the ways teachers work together. In nearly every detracking school we've studied, teachers report that it's neither technically nor emotionally possible to undertake the shift to heterogeneous grouping in isolation. Teaming is the most common solution we've encountered, although that does not always mean that teachers actually teach together.

Sometimes teaming means that teachers at a particular grade level or teachers of a particular subject pool their resources to create new lessons for heterogeneous classes, try them out individually, and then assess and revise them collectively. In other cases, teachers have joined together in cross-displinary teams that share responsibility for a group of students for one or more years. This approach seems particularly useful among middle school teachers, who then are able to make decisions together about their students' academic and social needs. Of course, productive cooperation imposes some special demands on the school schedule. Working together requires time, and at least some of that time must be available during the school day.

COMMITMENT OF LEADERS

Tracking is entrenched; sensible alternatives are complex, sometimes counter intuitive, and often controversial. Even when alternatives emerge from an inclusive and democratic process of inquiry and experimentation, steering the process of detracking through the inevitably troubled waters of school and community politics calls for strong leaders who unequivocally and unambiguously—if gently—assert the research, theory, and democratic values that support detracking.

At schools we've watched struggle over tracking, we've heard leaders identify specific ways in which their efforts are thwarted by traditions that hold tracking in place. They have openly, often courageously, acknowledged that curricular, administrative, teaching, and other traditions are more powerful than the profession's best knowledge of how children actually learn and that sometimes these traditions run contrary to deeply held democratic values.

Sometimes commitment requires telling a truth that everybody already knows. For example, recently Steve Leonard, principal of Boston's Martin Luther King Middle School and a member of the Boston school system's task force reviewing tracking practices, told reporters, "I would like to be able to look every parent in the eye and say, 'If you put your child in the Boston public schools, we will do everything we can to ensure that your child has a successful academic experience.' Right now, I couldn't honestly do that."[13]

We've heard other district and site administrators insist that new knowledge about intelligence and learning form the basis of instructional decisions. They speak out for a curriculum that provides all students with access to the most valued knowledge, they support evaluation that isn't easily summed up in a single test score, and they tell parents of gifted children that their sons and daughters will be well-served in heterogeneous classrooms. We've heard other administrators state unequivocally that teachers must have dramatically altered working conditions (e.g., time, support, resources, collegial work groups) if they are to make alternatives to tracking work.

Such assertions are a far cry from the pious and syrupy—if well-meant—statements of commitment to all children that garner widespread agreement and grace schools' mission statements. Confronting what's wrong with schools is a necessary—if risky—first step toward making changes. Successful leaders press their schools and communities to investigate, debate, and eventually move together toward practices that are consistent with research knowledge and democratic values. While these leaders are sensibly *strategic* as their schools implement new practices—perhaps taking a step back for each two forward or settling for half a loaf rather than none—they do not compromise the knowledge and democratic values that guide their professional commitments to children. And, by the way, they nearly always report the process to be professionally and personally invigorating.

THE CENTRAL LESSON

Research on tracking documents the negative consequences that these practices have for most children. Moreover, the research implicates a broad, complex, and interacting set of school characteristics and beliefs that sustain these practices. It's not surprising, then, that efforts to change a practice as deeply embedded as tracking necessarily address a broad array of normative and political concerns, as well as technical matters.

The anecdotal data about detracking call attention to a set of early commonalities in the cultures of detracking schools, while confirming that there is no simple "detracking" formula. Alternatives and the specific ways in which schools

go about detracking vary considerably. Like any other significant school reform, detracking is an extraordinarily difficult process that must fit the idiosyncrasies of local conditions.

Furthermore, while we have only a handful of completely detracked schools, partial solutions and compromises are springing up everywhere. Some of these efforts address fundamental tracking related problems (e.g., enrolling low-achieving high school students in extra "booster" classes so that they can keep up in rigorous heterogeneous core courses); some represent politically viable first steps in a long-term reform process (e.g., piloting detracking in a single subject within a school). Others are far less promising (e.g., "detracking" except for honors and remedial classes). The latter effort is unlikely to alter tracking's negative consequences or to lead to more substantial reforms, since it maintains the norms and structures that foster tracking and does little more than reshuffle the status quo.

CONCLUSION

Perhaps the central lesson to be drawn from our observations is that successful models can give schoolpeople confidence about the possibility and direction for change. But, as useful as these examples might seem, we should hesitate to trumpet too loudly any one school's specific alternative or implementation process as a model for others to follow. Ultimately, each school must find its own way to create a *culture for detracking* that enables it to make sense of its own situation and create alternatives that fit.

ENDNOTES

1. Adam Gamoran and Mark Berends, "The Effects of Stratification in Schools: Synthesis of Survey and Ethnographic Research," *Review of Educational Research,* vol. 57, 1987, pp. 415–35; Jeannie Oakes, *Keeping Track: How Schools Structure Inequality* (New Haven, Conn.: Yale University Press, 1985); idem, *Multiplying Inequalities: The Effects of Race, Social Class, and Tracking on Opportunities to Learn*

Mathematics and Science (Santa Monica, Calif.: RAND Corporation, 1990); Jeannie Oakes et al., *Educational Matchmaking: Toward a Better Understanding of High School Curriculum and Tracking Decisions* (Santa Monica, Calif.: RAND Corporation, in press); Robert Slavin, "Grouping for Instruction in the Elementary School," in idem, ed., *School and Classroom Organization* (Hillsdale, N.J.: Erlbaum, 1989); idem, "Ability Grouping and Student Achievement in Secondary Schools," *Review of Educational Research,* vol. 60, 1990, pp. 417–99; and idem, "Are Cooperative Learning and 'Untracking' Harmful to the Gifted?," *Educational Leadership,* March 1991, pp. 68–71.

2. Some preliminary work has been begun, however. In 1989 Robert Slavin and Jomills Braddock of the Center for Research on Effective Schooling for Disadvantaged Students conducted a survey of alternatives to tracking, and Anne Wheelock of the Massachusetts Advocacy Center has recently begun a project sponsored by the Edna McConnell Clark Foundation that will result in more comprehensive descriptions of detracked schools.

3. "Tracking: What Do You Think?," *English Journal,* March 1990, p. 75.

4. Ibid.

5. For a more elaborate discussion of approaches to restructuring these and other domains of schooling, see Jeannie Oakes and Martin Lipton, *Making the Best of Schools: A Handbook for Parents, Teachers, and Policymakers* (New Haven: Yale University Press, 1990).

6. Jean Caldwell, "A School on Track Without 'Tracking,' " *Boston Globe,* 5 August 1990, p. 57.

7. Slavin, "Ability Grouping . . ."; and idem, "Are Cooperative Learning and 'Untracking' Harmful?"

8. Elizabeth Cohen, *Designing Groupwork: Strategies for the Heterogeneous Classroom* (New York: Teachers College Press, 1986).

9. Deborah Stipek, "Children's Motivation to Learn," in Tommy M. Tomlinson and Herbert J. Walberg, eds., *Academic Work and Educational Excellence* (Berkeley, Calif.: McCutchan, 1986).

10. George Frey, "Equity in Student Placement in the San Diego Unified School District: The Good, the Bad, and the Ugly," paper presented at the annual meeting of the American Educational Research Association, New Orleans, 1988; and J. H. Lytle, "Minority Student Access to and Preparation for Higher Education," preliminary report presented at the annual meeting of the Council for Great City Schools, Miami, 1989.

11. Doreen Poupard-Tice, "Developing an Instructional Grouping Policy: A Participatory Model," paper presented at the annual meeting of the American Educational Research Association, New Orleans, 1988.

12. Carolyn S. Anderson and Rebecca Barr, "Teacher Response to Proposed Changes in Grouping: Impact on Policy and Practice," in Reba Page and Linda Valli, eds., *Curriculum Differentiation: Interpretive Studies* (New York: Teachers College Press, 1990).

13. Diego Ribadeneira, "School Chief Picks Panel on Tracking, Retention," *Boston Globe,* 12 October 1990.

DISCUSSION QUESTIONS

1. What modifications might be needed in subject matter content and instructional approaches to support detracking?

2. How would detracting impact the process of mainstreaming special needs students?

3. Can heterogeneous classes meet the needs of all students? Why? Why not?

4. What procedures will be necessary to successfully detrack a senior high school?

5. In what ways can administrators and organizational structures support or impede the process of detracking?

Synthesis of Research on Compensatory and Remedial Education

LORIN W. ANDERSON
LEONARD O. PELLICER

FOCUSING QUESTIONS

1. *What are the goals of compensatory and remedial education programs?*
2. *How do differences in staffing impact the effectiveness of such programs?*
3. *How does coordination with the regular education program influence student outcomes?*
4. *What are some of the disadvantages of compensatory and remedial education?*
5. *What role should educators play in reforming compensatory and remedial programs?*

Over the past quarter century, programs designed to provide quality education for children who are economically disadvantaged and educationally deficient have received substantial funding. The major federally-funded program of this type, Chapter 1, accounts for 20 percent of the U.S. Department of Education's total budget, or almost four billion dollars a year. Approximately one of every nine school-age children is enrolled in the Chapter 1 program (OERI 1987).

In recent years, individual states have begun to fund their own programs targeted toward students who fail to meet state achievement standards. In South Carolina, for example, at least one-fourth of the children enrolled in public schools are in state-funded compensatory and remedial programs.[1] Since 1985, the cost of the program in South Carolina has averaged over $55 million per year, a figure which represents approximately 20 percent of the total monies raised

in support of the school reform legislation (Anderson et al. 1989).

Whether the money is supplied by federal, state, or local funds, large amounts of money are spent on the education of these children. But what do we know about the operation and effectiveness of these programs? Do the academic gains made by the children served in these programs justify the large expenditure of funds? Are changes needed in the programs to increase their effectiveness? These are the issues we will examine in this paper, basing our generalizations on the results of numerous studies conducted during the past 15 years.

COSTS AND FUNDING

Compensatory and remedial programs are more costly than regular programs. Carter (1984) estimated that Chapter 1 services cost about $436 more per student than the services provided to non-Chapter 1 students. In South Carolina, services provided to students in compensatory and remedial programs cost approximately $362 and $159 more per student, respectively, than those provided to students not in special programs (Anderson et al. 1989). While these figures must be continually adjusted for increases in the cost of living, it is apparent that compensatory and remedial programs require substantial amounts of additional funds.

Compensatory and remedial programs are funding programs, not educational programs. The criteria and guidelines for these programs specify quite clearly *which* students are to be served, but tend to avoid specifying *how* students are to be served. For the federally-funded program, schools are selected on the basis of economic indicators (e.g., free or reduced price lunch status), while the eligibility of the students in those schools for the program depends on their levels of achievement. State-funded programs often rely exclusively on student achievement to determine which students are eligible for inclusion. In South Carolina, for example, all students who fail to achieve a passing score on one or more of the state's basic skills tests are eligible for placement in the program. Funding for both federal and state programs is based solely on the total number of students served.

The criteria and guidelines for monitoring the programs also have a funding orientation. School districts are expected to avoid co-mingling federal, state, and local funds. For example, Chapter 1 programs are intended to "supplement, not supplant" programs funded locally or at the state level. School districts are also expected to serve only those students who are eligible (OERI 1987).

The only educational advice provided to local educators concerns the available program models and the nature of the services provided to the students. The recommended models (e.g., in-class floating aide, special class or pull out, alternate class or replacement) are quite generic. District personnel are told that services should be

of "sufficient size, scope, and quality to give reasonable promise of substantial progress toward meeting students' needs" (OERI 1987, p. 54). As a consequence, any one model is staffed and implemented differently in different districts and schools (Rowan et al. 1986, Anderson et al 1989). Thus, it should not be surprising that the educational treatments provided to students in these programs are "as varied as can be imagined" (Carter 1984, p. 12).

ORGANIZATION AND ADMINISTRATION

Integration of compensatory and remedial programs into the total school program is often lacking. In addition, administrative leadership for these programs within the school often does not exist or exists at some minimal level. Schools' compensatory and remedial programs typically exist in isolation (Johnston et al. 1985, OERI 1987). Regular classroom teachers hold less than positive attitudes toward compensatory and remedial programs partly because of a perceived lack of coordination with the regular school program and partly because of a perceived lack of difficulty of the content and material included in the compensatory and remedial programs. (Anderson et al. 1989). Regular classroom teachers complain that the scheduling of compensatory and remedial programs takes precedence over the scheduling of regular classes (Rowan et al. 1986).

In addition, "weak or absent" coordination of the Chapter 1 program with the regular program tends to impede student learning (OERI 1987). District administrators usually make decisions concerning the models to use to deliver educational services to compensatory and remedial students without the involvement or even the knowledge of school principals. As a consequence, principals may not have a "clear understanding of the rationale for selecting particular remedial and compensatory models for their schools, much less an understanding of how to integrate these special programs within the regular school curriculum" (Anderson et al. 1989, p. 42).

Highlights of Research on Compensatory and Remedial Education

The research on compensatory and remedial educational programs shows that:
- Chapter 1 programs are often so poorly coordinated with regular programs that student learning is actually impeded. Along with some federal programs for the handicapped and state programs for the gifted, Chapter 1 programs contribute to a fragmentation of the curriculum.
- Although they generally lack qualifications, teacher's aides often serve as instructional staff in Chapter 1 programs because they are less expensive than certified teachers—they are chosen for pragmatic, rather than educational, reasons.
- Students in remedial and compensatory classes often spend inordinate amounts of time working alone at their desks.
- Chapter 1 teachers often have low expectations for their students and a tendency to teach to their present levels of functioning rather than to the levels they will need to be successful in the future. As a result, Chapter 1 students may do well on classroom tests and worksheets, but they often perform poorly on state or national tests.
- Chapter 1 programs are substantially less effective for students with severe learning problems than for "marginal" students, whose problems are associated with an inability or unwillingness to learn in regular classroom settings.
- Rather than exiting from the programs once they achieve better skills, Chapter 1 students often become "lifers." A primary cause of this phenomenon is the poor quality of instruction they receive.

The district administrators' decisions concerning the models to use often reflect their own preferences or the availability of resources (e.g., space, personnel) (OERI 1987, Anderson et al. 1989), rather than concerns for meeting the needs of students or evidence concerning the effectiveness of particular models. The models they choose usually remain quite stable from year to year (OERI 1987). Furthermore, in schools which operate both state-funded and federally-funded programs, the two programs generally use the same delivery model (Rowan et al. 1986).

Finally, in addition to the lack of coordination with the "regular" program, there may be a problem with the coordination of these programs with other special programs. For example, Anderson et al. (1989) found less effective state-funded programs in those schools which housed both federally-funded and state-funded compensatory and remedial programs. Along with federal programs for the handicapped and state programs for gifted and talented students, compensatory and remedial programs may be contributing to both a fragmentation of the school curriculum and an administrative nightmare for principals.

Staffing decisions may be more important to program effectiveness than decisions concerning the delivery model. There is increasing evidence that the delivery model chosen does not *by itself* affect the quality of the instruction provided (Rowan et al. 1986) or the effectiveness of the program (Anderson et al. 1989). Excellent instruction, as well as poor quality instruction, has been observed in all delivery models (Rowan et al. 1986, Anderson et al. 1989).

The selection of instructional staff, on the other hand, may be quite important in influencing the effectiveness of the model. Specifically, using aides in compensatory and remedial programs is particularly problematic because of their general lack of qualifications (OERI 1987) and training (Anderson and Reynolds 1990). Furthermore, aides vary greatly in the quality of instruction they provide to the students (Rowan et al. 1986).

Finally, less effective programs rely more on aides than do more effective programs (Anderson et al. 1989).

The two reasons for using aides are: (1) they are less expensive than certified teachers, and (2) they are less likely to cause role conflict between instructional personnel within the classroom (OERI 1987). Like the choice of models, the choice of personnel to staff the models seems more pragmatic than educational.

INSTRUCTION AND TEACHING

Students in compensatory and remedial programs receive instruction in smaller groups or classes, typically eight or fewer students. One thing we know about elementary compensatory and remedial programs, in general, is that the staff/student ratio is substantially lower than that of the regular program (Carter 1984, Rowan et al. 1986, OERI 1987). But, interestingly, some remedial high school classes in South Carolina have *larger* numbers of students than do the regular classes.

While classes with smaller numbers of students are likely to allow teachers to provide the type of instruction and teacher student interaction associated with higher levels of student achievement (OERI 1987), a simple reduction in class or group size does not necessarily guarantee quality teaching or higher levels of achievement. Some teachers use the same general approach to teaching regardless of class size or the achievement levels of their students (Robinson 1990).

Students in compensatory and remedial programs spend large amounts of time engaged in seatwork activities, particularly those students at the upper levels. Despite their smaller class or group sizes, students in compensatory and remedial programs (particularly those at the middle or junior high and high school levels) are seldom taught as a group. (Rowan et al. 1986). Their teachers spend little class time actively or interactively teaching, where the teacher explains material to a group of students and students interact

with the teacher and one another by asking questions and making comments. Instead, the students spend large amounts of time working by themselves at their seats on written assignments. During this time, teachers circulate among the students, monitor their work, and provide tutoring as necessary (OERI 1987, Anderson et al. 1989). And in elementary reading classes, students may work for extended periods of time *without* supervision as the teacher interacts with another reading group (Lee et al. 1986).

Students in compensatory and remedial programs have very high success rates (in terms of the percentage of correct responses to classroom questions and the percentage of correct answers or solutions to exercises included on worksheets or other written assignments). Unfortunately, however, the demands placed on these students by the academic content that is the basis for these questions and worksheets are often far lower than those typically included on the state or national tests they may have to pass to exit from the programs. Teachers of students enrolled in compensatory and remedial programs appear to be caught between the proverbial rock and a hard place. They want to target their instruction to the current levels at which their students are functioning. At the same time, however, they want to ensure that their students achieve those levels of learning they must achieve to do well on the end-of-year tests. Unfortunately, the data suggest that teachers teach to the students' present levels of academic functioning, rather than to the levels they will need to achieve to be successful in the future (Rowan et al. 1986, Anderson et al. 1989). As a consequence, many compensatory and remedial students appear to be very successful in the short term but remain largely unsuccessful over the long haul.

In general, expectations for students in compensatory and remedial programs are very low. In this regard, there is some evidence that these students would benefit greatly from increased expectations and demands. This generalization follows quite naturally from the previous one.

Teachers of students in compensatory and reme-dial programs tend to perceive that their students live in "intellectually deficient" home environ-ments, lack self-esteem, are unable to work with-out supervision, and are "slow learners" (Rowan et al. 1986). Furthermore, as we have mentioned, the assignments they give to students at the mid-dle or junior high and high school levels are fre-quently below the level at which they are functioning, let alone the level at which they need to function in order to pass the test which is the basis for exiting the programs (Anderson et al. 1989). Finally, compensatory and remedial pro-grams rarely teach the development of higher-order skills (Rowan et al. 1986). Rather, their emphasis is on the acquisition of basic facts and skills (Pogrow 1990).

Peterson (1989) suggests that when teachers hold higher expectations for remedial students' mathematics achievement (i.e., they teach algebra rather than review previously taught mechanical skills), the students actually do reach higher lev-els of achievement. Similarly, Anderson et al. (1989) concluded that giving middle or junior high school students more challenging assign-ments that result in a greater number of errors is more beneficial over the long term than giving them easier assignments on which they make fewer errors. Finally, Pogrow (1990) contends that emphasizing higher-order thinking skills (HOTS) "can develop the natural intellectual po-tential of at-risk students in a way that dramati-cally improves their basic skills" (p. 397).

THE EFFECTIVENESS OF COMPENSATORY AND REMEDIAL PROGRAMS

Compensatory and remedial programs are more effective for "marginal" students (those closest to the standard set for program inclusion) and substantially less effective for the remainder of the students enrolled in these programs. Clearly two distinct groups of students are served by compensatory and remedial programs: the com-pensatory students (who have severe learning

problems as a result of cumulative environmental and/or intellectual deficits) and the remedial stu-dents (who have less serious learning problems, problems associated with their inability or un-willingness to learn in regular classroom set-tings). Carter (1984) concluded that Chapter 1 has been effective for "students who were only mod-erately disadvantaged, but it did not improve the relative achievement of the most disadvantaged part of the school population" (p.7). As a conse-quence, Rowan et al. (1986) contend that the de-livery models and assignments provided to "marginal" remedial students vs. the compensa-tory students should be very different. Presently, they are not (Anderson et al. 1989).

The majority of students enrolled in compen-satory and remedial programs remain in or peri-odically return to those programs for the better part of their school lives. The percentage of stu-dents who remain in compensatory and remedial programs from one year to the next ranges from 40 percent to 75 percent (Carter 1984, Davidoff et al. 1989, Potter and Wall 1990). In addition, ap-proximately one-half of those who exit the pro-gram at the end of any given year qualify for re-entry to the program at the next testing date (Davidoff et al. 1989). As a consequence, almost one-half of the students initially enrolled in a compensatory and remedial program spend more of their school years in the program than out of the program (Potter and Wall 1990).

Many of these students experience particular difficulty negotiating the transition from one school level to the next. In a longitudinal study, Jenkins (1990) found that the number of students enrolled in the program increased by almost 40 percent from 5th grade (often the end of elemen-tary school) to 6th grade (often the beginning of middle school). Similarly, in a cross-sectional study, Anderson et al. (1989) found that the num-ber of students enrolled in Chapter 1 and state compensatory and remedial programs increased from 25 percent in 2nd grade to 38 percent by 7th grade. Possible reasons for this increase are higher passing standards on basic skills tests associated with higher school levels (Anderson et al. 1990) and generally less effective programs at the higher grade levels (Carter 1984).

RECOMMENDATIONS FOR CHANGE

There are three recommendations for change that we believe to be of primary importance in ameliorating some of the shortcomings of remedial and compensatory education programs.

Compensatory and remedial programs should be reconceptualized as educational programs rather than funding programs. The availability and allocation of sufficient funding for these programs is a necessary but not sufficient condition for their effectiveness. A number of researchers have documented a wide variety of approaches and strategies used in providing services to these students. As a consequence, there is no single identifiable educational program that we can reliably term "compensatory and remedial." Program input is the focus in the administration of these programs, not program implementation or outcomes. Thus, a student's *access* to a compensatory or remedial program is, in effect, of greater importance than his or her *exit* from it. In fact, many funding formulas actually reward school districts for having greater numbers of students *in* compensatory and remedial programs.

The use of the normal curve equivalent (NCE) metric in evaluating these programs should be reconsidered. An NCE gain of one unit (currently used as a standard in judging the success of federal and state programs in several states) requires that students, on the average, attain marginally higher test scores than they might have been expected to attain given their previous test scores. But for students to re-enter and achieve success in the regular school program they must attain substantially, *not* marginally, higher test scores. Program success should be equated with individual student success, not with the marginal success of students "on the average." Stated somewhat differently, compensatory and remedial programs should be judged successful only when large numbers of their students return to and remain in the academic mainstream.

Compensatory and remedial programs must be more completely integrated into the total school program. If the goals of these special programs are to be reached, they must achieve greater integration into the total school program. Several aspects of this needed integration must be addressed simultaneously.

Principals are the key players in integrating special programs into the total school program in individual schools. Presently, many building administrators are unfamiliar with compensatory and remedial programs and the students served by these programs. Principals must acquaint themselves with compensatory and remedial programs and actively involve themselves in important decisions about the programs.

Teachers also have a role to play in cross-program coordination. Rowan and his colleagues (1986) concluded that informal coordination was an important factor in program integration. However, regular classroom teachers and special program teachers must develop mutual respect and must function as colleagues if informal coordination is to occur. In the words of Rowan and his colleagues: "Schools that showed the tightest coupling between Chapter 1 and regular instruction were those in which staff endorsed a norm of collegiality and had developed shared beliefs about instruction" (p. 94).

Finally, several curriculum issues must be resolved if integration across programs is to be complete. Sufficient comparability of the curriculum across programs is necessary if students are to be able to move from program to program. The likelihood that students will remain in programs for the duration of their academic careers increases with curriculum diversity across programs because, quite literally, there is nowhere else to go. Teachers must increase the pace at which compensatory and remedial students move through the curriculum if these students are not to fall further behind their same-age peers.

The ultimate goal of compensatory and remedial programs—to bring academically deficient students back into the academic mainstream—will be better served if all administrators and teachers see these programs as an integral part of the total school program and as an important component in the school's educational mission. For programs to be seen in this light, principals and teachers must be better informed about the philosophical basis of and rationale for these programs as well as their organization, structure, integration, and evaluation. Once informed, they must use this knowledge to make important program and student decisions.

The quality of the education provided to compensatory and remedial students must be increased substantially. Once children are placed in compensatory and remedial programs, they usually remain in or return to those programs throughout their school careers. The evidence for this is so compelling that Anderson and his colleagues (1989) referred to these students as "lifers," while Pogrow (1990) termed them "professional Chapter 1 students." The specific reasons for this phenomenon are not completely clear, but there is ample reason to believe that the level and quality of instruction provided to these students are among the primary causes. (Anderson et al. 1990).

In order to improve the level and quality of instruction provided to compensatory and remedial students, we must first admit that smaller classes and greater individual student attention do not guarantee excellence in teaching or learning. The qualifications and training of those providing the services, the quality of the services provided (as opposed to whether the services have been provided), and the accomplishments of those receiving the services must be considered in determining program effectiveness.

Two aspects of quality instruction, expectations and teaching, need further elaboration. Many teachers hold low expectations for compensatory and remedial students. These teachers assign them less difficult work than necessary for students to develop the knowledge and skills needed to "pass the test" and move out of the program. Too often, these teachers accept effort ("they tried") rather than accomplishment ("they learned") in judging student success. They emphasize the learning of facts and discrete skills over the ability to think and reason. Students in these programs spend large amounts of time working on worksheets by themselves. Little interaction with peers has been observed; little whole-class or whole-group dialogue with teachers has been noted. Given the relatively smaller number of students in the classes, this level of student isolation is quite surprising.

Based on the above analysis, we suggest several changes in the level or quality of instruction provided to these students. First, students should be assigned more challenging content and associated tasks at a more rapid pace. Second, teachers should direct more active teaching to the entire class or to small groups of students. Third, at the very least, teachers and administrators should see that their programs incorporate higher-order thinking skills. Finally, schools should create substantially different instructional programs for compensatory and for remedial students.

CONCLUSION

In 25 years, we have apparently learned very little as a result of our efforts to provide appropriate educational experiences for culturally and educationally deprived children. Our neediest students are enrolled in the neediest programs. Rather than truly compensating or remediating these students, we have contented ourselves with merely slowing the rate at which they fall further and further behind. We continue to justify continuing huge financial commitments to programs that simply don't work very well, year after year after year. Those who make key decisions about compensatory programs are obviously reluctant to deviate very much from the established norms in program delivery, content, and measures of success. Unfortunately, the grim reality is that if you do what you did—you will get what you got!

This reluctance is inexplicable and tragic because we have both the technical expertise and sufficient resources to provide appropriate and effective services to compensatory and remedial students. But can we muster the necessary commitment, and are we willing to dedicate the resources and apply the know-how to ensure the educational success of a very large, but politically less than powerful, segment of our school population?

Throwing money at the problem in no way absolves policymakers and society in general, of the responsibility for providing these students with a set of educational experiences that are both appropriate and effective. In the final analysis, successful programs can be realistically defined only in terms of individual student success. And the ultimate measure of success can only be the ability of large numbers of remedial and compensatory students to exit these special programs and return to and remain in the academic mainstream.

ENDNOTES

1. The total number of students served in state compensatory and remedial programs is difficult to calculate precisely because the South Carolina Department of Education "double counts" students. That is, if a student is concurrently enrolled in both remedial reading and remedial mathematics, that student would appear twice in the overall total.

REFERENCES

Anderson, L.W., N.R. Cook, L.O. Pellicer, and R.L. Spradling. (1989). *A Study of EIA-Funded Remedial and Compensatory Programs in South Carolina.* Columbia, S.C.: The South Carolina Educational Policy Center.

Anderson, L.W., L.O. Pellicer, R.L. Spradling, N.R, Cook, and J.T. Sears. (1990). "No Way Out: Some Reasons for the Stability of Student Membership in State Compensatory and Remedial Programs," paper presented at the Annual Meeting of the American Educational Research Association, Boston.

Anderson, L.W., and E. Reynolds. (1990). "The Training, Qualifications, Duties, and Responsibilities of Teacher Aides in Compensatory and Remedial Programs in South Carolina," Unpublished manuscript, University of South Carolina.

Carter. L.F. (1984). "The Sustaining Effects Study of Compensatory and Elementary Education," *Educational Researcher,* 13, 7: 4–13.

Davidoff, S.H., R.J. Fishman, and E.M. Pierson. (1989). "Indicator Based Evaluation for Chapter 1," paper presented at the Annual Meeting of the American Educational Research Association, San Francisco.

Jenkins, B.S. (1990). "EIA Compensatory/Remedial Programs in Chesterfield County," paper presented at the annual Meeting of the South Carolina Educators for the Practical Use of Research, Columbia, S.C.

Johnston, P., R. Allington, and P. Afflerbach. (1985). "The Congruence of Classroom and Remedial Instruction." *Elementary School Journal,* 85, 4: 465–477.

Lee, G.V., B. Rowan, R. Allington, L.W. Anderson, S.T. Bossert, A. Harnischseger, and J.A. Stallings. (1986). *The Management and Delivery of Instructional Services to Chapter 1 Students: Case Studies of 12 Schools.* San Francisco: Far West Laboratory for Educational Research and Development.

Office of Educational Research and Improvement. (1987). *The Current Operation of the Chapter 1 Program.* Washington D.C.: OERI.

Peterson. J.M. (1989). "Remediation Is No Remedy," *Educational Leadership,* 46,6: 24–25.

Pogrow, S. (1990). "Challenging At-Risk Students: Findings From the HOTS Program." *Phi Delta Kappan,* 71: 389–397.

Potter, D., and M. Wall. (1990). "An Analysis of Five Years of State Remedial/Compensatory Program Evaluation Data," paper presented at the Annual Meeting of the South Carolina Educators for the Practical Use of Research, Columbia, S.C.

Robinson, G.E. (1990). "Synthesis of Research on the Effects of Class Size." *Educational Leadership* 47, 7:80–90.

Rowan, B., L.F. Guthrie, G.V. Lee, and G.P. Guthrie. (1986). *The Design and Implementation of Chapter 1 Instructional Services: A Study of 24 Schools.* San Francisco, Cal.: Far West Laboratory of Educational Research and Development.

DISCUSSION QUESTIONS

1. Are compensatory and remedial education programs effective? Why? Why not?
2. What organizational and administrative changes are needed to ensure the integrity of compensatory and remedial efforts?
3. How does the district administrator influence the success of such programs?
4. What types of programmatic changes might enhance the effectiveness of curriculum delivery and student outcomes?
5. What is the role of the teacher in cross-program coordination?

23

Home Culture—An Essential Curriculum

ELIOT WIGGINTON

FOCUSING QUESTIONS

1. *Why should schools teach students about their culture?*
2. *What are the goals of the Foxfire curriculum?*
3. *How does the Foxfire approach promote democracy?*
4. *What kind of thinking skills are fostered by Foxfire?*
5. *What types of learning activities and academic content are most appropriate for a curriculum that focuses on culture?*
6. *What methods of instruction are most likely to be associated with the Foxfire approach?*

The main thing you learn in these interviews is that there was a different life before our generation. A more self-sufficient life. Also that there is a lot to learn from our ancestors—our grandparents—and that they're really smarter and have a lot more knowledge than we thought. That is not captured without these interviews. . . . There's so much of heritage that is lost because things are not written down and saved. I guess every Foxfire student will tell you the same thing.

—Vaughn Rogers
Foxfire: 25 Years, p. 73

For a quarter century now, public high school students in at least three of my English classes every year have met their language arts requirements by studying their Appalachian mountain history, customs, and traditions.[1] They read books by Appalachian authors—Thomas Wolfe, James Agee, Wilma Dykeman, Jesse Stuart, Harriet Arnow, James Still—and are routinely amazed to discover that the region produced any authors at all. They also produce a quarterly magazine, *Foxfire,* whose contents are drawn from the extensive interviews they conduct with community elders. And they write books about

their heritage. To date, Doubleday has published 12 of these, and E. P. Dutton, 4, with total sales approaching 8 million copies.

All this is fact. Also fact is the nearly universal conviction among former students and their families that the work they did in the Foxfire project was abundantly worth doing. For *Foxfire: 25 Years,* 10th and 11th graders interviewed numerous former students to find out what impact, if any, their experience with Foxfire has had on their lives (Wigginton 1991). On one point there was unanimous agreement: through the program, they had confronted the national stereotype of the ignorant, shiftless Appalachian mountain hick, put it behind them, and entered into a new, unshakably proud relationship with their heritage.

And for 20 years, similar data have been flowing in, filling filing cabinets in our offices, from hundreds of similar projects based in nearly every conceivable school and community environment, from the Lower East Side of Manhattan to Bribri Indian classrooms in the Talamanca region of Costa Rica. That, too, is fact.

Inevitably, such work generates surprises, ironies, paradoxes, new convictions: *insights.* It is to those, at this point in my career, that I am most drawn. I'll share some of them here.

THE NEED TO KNOW OUR CULTURE

The fact that students are *of* a culture does not automatically mean that they will know very much about that culture or have more than superficial notions about its history or its worth. My native-born high school students routinely do not know that they are Appalachian—or even where the region is. How all that came to pass is grist for another article, but I find this condition shameful. More about this point later.

ONLY SUSTAINED EXPOSURE IS EFFECTIVE

When students are *told* by a teacher or a text that they should be proud of their culture, the impact is negligible. A guest speaker at an assembly doesn't remedy the situation nor do ethnic foods festivals or once-a-week "enlightenment" sessions. Rather, it is sustained exposure that is effective in an environment characterized by independent student research and inquiry, where aspects of culture are discovered (as in a scavenger hunt) and brought, as Maxine Greene would say, "to a level of consciousness" and examined.

Students in my introductory class spend a full school year of 55-minute periods immersed in Appalachian material, and that is barely enough. Given the continual interruptions, 180 state-mandated meetings over the course of a year usually translates into the equivalent of 17 eight-hour days. Not much.

Even so, when doctoral student John Puckett spent a year evaluating the Foxfire program and interviewing scores of former students selected at random, he heard the results of that sustained exposure loud and clear.[2] From one student:

> I never really knew what my heritage was until I got in Foxfire. Seems like I had a lot more in common with these old people than I had thought. It was like you've got a thumb here, but you've

never paid any attention to it. It was like something that's been there, but I never realized it was a part of me.

—Myra Queen Jones
Foxfire Reconsidered, p. 90

CULTURALLY APPROPRIATE TEXTS

The fact that time is so precious has led many educators to conclude that there simply is not enough room in the curriculum for subjects with a cultural focus. This belief has sometimes led to contrived half-remedies from well-meaning teachers: word problems with an Appalachian slant in a math class ("if three dogs tree a mother bear and two cubs . . .") or American history taught through a text revised to acknowledge a contribution or two from each of several ethnic groups.

Viewed from another angle, however, lack of time can impel us to make other kinds of compromises, which in retrospect turn out to be nearly elegant. The wedding of a language arts class and the examination of culture is one good example of such an "elegant compromise." In Georgia, the "mastery" of 92 Quality Core Curriculum (QCC) skills requirements in language arts, grades 9–12, is evaluated through a statewide testing program. Through constant trial and error, I've found that I can target, directly and effectively, every one of those requirements—be it in reading, research, writing, grammar, mechanics, even origins of the English language—through our study of the Appalachian region. Using a whole language approach, I can hit every one, hard, and prove it. And, often for the first time, largely because of the project and content focus, the kids begin to *like*—imagine that—English.

The experience of elementary teachers adds another dimension—and a degree of urgency and "fit"—to this point. Take Linda Oxendine, who teaches 2nd graders in the Appalachian coal field town of Barbourville, Kentucky. The district-mandated basal reader is full of alien elements that her kids can't relate to: brick homes, lawns and lawn sprinklers, and dogs that are allowed to come inside the house. Second grade, and they're starting to hate school.

As a compromise, Linda and her students attend to the basal on Mondays, but the rest of the week, in a whole language environment, they create their own text. And each year it is a wonder—published, bound, filled with personal experience narratives that are culturally based. They write about church singings, weekend rides with their fathers in coal trucks, hunting and fishing trips. The kids also create radio shows. Once a week, to an appreciative local audience, they read letters from their listeners and works in progress. And every year, the kids' scores on the Iowa Test of Basic Skills place them at or above grade level in reading and writing. Attention to culture, then, is not just an end in itself through a special class, but also a powerful catalyst to develop literacy. Double duty. (We teachers get good at this as we confront the realities of the clock.)

But here's an even bigger point: Linda's earlier problem with the basal would not be solved by a new reader filled with more culturally appropriate material produced by a text manufacturer. If such a reader existed, and Linda and her students used it, the world would go backwards. The kids' gains are the result of *creating* culturally appropriate texts. To replace that activity with a new, "better" reader would destroy all, for she now has one of those "elegant compromises" to which I referred earlier—a remarkable arrangement born of adversity, locally solved.

Similarly, I want no Appalachian text for my high schoolers. Each year, the kids create their own in the form of new *Foxfire* magazines and books. And that's the whole point. Text manufacturers, in other words, would only slow our progress and co-opt the potential of this opportunity. What we must be ever mindful of as teachers is that it is the act of creating a tangible product of substance, through *using* the skills to be learned, that students approach understanding and mastery. The personal investigation of culture—in part because it is something the kids can access so immediately and resonate to so deeply—can cause them to invest that budding tangible product with a sense of such importance that the classroom is lifted out of routine into another dimension.

TEACHERS AND STUDENTS, MEETING IN THE MIDDLE

The popular notion that a teacher must be from the same culture as his or her students in order to successfully navigate within and appreciate that culture is, to put it baldly, wrong. I am not from the part of the country where I have spent my whole career. I was not even trained in advance—"sensitized"—to work with rural Appalachian black and white kids. I just appeared in 1966 and started to teach. The 9th and 10th graders voted to start a magazine. They decided on its cultural focus; I followed their lead. They taught me how to work with them ("Let's *do* something real instead of sitting here!"); I taught them how to put the results of their research into publishable form. We met in the middle.

This year, *Minds Stayed On Freedom*, a fine oral history documenting the participation of Holmes County, Mississippi, adults in the civil rights movement, was published by Westview Press. The material was collected, compiled, and edited by local African-American teenagers as part of their Bloodlines project. The teacher who guided them through the process was a Harvard-educated northeastern Yankee white named Jay MacLeod. The Bribri Indian kids who wrote *Nuestra Talamanca Ayer y Hoy* were coached by Paula Palmer, who I know for a fact is not a Bribri Indian.

What is at issue here, in other words, is far more a style of working with people than a matter of ethnic background.

PREPARATION FOR THE LARGER WORLD

Another popular notion—the fear that attention to and celebration of culture may make the students more provincial, insulated, defensive, antagonistic, hostile, even revolutionary—may have some basis worth considering. Try as I might, however, I cannot find a shred of evidence to support that concern either among my former students, nor those who've worked on similar projects. (Friends, in fact, have told me that they wish there were more stirring among Foxfire students—tangible movement toward a Hillbilly revolution to reassert a cultural supremacy in the mountains.) It's not there. Rather, the prevailing pattern is that students appreciate their own culture, acknowledge its contributions, and move into the larger world to become reasonably responsible citizens: small business owners, teachers, journalists, builders, airline pilots. You know, *people.*

Apart from numerous other parental, societal, and environmental factors at work in these kids' lives, one reason for this positive outcome is that my colleagues in the Foxfire program and I search constantly for ways to put our students into direct working relationships with students from other cultures. We then help them process those experiences to gain insights.

Hundreds of our students, to give one example, have worked outside the mountains with other students and teachers to help start similar projects. Most recently, four just returned from Australia. I think particularly of Ronnie Welch, now foreman in a shop that repairs railroad cranes, who, as a 10th grader, accompanied me to the tiny fishing village of Togiak, Alaska. In *Foxfire: 25 Years,* he recalls:

> I learned a lot about Alaska and Alaskan people. Like some of the traditions that we have here, like making liquor, and rooster fighting, making quilts, making soap. . . . Up there they have the same thing, except different than we do. I mean . . . they fix fish completely different than we do. It's the same thing, except a different perspective of it all.
>
> It took some time to help the students understand how to go about getting a *Foxfire* started, and this one wasn't planned or nothing—three of the kids that was there was still really interested with what went on during the day, and we went out and talked to their daddy that evening. And he just naturally got off on stories because I wasn't familiar with it up there. . . . He showed me a differ-

ent way to smoke salmon than the other people did, you know, and just things like that.

> And it hit me all of a sudden. . . . They was looking at Foxfire . . . as being in a classroom, and they still wasn't getting the point. . . . But that right there let them know what it was all about . . . from that point . . . it was all natural . . . and I feel like we got accomplished what we were after. And now I have something I've done, something I'll always remember (pp. 232–233).

It's important to note at this point, in a time when so many classroom environments are multicultural, that not all of the students in Foxfire classes are, or have been, Appalachian. Some are sons and daughters of plant managers, for example, brought in from other areas to run the local rug mill. Sometimes the memories those students have of working with local elders are even more vivid than those of the local students. Their direct, positive immersion into a culture so different from their own is always a revelation and sometimes a life-changing experience.

I remember Gary Warfield, sent to Philadelphia, Mississippi, to spend a summer with Choctaw Indian students who were starting a magazine. One Saturday night, he went to town with his new friends to see a movie. At that time, Indians were required to use a separate entrance into the theater and to sit in the balcony. The theater owner, realizing instantly that Gary, as blond as a Norseman, was not Indian, tried to make him sit downstairs with the whites. But Gary stayed with his Indian friends, and up until his recent death in a tractor accident, he refused to tolerate racism or notions of cultural superiority.

Or take Bob Kugel, a wild, rebellious kid from Detroit whose connection with Aunt Arie (the elderly mountain woman played by Jessica Tandy in "Foxfire," the Broadway play and Hallmark television special) broadened his perspective of the world. Now a New York City cab driver, he says, in *Foxfire: 25 Years:*

> You can teach these kids about their community and about the outside world. Foxfire interviewed local people. There's local people everywhere.

There's local people in Rabun County, and local people in New York City. There are people that stay in their own little world. . . . They think, "I'm a New Yorker. This is where it's at. Ain't nothing out there." Which is a crock of bull-shit! That's America out there. So what Foxfire has done is open my eyes up to see the whole world. It helped me respect my fellow man (p. 299).

NOT ALL TRADITIONS WORTH CELEBRATING

Inevitably, as teachers and students examine traditions, they will uncover some that are not worth celebrating—some, in fact, that cannot be tolerated in this world. For example, would anyone want a return to the traditional role of the Appalachian woman? To traditional plumbing, as in an outhouse perched directly over a sparkling mountain stream? To traditional farming, with its steady, inexorable environmental degradation? To traditional childbirthing customs, with an axe placed under the bed to cut the pain? To a traditional, fatalistic acceptance of all misfortune? To blood-feuds? To Klan rallies? What kinds of people are going to salute that flag?

As we bring aspects of culture to that level of consciousness of which I spoke earlier, this skull-jarring paradox must be examined as well: a traditional culture probably does not exist that could not stand a good housecleaning. As David Whisnant eloquently said in a recent speech in Atlanta:

We all know, of course, that there are overtly reprehensible traditions: of violence, oppression, racism, sexism, bigotry, jingoism, xenophobia, and the like. Part of what is so disturbing about David Duke, Jesse Helms, Strom Thurmond, and their like is that so much of what they are and do is profoundly traditional. . . . One might indeed argue that as a source of mischief and grief in the world at present, traditional values, beliefs, practices, and structures easily hold their own with corporate cynicism, ideological rigidity, and nationalistic fervor.

Some might say at this point, "Wait. Examining these kinds of things, that's not for me. Once

it gets beyond red beans and rice, it's gone too far." I and many of my peers would argue, on the other hand, that this paradox presents us with an opportunity—another elegant compromise—that can be truly educational. We can gradually construct, *with* our students, a yardstick of ethical behavior against which we can measure those aspects of culture we are studying—treasuring, showcasing, celebrating, amplifying those that pass the test and discarding the rest. There is always much to honor and be proud of, as the more than 6,000 pages of printed material in the various *Foxfire* books confirm. And as we examine the outdated, and/or dishonorable, dysfunctional, and self-limiting, most of us will silently, simultaneously say to ourselves, "This practice or belief is one I will not carry forward with me into my life, or condone in others. We can do better than this."

A YARDSTICK OF ETHICAL BEHAVIOR

That yardstick. Where does it come from? Well, for starters we can look to the basic documents upon which this country was founded. "We hold these truths to be self-evident . . ." As we ask ourselves how we want to be treated by others, we can add homegrown convictions, such as: *We don't want to be made to feel stupid. We don't want to be lied to. We don't want our stuff to get stolen or messed with. We want to feel important, special.*

Added to and revised over the course of a year, the list can become pretty impressive—and persuasive. And if we turn the activity of looking for a yardstick of behavior a few degrees, and we begin to examine our guidelines for a decent society; and if we turn it a few degrees more, and we discuss what obstacles prevent us from achieving such a society; and if we turn it a bit further to intersect with our study of culture, and we examine practices that foster or discourage the kind of society we all want; and if we turn it a bit further to embrace a multicultural classroom, with lessons to be learned, positive and negative, from all cultures; and if we then connect all this to the study of American history, things begin to get interesting.

And if we determine from the start that our classroom will model the kinds of behaviors we have identified together for that yardstick, and we affirm that as we work together, we will refer to that yardstick constantly for guidance, things get even more interesting. We become, in other words, the society we envision for America: respectful and enthusiastic of the traditions of others that serve and advance the vision, and intolerant of those traditions that retard it.

In such a classroom, the endless, droning dichotomous discussion between those who advocate the study of culture and those who would protect the American values that originally brought various immigrant cultures to this new democratic experiment becomes pointless background noise. The elegant blend of both agendas in the context of a democratic classroom is all.

CONCLUSION

"But it can't happen." Yes, it can. It is. It's happening in lots of places. And I can prove it.

This brings me back to an earlier point, that not knowing about one's culture is shameful. It's shameful because ignorance of our culture leads us to be blind to some of the forces that control our behavior and attitudes. If we are not led to

examine our culture and background, we are denied the potential such study has to influence the acquisition of certain academic skills and content, to evaluate our beliefs in comparison with those of others, to select the best against certain unassailable principles, and to change society.

It—the study of culture—is exactly that important.

ENDNOTES

1. One of these courses is described in week-by-week detail in *Sometimes A Shining Moment* (Wigginton, 1985).
2. John Puckett evaluated the Foxfire program for his Ph.D. dissertation in education from the University of North Carolina at Chapel Hill.

REFERENCES

Oxendine, L. (Fall/Winter 1990). "Dick and Jane Are Dead. Let's Begin Anew." *Hands On: A Journal for Teachers:* 32.

Puckett, J. (1989). *Foxfire Reconsidered.* Chicago: University of Illinois Press.

Wigginton, E. (1991). *Foxfire: 25 Years.* New York: Doubleday.

Wigginton, E. (1985). *Sometimes A Shining Moment: The Foxfire Experience.* New York: Doubleday.

Youth of the Rural Organizing and Cultural Center. (1991). *Minds Stayed on Freedom.* San Francisco: Westview Press.

DISCUSSION QUESTIONS

1. How does the Foxfire method differ from curriculum approaches that are integrative, multidisciplinary, and correlational?
2. What is the relationship between the goals of the Foxfire curriculum and the aims of education?
3. What implications are suggested by the Foxfire approach concerning curriculum development?
4. How might the Foxfire method be used to guide professional development for teachers, principals, and curriculum specialists?
5. How does the Foxfire program put students into working relationships with students from other cultures?

Teaching, Instruction, and Technology

SIMON HOOPER
LLOYD P. RIEBER

FOCUSING QUESTIONS

1. *How does educational technology differ from teaching with technology?*
2. *In what ways is teaching with technology affecting classroom instruction?*
3. *What roles do the familiarization, utilization, integration, reorientation, and evolution phases play in applications of technology in education?*
4. *What are the advantages and disadvantages of product technologies?*
5. *What pedagogical principles are likely to guide effective technology-based teaching?*

Classroom teaching is a demanding job. Most people outside education probably think teachers spend most of their time teaching, but teachers are responsible for many tasks that have little to do with classroom instruction. Beyond planning and implementing instruction, teachers are also expected to be managers, psychologists, counselors, custodians, and community "ambassadors," not to mention entertainers. If teaching sounds like an unreasonable almost impossible job, perhaps it is.

It is easy to understand how a teacher might become frustrated and disillusioned. Most teachers enter the profession expecting to spark the joy of learning in their students. Unfortunately, the other demands of the classroom are very distracting and consuming. We envision technology as a teacher's liberator to help reestablish the role and value of the individual classroom teacher. To do so, two things must happen. First the perspective of the classroom must change to become learner-centered. Second, students and teachers must en-

ter into a collaboration or partnership with technology to create a "community" that nurtures, encourages, and supports the learning process (Cognition and Technology Group at Vanderbilt, 1992).

It is important to note that the focus in this chapter is on *educational technology* as compared to technology in education. There is a difference. Technology in education is often perceived in terms of how many computers or videocassette recorders are in a classroom and how they might be used to support traditional classroom activities, but this is a misleading and potentially dangerous interpretation. It not only places an inappropriate focus on hardware, but fails to consider other potentially useful "idea" technologies that result from the application of one or more knowledge bases such as learning theory. Educational technology involves applying ideas from various sources to create the best learning environments possible for students. Educational technologists also ask questions such as how a classroom might change or adapt when a computer is integrated into the curriculum. This integration means that the curriculum and setting may also need to change to meet the opportunities that the technology may offer.

There are four purposes to this chapter. First, we will examine several different stages of technology adoption. Second, we will review national roles that technology has served in the classroom. Third, we will examine what a classroom might be like when attention is given to educational technology. Fourth, we will provide some specific examples that incorporate contemporary educational principles. This chapter will try to present ways in which educational technology may be useful to teachers given current classroom conditions as well as how it might influence the course that many schools may chart in the future.

A MODEL OF TECHNOLOGY ADOPTION IN THE CLASSROOM

Educational technology is often considered, erroneously, as synonymous with instructional innovation. Technology, by definition, applies current knowledge to some useful purpose. Therefore, technology uses evolving knowledge (whether about a kitchen or a classroom) to adapt and improve the system to which the knowledge applies (such as a kitchen's microwave oven or educational computing). In contrast, innovations represent only change for change sake. Given this distinction, it is easy to argue that educators are correct to resist mere innovation, but they should welcome educational technology. Unfortunately, the history of educational technology does not support this hypothesis (Saettler, 1990).

Although education has witnessed a multitude of both technology and innovation over the past fifty years (Reiser, 1987), the educational system has scarcely changed during that time. Few would argue that doctors and dentists of fifty years ago would be competent and capable enough to practice with the technology of today. Yet, a teacher from fifty years ago would prob-

ably feel right at home in most of today's classrooms as most technologies and innovations introduced during this time have been discarded. It is difficult to account for the rapid abandonment of technologies and innovations in education over the past fifty years. Has the educational system reached the point of development at which no further improvement can be expected from current educational technology? Have all educational technologies really just been fads of innovation that educators have correctly denounced as irrelevant and unnecessary? We think not in both cases. It seems appropriate to consider these questions as a way to understand both traditional and contemporary roles of educational technology. We will use a simple model as a tool to help explain the patterns of adoption by teachers after they are first introduced to educational technology. Understanding these adoption patterns of the past may give us insights to which technologies may be adopted or discarded in the future.

There have been many attempts to understand patterns of adoption in education (Dalton, 1989; Dwyer, Ringstaff, & Sandholtz, 1991). In this section, we present one such model in simplified form in order to better understand both traditional and contemporary applications of technology in education. The model, as illustrated in Figure 24.1, has five steps or phases: familiarization, utilization, integration, reorientation, and evolution. The full potential of any educational technology can only be realized when educators progress through all five phases, otherwise, the technology will likely be misused or discarded (Rieber & Welliver, 1989; Marcinkiewicz, in press). The *traditional* role of technology in education is necessarily limited to the first three phases, whereas contemporary views hold the promise to reach the evolution phase.

Familiarization

The familiarization phase is concerned with one's initial exposure to and experience with a technology. A typical example of familiarization is a

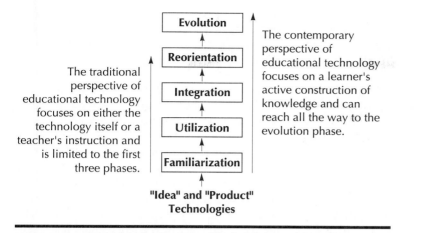

The traditional perspective of educational technology focuses on either the technology itself or a teacher's instruction and is limited to the first three phases.

The contemporary perspective of educational technology focuses on a learner's active construction of knowledge and can reach all the way to the evolution phase.

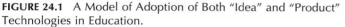

FIGURE 24.1 A Model of Adoption of Both "Idea" and "Product" Technologies in Education.

teacher participating in an in-service workshop covering the "how to's" of a technology, such as word processing, spreadsheets, assertive discipline, cooperative learning, motivational strategies, etc. In this phase, the teacher simply becomes acquainted with a technology. Once the workshop ends, so too does the teacher's experience and growth with the technology. All that remains is a memory of the experience. The teacher may discuss the experience and the ideas represented in the experience, even with some degree of authority, but no further action takes place. A great deal of instructional innovation begins and ends with this phase.

Utilization

The utilization phase, in contrast, occurs when the teacher tries out the technology or innovation in the classroom. An example is a social studies teacher who uses role-playing simulations learned in a workshop or graduate course. Obviously, teachers who reach this phase have progressed further than familiarization, but there is the inherent danger that a teacher will become prematurely satisfied with their limited use of the technology. The attitude of "At least I gave it a

try" will likely interfere with any enduring and long-term adoption of the technology. Teachers who progress only to this phase will probably discard the technology at the first sign of trouble because they have made no commitment to it. This is probably the highest phase of adoption reached by most teachers who use contemporary educational media, including the computer. If the technology were taken away on Monday, hardly anyone would notice on Tuesday.

Integration

Integration represents the "break through" phase. This occurs when a teacher consciously decides to designate certain tasks and responsibilities to the technology, so, if the technology is suddenly removed or is unavailable, the teacher cannot proceed with the instruction as planned. The most obvious technology that has reached this phase of adoption in education is the book and its derivatives, such as worksheets and other handouts. Most teachers could not function without the support of such print-based technologies. Another example, though perhaps amusing to some, is the chalkboard. Most teachers would find it extremely difficult to teach without it. Hence, the "expendability" of the technology is the most critical attribute or characteristic of this phase (Marcinkiewicz, in press). Although integration is the end of the adoption model for many, it really only represents the beginning of understanding educational technology. For some teachers, the integration phase marks the beginning of a professional "metamorphosis," but only if they progress even further in their adoption pattern.

Reorientation

The reorientation phase requires that educators reconsider and reconceptualize the purpose and function of the classroom. It is marked by many characteristics, probably the most important of which is that the focus of the classroom is now centered on a student's learning, as opposed to the teacher's instruction. A teacher who has reached the reorientation phase does not view good teaching as the delivery of content (i.e., the teaching "acts" of explaining, managing, or motivating). Instead, the teacher's role is to establish a learning environment that supports and facilitates students as they construct and shape their own knowledge. In this phase, the learner becomes the *subject* rather than the *object* of education.

Teachers in the reorientation phase are open to technologies that enable this knowledge construction process and they are not threatened by being "replaced" by technology. In fact, these teachers will probably include technology in their classrooms without necessarily feeling the need to be an "expert" themselves. Their interest is on how technology allows their students to engage the subject matter. It would not be unusual for the students to be more competent than their teachers with the technology. For example, consider a history teacher who discovers that students prefer to create HyperCard stacks, replacing the traditional term paper assignment (Hoffmeister, 1990). If the teacher has a reoriented view of education that is student-centered, the teacher will focus on how intensely the student has engaged the content, not on how well the stack is "programmed." The

teacher will emphasize (and evaluate) how well the student has become both a researcher and explorer because of the availability of the computing tool. Whether the teacher possesses more or less technical skill with HyperCard than the student is inconsequential. In addition, the teacher learns about history and HyperCard along with the student. Of course, the teacher's greater experience is an indispensable resource and guide to the student. Rather than view a technology as something that must be mastered beforehand and presented to students in a controlled and systematic way, a teacher at the reorientation phase would encourage and expect students to appropriate the technology in ways that could not be anticipated.

Evolution

The final phase, evolution, serves as a reminder that the educational system must continue to evolve and adapt to remain effective. There will never be a final solution or conclusion and to be searching for one means that one is missing the point. The classroom learning environment should constantly change to meet the challenge and potential provided by new understandings of how people learn. As previously discussed, this appropriate application of basic knowledge for some useful purpose is what defines educational technology, and living up to this definition is the hallmark of the evolution phase.

TRADITIONAL ROLE OF TECHNOLOGY IN EDUCATION

There have been two main types of technology in education that we choose to label as "product technologies" and "idea technologies." Product technologies include (1) hardware, or machine-oriented, technologies that people most often associate with educational technology, such as the range of audiovisual equipment, both traditional (i.e., film strips, movies, audiocassette player/recorders) and contemporary (i.e., videocassette players/recorders, laserdiscs, computers,

CD-ROM) and (2) software technologies such as print-based material (i.e., books, worksheets, overhead transparencies) and computer software (i.e., computer-assisted instruction). In contrast, idea technologies do not have such tangible forms.

Of course, idea technologies are usually represented in or through some product technology. For example, simulations are, by and large, idea technologies. Simulations try to give people experiences with events and concepts not generally possible (e.g., travel back in time), probable (e.g., ride aboard the space shuttle), or desirable (e.g., the greenhouse effect) under normal conditions. The idea of a simulation must be realized through some product, such as computer software. In this way, the idea is supported or made possible by the product. A classic example of the distinction between product and idea technologies is Henry Ford's assembly line. The concept of the assembly line is an idea technology that transformed industry in the United States. However, the conveyor belts, workstations, and factories that one sees in old photographs show the product technologies that were used to support the original idea.

The distinction between product technologies and idea technologies is important because most of the historical attempts to use technology in education have focused on product technologies such as teaching machines, educational television and films, and, most currently, computers (Reiser, 1987). Consequently, the role and value of these product technologies were defined by how they supported the established beliefs and practices of classroom teachers. These established practices were largely based on behavioral models that emphasized the transmission and delivery of predetermined content. These approaches exemplify the "student as bucket" metaphor in which the emphasis is on "pouring knowledge" into students' minds by designing and delivering well-planned and controlled instruction. Learning is viewed as a consequence of receiving the information. We believe that contemporary notions of educational technology must go well beyond this philosophy of learning and education. Teachers who adopt technologies without considering the belief structure into which these products and ideas are introduced are necessarily limited to the third phase of integration, though, as previously mentioned, few progress that far.

Consider an example of a product technology reaching the integration phase of adoption—the hand-held graphing calculator. Many high school math teachers use graphing calculators in their teaching. In fact, there are several brands on the market that use a transparent liquid crystal display (LCD) so that the calculator can be placed on an overhead projector. The use of these calculators easily passes the expendability test for many teachers—their teaching would be seriously disrupted if the calculators were removed. They would be unable to convey the same information given a quick and sudden return to the static medium of the overhead or chalkboard.

However, the degree to which the teacher's instruction has been altered because of the graphing calculator is critical to determining if the teacher is on the verge of entering the reorientation phase. If the calculator allows the teacher to focus on a student's conceptual understanding of the mathematical function, perhaps because of the calculator's ability to draw a graph using real-time animation, then the teacher has begun to rethink and reflect on the partnership between how product and idea technologies can help a student's learning. The teacher will derive satisfaction from how the technology was harnessed to enable and empower students to understand and apply the mathematical ideas. This teacher is on the brink of entering the reorientation phase. Such a teacher will probably seek to turn the technology (i.e., the calculator) over to the students so that they can begin constructing mathematics.

On the other hand, if the instructional strategies employed by the teacher are virtually the same as those used before the graphing calculator was introduced, then it is very likely that the teacher's adoption of the technology will end with integration because nothing has changed or improved other than the mode of delivery. In this case, although the product technology of the calculator has been integrated, the underlying idea technology of "present, practice, and test" remains unchanged and unchallenged.

The distinction between educators who enter and stall at the integration phase versus those who are "transformed" and enter the reorientation phase is best characterized as a magical line on an "instruction/construction" continuum, as illustrated in Figure 24.2. The utilization and integration of any one technology can be defined by this continuum. The technology of a computer spreadsheet, for example, when used only by a teacher for grade management or as part of an instructional presentation of, say, the principle of averages in a math class, is integrating only the product technology without changing the underlying philosophical base in which it is applied. The philosophical base, in this example, would be an instruction-centered classroom in which a teacher manages the presentation and practice of predetermined and preselected content.

Consider instead a teacher who uses the same spreadsheet to have students build and construct the knowledge themselves, whether it be the principle of mathematical average or a range of "what if" relationships in economics or history. In this case, the product technology of the spreadsheet directly supports the idea technology of a "microworld" in which students live and experience the content rather than just study it (Dede, 1987; Papert 1981; Rieber, 1992).

What fundamental principles of learning underlie the most contemporary views of idea technologies that help all educators enter into the reorientation phase of adoption? This is the goal of the next section.

CONTEMPORARY ROLE OF TECHNOLOGY IN EDUCATION

Among the many educational goals are three cognitive outcomes, and they are that students should be able to remember, understand, and use information (Perkins, 1992). One of these outcomes is apparently very difficult to achieve. After more

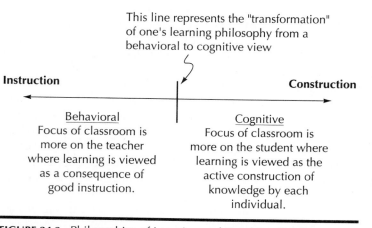

FIGURE 24.2 Philosophies of Learning and Teaching Can Be Viewed as a Continuum with Extreme Educational Interpretations of Behaviorism (e.g., Instruction) and Cognitivism (e.g., Construction) at Either End. Any One Educator's Philosophy Resides Somewhere on this Line. The Threshold Between the Two Views Marks a Critical Point of "Transformation" for an Educator.

than a decade of schooling, many students leave school unable to use much of the content that they have learned.

Students' inability to apply their learning is attributable to the shallow processing that often occurs in school. Schoolwork often focuses on remembering and organizing lesson content, but rarely on making information meaningful. Meaningful learning is the product of building external connections between existing and new information. Mayer (1984) identified three learning strategies that affect meaningfulness: selection, organization, and integration. Information must initially be selected. Selected information must be organized in working memory if it is to be transferred to long-term memory. Information that is not organized is meaningless. The nature of the organization determines the degree of meaningfulness. Information that is integrated within familiar knowledge or experiences is more durable than information that is not associated to prior knowledge. In school, students select information that they memorize and organize sufficiently to enable satisfactory performance on tests, but they often fail to integrate the information by relating it to previous experiences or knowledge stored in long-term memory. Consequently, one outcome of education, it seems, is a large reserve of inert information that is eventually forgotten (Cognition and Technology Group at Vanderbilt, 1992). For example, how many of us can remember how to compute the sine of a triangle?

How can teaching with technology facilitate deeper, more meaningful cognitive processing? Moreover, what framework should be used to inform such decisions? In a sense, teaching with technology is unlikely to differ greatly from teaching in general. Effective technology-based teaching is more likely the result of teachers' abilities to design lessons based upon robust instructional principles than of the technology per se (Savenye, Davidson, & Smith, 1991). Consequently, guidance for designing effective technology-based classrooms should be grounded in the literature on effective pedagogy in general.

Recently, researchers have identified several principles to guide effective teaching (Koschman, Myers, Feltovich, & Barrows, in press). Although designed primarily for instruction in complex and ill-structured domains, the principles are relevant for many instructional tasks. Most real-world tasks are ill-structured. Problems that are "well-structured" generally occur only in classroom settings. In the following section we will examine three principles and consider the implications of each for using technology in the classroom.

Principle 1: Effective Learners Actively Process Lesson Content

During the past thirty years the shift from behaviorism to cognitivism has modified our conceptions of effective learning and instruction. One of the most consistent themes to emerge from the transition is that learning is an active process. By this it is meant that effective learning requires students to do more than simply respond to stimuli. Instead, learners must actively seek and generate relationships between lesson content and prior knowledge.

One common myth is that product technologies increase interactivity and thereby improve learning. The source of this perception is not difficult to trace. The results of research on students attitudes toward working with product technologies, especially computers, are generally positive (Martin, Heller, & Mahmoud, 1991). Furthermore, research appears to support the belief that product technologies improve learning (Kulik, Bangert, & Williams, 1983). Yet product technologies alone do not ensure learning (Clark, 1983). Indeed, in some cases they may detract from learning by diminishing the amount of effort a student invests.

In general, learning requires students to invest considerable mental effort in the task. However, students appear to vary the effort they invest during learning according to their self-perceptions and their beliefs gained from different media about the difficulty of learning. Salomon (1984) found that children who believed themselves to be effective learners invested greater effort when a learning task was perceived to be challenging than when it was perceived to be easy. However, children with low self-efficacy invested greater effort when learning was perceived to be more attainable than challenging. In other words, high-ability learners may invest more mental effort in a challenging task, such as reading a book, than in a task perceived to be easy, such as learning from television. Low-ability students may invest more effort in a task that they believe to be attainable than one that they perceive to be challenging.

We are by no means opponents of product technologies in education. However, we recognize the importance of blending product and idea technologies into "technological partnerships." An example of an effective technological marriage is that of a musical symphony. A good symphony combines an ideal blend of musical instruments (product technologies) and musical compositions (idea technologies). Misusing the capabilities of the instruments or underemphasizing the composition of the musical score will detract from the final production of the symphony. Similarly, effective uses of technology in education require a blend of product and idea technologies. Together, they form environments that unite technological capability with pedagogical necessity—combining what can be done with what should be done.

Too often in education we have failed to find the right blend of technologies. In particular, the capabilities of product technologies are overemphasized. For example, product technologies are often used to increase cost efficiency by replacing the classroom teacher or by transmitting lessons to larger audiences via satellites and telephone lines. Such approaches are often misdirected. Although the importance of increasing access to education should not be devalued, reproducing existing materials is unlikely to improve educational quality. Rather, using technology as delivery media may perpetuate or even exacerbate existing problems. The benefit of technology is not simply its potential to replicate existing educational practice, but its ability to combine idea and product technologies to encourage students to engage in deeper cognitive activity.

Principle 2: Presenting Information from Multiple Perspectives Increases the Durability of Instruction

Although instruction has traditionally focused on learning specific content, much of contemporary curriculum development focuses on solving problems that require learners to develop ever evolving networks of facts, principles, and procedures. The National Council of Teachers of Mathematics (1989), for example, suggested that greater emphasis be placed on solving open-ended "real world" problems in small groups, connecting mathematics with other content areas and using computer-based tools to allow students to speculate and explore interrelationships among concepts rather than to spend time on time-consuming calculations. To achieve such goals, learning should take place in environments that emphasize the interconnectedness of ideas across content domains and that help learners develop flexible networks of propositions and productions (Gagné, 1985). Presenting content from a single perspective is unlikely to reflect the complexity inherent in many concepts. In contrast, repeated exposure to information from varying perspectives helps learners to establish the interrelationships necessary to mediate deep processing and effective retrieval of lesson concepts.

Cooperative learning and hypermedia represent technologies with significant potential for developing multiple perspectives. Cooperative learning is an idea technology that stimulates the development of alternative perspectives through exposure to multiple viewpoints. Two important differences exist between cooperative learning and traditional instruction. First, information to be learned by the students is not transmitted by the teacher. Instead, students teach each other in small groups of between two and five students. Second, students are made responsible for each other's learning. Students must ensure that every member of their group achieves the lesson's objectives. These experiences appear to benefit students of all abilities. More able students gain from the cognitive restructuring associated with teaching, and less able students benefit from the personalized attention available from group members. Moreover, groups appear to create environments in which all members benefit from exposure to diverse attitudes and opinions that are often unavailable in the traditional classroom.

Hypermedia is a product technology that represents a shift in beliefs about how information should be presented to and accessed by students. Hypermedia refers to computer programs that organize information nonsequentially. Information is structured around series of nodes that are connected through associative links. Node is the term used to describe an information chunk that is stored in the hypermedia program. Information in a node may be represented through text, illustrations, or sounds. Associative links, which allow users to navigate among nodes, represent the main difference between traditional ways of presenting information on the computer and hypermedia (Jonassen, 1991).

Whereas traditional instruction often presents information sequentially to make the content easier to comprehend, hypermedia allows users to browse through an information base and to construct relationships between their personal experiences and the lesson. It is often claimed that in doing so learning becomes more meaningful as students generate webs of semantically and logically related information that accommodate the knowledge structure of the learner rather than that of the teacher or designer. Although hypermedia environments can be used to present information sequentially to students, when carefully designed users can create different diverse pathways through a lesson resulting in multiple cognitive representations of the content. By allowing exploration, students are encouraged to discover interrelationships that are often missed in traditional presentations of lesson content and to search for information that meets individual needs. Hypermedia is especially effective when

users are encouraged to explore a database, to create links among information nodes, and even to modify a knowledge base based on new insight into content structure (Nelson & Palumbo, 1992).

Hypermedia and cooperative learning represent technologies that can make learning more meaningful. However, both must be managed carefully to achieve the intended outcomes. In cooperative learning, potentially damaging social effects often occur when individual accountability is not maintained. Similarly, hypermedia projects often focus on presenting information and rarely fulfill their promise as knowledge construction kits. Furthermore, although each can be used independently, the learning benefits may be magnified when they are combined. Although many computer lessons are designed for single users, the benefits appear to multiply when used collaboratively (Hooper, 1992).

Principle 3: Effective Instruction Should Build upon Students Knowledge and Experiences and Be Grounded in Meaningful Contexts

Philosophical beliefs about how educational goals can best be achieved have shifted from emphasizing curriculum content to focusing on learners' knowledge and experiences (Pea & Gomez, 1992; Tobin & Dawson, 1992). During the 1960s and 1970s considerable emphasis was placed on curriculum projects that focused on the structural analysis of content. These projects produced curriculum materials that emphasized helping learners better understand lesson content. For many years, education followed a correspondingly curriculum-centered approach. Teaching focused on analyzing learning tasks and on identifying strategies to achieve specific learning outcomes.

Recently, research emphasis has shifted from examining the structure of curriculum materials to determining the cognitive state of the learner. Education is presently concerned less with transmitting the "optimal" structure of lesson content than on building onto the current knowledge level of the student. This perspective has implications for teaching with technology. First, instruction should attempt to build upon the experiential base of each student. What a student learns from education is, to a large extent, a function of prior knowledge. One role of technology, therefore, is to bridge personal experiences and formal instruction. Technology should also be sufficiently flexible to adapt to students' ongoing instructional needs. One of the hallmarks of a master teacher is the ability to recognize and repair student misunderstandings and misconceptions. When learning difficulties arise, therefore, technology-based instruction should be sufficiently flexible to adapt to student experiences.

Closely related to building upon the knowledge and experiences of students is the belief that instruction should be grounded in familiar contexts. Teachers often decontextualize instruction to stimulate transfer and to improve instructional efficiency (Merrill, 1991). Recently, however, researchers have argued that such practices actually hinder transfer. Instead, they claim, instruction should be rooted in real-life problem-solving contexts. One such approach, known as situated cognition (Brown, Collins, & Duguid, 1989) involves teaching across multiple contexts before generating rules. Grounding instruction in meaningful contexts appears to have both cognitive and affective benefits. One of the axioms of cognitive psychology is that learning occurs by building upon previously learned experiences. Teaching in familiar contexts appears to help learners to relate new information to those experiences. Contextualization also appears to have a strong motivational component. Learning in a familiar context may make learning more personally relevant than decontextualized learning (Keller & Suzuki, 1988).

Microworlds illustrate how technology can improve meaningfulness by building upon students' experiences and by providing a relevant learning environment. A microworld is a special learning environment that accurately models a phenomenon and adapts the complexity of instruction to match the learner's level of understanding. Rieber (1992) designed Space Shuttle Commander, a computer microworld to teach Newton's Laws of Motion. By exploring the microworld, students generate a visceral understanding of the interrelationships that exist among lesson concepts. Microworlds offer opportunities for students to transfer understanding to the real world and to examine and manipulate concepts in a manner that would otherwise be impossible. The microworld contains several levels of difficulty to accommodate varying levels of user expertise and introduces an element of fantasy to motivate learners by using the scenario of traveling through frictionless space in a space shuttle.

THEORY INTO PRACTICE

In this section we present three examples of educational products that incorporate many of the principles outlined earlier in the chapter. None of these products ensures that learning will take place. The key ingredient in each case is the idea technology employed by the teacher.

The Jasper Woodbury Problem Solving Series

The Adventures of Jasper Woodbury (Cognition and Technology Group at Vanderbilt, 1992) is a video package that reflects contemporary beliefs about learning and instruction. Important differences exist between the Jasper series and traditional educational television. Each episode of the Jasper videos presents instruction in a motivating and realistic environment that encourages students to explore and to identify and solve real problems. Furthermore, teachers are encouraged to blend idea technologies such as cooperative grouping and problem-based learning with the videos to make learning active, meaningful, and motivating. Perhaps the most striking difference between the Jasper materials and national educational television concerns the role played by the students. Educational television often transmits information to students who may, or may not, participate in the learning experience. In contrast, the Jasper series requires students to be actively engaged. While watching the video, students must collect information. Following each episode, a problem is presented. The problem challenges the students to use the information collected during the lesson to identify and solve sub-problems en route to solving the larger problem.

The Voyage of the Mimi

The Voyage of the Mimi is a multimedia curriculum package developed at the Bank Street College of Education that integrates print, video, and computer materials in learning about science and mathematics. Video is used to present the package's context for learning: a realistic, fictional account of the adventures of the crew of the Mimi, a boat hired by a team of scientists to study humpback whales (a second Mimi series has also been produced using the context of Mayan archaeology). The context was chosen based on research conducted at Bank Street that indicated that people, and especially children, share a general fascination with whales. Mathematics and science become the crew's most important tools as they conduct their whale research or engage in many other problem-solving activities. Video is also used to present a series of documentaries showing real scientists at work using many of the principles introduced in the dramatic episodes. The computer materials provide students with interactive activities, usually simulations and games, that closely mirror the adventures of the Mimi's crew in the video. The print-based materials include a text version of the video and consumable workbooks for the students to complete. The Mimi materials were developed to be sufficiently flexible to provide teachers with multiple entry levels to the materials (Martin, 1987). Teachers can choose to use the materials to augment or to replace all or part of their curriculum.

The materials provide for the range of learning outcomes from initial concept formation to problem solving. The materials can also be used individually by students or cooperatively in groups.

The Geometric Supposer

The Geometric Supposer (Schwartz & Yerushalmy, 1985a) is a computer-based geometry tool that teaches deductive reasoning by providing students with opportunities to experiment with geometry. Traditionally, geometry teaching has employed passive instructional strategies by focusing on definitions, theorems, and proofs. In contrast, the Geometric Supposer stimulates active learning by encouraging learners to discover geometric properties (Schwartz, Yerushalmy, & Wilson, 1993).

The program allows students to perform two functions that are difficult to achieve in non-computer-based environments. First, it allows students to construct electronically any geometric shape that can be made with a straight edge and a compass. Moreover, the program "remembers" the construction and will repeat the procedure on similar shapes when instructed to do so. Second, the program can automatically measure and report any element of a construction thus allowing users to instantaneously observe the outcomes of any manipulations of the geometric figures. Together, these features allow students to create constructions, hypothesize about geometric relationships, and test and observe the validity of their conjectures. For example, students studying relationships among the medians of a triangle may attempt to identify and test principles by examining results across several different cases (Schwartz & Yerushalmy, 1985b).

Putting It Together

It is important to recognize that the learning outcomes achieved using any of the materials outlined above will reflect the idea technology employed. The idea technology will also indicate the level of technology adoption to which the teacher has risen. Three idea technologies have been outlined by the Cognition and Technology Group at Vanderbilt (1992).

1. *Basics First* advocates mastering basic skills before attempting similar problems embedded in the video. Teachers who use this approach may have entered the utilization phase, but have not entered the integration phase. Few instructional differences would result if the videos were removed from the classroom. Similar problems could easily be generated from other sources.

2. *Structured Problem Solving* involves capitalizing on the design features inherent in the videos but restricts students' progress to prevent errors and disorientation. For example, teachers might use structured worksheets to guide students' progress. Teachers who focus on rigid lesson structuring may have reached the integration phase, but probably have not entered into reorientation.

3. *Guided Generation* involves using activities that reflect many of the principles outlined earlier in the chapter, that is, activities that help students to generate meaningful relationships. The teacher focuses on guiding students and exploring issues that may be novel or unfamiliar to both teacher and student. Teachers who use Guided Generation would probably have entered the reorientation or evolution adoption phases.

CONCLUSION

In this chapter we have examined why technology has failed to impact education in the past and have outlined the conditions necessary for technology to be used effectively in the future. To be used effectively, idea and product technologies must be united and teachers must venture beyond familiarization and utilization and into the integration, reorientation, and evolution phases of technology use. Teachers who learn to integrate technology may go on to reconceptualize their roles in the classroom. Guided by research findings from cognitive psychology and other related areas, teachers can create environments in which students actively engage in cognitive partnerships with technology.

REFERENCES

Brown, John, Allan Collins, and Paul Duguid. (1989). "Situated Cognition and the Culture of Learning." *Educational Researcher, 18*(1), 32–42.

Clark, Richard. (1983). "Reconsidering Research on Learning From Media." *Review of Educational Research, 53,* 445–459.

Cognition and Technology Group at Vanderbilt. (1992). "The Jasper Experiment: An Exploration of Issues in Learning and Instructional Design." *Educational Technology Research and Development, 40*(1), 65–80.

Dalton, David. (1989). "Computers in the Schools: A Diffusion/Adoption Perspective." *Educational Technology, 29*(11), 20–27.

Dede, Christopher. (1987). "Empowering Environments, Hypermedia and Microworlds." *The Computing Teacher, 15*(3), 20–24, 61.

Dwyer, David, Cathy Ringstaff, and Judy Sandholtz. (1991). "Changes in Teachers' Beliefs and Practices in Technology-Rich Classrooms." *Educational Leadership, 48*(8), 45–52.

Gagné, Ellen. (1985). *"The Cognitive Psychology of School Learning."* Boston: Little, Brown and Company.

Hoffmeister, Joseph. (1990). "The Birth of Hyper-School." In S. Ambron, and K. Hooper (Eds.). *Learning with Interactive Multimedia: Developing and Using Multimedia Tools in Education* (pp. 199–221). Redmond, WA: Microsoft Press.

Hooper, Simon. (1992). "Cooperative Learning and Computer-Based Instruction." *Educational Technology Research and Development, 40*(3), 21–38.

Jonassen, David. (1991). "Hypertext as Instruction Design." *Educational Technology Research and Development, 39*(1), 83–92.

Keller, John, and Katsuaki Suzuki. (1988). "Using the ARCS Motivation Model in Courseware Design." In D. Jonassen (Ed.), *Instructional Designs for Microcomputer Courseware,* (pp. 401–434). Hillsdale, NJ: Lawrence Erlbaum Associates.

Kulik, James, Robert Bangert, and George Williams. (1983). "Effects of Computer-Based Teaching on Secondary School Students." *Journal of Educational Psychology, 75,* 19–26.

Marcinkiewicz, Heinrich. (1991). "The Relationships of Selected Personological Variables to the Use of Available Microcomputers by Elementary School Teachers." Doctoral dissertation, Pennsylvania State University.

Marcinkiewicz, Heinrich. (in press). "Computers and Teachers: Factors Influencing Computer Use in the Classroom." *Journal of Research on Computing in Education.*

Martin, C. Dianne, Rachelle Heller, and Emad Mahmoud. (1991). "American and Soviet Children's Attitudes Toward Computers." *Journal of Educational Computing Research, 8*(2), 155–185.

Martin, L. (1987). "Teachers' Adoption of Multimedia Technologies for Science and Mathematics Instruction." In R. D. Pea, and K. Sheingold (Eds.). *Mirrors of Minds: Patterns of Experience in Educational Computing* (pp. 35–56). Norwood, NJ: Ablex Publishing Corporation.

Mayer, Richard. (1984). "Aids to Text Comprehension." *Educational Psychologist, 19,* 30–42.

Merrill, M. David. (1991). "Constructivism and Instructional Design." *Educational Technology, 31*(5), 45–53.

National Council of Teachers of Mathematics. (1989). *"Curriculum and Evaluation Standards for School Mathematics."* Reston, VA: National Council of Teachers of Mathematics.

Nelson, Wayne, and David Palumbo. (1992). "Learning, Instruction, and Hypermedia." *Journal of Educational Multimedia and Hypermedia, 1,* 287–299.

Papert, Seymour. (1981). "Computer-Based Microworlds as Incubators for Powerful Ideas." In R. Taylor (Ed.). *The Computer in the School: Tutor, Tool, Tutee* (pp. 203–210). New York: Teachers College Press.

Pea, Roy, and Louis Gomez. (1992). "Distributed Multimedia Learning Environments: Why and How?" *Interactive Learning Environments, 2*(2), 73–109.

Perkins, David. (1992). "Technology Meets Constructivism: Do They Make a Marriage?" *Educational Technology, 31*(5), 18–23.

Reiser, Robert. (1987). "Instructional Technology: A History." In R. Gagné (Ed.). *Instructional Technology: Foundations* (pp. 11–48). Hillsdale, NJ: Lawrence Erlbaum Associates.

Rieber, Lloyd. (1992). "Computer-Based Microworlds: A Bridge Between Constructivism and Direct Instruction." *Educational Technology Research and Development, 40(1),* 93–106.

Rieber, Lloyd, and Paul Welliver. (1989). "Infusing Educational Technology into Mainstream Educational Computing." *International Journal of Instructional Media, 16*(1), 21–32.

Saettler, Paul. (1990). *"The Evolution of American Educational Technology."* Denver, CO: Libraries Unlimited.

Salomon, Gavriel. (1984). "Television Is "Easy" and Print Is "Tough": The Differential Investment of Mental Effort in Learning as a Function of Perceptions and Attributions." *Journal of Educational Psychology, 76,* 647–658.

Savenye, Wilhelmina, Gayle Davidson, and Patricia Smith. (1991). "Teaching Instructional Design in a Computer Literacy Course." *Educational Technology Research and Development 39*(3), 49–58.

Schwartz, Judah, and Michel Yerushalmy. (1985a). "The Geometric Supposer." Pleasantville, N.Y.: Sunburst Communications.

Schwartz, Judah, and Michel Yerushalmy. (1985b). "The Geometric Supposer: An Intellectual Prosthesis for Making Conjectures." *The College Mathematics Journal, 18,* 58–65.

Schwartz, Judah, Michel Yerushalmy, and B. Wilson (Eds.). (1993). *"The Geometric Supposer: What Is It a Case Of?"* Hillsdale, NJ: Lawrence Erlbaum Associates.

Tobin, Kenneth, and George Dawson. (1992). "Constraints to Curriculum Reform." *Educational Technology Research and Development, 40*(1), 81–92.

DISCUSSION QUESTIONS

1. How do idea technologies and product technologies exemplify teachers' philosophical beliefs?

2. Can product technologies and idea technologies be integrated to provide effective use of educational technology? Why? Why not?

3. How can educational technology be effectively integrated with instructional approaches?

4. How does educational technology facilitate higher order thinking skills?

5. How might educational technology result in a reconceptualization of teachers' roles?

25

Curriculum Trends Revisited

ALLAN C. ORNSTEIN

FOCUSING QUESTIONS

1. *What are some of the trends affecting curriculum?*
2. *How have these trends affected curricularists' thinking?*
3. *How might the integration of advanced technology into school-based curriculum impact student achievement?*
4. *What procedures will curricularists employ to design a relevant curriculum?*
5. *Which time-tested aspects of the curriculum are likely to continue in the future?*

Opinions differ on the directions education will take, and library shelves are filled with volumes describing current and anticipated changes in society and education. Despite disagreements, however, it is likely that certain trends in particular will increasingly affect curriculum planning in the near future. Some of the most important of these trends are noted in the discussion that follows.

The emerging curriculum responds to the urge to break away from traditional disciplines, to develop more interdisciplinary approaches. In the curriculum of the future, subject matter most likely will be less compartmentalized and more integrated and holistic. Although traditional subject boundaries will remain, there will be increased cross-subject material; knowledge will no longer be considered fragmented or linear but multidisciplinary and multidimensional; it will also be integrated with more visual and auditory resources and will rely less on verbal and reading materials.

ELECTRONIC EDUCATION

The advent of video technology has made available another valuable tool for instruction. Video-

tapes, cassettes, and disks can be used for instruction in classrooms, libraries, resource centers, and the student's home. Because the video can be played at any convenient time, the students never have to miss a lesson. Hundreds of catalogs offer videos on a wide range of subjects; in addition, many school systems and teachers have begun to produce their own videos for specific instructional purposes. With the help of a videoprinter, individual images from the screen—photographs, tables, graphs, or any other useful picture—can be printed on paper for further study.

Many videos interact with the viewer when used in conjunction with a computer. Realistic simulations and action-reaction situations can be presented as part of an instructional program. The program can tell the viewer whether a response is right or wrong—or the viewer can be offered a choice of options, and the program will then display the outcome of the option chosen. Interactive videos have an enormous teaching potential that educators are just beginning to explore. Such videos can be used either for individual lessons or for instruction in small groups.

Educators need to investigate ways to use the popularity of videogames for teaching purposes. Although videogames have been criticized for their escapism, they are by nature interactive: to each move by the player, the machine responds with a move of its own. Math, reading, and writing lessons can be written in a videogame format, and the student will find practice and drill more lively in a game atmosphere.

According to one estimate, by the year 2000 more than 20 percent of instructional tools will include computers and videos. Teachers must not only keep abreast of this changing video technology, but must also plan ways to integrate it into the curriculum. In an era when the number of videos rented from video stores surpasses the total number of books checked out of libraries, teachers should help students to become critical video consumers and to be aware of how visual images affect us as individuals and as a society (Ornstein, 1990, 1991).

Today, schools may select television programs specifically developed for educational purposes and have them beamed into the classroom by satellite. This is particularly useful for small, rural schools with limited local resources. Some home cable systems also carry educational programming, but its quantity and quality will increase only if educators demand this resource and use it.

Widely used in business and industry, teleconferences have begun to appear in school systems, usually as an experiment on the secondary level. In a typical conference, a resource person, teacher, or group of students is viewed through the television screen, talking to or instructing other students or participants. Viewers can watch as if they were across the table, although they may be thousands of miles away. The viewing audience can ask questions and make decisions about what further information should be presented.

The curriculum is going to come alive with interactive videos, satellite and cable networks, and teleconferences for most subject areas. The fact that there are already some two million computers in classrooms, and increasing at a rate of 100,000 per year, suggests the demise of what

some call "pencil technology." The point will no longer be made by the pencil. And, similarly, the textbook as we know it is doomed to obsolescence. It will become incidental and probably take on different forms: talking to the student, monitoring his or her progress, and modifying content accordingly.

New forms of electronic knowledge will take shape—more personal, immediate, graphic, and rapid. Acquiring new knowledge will not be crucial, because no one will be able to keep pace with it, rather being able to access it and being networked into a call system will be critical. People who lack information or who are unable to call for it and use it, will become impotent on the job and in dealing on a daily basis with other people, service agencies, or institutions that have information.

TECHNICAL LITERACY

Because of the revolution in technology, the schools must now educate citizens to become familiar with computers, electronics, lasers, and robots. Computer literacy stands beside the three Rs as a fundamental skill. According to government projections to 1995, of the ten fastest-growing occupations, four require knowledge of computers (technician, systems analyst, programmer, and operator). Other trends suggest high-tech influence in such growth areas as biogenetics, computer/video software, robotics, telecommunications, microelectronics, toxic waste and pollution, space, and the oceans (Klode, 1991; *Occupational Projections and Training Data,* 1990). Soon there will exist technical occupations for which we do not yet even have names.

In a high-tech economy, workers will need to be better educated (compared to the industrial economy) and to have better cognitive, communication, and cooperative team skills. People at home and on the job will have calculators, computers, fax machines, and other technical tools to do their symbol crunching for them; however, they will have to decide what buttons to push and what the symbols mean. As the pace of technology accelerates, whole industries may be born, expand, and die in terms of peaks and valleys of the stock market; it will be impossible to predict the precise skills employees will need on the job, but they will need to be retrained periodically in order to compete on a global basis. In such an environment, it is likely that workers will be displaced from one job to another and will be required to retool and relearn new skills on the job; education will become a lifelong enterprise.

In cooperation with industry and government, schools must identify the emerging technologies and services and provide a curriculum that prepares students for viable careers. In part, this means educating future scientists who can design, develop, and apply the new technology. But not everyone needs to become a scientific expert. For many occupations, people simply need to understand the technological basics— what buttons to push under what conditions and how to make machines provide the service or information that they were designed to offer. Only a small percentage of the work force will require sophisticated technical or scientific knowledge, but many will need better cognitive and communication skills.

The National Science Teachers Association (NSTA) has endorsed a curricular approach called Science/Technology/Society, which emphasizes the social and technical aspects of science rather than pure science. One of the purposes of such programs is to help students prepare for the impact of technology on daily life. Some traditional vocational/industrial programs are also being enriched with a focus on technology, especially on computers and robotic design. In still other cases, the entire vocational and industrial arts program is being revamped to meet new technological requirements; this demands updated equipment, the integration of computers into courses, and continual interaction among schools, government, and the work force.

As the pace of technology accelerates, there is increasing need to develop a nationwide plan—

involving education, industry, and government—that assesses the future occupational needs of society and establishes corresponding guidelines for schools. Cooperative planning is needed— now.

LIFELONG LEARNING

The trend toward lifelong learning is occurring in all modern societies as a result of the knowledge explosion and the rapid social, technological, and economic changes that force people to prepare for second or third careers and to keep themselves updated on new developments that affect their personal and social goals. Education will continue to become more a lifelong enterprise and increasingly will take place outside the confines of the traditional school. Taking note of these trends, the Carnegie Commission has developed the concept of a "step-in, step-out" educational system for lifelong learning. This means that people could move in and out of educational programs throughout their lives.

Some observers believe that much of the learning that has been provided by elementary, secondary, and postsecondary schools may be provided in the future by business and industry, especially to meet the needs of a skilled work force in high-tech and information-based industries (Hoyt, 1991; Magaziner and Clinton, 1992; Weisman, 1993). By 1989, in fact, employers were spending $250 billion annually in training; in comparison, colleges and universities spent only $120 billion (*Condition of Education,* 1991; *Digest of Education and Statistics,* 1990). Still other scenarios envision educating adolescents and adults through a network of community resources as well as small learning centers and libraries.

There is also growing concern about the rate of international illiteracy, about 1.1 billion (or 20%) worldwide (mostly involving Third World countries), including 23 to 25 million in the United States, which is the highest number in the industrialized world. Methods for eliminating illiteracy in the United States are mainly tied to adult education courses in basic education. Spending for adult education at the state and local levels increased 379 percent between 1980 and 1988, and the number of participants increased from 2 million to 3.1 million (*Adult Literacy,* 1990; *Digest of Education Statistics,* 1990). Adult education is expected to increase in the 1990s, especially in states in which there are large minority and immigrant populations.

INTERNATIONAL EDUCATION

Although historically the United States has taken a relatively isolationist position, the increasing interdependence among nations demands that Americans become knowledgeable about developments in distant lands. Oil prices in Saudi Arabia and Iran affect job opportunities in Houston, Denver, and Tulsa. Auto and steel production in Japan and Korea influence the local economy in Detroit and Pittsburgh. Deforestation in Brazil and Malaysia affects the atmosphere in New York and San Francisco. We truly inhabit a "global village" in which our standard of living and our national economy are virtually connected to events in other parts of the world.

Satellite and aerospace communications, instant television reporting, supercomputer networks, laser technology, and jet travel have made this planet seem smaller, and other peoples' problems (or strengths) are harder to ignore. About 20 million children in Third World countries die of starvation each year, and another 800 million (about 15% of humanity) go to bed hungry or malnourished. Considering the rapid worldwide growth in population and the increasing scarcity of world resources, these figures indicate a planet in transition that may soon be unable to sustain even the industrialized nations.

Another area of international education that U.S. schools may need to address in the future is foreign language instruction. The most common spoken language in the world is Mandarin, followed by English, Hindi, and Spanish. Japanese ranks tenth, and German and French rank much lower. Nearly all foreign language programs in American schools offer Spanish and French; in fact, 58 percent of secondary students enrolled in a foreign language study Spanish (Met, 1989). But fewer than .01 percent of U.S. high school students study Japanese, and about .001 percent attempt Mandarin (Ornstein & Hunkins, 1993). Failure to train students in these languages may severely limit the future growth of U.S. trade and our understanding of other economic market places.

Education in America must become more widely international in scope. Educators might expand travel exchange programs and perhaps make study in another culture a requirement for graduation. There should be emphasis on international geography, history, political science, and economics. As the world becomes more interconnected and interdependent, such needs will become more evident and more funds may be devoted to the area of global curriculum.

ENVIRONMENTAL EDUCATION

Mounting concern over such problems as pollution, toxic waste, overpopulation, and depletion of food and natural resources has created demands for more knowledge and new programs in ecology and environmental education. Much of the relevant content has long been included in traditional earth sciences, biology, and geography courses and in conservation programs. The new demand calls for a more meaningful and better coordinated program that raises the theme of crisis.

The parade of grim environmental realities is a long one and is continually expanding. Scientists believe that the depletion of the earth's ozone layer (already depleted some 5%), caused chiefly by man-made chemicals used in the manufacture of some plastics and in aerosol sprays and cleaning solvents, will increase the incidence of skin cancer, cataracts, and immune system disorders; it may also damage crops, trees, and marine organisms worldwide. If the ozone layer fades over populated regions (there is evidence that such a hole may already exist over Northeast portions of the United States), the results could be devastating. The greenhouse effect, which may warm the atmosphere and increase the sea level, may result in substantial harm to both farmlands and cities.

In addition, fish and wildlife, soil, water, and the air we breathe are often contaminated; the only debatable point is when the cumulative effects of all these poisons and toxic substances begin to affect our health. Many people believe that the entire ecological chain is in jeopardy; and some even predict that the great wars of the twenty-first century will be fought for clean water and soil.

Rather than terrifying students about ecological disaster, however, schools should prepare students for tomorrow's world by helping them understand how scientific, social, and political issues interact. Because mere possession of knowledge does not ensure proper action, the curriculum must also deal with the attitudes, values, and moral thinking that lead to responsible environmental behavior. Ecological literacy requires a comprehensive view of the modern world, of how fragile it is, and of how scientific, social, and political issues combine and lead to problems and or solutions. It requires that schools take a more active role in requiring students to study the environment rather than expect government agencies and activist groups to manage or protect people from other people.

NUCLEAR EDUCATION

The nuclear standoff between the United States and the Soviet Union has ended, and we are now less vulnerable to world nuclear confrontation than we were during the last fifty years. Indeed, the threat of computer malfunction and subsequent nuclear disaster has declined dramatically. But the nuclear bomb club, which now includes more than twelve nations, is expanding. Some countries such as China, and private corporations in Germany and France, continue to sell their nuclear knowledge to Third World countries. Considering the possibility that terrorists

may use nuclear devices for their own purposes, the world may not be that safe from nuclear threat after all.

Even peaceful uses of nuclear energy—power plants, medical facilities, radiation therapy, and nuclear medicines—have come to seem more problematical, especially since the disasters at Three Mile Island and Chernobyl. The entire world is affected by a serious meltdown—in terms of air, food, and water quality. Global weather patterns know no national boundaries; concentrated radiation can affect human populations thousands of miles away.

The waste products of nuclear facilities and toxic chemicals also present a continuing problem; where in this world can we bury them? Try to convince the residents of Maine or Michigan that it is to their advantage, or that it is their patriotic duty, to have a nuclear (or toxic) dump site in their backyards. For children to realize that nuclear destruction comes in various forms, and that they cannot always rely on adults to watch for their future, is very painful and fearsome.

Concern about nuclear energy has reached schools under such rubrics as "nuclear-sane programs," "peace education," and "peace-making strategies." In coming years these will continue to be important elements in a globally oriented curriculum. We must not reduce our concern about nuclear energy because of the demise of the Soviet Union; nuclear energy will play a great role in the future—and we will need a nuclear education program.

HEALTH EDUCATION AND
PHYSICAL FITNESS

Trends in the health of the U.S. population are producing new pressures to expand or reorient the curriculum. For example, the epidemic of AIDS (acquired immunodeficiency syndrome), with its dire risk to sexually active adolescents, has forced educators to confront the issue of student health in a new way. Predictions are that by the year 2000 some 40 to 50 million people around the world will be affected by the disease; the majority will be from Africa, but some four to five million will be Americans (Altman, 1991; Popham, 1993). Some educators see the AIDS epidemic as literally a life-or-death matter for their students. Schools have been slow, however, to include AIDS education in the curriculum.

One reason for the lack of AIDS education is the continued controversy over the disease and the recommended preventive measures. Many parents and educators have been particularly incensed by programs involving the distribution of condoms in big-city schools. A more basic reason for the lack of AIDS education, however, is that only twenty-seven states require any form of health or sex education, and American students average only 13.9 hours of such education annually. Moreover, nationwide there is only one certified health teacher for every 21,500 students (Manna & Symons, 1990; Miller & Becker-Dunn, 1993). Many educators believe that this shortage must and will be addressed in the future. Certainly AIDS education is going to be incorporated into the curriculum, as early as at the elementary grade level.

Dietary habits and exercise comprise another health concern. Citing medical evidence of high blood pressure and elevated blood fats and cholesterol counts among American youngsters, physicians have criticized the high-fat, burgers-and-fries diet common among school-age children. Many young students appear to be eating their way toward heart disease and other maladies. In addition, school children have been increasingly unable to pass basic physical fitness tests; they do poorly on measures of body development, strength, and flexibility. Television and video viewing habits (including salt and sugar-coated snacks) among American children and youth have contributed to this lack of fitness, and what we might call the "fat and flabby" generation.

Although the American adult population appears to have a love affair with physical fitness and sports, the schools ironically have cut back physical education and fitness programs because of budget considerations and the renewed stress on academic excellence. Educators frequently assert that we will need to rebuild these programs in the curriculum of the future. Some schools are already recognizing the need to provide better guidance for diet and exercise.

Sports, too, should be reoriented to increase the emphasis on aerobic and rhythmic activities (running, jumping, jogging, bicycling). By the end of the 1990s, progressive and far-sighted schools should be deemphasizing traditional competitive sports, which tend to cater to only a few students and involve activities that only the young pursue. Instead, schools increasingly should emphasize lifelong sports such as tennis, golf, biking, and swimming, as well as noncompetitive intramural activities in which the average athlete and even the nonathlete can participate.

The primary goal for physical and health programs is to have fun and socialize in sporting activities, not to compete and win, and to adopt lifelong exercise behavior. Some type A parents and coaches are going to have to be reprogrammed; winning and working out for three hours a day is appropriate for a very small percentage of students.

IMMIGRANT EDUCATION

Legal immigration now accounts for up to one-half of the annual growth in the U.S. population. It has already surpassed post–World War II rates and is approaching the peaks reached in the years prior to World War I. Despite its present economic ills, the United States still looks like the promised land to many people who are searching for a better life.

The new immigrant population differs in ethnic origins from that of the past. From 1930 to 1950, 80 percent of immigrants to the United States came from Western Europe and Canada. From 1970 through 1985, only 10 percent came from these countries; the leading source countries, with the highest first, were Mexico, the Philippines, South Korea, Taiwan, Vietnam, Jamaica, India, the Dominican Republic, and Guatemala. In tenth place, with two percent of the total, was Great Britain. Today as many as 90 to 95 percent of immigrants come from non-Western or Third World countries. Moreover, estimates of *illegal* immigration, mainly from Mexico, Central America, and the Caribbean, total about 1 million people per year, with approximately 500,000 establishing permanent residence (Fallows, 1991; Juffus, 1991). Partly as a result of these immigration trends, by the year 2000 nearly one-third of the U.S. population will be nonwhite and Hispanic, and in Arizona, California, Colorado, Texas, and New Mexico the proportion will approach 50 percent (Ornstein, 1984, 1989).

For some recent immigrants, life in America has been a remarkable success story. Many, however, face language barriers, ethnic prejudice, health problems, and a lack of good jobs. One difference is that the newcomers now enter a country that is vastly different from the open, economically booming America that absorbed the European masses with ease in prior decades. Moreover, hostility toward immigrants, especially illegal immigrants, is common, and born of economic and population pressures. Jobs are scarce in many parts of the country, and wages and unemployment trends in many sectors of the economy are affected by immigrants who are willing to work harder and for less money than Americans.

A significant number of immigrant families are "structurally poor," meaning that the family conditions are unstable or disorganized and the children have few chances to escape from poverty. Because of cultural differences in learning styles or thinking patterns, the children may be labeled "learning disabled" or "slow." Even when this is not the case, value hierarchies vary widely across cultures, so that immigrant children have diverse attitudes about school, teacher authority, gender differences, social class, and behavior in general.

To assist these new immigrants, many educators are suggesting an increase in compensatory and bilingual programs in the schools. A multicultural curriculum can also help immigrant children achieve acceptance and respect in their new country. But in the future, if present immigration trends continue, schools will have to go even further in adapting their curricula for students who have been transplanted from another land and another culture. We can expect our school budgets to be strained while we try to resolve the learning and linguistic problems that these children bring to school, and we will need to sensitize our teachers to immigrant customs and values, rather than mislabel many with such terms as "learning disabled," "behavioral disordered," "handicapped."

THE RETURN OF GEOGRAPHY

Most adults over forty remember geography as a required unit in their elementary school days and as a separate subject in high school that was taken for a half year along with civics or economics for the remaining half year. Those of us with good spatial relations and abstract abilities were able to appreciate the concept of longitude and latitude, topography and climate maps, and great circle routes. For others geography was a drudgery-filled requirement with names of far-off rivers and mountain ranges and hard-to-pronounce capitals that had little meaning to us.

During World War II and the Cold War period, geography was considered important for understanding international relations, economic power, military warfare, and U.S. and Allied activities in Europe and Asia. The subject was considered useful for explaining current events in the elementary grades and was considered one of the "essential" subjects needed for transmitting the nation's heritage and for guaranteeing international leadership.

However, geography gradually disappeared from the school curriculum; absorbed into social studies, it was often delegated to teachers who preferred to emphasize history. By 1960 only 14 percent of U.S. students in grades 7 to 12 were enrolled in geography courses, and in the mid-1970s the proportion dropped to 9 percent—a low point for the entire century (Gardner, 1986; Stoltman, 1990). Not only had geography been consolidated into social studies, it also was no longer a requirement for college admission.

As a result of this neglect, American high school and college students became geographically illiterate. A recent NAEP assessment of the nation's high school students revealed that only 42 percent could locate Nigeria on a map of Africa, and only 37 percent could find Southeast Asia on a world map (*The Geography Learning of High School Seniors,* 1990). In another survey, 39 percent of young adults living in Boston could not name the six New England states; in Dallas 25 percent could not identify the country that borders the United States to the South (Kearns, 1988).

The reform movement in education, starting with the publication of *A Nation at Risk* in 1983, has sounded the alarm. For the United States to remain a worldwide power, U.S. students must learn about the world around them, including its basic geography. Renewed emphasis on geography has become part of several different curriculum focuses, such as back-to-basics, cultural literacy, environmental education, and global education. As the drive toward restoring substantive content to the curriculum continues, geography will play an increasing role.

MIDDLE-GRADE EDUCATION

There is a growing recognition today that students between the ages of ten and fifteen are often distracted from their schoolwork because they are going through a time of rapid growth and development. Enormous variability exists among these students, even within the same age group and in the same classroom. The differences in physical, intellectual, and emotional development are so great that averages have little meaning. One eighth-grade student may be six feet and weigh two hundred pounds, and the student sitting next to him may be nearly two feet smaller and weigh half that amount.

The expanding use of middle schools is an attempt to make education more responsive to these students' social and psychological needs. Middle schools comprising grades 6 to 8 now enroll as many as 40 percent of U.S. students in this grade span. Schools concentrating on grades 7 and 8—also called middle schools—account for another 25 percent. Today only 17 percent of U.S. students in this grade range attend a school comprising grades 7 through 9, the traditional junior high school (Epstein & MacIver, 1988; Ornstein, 1992).

The difference between middle schools and junior highs is often confusing. Many middle schools were originally established for administrative reasons, such as the need to alleviate overcrowded elementary or high schools. Since the 1980s, however, middle schools have tended to represent a distinct way of thinking about the education of preadolescents and early adolescents. Compared to other secondary schools, middle schools put more emphasis on socialization, less on academics; more emphasis on intramural sports, less on interscholastic or competitive sports. There is more emphasis on the students' growth and development, not only on cognitive domains of learning. Their curricula are more interdisciplinary, and they offer more exploratory subjects, such as sex education, creative writing, and drama in blocks of ten to twelve weeks as opposed to traditional academic subjects for the entire term. Cooperative learning, heterogeneous grouping, flexible scheduling, and extended advisory periods are more common in middle schools than in junior high and high schools.

As middle schools become even more widespread, new curriculum approaches will continue to develop. Teacher education programs will also reflect the change. Until now, only a tiny percentage of teacher education programs have distinguished middle schools from elementary and secondary schools in their preservice programs. In the new future, however, teacher training institutions will focus increasingly on the skills and knowledge needed to teach in a middle school.

AGING EDUCATION

Unless the U.S. birth and death rates both dramatically increase, we are heading for a society in which the young will play a diminished role. Our society is rapidly aging, and all of us are on the same conveyor belt—the only difference being that we got on at different times. By the year 2020, increased longevity and the aging of the post–World War II baby-boom group will increase the number of elderly Americans (age 65 or older) to an estimated 51.4 million, or 17.3 percent of the projected U.S. population. By comparison, this age group included only 25.5 million people, or 11.3 percent of the population, in 1980 (*U.S. Population, Where We Are, Where We're Going,* 1992; Van Wishard, 1990).

The costs for medical and custodial care of elderly people will likely create an increasing burden on the younger working population. Moreover, the aging members of society constitute a growing political force, able to shift social spending dollars toward their own needs at the expense of school budgets. According to some projections, the increases in federal spending for Medicaid, Social Security, and old-age benefits will increase 73 percent between 1990 and 1995, after a 52 percent hike during the previous ten years, while spending on education dips 4 percent (Hadley & Zuckerman, 1990; Kaplan, 1991).

Given this "graying of America" and the issues it raises, some educators believe that schools must teach students to understand the problems and prospects of aging: how to cope with aging personally (even though it may seem distant when we are young) and how to help loved ones (parents and grandparents) successfully confront this stage of life. On another level, schools should attempt to counter many of the existing stereotypes about the elderly. Retirement ages are changing as people stay in the work force well past the age of sixty-five. We see more and more people in their seventies playing tennis and being actively involved in business and community affairs. Soon the curriculum may treat age stereotypes and age discrimination as another "ism," like racism and sexism, that students should learn to overcome.

Schools themselves should integrate semiretired and retired people into the school work force, as volunteers, teacher aides, and resource people. The collective wisdom of these people is immense, and their political support for schools will become increasingly important. Most important, schools may be required to deal with shrinking budgets as our nation's priorities change from the youth to aging group.

FOR-PROFIT EDUCATION

A new form of separate and unequal schooling may increase in the years ahead. Privatization and profitization of education have appeared in the form of nationwide nursery schools, day-care and after-school centers, private coaching and sports centers, franchised tutoring centers, private college counseling services (aimed at selected colleges), private coaching for SAT and professional tests, corporate training schools, and contracted out-of-school services. All of these trends have one thing in common: they turn education into business by marketing educational services for a fee.

Although we have always had private alternatives to public education, a growing number of affluent families are willing to pay for various types of educational services to enhance their children's education and opportunities. Because of parental emphasis on the importance of education for their children's success, and fueled by the school choice and private school movements, entrepreneurs have rightly judged that there is a market for supplementary services—especially among well-to-do, high-driven parents.

The largest private learning centers, as of 1991, were the Britannica Learning Centers, with 86 centers in 8 states; Huntington Learning Centers, with 100 centers in 26 states; Kinder Learning Centers, with 1,250 centers in 41 states and 2 Canadian provinces; and Stanley Kaplan Educational Centers, with 125 permanent centers and nearly 500 temporary centers (Telephone conversations, 1991). About 3 to 5 percent of the U.S. school population participates in this type of proprietary school, twice the percentage that did so in 1987; the percentage is expected to increase further as the learning centers expand.

Some commentators have welcomed these private and profit-making schools as a means for radically changing American education. The present school structure, they contend, hinders school reform; educational services can be delivered more efficiently by the market system than by the government. Other observers argue that public education discriminates against taxpayers who do not have children in school. Some proponents of profit-making schools see a worldwide movement in industrialized countries to privatize education. In fact, it would not be surprising to see large computer or publishing companies such as Apple, IBM, Macmillan, and World Encyclopedia enter the market or even begin to franchise education for-profit centers.

On the other hand, many educators believe the rise of for-profit education will widen the gap between "have" and "have-not" children. Hourly fees for many learning centers and tutoring courses range from $15 to $50, a cost that prices out the great majority of parents. The price will probably increase as the demand for such services rises. To counter the trend, critics argue that public schools should offer more remedial education, supplementary help, and enrichment programs—services that would benefit students and increase parents' confidence in local schools. In this way, the rise of private learning centers may soon stimulate changes in curriculum and instruction in the public schools.

FUTURISTIC EDUCATION

According to Toffler (1970), many people are susceptible to "future shock," that is, they are unable to cope with the rapid change of today's society. As he puts it, "To survive, [and] to avert . . . future shock, the individual must become infinitely more adaptable and capable than ever before." The principal aim of education "must be to increase the individual's 'cope-ability'—the speed and economy with which the person can adapt to continual change (pp. 35, 402).

One way of preparing students for the future is through studying the future itself. New courses or programs, called futuristic studies, futuristics, or futurism, are now being offered at the college level, and they should soon filter down to secondary schools. This field of study considers technological developments and social events not as separate but rather as twin components that will determine our future. To generate accurate conceptions of the future is no small task, but presenting the future as a formal object of study helps students learn the implications of rapid change and how society can adjust to these changes.

Educators have identified several areas of competence that are important in a future-oriented curriculum. An understanding of technology is critical, of course, particularly communications technology. Other subjects of study include planning procedures, the organization of information, forecasting techniques, decision making, and working in groups and institutions. Students would be taught to think in multidimensional as well as linear ways. Finally, the curriculum would enhance students' self-concepts so they do not feel powerless in a powerful society and would equip them to deal with the complexity of international power shifts and rapid change (Ornstein & Hunkins, 1989, 1993).

The future is always evolving; therefore, the curriculum must also be evolving. Whether in futuristic courses or in more standard ones, educators must begin to confront the twenty-first century. We must plan it now, but we must keep in mind that there are valuable historical lessons to remember and a rich culture that needs to be preserved.

CONCLUSION

Although the curriculum must evolve to serve a changing society, we caution the reader on several fronts. Change for the sake of change is not good; it must be tempered with wisdom, compassion, and justice. Schools throughout the ages have viewed their programs as being on the cutting edge of progress, and they have often been wrong. We may be misguided again as we view our schools and society; only the future will tell.

New knowledge, indeed, is not necessarily better than old knowledge. Are we to throw away most of Aristotle, Galileo, Kepler, Darwin, and Newton merely because they are no longer part of this century? If we stress only scientific and technological knowledge, we could languish physically, aesthetically, morally, and spiritually. As we try to maintain curriculum relevancy and plan for the future, there is no guarantee that we will not repeat the mistakes of the past; as educators, we should never lose historical perspective.

What knowledge we select and how we organize the curriculum requires continual attention; we must learn to prune away old and irrelevant knowledge and to balance and integrate new knowledge into the curriculum. As we modify and update content, we must not throw away time-tested, enduring subjects such as literature, history, even music or art (or the three Rs at the elementary school level). Teachers, and especially curriculum specialists, must protect the schools and their students against fads and frills, and especially against extremism. They must keep in perspective the type of society we are, the values we cherish, and the educational aims we wish to achieve.

REFERENCES

Adult Literacy (1990). *Education Digest,* 56 (October), 42.

Altman, L.K. (1991). W.H. says 40 million will be infected with AIDS. *New York Times.* June 18, B8.

Condition of Education (1991). Washington, D.C.: U.S. Dept. of Education, Table 1:25-2, p. 225.

Digest of Education Statistics (1990). Washington, D.C.: U.S. Dept. of Education, Tables 229, 321, pp. 302, 322.

Epstein, J.L. and D.J. MacIver (1988). The middle school grades: Is grade span the most important issue? *Educational Horizons.* 67 (Winter), 88–94.

Fallows, J. (1983). The new immigrants. *Atlantic* (November), 45–68, 85–89.

Gardner, D.P. (1986). Geography in the school curriculum. *Annals of the Association of American Geographers.* Washington, D.C.: The Association.

The Geography Learning of High School Seniors (1990). Washington, D.C.: U.S. Dept. of Education.

Hadley, J. and S. Zuckerman (1990). Rising hospital costs. *Urban Institute Policy and Research Report,* 20 (Winter-Spring), 9–10.

Hoyt, K. (1991). Education reform and relationships between the private sector and education. *Phi Delta Kappan,* 72 (February), 450–452.

Juffus, J. (1991). *The Impact of the Immigration Reform and Control Act on Immigration.* Washington, D.C.: Urban Institute.

Kaplan, G. (1991). Suppose they gave an intergenerational conflict and nobody came. *Phi Delta Kappan,* 72 (May), K1–K12.

Kearns, D.T. (1988). An education recovery plan for America. *Phi Delta Kappan,* 69 (April), 565–570.

Klode, R.F. (1991). Integrated learning for a competitive workforce. *Phi Delta Kappan,* 72 (February), 453–455.

Magaziner, I. and H.R. Clinton (1992). Will America choose high skills or low wages? *Educational Leadership,* 49 (March), 10–14.

Manna, A.L. and C.W. Symons (1990). Promoting student health through children's literature. *Educational Horizons,* 69 (Fall), 37–43.

Met, M. (1989). Which foreign languages should students learn? *Educational Leadership,* 47 (September), 54–58.

Miller, L. and Becker-Dunn, E. (1993). HIV at school. *American School Board Journal,* 180 (February), 42–45.

Occupational Projections and Training Data (1990). Washington, D.C.: U.S. Dept. of Labor.

Ornstein, A.C. (1984). Urban demographics with educational implications. *Education and Urban Society,* 16 (August), 477–496.

Ornstein, A.C. (1989). Enrollment trends in big-city schools. *Peabody Journal of Education,* 66 (Summer), 64–71.

Ornstein, A.C. (1990). Bring telecommunications and videos into the classroom. *High School Journal,* 73 (April-May), 252–257.

Ornstein, A.C. (1991). Video technology and the urban curriculum. *Education and Urban Society,* 23 (May), 335–341.

Ornstein, A.C. (1992). Middle school notes: The troubled world of the adolescent. *Principal,* 72 (September), 49–52.

Ornstein, A.C. and F.P. Hunkins (1989). Curriculum futures: Review and outlook. *Kappa Delta Pi Record,* 25 (Summer), 107–111.

Ornstein, A.C. and F.P. Hunkins (1993). *Curriculum: Foundations, Principles, and Issues.* Needham Heights, Mass. Allyn and Bacon.

Popham, W.J. (1993). Wanted: AIDS education that works. *Phi Delta Kappan,* 74 (March), 559–562.

Stoltman, J.P. (1990). Geography in the secondary schools: 1945–1990. *NASSP Bulletin,* 74 (December), 9–13.

Telephone conversations (1991). With David Hiatt, Vice President of Development, Kinder Learning Centers, July 11; Susan Meutchen, Manager of Franchise Services, Huntington Learning Centers, June 21; and Mary Verdon, Director of Public Relations, Britannica Learning Center, June 24.

Toffler, A. (1970). *Future Shock.* New York: Bantam Books.

U.S. Population: Where We Are, Where We're Going. (1992). Washington, D.C.: Population Reference Bureau.

Van Wishard, W. (1990). What in the world is going on? *Vital Speeches of the Day,* 74 (March), 314.

Weisman, J. (1993). Skills in the schools: Now it's business' turn. *Phi Delta Kappan,* 74 (January), 367–369.

DISCUSSION QUESTIONS

1. How can curricularists effectively integrate technology into curriculums for early childhood, elementary, middle school/junior high, secondary, and special education students?

2. What implications does the influx of electronic and technological capabilities have for lifelong learning?

3. What kinds of curricular changes will be needed to ensure that students can actively participate in a global economy?

4. How can schools and businesses work together to provide student learning?

5. What alternative conceptions of curriculum might be considered to effectively integrate the trends addressed in this article?

PRO-CON CHART 4

Should academic achievement be the main criteria for assessing student outcomes?

<table>
<tr><th>PRO</th><th>CON</th></tr>
<tr>
<td>1. Academic achievement standards provide an objective means for evaluating student outcomes.</td>
<td>1. Alternative forms of assessment provide a more comprehensive view of how well students are performing in school.</td>
</tr>
<tr>
<td>2. Achievement measures can be used to group students for instructional purposes or as objective criteria for college admission.</td>
<td>2. Teachers become locked into presenting content that they anticipate will be assessed by tests; subsequently, achievement tests drive the curriculum.</td>
</tr>
<tr>
<td>3. Measures of achievement provide feedback to teachers about effectiveness of their instruction.</td>
<td>3. Pressures of instructional assessment constrain the teachers' creativity and lead to trivialization of learning.</td>
</tr>
<tr>
<td>4. Academic achievement measures let students know how well they are doing in school and can serve as a motivator to do good work.</td>
<td>4. Students need different kinds of feedback and should receive praise for quality work in cognitive as well as in noncognitive domains.</td>
</tr>
<tr>
<td>5. The essence of schooling boils down to academic excellence.</td>
<td>5. Schools should address the cognitive, social, personal, and moral domains of learners.</td>
</tr>
</table>

CASE STUDY 4

An Advocate for Longer School Days

Jack Pierce, curriculum coordinator of Ipsid Elementary District handed a written proposal to the superintendent, Dick Bosio, which suggested that the district lengthen the school day by forty minutes beginning in the fall. Pierce cited research to support his claim that academic learning time is the most important variable associated with student learning for most types of learners. He also reported research that showed significant relationships between increased academic time and gains in student achievement. While explaining his rationale for increasing the length of the school day, Pierce said he felt confident that overall the district would demonstrate an increase in students' Iowa Test of Basic Skills scores. He suggested that this change would probably satisfy the public that Ipsid was promoting excellence in education.

Pierce emphasized that since time spent on relevant academic tasks is measurable the district would be able to show that better test scores were the result of the increased academic instruction. Furthermore, he said that increased instructional time was advisable according to the research on teaching that emphasized student outcomes.

The Ipsid superintendent listened closely to Pierce's proposal. He had some concerns, but decided that Pierce had analyzed almost all the critical factors. Noting some of the considerations that might need to be addressed, Bosio thought to himself that because engaged time was equivalent to time devoted to actual work, asking teachers to stay a little longer each day would not be an issue. Bosio turned to Pierce and said, "I think this is a good idea. Go ahead and implement this change."

1. Assume you are Bosio and discuss how you would implement an extension of your school's instructional day by forty minutes.

2. Do you think that student achievement is directly correlated with academic engaged time? Why? Why not?

3. Based on your experience, what factors other than time on task influence student outcomes?

4. In what ways do the use of different instructional models influence student outcomes?

5. What alternatives might be considered to promote student outcomes instead of lengthening the school day?

6. What is the relationship between content, quality of teaching, academic engaged time and student outcomes?

7. How do subject matter content and social atmosphere of the classroom affect academic engaged time?

PART FIVE

Curriculum and Supervision

INTRODUCTION

How do developments in supervision influence curriculum? What are the issues impacting views of supervision and leadership?

In Chapter 26, Allan Ornstein explores the relationship between curriculum, instruction, and supervision as well as the issues related to the absence of a curriculum certification. He suggests that supervisory decision making is the foundation for curriculum and instruction and that the relationships among and between all three components should be of concern to educators. In the next chapter, Allan Glatthorn suggests a new model for supervision, referred to as professional development. Comprised of four related tasks, including staff development, information observations, rating, and individual development, this approach acknowledges the integrity of the individual and focuses on helping teachers grow professionally.

In Chapter 28, Dennis Sparks and Susan Loucks-Horsely provide an overview of the models that characterize effective staff development. They discuss the theory and research that supports each model. The authors also consider how organizational climate, administrative structures, policy, and participant involvement support or impede the implementation of each approach. Next, in Chapter 29, Mary Phillips and Carl Glickman highlight the contribution of the peer coaching approach to staff development models. They point out that the effectiveness of staff development programs rests upon allowing teachers to work and make decisions together as colleagues in learning about, planning, implementing, and evaluating instruction.

Matthew Miles and Karen Seashore Louis, in Chapter 30, discuss which issues are essential to the change process. They describe how change agents can use context, vision building, resources, and coping with problems as vehicles for implementing successful change. In the final chapter of Part Five, Thomas Sergiovanni explains how effective and ineffective schools differ in the kind of education they offer. He discusses the relationship between leadership and students' outcomes. He also considers how leadership styles affect school climate and staff morale.

Curriculum, Instruction, and Supervision: Their Relationship and the Role of the Principal

ALLAN C. ORNSTEIN

FOCUSING QUESTIONS

1. *What issues have been created by the absence of a curriculum certification?*
2. *What are the advantages and disadvantages of providing different definitions for the terms curriculum and instruction?*
3. *What implications do agreed-upon definitions for curriculum, instruction, and supervision have for curriculum delivery?*
4. *Should the states establish minimum requirements for graduate training in the field of curriculum? Why? Why not?*
5. *What implications do agreed-upon definitions for curriculum, instruction, and supervision have for graduate programs in curriculum, supervision, or administration?*

Clarifying the relationship of curriculum, instruction, and supervision, this educator believes, will not only help the teaching/learning situation in general, but will also help principals in their decision-making role by knowing the dynamic nature of the three components and how they interact.

Most theoreticians and practitioners of curriculum find the relationship between curriculum, instruction, and supervision ill defined.

Part of the problem is related to certification, the fact that the degrees of specialization (curriculum, instruction, and supervision) are not well defined and that too many different programs and functions of curriculum leadership prevail.

Although some members of the field want to clarify the relationship between curriculum, in-

struction, and supervision, the descriptions are still in flux and fragmented.

Professional organizations avoid the issue in the literature; and principals, while they recognize their importance as the "curriculum leader," "instructional leader," and "supervisory leader," rarely have time to act on their concerns because of pressing managerial, community, and fiscal responsibilities.

The need to examine this relationship is important for everyone concerned with curriculum, instruction, and supervision.

CURRICULUM CERTIFICATION

The fact that curriculum lacks certification, whereby requirements are specified on a statewide or professional basis, adds to the problem of defining the field and agreeing on the scope and content of curriculum knowledge and on curriculum courses at the college and university level.

Not only do minimum requirements for curriculum personnel vary among school systems within states, not to mention among states, the programs vary considerably among colleges and universities. Because there are no state regulations, each school of education usually decides on its own requirements.

The result is a proliferation of elective courses in the curriculum program at the expense of specialized courses and common, agreed-upon courses. Even when curriculum course titles are similar, there are often wide differences in content, level of instruction, and competencies required.

The irony is that there is great confusion in content and experiences in a field that should be very clear about its curriculum. Moreover, there is little guarantee that curriculum specialists who graduate from a program know how to develop, implement, and evaluate a curriculum. And, there is no test or screening device to help school systems make choices about curriculum personnel and their expertise in curriculum.

This also adds to the problem of who are curriculum specialists or generalists and what are their respective job titles, roles, and responsibilities. Is a supervisor a curriculum generalist or specialist? What about the principal who is supposed to be a curriculum and instruction leader? Is a resource teacher, consultant, director, etc., a curriculum person? And what about the classroom teacher?

Professionals are certified in teaching, counseling, school psychology, supervision, or administration, with job descriptions and related course requirements all defined. Students can major in curriculum, but they are at risk since curriculum jobs are not well-defined and there are no certification requirements or licenses that protect their jobs.

Actually many curriculum specialists in the schools are certified in other fields. This means that their loyalties and professional reading habits may be closely aligned to other fields. Similarly,

professors of curriculum are usually schooled in many disciplines, not only curriculum per se.

Thus, the field is open to several interpretations by the experts themselves—to what curriculum should encompass, what knowledge is of tangible substance, and what content and processes are essential.

AN UNCLEAR RELATIONSHIP

The relationship between curriculum, instruction, and supervision is not clearly defined in the professional literature; moreover, the instructional-supervisional aspects of curriculum in terms of how much weight or consideration they should have is unclear.[1]

While there is much discussion about the relationship between curriculum and instruction, reflected in the historical roots of curriculum as well as in current curriculum textbooks, the discussion about curriculum and supervision in the past few years has declined considerably in curriculum texts compared to earlier periods.

Curriculum and Instruction

The eighteenth and nineteenth century European pioneers, from Locke and Rousseau to Spencer and Herbart, were pioneers in pedagogical principles. Their concern was not curriculum as we know it, since the term was unknown until the twentieth century, but rather with content and teaching methods, which they attempted to explore as scientific principles. But what they had to say was related to curriculum, even though the field of study did not exist.

The actual relationship between curriculum and instruction was not examined until 1930, when the famous committee for the 26th Yearbook of the National Society for the Study of Education (NSSE) formulated a composite statement about curriculum making. Twelve steps were developed and two were linked to instruction: "the place of school subjects in instruction" and "measuring the outcomes of instruction."

Both Tyler and Taba were concerned with instruction in their classic texts. This was especially true of Tyler who saw instruction as a plan for teaching the curriculum and as "the procedures for organizing learning experiences into units, courses, and programs."[2]

By entitling his book *Basic Principles of Curriculum and Instruction,* he took the position that both components were equally important and part of a continuous cyclical process, involving constant replanning and reappraisal. One of his four major chapters examined "how learning experiences [can] be organized for effective instruction."

Taba saw curriculum in a broader context than teaching, and teaching in a broader context than instruction. Curriculum represented the substance and content of what was to be learned; teaching was identified with the general behavior and methods of the teacher for imparting the subject matter to the learner; and instruction was viewed as the specific activities introduced at various stages of the curriculum.

By taking this approach, Taba saw instruction as something apart from curriculum—and something that did not have equal weight with curriculum.[3]

In the 1960s a good deal of activity occurred over theories of instruction and how curriculum and instruction were related. Curriculum and instruction were also defined by Jerome Bruner, who developed a theory of instruction that focused on four factors: (1) facilitating learning, (2) structuring of knowledge, (3) sequencing of learning experiences, and (4) pacing of rewards and punishments in the process of learning and teaching.[4] In this context, curriculum and instruction were considered as separate disciplines of education and both had equal weight.

James MacDonald argued for clarification of terms associated with curriculum, instruction, teaching, and learning. Curriculum was defined as the "plans for action," instruction was "putting plans into action" (similar to Tyler), teaching was "the behavior of the teacher" (similar to Taba), and learning was the "desired responses" of the learner (similar to both Tyler and Taba).[5] Singling out instruction as a unique concept among

the four terms, and basically as the "implementation" stage of curriculum, he advocated further research on instruction.

Finally, Harry Broudy and his colleagues spoke of curriculum as a total system, with instruction and teaching as subsystems and therefore not as important. Instruction was further categorized into five content or subject areas, what they termed "study areas"; and teaching was further categorized into two methods or strategies, what they termed "modes."[6]

They further claimed that while "modes of teaching are not, strictly speaking, a part of curriculum, for practical purposes it is not useful to ignore them entirely in curriculum theory."[7] This statement would not differ significantly from most current theories of curriculum.

While Tanner and Tanner today devote limited space on the relationship between curriculum and instruction, they assert that to describe both as separate components is misleading, and even breaks down when the curriculum is implemented at the classroom or school level.[8] To examine them as separate components, they are likened to the old "doctrine of dualism" which was once criticized by John Dewey.[9]

This doctrine conceives curriculum as a "means" for achieving the "ends" of education, whereby the ends and means are artificially separated or viewed as discontinuous functions. The Tanners conclude that the need is to *synthesize* curriculum and instruction as one problem, not to analyze them as separate problems. His view corresponds with Tyler's.

At the other extreme, among current textbook writers, is Robert Zais. He *separates* curriculum and instruction along the views of Broudy and Taba, viewing curriculum as a broad concept and instruction as a specific phenomenon (with less importance). Instruction is to be introduced at some point along a curriculum continuum. The point of introduction is flexible, permitting subjective judgment on the part of the teacher; it "is to be selected according to the teacher's personality and teacher style, and the students' needs and interests."[10]

Most curriculum specialists today take a middle position between the Tanners and Zais. Although they separate curriculum and instruction for purposes of discussion, one without the other is considered incomplete. The two components are *fused*—a view similar to Beauchamp and MacDonald. The two components retain their original characteristics or independence.

The three approaches to curriculum and instruction have their own perspectives: the first (synthesis) is an interdisciplinary perspective; the second (separation) reflects a discipline approach to subject matter or a field of study; the third (fusion) is a more fluid approach.

They all have their shortcomings. Those who wish to synthesize both components fail to provide us with answers about how curriculum and instruction can be combined; they merely provide us with theoretical insights without dealing with practice; they raise more questions than they resolve. A total synthesis of both components, for example, could blur the principles and processes of curriculum and instruction.

Furthermore, it is somewhat premature to synthesize something as elusive as curriculum and instruction, since the experts cannot agree on definition of terms or on the exact relationship. In fact, they really do not know to what extent these two components can be synthesized.

Those who separate the components fail to recognize that it is too simple and rigid to claim one is the subsystem of the other or one takes place prior to the other. The separation of one component from the other does harm to both, since both become incomplete. Curriculum specialists who separate both components tend to overemphasize curriculum at the expense of instruction, and instructional theorists and educational psychologists tend to overemphasize instruction at the expense of curriculum.

On a theoretical level, we can make a good case for the fusion viewpoint, because it represents a compromise between synthesis and separation but on a practical level, especially in the classroom, events come and go at a very rapid, complex, and multidimensional level. The two components do not remain still in the classroom; they move around and interface in different ways under different circumstances (with different teachers, students, and subjects).

Sometimes the two components fuse—sometimes they are exclusive of one another—when and where varies with the situation. Sometimes fusing is not productive and sometimes it makes sense. Actually, no one can really pinpoint the relationship or when it is best to fuse, synthesize, or separate, especially in the classroom where most teaching and learning take place in school.

Whether people wish to synthesize curriculum and instruction, treat them as separate components, or take the middle position and fuse them reflects their philosophical and psychological views on education. Curriculum experts and school principals do not have strong views on this subject.

Instructional experts have a definite position; their ideas reflect the growing influence of educational psychologists in the field of curriculum who have associated instruction with learning theory, theory-based matching of students and teachers, testing and evaluation, and scientific principles of teaching.

It is the psychological school represented by David Berliner, Benjamin Bloom, Jere Brophy, Nate Gage, and Thomas Good, who now dominate the field of instruction, not the curriculum specialist school, and who now provide much purpose and direction in the relationship between curriculum and instruction.[11]

Curriculum and Supervision

For about 25 years, starting during the post World War II era, ASCD published a number of yearbooks linking curriculum and supervision (specifically in 1946, 1951, 1960, 1965, and 1971) as well as monographs. In these publications, administrators and supervisors were seen as instructional and curriculum leaders who also assumed leadership roles in their own areas of competence in content fields. They were viewed as designers of inservice education, designers of curriculum materials, change agents, and innovators. They were responsible for selecting and organizing common relationships among various subjects, for scheduling and programming classrooms, subjects, materials, media, etc., and responsible for setting instructional standards and improving the educational program of learners.

During the last 20 or 25 years, the supervisory component in curriculum has diminished in the professional literature and in the attitudes and perceptions of curriculum specialists. Most curriculum texts today briefly examine the relationship in no more than one chapter, and in still other cases ignore the relationship entirely.

Only Ronald Doll devotes considerable space to curriculum and supervision, envisioning curriculum as a process entailing decisions that supervisors must make; the supervisor is viewed as a curriculum worker and leader for curriculum change and improvement.[12] His discussion coincides with the views of most school principals.

Coinciding with the declining relationship between curriculum and supervision in the field of curriculum, supervision has shifted to departments of administration. The trend is rooted in the theoretical discussions of the University Council for Educational Administration, based at Ohio State University,[13] and the Institute of Administrative Research at Teachers College, Columbia University,[14] which in the early 1960s explored the relationship between supervision and administration, and then curriculum and supervision as they related to administration.

The relationship between supervision and administration has intensified in recent years because there has been a dramatic decline in supervisory personnel in curriculum fields, exasperated by two trends since the early 1980s:

- Eliminating non-specialized and noncertified personnel in curriculum at the local school and school district levels, and
- Transferring many curriculum tasks to administrators, especially principals, to fill this void.[15]

Put in different words, as schools drop curriculum specialists, principals and other administrators absorb their roles.

Supervisors who might have specialized in curriculum have opted in large numbers to enhance their professional education at the university level in the area of administration—where there is certification and expanding job opportunities. The result is that in a growing number of schools of education, curriculum and supervision courses and departments are in decline and supervision and administration courses and departments are on the rise.

Indeed, few teachers, chairpeople, and vice principals enroll in curriculum departments: most see their career advancement in terms of studying for a principalship, and enroll in departments of administration.

Just as the supervision and administrative relationship has increased at theoretical and practical levels, most supervisory texts have continued over the years to discuss the relationship between supervision and curriculum. In this discussion, supervision is usually seen as the major system and curriculum as a subsystem.

In this context, the supervisor is seen as a policymaker and implementer of curriculum, involved in planning and designing the curriculum, from clarifying the goals and objectives of the school (or school district) to evaluating personnel as well as the ongoing curriculum. This is reflected in the traditional view that sees the supervisor (along with the administrator) as the curriculum and instructional leader, and is keenly illustrated in the recent expansion of the supervisory role which includes staff development, commitment to curriculum change, selecting and organizing curriculum resources, improving curriculum communication, and working with teachers in and outside classrooms to organize and improve instruction and learning.

In this context, Lucio and McNeil, in a classic text on supervision, claimed that there were six major tasks of the supervisor, including "curriculum development" in which the person "participated directly in the formulation of objectives, selection of school experiences, preparation of teacher studies, and selection of instructional aids."[16]

Ten years later, Mosher and Purpel discussed the evolution of supervision in terms of schools of thought or approaches. Five historical trends were examined: the most recent was identified as "supervision as curriculum and development," which according to the authors, "seems to stress the materials, units, and content of instruction." As a curriculum developer, "the supervisor . . . organizes curriculum materials, involves teachers in their production and implementation and acts as a resource person for individual teachers."[17]

By 1980 the use of systems analysis in supervision was fashionable, and Neagley and Evans outlined a "systems approach in supervision with implications for improving the curriculum and instruction." It included nine supervisory concepts or roles, including: "organizing for instruction . . . solving instructional problems, developing media systems for instruction . . . planning the curriculum . . . developing instructional models, [and] budgeting, and cost studies related to instruction and curriculum."[18]

And, in a classic supervisory text that has been popular for more than 20 years, Ben Harris emphasized 10 tasks of the supervisor, for purposes of assessing the supervisor, which included "developing curriculum [on top of the list], providing materials [for implementing the curriculum], providing staff for instruction, organizing for instruction . . . [and] evaluating instruction."[19] What seems to be happening is that supervision is not only digesting curriculum but also instruction in the past few years as subcomponents that relate to its field.

CONCLUSION

It is foolish to get into a debate whether curriculum, instruction, or supervision are major systems or subsystems, or which one is the major field and which are the minor fields. It really depends on one's perspective and professional background on how the relationship is viewed.

The author takes the view that they are all related, pretty much equally, with room for variation depending on what theories and practices are considered. They interact in various ways, but the exact interaction is impossible to determine because of the dynamic nature of the three components.

Curriculum, instruction, and supervision should have similar weight, and no particular significance or importance should be given to one over the other components. Although all three components do not unfold equally at the same time, the planning and organization of the three components go hand in hand, and one without the other two is incomplete.

This relationship implies that curriculum decisions are related and implemented together with instructional and supervisory decisions, that instructional decisions are related and implemented together with curriculum and supervisory decisions. It further implies that supervisory decision making is the basis for curriculum and instruction, and that the relationship between and among all three components should be of major concern to all school principals.

ENDNOTES

1. There are about 80 departments in curriculum at the graduate level in universities across the country. Based on a review of the first 50 at random, about 40 percent of the curriculum departments use only the word "curriculum" in their department name, 30 percent refer to "curriculum and instruction," 25 percent use the term "educational leadership" or "curriculum leadership" suggesting a curriculum-supervisory-administrative program, and about 5 percent use the term "curriculum and supervision."
2. Ralph W. Tyler, *Basic Principles of Curriculum and Instruction* (Chicago: University of Chicago Press, 1949) p. 83.
3. Hilda Taba, *Curriculum Development: Theory and Practice* (New York: Macmillan, 1962).
4. Jerome S. Bruner, *Toward a Theory of Instruction* (New York: W. W. Norton, 1968).
5. James B. MacDonald, "Educational Models for Instruction—Introduction." in *Theories of Instruction,*

edited by J. B. MacDonald (Washington. D.C.: Association for Supervision and Curriculum Development, 1965), pp. 5–6.

6. Harry S. Broudy, B. Othaniel Smith, and Joe R. Burnett, *Democracy and Excellence in American Secondary Education* (Chicago: Rand McNally, 1964), p. 78.

7. Ibid., p. 79.

8. Daniel Tanner and Laurel N. Tanner. *Curriculum Development: Theory into Practice,* 2nd ed. (New York: Macmillan, 1980).

9. John Dewey, *Democracy and Education* (New York: Macmillan, 1916).

10. Robert S. Zais, *Curriculum: Principles and Foundations* (New York: Harper & Row, 1976), p. 12.

11. Allan C. Ornstein, "A Difference Teachers Make," *Educational Forum* (Fall 1984), pp. 109–118; Ornstein, "Teacher Effectivenes Research," *Education and Urban Society* (February 1986), pp. 168–175.

12. Ronald C. Doll, *Curriculum Improvement: Decision Making and Process,* 4th ed. (Boston: Allyn and Bacon, 1979).

13. Jack Culbertson, "Recruiting Candidates To Prepare for Positions of Educational Leadership," Paper presented to the University Council for Educational Administration, Columbus, Ohio, April 1962; John A. Ramseyer, "Supervisory Personnel," in *Preparation Programs for School Administrators: Common and Specialized Learnings,* edited by D. J. Leu and H. C. Rudman, Seventh UCEA Career Development Seminar (East Lansing, Mich.: Michigan State University, 1963), pp. 155–168.

14. Bernard H. McKenna. "Do You Have Enough Staff To Do a Proper Job?," *IAR-Research Bulletin* (April 1961), pp. 1–4; Harold T. Shafer, *A Study of Administrative Procedures Influencing the Evolvement of the Curriculum Director's Role in Seven Selected New Jersey School Systems* (New York: Teachers College Press, Columbia University, 1959).

15. Allan C. Ornstein, "Thinking Small for the 1980s," *Clearing House* (February 1982), pp. 279–280.

16. William H. Lucio and John D. McNeil, *Supervision: A Synthesis of Thought and Action* (New York: McGraw-Hill, 1962), p. 26.

17. Ralph L. Mosher and David E. Purpel, *Supervisor: The Reluctant Profession* (Boston: Houghton Mifflin, 1972), pp. 20–21.

18. Ross L. Neagley and N. Dean Evans, *Handbook for Effective Supervision of Instruction,* 3rd ed. (Englewood Cliffs, N.J.: Prentice-Hall, 1980), p. 48.

19. Ben M. Harris, *Supervisory Behavior in Education,* 3rd ed. (Englewood Cliffs, N.J.: Prentice-Hall, 1985), p. 18.

DISCUSSION QUESTIONS

1. How do you view the relationship between curriculum, instruction, and supervision?

2. How might clarifying the relationship between curriculum, instruction, and supervision aid principals?

3. Who should seek to clarify the relationship between curriculum, instruction, and supervision? Scholars or practitioners? Or both?

4. Should curriculum, instruction, and supervision be defined in terms of behaviors and tasks or performance competencies? Why? Why not?

5. What procedural steps would be necessary to establish a curriculum certification?

6. As a result of their training, should graduate students in administration and supervision be required to demonstrate a knowledge of processes that are characteristic of curriculum? Why? Why not?

A New Concept of Supervision

ALLAN A. GLATTHORN

FOCUSING QUESTIONS

1. *What is staff development?*
2. *How does professional development differ from supervision?*
3. *What are the essential components of professional development?*
4. *What are some potential problems associated with informal observations?*
5. *How does the use of a rating system differ from evaluation?*

What is the nature of effective teaching? How do we encourage greater effectiveness in classrooms today? The wealth of new knowledge available to us about how teachers think and the numerous attempts by educators to restructure the teacher's role lead us to examine our assumptions, to criticize our practices, and to develop new ways of thinking about our profession.

In particular we need to rethink the concept of supervision. In an attempt to do this, I find it useful to substitute the term *professional development* for the more restrictive term *supervision.* Professional development, then, means all those systematic processes used by school administrators, supervisors, and teachers to help teachers grow professionally.

THE COMPONENTS OF PROFESSIONAL DEVELOPMENT

Professional development processes are divided into four related tasks: staff development, informal observations, rating, and individual development.

Staff Development

Staff development can be defined as all formal and informal programs that are offered to groups of teachers in response to organizational needs.

Formal staff development programs have specific agendas, a set schedule, and a structured set of experiences. They focus on specific instructional skills. Research suggests that they will be more effective if they include tested practices identified in reviews by Sparks and others.[1] Unfortunately, too many formal programs are offered on the assumption that research can be directly translated into practice by consultants. I contend that we would achieve better results by using an approach which Buchmann calls "conversation about teaching," a dialog among peers.[2]

For example, a staff development session might involve a linguist, a district language arts coordinator, an English department chairperson, a principal, and several English teachers discussing together the teaching of grammar. Topics might include the contributions of contemporary grammar, the functions of teaching grammar, the implications of research on the teaching of grammar, and the possibilities of conducting class-room-based research on students' use of language.

Another fault of formal programs is that they tend to be too individualistic and neglect organizational needs. Central office staff should base inservice activities for teachers on the long-range goals of the school district.[3]

In summary, staff development programs can be effective if they reflect sound research, create a spirit of dialog, and respond to district goals. However, they should be implemented with an array of informal staff development approaches. Ineffective principals and supervisors complain that they do not have time for staff development; effective leaders use whatever time is available. They work with small groups of teachers during preparation periods, over lunch, and in faculty meetings in a less systematic and structured fashion. They share ideas, discuss current educational issues, and solve problems informally.

Informal Observations

Brief, unannounced classroom visits, which last from 5 to 15 minutes, were previously called *administrative monitoring*. However, because the term has negative connotations, we can use the term *informal observation* instead. Supervisors in business might use the term *managing by walking around*.

Informal observations serve several purposes. The principal and supervisor become less office bound and more visible and thus reduce the isolation that teachers tend to feel. It provides excellent opportunities for principals and supervisors to reinforce and praise good teaching, gather data regarding curriculum implementation, and head off instructional problems before they become critical.

The value of informal observations has been questioned. Many standard texts on supervision disparage them and insist that all observations should be for a full period and should be preceded by a conference. However, many researchers conclude that in effective schools the educational leader is highly visible, frequently monitors classrooms, stays well informed about day-to-day school activities, and demonstrates an interest in instruction by spending much time in the classroom.[4] In school systems where I have helped implement a program of informal observations, teachers welcomed the process unless it was linked to a rating system.

Guidelines should be established for the use of informal observations by supervisors and teachers together:

- Do not link teacher evaluations with information gleaned by informal observation.
- Conduct informal observations frequently.
- Provide immediate feedback with a smile, a gesture of approval, or a brief note. A face-to-face conference may be needed; if so, concerns should be expressed tentatively: "I was there for only five minutes, but I did note that many of the small groups seemed not to be on task. What is your perception?"
- Be systematic. Observations should focus on a particular subject area, grade level, group of students, or instructional method.

Rating

The term *rating* can be defined as the process of making formative and summative assessments of teacher performance for purposes of making administrative decisions. In light of this new concept of professional development, rating is distinguished from evaluation in that rating is tied to explicit criteria, whereas evaluation is a judgment about the overall quality of performance on any occasion.

Consider the following examples. The supervisor or principal informally observes a teacher with a disorderly class and makes a negative judgment. An observation is made to diagnose the teaching style. An attempt is made to be objective, but the supervisor can't help smiling in approval. In a staff development session, a teacher gives an ineffective demonstration.

In each of these examples a judgment was made about quality, despite attempts to be objective. It is difficult for supervisors to pretend not to have made judgments about teacher performance; in fact, there is some evidence that those who are candid about assessments are more effective than those who do not provide evaluative feedback.[5]

Now consider the following example. A teacher's class is visited by a principal carrying a rating form listing explicit criteria. The form is completed. A conference is held at which the principal says, "Your performance in that class was not satisfactory; I hope your supervisor will be able to help you improve before the next rating observation." Several more *formative* ratings are made throughout the year. In May a summative assessment is made based on all data collected during the year. The principal says, "Your performance this year was unsatisfactory; your contract will not be renewed."

The following analogy clarifies the difference between evaluation and rating: A gymnast performs a set of exercises in a meet. The coach watches and makes the *evaluation,* "Your approach was faulty; we'll have to work on that." The judges, who were also watching, hold up their scorecards. They have made a *rating.*

What kinds of rating systems are most effective? After studying 32 school districts reported to have effective evaluation systems, Wise and his colleagues reached five conclusions:

- To succeed, the teacher evaluation system must suit the goals, management style, concept of teaching, and community values of the school district.
- Administrative commitment and resources for evaluation are more important than the particular kind of checklist or procedures used.
- The school district should decide about the main purpose of the rating system and then match the process to the purpose.
- The evaluation process must be seen to have utility. It must be cost effective, valid, and reliable.

- Teacher involvement and responsibility for the process improves the quality of teacher evaluation.[6]

If rating systems are to be used for making administrative decisions, a criterion based system using multiple observations will be preferable. Here is one process.

Administrators, supervisors, and teachers analyze the role of the teacher and the research on effective teaching, after which they develop a comprehensive set of criteria including three types of measures. The measures are non-instructional aspects of role performance, such as supervising students in non-instructional settings; the essential instructional skills that are not always directly observable, such as making valid tests; and the essential instructional skills that can be observed, such as sustaining a desirable learning environment.

The scenario includes informing the teacher of the date and time of the rating, the actual rating using criteria agreed upon, and, last, holding a rating conference in which the teacher is informed of the general rating. Specific strengths and weaknesses are reviewed, and the supervisor lays out a professional development plan for remedying perceived deficiencies.

An extensive amount of time is required of administrators and supervisors if such a rating is to be thorough and valuable. Therefore, it may be useful to develop two rating tracks, one standard and one intensive. The standard track can be used with career teachers whose performance clearly is satisfactory. In this case, the rating is a formality used to comply with the state school code and includes one observation and a final conference. Intensive ratings should be used with all probationary teachers, those being considered for promotion, and those whose performance is questionable. Intensive ratings involve several observations by two or more observers, each of which is followed by a conference to assess non-observable skills and to monitor non-instructional responsibilities.

Individual Development

Most principals are too busy to provide clinical supervision to all teachers, and teachers vary significantly in their conceptual development, in learning styles, and in their professional needs. Therefore, a differentiated system of professional development gives each teacher options in the types of developmental processes used to aid professional growth. Such a system offers intensive, cooperative, and self-directed options.

1. *Intensive development is a process in which a supervisor, an administrator, or an expert teacher works closely with an individual teacher in order to effect significant improvement in the essential skills of teaching.* It is more comprehensive than clinical supervision and is geared to significant improvement in teaching performance. Intensive development may include the following:

— planning conferences: conferring with the teacher on yearly planning, semester planning, unit planning, and daily planning;
— student assessment conferences: conferring with the teacher about assessing student progress, testing, grading, record keeping, and using data;
— diagnostic observations and feedback: observing all significant transactions in a classroom in order to diagnose developmental needs and determine a developmental agenda;
— focused observation and feedback: observing one particular aspect of teaching and learning and providing appropriate feedback;
— videotape analysis: making a videotape of teaching and analyzing it with the teacher as a complement to direct observation;
— coaching: developing a particular teaching skill by providing a rationale, explaining the steps, demonstrating, and providing a supportive environment in which the teacher can try the skill, and giving the teacher feedback about that trial;
— descriptive student feedback: surveying students for their perceptions of the classroom by asking them to offer descriptive (not evaluative) feedback;

— directed observation of a colleague: structuring and guiding an opportunity for the teacher to observe a colleague and to learn from that observation.

Differentiated intensive staff development is provided mainly to probationary teachers or others who the principal feels need intensive help.

2. *Cooperative development allows experienced teachers to work together in small groups for mutual growth.* It is teacher centered, teacher directed, and respects the professionalism of competent teachers. It takes administrative support but little administrative time. Teams are encouraged to consider at which of the following levels of collaboration they feel ready to begin:

— Level 1. Cooperative dialogs: Teachers meet in small groups to discuss professional issues, share their reactions to professional books, and exchange ideas about teaching.
— Level 2. Cooperative planning: Teachers meet in small groups to help each other plan. They discuss planning strategies, critique each other's plans, and offer suggestions about methods and materials.
— Level 3. Cooperative observation: Teachers observe each other's classes, give each other objective feedback, and discuss the observations in a nonjudgmental manner.
— Level 4. Cooperative production: Teachers work in small groups to produce instructional materials that they will test and use in their classrooms.
— Level 5. Cooperative research: Teachers work together in an action research mode to solve common problems.

3. *Self-directed development options provide opportunities for experienced and competent teachers to work independently.* One or two professional growth goals are selected, and the administrator acts as a supportive resource. The model is similar to McGreal's "practical goal setting approach" except that it is completely divorced from the rating function.

CONCLUSION

The processes of staff development, informal observations, rating, and individual development are closely related. Data derived from informal observations can be used to supplement the information derived from rating observations, can suggest the need for intensive development, and can play an important part in assisting staff development needs. The rating process can help the supervisor or principal identify teachers who need intensive development. Individual development options can be linked with ongoing staff development programs.

However, administrators and supervisors should examine the processes separately and analytically. Because each requires different skills, provides different kinds of information, and employs different processes, I have found it useful to help individual districts develop their own models that link the processes according to their needs. Their models then tend to be affected by district size, administrative preferences, and available resources.

Even though models are designed locally, it is important that each district determine who will be primarily responsible for each component. Some districts limit the informal observations to administrators; others want supervisors and department chairpersons involved. Some require administrators to rate; others expect input from the supervisory staff. It is important to resolve all these issues in ways that make the most sense to administrators, supervisors, and teachers.

Although it has not been possible to assess the effectiveness of the model through quasi-experimental studies, several evaluations conducted by the districts themselves suggest that their unique models have been judged by their administrators, supervisors, and teachers to be more professionally useful than the standard clinical model.

ENDNOTES

1. G. M. Sparks, "Synthesis of Research on Staff Development for Effective Teaching," *Educational Leadership* 41 (1984): 65–72.
2. M. Buchmann, "Improving Teaching by Talking: Argument or Conversation?" *Teachers College Record* 86 (1985): 441–453.
3. G. D. Fielding and H. D. Schalock, *Promoting the Professional Development of Teachers and Administrators* (Eugene: Center for Educational Policy and Management, University of Oregon, 1985): 55–57.
4. D. A. Squires, W. G. Huitt, and J. K. Segars, "Improving Classrooms and Schools: What's Important," *Educational Leadership* 39 (1981): 174–179.
5. R. Gersten, W. Green, and G. Davis, "The Realities of Instructional Leadership: An Intensive Study of Four Inner City Schools" (Paper delivered at the annual meetings of the American Educational Research Association, Chicago, April, 1985).
6. A. E. Wise, et al., *Teacher Evaluation: A Study of Effective Practice* (Santa Monica, CA: Rand Corporation, 1984): 66–80.

DISCUSSION QUESTIONS

1. What are some of the advantages associated with informal observations?
2. Compare and contrast the individual and group development models of staff development. Which approach do you prefer? Why?
3. How are the individual and group development models of staff development similar to and different from the clinical model of supervision?
4. Which approach is most effective for novice teachers? Expert teachers?
5. What kind of rating systems are most effective?

Five Models of Staff Development for Teachers

DENNIS SPARKS
SUSAN LOUCKS-HORSLEY

FOCUSING QUESTIONS

1. *How are staff development and school restructuring initiatives related?*
2. *For what kind of person is the individually guided model of staff development most suitable?*
3. *How are cognitive levels and types of feedback related?*
4. *What activities are characteristic of the peer-coaching, clinical supervision, and evaluation supervisory approaches?*
5. *How can training facilitate school improvement efforts?*
6. *What are the common elements within organizations that have successful staff development programs?*
7. *How can staff development contribute to the professionalization of teaching?*

In the early 1970s, a growing concern about the effectiveness of inservice education resulted in a spate of studies to determine the attitudes of educators about these programs (Ainsworth, 1976; Brim & Tollett, 1974; Joyce & Peck, 1977; Zigarmi, Betz, & Jensen, 1977). The findings indicated nearly unanimous dissatisfaction with current efforts, but a strong consensus that inservice was critical if school programs and practices were to be improved (Wood & Kleine, 1987).

During the late 1970s and early 1980s, several major studies and reviews contributed to our understanding of the characteristics of effective staff development, focusing not on attitudes, but on actual practices (Berman & McLaughlin, 1978; Kells, 1980; Lawrence, 1974; Yarger, Howey, & Joyce, 1980). The resulting list of effective practices, well known by now, included:

- Programs conducted in school settings and linked to school-wide efforts
- Teachers participating as helpers to each other and as planners, with administrators, of inservice activities
- Emphasis on self instruction, with differentiated training opportunities
- Teachers in active roles, choosing goals and activities for themselves
- Emphasis on demonstration, supervised trials, and feedback; training that is concrete and ongoing over time
- Ongoing assistance and support available on request

Staff development came of age in the 1980s. It was the focus of countless conferences, workshops, articles, books, and research reports. State legislators and administrators of local school districts saw staff development as a key aspect of school improvement efforts. Many school districts initiated extensive staff development projects to improve student learning. Research on these projects and craft knowledge generated by staff developers have substantially advanced our understanding of effective staff development practices beyond the overview studies of the early 1980s referred to above.

INTRODUCTION

In spite of this recent intense, widespread interest in staff development, much remains to be learned about the process. This article organizes what is known about effective staff development into five models currently being espoused and used by staff developers. A review of the supporting theory and research on these models is followed by a description of what is currently known about the organizational context that is required to support successful staff development efforts. The conclusion discusses what can be said with confidence about effective staff development practice and what remains to be learned. First, however, are definitions of the key terms and a description of the literature that is used throughout the article.

Definitions

Staff development is defined as those processes that improve the job-related knowledge, skills, or attitudes of school employees. While participants in staff development activities may include school board members, central office administrators, principals, and non-certified staff, this article focuses on staff development for teachers. In particular, it examines what is known about staff development that is intended to improve student learning through enhanced teacher performance.

Two uses of the word "model" have been combined in an effort to both conceptualize staff development and make this conceptualization useful to staff developers. First, borrowing from Ingvar-

son's (1987) use of the term, a model can be seen as a design for learning which embodies a set of assumptions about (a) where knowledge about teaching practice comes from, and (b) how teachers acquire or extend their knowledge. Models chosen for discussion differ in their assumptions. Second, adapting Joyce and Weil's (1972) definition of a model of teaching, a staff development model is a pattern or plan which can be used to guide the design of a staff development program.

Each staff development model presented below is discussed in terms of its theoretical and research underpinnings, its critical attributes (including its underlying assumptions and phases of activities), and illustrations of its impact on teacher growth and development. The literature supporting these models is of several types. First, for each model, the theoretical and research bases that support its use in improving teachers' knowledge, skills, or attitudes are considered. The question asked was: Why should one believe that this model *should* affect teachers' classroom behavior? Second, program descriptions were reviewed in which these models were applied. The question asked was: What evidence exists that demonstrates that this model can be implemented by staff developers in schools and school districts? Third, data about outcomes was sought. The question asked was: What evidence indicates that this model actually makes a difference in teacher performance?

An Overview

This article presents five models of staff development: (a) individually-guided staff development, (b) observation/assessment, (c) involvement in a development/improvement process, (d) training, and (e) inquiry.

Individually-guided staff development refers to a process through which teachers plan for and pursue activities they believe will promote their own learning. The observation/assessment model provides teachers with objective data and feedback regarding their classroom performance. This process may in itself produce growth or it can provide information that may be used to select areas for growth.

Involvement in a development/improvement process engages teachers in developing curriculum, designing programs, or engaging in a school improvement process to solve general or particular problems. The inquiry model requires that teachers identify an area of instructional interest, collect data, and make changes in their instruction based on an interpretation of those data. The training model (which may be synonymous with staff development in the minds of many educators) involves teachers in acquiring knowledge or skills through appropriate individual or group instruction.

Next, this article examines the organizational context that is required to support these models. Our discussion includes organizational climate, leadership and support, district policies and systems, and participant involvement.

The final section looks for gaps in the knowledge base of staff development, identifying areas about which there is still more to learn and areas that as yet remain unexplored by researchers. The hope is that this chapter will serve as both a signpost for how far we have come in the past 20 years in our understanding of effective staff development practices and a spring-board for future research in this vital area.

Five Models of Staff Development

1. Individually-Guided Staff Development

Teachers learn many things on their own. They read professional publications, have discussions with colleagues, and experiment with new instructional strategies, among other activities. All of these may occur with or without the existence of a formal staff development program.

It is possible, however, for staff development programs to actively promote individually-guided activities. While the actual activities may vary widely, the key characteristic of the individually-guided staff development model is that the learning is designed by the teacher. The teacher determines his or her own goals and selects the activities that will result in the achievement of those goals. Perhaps a sense of this model is best represented in an advertisement for the Great Books Foundation which reads: "At 30, 50, or 70, you are more self-educable than you were at 20. It's time to join a Great Books reading and discussion group."

Underlying assumptions. This model assumes that individuals can best judge their own learning needs and that they are capable of self direction and self-initiated learning. It also assumes that adults learn most efficiently when they initiate and plan their learning activities rather than spending their time in activities that are less relevant than those they would design. (It is, however, true that when individual teachers design their own learning there is much "reinventing of the wheel," which may seem inefficient to some observers.) The model also holds that individuals will be most motivated when they select their own learning goals based on their personal assessment of their needs.

Theoretical and research underpinnings. According to Lawrence's (1974) review of 97 studies of inservice programs, programs with individualized activities were more likely to achieve their objectives than were those that provided identical experiences for all participants. Theory supporting the individually-guided model can be found in the work of a number of individuals. Rogers' (1969) client-centered therapy and views on education are based on the premise that human beings will seek growth given the appropriate conditions. "I have come to feel," Rogers wrote, "that the only learning which significantly influences behavior is self-discovered, self-appropriated learning" (p. 153).

The differences in people and their needs are well represented in the literature on adult learning theory, adult development, learning styles, and the change process. Adult learning theorists

(Kidd, 1973; Knowles, 1980) believe that adults become increasingly self-directed and that their readiness to learn is stimulated by real life tasks and problems. Stage theorists (Levine, 1989) hold that individuals in different stages of development have different personal and professional needs. Consequently, staff development that provides practical classroom management assistance to a 22-year-old beginning teacher may be inappropriate for a teaching veteran who is approaching retirement.

Learning styles researchers (Dunn & Dunn, 1978; Gregorc, 1979) argue that individuals are different in the ways they perceive and process information and in the manner in which they most effectively learn (e.g., alone or with others, by doing as opposed to hearing about). Research on the Concerns-Based Adoption Model (CBAM) (Hall & Loucks, 1978) indicates that as individuals learn new behaviors and change their practice, they experience different types of concerns that require different types of responses from staff developers. For instance, when first learning about a new instructional technique, some teachers with personal concerns require reassurance that they will not be immediately evaluated on the use of the strategy, while a teacher with management concerns wants to know how this technique can be used in the classroom.

Taken together, these theorists and researchers recognize that the circumstances most suitable for one person's professional development may be quite different from those that promote another individual's growth. Consequently, individually-guided staff development allows teachers to find answers to self-selected professional problems using their preferred modes of learning.

Phases of activity.   Individually-guided staff development consists of several phases: (a) the identification of a need or interest, (b) the development of a plan to meet the need or interest, (c) the learning activity(ies), and (d) assessment of whether the learning meets the identified need

or interest. These phases might be undertaken informally and almost unconsciously, or they may be part of a formal, structured process. Each phase is explained in greater detail below.

With the identification of a need or interest, the teacher considers what he or she needs to learn. This assessment may be done formally (e.g., the completion of a needs assessment process or as a result of evaluation by a supervisor) or occur more spontaneously (e.g., a conversation with a colleague or reflection upon an instructional problem). The need or interest may be remedial (e.g., "I've really come to dislike my work because of the classroom management problems I'm having") or growth-oriented (e.g., "I'm intrigued by recent research on the brain and want to better understand its implications for student learning").

Having identified the need or interest, the teacher selects a learning objective and chooses activities that will lead to accomplishing this objective. Activities may include workshop attendance, reading, visits to another classroom or school, or initiation of a seminar or similar learning program.

The learning activity may be single session (e.g., attendance at a workshop on new approaches to reading in the content areas) or occur over time (e.g., examination of the research on retaining students in grade). Based on the individual's preferred mode of learning, it may be done alone (e.g., reading or writing), with others (e.g., a seminar that considers ways of boosting the self-esteem of high school students), or as a combination of these activities.

When assessing formal individually-guided processes the teacher may be asked to make a brief written report to the funding source or an oral report to colleagues. In other instances the teacher may simply be aware that he or she now better understands something. It is not uncommon that as a result of this assessment phase the teacher may realize how much more there is to be learned on the topic or be led to a newly emerging need or interest.

Illustrations and outcomes. Individually-guided staff development may take many forms. It may be as simple as a teacher reading a journal article on a topic of interest. Other forms of individually-guided staff development are more complex. For instance, teachers may design and carry out special professional projects supported by incentive grants such as a competitive "teacher excellence fund" promoted by Boyer (1983) or "mini-grants" described by Mosher (1981). Their projects may involve research, curriculum development, or other learning activities. While evidence of outcomes for such programs is not substantial, there are indications that they can empower teachers to address their own problems, create a sense of professionalism, and provide intellectual stimulation (Loucks-Horsley, Harding, Arbuckle, Dubea, Murray, & Williams, 1987). This strategy proved effective in New York City and Houston, where teachers were supported to develop and disseminate their own exemplary programs through Impact II grants. They reported changes in their classroom practices, as well as increases in student attendance, discipline, and motivation (Mann, 1984–85).

Teacher evaluation and supervision can be a source of data for individually guided staff development. McGreal (1983) advocates that goal setting be the principal activity of teacher evaluation. Supervisors would assist in the establishment of those goals based on the motivation and ability of the teacher. The type of goals, the activities teachers engage in to meet the goals, and the amount of assistance provided by supervisors would differ from teacher to teacher based upon developmental level, interests, concerns, and instructional problems.

Similarly, Glatthorn's (1984) "differentiated supervision" calls for "self-directed development" as one form of assistance to teachers. Self-directed development is a goal-based approach to professional improvement in which teachers have access to a variety of resources for meeting their collaboratively identified needs.

Research on teacher centers also demonstrates the value of individually guided staff development. Hering and Howey (1982) summarized research conducted on 15 teacher centers sponsored by the Far West Laboratory for Educational Research and Development from 1978 to 1982. They concluded that, "the most important contribution of teachers' centers is their emphasis on working with individual teachers over time" (p. 2). Such a focus on individual teachers is absent from many traditional staff development programs, which teacher centers appear to complement quite effectively.

Hering and Howey (1982) reported that mini-grants of up to $750 provided by the St. Louis Metropolitan Teacher Center were used to fund a variety of classroom-oriented projects. Interviews with participants found that teachers made extensive use of the ideas and products they developed. Some of these projects eventually affected not only an individual classroom, but a school or the entire district. Regarding this project, Hering and Howey concluded:

> As would be expected, teachers who were given money and support reported high levels of satisfaction and a sense of accomplishment. Also not surprisingly, they developed projects anchored in the realities of the classroom and responsive to the needs and interests of their students. Perhaps most important, however, is the strong suggestion that they can, indeed, influence change and innovation in other classrooms, as well as their own, through projects they design at minimal costs. (p. 6)

Hering and Howey (1982) also report the findings for a study done on individualized services provided at the Northwest Staff Development Center in Livonia, Michigan. Even though these awards rarely exceeded $50, 78 percent of the recipients reported that they had considerable control over their own learning and professional development. Almost 85 percent of the recipients thought that these services made a substantive difference in their classrooms. In summarizing the value of individualized services, the researchers wrote, "Individual teacher needs and concerns have to be attended to, as well as schoolwide collective ones, or enthusiasm for the collective approach will quickly wane" (p. 6).

While there are many illustrations of an individualized approach to staff development in the literature and many more in practice, research on its impact on teaching is largely perceptual and self-report. Perhaps as more resources are directed to supporting this strategy—particularly in the form of incentive grants to teachers—more will be learned about its contribution to teacher, as well as student, growth.

2. Observation/Assessment

"Feedback is the breakfast of champions" is the theme of Blanchard and Johnson's (1982) popular management book, *The One Minute Manager.* Yet many teachers receive little or no feedback on their classroom performance. In fact, in some school districts teachers may be observed by a supervisor as little as once every 3 years, and that observation/feedback cycle may be perfunctory in nature.

While observation/assessment can be a powerful staff development model, in the minds of many teachers it is associated with evaluation. Because this process often has not been perceived as helpful (Wise & Darling-Hammond, 1985), teachers frequently have difficulty understanding the value of this staff development model. However, once they have had an opportunity to learn about the many forms this model can take (for instance, peer coaching and clinical supervision, as well as teacher evaluation), it may become more widely practiced.

Underlying assumptions. One assumption underlying this model, according to Loucks-Horsley and her associates (1987), is that "Reflection and analysis are central means of professional growth" (p. 61). Observation and assessment of instruction provide the teacher with data that can be reflected upon and analyzed for the purpose of improving student learning.

A second assumption is that reflection by an individual on his or her own practice can be enhanced by another's observations. Since teaching is an isolated profession, typically taking place in the presence of no other adults, teachers are not able to benefit from the observations of others. Having "another set of eyes" gives a teacher a different view of how he or she is performing with students.

Another assumption is that observation and assessment of classroom teaching can benefit both involved parties—the teacher being observed and the observer. The teacher benefits by another's view of his or her behavior and by receiving helpful feedback from a colleague. The observer benefits by watching a colleague, preparing the feedback, and discussing the common experience.

A final assumption is that when teachers see positive results from their efforts to change, they are more apt to continue to engage in improvement. Because this model may involve multiple observations and conferences spread over time, it can help teachers see that change is possible. As they apply new strategies, they can see changes both in their own and their students' behavior. In some instances, measurable improvements in student learning will also be observed.

Theoretical and research underpinnings.   Theoretical and research support for the observation/assessment model can be found in the literature on teacher evaluation, clinical supervision, and peer coaching. Each of these approaches is based on the premise that teaching can be objectively observed and analyzed and that improvement can result from feedback on that performance.

McGreal's (1982) work on teacher evaluation suggests a key role for classroom observation, but expresses a major concern about reliability of observations. The author points to two primary ways to increase the reliability of classroom observations. The first is to narrow the range of what is looked for by having a system that takes a narrowed focus on teaching (for instance, an observation system based on the Madeline Hunter approach to instruction), or by using an observation guide or focusing instrument. The second way is to use a pre-conference to increase the kind and amount of information the observer has prior to the observation. Glatthorn (1984) recommends that clinical supervisors (or coaches) alternate unfocused observations with focused observations. In unfocused observation the observer usually takes verbatim notes on all significant behavior. These data are used to identify some strengths and potential problems that are discussed in a problem-solving feedback conference. A focus is then determined for the next observation, during which the observer gathers data related to the identified problem.

Glickman (1986) suggests that the type of feedback provided teachers should be based on their cognitive levels. Teachers with a "low abstract" cognitive style should receive directive conferences (problem identification and solution come primarily from the coach or supervisor); "moderate-abstract" teachers should receive collaborative conferences (an exchange of perceptions about problems and a negotiated solution); and "high-abstract" teachers should receive a non-directive approach (the coach or supervisor helps the teacher clarify problems and choose a course of action).

Peer coaching is a form of the observation/assessment model that promotes transfer of learning to the classroom (Joyce & Showers, 1982). In peer observation, teachers visit one another's classrooms, gather objective data about student performance or teacher behavior, and give feedback in a follow-up conference. According to Joyce and Showers (1983):

> Relatively few persons, having mastered a new teaching skill, will then transfer that skill into their active repertoire. In fact, few will use it at all. Continuous practice, feedback, and the companionship of coaches is essential to enable even highly motivated persons to bring additions to their repertoire under effective control. (p. 4)

Joyce (Brandt, 1987) says that up to 30 trials may be required to bring a new teaching strategy under "executive control." Similarly, Shalaway (1985) found that 10 to 15 coaching sessions may be necessary for teachers to use what they have learned in their classrooms.

Phases of activity. The observation/assessment model—whether implemented through evaluation, clinical supervision, or peer coaching—usually includes a pre-observation conference, observation, analysis of data, post-observation conference, and (in some instances) an analysis of the observation/assessment process (Loucks-Horsley et al., 1987). In the pre-observation conference, a focus for the observation is determined, observation methods selected, and any special problems noted.

During the observation, data are collected using the processes agreed upon in the pre-observation conference. The observation may be focused on the students or on the teacher, and can be global in nature or narrowly focused. Patterns found during instruction may become evident. Hunter (1982) recommends three points of analysis: (a) behaviors that contribute to learning, (b) behaviors that interfere with learning, and (c) behaviors that neither contribute nor interfere, but use time and energy that could be better spent.

In the post-observation conference both the teacher and observer reflect on the lesson and the observer shares the data collected. Strengths are typically acknowledged and areas for improvement suggested (by either the teacher or observer, depending upon the goals established in the pre-observation conference). An analysis of the supervisory (or coaching) process itself, while not necessarily a part of all forms of this model, provides participants with an opportunity to reflect on the value of the observation/assessment process and to discuss modifications that might be made in future cycles.

Illustrations and outcomes. Acheson and Gall (1980) report a number of studies in which the clinical supervision model has been accepted by teachers when they and their supervisors are taught systematic observation techniques. They further note that this process is viewed as productive by teachers when the supervisor uses "indirect" behaviors (e.g., accepting feelings and ideas, giving praise and encouragement, asking questions). While the authors report that trained supervisors helped teachers make improvements in a number of instructional behaviors, they were unable to find any studies that demonstrated student effects.

The most intensive and extensive studies of the impact of observation/assessment on learning comes from the work of Showers and Joyce. Discussed in more detail in the training section, these authors and their associates have found that powerful improvements have been made to student learning when the training of teachers in effective instructional practices is followed by observations and coaching in their classrooms (Joyce & Showers, 1988). In a study that contrasted different sources of coaching, Sparks (1986) contrasted a workshop-only approach with peer coaching and with consultant coaching. Her findings indicated that peer coaching was most powerful in improving classroom performance.

The research, then, provides reason to believe that teacher behaviors can be positively influenced by the use of an observation/assessment model of staff development. It still remains to be learned, however, whether this model must be combined with particular kinds of training if student learning is to be enhanced.

3. Involvement in a Development/Improvement Process

Teachers are sometimes asked to develop or adapt curriculum, design programs, or engage in systematic school improvement processes that have as their goal the improvement of classroom instruction and/or curriculum. Typically these projects are initiated to solve a problem. Their successful completion may require that teachers acquire specific knowledge or skills (e.g., curriculum planning, research on effective teaching, group problem-solving strategies). This learning

could be acquired through reading, discussion, observation, training, and/or trial and error. In other instances, the process of developing a product itself may cause significant learnings (e.g., through experiential learning), some of which may have been difficult or impossible to predict in advance. This model focuses on the combination of learnings that result from the involvement of teachers in such development/improvement processes.

Underlying assumptions. One assumption on which this model is based is that adults learn most effectively when they have a need to know or a problem to solve (Knowles, 1980). Serving on a school improvement committee may require that teachers read the research on effective teaching and that they learn new group and interpersonal skills. Curriculum development may demand new content knowledge of teachers. In each instance, teachers' learning is driven by the demands of problem solving.

Another assumption of this model is that people working closest to the job best understand what is required to improve their performance. Their teaching experiences guide teachers as they frame problems and develop solutions. Given appropriate opportunities, teachers can effectively bring their unique perspectives to the tasks of improving teaching and their schools.

A final assumption is that teachers acquire important knowledge or skills through their involvement in school improvement or curriculum development processes. Such involvement may cause alterations in attitudes or the acquisition of skills as individuals or groups work toward the solution of a common problem. For instance, teachers may become more aware of the perspectives of others, more appreciative of individual differences, more skilled in group leadership, and better able to solve problems. While the learnings may be unpredictable in advance, they are often regarded as important by teachers.

Theoretical and research underpinnings. We have chosen to represent curriculum development and school improvement as types of staff development; involvement in these processes nurtures teachers' growth. Others see staff development (perhaps viewed more narrowly as training) as a key component of effective curriculum development and implementation. As Joyce and Showers (1988) write, "It has been well established that curriculum implementation is demanding of staff development—essentially, without strong staff development programs that are appropriately designed a very low level of implementation occurs" (p. 44).

Whichever perspective one has, staff development and the improvement of schools and curriculum go hand in hand. Glickman (1986), who argues that the aim of staff development should be to improve teachers' ability to think, views curriculum development as a key aspect of this process. He believes that the intellectual engagement required in curriculum development demands that teachers not only know their content, but that they must also acquire curriculum planning skills. He recommends that curriculum development be conducted in heterogeneous groups composed of teachers of low, medium, and high abstract reasoning abilities. According to Glickman, the complexity of the curriculum development task should be matched to the abstract reasoning ability of the majority of teachers in the group.

Glatthorn (1987) describes three ways in which teachers can modify a district's curriculum guide. They may operationalize the district's curriculum guide by taking its lists of objectives and recommended teaching methods and turning them into a set of usable instructional guides. Or they may adapt the guide to students' special needs (e.g., remediation, learning style differences, etc.). Finally, teachers may enhance the guide by developing optional enrichment units. Glatthorn recommends that these activities be done in groups, believing that, in doing so, teachers will become more cohesive and will share ideas about teaching and learning in general, as well as on the development task at hand.

The involvement of teachers in school improvement processes, while similar in its assumptions and process to curriculum development, finds its research and theory base in other sources. General approaches to school improvement come from the literature on change and innovation. For example, Loucks-Horsley and Hergert (1985) describe seven action steps in a school improvement process that are based in research on implementation of new practices in schools (Crandall & Loucks, 1983; Hall & Loucks, 1978; Louis & Rosenblum, 1981). The research on effective schools underpins other approaches to school improvement (Cohen, 1981). Finally, an approach to school improvement through staff development developed by Wood and his associates was derived from an analysis of effective staff development practices as represented in the research and in reports from educational practitioners (Thompson, 1982; Wood, 1989). The result is a five-stage RPTIM model (Readiness, Planning, Training, Implementation, and Maintenance) used widely in designing and implementing staff development efforts (Wood, Thompson, & Russell, 1981). As a result of involvement in such improvement efforts, schools (and the teachers within them) may develop new curriculum, change reporting procedures to parents, enhance communication within the faculty, and improve instruction, among many other topics.

Phases of activity.   This model begins with the identification of a problem or need by an individual, a group of teachers (e.g., a grade-level team or a secondary department), a school faculty, or a district administrator. The need may be identified informally through discussion or a growing sense of dissatisfaction, through a more formal process such as brainstorming or the use of a standardized instrument (such as a school improvement survey or needs assessment), or through examination of student achievement or program evaluation data.

After a need has been identified, a response is formulated. This response may be determined informally or formally. In some cases, the necessary action may become immediately evident (e.g., the need for new lunchroom rules). At other times, teachers may need to brainstorm or search out alternatives, weigh them against a set of predetermined criteria, develop an action plan, and determine evaluation procedures. This process may take several sessions to complete and require consultation with a larger group (e.g., the school-wide staff development committee may receive feedback on the tentative plan from the entire faculty).

Typically it becomes evident during this phase that specific knowledge or skills may be required to implement the plan. For instance, the faculty may decide that it wants to study several discipline systems before implementing the new lunchroom management system. The improvement of students' higher-order thinking may involve the selection of new textbooks, requiring that committee members better understand which features to look for in a textbook to support this goal. The development or selection of a new elementary science curriculum may require study of the latest research on science teaching and the examination of other curricula.

At this point the plan is implemented or the product developed. This process may take several days, several months, or several years. As a final step, the success of the program is assessed. If teachers are not satisfied with the results, they may return to an earlier phase (e.g., acquisition of knowledge or skills) and repeat the process.

Illustrations and outcomes. While teachers have long been involved in curriculum development, little research on the impact of these experiences on their professional development has been conducted. The research that has been done has assessed the impact of such involvement on areas other than professional development (for example, job satisfaction, costs, and commitment to the organization) (Kimpston & Rogers, 1987). Similarly, although the engagement of teachers in school improvement processes has increased in the last few years, little research has been conducted on the effects of that involvement on their professional development. There are, however, numerous examples that illustrate the various

ways schools and districts have enhanced teacher growth by engaging them in the development/improvement process.

In the past few years, many state education agencies have supported implementation of state-initiated reforms through the encouragement (and sometimes mandating) of school improvement processes. For example, the Franklin County (Ohio) Department of Education used a staff development process to assist five school districts to meet mandated state goals (Scholl & McQueen, 1985). Teachers and administrators from the districts learned about the state requirements and developed goals and planning strategies for their districts. A major product of the program was a manual that included a synthesis of information and worksheets that could be used to guide small group activities in the five districts.

School districts have also initiated programs which involved teachers in improvement planning. In the Hammond (Indiana) Public Schools, decision making is school based (Casner-Lotto, 1988). School improvement committees (each composed of 15–20 members, including teachers, administrators, parents, students, and community members) received training in consensus building, brainstorming, creative problem solving, and group dynamics. After this training, each committee develops a "vision of excellence" for its school. As a result, schools have initiated projects in individualized learning, peer evaluation, cross-grade-level reading, and teacher coaching/mentoring.

Sparks, Nowakowski, Hall, Alec, and Imrick (1985) reported on two elementary school improvement projects that led to large gains on state reading tests. The first school's staff decided to review the reading curriculum and to investigate alternative instructional approaches. Teachers task-analyzed the six lowest-scoring objectives on the state test, studied effective instructional techniques, and participated in self-selected professional growth activities. In 2 years the number of students who scored above the average rose from 72 percent to 100 percent. In the second school, teachers adopted a new reading series, revised the kindergarten program, and created a booklet that included practice test items and effective instructional practices for improving student achievement. The percentage of students achieving the reading objectives increased almost 20 percent in 3 years.

The Jefferson County (Colorado) School District has long involved teachers in curriculum development and adaptation (Jefferson County Public Schools, 1974). A cyclical process of needs assessment, curriculum objective statements, curriculum writing, pilot testing and evaluation, and district-wide implementation has been used on a regular basis in the major content areas. Teachers involved in writing and pilot test teams hone their skills as curriculum planners and developers and as masters of the new techniques that are incorporated into the curriculum (these have included such strategies as cooperative learning and individualized instruction). They also often take on the role of teacher trainers for the district-wide implementation that follows pilot and field tests (Loucks & Pratt, 1979).

E. J. Wilson High School in Spencerport (New York) is one of many across the country that has implemented elements of effective schools through a systematic school improvement process. Teachers in the school participate with building administrators on a Building Planning Committee which spearheads the achievement of "ideal practices" within the school through a seven-step process that engages the entire faculty in assessment, planning, implementation, and evaluation. As a result, the school climate and student achievement have improved, as have the knowledge, skills, and attitudes of the teachers involved. This school's outcome is representative of other schools that have implemented similar improvement processes (Kyle, 1985).

These state, school, and district-level efforts illustrate the wide variety of ways in which this model of staff development is being used. While the research and evaluation evidence regarding the impact of these processes on teacher knowledge and skills is not substantial, research does support many of the ingredients contained within these processes. These include commitment to the process by school and building administrators, which includes giving authority and resources to the team to pursue and then implement its agenda; development of knowledge and skills on the part of the teacher participants; adequate, quality time to meet, reflect, and develop; adequate resources to purchase materials, visit other sites, hire consultants to contribute to informed decision making; leadership that provides a vision, direction and guidance, but allows for significant decision making on the part of the teacher participants; and integration of the effort into other improvement efforts and into other structures that influence teaching and learning in the school (Loucks-Horsley et al., 1987). When these factors are present, a limited amount of research data and a great deal of self-report data indicate clearly that the desired outcomes of staff development are achieved.

4. *Training*

In the minds of many educators, training is synonymous with staff development. Most teachers are accustomed to attending workshop-type sessions in which the presenter is the expert who establishes the content and flow of activities. Typically the training session is conducted with a clear set of objectives or learner outcomes. These outcomes frequently include awareness or knowledge (e.g., participants will be able to explain the five principles of cooperative learning) and skill development (e.g., participants will demonstrate the appropriate use of open-ended questions in a class discussion). Joyce and Showers (1988) cite changes in attitudes, transfer of training, and "executive control" (the appropriate and consistent use of new strategies in the classroom) as additional outcomes. It is the trainer's role to select activities (e.g., lecture, demonstration, role-playing, simulation, micro-teaching) that will aid teachers in achieving the desired outcomes.

Whatever the anticipated outcomes, the improvement of teachers' thinking is an important goal. According to Showers, Joyce, and Bennett (1987):

> ... the purpose of providing training in any practice is not simply to generate the external visible teaching "moves" that bring that practice to bear in the instructional setting but to generate the conditions that enable the practice to be selected and used appropriately and integratively.... a major, perhaps the major, dimension of teaching skill is cognitive in nature. (pp. 85–86)

Underlying assumptions. An assumption that undergirds the training model of staff development is that there are behaviors and techniques that are worthy of replication by teachers in the classroom. This assumption can certainly be supported by the large number of research-based effective teaching practices that have been identified and verified in the past 20 years (Sparks, 1983).

Another assumption underlying this model is that teachers can change their behaviors and learn to replicate behaviors in their classroom that were not previously in their repertoire. As Joyce and Showers (1983) point out, training is a powerful process for enhancing knowledge and skills. "It is plain from the research on training," they say, "that teachers can be wonderful learners. They can master just about any kind of teaching strategy or implement almost any technique as long as adequate training is provided" (p. 2).

Because of a high participant-to-trainer ratio, training is usually a cost-efficient means for teachers to acquire knowledge or skills. Many instructional skills require that teachers view a demonstration of their use to fully understand their implementation. Likewise, certain instructional techniques require for their classroom implementation that teachers have an opportunity to practice them with feedback from a skilled observer. Training may be the most efficient means for large numbers of teachers to view these demonstrations and to receive feedback as they practice.

Theoretical and research underpinnings. The theoretical and research underpinnings for the training model come from several sources, but the most recent and intensive research has been conducted by Joyce and Showers (1988). They have determined that, depending upon the desired outcomes, training might include exploration of theory, demonstration or modeling of a skill, practice of the skill under simulated conditions, feedback about performance, and coaching in the workplace. Their research indicates that this combination of components is necessary if the outcome is skill development.

In addition to those components identified by Joyce and Showers, Sparks (1983) cites the importance of discussion and peer observation as training activities. She notes that discussion is useful both when new concepts or techniques are presented and as a problem-solving tool after teachers have had an opportunity to try out new strategies in their classrooms. Training sessions that are spaced 1 or more weeks apart so that content can be "chunked" for improved comprehension and so that teachers have opportunities for classroom practice and peer coaching are shown to be more effective than "one-shot" training (Loucks-Horsley et al., 1987; Sparks, 1983).

Sparks (1983), Wu (1987), and Wood and Kleine (1987) point out the value of teachers as trainers of their peers. Sparks indicates that teachers may learn as much from their peers as from "expert" trainers. She also argues that school districts can afford the type of small-group training that she recommends when peers are used rather than more expensive external consultants. In reviewing the research, Wood and Kleine found that teachers preferred their peers as trainers. Wu's review of the research also confirmed this, finding that when their peers are trainers, teachers feel more comfortable exchanging ideas, play a more active role in workshops, and report that they receive more practical suggestions. There is, however, evidence that indicates that expert trainers who have the critical qualities teachers value in their peers (e.g., a clear understanding of how a new practice works with real students in real classroom settings) can also be highly effective (Crandall, 1983).

Phases of activities. According to Joyce and Showers (1988), "Someone has to decide what will be the substance of the training, who will provide training, when and where the training will be held and for what duration" (p. 69). While training content, objectives, and schedules are often determined by administrators or by the trainer, Wood, McQuarrie, and Thompson's (1982) research-based model advocates involving participants in planning training programs. Participants serve on planning teams which assess needs (using appropriate sources of data), explore various research-based approaches, select content, determine goals and objectives, schedule training sessions, and monitor implementation of the program.

Joyce and Showers (1988) point out that there are specific "learning-to-learn" attitudes and skills that teachers possess or can develop that aid the training process. They cite persistence, acknowledgment of the transfer problem (the need for considerable practice of new skills in the classroom), teaching new behaviors to students, meeting the cognitive demands of innovations (developing a "deep understanding" of new practices), the productive use of peers, and flexibility. The authors list several conditions of training sessions that foster these aptitudes and behaviors: adequate training, opportunities for collegial problem solving, norms that encourage experimentation, and organizational structures that support learning. Sparks' (1983) review of staff development research suggests that a diagnostic process (such as detailed profiles of teaching behaviors based upon classroom observations) may be an important first step in the training process.

After training, in-classroom assistance in the form of peer observation and coaching is critical to the transfer of more complex teaching skills (Joyce & Showers, 1988). The process of data gathering and analysis that accompanies most forms of peer observation is valuable to the observer as well as the observed teacher (Brandt, 1987; Sparks, 1986). A more thorough discussion of this topic can be found in the observation/assessment model described earlier in this article.

Illustrations and outcomes. The power of training to alter teachers' knowledge, attitudes, and instructional skills is well established. Its impact on teachers, however, depends upon its objectives and the quality of the training program. Joyce and Showers (1988) have determined that when all training components are present (theory, demonstration, practice, feedback, and coaching), an effect size of 2.71 exists for knowledge-level objectives, 1.25 for skill-level objectives, and 1.68 for transfer of training to the classroom. (The effect size describes the magnitude of gains from any given change in educational practice; the higher the effect size, the greater the magnitude of gain. For instance, an effect size of 1.0 indicates that the average teacher in the experimental group outperformed 84% of the teachers in the control group.) "We have concluded from these data," Joyce and Showers (1988) report, "that teachers can acquire new knowledge and skill and use it in their instructional practice when provided with adequate opportunities to learn" (p. 72). Coaching and peer observation research cited earlier in the observation/assessment model also supports the efficacy of training.

Wade (1985) found in her meta-analysis of inservice teacher education research that training affected participants' learning by an effect size of .90 and their behavior by .60. An effect size of .37 was found for the impact of teacher training on student behavior. Wade also concluded that training groups composed of both elementary and secondary teachers achieved higher effect sizes than did those enrolling only elementary or only secondary teachers.

Gage (1984) traces the evolution of research on teaching from observational and descriptive studies to correlational studies to nine experiments that were designed to alter instructional practices. "The main conclusion of this body of research," Gage wrote, "is that, in eight out of the nine cases, inservice education was fairly effective—not with all teachers and not with all teaching practices but effective enough to change teachers and improve student achievement, or attitudes, or behavior" (p. 92).

Numerous specific illustrations of training programs are available that have demonstrated impact on teacher behavior and/or student learning. For instance, studies indicate that teachers who have been taught cooperative learning strategies for their classrooms have students who have higher achievement, display higher reasoning and greater critical thinking, have more positive attitudes toward the subject area, and like their fellow students better (Johnson, Johnson, Holubec, & Roy, 1984).

Good and Grouws (1987) describe a mathematics staff development program for elementary teachers. In this 10-session program teachers learned more about mathematics content and about instructional and management issues. As a result of the training, the researchers found changes in teachers' classroom practice and improved mathematics presentations. Student mathematics performance was also improved.

Kerman (1979) reports a 3-year study in which several hundred K-12 teachers were trained to improve their interactions with low-achieving students. The five-session training program included peer observation in the month interval between each session. The researchers found that low-achieving students in experimental class made significant academic gains over their counterparts in control groups.

Rauth (1986) describes an American Federation of Teachers training program that brought research on teaching to its members. Teacher Research Linkers (TRLs) first determine which aspects of the research will be most valuable in their teaching. Between sessions they carry out implementation plans in their own classrooms. TRLs are then taught how to effectively share this research with their colleagues. A study of this program indicated that teachers made significant changes in their practice and that, in addition, their morale and collegiality increased dramatically.

Robbins and Wolfe (1987) discuss a 4-year staff development project designed to increase elementary students' engaged time and achievement. Evaluation of the training program documented steady improvement for 3 years in teachers' instructional skills, student engaged time, and student achievement in reading and math. While scores in all these areas dropped in the project's fourth and final year, Robbins and Wolfe argue that this decline was due to insufficient coaching and peer observation during that year.

As the preceding discussion indicates, there is a much more substantial research literature on training than on the models presented earlier. Under the appropriate conditions, training has the potential for significantly changing teachers' beliefs, knowledge, behavior, and the performance of their students.

5. *Inquiry*

Teacher inquiry can take different forms. A high school teacher wonders if an alteration in her lesson plan from her first period class will produce improved student understanding in second period. A brief written quiz given at the end of the class indicates that it did. A group of teachers gathers weekly after school for an hour or two at the teacher center to examine the research on ability grouping. Their findings will be shared with the district's curriculum council. Several elementary teachers study basic classroom research techniques, formulate research questions, gather and analyze data, and use their findings to improve instruction in their classrooms.

Teacher inquiry may be a solitary activity, be done in small groups, or be conducted by a school faculty. Its process may be formal or informal. It may occur in a classroom, at a teacher center, or result from a university class. In this section teacher inquiry is explored as a staff development model.

Underlying assumptions.   Inquiry reflects a basic belief in teachers' ability to formulate valid questions about their own practice and to pursue objective answers to those questions. Loucks-Horsley and her associates (1987) list three assumptions about a teacher inquiry approach to staff development:

- Teachers are intelligent, inquiring individuals with legitimate expertise and important experience.
- Teachers are inclined to search for data to answer pressing questions and to reflect on the data to formulate solutions.
- Teachers will develop new understandings as they formulate their own questions and collect their own data to answer them.

The overarching assumption of the model is that

the most effective avenue for professional development is cooperative study by teachers themselves into problems and issues arising from their attempts to make their practice consistent with their educational values. . . . [The approach] aims to give greater control over what is to count as valid educational knowledge to teachers. (Ingvarson, 1987, pp. 15, 17)

Theoretical and research underpinnings. The call for inquiry-oriented teachers is not new. Dewey (1933) wrote of the need for teachers to take "reflective action." Zeichner (1983) cites more than 30 years of advocacy for "teachers as action researchers," "teacher scholars," "teacher innovators," "self-monitoring teachers," and "teachers as participant observers."

More recently, various forms of inquiry have been advocated by a number of theorists and researchers. Tikunoff and Ward's (1983) model of interactive research and development promotes teacher inquiry into the questions they are asking through close work with researchers (who help with methodology) and staff developers (who help them create ways of sharing their results with others). Lieberman (1986) reports on a similar process in which teachers serving on collaborative teams pursued answers to school-wide

rather than classroom problems. Watts (1985) discusses the role of collaborative research, classroom action research, and teacher support groups in encouraging teacher inquiry. Simmons and Sparks (1985) describe the use of action research to help teachers better relate research on teaching to their unique classrooms.

Glickman (1986) advocates action research in the form of quality circles, problem-solving groups, and school improvement projects as means to develop teacher thought. Cross (1987) proposes classroom research to help teachers evaluate the effectiveness of their own teaching. Glatthorn (1987) discusses action research by teams of teachers as a peer-centered option for promoting professional growth. Loucks-Horsley and her colleagues (1987) discuss teachers-as-researchers as a form of teacher development that helps narrow the gap between research and practice. Sparks and Simmons (1989) propose inquiry-oriented staff development as a means to enhance teachers' decision-making abilities.

One of the important tenets of the inquiry approach is that research is an important activity in which teachers should be engaged, although they rarely participate in it other than as "subjects." Gable and Rogers (1987) "take the terror out of research" by describing ways in which it can be used as a staff development tool. They discuss both qualitative and quantitative methodology, providing specific strategies that teachers can use in their classrooms. They conclude by saying ". . . the desire and ability to do research is an essential attribute of the professional teacher of the Eighties" (p. 695).

Phases of activity. While the inquiry model of staff development can take many forms, these forms have a number of elements in common. First, individuals or a group of teachers identify a problem of interest. Next, they explore ways of collecting data that may range from examining existing theoretical and research literature to gathering original classroom or school data. These data are then analyzed and interpreted by an individual or the group. Finally, changes are made, and new data are gathered and analyzed to determine the effects of the intervention.

This process can be adapted to the unique needs of a particular approach to inquiry. For instance, Hovda and Kyle (1984) provide a 10-step process for action research that progresses from identifying interested participants, through sharing several study ideas, to discussing findings, to considering having the study published or presented. Glatthorn (1987) describes a four-step process for action research. Collaborative research teams (a) identify a problem, (b) decide upon specific research questions to be investigated and methodology to be used, (c) carry out the research design, and (d) use the research to design an intervention to be implemented in the school.

Watts (1985) describes "reflective conversations" in which teachers carefully observe and thoughtfully consider a particular child or practice. Using a standard procedure, the group shares observations, reviews previous records and information, summarizes their findings, and makes recommendations. As a final step, the group reviews the process to assess how well it went, looks for gaps, and identifies ideas to repeat in future conversations.

Organizational support and/or technical assistance may be required throughout the phases of an inquiry activity. Organizational support may take the form of structures such as teacher centers or study groups, or of resources such as released time or materials. Technical assistance may involve training in research methodologies, data-gathering techniques, and other processes that aid teachers in making sense of their experiences.

Illustrations and outcomes.   The forms inquiry as a staff development model may take are limited only by the imagination. Simmons and Sparks (1985) describe a "Master of Arts in Classroom Teaching" degree designed to help teachers meet their individually identified improvement goals. Teachers in this program learn about educational research, identify and analyze

classroom problems, pursue topics of professional interest, and improve their overall teaching ability. The authors report evidence of change in participant knowledge (e.g., concerning effective teaching-learning), thinking (e.g., enhanced problem-solving skills, increased cognitive complexity), and patterns of communication and collegiality.

Watts (1985) presents a number of ways in which teachers act as researchers. She discussed collaborative research in teacher centers funded by the Teachers' Center Exchange (then located at the Far West Laboratory for Educational Research and Development) that was conducted in the late 1970s and early 1980s. Fourteen projects were funded in which teachers collaborated with researchers on topics of interest to the individual teachers' center. Watts also described ethnographic studies of classrooms conducted collaboratively by teachers and researchers. In addition, she provided examples of classroom action research and teachers' study groups as forms of inquiry. Watts concluded that these three approaches share several outcomes. First, as a result of learning more about research, teachers make more informed decisions about when and how to apply the research findings of others. Second, teachers experience more supportive and collegial relationships. And third, teaching improves as teachers learn more about it by becoming better able to look beyond the immediate, the individual, and the concrete.

The effects of the teacher inquiry model of staff development may reach beyond the classroom to the school. An example of school-wide impact comes from the report of a high school team convened to reflect on a lack of communication and support between teachers and administrators (Lieberman & Miller, 1984). As a result of working together to define the problem, learn each other's perspectives, gather evidence, and formulate solutions, teachers and administrators address important school problems collaboratively. Note that there is a substantial overlap between this kind of "school-based" inquiry and some of the school improvement processes discussed earlier in the model described as involvement in a development/improvement process.

ORGANIZATIONAL CONTEXT

Teacher development in school districts does not take place in a vacuum. Its success is influenced in many ways by the district's organizational context (McLaughlin & Marsh, 1978; Sparks, 1983). Key organizational factors include school and district climate, leadership attitudes and behaviors, district policies and systems, and the involvement of participants.

While staff development fosters the professional growth of individuals, organizational development addresses the organization's responsibility to define and meet changing self improvement goals (Dillon-Peterson, 1981). Consequently, effective organizations have the capacity to continually renew themselves and solve problems. Within this context, individuals can grow.

In earlier sections of this article, five models of staff development were discussed that have solid foundations in research and/or practice, and are being used in increasingly robust forms throughout the country today. While each model requires somewhat different organizational supports to make it successful, it is also true that research points to a common set of attributes of the organizational context without which staff development can have only limited success (Loucks-Horsley et al., 1987). In organizations where staff development is most successful:

- Staff members have a common, coherent set of goals and objectives that they have helped formulate, reflecting high expectations of themselves and their students.
- Administrators exercise strong leadership by promoting a "norm of collegiality," minimizing status differences between themselves and their staff members, promoting informal communication, and reducing their own need to use formal controls to achieve coordination.

- Administrators and teachers place a high priority on staff development and continuous improvement.
- Administrators and teachers make use of a variety of formal and informal processes for monitoring progress toward goals, using them to identify obstacles to such progress and ways of overcoming these obstacles, rather than using them to make summary judgments regarding the "competence" of particular staff members (Conley & Bacharach, 1987).
- Knowledge, expertise, and resources, including time, are drawn on appropriately, yet liberally, to initiate and support the pursuit of staff development goals.

This section briefly highlights the research that supports these organizational attributes.

Organizational Climate

Little (1982) found that effective schools are characterized by norms of collegiality and experimentation. Simply put, teachers are more likely to persist in using new behaviors when they feel the support of colleagues and when they believe that professional risk taking (and its occasional failures) are encouraged. Fullan (1982) reports that the degree of change is strongly related to the extent to which teachers interact with each other and provide technical help to one another. "Teachers need to participate in skill-training workshops," Fullan writes, "but they also need to have one-to-one and group opportunities to receive and give help, and more simply to converse about the meaning of change" (p. 121).

Joyce and Showers (1983) point out that "in a loose and disorganized social climate without clear goals, reticent teachers may actually subvert elements of the training process not only for themselves but also for others" (p. 31). While teacher commitment is desirable, it need not necessarily be present initially for the program to be successful. Miles (1983) found that teacher/administrator harmony was critical to the success of improvement efforts, but that it could develop over the course of an improvement effort. Initially, working relationships between teachers and administrators had to be clear and supportive enough so that most participants could "suspend disbelief," believing that the demands of change would be dealt with together (Crandall, 1983). In their study of school improvement efforts that relied heavily on staff development for their success, both Miles and Crandall found that in projects where a mandated strategy caused some initial disharmony between teachers and administrators, the climate changed as the new program's positive impact on students became clear. When a new program was selected carefully and teachers received good training and support, most who were initially skeptical soon agreed with and were committed to the effort. Showers, Joyce, and Bennett (1987) support the position that, at least initially, teachers' ability to use a new practice in a competent way may be more important than commitment.

Few would disagree with the importance of a school and district climate that encourages experimentation and supports teachers to take risks, i.e., establishes readiness for change (Wood, Thompson, & Russell, 1981). Yet a supportive context consists of more than "good feelings." The quality of the recommended practices is also critical. Research conducted by Guskey (1986) and Loucks and Zacchei (1983) indicates that the new practices developed or chosen by or for teachers need to be effective ones—effective by virtue of evaluation results offered by the developer or by careful testing by the teachers who have developed them. These researchers found that only when teachers see that a new program or practice enhances the learning of their students will their beliefs and attitudes change in a significant way.

Leadership and Support

According to the Rand Change Agent Study (McLaughlin & Marsh, 1978) active support by principals and district administrators is critical to the success of any change effort. According to McLaughlin and Marsh (1978):

The Rand research sets the role of the principal as instructional leader in the context of strengthening the school improvement process through team building and problem solving in a "project-like" context. It suggests that principals need to give clear messages that teachers may take responsibility for their own professional growth. (p. 92)

Stallings and Mohlman (1981) determined that teachers improved most in staff development programs where the principal supported them and was clear and consistent in communicating school policies. Likewise, Fielding and Schalock (1985) report a study in which principals' involvement in teachers' staff development produced longer-term changes than when principals were not involved.

In their discussion of factors that affect the application of innovations, Loucks and Zacchei (1983) wrote ". . . administrators in successful improvement sites take their leadership roles seriously and provide the direction needed to engage teachers in the new practices" (p. 30).

According to Huberman (1983), teachers' successful use of new skills often occurs when administrators exert strong and continuous pressure for implementation. He argues that ". . . administrators, both at the central office and building levels, have to go to center stage and stay there if school improvement efforts are to succeed" (p. 27). While administrator presence is important, administrators must also act as gatekeepers of change so that "innovation overload" can be avoided (Anderson & Odden, 1986).

While much research points to administrators as being key leaders in staff development and change, it is also true that others can take on leadership and support roles—and may in fact be better placed to do so. Research on school improvement indicates that a team approach can help orchestrate leadership and support "functions" which can be shared by administrators (building and district level), district coordinators or staff developers, teachers, and external trainers and consultants (Loucks-Horsley & Hergert, 1985). For example, Cox (1983) reports that while principals seem to play an important role in clarifying expectations and goals and stabilizing the school organization, central office coordinators, who often know more about a specific practice, can effectively coach teachers in their attempts to change their classroom behavior. Coordinated leadership can also help avoid situations such as a school's textbooks and curriculum not matching the instructional models teachers are being taught to use (Fielding & Schalock, 1985).

District Policies and Systems

Staff development activities occur within the context of a school district's staff development program. According to Ellis (1988), a comprehensive staff development program includes a philosophy, goals, allocation of resources, and coordination. The philosophy spells out beliefs that guide the program. District, school, and individual goals (and their accompanying action plans) provide direction to staff development efforts. Resources need to be allocated at the district, school, and individual levels so that these goals have a reasonable chance of being achieved. Staff development programs need to be coordinated by individuals who have an assigned responsibility for this area. Ellis also supports the use of a district-level staff development committee to aid in coordination of programs.

The selection, incorporation, or combination of the models of staff development described in this article are the responsibility of the district's staff development structure. Decisions about their use need to match the intended outcomes if they are to be effective (Levine & Broude, 1989), but these decisions are also influenced by state and/or community initiatives aimed at the improvement of schools and/or teaching (Anderson & Odden, 1986).

Participant Involvement

Research clearly indicates that involving participants in key decisions about staff development is necessary for a program to have its greatest impact. According to Lieberman and Miller (1986), a supportive context for staff development requires both a "top-down" and "bottom-up" approach. The top-down component sets a general direction for the district or school and communicates expectations regarding performance. The bottom-up processes involve teachers in establishing goals and designing appropriate staff development activities.

The establishment of common goals is important to the success of staff development efforts (Ward & Tikunoff, 1981). Odden and Anderson's (1986) research indicates that a clearly defined process of data collection, shared diagnosis, and identification of solutions to problems must be employed during the planning phase. Collaboration, from initial planning through implementation and institutionalization, is a key process in determining these goals and in influencing lasting change (Lambert, 1984; McLaughlin & Marsh, 1978; Wood, Thompson, & Russell, 1981).

Lortie (1986) argues that when teachers perceive that they can participate in important school-level decisions, the relationship between the extra efforts required by school improvement and the benefits of these efforts becomes clearer. Following this argument, he recommends that schools be given relatively little detailed supervision, but be monitored instead for results based on explicit criteria.

Others report that, when teachers cannot be involved in initial decisions regarding staff development (e.g., when it is mandated by state legislation or when it supports the use of district-wide curriculum), their involvement in decisions about the "hows" and "whens" of implementation can be important to success. Furthermore, teachers' involvement in developing curriculum and as trainers for staff development programs can contribute in important ways to the success of an effort (Loucks & Pratt, 1979).

Odden and Anderson (1986) capture the reciprocal relationship between organization and individual development in this discussion of their research:

> When instructional strategies, which aim to improve the skills of individuals, were successful, they had significant effects on schools as organi-

zations. When school strategies, which aim to improve schools as organizations, were successful, they had significant impacts on individuals. (p. 585)

The importance of paying attention to the context of staff development is underscored by Fullan (1982). He responds to educators who say that they cannot provide the elements required to support change (e.g., supportive principals, a 2- or 3-year time period for implementation):

> Well don't expect much implementation to occur . . . I say this not because I am a cynic but because it is wrong to let hopes blind us to the actual obstacles to change. If these obstacles are ignored, the experience with implementation can be harmful to the adults and children directly involved—more harmful than if nothing had been done. (p. 103)

CONCLUSION

Staff development is a relatively young "science" within education. In many ways the current knowledge base in staff development is similar to what was known about teaching in the early 1970s. During the 1970s and early 1980s research on teaching advanced from descriptive to correlational to experimental (Gage, 1984). With the exception of research on training, much of the staff development literature is theoretical and descriptive rather than experimental. The remaining two sections describe what can be said with some confidence about the research base for the staff development models and what remains to be learned.

What Can Be Said with Confidence

Staff development possesses a useful "craft knowledge" that guides the field. This craft knowledge includes ways to organize, structure, and deliver staff development programs (Caldwell, 1989). It has been disseminated in the past decade through publications such as *The Journal of Staff Development, Educational Leadership,* and *Phi Delta Kappan,* and through thou-

sands of presentations at workshops and conventions. As a result, in the past 20 years hundreds of staff development programs have been established in urban, suburban, and rural school districts throughout the United States and Canada. This craft knowledge serves another useful purpose: It can guide researchers in asking far better questions than they could have asked a decade ago.

Of the five models discussed in this article, the research on training is the most robust. It is the most widely used form of staff development and the most thoroughly investigated. As a result, it is possible to say with some confidence which training elements are required to promote the attainment of specific outcomes. Likewise, research on coaching has demonstrated the importance of in-classroom assistance to teachers (by an "expert" or by a peer) for the transfer of training to the classroom.

The consensus of "expert opinion" is that school improvement is a systemic process (Fullan, 1982). This ecological approach recognizes that changes in one part of a system influence the other parts. Consequently, staff development both influences and is influenced by the organizational context in which it takes place. The impact of the staff development models that have been discussed depends not only upon their individual or blended use, but upon the features of the organization in which they are used.

While this appears to relate to the "art" of making staff development work (i.e., the judgment with which one combines and juggles the various organizational interactions), there is also much "science" that can be drawn from when it comes to the organizational supports necessary for effective staff development. Study after study confirms the necessity of:

- Schools possessing norms that support collegiality and experimentation
- District and building administrators who work with staff to clarify goals and expectations, and actively commit to and support teachers' efforts to change their practice

- Efforts that are strongly focused on changes in curricular, instructional, and classroom management practices with improved student learning as the goal
- Adequate, appropriate staff development experiences with follow-up assistance that continues long enough for new behaviors to be incorporated into ongoing practice

Interestingly enough, it appears that these factors apply to a wide variety of school improvement and staff development efforts. While there are little hard research data on some of the models discussed above (see next section), most if not all of these factors will certainly persist as being important, regardless of what is learned about other models.

What We Need to Learn More About

While the work of staff developers during the past decade has been grounded in theory and research from various disciplines (e.g., adult learning, organization development, training), the scientific base of their own practice (with the exception of training and coaching) is quite thin. Unfortunately, the systematic study of some of the models discussed earlier is difficult because their use is not widespread or because they have been implemented only recently as part of comprehensive staff development programs. Listed below are areas for further study.

1. We need research to determine the potency of the models described above (with the exception of training).   We need to learn which models are most effective for which outcomes with which teachers. For instance, we might ask: How effective is individually-guided staff development for knowledge level outcomes for self-directed experienced teachers? Or: How effective is an inquiry approach in helping beginning teachers learn their craft?

2. We need a better understanding of the impact on student learning of the four non-training

staff development models.   Do non-training models alter teacher knowledge or skills in a way that improves student learning?

3. We need to know more about the impact on teachers of blending the models described above in a comprehensive staff development program.   How are teachers' attitudes, knowledge, and skills altered when they choose among and blend various models as the means of reaching one or more "growth" goals? For instance, what would be the result if a teacher blended individually-guided staff development (e.g., reading research on tracking), observation/assessment (e.g., peer observation), and training (e.g., in cooperative learning) as means to alter classroom practices that are viewed as disadvantageous to a subgroup of students?

4. We need a systemic view of comprehensive staff development at the district level.   Most districts provide a variety of staff development opportunities to teachers. Some purposely support individual, school-based, and district-based activities. We need descriptive studies of what these programs look like, both from the overall, coordination point of view, and from the individual teacher point of view. We need to know: How are goals set and coordinated? How are resources allocated? How equitable are opportunities for individual teachers? How do different contextual factors (e.g., resources, state mandates) influence success?

5. We need to understand more about the relative costs of different staff development models and combinations of the models.   Moore and Hyde (1978, 1979, 1981) have conducted some useful analyses of how many school district resources actually go for staff development purposes. But more micro-analyses would be useful to understand the cost-effectiveness of relatively labor-intensive models (e.g., coaching) versus those that rely only on the activity of a single teacher (e.g., individually-guided staff development).

6. Finally, we need to look at staff development as it contributes to teacher professionalism and teacher leadership. Many believe that teacher professionalism and leadership must characterize our education system in the future if that system is to survive. Yet there are as many different definitions of the terms as there are ideas of how to implement them. One role of staff development research is to help identify and clarify the various meanings given to these concepts. We then need descriptive studies of staff development's contributions to these efforts, with special attention to how these efforts influence the conduct of staff development.

It is possible that future research may contradict current craft knowledge (this, for example, has occurred with the learning that attitude change does not always have to precede behavior change), or, as is likely, future research will support current practice. Many questions about effective staff development remain unanswered. The need is great for well-designed, long-term studies of school improvement efforts that are based on staff development. The field of staff development seeks a solid base that moves beyond description and advocacy to a better understanding of those factors that support and improve classroom practice.

ENDNOTE

This article was adapted from "Models of Staff Development," in W. Robert Houston (Ed.), *Handbook of Research on Teacher Education.* New York: Macmillan, 1990.

REFERENCES

Ainsworth, A. (1976). Teachers talk about in-service education. *Journal of Teacher Education, 27,* 107–109.

Anderson, B., & Odden, A. (1986). State initiatives can foster school improvement. *Phi Delta Kappan, 67*(8), 578–581.

Berman, P., & McLaughlin, M. (1978). *Federal programs supporting educational change: Vol. 8. Implementing and sustaining innovation.* Santa Monica, CA: Rand Corporation.

Blanchard, K., & Johnson, S. (1982). *The one minute manager.* New York: William Morrow.

Boyer, E. (1983). *High school: A report on secondary education in America.* New York: Harper & Row.

Brandt, R. (1982). On improving teacher effectiveness: A conversation with David Berliner. *Educational Leadership, 40*(1), 12–15.

Brandt, R. (1987). On teachers coaching teachers: A conversation with Bruce Joyce. *Educational Leadership, 44*(5), 12–17.

Brim, J., & Tollett, D. (1974). How do teachers feel about inservice education? *Educational Leadership, 31,* 21–25.

Caldwell, S. (Ed.) (1989). *Staff development: A handbook of effective practices.* Oxford, OH: National Staff Development Council.

Casner-Lotto, J. (1988). Expanding the teacher's role: Hammond's school improvement process. *Phi Delta Kappan, 69*(5), 349–353.

Cohen, M. (1981). Effective schools: What the research says. *Today's Education, 70,* 466–469.

Conley, S., & Bacharach, S. (1987). The Holmes Group report: Standards, hierarchies, and management. *Teachers College Record, 88*(3). 340–347.

Crandall, D. The teacher's role in school improvement. *Educational Leadership, 41*(3), 6–9.

Crandall, D., & Loucks. S. (1983). *A roadmap for school improvement.* Executive summary of *People, policies, and practices: Examining the chain of school improvement.* Andover, MA: The NETWORK, Inc.

Cross, P. (1987). The adventures of education in wonderland: Implementing education reform. *Phi Delta Kappan, 68*(7), 496–502.

Dewey, J. (1933). *How we think.* Chicago, IL: Henry Regnery Co.

Dillon-Peterson, B. (1981). Staff development/organizational development—perspective 1981. In B. Dillon-Peterson (Ed.), *Staff development/organization development* (pp. 1–10). Alexandria, VA: Association for Supervision and Curriculum Development.

Dunn, R., & Dunn, K. (1978). *Teaching students through their individual learning styles: A practical approach.* Reston, VA: Reston Publishing Co.

Ellis, S. (1989). Putting it all together: An integrated staff development program. In S. Caldwell (Ed.), *Staff development: A handbook of effective practices* (pp. 58–69). Oxford, OH: National Staff Development Council.

Fielding, G., & Schalock, H. (1985). *Promoting the professional development of teachers and administrators.* Eugene, OR: ERIC Clearinghouse on Educational Management. (ERIC Document Reproduction Service No. EA 017 747)

Fullan, M. (1982). *The meaning of educational change.* Toronto: OISE Press.

Gable, R., & Rogers, V. (1987). Taking the terror out of research. *Phi Delta Kappan, 68*(9), 690–695.

Gage, N. (1984). What do we know about teaching effectiveness? *Phi Delta Kappan, 66*(2), 87–93.

Glatthorn, A. (1984). *Differentiated supervision.* Alexandria, VA. Association for Supervision and Curriculum Development.

Glatthorn, A. (1987). Cooperative professional development: Peer-centered options for teacher growth. *Educational Leadership, 45*(3), 31–35.

Glickman, E. (1986). Developing teacher thought. *Journal of Staff Development, 7*(1), 6–21.

Good, T. (1981). Teacher expectations and student perceptions: A decade of research. *Educational Leadership, 38*(5), 415–422.

Good, T., & Grouws, D. (1987). Increasing teachers' understanding of mathematical ideas through inservice training. *Phi Delta Kappan, 68*(10), 778–783.

Gregorc, A. (1970). Learning/teaching styles: Their nature and effects. In *Student learning styles: Diagnosing and prescribing programs.* Reston, VA: National Association of Secondary School Principals.

Guskey, T. (1986). Staff development and the process of teacher change. *Educational Researcher, 15*(5), 5–12.

Hall, G., & Loucks, S. (1978). Teacher concerns as a basis for facilitating and personalizing staff development. *Teachers College Record, 80*(1), 36–53.

Hering, W., & Howey, K. (1982). *Research in, on, and by teachers' centers.* Occasional Paper No. 10. San Francisco, CA: Teachers' Center Exchange,

Far West Laboratory for Educational Research and Development.

Hovda, R., & Kyle, D. (1984). A strategy for helping teachers integrate research into teaching. *Middle School Journal, 15*(3), 21–23.

Huberman, A. (1983). School improvement strategies that work: Some scenarios. *Educational Leadership, 41*(3), 23–27.

Hunter, M. (1982). *Mastery teaching.* El Segundo, CA: TIP Publications.

Ingvarson, L. (1987). *Models of inservice education and their implications for professional development policy.* Paper presented at a conference on "Inservice Education: Trends of the Past, Themes for the Future," Melbourne, Australia.

Jefferson County Public Schools (1974). *Report of the task force to define the process of developing curriculum.* Lakewood, CO: Author.

Johnson, D., Johnson, R., Holubec, E., & Roy, P. (1984). *Circles of learning.* Alexandria, VA: Association for Supervision and Curriculum Development.

Joyce, B., & Peck, L. (1977). *Inservice teacher education project report II: Interviews.* Syracuse, NY: Syracuse University.

Joyce, B., & Showers, B. (1982). The coaching of teaching. *Educational Leadership, 40*(1), 4–10.

Joyce, B., & Showers, B. (1983). *Power in staff development through research in training.* Alexandria, VA: Association for Supervision and Curriculum Development.

Joyce, B., & Showers, B. (1988). *Student achievement through staff development.* New York: Longman.

Joyce, B., & Weil, M. (1972). *Models of teaching.* Englewood Cliffs, NJ: Prentice-Hall.

Kells, P. (1981, January). Quality practices in inservice education. *The Developer.* Oxford, OH: National Staff Development Council.

Kerman, S. (1979). Teacher expectations and student achievement. *Phi Delta Kappan, 60*(10), 716–718.

Kidd, J. (1973). *How adults learn.* Chicago, IL: Follett Publishing Co.

Kimpston, R., & Rogers, K. (1987). The influence of prior perspectives, differences in participatory roles, and degree of participation on views about curriculum development: A case study. *Journal of Curriculum and Supervision, 2*(3), 203–220.

Knowles, M. (1980). *The modern practice of adult education.* Chicago, IL: Association/Follett Press.

Kyle, R. (Ed.) (1985). *Reaching for excellence: An effective school sourcebook.* Washington, DC: U.S. Government Printing Office.

Lambert, L. (1984). *How adults learn: An interview study of leading researchers, policy makers, and staff developers.* Paper presented at the annual meeting of the American Educational Research Association, New Orleans, LA.

Lawrence, G. (1974). *Patterns of effective inservice education: A state of the art summary of research on materials and procedures for changing teacher behaviors in inservice education.* Gainesville: University of Florida College of Education. (ERIC Document Reproduction Service No. ED 176 424)

Levine, S. (1989). *Promoting adult growth in schools: The promise of professional development.* Lexington, MA: Allyn & Bacon.

Levine, S., & Broude, N. (1989). Designs for learning. In S. Caldwell (Ed.), *Staff development: A handbook of effective practices.* Oxford, OH: National Staff Development Council.

Levine, S., & Jacobs, V. (1986). Writing as a staff development tool. *Journal of Staff Development, 7*(1), 44–51.

Lieberman, A. (1986). Collaborative research: Working with, not working on. *Educational Leadership, 43*(5), 28–32.

Lieberman, A., & Miller, L. (1984). *Teachers, their world and their work: Implications for school improvement.* Alexandria, VA: Association for Supervision and Curriculum Development.

Lieberman, A., & Miller, L. (1986). School improvement: Themes and variations. In A. Lieberman (Ed.), *Rethinking school improvement: Research, craft, and concept.* New York: Teachers College Press.

Little, J. (1982). Norms of collegiality and experimentation: Work-place conditions of school success. *American Educational Research Journal, 19*(3), 325–340.

Lortie, D. (1986). Teacher status in Dade County: A case of structural strain? *Phi Delta Kappan, 67*(8), 568–575.

Loucks, S., & Pratt, H. (1979). A concerns-based approach to curriculum change. *Educational Leadership, 37*(3), 212–215.

Loucks, S., & Zacchei, D. (1983). Applying our findings to today's innovations. *Educational Leadership, 41*(3), 28–31.

Loucks-Horsley, S., Harding, C., Arbuckle, M., Murray, L., Dubea, C., & Williams, M. (1987). *Continuing to learn: A guidebook for teacher development.* Andover, MA: Regional Laboratory for Educational Improvement of the Northeast and Islands, and the National Staff Development Council.

Loucks-Horsley, S., & Hergert, L. (1985). *An action guide to school improvement.* Alexandria, VA: Association for Supervision and Curriculum Development and Andover, MA: The NETWORK, Inc.

Louis, K., & Rosenblum, S. (1981). *Linking R & D with schools: A program and its implications for dissemination and school improvement policy.* Washington, DC: National Institute of Education.

Mann, D. (1984–85). Impact II and the problem of staff development. *Educational Leadership, 42*(4), 44–47.

Mathieson, D. (1987, December). Writing for professional growth. *The Developer.* Oxford, OH: National Staff Development Council.

McGreal, T. (1982). Effective teacher evaluation systems. *Educational Leadership, 39*(4), 303–305.

McGreal, T. (1983). *Successful teacher evaluation.* Alexandria, VA: Association for Supervision and Curriculum Development.

McLaughlin, M., & Marsh, D. (1978). Staff development and school change. *Teachers College Record, 80*(1), 69–94.

Miles, M. (1983). Unraveling the mystery of institutionalization. *Educational Leadership, 41*(3), 14–19.

Mosher, W. (1981). *Individual and systemic change mediated by a small educational grant program.* San Francisco, CA: Far West Laboratory for Educational Research and Development.

Odden, A., & Anderson, B. (1986). How successful state education improvement programs work. *Phi Delta Kappan, 67*(8), 582–585.

Rauth, M. (1986). Putting research to work. *American Educator, 10*(4), 26–31.

Robbins, P., & Wolfe, P. (1987). Reflections on a Hunter-based staff development project. *Educational Leadership, 44*(5), 56–61.

Rogers, C. (1969). *Freedom to learn.* Columbus, OH: Charles E. Merrill.

Scholl, S., & McQueen, P. (1985). The basic skills articulation plan: Curriculum development through staff development. *Journal of Staff Development, 6*(2), 138–142.

Shalaway, T. S. (1985). Peer coaching . . . does it work? *R & D Notes.* Washington, DC: National Institute of Education.

Showers, B. (1984). *Peer coaching: A strategy for facilitating transfer of training.* Eugene, OR: Center for Educational Policy and Management, University of Oregon.

Showers, B., Joyce, B., & Bennett, B. (1987). Synthesis of research on staff development: A framework for future study and a state-of-art analysis. *Educational Leadership, 45*(3), 77–87.

Simmons, J., & Parks, G. (1985). Using research to develop professional thinking about teaching. *Journal of Staff Development, 6*(1), 106–116.

Sparks, G. (1983). Synthesis of research on staff development for effective teaching. *Educational Leadership, 41*(3), 65–72.

Sparks, G. (1986). The effectiveness of alternative training activities in changing teaching practices. *American Educational Research Journal, 23*(2), 217–225.

Sparks, G., Nowakowski, M., Hall, B., Alec, R., & Imrick, J. (1985). School improvement through staff development. *Educational Leadership, 42*(6), 59–61.

Sparks, G., & Simmons, J. (1989). Inquiry-oriented staff development: Using research as a source of tools, not rules. In S. Caldwell (Ed.), *Staff development: A handbook of effective practices* (pp. 126–139). Oxford, OH: National Staff Development Council.

Stallings, J., & Mohlman, G. (1981). *School policy, leadership style, teacher change, and student behavior in eight schools, final report.* Washington, DC: National Institute of Education.

Thompson, S. (1982). *A survey and analysis of Pennsylvania public school personnel perceptions of staff development practices and beliefs with a view to identifying some critical problems or needs.* Unpublished Dissertation, The Pennsylvania State University, University Park, PA.

Tikunoff, W., & Ward, B. (1983). Collaborative research on teaching. *The Elementary School Journal, 83*(4), 453–468.

Wade, R. (1985). What makes a difference in inservice teacher education? A meta-analysis of research. *Educational Leadership, 42*(4), 48–54.

Wanous, D., & Sparks, D. (1981). *Analysis of individualized teacher center services.* San Francisco, CA: Far West Laboratory for Educational Research and Development.

Ward, B., & Tikunoff, W. (1981, September). The relationship between inservice training, organizational structure and school climate. *Inservice, 7–8.*

Watts, H. (1985). When teachers are researchers, teaching improves. *Journal of Staff Development, 6*(2), 118–127.

Westbrook, C., Loomis, A., Coffina, J., Adelberg, J., Brooks, S., & Ellis, S. (1985). Classroom research: A promising model for staff development. *Journal of Staff Development, 6*(2), 128–132.

Wise, A., & Darling-Hammond, L. (1985). *Educational Leadership, 42*(4), 28–33.

Wood, F. (1989). Organizing and managing school-based staff development. In S. Caldwell (Ed.), *Staff development: A handbook of effective practices* (pp. 26–43). Oxford, OH: National Staff Development Council.

Wood, F., & Kleine, P. (1987). *Staff development research and rural schools: A critical appraisal.* Unpublished paper, University of Oklahoma, Norman.

Wood, F., McQuarrie, F., & Thompson, S. (1982). Practitioners and professors agree on effective staff development practices. *Educational Leadership, 43,* 63–66.

Wood, F., Thompson, S., & Russell, F. (1981). Designing effective staff development programs. In B. Dillon-Peterson (Ed.), *Staff development/organization development* (pp. 59–91). Alexandria, VA: Association for Supervision and Curriculum Development.

Wu, P. (1987). Teachers as staff developers: Research, opinions, and cautions. *Journal of Staff Development, 8*(1), 4–6.

Yarger, S., Howey, K., & Joyce, B. (1980). *Inservice teacher education.* Palo Alto, CA: Booksend Laboratory.

Zeichner, K. (1983). Alternative paradigms of teacher education. *Journal of Teacher Education, 34*(3), 3–9.

Zigarmi, P., Betz, L., & Jensen, D. (1977). Teacher preference in and perceptions of inservice. Educational Leadership, 34, 545–551.

DISCUSSION QUESTIONS

1. How is knowledge of adult learning theory integrated into the underlying assumptions of the five staff development models described?

2. In what ways can staff development programs aid teachers in school improvement or curriculum development?

3. What kind of staff development program would you design to assist your colleagues in mainstreaming students?

4. Discuss the similarities and differences between the inquiry model of staff development, reflective action, and an independent research initiative.

5. How do school district attitudes and climate variables influence staff development program efforts?

Peer Coaching: Developmental Approach to Enhancing Teacher Thinking

MARY D. PHILLIPS
CARL D. GLICKMAN

FOCUSING QUESTIONS

1. *How would you describe past staff development program efforts?*
2. *What characteristics typify recent staff development programs?*
3. *How are Glickman's supervisory approaches, Hunt's conceptual level, and developmental matching models related?*
4. *What are the advantages and disadvantages of the peer coaching model?*
5. *In your opinion, were the methods used to assess the impact of this staff development program valid approaches? Why? Why not?*

Teachers in the past have been typically viewed as recipients rather than as decision-makers or active participants in staff development programs (Lambert, 1989). A peer coaching program offered in Georgia was designed to involve teachers as active participants in their professional development and to stimulate their cognitive development.

CHALLENGE

Past staff development programs have contributed to the mental stagnation of teachers (Glickman, 1990), to isolation, and to lowered teacher morale (Lieberman & Miller, 1984). This in turn, has led to teachers' negative attitudes toward staff development and, thus, to minimal use of newly learned skills or knowledge (Goodlad, 1984).

Such staff development programs might have worked if teaching were simple and teachers could easily integrate newly learned instructional strategies into their existing repertoires. However, research findings reveal that teaching is complex (Good & Brophy, 1987; Shavelson, 1983). Teachers daily make difficult decisions about students' abilities and needs and about the most appropriate approaches to planning, teaching, and evaluating. A recent meta-analysis of staff development research (Showers, Joyce, & Bennett, 1987) concluded that "An extremely important yield from the research is that a major, perhaps *the* major, dimension of teaching skill is cognitive in nature" (pp. 85–86).

A strong positive relationship has been shown between teachers' thinking at higher conceptual levels (Hunt, 1975) and (a) transfer of training (Showers, 1982), (b) quality of communication to students (Calhoun, 1985), (c) information-handling behavior (Rathbone, 1971), (d) teaching toward inquiry (Eggleston, 1977), (e) instructional planning (Mintz & Yarger, 1980), (f) teaching approaches and classroom atmosphere (Harvey, White, Prather, Alter, &

Hoffmeister, 1966), and (g) mastery of teaching models (Joyce, Wald, & Weil, 1981).

Therefore, the challenge is to provide staff development that gives strong consideration to the thinking part of teaching and to the contextual elements of teaching and learning. The emphasis should not be on simply increasing their knowledge and skill levels.

CONCEPTUAL LEVELS

Harvey, Hunt, and Schroder (1961) developed the Conceptual Systems Theory (CST) which provides a framework for studying progressive stages of cognitive development. From the CST, Hunt (1970) redefined cognitive development as a personality dimension and delineated three conceptual levels (low, moderate, and high) of thought development which varied along a concreteness-abstractness continuum.

Glickman (1990) adapted Hunt's conceptual level (CL) stages to teachers' thinking about their teaching. Concretely thinking teachers (who are at the low conceptual level) are confused about instructional problems, lack ideas about what to do, often ask to be shown, and use habitual and unilateral responses to varying situations. Highly abstract teachers (who are at the high conceptual level) can identify instructional problems from various sources of information, seek and generate multiple sources of ideas about what can be done, visualize and verbalize consequences of various actions, choose action(s), plan implementation, and then make changes for which they accept responsibility. Moderately abstract teachers (moderate CL) fall between these two.

Hunt (1975) proposed a Developmental Matching Model as a means of raising a person's conceptual level. Low CL individuals need experiences with high structure (e.g., a lecture); high CL individuals profit from low structure (e.g., a discovery approach). In order for individuals to progress to a higher CL stage, Hunt suggested that instructors must not only take into account a person's current need for structure but also move

in the direction of less structure to encourage independence and autonomy in learning.

While this plan for promoting conceptual level of thought development is logical and relatively straightforward to use, it does not take other environmental conditions into account which might stimulate a person's conceptual level development (Macrostie, in progress). Thies-Sprinthall (1984) extracted guidelines for stimulating cognitive development from research she conducted with both inservice and preservice teachers (see the left column of Figure 29.1). In the right column of Figure 29.1 an explanation is given of how the Thies-Sprinthall guidelines were incorporated into the peer coaching that is discussed later.

Glickman (1990) suggested that different supervisory approaches, (including directive, collaborative, and non-directive) be used with teachers at different developmental stages to facilitate positive changes in their cognitive developmental growth. He recommended that only collaborative and non-directive approaches be used with peer teachers. The directive approach is used when the supervisor is considered the expert and tells the teacher what to do; the assumption is that the teacher has a deficit which needs to be corrected. The assumption underlying the peer coaching program is that both teachers are competent, but are helping each other improve their teaching through the coaching process. For instance, a collaborative approach is used when supervisor and teacher are considered equals in degree of expertise. They exchange perceptions about teaching concerns, generate possible actions the teacher might take, and then negotiate an agreement about changes to be made.

A non-directive approach is used when the teacher is considered by the supervisor to be more knowledgeable about the particular aspect of teaching being discussed. The supervisor serves as a facilitator, helping the teacher to recognize instructional concerns, questioning the teacher regarding possible actions to take with students, and asking the teacher to choose a course of

Thies-Sprinthall Guidelines for Stimulating Cognitive Development	How the Guidelines were Applied in the Peer Coaching Program
1. Role-Taking Experiences Persons need to be placed in qualitatively significant role-taking experiences, stretching their functioning somewhat, but not much beyond their currently preferred style.	Teachers experience two roles: (1) coach, and (2) teacher being coached, affording what Thies-Sprinthall called an "optimal mismatch" which stretches their thinking somewhat, but not too far.
2. Careful and Continuous Guided Reflection . . . In a Deweyan sense, unexamined experience misses the point. To insure that reflection occurs, there is often a need to provide careful feedback to aid in the process of examining the experiences.	Following each classroom observation, the coach spends time alone, analyzing the data collected in order to assist the teacher in examining the teaching experience. In the post-observation conference, he gives the teacher feedback about the classroom observation, and together they consider alternative actions and consequences and develop a plan for instructional improvement.
3. Balance Between Real Experience and Discussion/Reflection There should be cycles of experiential application and intellectual analysis.	The four staff development sessions include this balance with discussion, guided practice, and reflection on that practice. The clinical supervision already has this balance incorporated into its structure with pre-conference, classroom observation, and post-conference.
4. Personal Support and Challenge Any effective training approach must offer major personal support as a direct part of the instruction. The participants are required to "do" the role-taking. That is the challenge. The instructor must supply the requisite personal support to overcome the dissonance and fear involved in such new learning.	Challenge is inevitable as teacher and coach each become students of the instructional process. Teachers are asked to focus on a specific aspect of teaching and instructional concerns. Laters, coach and teacher consider many alternatives and develop a plan for instructional improvement. Support is provided throughout the staff development sessions with an abundance of guided practice. Peers support each other as they experience the peer coaching cycles. Group sessions allow concerns and problems to be addressed.
5. Continuity At least six months is required for congitive-developmental to occur.	The peer coaching program extends over at least a seven-month period.

FIGURE 29.1   Thies-Sprinthall's Guidelines Incorporated into a Peer Coaching Program

action. The Thies-Sprinthall (1984) guidelines, Glickman's (1990) developmental supervision, and Hunt's Matching Model (1975) were all incorporated into the peer coaching program described here.

THE PEER COACHING PROGRAM

Twenty-two teachers (out of 52) at an elementary school in northeast Georgia volunteered in the fall of 1987 to participate in a peer coaching program following a school-based needs assessment in the spring of 1987 and the drafting by the faculty of a staff development plan. The program began in late October, 1987.

Peer coaching is defined as a process in which classroom teachers observe one another, teach, give feedback concerning the observation, and together develop an instructional improvement plan (Phillips, 1989). The peer coaching program was designed by Carl Glickman of the University of Georgia's Program for School Improvement. He also conducted the staff development sessions. The program was intended to meet teachers' needs which were ignored in previous staff development programs and to stimulate the teachers' cognitive development and conceptual levels of thought development.

PROGRAM FEATURES

Teachers were allowed to choose (a) whether or not they would participate in the peer coaching program, (b) their partners for the four cycles of coaching, (c) the focal points for classroom observations, (d) observation techniques for the classroom observation, and (e) their own plans for instructional improvement.

Teachers were not taught, nor were they expected to use, any particular instructional strategy. The program was based on an assumption that participants were competent teachers who could choose their own agendas for instructional

improvement. The non-evaluative nature of the peer coaching program was communicated to the teachers throughout the staff development process.

The coaching program, which lasted from October 1987 to May 1988, was divided into two parts: (a) learning the peer coaching process, and (b) participating in four peer coaching cycles (each being two weeks in duration).

Learning the Process

Teachers learned about the peer coaching process in four sessions spaced at two-to-three week intervals. In the first session the steps in clinical supervision were presented (Goldhammer, 1969). Teachers observed a demonstration of three steps in the clinical supervision cycle: (a) the pre-observation conference, (b) the classroom observation, and (c) the post-observation conference. Teachers then practiced active listening strategies in pairs. They also were taught both qualitative and quantitative observation techniques, such as open-ended narrative, visual diagramming, and recording information on frequency charts (Glickman, 1990).

In the second session, teachers were guided in conducting a simulated preconference prior to viewing a videotaped teaching episode in which they practiced their newly learned observation skills. The non-evaluative nature of peer coaching was emphasized in an exercise that emphasized the differences between the descriptive and interpretative recording of observation data.

The third and fourth sessions were devoted to learning how to conduct post-observation conferences using the non-directive and collaborative approaches already mentioned (Glickman, 1990). Teachers were guided through three phases of the postobservation conference: (a) goal identification, (b) planning, and (c) critique. Goal identification involves determining a focus for the improvement of teaching based on information from the classroom observation provided by the coach. Planning for instructional improvement includes determining teaching activities related to the identified focus. During the critique teachers gave feedback to coaches about the conferencing approach used (see Glickman, 1990).

In all four staff development sessions, special attention was paid to the Thies-Sprinthall (1984) guidelines for facilitating cognitive developmental growth. One of the most important components was the involvement of teachers in significant role-taking experiences in both their roles as coaches and teachers.

Several instructional approaches were used by the instructor, including lecture, demonstration and modeling, practice in using classroom observation and conferencing skills, and outside readings. In this way, teachers were provided with different degrees of structure as suggested by Hunt's (1975) Developmental Matching Model.

Participating in Coaching Cycles

There were four cycles of peer coaching, with each coaching pair determining who would initially take the role of coach. Both the teacher and

coach experienced two clinical supervision cycles and then switched roles so that the other teacher became the coach. In this manner both teachers served as a "mirror" of the other's teaching, and each supported the other in attempting a new instructional strategy or refining an old one. The instructor also held debriefing group sessions after each coaching cycle. Figure 29.2 illustrates the cycles of peer coaching.

PROGRAM EVALUATION

Since teachers who participated were volunteers, an exploratory case study method was used in the research design. The research design was a two-phase process: (a) a description of the effects on the 22 teacher volunteers who participated in the peer coaching program, and (b) a comparison of 14 of the peer coaching teachers with 14 other teachers in the school who did not participate in the program. Because of space limitations, the results from only the first phase of the study (i.e., the description of peer coaching teachers) will be reported here.

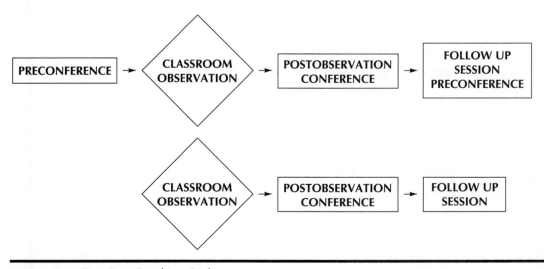

FIGURE 29.2 Two Peer Coaching Cycles

Evaluation Procedures

Research in staff development has not sufficiently answered questions about program impact, with most program evaluations taking the form of program descriptions (Yarger, 1982). In this staff development program, five different data collection methods were used so that substantial data might be uncovered to aid practitioners in making decisions regarding their staff development programming.

First, the *Paragraph Completion Method* (PCM) developed by Hunt, Butler, Noy, and Rosser (1978) was used to assess teachers' conceptual level. Teachers were asked to complete open-ended statements such as "When I think about rules. . ." or "When I am criticized. . ." Teachers were then categorized as possessing low, moderate, or high conceptual levels of thought development.

Second, teachers' conceptual levels were also assessed through the level of their talk about teaching (verbal behavior). Transcripts of audiotaped post-observation conferences from five teacher-coach pairs (randomly selected) during their first cycles of peer coaching were matched with transcripts from the same pairs during their last cycles of peer coaching.

The statements of the five pairs were categorized into one of four basic discourse categories. In a 1985 study, Zeichner and Liston found a statistically significant relationship between student teachers' higher conceptual levels of thought development and three discourse categories which they called the Reflective Teaching Index. Transcripts were analyzed to determine if there were an increase in teacher talk in these three categories between the first and last peer coaching cycles.

Third, an interview was conducted before the peer coaching began and after it was concluded to determine if teachers felt less isolated and more collegiality following the peer coaching experience. Each teacher in the program was questioned to determine (a) the kinds of assistance they gave to and received from other teachers in the school,

(b) teachers from whom assistance was received, (c) the frequency and amounts of teacher-teacher interactions, and (d) the time spent in these interactions. The questions were adapted from an interview guide used by Zahorik (1987) in a study of teacher interactions.

Fourth, a portion of the *Supervisory Practices for Promoting Instructional Improvement* questionnaire (Jones, 1986) was used to measure teachers' perceptions of instructional supervisory support to determine if these perceptions would change between the beginning of the program and the last peer coaching cycle. Ten supervisory services were ranked by teachers on a 10-point Likert scale as being of "little value," of "some value," or of "least value." These services included such items as "consultation on instructional problems and concerns," "conferences to schedule and plan observations," and "supportive and helpful assistance."

Fifth, teachers were asked to complete a questionnaire at the end of each coaching cycle to determine their perceptions of the peer coaching program and whether or not they felt it would change their teaching. Responses to two questions on the questionnaire were analyzed: (a) What do you think of the peer coaching process in which you just participated? and (b) Will the peer coaching process result in a change in the way you teach?

Findings

A statistically significant difference was found between the peer coaching teachers' scores *before* the coaching program (1.89) and their scores (2.033) *following* coaching (p < .05) as measured by the *Paragraph Completion Method* (Hunt et al., 1978). This difference was important because Hunt et al. (1978) assert that conceptual changes are unlikely to occur in periods of less than one year.

Three of five teacher coach pairs showed a gain (but not a statistically significant gain) in their use of discourse in the Reflective Teaching Index (Zeichner & Liston, 1985), which has been shown to correspond with higher conceptual levels of thought development. It is another possible indicator of the teachers' rise in conceptual level of thought development.

Responses in the teacher interviews showed that teachers had a slight increase in the number of interactions with other teachers (not counting peer coaching interactions), a substantial decrease in the mean number of minutes they reported interacting with other teachers (perhaps due to time now spent with peer coaching), and a small increase in average number of instances they gave help to and received help from other teachers in the school. Any increase was considered important since other research has reported that teachers have generally not supported the giving or receiving of help from other teachers (Feiman-Nemser & Floden, 1986).

Teachers' perceptions of supervisory support services in the school (measured on a scale of 1 to 10) were high both before ($M = 9.061$) and following ($M = 8.743$) coaching. No specific conclusion was drawn from this slight decrease in teachers' positive perceptions of supervisory support other than that teachers might now be contrasting their own peer supervision with other supervision. The willingness of all peer coaching teachers to voluntarily continue peer coaching, and the expressed desire of 17 other teachers to participate the following year were strong indicators of their positive perceptions of this type of staff development.

Eighteen of 22 teachers reported in a questionnaire that the peer coaching process would change their teaching. They said that it was already helping them to: (a) focus on the specifics of teaching, (b) gain new ideas and/or information, and (c) develop new insight or awareness about the teaching process (reported most frequently). The peer coaching program obviously helped teachers develop a more elaborate view of teaching than was held by classroom teachers in studies by Good and Brophy (1987) and Jackson (1968). Teachers also reported that they were willing toward the end of the program for peers to see them teach lessons that were more open-ended and involved more creativity and risk-taking.

RECOMMENDATIONS TO OTHER STAFF DEVELOPERS

Based on the experiences with this peer coaching program, we offer the following recommendations to staff developers.

1. *Staff development planners need to consider teachers' cognitive growth as a possible outcome of staff development programs.* There is ample research to show that teachers who think at high conceptual levels can diagnose instructional problems more effectively, think of more ideas when planning, project the consequences of their actions, use a variety of teaching approaches, and have higher quality communication with their students.

2. *Staff development program should have continuity over time and provide support as well as challenge to participants.* The length of this peer coaching program and its supportive nature appear to have given teachers the time and opportunity to grow conceptually and to take risks when designing lessons for their peers to observe.

3. *Staff developers should establish programs developed by and for teachers.* Staff development is often portrayed and implemented as a "training" or "inservicing" set of activities in which experts teach teachers predetermined instructional methods. This study suggests that teachers need not be "trained," but rather be given the tools for determining their own instructional priorities. In doing so, they became more thoughtful and resourceful about teaching.

4. *Any staff development program, regardless of its content, should include components which allow teachers to work and make decisions together as colleagues in learning about, planning, implementing, and evaluating instruction.* Little's (1982) study of successful schools provides evidence that teachers in more collegial schools are more effective in achieving their goals than teachers in non-collegial school.

CONCLUSION

While statements about the effects of this program must be viewed with caution due to the small sample size and its voluntary basis, it raised teachers' conceptual levels, helped reduce teacher isolation, and developed more positive teacher attitudes toward their own professional growth experiences. The peer coaching program gave teachers the opportunity to come together in collegial groups, assume more complex roles, reflect together on their work, and take an important step toward lasting professional growth. It is hoped that all teachers could have these experiences.

REFERENCES

Bernier, Jr. J. E. (1976). A psychological education intervention for teacher development. (Doctoral dissertation, University of Minnesota, 1976) *Dissertation Abstracts International, 37,* 6266A-6267A.

Calhoun, E. F. (1985). *Relationship of elementary school teachers to the utilization of supervisory and to the classroom instructional environment.* Unpublished doctoral dissertation, University of Georgia.

Eggleston, A. (1977). Conceptual level and other selected variables as predictors of teacher success in teaching toward inquiry. (Doctoral dissertation, University of Southern California, 1977) *Dissertation Abstracts International, 37,* 7099A.

Feiman-Nemser, S., & Floden, R. D. (1986). The cultures of teaching. In M. C. Wittrock (Ed.), *The handbook of research on teaching* (pp. 505–526). New York: Macmillan.

Glassberg, S. (1977). *Peer supervision for student teachers: A cognitive developmental approach.* Unpublished doctoral dissertation, University of Minnesota.

Glickman, C. D. (1990). *Supervision of instructions: A developmental approach* (2nd ed.). Boston: Allyn and Bacon.

Goldhammer. R. (1969). *Clinical supervision: Special methods for the supervision of teachers.* New York: Holt, Rinehart and Winston.

Good, T., & Brophy, J. (1987). *Looking in classrooms* (4th ed.). New York: Harper and Row.

Goodlad, J. I. (1984). *A place called school: Prospects for the future.* New York: McGraw-Hill.

Harvey, O. J., Hunt, D. E., & Schroder, H. M. (1961). *Conceptual systems and personality organization.* New York: John Wiley & Sons.

Harvey, O. J., Prather, M., White, B. J., Alter, R., & Hoffmeister, J. (1966). Teachers' belief systems and preschool atmospheres. *Journal of Educational Psychology, 57*(6), 373–381.

Hunt, D. E. (1970). A conceptual level matching model for coordinating learner characteristics with educational approaches. *Interchange, 1*(3), 68–82.

Hunt, D. E. (1975). A person-environment interaction: A challenge found wanting before it was tried. *Review of Educational Research, 45*(2), 209–229.

Hunt, D. E., Butler, L. F., Noy, J. E., & Rosser, M. E. (1978). *Assessing conceptual level by the paragraph completion method.* Toronto: The Ontario Institute for Studies in Education.

Jackson, P. W. (1968). *Life in classrooms.* New York: Holt, Rinehart and Winston.

Jones, J. W. (1986). *A data collection system for describing research-based supervisory practices for promoting instructional improvement in a local school district.* Unpublished doctoral dissertation, University of Georgia.

Joyce, B. R., Wald, R., & Weil, M. (1981). Can teachers learn repertoires of models of teaching? In B. R. Joyce, C. C. Brown, & L. Peck (Eds.), *Flexibility in teaching* (pp. 141–156). New York: Longman.

Lambert, L. (1989). The end of an era of staff development. *Educational Leadership, 7*(1), 78–91.

Lieberman, A., & Miller, L. (1984). *Teachers, their world and their work: Implications for school improvement.* Alexandria, VA: Association for Supervision and Curriculum Development.

Little, J. W. (1982). Norms of collegiality and experimentation: Workplace conditions of school success. *American Educational Research Journal, 19*(3), 325–340.

Macrostie (in progress). *Through development: The aim of a teacher inservice education program.* Unpublished doctoral dissertation, University of Tasmania, Australia.

Mintz, S. L., & Yarger, S. J. (1980, April). *Conceptual level and teachers' written plans.* Paper presented at the annual meeting of the American Education Research Association, Boston, MA.

Oja, S. (1978). A cognitive-structural approach to adult ego, moral, and conceptual development through inservice teacher education. (Doctoral dissertation, University of Minnesota, 1978). *Dissertation Abstracts International, 39,* 5356A.

Phillips, M. D. (1989). *A case study evaluation of the impact on teachers of a school-based staff development program in an elementary school.* Unpublished doctoral dissertation, University of Georgia.

Rathbone, C. (1971). Teachers' information handling behavior when grouped with students by conceptual level. (Doctoral dissertation, Syracuse University, 1970). *Dissertation Abstracts International, 32,* 798A.

Shavelson, R. J. (1983). Review of research on teachers' pedagogical judgments, plans, and decisions. *The Elementary School Journal, 83*(4), 392–413.

Showers, B. (1982). *Transfer of training: The contribution of coaching.* Eugene, OR: University of Oregon, Center for Educational Policy and Management.

Showers, B., Joyce, B., & Bennett, B. (1987). Synthesis of research on staff development: A framework for future study and state-of-the-art analysis. *Educational Leadership, 45*(3), 77–87.

Thies-Sprinthall, L. (1984). Promoting the developmental growth of supervising teachers: Theory, research programs, and implications. *Journal of Teacher Education, 35*(3), 53–60.

Yarger, S. J. (1982). *Inservice education.* Washington, DC: National Commission on Excellence in Education. (ERIC Document Reproduction Service No. ED 227 075).

Yarger, S., Howey, K., & Joyce, D. (1980). *Inservice teacher education.* Palo Alto, CA: Booksend Laboratories.

Zahorik, J. A. (1987). Teachers' collegial interactions: An exploratory study. *The Elementary School Journal, 87*(4), 386–396.

Zeichner, K. M., & Liston, D. (1985). Varieties of discourse in supervisory conferences. *Teaching and Teacher Education, 1*(2), 155–174.

DISCUSSION QUESTIONS

1. What are the implications of Hunt's conceptual level stages for staff development programs?

2. What are the implications of Hunt's Developmental Matching Model for staff development programs?

3. What components are common to effective staff development programs?

4. How would teachers' involvement in the development of a staff development program most likely influence program goals and potential outcomes?

5. Which kind of staff development program would be most appropriate for you and your colleagues?

Mustering the Will and Skill for Change

MATTHEW B. MILES
KAREN SEASHORE LOUIS

FOCUSING QUESTIONS

1. *How might the process of change differ for schools located in urban, suburban, and rural sectors?*
2. *What are the issues that transform knowledge into action that are involved in change?*
3. *How does autonomy influence individual schools involved in the process of change?*
4. *How does having vision impact change efforts?*
5. *In what way can internal coordination multiply a school's resources?*

It's like a different school now. It's entirely different in terms of attitude and commitment that weren't here when I first came.

99 and 44/100 percent of efforts to change things here have conked out.

These comments came from two schools in our four-year study of high school renewal.[1] We focused on what lay behind such different degrees of success in improving schools. Others have done good studies of "excellent," "recognized" schools (Corcoran and Wilson 1988). But the missing piece for most school people is *how to get there:* how to lead and manage the process of school reform.

We chose to look at urban high schools—really difficult settings for improvement. Buildings are decaying, teachers are frustrated with an outmoded curriculum and school structure, administrators are harried, parents are desperate, and students—poor, minority, and immigrant—are often shortchanged. We believed that if we could understand how real improvement takes place in

such settings, the lessons would be generic, useful in less difficult schools.

During 1985–86 we did five in-depth case studies of high schools in Boston, New York, New Jersey, Cleveland, and Los Angeles—high schools that were improving; we returned to them briefly in 1988. We also did a national survey of 178 big-city high school principals whose schools had been carrying out serious improvement efforts for one to four years. We were able to draw clear, compelling lessons about what makes for successful change efforts.[2] We saw repeatedly that the leadership and management of change was a matter of dealing with uncertainty, complexity, turbulence, and the cussedness of many different people. Narrow blueprints or "rules for change" did not work. As Fullan (1982) points out, the issue is developing "a feel for the process" and "learning to get better at change."

In this article, we summarize a few of our key conclusions about successful change and outline what may be involved in *using* them effectively.

FROM KNOWLEDGE TO ACTION

We believe that at least five issues are involved in getting from knowledge to action (Miles 1987, Louis and Miles 1990a):

- *Clarity.* The knowledge must be understood clearly—not be fuzzy, vague, or confusing.
- *Relevance.* The knowledge must be seen as meaningful, as connected to one's normal life and concerns—not irrelevant, inapplicable, impractical.
- *Action images.* The knowledge must be exemplified in specific actions, clearly visualized. People must have an image of "what to do to get there."
- *Will.* There must be motivation, interest, action orientation, a will to *do* something with the knowledge.
- *Skill.* There must be actual behavioral ability to *do* the action envisioned.

But even clear, relevant, action-focused findings (like those we describe below) often go unused. So we'd like to share ideas about mustering will and skill for real school improvement. Many research-to-practice efforts founder on the issues of will and skill.

First, *will.* Do you really want to do it? This is such a primitive, old-fashioned, even trite question that we often don't even ask it. People in schools often complain that nothing can be done, that all power resides elsewhere (in the union, in the central office, in the principal, in the department heads . . .). Yet in our study, we often saw action taken on near-intractable problems when someone simply decided to act.

Where does will come from? It comes in part from success experiences and in part from environmental encouragement of change efforts, both of which lead people to believe that their actions can make a difference. There is also a personal factor composed of sheer courage and assertion.

Questions of *skill* are also often ignored. Knowing *that* X is a workable action you want to take does not mean knowing *how* to deliver X.

The paths to educational improvement are strewn with examples of behavior that no one knew how to deliver: the team teaching project where no one knew how to make good group decisions; the clinical supervision program where principals had no practice in giving effective feedback; the science inquiry project where teachers kept on using closed-end questions.

Furthermore, skill can't be developed through reading, explanations, or videotapes. Improving skill requires *doing:* practice, getting feedback, and reshaping the doing until the action makes sense, is smooth, and gets you where you want to go. Most people know this about skiing or tennis, but don't consider it in relation to the behaviors involved in educational change. Good skill-development models (for example, Joyce and Showers 1983) often go unused in day-to-day school improvement work.

OUR FINDINGS AND HOW TO USE THEM

We'll talk about four topics from our study (the context, vision building, resources, and problem coping), discuss some of the will and skill issues involved, and suggest some advice.[3]

The Context

Our basic findings here were that turbulence in the external context is the norm (five new chancellors in New York since 1980, for example) and that school improvement is most successful when schools and their districts are actively engaged with each other—but with few strict rules and much autonomy for the school in choosing change goals and strategies. Our least successful site, for example, was "micro-managed" by the district office down to the level of who should do cafeteria duty.

It's clear that district offices will have to learn to rely more on their working relationships with schools, and less on rules and mandates, to steer a course through the turbulent waters.

Schools have to have room, a good deal of local decision-making power, and help with the problems they face. That means a well-coupled relationship, not a distant one. And when there is pressure to carry out a particular improvement program, it must be accompanied by plenty of support (Huberman and Miles 1984) if it is to succeed.[4]

Schools also have an *internal* context, which may include weak cohesiveness, staff cynicism about past innovation failures, or disgruntlement about the present, in contrast to a prior "golden age" ("good kids were here in the '50s and '60s . . . not a mark on the walls . . . they could get into any college they wanted. Now it's a zoo."). These issues need to be addressed early in the improvement process.

Issues of will. Central office people often worry that empowering schools will just lead to chaos (read "central office powerlessness"). There is often a zero-sum view (more for them means less for us), but real empowerment usually expands the pie, with more coherent control on everyone's part. Also, when school-based management is launched, district staff may not be tenacious enough to make it work—or may just abandon schools, leaving them to their own devices.

People in schools sometimes feel unwilling to stick their necks out, ask for the autonomy they need, bid for the type of working relationship that will get things done. It's safer to blame "downtown" than to take responsibility for working things through with the central office. And it's also easy to avoid taking a square look at the school's own internal context and doing direct work on less-than-optimal conditions. *Advice: Getting focused help through organization development, school-based review, or effective school programs is useful.*

Key skills. The skills of empowerment are not easy ones. One needs to learn how to take active initiative without shutting others out—and to support others' initiative without becoming paternal. It can help central office people to realize that they are not necessarily sharing or delegating decision-making power over every aspect of school life.

Another key skill is clear decision *allocation* (this one is non-negotiably ours; I will decide this one but need your advice; that one belongs to the school; this one we should discuss and decide jointly in a principals' meeting; that one is properly a board decision). *Advice: Coaching on decision allocation helps—even for central office people.*

The skills of relationship-building between previously unequal partners are not minor. How does one build trust and supply/receive help if the history is one of rules and control/compliance/avoidance? On the school side of the relationship, key skills include assertiveness (how to ask for what's wanted directly without aggression, game-playing, or blaming) and how to negotiate effectively when resources are scarce or there are competing claims. *Advice: Assertiveness training, as well as training in negotiation and conflict resolution for principals and department heads—since the same issues appear internally when school-based management is under way—is money well spent.[5]*

Vision Building

Our findings were that broad, ennobling, passionate, *shared* images of what the school should become do much to guide successful improvement. People in one of our successful schools said, "We are not only a school for kids, but a university for teachers"—a vision that led to a strong internal cadre's running an immense and rich range of staff development. Visions may either emerge from or lead to smaller "change themes," such as "get successful small projects going" or "model improved supervision and teaching." Gaining real ownership of visions by school staff is critical and requires serious time investment, patience, and empowerment for success. Visioning is a joint process; hope depends on successful and optimistic interaction among people.

Issues of will.   Will looms very large in vision building. Many people experience fear and uncertainty about the future, since they feel it cannot be known. *Advice: Asking people to look back on the future, as if it had already happened, is very helpful.* An example: "It's October 6, 1992. The governor's office has just cited this school as one of 10 outstanding schools in the state. Write the citation." Furthermore, people often stop themselves from vision building by doubting themselves and their ability to be out front, leading, making a commitment. And they weaken the power of their visions by taking present structures and procedures as givens, not as things to be transcended.

Key skills.   Here we can point to the skill of "going outside the frame," thinking laterally and creatively. An associated skill is the ability to *design,* invent new structures and procedures.[6]

The basic skills of collaboration are key. Visions can't be shared without direct, joint work on decisions that matter, nor without the ability to support and encourage others in dreaming. *Advice: Spend time on team building and on training in group problem solving and decision making.*

Resources

Effective change takes money and time. We found that a floor of funds (from $50–100,000 annually for several years) is needed for serious change efforts in big-city high schools. Such funds may be "add-ons," or reallocations within the budget, or in-kind donations of services. Most of these funds should go to internal coordination and shared planning (our average survey principal spent 70 days a year on improvement work; the average teacher spent 70 days over three to four years) and to intense, sustained, focused external assistance (more-successful schools used more than 50 days a year of external

assistance for training, coaching, and capacity-building).[7]

Successful schools also scanned actively for a broad range of resources (time, the right people, services, educational programs and materials, support and influence) that furthered their vision. We also saw much assertive, imaginative negotiation to get what was needed. ("The central office wanted to fix the boiler, but I knew that paint and cleanup was much more critical for staff morale. I knew they'd fix the boiler anyway if it broke.") Building permanent internal resource structures (for example, cadres, coordinators, program managers, steering groups) was also important.

Although money is a master resource for buying other resources, assistance and internal coordination are really "multiplier" resources. Good assistance and coordination multiply resources through better decisions on other resources: staffing, time use, and educational practices and materials. They also build internal assistance capacity.

Issues of will.   One of the biggest issues is facing up to the fact that changes cost money and confronting a second fact: powerful others may lack that realization—and may have to be persuaded (for example, through reminders that $50,000 a year is usually less than 1 percent of a school's budget), converted to supporters, or even bypassed. Finding and getting resources takes tenacity—hanging in there and persisting against obstacles.

A second big issue is false pride and mistaken self-sufficiency. The basic feeling that "we can do it ourselves" is sometimes reinforced by a mistaken belief that our school system is unique and ideas from elsewhere won't work. *Advice: Seeking assistance has to be reframed as a sign of intelligence and strength, not of weakness.*

Key skills.   Negotiating skills, "getting to yes" in Fisher and Ury's (1981) terms, loom very large. A less focused but equally important skill is the "garage sale junkie" stance: the ability to scan regularly and automatically for whatever looks good and fits with the vision. Here too the skill of "going outside the frame" is crucial, not only in reworking existing resources in creative ways but in looking in odd places for what you need.

In the special case of assistance resources, key skills are those of how to broker the right assistance to needy parts of the improvement program; how to develop a clear contract with assistance providers, especially outsiders; and how to design and strengthen internal assistance capacity. *Advice: Put this motto on the wall: "No training without training trainers."*

Problem Coping

The problems arising during school improvement efforts are multiple, pervasive, and sometimes nearly intractable. In our schools, they ranged from "no place for seven new counselors to sit" to "delayed funding" to "staff skepticism," "the vice-principal's heart attack," and "conflicts in the cabinet." Good problem coping (dealing with problems promptly, actively, and with some depth) is the *single biggest determinant* of program success. *Depth* means thinking structurally, or in terms of capacity-building, rather than in a "business as usual" or "push a little harder" or "fire fighting" style. (For example, instead of exhorting overloaded teachers to be more dedicated and "professional," rearrange the schedule to permit shared planning periods and added technical assistance.)

It pays to become aware of one's own typical coping style—and the styles typical in the school. Reviewing recent problems, what was done about them, and whether they stayed solved can be illuminating. *Advice: Routinize problem scanning (for example, beginning meetings with a "worry list"), as well as solution generation (always getting a range of brainstormed alternatives before deciding on one) and follow-up (reviewing consequences of each past coping effort).*

Issues of will.   Passivity and denial are the main enemies of good coping. Doing nothing, and its

partner procrastination, rarely work unless done deliberately with good reasons. Pretending or believing that the problem doesn't really exist or will go away are also ways to fail.

Here, too, refusal to "go outside the frame" hinders success. A dogmatic preference for low-risk, incremental coping (sometimes expressed as fear of seeming too radical) means that the deep coping required for difficult, persistent problems won't happen.

Key skills.   One essential skill is the ability to locate and state problems as natural, even helpful occurrences ("Problems are our friends") without blaming anyone, arousing defensiveness, or implying a predetermined solution.

As we've seen repeatedly, creativity, invention, and design skills are critical in generating coping alternatives that go deeper than "trying harder," go to the roots of the problem—and build others' capability for future problem-coping.

CONCLUSION

This review of our findings and the associated issues of will and skill show the limits of what can be done with words on paper. But words and ideas shape beliefs about what is possible in school reform and lead toward the skilled actions that will bring it about. Mustering of will and skill, judging from the successful school improvement efforts we have studied, unlocks and focuses a great deal of energy—and it does not require heroic, superhuman effort. Working smarter, not just harder, can get us there.

ENDNOTES

1. The Project on Improving Urban High Schools staff included Matthew B. Miles, Karen Seashore Louis, Sheila Rosenblum, Tony Cipollone and the late Eleanor Farrar (1986). Early results were reported in Louis and Cipollone (1986), Miles et al. (1986), Miles (1987), and Farrar (1987, 1988). Final reports are Louis and Miles (1990a) and Louis and Miles (1990b).

2. They are reported in *Improving the Urban High School: What Works and Why* (Louis and Miles 1990a). "Success" was defined in survey sites as improved student outcomes (achievement, behavior, drop-out reduction, employment of graduates, etc.); improved organizational outcomes (problem solving, etc.); and improved teacher outcomes (new teaching methods, skills, commitment, etc.). Our cases used the same criteria, plus completeness of implementation and continuation of the change effort.

3. These findings are drawn both from our intensive case studies and from the national survey data. The two sources had many areas of agreement and never produced contradictory conclusions.

4. This discussion deals only with the main issues we found critical in district-school relationships. For a full and helpful discussion, see Patterson, Parker, and Purkey (1986).

5. For further helpful material along these lines, see Block's directly written book *The Empowered Manager* (1987). Helpful work on conflict resolution appears in Cole (1983). Caldwell and Spinks (1988) have described some very useful methods for school-based management.

6. A very useful sourcebook of ideas and techniques on both creativity and design skills is Koberg and Bagnall (1976).

7. Our survey principals said their programs ran on an average of $800 per year, but the time use figures show that a very large amount of coordination and assistance was involved from both school and central office, as well as from external business and university partners.

REFERENCES

Block, P. (1987). *The Empowered Manager.* San Francisco: Jossey-Bass.

Caldwell, B. J., and J. M. Spinks. (1988). *The Self-Managing School.* London: Falmer Press.

Cole, D. W. (1983). *Conflict Resolution Technology.* Cleveland, Ohio: The Organization Development Institute.

Corcoran, T. B., and B. L. Wilson. (1988). *Research for Successful Secondary Schools: The First Three Years of the Secondary School Recognition Program.* Philadelphia: Research for Better Schools.

Farrar, E. (1987). "Improving the Urban High School: The Role of Leadership in the School, District,

and State." Paper read at American Educational Research Association meeting, Washington, D.C.

Farrar, E. (1988). "Environmental Contexts and the Implementation of Teacher and School-Based Reforms." Paper read at American Educational Research Association meeting, San Francisco.

Fisher, R., and W. Ury. (1981). *Getting to Yes: Negotiating Agreement Without Giving In.* Boston: Houghton Mifflin.

Fullan, M. (1982). *The Meaning of Educational Change.* New York: Teachers College Press.

Huberman, A. M., and M. B. Miles. (1984). *Innovation Up Close.* New York: Plenum.

Joyce. B. R., and B. Showers. (1983). *Power in Staff Development Through Research on Training.* Alexandria, Va.: Association for Supervision and Curriculum Development.

Koberg, D., and J. Bagnall. (1976). *The Universal Traveller: A Soft-Systems Guide to Creativity, Problem-Solving and the Process of Reaching Goals.* Los Altos, Calif: William Kaufmann, Inc.

Louis, K. S., and A. Cipollone. (1986). "Reforming the Urban High School: Reports from a Survey." Paper read at American Educational Research Association meeting, San Francisco.

Louis, K. S., and M. B. Miles. (1990a). *Improving the Urban High School: What Works and Why.* New York: Teachers College Press.

Louis, K. S., and M. B. Miles. (1990b). "Managing Reform: Lessons from a Survey of High Schools." Madison, Wis.: Department of Educational Policy and Administration, University of Wisconsin.

Miles, M. B. (1987). "Practical Guidelines for School Administrators: How To Get There." Paper read at American Educational Research Association meeting, Washington. D.C.

Miles, M. B., K. S. Louis, S. Rosenblum. A. Cipollone, and E. Farrar. (1986). *Lessons for Managing Implementation.* [Improving the Urban High School: a Preliminary Report.] Boston: Center for Survey Research, University of Massachusetts.

Patterson J., J. Parker, and S. Purkey. (1986). *Productive School Systems for a Non-Rational World.* Alexandria, Va.: Association for Supervision and Curriculum Development.

Copyright © 1990 by Matthew B. Miles and Karen Seashore Louis.

DISCUSSION QUESTIONS

1. How is planning related to change?
2. What role does communication play in the change process?
3. Why do educators tend to resist change?
4. To what extent does the process of change correspond to curriculum implementation?
5. What are the most effective methods for helping aspiring school leaders acquire the skills essential to promoting successful change?

Leadership and Excellence in Schooling

THOMAS J. SERGIOVANNI

FOCUSING QUESTIONS

1. *How do excellent, effective, and ineffective schools differ in the kind of education offered to students?*
2. *How do leadership forces influence student outcomes?*
3. *What is purposing?*
4. *How does the school culture's influence student outcomes?*
5. *How do the notions of tight structure and loose structure coincide with excellent schools?*

It is in and through symbols that man, consciously or unconsciously, lives, works and has his meaning.

—Thomas Carlyle

Is your school a good school? When Joan Lipsitz posed this question to principals of the excellent middle schools she studied, she found that they had difficulty defining what made their schools special or what the dimensions of excellence in schooling were. "You will have to come and see my school," was the typical response.[1]

Excellence is readily recognized in our ordinary experiences. It is difficult to put our finger on what makes a particular athletic or artistic performance excellent. But we know excellence when we see it. The earmarks of an excellent piano performance may be found not in the notes played but in the pauses between them. Clearly, excellence is multidimensional, holistic.

Competence, by contrast, is marked by mastery of certain predetermined, essential fundamentals. The piano student achieves mastery and thus is able to play the notes flawlessly and deliver a performance recognized as technically competent.

Similarly, we know excellent schools when we experience them, despite difficulties in definition. In excellent schools things "hang together"; a sense of purpose rallies people to a common cause; work has meaning and life is significant; teachers and students work together and with spirit; and accomplishments are readily recognized. To say excellent schools have high morale or have students who achieve high test scores or are schools that send more students to college misses the point. Excellence is all of these and more.

EXCELLENCE, NOT COMPETENCE

Should we expect more from our schools than the satisfaction of knowing they're performing "up to standard" and that students are competent performers? Most surveys indicate that basic skill learning and developing fundamental academic competence—the indicators of effectiveness common to the school effectiveness literature—are paramount goals in the minds of most parents and teachers. But, pushed a bit further, parents and teachers provide a more expansive view of excellence, which includes developing a love of learning, critical thinking and problem-solving skills, aesthetic appreciation, curiosity and creativity, interpersonal competence, and so on. Parents want a complete education for their children. Indeed our society requires it. Our young need to become cultured, educated citizens able to participate fully in society, not just trained workers with limited potential for such participation.

Important differences exist among incompetent, competent and excellent schools and their leaders. Schools managed by incompetent leaders simply don't get the job done. Typically, such schools are characterized by confusion and inefficiency in operation and malaise in human climate. Student achievement is lower in such schools. Teachers may not be giving a fair day's work for a fair day's pay. Student absenteeism, discipline, and violence may be a problem. Conflict may characterize interpersonal relationships among faculty or between faculty and supervisors. Parents may feel isolated from the school. Competent schools, by contrast, measure up to these and other standards of effectiveness. They get the job done in a satisfactory manner. Excellent schools, however, exceed the expectations necessary to be considered satisfactory. Students in such schools accomplish far more and teachers work much harder than can ordinarily be expected.

LEADERSHIP FORCES AND EXCELLENCE

Leadership has several aspects, each of which contributes uniquely to school competence and to school excellence. The current focus in leadership theory and practice provides a limited view, dwelling excessively on some aspects of leadership to the virtual exclusion of others. Unfortunately, these neglected aspects of leadership are linked to excellence—a revelation now unfolding from recent research on school effectiveness and school excellence.

Aspects of leadership can be described metaphorically as forces available to administrators, supervisors, and teachers as they influence the events of schooling. Force is the strength or energy brought to bear on a situation to start or stop motion or change. Leadership forces can be thought of as the means available to administrators, supervisors, and teachers to bring about or preserve changes needed to improve schooling.

At least five leadership forces can be identified:

- *Technical*—derived from sound management techniques
- *Human*—derived from harnessing available social and interpersonal resources
- *Educational*—derived from expert knowledge about matters of education and schooling
- *Symbolic*—derived from focusing the attention of others on matters of importance to the school
- *Cultural*—derived from building a unique school culture.

The first two forces have dominated the leadership literature in recent years and loom large in training programs offered through ASCD's National Curriculum Study Institutes.

1. *The technical leader assumes the role of "management engineer."* By emphasizing such concepts as planning and time management technologies, contingency leadership theories, and organizational structures, the leader provides planning, organizing, coordinating, and scheduling to the life of the school. An accomplished management engineer is skilled at manipulating strategies and situations to ensure optimum effectiveness.

2. *The human leader assumes the role of "human engineer."* By emphasizing such concepts as human relations, interpersonal competence, and instrumental motivational technologies, she or he provides support, encouragement, and growth opportunities to the school's human organization. The skilled engineer is adept at building and maintaining morale and using such processes as participatory decision making.

3. *The educational leader assumes the role of "clinical practitioner," bringing expert profes-*

sional knowledge and bearing as they relate to teaching effectiveness, educational program development, and clinical supervision. The clinical practitioner is adept at diagnosing educational problems; counseling teachers; providing for supervision, evaluation, and staff development; and developing curriculum. One wonders how such essential concerns of *school* leadership could, for so long, have been neglected in the literature of educational administration.

In an earlier era the *educational* aspects of leadership were center stage in the literature of educational administration and supervision. Principals were considered to be instructional leaders, and an emphasis on schooling characterized university training programs. However, advances of management and social science theory in educational administration and supervision soon brought to center stage technical and human aspects. John Goodlad has been a persistent critic of the displacement of education aspects of leadership in favor of technical and human. He argues, "But to put these matters at the center, often for understandable reasons of survival and expediency, is to commit a fundamental error which ultimately, will have a negative impact on both education and one's own career. *Our work, for which we will be held accountable, is to maintain, justify, and articulate sound, comprehensive programs of instruction for children and youth.*"[2]

He states further, "It is now time to put the right things at the center again. And the right things have to do with assuring comprehensive, quality educational programs in each and every school under our jurisdiction."[3]

The technical, human, and educational forces of leadership, brought together in an effort to maintain or improve schooling, provide the critical mass needed for *competent* schooling. A deficit in any one of the three upsets this critical mass, and less effective schooling is likely to occur. Recent studies of excellence in organizations suggest that despite the link between these three aspects of leadership and competence in schooling, their presence does not guarantee excellence. Excellent organizations, schools among them, are

characterized by other leadership qualities: forces described here as *symbolic* and *cultural*.

4. *The symbolic leader assumes the role of "chief" and by emphasizing selective attention (the modeling of important goals and behaviors) signals to others what is of importance and value.* Touring the school; visiting classrooms; seeking out and visibly spending time with students; downplaying management concerns in favor of educational ones; presiding over ceremonies, rituals, and other important occasions; and providing a unified vision of the school through proper use of words and actions are examples of leader activities associated with this fourth force.

Purposing is of major concern to the symbolic force. Peter Vaill defines purposing as "that continuous stream of actions by an organization's formal leadership which has the effect of inducing clarity, consensus, and commitment regarding the organization's basic purposes."[4] Students and teachers alike want to know what is of value to the school and its leadership; desire a sense of order and direction; and enjoy sharing this sense with others. They respond to these conditions with increased work motivation and commitment.

Of less concern to the symbolic force is the leader's behavioral style. Instead, what the leader stands for and communicates to others is emphasized. The object of symbolic leadership is the stirring of human consciousness, the integration and enhancing of meaning, the articulation of key cultural strands that identify the substance of a school, and the linking of persons involved in the school's activities to them. As Lou Pondy suggests "What kind of insights can we get if we say that the effectiveness of a leader lies in his ability to make activity meaningful for those in his role set—not to change behavior but to give others a sense of understanding what they are doing, and especially to articulate it so they can communicate about the meaning of their behavior?"[5] Providing meaning and rallying people to a common cause constitute effectiveness in symbolic leadership.

Leaders typically express symbolic aspects of leadership by working beneath the surface of events and activities and searching for deeper meaning and value. As Robert J. Starrat suggests, leaders seek to identify the roots of meaning and the flow and ebb of daily life in schools so that they might provide students, teachers, and members of the community with a sense of importance, vision, and purpose about the seemingly ordinary and mundane. Indeed, these leaders bring to the school a sense of drama in human life that permits persons to rise above the daily routine. They are able to see the significance of what a group is doing, and indeed *could* be doing. They have a feel for the dramatic possibilities inherent in most situations and are able to urge people to go beyond the routine, to break out of the mold into something more lively and vibrant. And finally, symbolic leaders are able to communicate their sense of vision by words and examples. They use easily understood language symbols, which communicate a sense of excitement, originality, and freshness. These efforts provide opportunities for others in the school to experience this vision and to obtain a sense of purpose so that they might come to share in the ownership of the school enterprise more fully.[6]

Warren Bennis argues that a compelling vision is the key ingredient of leadership in the excellent organizations he studied. Vision refers to the capacity to create and communicate a view of a desired state of affairs that induces commitment among those working in the organization.[7] Vision, then, becomes the substance of what is communicated as symbolic aspects of leadership are emphasized.

5. *The cultural leader assumes the role of "high priest," seeking to define, strengthen, and articulate those enduring values, beliefs, and cultural strands that give the school its unique identity.* As high priest the leader is engaged in legacy building, and in creating, nurturing, and teaching an organizational saga,[8] which defines the school as a distinct entity within an identifiable culture. The words clan or tribe come to mind. Leader activities associated with the cultural force include articulating school purposes and mission; socializing new members to the culture; telling stories and maintaining or reinforcing myths, traditions, and beliefs; explaining "the way things operate here"; developing and displaying a system of symbols over time; and rewarding those who reflect this culture.

The net effect of the cultural force of leadership is to bond together students, teachers, and others as believers in the work of the school. Indeed, the school and its purposes are somewhat revered as if they resembled an ideological system dedicated to a sacred mission. As persons become members of this strong and binding culture, they are provided with opportunities for enjoying a special sense of personal importance and significance. Their work and their lives take on a new importance, one characterized by richer meanings, an expanded sense of identity, and a feeling of belonging to something special—all highly motivating conditions.[9]

Before further pursuing the powerful forces of symbolic and cultural leadership, let's view the five forces in the form of a leadership hierarchy as depicted in Figure 31.1. The following assertions can be made about the relationship of these forces:

1. Technical and human leadership forces are generic and thus share identical qualities with competent management and leadership wherever they are expressed. They are not, therefore, unique to the school and its enterprise regardless of how important they may be.

2. Educational, symbolic, and cultural leadership forces are situational and contextual, deriving their unique qualities from specific matters of education and schooling. These qualities differentiate educational leadership, supervision, and administration from management and leadership in general.

3. Technical, human, and educational aspects of educational leadership forces are essential to competent schooling, and their absence contributes to ineffectiveness. The strength of their presence alone, however, is not sufficient to bring about excellence in schooling.

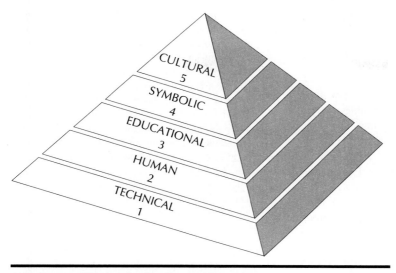

FIGURE 31.1 The Leadership Forces Hierarchy

4. Cultural and symbolic aspects of substantive leadership forces are essential to excellence in schooling. Their absence, however, does not appear to negatively affect routine competence.

5. The greater the presence of a leadership force higher in the hierarchy, the less important (beyond some unknown minimum presence) are others below.

CULTURE AND PURPOSE: ESSENTIALS OF EXCELLENCE

Culture building and practicing the art of purposing are the essentials of symbolic and cultural leadership forces. Culture can be described as the collective programming of the mind that distinguishes the members of one school from another.[10] Cultural life in schools is constructed reality, and leaders play a key role in building this reality. School culture includes values, symbols, beliefs, and shared meanings of parents, students, teachers, and others conceived as a group or community. Culture governs what is of worth for this group and how members should think, feel, and behave. The "stuff" of culture includes a school's customs and traditions; historical accounts; stated and unstated understandings; habits, norms, and expectations; common meanings and shared assumptions. The more understood, accepted, and cohesive the culture of a school, the better able it is to move in concert toward ideals it holds and objectives it wishes to pursue.

All schools have cultures: strong or weak, functional or dysfunctional. Successful schools seem to have strong and functional cultures aligned with a vision of excellence in schooling. This culture serves as a compass setting to steer people in a common direction; provides a set of norms that defines what people should accomplish and how; and provides a source of meaning and significance for teachers, students, administrators, and others as they work. Strong, functional cultures are domesticated in the sense that they emerge deliberately—they are nurtured and built by the school leadership and membership.

Weak cultures, by contrast, result in a malaise in schools characterized by a lack of understanding of what is to be accomplished and a lack of excitement for accomplishment itself. Sometimes cultures are strong *and* dysfunctional. In this case, students may have banded together to build a strong culture directed at disrupting the school or coercing other students to misbehave or perform poorly. Teachers, too, can be sources of problems in strong, dysfunctional cultures if they place their own interests first. In some schools, for example, an informal culture may exist with strong norms that dictate to faculty how they should behave. It might be unacceptable, for example, for teachers to take work home with them or to visit with students after school. Teachers who are working very hard might be considered "eager beavers" or "rate busters," and as a result find themselves distanced from this culture. Cultures of this sort might be referred to as *wild.* Wild cultures are not in control of administrators, supervisors, parents, teachers, and students as a cohesive group. They develop more informally or willy-nilly. When a dysfunctional wild culture exists in a school, excellence requires the building of a new, strong culture.

Culture building requires school leaders to give more attention to the informal, subtle, and symbolic aspects of school life. Teachers, parents, and students need answers to some basic questions: What is the school about? What is important here? What do we believe in? Why do we function the way we do? How are we unique? How do I fit into the scheme of things? Answering such question provides an orderliness to one's school life derived from a sense of purpose and enriched meanings.

"The task of leadership is to create the moral order that binds them . . . and the people around them," notes Thomas B. Greenfield.[11]

James Quinn states, "The role of the leader, then, is one of orchestrator and labeler: taking what can be gotten in the way of action and shaping it—generally after the fact—into lasting commitment to a new strategic direction. In short, he makes meanings."[12]

Leadership as culture building is not a new idea, but one solidly embedded in our history and well known to successful school and other leaders. In 1957, Phillip Selznick wrote:

> The art of the creative leader is the art of institution building, the reworking of human and tech-

nological materials to fashion an organism that embodies new and enduring values. . . . To institutionalize is to *infuse with value* beyond the technical requirements of the task at hand. The prizing of social machinery beyond its technical role is largely a reflection of the unique way it fulfills personal or group needs. Whenever individuals become attached to an organization or a way of doing things as persons rather than as technicians, the result is a prizing of the device for its own sake. From the standpoint of the committed person, the organization is changed from an expendable tool into a valued source of personal satisfaction. . . . The institutional leader, then, is *primarily an expert in the promotion and protection of values.*[13]

And in 1938, the noted theorist, Chester Barnard, stated the following about executive functions:

> The essential functions are, first to provide the system of communications; second, to promote the securing of essential efforts; and third, to formulate and define purpose. . . . It has already been made clear that, strictly speaking, purpose is defined more nearly by the aggregate of action taken than by any formulation in words.[14]

FREEDOM WITH RESTRICTIONS

Excellent schools have central zones composed of values and beliefs that take on sacred or cultural characteristics. Indeed, it might be useful to think of them as having an official "religion," which gives meaning and guides appropriate actions. As repositories of values, these central zones become sources of identity for teachers and students, giving meaning to their school lives. The focus of leadership, then, is on developing and nurturing these central zone patterns so that they provide a normative basis for action within the school.

In some respects, the concept of central zone suggests that effective schools are tightly structured. That is, they are organized in a highly disciplined fashion around a set of core ideas, which spell out the way of life in the school and govern behaviors. This is in contrast to recent developments in organizational theory which describe schools as being loosely structured entities. James G. March, a noted organizational theorist, speaks of educational organizations as being organized anarchies.[15] Similarly, Karl Weick uses the phrase loose coupling to describe the ways in which schools are organized.[16] Indeed Weick believes that one of the reasons for ineffectiveness in schooling is that schools are managed with the wrong theory in mind.

Contemporary thought, Weick argues, assumes that schools are characterized by four properties: the existence of a self-correcting rational system among people who work in a highly interdependent way; consensus on goals and the means to obtain these goals; coordination by the dissemination of information; and predictability of problems and responses to these problems. In fact, he notes, none of these properties are true characteristics of schools and how they function. Effective school administrators in loosely coupled schools, he observes, need to make full use of symbol management to tie together the system. In his words:

> People need to be part of sensible projects. Their action becomes richer, more confident, and more satisfying when it is linked with important underlying themes, values and movements. . . . administrators must be attentive to the 'glue' that holds loosely coupled systems together because such forms are just barely systems.[17]

Weick continues:

> The administrator who manages symbols does not just sit in his or her office mouthing clever slogans. Eloquence must be disseminated. And since channels are unpredictable, administrators must get out of the office and spend lots of time one on one—both to remind people of central visions and to assist them in applying these visions to their own activities. The administrator teaches people to interpret what they are doing in a common language.[18]

Recent observations about the school effectiveness literature point out that effective schools are not loosely coupled or structured at all but instead are tightly coupled.[19] My interpretation of the school effectiveness excellence literature leads me to believe that these schools are *both* tightly coupled and loosely coupled, an observation noted as well by Peters and Waterman in their studies of America's best-run cooperations. There exists in excellent schools a strong culture and clear sense of purpose, which defines the general thrust and nature of life for their inhabitants. At the same time, a great deal of freedom is given to teachers and others as to how these essential core values are to be honored and realized. This combination of tight structure around clear and explicit themes, which represent the core of the school's culture, and of autonomy for people to pursue these themes in ways that make sense to them, may well be a key reason for their success.

The combination of tight structure and loose structure corresponds very well to three important characteristics associated with motivation: commitment, enthusiasm, and loyalty to school. Teachers, students, and other school staff need to:

1. Find their work and personal lives meaningful, purposeful, sensible, and significant

2. Have some reasonable control over their work activities and affairs and to be able to exert reasonable influence over work events and circumstances

3. Experience success, think of themselves as winners, and receive recognition for their success.

People are willing to make a significant investment of time, talent, and energy in exchange for enhancement and fulfillment of these three needs.[20]

CONCLUSION

Figure 31.2 provides a summary of the relationship between the five forces of leadership and excellence in schooling. Included for each force are the dominant metaphor for leadership role and behavior; important theoretical constructs from

Force	Leadership Role Metaphor	Theoretical Constructs	Examples	Reactions	Link to Excellence
1. Technical	"Management engineer"	▬ Planning and time management technologies ▬ Contingency leadership theories ▬ Organizational structure	▬ Plan, organize, coordinate, and schedule ▬ Manipulate strategies and situations to ensure optimum effectiveness	People are managed as objects of a mechanical system. They react to efficient management with indifference but have a low tolerance for inefficient management.	Presence is important to achieve and maintain routine school competence but not sufficient to achieve excellence. Absence results in school ineffectiveness and poor morale.
2. Human	"Human engineer"	▬ Human relation supervision ▬ "Linking" motivation theories ▬ Interpersonal competence ▬ Conflict management ▬ Group cohesiveness	▬ Provide needed support ▬ Encourage growth and creativity ▬ Build and maintain morale ▬ Use participatory decision making	People achieve high satisfaction of their interpersonal needs. They like the leader and the school and respond with positive interpersonal behavior. A pleasant atmosphere exists that facilitates the work of the school.	
3. Educational	"Clinical practitioner"	▬ Professional knowledge and bearing ▬ Teaching effectiveness ▬ Educational program design ▬ Clinical supervision	▬ Diagnose educational problems ▬ Counsel teachers ▬ Provide supervision and evaluation ▬ Provide inservice ▬ Develop curriculum	People respond positively to the strong expert power of the leader and are motivated to work. They appreciate the assistance and concern provided.	Presence is essential to routine competence. Strongly linked to, but still not sufficient for, excellence in schooling. Absence results in ineffectiveness.
4. Symbolic	"Chief"	▬ Selective attention ▬ Purposing ▬ Modeling	▬ Tour the school ▬ Visit classrooms ▬ Know students ▬ Preside over ceremonies and rituals ▬ Provide a unified vision	People learn what is of value to the leader and school, have a sense of order and direction and enjoy sharing that sense with others. They respond with increased motivation and commitment.	Presence is essential to excellence in schooling though absence does not appear to negatively impact routine competence.
5. Cultural	"High priest"	▬ Climate, clan, culture ▬ Tightly structured values—loosely structured system ▬ Ideology ▬ "Bonding" motivation theory	▬ Articulate school purpose and mission ▬ Socialize new members ▬ Tell stories and maintain reinforcing myths ▬ Explain SOPs ▬ Define uniqueness ▬ Develop and display a reinforcing symbol system ▬ Reward those who reflect the culture	People become believers in the school as an ideological system. They are members of a strong culture that provides them with a sense of personal importance and significance and work meaningfulness, which is highly motivating.	

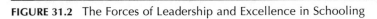

FIGURE 31.2 The Forces of Leadership and Excellence in Schooling

which such behavior is derived; examples of the behaviors in school leadership; reactions of teachers and others to the articulation of leadership forces; and links of each force to school competence and excellence.

As leaders are able to better understand and incorporate each of the five forces, they must be prepared to accept some additional burden. Symbolic and cultural forces are very powerful influences of human thought and behavior. People respond to these forces by bonding together into a highly normative-cohesive group, and this group in turn bonds itself to the school culture in an almost irrational way. The "cult" metaphor communicates well the nature of and effect of extremely strong bonding. How strong is the bonding of excellent schools? Is it possible that there are limits beyond which bonding works against excellence? As bonding grows, one is apt to "think" less and "feel" more about work and commitments to school.

No easy answer exists to this problem. But the burdens of leadership will be less if leadership functions and roles are shared and if the concept of *leadership density* were to emerge as a viable replacement for principal leadership. The moral and ethical foundation for leadership will be strengthened if leaders place outer world concerns (such as the welfare of schooling) before inner concerns for self-expression and personal success. Leaders might select as their slogan Kant's admonition. "Act so that you treat humanity, whether in your own person or in that of another, always as an end and never as a means only."

ENDNOTES

1. Joan Lipsitz, *Successful Schools for Young Adolescents* (New Brunswick, N.J.: Transaction Books, 1983). (Available from the Center for Early Adolescence at the University of North Carolina-Chapel Hill in Carrboro, N.C.)

2. John Goodlad, "Educational Leadership: Toward the Third Era," *Educational Leadership, 35,* (January 1978): 326.

3. Ibid., p. 331.

4. Peter B. Vaill, "The Purposing of High Performing Systems," in *Leadership and Organizational Culture,* eds., Thomas J. Sergiovanni and John E. Corbally (Urbana-Champaign: University of Illinois Press, 1984).

5. Louis Pondy, "Leadership Is a Language Game," in *Leadership Where Else Can We Go?* eds. Morgan W. McCall, Jr., and Michael M. Lombardo (Durham, N.C.: Duke University Press, 1978), p. 94.

6. See, for example, his "Apostolic Leadership," Jesuit Commission on Research and Development, San Jose, Ca., June, 1977 (available from the Commission of Fordham University, Lincoln Center, New York, N.Y.); and "Contemporary Talk on Leadership: Too Many Kings in the Parade?" *Notre Dame Journal of Education* 4, 1 (1973).

7. Warren Bennis, "Transformation Power and Leadership" in T. J. Sergiovanni and J. E. Corbally, op. cit.

8. Burton R. Clark, "The Organizational Saga in Higher Education," *Administrative Science Quarterly* 17, 2 (1972).

9. See, for example, Thomas J. Peters and Robert H. Waterman, Jr., *In Search of Excellence* (N.Y.: Harper & Row, 1982), particularly Chapter 4; and T. J. Sergiovanni, "Motivation to Work, Satisfaction and Quality of Life in Schools," *Issues in Education: A Forum of Research and Opinion* 1, 2 (1984).

10. G. Hofstede, *Cultures Consequences* (Beverly Hills: Sage Publications, 1980), p. 13.

11. Thomas B. Greenfield, "Leaders and Schools: Willfulness and Non-Natural Order in Organization," in T. J. Sergiovanni and J. E. Corbally, op. cit.

12. James B. Qwinn, "Formulating Strategy One Step at a Time," *Journal of Business Strategy* (Winter 1981): 59.

13. Phillip Selznick, *Leadership and Administration: A Sociological Interpretation* (N.Y.: Harper & Row, 1957).

14. Chester I. Barnard. *The Functions of the Executive.* Cambridge, Mass.: Harvard University Press, 1968, p. vii.

15. Michael D. Cohen, James G. March, and Johan Olson, "A Garbage Can Model of Organizational Choice," *Administrative Science Quarterly* 17, 1 (1972): 1–25.

16. Karl E. Weick, "Administering Education in Loosely Coupled Schools," *Phi Delta Kappan* 27, 2 (June 1982): 673–676.

17. Ibid., p. 675.

18. Ibid., p. 676.

19. See, for example, Michael Cohen, "Instructional Management and Social Conditions in Effective Schools," in *School Finance and School Improvement; Linkages in the 1980's,* eds. Allan Odden and L. Dean Webb. 1983 Yearbook of the American Educational Finance Association.

20. See, for example, Peters and Waterman, op. cit.; Sergiovanni, op. cit.; and J. Richard Hackman and Greg R. Oldham, *Work Redesign* (Reading, Mass.: Addison-Wesley, 1980).

DISCUSSION QUESTIONS

1. What roles are associated with the technical, human, educational, symbolic, and cultural leadership forces?
2. In what way is leadership related to excellent and competent schools?
3. How does leadership impact school climate?
4. How does the nature of leadership influence staff morale?
5. In what ways are curriculum implementation and leadership forces related?

PRO-CON CHART 5

Does site-based management improve staff morale?

PRO	CON
1. Site-based management encourages collaborative working relationships between teachers and administrators.	1. Teachers are not trained for shared leadership; instead of cooperating they often reopen old disagreements and old wounds.
2. Most teachers welcome the increased involvement and reach greater professional maturity; the result is improved school effectiveness.	2. Considerable time is devoted to discussing daily problems such as equipment needs, clerical routines, and working conditions; little time remains for the larger issue of school effectiveness.
3. Site-based management promotes participatory decision making between teachers and administrators as well as a commitment to long-range planning and budgeting.	3. School organizations ensure a clear division of administrative and teacher roles as well as an emphasis on short-term goals, often evidenced by achievement test scores and budget constraints.
4. Site-based management fosters improved school-community relations among teachers, administrators, parents, and community members.	4. Because of differences in expectations among participants, site based management often leads to conflict or to interference by individuals who lack expertise in school matters.
5. Site-based management empowers teachers and further enhances their professional status; it is important for teachers and administrators to work together for a common goal.	5. Teacher organizations empower teachers and enhance their professional status; it is important for teachers to retain their autonomy through professional associations.

CASE STUDY 5

Principals to Assume New Role as Curriculum Leaders

A memo from District Superintendent Harry Shaffer was sent to all of the district principals. The principals knew that Shaffer and the board expected them to begin directing all aspects of the curriculum including the planning, implementation, and evaluation components next year. The fifteen veteran principals, who had administrative experience in the range of five to twelve years, were not happy about receiving this mandate.

After describing his expectations, Shaffer asked if there were any questions. Sharon Flamb, who spoke on behalf of the principal group voiced several problems with the new expectations. Flamb indicated that she had already assigned the curriculum planning and evaluation functions to her department chairpersons. She stated that curriculum implementation was the teacher's domain and any concerns about instructional practice could be addressed in teacher evaluation assessments. Flamb pointed out that the principals had not had any input on this decision and that Shaffer's action was felt both as a top-down mandate and as professionally insensitive to their roles. Finally, Flamb suggested that asking principals to assume the role of instructional leader might be sound from a theoretical perspective, but it was not practical given all the responsibilities already assigned to the principals. Shaffer listened impatiently while Flamb spoke.

1. Using the information in this case study, indicate some of the actions that probably influenced Flamb's response.

2. Assume you are Shaffer, what actions will you take now?

3. What are some ways that the principals could have been involved in the decision-making process that was going to impact their responsibilities?

4. What are the advantages and disadvantages of having principals assume the responsibilities of an instructional leader?

5. What type of skills do principals need to supervise the curriculum?

6. What steps can be taken to train principals who lack adequate preparation in and knowledge of curriculum?

7. What should be the role of teachers in curriculum development and design?

8. Many perceive the role of the high school principal as akin to a manager. Do you agree with this perception? Why? Why not?

PART SIX

Curriculum and Policy

INTRODUCTION

In Part Six, the relationship between policy and curriculum is considered. How are issues of diversity, gender, and the movement toward national standards impacting the curriculum? How are school reform and restructuring efforts affecting the curriculum? What can we learn from other nations about curriculum implementation?

In Chapter 32, John Ogbu explores the debate between core and multicultural curriculum movements. He points out that the crucial issue really concerns cultural frames of reference. Ogbu contends that educators could facilitate the success of minority students if they understood the cultural and language differences that influence their academic achievement. Next, Nel Noddings points out how the male experience as a standard has influenced schooling. She suggests that school cultures need to change to reflect women's and men's experiences. Noddings claims that using standards in curricular planning that arise in women's culture will promote community, safety, and caring.

In Chapter 34, Diane Ravitch stresses the need for establishing national goals. She suggests that the adoption of national standards will promote student success, educational excellence, and equity. In Chapter 35, Harold Hodgkinson describes how changes in family and the increases in the diversity of the school-age population are affecting educational delivery. He offers suggestions concerning how education can facilitate the success of at-risk and disadvantaged students. In Chapter 36, Elliot Eisner considers the factors that influence the success of school reform including teacher, parent, and community views of education and the organization dynamics within schools. He highlights how action research, qualitative forms of evaluation, and giving teachers a greater role in creating local policy might reform initiatives.

In the following chapter, Michael Fullan and Matthew Miles identify the factors that often cause change efforts to fail. They offer several propositions that support successful change. In the final chapter of this book, Chapter 38, Gerald Unks explores the curriculum design models that guide educational delivery in Germany, Japan, and Great Britain. He considers the political, social, economic, and philosophical issues that influence curriculum implementation within a nation. Unks examines various components that characterize international curricula and considers what we learn from them.

32

Understanding Cultural Diversity and Learning

JOHN U. OGBU

FOCUSING QUESTIONS

1. *What are the implications of the core curriculum educational movement for minority students?*
2. *What are the implications of a multicultural educational movement for minority students?*
3. *What is multicultural education?*
4. *How can contextualized research of minority groups lead to improved classroom instruction?*
5. *In what ways do school systems impede the educational success of minority students?*
6. *How do cultural and language differences influence academic success of minority students?*
7. *How do secondary cultural differences impact learning of involuntary minorities?*

Core curriculum and multicultural education are two major approaches advocated in the current school reform movement. This article argues that neither of these approaches adequately addresses the problem of those minority groups who have not traditionally done well in the public school. Core curriculum advocates falsely assume that as a result of instituting a core curriculum, demanding higher standards, and patching up supposed individual deficiencies, all students will perform as expected. Multicultural education advocates inadequately design their program to focus on cultural differences in content and form. This chapter contends that the crucial issue in cultural diversity and learning is the relationship between the minority cultures and the American mainstream culture. Minorities whose cultural frames of reference are oppositional to the cultural frame of reference of American mainstream culture have greater difficulty crossing cultural boundaries at school to learn. Core curriculum and mul-

ticultural advocates have yet to understand and take this into account.

Educational Researcher, Vol. 21, No. 8, pp. 5–14

Cultural diversity has become a household phrase in education, especially minority education. I suspect, however, that there is some misunderstanding about what it means and its relevance to minority education. As an anthropologist, I am sensitive to the use of the phrase *cultural diversity;* as a student of minority education, I am concerned about its application or misapplication with respect to the school adjustment and performance of minority children.

This chapter addresses two contrasting educational responses to the cultural diversity: (a) a core curriculum education movement and (b) a multicultural education movement. I argue that neither of the two responses will have an appreciable impact on the school-learning problems of those minorities who have not traditionally done well in school. The reason is that they are not based on a good understanding of the nature of the cultural diversity or cultural differences of minority groups.

I first summarize the two responses and their shortcomings. Second, I attempt to explain the nature of the cultural diversity and its implications for minority schooling. I do so by first distinguishing and describing different types of minorities and the difference in the relationship between their cultures and the mainstream American culture. Third, I examine their differing educational implications. I will conclude with some recommendations.

RESPONSES TO CULTURAL DIVERSITY

Core Curriculum Education

Explicit advocates of a core curriculum for the U.S. public schools come largely from the humanities (Bennett, 1984; Bloom, 1987; Finn, 1989; Hirsch, 1987, 1988). Their critics call them "assimilationists" (Carroll & Schensul, 1990). I believe, however, that core curriculum advocates are more concerned about U.S. economic and technological status in international competition than about assimilating culturally diverse groups into the mainstream culture. They think that U.S. schools should teach a core curriculum like German, Japanese, South Korean, and Taiwanese schools, countries that have made remarkable economic and technological advances. Americans attribute the technological advances to their superior education as evidenced by the fact that their students outperform American students by every academic measure.

Will this movement improve the school performance of those minorities who have not traditionally done well in school? One assumption in the core curriculum movement (and in related school reform movements) is that the academic performance of both the majority and the minority students depends on what goes on inside the schools and that what needs to be done is to "fix"

the schools (Ogbu, 1988; Weis, 1985). Fixing the school will certainly have some positive effects, as can be seen from increasing numbers of minorities graduating from high school and college as well as entering the fields of math and science due to intervention programs.

However, the ability of a core curriculum to increase the school performance of some minority groups will be limited because it does not address the nature of minority cultural diversity. Past experience with compensatory education and other remedial programs suggests that it is not enough to simply announce higher academic standards and expectations (Passow, 1984). What goes on inside the schools, including the kind of curriculum taught, is very important for minority students (Edmonds, 1986; Ogbu, 1974), but more is involved. What the children bring to school— their communities' cultural models or understandings of "social realities" and the educational strategies that they, their families, and their communities use or do not use in seeking education are as important as within-school factors (Ogbu, 1988).

Multicultural Education

The other response is multicultural education. The current movement, led largely by minorities, emerged primarily in the 1960s, initially in response to cultural deprivation theory. Before then, minorities, such as Black Americans, protested against a differential and inferior curriculum; they wanted the same curriculum that was available to Whites (Bullock, 1970; Ogbu, 1978). Today, however, multicultural education is linked to cultural diversity (Yee, 1991). Moreover, the current demand for multicultural education is for both minorities who are doing relatively well in school and those who are not.

There is, however, no clear definition of multicultural education (see Appleton, 1983; Banks, 1989a, 1989b; Bullivant, 1981; Gay, 1979; Gibson, 1976; Grant & Sleeter, 1986; Suzuki, 1994). Furthermore, many writers propose diverse "models" of multicultural education that are rarely based on ethnographic or empirical studies of minorities' cultures. Gibson's (1976) survey found five models in the mid-1970s: (a) multicultural education for cross-cultural understanding, which, among other things, stresses teaching strategies affirming the right to be different and the need for members of different cultures to respect one another; (b) "culturally responsive education" at the elementary and secondary schools to enhance minority school learning by including minority cultures in the content of the curriculum and as a medium of instruction; (c) bicultural education, often associated with bilingual education programs, designed to reinforce minority students' cultures, languages, and identities while teaching the language and other skills functional in mainstream culture; (d) cultural pluralism in education, designed to preserve and strengthen ethnic-group identity and to increase minority groups' social, political, and economic participation in society; (e) multicultural education as the normal human experience, enabling individuals to participate competently in a multicultural society.

James Banks, probably the most prolific theorist, has also reviewed various models of multicultural education (Banks, 1981). He criticizes them for emphasizing cultural differences and deficiencies. He proposes a "multiple acculturation" model that would promote "cross-cultural competency" (Banks & Shin, 1981). Sleeter and Grant (1987) classify multicultural education into four types and added a fifth: (a) teaching the "culturally different," an assimilationist approach; (b) a human relations approach to improve interpersonal relations; (c) single-group studies to promote cultural pluralism by raising consciousness; (d) multicultural education within the regular curriculum to reflect diversity and thereby enhance pluralism and equality; (e) education that is multicultural and social reconstructionist (p. 423), proposed by the authors to encourage students to challenge social inequality and to promote cultural diversity. Baker (1978), Baptiste (1979), Gay (1979, 1988, 1990), and Suzuki (1984) have proposed other models.

Taken together, multicultural education fosters pride in minority cultures, helps minority students develop new insights into their culture, reduces prejudice and stereotyping, and promotes intercultural understandings (Rubalcava, 1991). But the crucial question is to what extent will multicultural education improve the academic performance of those minorities who have not traditionally done well in school? Rarely do multicultural education models address this question explicitly. Two exceptions are bicultural education and culturally responsive education (Gibson, 1976).

Multicultural education may indeed improve school learning for some minority children. However, for several reasons it is not an adequate strategy to enhance the academic performance of those minorities who have traditionally not done well in school. One reason is that multicultural education generally ignores the minority students' own responsibility for their academic performance. Multicultural education models and actual programs convey the impression that educating minority students is a process whereby teachers and schools must change for the benefit of the students. They should acquire knowledge of minority cultures and languages for teaching minority children, promoting cross-cultural understanding, reinforcing ethnic identity, and so on. Multicultural education generally emphasizes changing teacher attitudes and practices. Yet a comparative study of the situation will show that school success depends not only on what schools and teachers do but also on what students do (Ogbu & Matute-Bianchi, 1986).

Second, we suspect that multicultural education theories and programs are rarely based on actual study of minority cultures and languages. To our knowledge, many proponents of multicultural education models have not studied minority cultures in *minority communities,* although some have studied minority children at school and some are minority-group members. However, membership in a minority group is not a sufficient basis for theorizing about cultural influences on learning. For example, I have found that some members of my research team studying their own local communities initially did not recognize some relevant cultural data, including cultural assumptions underlying their own behaviors. Research with minority children at school provides a very limited access to the cultural assumptions underlying the children's distinctive attitudes and behaviors. Furthermore, a good study of a minority group's culture or language may turn up some cultural/language differences that actually cause learning problems that cannot be remedied through cultural infusion into the curriculum or teaching and learning styles (Closs, 1986; Orr, 1987). What is also instructive is that there are minority groups whose language expressions, mathematical or number systems, and overt cultural behaviors might be different enough from those of White Americans to be considered barriers to learning math and science but whose members, nevertheless, learn more or less successfully. That is, they are able, eventually, to cross cultural and language boundaries and succeed academically. Thus, a third reason for the inadequacy of the multicultural education solution is that it fails to separate minority groups that are able to cross cultural and language boundaries and learn successfully, in spite of initial cultural barriers, from those that are not able to do so (Gibson & Ogbu, 1991; Ogbu, 1987, 1990).

The question of who needs multicultural education to enhance academic success and who does not becomes more important when one looks at the increasing diversity in U.S. schools and classrooms (Yee, 1991). For example, we found only 5 or 6 ethnic groups represented in our initial study of Stockton, California, schools in 1968–1970. However, by 1986 the ethnic representation increased to 12 at the elementary, 11 at the junior high, and 16 at the senior high schools. As in earlier years, in 1986 some of the minority groups were doing very well in school in spite of their language and cultural differences, and some were not.

In summary, neither the core curriculum response nor the multicultural education response in its various forms is likely to enhance appreciably the academic achievement of those minority groups who have not traditionally done well in school. Like the core curriculum movement, the multicultural education movement is based on the erroneous assumption that academic achievement is primarily the result of the transaction between the specific skills and abilities of the students and the teaching of the curriculum and the process of the classroom environment, including teacher attitudes. These movements fail to recognize that the meaning and value students associate with school learning and achievement play a very significant role in determining their efforts toward learning and performance. Furthermore, the meaning and value that students from different cultural groups associate with the process of formal education vary and are socially transmitted by their ethnic communities. The important point here is that neither the core curriculum approach nor the multicultural education approach will appreciably improve the school performance of some minority groups until they and other school interventions, innovations, and reforms are informed by an understanding of *why* children from specific minority groups are experiencing learning and performance difficulty.

The problem is not merely one of cultural and language differences, although these differences are important. What is even more significant, but thus far unrecognized, is the nature of the relationship between minority cultures/languages and the culture and language of the dominant White Americans and the public schools they control. The relationship between the minority cultures/languages and the mainstream culture and language is different for different minorities. And it is this difference in the relationship that is problematic in the ability of the minorities to cross cultural and language boundaries and that calls for understanding in order to enhance the success of intervention and other efforts. What is the nature of this intercultural relationship and what are its implications for minority education?

CULTURAL DIVERSITY AND DIFFERENTIAL SCHOOL SUCCESS

Societal and School Influences on Minority Education

The school learning and performance of minority children are influenced by complex social, economic, historical, and cultural factors. Therefore, before describing the cultural forces, I want to make it categorically clear that I am focusing on only one group of forces. I have described elsewhere other forces at work, namely, how American society at large, the local communities, and the schools all contribute to minority problems in school learning and performance. Societal contributions include denying the minorities equal access to good education through societal and community educational policies and practices and denying them adequate and/or equal rewards with Whites for their educational accomplishments through a job ceiling and other mechanisms. Schools contribute to the educational problems through subtle and not so subtle policies and practices. The latter include tracking, "biased" testing and curriculum, and misclassification (see Ogbu, 1974, 1977, 1978, 1991). Here we are focusing on cultural forces, specifically, on the relationship between minority cultures and mainstream culture and the implications of that relationship for minority schooling.

Differential Influence of Cultural Forces

There is evidence from comparative research suggesting that differences in school learning and performance among minorities are not due merely to cultural and language differences. Some minority groups do well in school even though they do not share the language and cultural backgrounds of the dominant group that are reflected in the curriculum, instructional style, and other practices of the schools. Such minorities may initially experience problems due to the cultural and language difference, but the problems do not persist.

The reason some minorities do well in school is not necessarily because their cultures are similar to the mainstream culture. For example, Gibson (1988) reports that in Valleyside, California, the Punjabis do well even though judged by mainstream culture they would be regarded as being academically at risk.

One cultural feature, namely, differential interpretation of eye contacts by White teachers and minority-group members, has been offered as an explanation for the learning difficulties among Puerto Rican children in New York (Byers & Byers, 1972) but has not had similar adverse effects on the Punjabis. Other examples of differential academic influence of minority cultural differences have been found in studies of minority education in Stockton (Ogbu, 1974), Watsonville (Matute-Bianchi, 1986; see also Woolard, 1981), and San Francisco (Suarez-Orozco, 1988).

Studies outside the United States have also found that minority children do not fail in school because of mere cultural/language differences or succeed in school because they share the culture and language of the dominant group. In Britain, students of East Asian origins, for whom the British language and culture are different, do considerably better in school than West Indian students, who have much longer been privy to the British language and culture (Ogbu, 1978; Taylor & Hegarty, 1985). In Japan (DeVos & Lee, 1981) and New Zealand (Penfold, conversation with author, 1981), minority groups—even if they have similar cultures and languages but different histories—differ in school learning and academic success.

There are cases where a minority group does better in school when it is away from its country of origin, residing in a host society where its language and culture differ greatly from the language and culture of the dominant group. Take the case of the Japanese Buraku outcaste. In Japan itself, Buraku students continue to do poorly in school when compared with the dominant Ippan students (Hirasawa, 1989; Shimahara, 1991). But the Buraku immigrants in the United States are doing just as well as the Ippan immigrants (De-Vos, 1973; Ito, 1967). The Koreans in Japan are another example. In Japan, where they went originally as colonial forced labor, they do very poorly in school. But in Hawaii and the continental United States, Korean students do as well as other Asians; yet Korean culture is more to Japanese culture than to American mainstream culture (De-Vos, 1984; DeVos & Lee, 1981; Lee, 1991; Rohlen, 1981). The Koreans' case is further instructive because of their differential school success as a minority group in the United States, Japan, and China (see Kristoff, 1992, for Koreans in China). Korean peasants relocated to these three countries about the same time as emigrants, except the group that went to Japan. The Koreans are academically successful in China and Hawaii, but not in Japan. West Indians are a similar example. They are academically successful in the continental United States and in the U.S. Virgin Islands, where they regard themselves as "immigrants" (Fordham, 1984; Gibson, 1991); less successful in Canada, where they regard themselves as members of "the Commonwealth" (Solomon, 1992); and least successful in Britain, which they regard as their "motherland" (Ogbu, 1978; Tomlinson, 1982).

As these studies suggest, mere cultural and language differences cannot account for the relative school failure of some minorities and the school success of others. Minority status involves complex realities that affect the relationship between the culture and language of the minority and those of the dominant groups and thereby influence the school adjustment and learning of the minority.

TYPES OF MINORITY STATUS: A PREREQUISITE FOR UNDERSTANDING CULTURAL DIVERSITY AND LEARNING

To understand what it is about minority groups, their cultures and languages that makes crossing cultural boundaries and school learning difficult for some but not for others, we must recognize that there are different types of minority groups or minority status. Our comparative study has led us to classify minority groups into (a) autonomous, (b) immigrant or voluntary, and (c) castelike or involuntary minorities.

1. Autonomous minorities are people who are minorities primarily in a numerical sense. American examples are Jews, Mormons, and the Amish. There are no non-White autonomous minorities in the United States, so we will not discuss this type further (see Ogbu, 1978).

2. Immigrant or voluntary minorities are people who have moved more or less voluntarily to the United States—or any other society—because they desire more economic well-being, better overall opportunities, and/or greater political freedom. Their expectations continue to influence the way they perceive and respond to events, including schooling, in the host society. Voluntary minorities usually experience initial problems in school due to cultural and language differences as well as lack of understanding of how the education system works. But they do not experience lingering, disproportionate school failure. The Chinese and Punjabi Indians are representative U.S. examples. Refugees are not voluntary minorities; they are not a part of this classification or the subject of this paper (see Ogbu, 1990, for a full discussion of the distinction).

3. Castelike or involuntary minorities are people who were originally brought into the United States or any other society against their will. For example, through slavery, conquest, colonization, or forced labor. Thereafter, these minorities were often relegated to menial positions and denied true assimilation into the mainstream society. American Indians, Black Americans, early Mexican-Americans in the Southwest, and native Hawaiians are U.S. examples. Puerto Ricans may qualify for membership in this category if they consider themselves "a colonized people." The Burakumin and Koreans in Japan and the Maoris in New Zealand are examples outside the United

States. It is involuntary minorities that usually experience greater and more persistent difficulties with school learning.

MINORITY STATUS, CULTURE, AND IDENTITY

The different types of minorities are characterized by different types of cultural differences as well as social or collective identities. Voluntary minorities are characterized by primary cultural differences and involuntary minorities by secondary cultural differences.

Primary cultural differences are differences that existed before two groups came in contact, such as before immigrant minorities came to the United States. For example, Punjabi Indians in Valleyside, California, spoke Punjabi; practiced the Sikh, Hindu, or Muslim religion; had arranged marriages, and wore turbans, if they were male, before they came to the United States. In Valleyside they continue these beliefs and practices to some extent (Gibson, 1988). The Punjabis also brought with them their distinctive way of raising children, including teaching children how to make decisions and how to manage money.

We gain a better understanding of primary cultural differences when we examine non-Western children who attend Western-type schools in their own countries. The Kpelle of Liberia are a good example. John Gay and Michael Cole (1967) found that the arithmetic concepts in Kpelle culture were similar in some respects to those used in the American-type school but differed in other ways. The Kpelle had few geometrical concepts, and although they measured time, volume, and money, their culture lacked measurements of weight, area, speed, and temperature. These differences in mathematical concepts and use existed *before* the Kpelle were introduced to Western-type schools.

Secondary cultural differences are differences that arose after two populations came into contact or after members of a given population began to participate in an institution controlled by members of another population, such as the schools controlled by the dominant group. Thus, secondary cultural differences develop as a response to a contact situation, especially one involving the domination of one group by another.

At the beginning of the culture contact the two groups are characterized by primary cultural differences; later, the minorities develop secondary cultural differences to cope with their subordination. The secondary culture develops in several ways: from a reinterpretation of previous primary cultural differences or through the emergence of new types of cultural norms and behaviors.

Several features of secondary cultural differences are worth noting for their effects on schooling. First, it is the differences in style rather than in content that involuntary minorities emphasize: cognitive style (Ramirez & Castenada, 1974; Shade, 1982), communication style (Gumperz, 1981; Kochman, 1982; Philips, 1972, 1983), interaction style (Erickson & Mohatt, 1982), and learning style (Au, 1981; Boykin, 1980; Philips, 1976).

Another feature is cultural inversion. Cultural inversion is the tendency for involuntary minorities to regard certain forms of behavior, events, symbols, and meanings as inappropriate for them because these are characteristic of White Americans. At the same time the minorities value other forms of behavior, events, symbols and meanings, often the opposite, as more appropriate for themselves. Thus, what is appropriate or even legitimate behavior for in-group members may be defined in opposition to White out-group members' practices and preferences.

Cultural inversion may take several forms. It may be in-group meanings of words and statements (Bontemps, July 1969, conversation with author), different notions and use of time (Weis, 1985), different emphasis on dialects and communication style (Baugh, 1984; Holt, 1972; Luster, 1992), or an outright rejection of White American preferences or what Whites consider appropriate behavior in a given setting (Fordham & Ogbu, 1986; Petroni, 1970). Cultural inversion, along with other oppositional elements, results in the coexistence of two opposing cultural frames of reference or ideals orienting behavior, from the perspectives of involuntary minorities.

Involuntary minorities sometimes use cultural inversion to repudiate negative White stereotypes or derogatory images. Sometimes they use it as a strategy to manipulate Whites, to get even with Whites, or, as Holt (1972) puts it for Black Americans, "to turn the table against whites."

Secondary cultural differences seem to be associated with ambivalent or oppositional social or collective identities vis-à-vis the White American social identity. Voluntary minorities seem to bring to the United States a sense of who they are from their homeland and seem to retain this different but non-oppositional social identity at least during the first generation. Involuntary minorities, in contrast, develop a new sense of social or collective identity that is in opposition to the social identity of the dominant group after they have become subordinated. They do so in response to their treatment by White Americans in economic, political, social, psychological, cultural, and language domains. Whites' treatment included deliberate exclusion from true assimilation or the reverse, namely, forced superficial assimilation (Castile & Kushner, 1981; DeVos, 1967, 1984; Spicer, 1966, 1971). Involuntary minorities, such as Black Americans, developed oppositional identity because for many generations they realized and believed that the White treatment was both collective and enduring. They were (and still are) not treated like White Americans regardless of their individual differences in ability, training, education, place of origin or residence, economic status, or physical appearance. They could not (and still cannot) easily escape from their birth ascribed membership in a subordinate and disparaged group by "passing" for White or by returning to a "homeland" (Green, 1981). Native Americans and native Hawaiians have no other "homeland" to return to. In the past some Black Americans sought an escape by returning to Africa (Hall, 1978) and, more recently, by converting to the Muslim religion (Essien-Udom, 1964).

CULTURAL DIFFERENCES, IDENTITY, AND SCHOOL LEARNING

I have identified different types of cultural differences characteristic of the voluntary and involuntary minorities and have described the relationship between these cultural differences and mainstream (White) American culture. I turn now to the way the relationship between the minority cultures and mainstream culture affects minority schooling.

The primary cultural differences of voluntary minorities and the secondary cultural differences of involuntary minorities affect minority school learning differently. My comparative research suggests that involuntary minorities experience more difficulties in school learning and performance partly because of the relationship between their cultures and the mainstream culture. As I have come to understand it, they have greater difficulty with school learning and performance partly because they have greater difficulty crossing cultural/language boundaries in school than voluntary minorities with primary cultural differences.

Primary Cultural Differences and Schooling

What kinds of school problems are associated with primary cultural differences and why do the bearers of these differences overcome these problems and learn more or less successfully? Why do voluntary minorities successfully cross cultural boundaries?

In school, primary cultural differences may initially cause problems in interpersonal and intergroup relations as well as difficulties in academic work for several reasons. One is that children from different cultural backgrounds may begin school with different cultural assumptions about the world and human relations. Another is that the minorities may come to school lacking certain concepts necessary to learn math and science, for instance, because their own cultures do not have or use such concepts. Still another problem is that the children may be non-English-speaking. Finally, there may be differences in teaching and learning styles.

However, the relationship between the primary cultural differences and White American mainstream culture helps voluntary minority children to eventually overcome the initial problems, adjust socially, and learn and perform academically more or less successfully. First, the cultural differences existed before the minorities came to the United States or entered the public schools; the differences did not arise to maintain boundaries between them and White Americans. They are different from, but not necessarily oppositional to, equivalent features in mainstream culture in the schools.

Furthermore, because cultural differences did not develop in opposition or to protect their collective identity and sense of security and self-worth, voluntary minorities do not perceive learning the attitudes and behaviors required for school success as threatening their own culture, language, and identities. Instead, they interpret such learning (e.g., English) instrumentally and as additive, as adding to what they already have (their own language), for use in the appropriate context (Chung, 1992). They also believe that the learning will help them succeed in school and later in the labor market. Voluntary minorities, therefore, tend to adopt the strategy of "accommodation without assimilation" (Gibson, 1988) or "alternation strategy" (Ogbu, 1987). That is, while they may not give up their own cultural beliefs and practices, voluntary minorities are willing, and may even strive, to play the classroom game by the rules and try to overcome all kinds of schooling difficulties because they believe so strongly that there will be a payoff later (Gibson, 1987). With this kind of attitude, they are able to cross cultural boundaries and do relatively well in school.

Still another factor in favor of voluntary minorities is that they interpret the cultural and language differences they encounter as barriers to be overcome in order for them to achieve their long-range goals of obtaining good school credentials for future employment. They did not come to the United States expecting the schools to teach them in their own culture and language, although they are grateful if the schools do. Usually, they go to the school expecting and willing to learn the culture and language of the schools, and they also expect at least some initial difficulty in doing so.

Finally, primary cultural differences and the problems they cause are often specific enough to be identified through careful ethnographic research. This specificity and identifiability facilitate developing educational policies, programs, and practices to eliminate their negative impact.

Secondary Cultural Differences and Schooling

Many of the "cultural problems" caused by secondary cultural differences are on the surface similar to those caused by primary cultural differences: conflicts in interpersonal/intergroup relations due to cultural misunderstandings, conceptual problems due to absence of certain concepts in the ethnic-group cultures, lack of fluency in standard English, and conflicts in teaching and learning style.

However, the underlying factor that distinguishes these problems from those of primary cultural differences is the style, not the content. Sociolinguists stress differences in communication style; cognitive researchers emphasize cognitive styles, styles of thought, or a mismatch between teacher and minority students in cognitive maps; interactionists and transactionists locate the problem in differences in interactional style. Researchers working among native Hawaiians traced their reading problems to differences in learning style.

What needs to be stressed is that secondary cultural differences do not merely cause initial problems in the social adjustment and academic performance of involuntary minorities but the problems appear to be extensive and persistent.

One reason for this is that these minorities find it harder to cross cultural and language boundaries.

This difficulty occurs because of the nature of the relationship between the minority culture and the dominant White American culture. The cultural differences arose initially to serve boundary-maintaining and coping functions under subordination. As boundary-maintaining mechanisms, they do not necessarily disappear or change when involuntary minorities and Whites are brought together, as in desegregated schools. Secondary cultural differences evolved as coping mechanisms under "oppressive conditions," and the minorities have no strong incentives to give up these differences as long as they believe that they are still oppressed; some of the cultural differences have taken on a life of their own, and the minorities are not necessarily aware of their boundary-maintaining functions or oppositional quality.

Involuntary minorities interpret the cultural and language differences as markers of their collective identity to be maintained, not as barriers to be overcome. This results partly from coexistence of opposing cultural frames of reference discussed earlier. There is, again, no incentive to learn or behave in a manner considered consciously and unconsciously as inappropriate for the minorities.

Among involuntary minorities, school learning tends to be equated with the learning of the culture and language of White Americans, that is, the learning of the cultural and language frames of reference of their "enemy" or "oppressors." Consider the current argument by some that school curriculum and textbooks are reflective of White culture. (Note that for their part, White Americans also define minority school learning in terms of learning White culture and language as reflected in the school curriculum and practices.) Thus, involuntary minorities may consciously or unconsciously interpret school learning as a displacement process detrimental to their social identity, sense of security, and self-worth. They fear that by learning the White cultural frame of reference, they will cease to act like minorities and lose their identity as minorities and their

sense of community and self-worth. Furthermore, reality has demonstrated that those who successfully learn to act White or who succeed in school are not fully accepted by the Whites; nor do such people receive rewards or opportunity for advancement equal to those open to Whites with similar education.

The important point here is that unlike voluntary minorities, involuntary minorities do not seem to be able or willing to separate attitudes and behaviors that result in academic success from those that may result in linear acculturation or replacement of their cultural identity with White American cultural identity.

There are social pressures discouraging involuntary minority students from adopting the standard attitudes and behavior practices that enhance school learning because such attitudes and behaviors are considered "White." In the case of Black students, for example, the social pressures against "acting White" include accusations of Uncle Tomism or disloyalty to the Black cause and to the Black community, fear of losing one's friends and one's sense of community (Fordham & Ogbu, 1986; Luster, 1992; Ogbu, 1974; Petroni, 1970).

The same phenomenon has been described for American Indian students—the tendency to "resist" adopting and following school rules of behavior and standard practices (Deyhle 1989; Dumont, 1972; Kramer, 1991; Philips, 1972, 1983). According to some studies, Indian students enter the classroom with a cultural convention that dictates that they should not adopt the expected classroom rules of behavior and standard practices. A good illustration is Philips's study of Indian children in Warm Springs Reservation in Oregon referred to earlier. She found that the Indian students and their White teachers in an elementary school held different views about how students should interact with teachers and among themselves; they also held different views about how students should participate in classroom activities. Although the teachers' views apparently prevailed, the teachers were not particularly effective in classroom management and in getting the children to learn and perform.

There are also psychological pressures against "acting White" that are just as effective in discouraging involuntary minority students from striving for academic success. An involuntary minority individual who desires to do well in school may also define the behavior enhancing school success or the success itself as "acting White." Thinking that attitudes and behaviors associated with academic success and the success itself may result in loss of peer affiliation and support and at the same time uncertain of White acceptance and support if he or she succeeds in learning to act White, a student may feel a personal conflict. Put differently, an involuntary minority student desiring and striving to do well in school is faced with the conflict between loyalty to the minority peer group, which provides a sense of community and security, and the desire to behave in ways that may improve school performance but that the peer group defines as "White."

The dilemma of involuntary minority students, then, is that they may have to choose between "acting White" (i.e., adopting "appropriate" attitudes and behaviors or school rules and standard practices that enhance academic success but that are perceived and interpreted by the minorities as typical of White Americans and therefore negatively sanctioned by them) and "acting Black," "acting Indian," "acting Chicano," and so on (i.e., adopting attitudes and behaviors that the minority students consider appropriate for their group but that are not necessarily conducive to school success).

We noted earlier that researchers among involuntary minorities repeatedly emphasize conflicts and discontinuities in teaching and learning due to differences in style, rather than content. Stylistic differences are more diffuse and less specific than the content differences of primary cultural differences. The differences in manifest contents are not the overriding problem, because they also exist within the primary cultural differences of voluntary minorities. Rather, the differences that are more problematic among involuntary minorities are differences in style and are oppositional in relation to White or mainstream culture. Moreover, it is more difficult for

interventionists and teachers without special training to detect the problems and help the students.

Involuntary minorities lack some instrumental factors that motivate voluntary minorities to cross cultural boundaries. The latter try to overcome cultural, language, and other barriers because they strongly believe that there will be a material payoff later. Involuntary minorities—who did not choose to come to the United States motivated by hope of economic success or political freedom—believe less strongly. Furthermore, they lack the positive dual frame of reference of the immigrants, who compare their progress in the United States with that of their peers "back home." Involuntary minorities compare their progress—if at all—with that of White Americans, and they usually conclude that they are worse off than they should be and blame Whites, the schools, and other societal institutions controlled by Whites. Thus, these minorities do not have as strong incentives merely to play the classroom game by the rules (Gibson, 1988).

THE INDIVIDUAL IN COLLECTIVE ADAPTATION

We have described what appears to be the dominant pattern for each type of minority. But when we enter a minority community, whether of voluntary or involuntary minorities, we usually find some students who are doing well in school and other students who are not. We also find that the members of each community know that some strategies enhance school success and other strategies do not. We may even learn about the kinds of individuals and subgroups who use the different strategies. However, the strategies of a voluntary minority community are not necessarily the same as those of the involuntary minorities (Ogbu, 1989).

Among the voluntary minorities there appears to be a collective orientation toward making good grades in school and there also appear to be social pressures, including peer pressures, that encourage making good grades. In addition, community gossips promote striving for school success. Partly to avoid ridicule (which may extend to one's family), criticism, and isolation, voluntary minority youths tend to utilize those strategies that enhance their chances to succeed in school. The community also appears to use both tangible and symbolic means to encourage school striving. While successful members of the group may live outside the ethnic neighborhood, they tend to maintain social membership there and participate in activities in which they mix informally with the residents. They thus provide concrete evidence to the youth both that they can succeed through education and that they can be bona fide members of the community in spite of their success. Finally, voluntary minority students are eager to utilize information and resources available in school.

For involuntary minorities the situation is somewhat different. Although making good grades is strongly verbalized by students, parents, and the community as a desirable goal, there is less community and family pressure to achieve it. For example, there rarely is any stigma attached to being a poor student, and there are no community gossips criticizing a poor student or his or her family. As for peer groups, their collective orientation is probably against academic striving. Therefore, peer pressures discourage making good grades. Students who adopt attitudes and behaviors enhancing school success or who make good grades may be subjected to negative peer pressures, including criticism and isolation.

Under this circumstance, involuntary minority youths who want to succeed academically often consciously choose from a variety of secondary strategies to shield them from the peer pressures and other detracting forces of the community. The secondary strategies are over and above the conventional strategy of adopting proper academic attitudes, hard work, and perseverance. These strategies provide the context in which the student can practice the conventional strategy.

I will use Black students as an example of involuntary minorities employing secondary strategies. I have identified among them the following strategies, some promoting school success, some not.

1. Emulation of Whites or cultural passing (i.e., adopting "White" academic attitudes and behaviors or trying to behave like middle-class White students). Some students say, "If it takes acting like White people to do well in school, I'll do that." Such students get good grades. The problem is, however, that they usually experience isolation from other Black students, resulting in high psychological costs.

2. Accommodation without assimilation—an alternation model—a characteristic strategy among voluntary minorities. A student adopting this strategy behaves according to school norms while at school, but at home in the community behaves according to Black norms. One school counselor in Stockton described this strategy this way: "Their motto seems to be 'Do your Black thing [in the community] but know the White man thing [at school]'." Black students who adopt this strategy do not pay the psychological costs that attend White emulators.

3. Camouflage (i.e., disguising true academic attitudes and behaviors), using a variety of techniques. One technique is to become a jester or class clown. Since peer group members are not particularly interested in how well a student is doing academically, the student claims to lack interest in school, that schoolwork/homework or getting good grades is not important. The camouflaging student studies in secret. The good grades of camouflaging students are attributed to their "natural smartness." Another way of camouflaging is to become involved in "Black activities." If a Black athlete gets As, there's no harm done.

4. Involvement in church activities. This also promotes school success.

5. Attending private schools. For some, this is a successful way to get away from peer groups.

6. Mentors. Having a mentor is another success-enhancing strategy.

7. Protection. A few students secure the protection of bullies from peer pressures in return for helping the bullies with their homework.

8. Remedial and intervention programs. Some students succeed because they participate in such a program.

9. Encapsulation. Many Black youths, unfortunately, become encapsulated in peer group logic and activities. These students don't want to do the White man's thing or don't consider schooling important for a variety of reasons. They don't do their schoolwork. Many fail.

WHAT CAN BE DONE

Prerequisites

Recognize that there are different kinds of cultural/language differences and that the different types arise for different reasons or circumstances.

Recognize that there are different types of minority groups and that the minority types are associated with the different types of cultural/language differences.

Recognize that all minority children face problems of social adjustment and academic performance in school because of cultural/language differences. However, while problems faced by bearers of primary cultural differences are superficially similar to those of bearers of secondary cultural differences, they are fundamentally different. The reason lies in the difference in the relationship between the two types of cultural differences and White American mainstream culture.

Helping Children With Primary Cultural/Language Differences

Most problems caused by primary cultural differences are due to differences in cultural content and practice. One solution is for teachers and interventionists to learn about the students' cultural backgrounds and use this knowledge to organize their classrooms and programs, to help students learn what they teach, to help students get along with one another, to communicate with parents, and the like. Teachers and interventionists can learn about the students' cultures through

(a) observation of children's behavior in the classroom and on playgrounds, (b) asking children questions about their cultural practices and preferences, (c) talking with parents about their cultural practices and preferences, (d) doing research on various ethnic groups with children in school, and (e) studying published works on children's ethnic groups.

Some problems caused by primary cultural differences can also be solved through well-designed and implemented multicultural education. Such multicultural education must be based on actual knowledge of the cultures and languages of the children's ethnic groups, how they differ from mainstream culture and language, and the kinds of problems they generate.

Helping Children With Secondary Cultural/Language Differences

First, teachers and interventionists must recognize that involuntary minority children come to school with cultural and language frames of reference that are not only different from but probably oppositional to those of the mainstream and school. Second, teachers and interventionists should study the histories and cultural adaptations of involuntary minorities in order to understand the bases and nature of the groups' cultural and language frames of reference as well as the children's sense of social identity. This knowledge will help them understand why these factors affect the process of minority schooling, particularly their school orientations and behaviors.

Third, special counseling and related programs should be used (a) to help involuntary minority students learn to separate attitudes and behaviors enhancing school success from those that lead to linear acculturation or "acting White" and (b) to help the students to avoid interpreting the former as a threat to their social identity and sense of security.

Fourth, programs are needed to increase students' adoption of the strategy of "accommodation without assimilation," "alternation model," or "playing the classroom game." The essence of this strategy is that students should recognize and accept the fact that they can participate in two cultural or language frames of reference for different purposes without losing their own cultural and language identity or undermining their loyalty to the minority community. They should learn to practice "when in Rome, do as the Romans do," without becoming Romans.

We have found from ethnographic studies (Ogbu & Hickerson, 1980) that whereas voluntary minority students try to learn to act according to school norms and expectations, involuntary minority students do not necessarily do so. Instead, they emphasize learning how to manipulate "the system," how to deal with or respond to White people and schools controlled by White people or their minority representatives. This problem should be addressed. A related approach that can be built into multicultural education programs is teaching the students their own responsibility for their academic performance and school adjustment.

Finally, society can help reorient minority youths toward more academic striving for school credentials for future employment by (a) creating more jobs in general, (b) eliminating the job ceiling against minorities, and (c) providing better employment opportunities for minorities.

The Role of the Involuntary Minority Community

The involuntary minority community can and should play an important part in changing the situation for three reasons. First, some of the needed changes can be most effectively brought about through community effort. Second, minority children do not succeed or fail only because of what schools do or do not do, but also because of what the community does. Third, our comparative research suggests that the social structure and relationship within the minority communities could be a significant influence on students' educational orientations and behaviors.

At this point in my research I suggest four ways in which the involuntary minority community can encourage academic striving and success

among its children. One is to teach the children to separate attitudes and behaviors that lead to academic success from attitudes and behaviors that lead to a loss of ethnic identity and culture or language. This can be achieved partly by successful members of the group retaining their social membership in the community and not dissociating themselves from the neighborhood, labeling the less successful invidiously as "underclass," and so on. Second, the involuntary minority community should provide the children with concrete evidence that its members appreciate and value academic success as much as they appreciate and value achievements in sports, athletics, and entertainment.

Third, the involuntary minority community must teach the children to recognize and accept the responsibility for their school adjustment and academic performance. One difference between voluntary and involuntary minorities is that the former place a good deal of responsibility on the children for their school behavior and academic performance (Gibson, 1988).

Finally, the involuntary minority middle class needs to reevaluate and change its role vis-à-vis the community. We have discovered in our comparative research two contrasting models of middle class relationship with minority community which we suspect have differential effects on minority school success. The first model is, apparently, characteristic of voluntary minorities. Here successful, educated, and professional individuals, such as business people, doctors, engineers, lawyers, social workers, and university professors, appear to retain their social membership in the community, although they generally reside outside predominantly minority neighborhoods. Such people regard their accomplishments as a positive contribution to their community, a community, not just individual, achievement. The community, in turn, interprets their accomplishments in a similar manner. The successful members participate in community events where they interact with the youth and less successful adults informally and outside their official roles as representatives of the welfare, police, school district, or White-controlled companies. In this community, the middle class provides concrete evidence to young people that school success pays *and* that school success and economic and professional success in the wider society are compatible with collective identity and bona fide membership in the minority community.

CONCLUSION

Involuntary minorities seem to have a model that probably does not have much positive influence on schooling. Members of involuntary minorities seem to view professional success as "a ticket" to leave their community both physically and socially, to get away from those who have not "made it." People seek education and professional success, as it were, in order to leave their minority community. White Americans and their media reinforce this by praising those who have made their way out of the ghetto, barrio, or reservation. The middle-class minorities do not generally interpret their achievements as an indication that "their community is making it"; neither does the community interpret their achievements as an evidence of the "development" or "progress" of its members. The middle class may later return to or visit the community with "programs," or as "advocates" for those left behind or as representatives of White institutions. They rarely participate in community events where they interact outside these roles with the youth and the less successful community members. Thus, the involuntary minority middle class does not provide adequate concrete evidence to the youth and the less successful that school success leads to social and economic success in later adult life. The involuntary minority middle class must rethink its role vis-à-vis the minority youth. What is needed is for the middle class to go beyond programs, advocacy, and institutional representation to reaffiliate with the community socially.

ENDNOTE

An earlier version of this article was presented as an invited address to Division D, AERA, Annual Meet-ing, Chicago, March 1991. This article was revised June 1992.

REFERENCES

Appleton, N. (1983). *Cultural pluralism in education: Theoretical foundations.* New York: Longmans.

Au, K. H. (1981). Participant structure in a reading lesson with Hawaiian children: Analysis of a culturally appropriate instructional event. *Anthropology and Education Quarterly, 10*(2), 91–115.

Baker, G. C. (1978). The role of the school in transmitting the culture of all learners in a free and democratic society. *Educational Leadership, 36,* 134–138.

Banks, J. (Ed.). (1981). *Multicultural education: Theory and practice.* Boston: Allyn & Bacon.

Banks, J. (1989a). Integrating the curriculum with ethnic content: Approaches and guidelines. In J. A. Banks & C. A. Banks (Eds.), *Multicultural education* (pp. 189–207). Needham Heights, MA: Allyn & Bacon.

Banks, J. (1989b). Multicultural education: Characteristics and goals. In J. A. Banks & C. A. Banks (Eds.), *Multicultural education* (pp. 2–26). Needham Heights, MA: Allyn & Bacon.

Banks, J. A., & Shin, B. J. (1981). The nature of multiethnic education. In J. A. Banks & B. J. Shin (Eds.), *Multiethnic education.* Washington, DC: National Education Association.

Baptiste, H. P., Jr. (1979). The rekindling of cultural pluralism. In H. P. Baptiste & M. L. Baptiste (Eds.), *Developing multicultural education process in classroom instruction: Competencies for teachers* (pp. 9–17). Washington, DC: University Press of America.

Baugh, J. (1984). *Black street speech: Its history, structure, and survival.* Austin, TX: University of Texas Press.

Bennett, W. J. (1984). *To reclaim a legacy: A report on the humanities in higher education.* Washington, DC: National Endowment for the Humanities.

Bloom, A. (1987). *The closing of the American mind: How higher education has failed democracy and impoverished the souls of today's students.* New York: Simon & Schuster.

Boykin, A. W. (1980, November). *Reading achievement and the sociocultural frame of reference of Afro American children.* Paper presented at NIE Roundtable Discussion on Issues in Urban Reading: Washington, DC: The National Institute of Education.

Bullivant, B. M. (1981). *The pluralist dilemma in education.* Sydney, Australia: George Allen & Unwin.

Bullock, H. A. (1970). *A history of Negro education in the South from 1619 to the present.* New York: Praeger.

Byers, P., & Byers, H. (1972). Non-verbal communication and the education of children. In C. B. Cazden, D. Hymes, & V. John (Eds.), *Functions of language in the classroom.* New York: Teachers College Press.

Carroll, T. G., & Schensul, J. J. (Eds.). (1990). Cultural diversity and American education: Visions of the future [Special issue]. *Education and Urban Society, 22*(4).

Castile, G. P., & Kushner, G. (Eds.). (1981). *Persistent peoples: Cultural enclaves in perspective.* Tucson, AZ: University of Arizona Press.

Chung, J. P-L. (1992). *The out-of-language and social experience of a clique of Chinese immigrant students: An ethnography of a process of social identity formation.* Unpublished Doctoral Dissertation, State University of New York at Buffalo.

Closs, M. P. (Ed.). (1986). *Native American mathematics.* Austin, TX: University of Texas Press.

DeVos, G. A. (1967). Essential elements of caste: Psychological determinants in structural theory. In G. A. DeVos & H. Wagatsuma (Eds.), *Japan's invisible race: Caste in culture and personality* (pp. 332–384). Berkeley, CA: University of California Press.

DeVos, G. A. (1973). Japan's outcastes: The problem of the Burakumin. In B. Whitaker (Ed.), *The fourth world: Victims of group oppression* (pp. 307–327). New York: Schocken.

DeVos, G. A. (1984, April). *Ethnic persistence and role degradation: An illustration from Japan.* Paper presented at the American-Soviet Symposium on Contemporary Ethnic Processes in the USA and the USSR. New Orleans, LA.

DeVos, G. A., & Lee, C. (1981). *Koreans in Japan.* Berkeley, CA: University of California Press.

Dumont, R. V., Jr. (1972). Learning English and how to be silent: Studies in Sioux and Cherokee classrooms. In C. B. Cazden, D. Hymes, & V. John (Eds.), *Functions of language in the classroom.* New York: Teachers College Press.

Edmonds, R. (1986). Characteristics of effective schools. In U. Neisser (Ed.), *The school achievement of minority children: New perspectives* (pp. 93–104). Hillsdale, NJ: Erlbaum.

Essien-Udom, E. U. (1964). *Black nationalism: A search for identity in America.* New York: Dell.

Erickson, F., & Mohatt, G. (1982). Cultural organization of participant structure in two classrooms of Indian students. In G. D. Spindler (Ed.), *Doing the ethnography of schooling: Educational anthology in action* (pp. 132–175). New York: Holt.

Finn, C. E. (1989, July 16). Norms for the nation's schools. *The Washington Post,* p. B7.

Fordham, S. (1984, November). *Ethnography in a Black high school: Learning not to be a native.* Paper presented at the 83rd Annual Meeting of the American Anthropological Association, Denver.

Fordham, S., & Ogbu, J. U. (1986). Black students' school success: Coping with the "burden of 'acting white.' " *The Urban Review, 18*(3), 176–206.

Gay, G. (1979). Changing conceptions of multicultural education. In H. P. Baptiste and M. L. Baptiste (Eds.), *Developing multicultural process in classroom instruction: Competencies for Teachers.* (pp. 18–27). Washington, DC: University Press of America.

Gay, G. (1988). Designing relevant curricula for diverse learners. *Education and Urban Society, 20*(4), 327–340.

Gay, C. (1990). Achieving educational equality through curriculum design. *Phi Delta Kappan, 70,* 56–62.

Gay, J., & Cole, M. (1967). *The new mathematics and an old culture: A study of learning among the Kpelle of Liberia.* New York: Holt.

Gibson, M. A. (1976). Approaches to multicultural education in the United States: Some concepts and assumptions. *Anthropology Education Quarterly, 7*(4), 7–18.

Gibson, M. A. (1987). Playing by the Rules. In G. D. Spindler (Ed.), *Education and cultural process* (2nd ed., pp. 274–281). Prospect Heights, IL: Waveland Press.

Gibson, M. A. (1988). *Accommodation without assimilation: Sikh immigrants in an American high school.* Ithaca, NY: Cornell University Press.

Gibson, M. A. (1991). Ethnicity, gender, and social class: The social adaptation patterns of West Indian youths. In M. A. Gibson & J. U. Ogbu (Eds.), *Minority status and schooling: A comparative study of immigrants and involuntary minorities* (pp. 169–203). New York: Garland.

Gibson, M. A., & Ogbu, J. U. (Eds.). (1991). *Minority status and schooling: A comparative study of immigrants and involuntary minorities.* New York: Garland.

Grant, C., & Sleeter, C. E. (1986). Educational equity: Education that is multicultural and social reconstructionist. *Journal of Educational Equity and Leadership, 6*(2), 105–118.

Green, V. (1981). Blacks in the United States: The creation of an enduring people? In G. P. Castile & G. Kushner (Eds.), *Persistent peoples: Cultural enclaves in perspective* (pp. 69–77). Tucson, AZ: University of Arizona Press.

Gumperz, J. J. (1981). Conversational inference and classroom learning. In J. Green & C. Wallat (Eds.), *Ethnographic approaches to face-to-face interaction* (pp. 3–23). Norwood, NJ: Ablex.

Hall, R. A. (1978). *Black separatism in the United States.* Hanover, NH: The New England University Press.

Hirasawa, Y. (1989). *A policy study of the evolution of Dowa education in Japan.* Unpublished Doctoral Dissertation, Harvard University.

Hirsch, E. D. (1987). *Cultural literacy: What every American needs to know.* Boston: Houghton Mifflin.

Hirsch, E. D. (1988, July/August). *Cultural literacy: What every American needs to know,* E. D. Hirsch, Jr.: A post script by E. D. Hirsch, Jr. *Change,* pp. 22–26.

Holt, G. S. (1972). "Inversion" in Black communication. In T. Kochman (Ed.), *Rappin' and stylin' out: Communication in urban Black America* (pp. 152–159). Chicago: University of Illinois Press.

Ito, H. (1967). Japan's outcastes in the United States. In G. A. DeVos & H. Wagatasuma (Eds.), *Japan's invisible race: Caste in culture and personality* (pp. 200–221). Berkeley, CA: University of California Press.

Kochman, T. (1982). *Black and White styles in conflict.* Chicago: University of Chicago Press.

Kramer, B. J. (1991). Education and American Indians: The experience of the Ute Indian tribe. In M. A. Gibson & J. U. Ogbu (Eds.), *Minority status and schooling: A comparative study of immigrants and involuntary minorities* (pp. 287–307). New York: Garland.

Kristof, N. D. (1992, February 7). In China, the Koreans shine ("It's Our Custom"). *New York Times,* p. A7.

Lee, Y. (1991). *Koreans in Japan and United States.* In M. A. Gibson & J. U. Ogbu (Eds.), *Minority status and schooling: A comparative study of immigrants and involuntary minorities* (pp. 131–167). New York: Garland.

Luster, L. (1992). *Schooling, survival, and struggle: Black women and the GED.* Unpublished Doctoral Dissertation, Stanford University.

Matute-Bianchi, M. E. (1986). Ethnic identities and patterns of school success and failure among Mexican-descent and Japanese-American students in a California high school: An ethnographic analysis. *American Journal of Education, 95*(1), 233–255.

Ogbu, J. U. (1974). *The next generation: An ethnography of education in an urban neighborhood.* New York: Academic Press.

Ogbu, J. U. (1977). Racial stratification and education: The case of Stockton, California. *ICRD Bulletin, 12*(3), 1–26.

Ogbu, J. U. (1978). *Minority education and caste: The American system in cross-cultural perspective.* New York: Academic Press.

Ogbu, J. U. (1987). Variability in minority school performance: A problem in search of an explanation. *Anthropology and Education Quarterly, 18*(4), 312–334.

Ogbu, J. U. (1988). Diversity and equity in public education: Community forces and minority school adjustment and performance. In R. Haskins and D. Macrae (Eds.), *Policies for America's public schools: Teachers, equity, and indicators* (pp. 127–170). Norwood, NJ: Ablex.

Ogbu, J. U. (1989). The individual in collective adaptation: A framework for focusing on academic under performance and dropping out among involuntary minorities. In L. Weis, E. Farrar, & H. G. Petrie (Eds.), *Dropouts from schools: Issues, dilemmas and solutions* (pp. 181–204). Buffalo, NY: State University of New York Press.

Ogbu, J. U. (1990). Minority status and literacy in comparative perspective. *Daedalus, 119*(2), 141–168.

Ogbu, J. U. (1991). Low school performance as an adaptation: The case of Blacks in Stockton, California. In M. A. Gibson & J. U. Ogbu (Eds.), *Minority status and schooling: A comparative study of immigrants and involuntary minorities* (pp. 249–285). New York: Garland.

Ogbu, J. U., & Hickerson, R. (1980). *Survival strategies and role models in the ghetto.* University of California–Berkeley, Department of Anthropology, Special Project.

Ogbu, J. U., & Matute-Bianchi, M. E. (1986). Understanding factors in education: Knowledge, identity, and adjustment in schooling. In California State Department of Education, Bilingual Education Office, *Beyond language: Social and cultural factors in schooling language minority students* (pp. 73–142). Sacramento, CA: California State University–Los Angeles, Evaluation, Dissemination and Assessment Center.

Orr, E. W. (1987). *Twice as less: Black English and the performance of Black students in mathematics and science.* New York: Norton.

Passow, A. H. (1984). *Equity and excellence: Confronting the dilemma.* Paper presented at the First International Conference on Education in the 1990s, Tel Aviv, Israel.

Petroni, F. A. (1970). Uncle Toms: White stereotypes in the Black movement. *Human Organization, 29,* 260–266.

Philips, S. U. (1972). Participant structure and comunicative competence: Warm Springs children in community and classroom. In C. B. Cazden, D. Hymes, & V. John (Eds.), *Functions of language in the classroom.* New York: Teachers College Press.

Philips, S. U. (1976). Commentary: Access to power and maintenance of ethnic identity as goals of multi-cultural education. *Anthropology and Education Quarterly, 7*(4), 30–32.

Philips, S. U. (1983). *The invisible culture: Communication in classroom and community on the Warm Springs Indian Reservation.* New York: Longman.

Ramirez, M., & Castenada, A. (1974). *Cultural democracy, bicognitive development and education.* New York: Academic Press.

Rohlen, T. (1981). Education: Policies and prospects. In C. Lee & G. A. DeVos (Eds.), *Koreans in Japan: Ethnic conflicts and accommodation* (pp. 182–222). Berkeley, CA: University of California Press.

Rubalcava, M. (1991). *Locating transformative teaching in multicultural education.* Unpublished manuscript. University of California–Berkeley, Department of Anthropology, Special Project.

Shade, B. J. (1982). *Afro-American patterns of cognition.* Unpublished manuscript, Wisconsin Center for Educational Research, Madison, WI.

Shimahara, N. K. (1991). *Social mobility and education: Buraku in Japan.* In M. A. Gibson & J. U. Ogbu (Eds.), *Minority status and schooling: A comparative study of immigrants and involuntary minorities* (pp. 249–285). New York: Garland.

Sleeter, C. E., & Grant, C. A. (1987). An analysis of multicultural education in the United States. *Harvard Educational Review, 57*(4), 421–444.

Solomon, R. P. (1992). *The creation of separation: Black culture and struggle in an American high school.* Albany, NY: State University of New York Press.

Spicer, E. H. (1966). The process of cultural enslavement in Middle America. *36th Congress of International de Americanistas, Seville, 3,* 267–279.

Spicer, E. H. (1971). Persistent cultural systems: A comparative study of identity systems that can adapt to contrasting environments. *Science, 174,* 795–800.

Suarez-Orozco, M. M. (1987). Becoming somebody: Central American immigrants in U.S. inner-city schools. *Anthropology & Education Quarterly, 18*(4), 287–299.

Suzuki, B. H. (1984). Curriculum transformation for multicultural education. *Education and Urban Society, 16*(3), 294–322.

Taylor, M. J. & Hegarty, S. (1985). *The best of both worlds: A review of research into the education of pupils of South Asian origin.* Windsor, UK: National Foundation for Educational Research-Nelson.

Tomlinson, S. (1982). *A sociology of special education.* London, UK: Routledge & Kegan Paul.

Weis, L. (1985). *Between two worlds: Black students in an urban community college.* Boston: Routledge & Kegan Paul.

Woolard, K. A. (1981). *Ethnicity in education: Some problems of language and identify in Spain and the United States.* Unpublished manuscript. University of California–Berkeley, Department of Anthropology.

Yee, G. (1991). *The melting pot revisited: A literature review of current literature in multicultural education.* Unpublished manuscript. University of California–Berkeley Department of Anthropology, Special Project.

DISCUSSION QUESTIONS

1. In what ways does cultural inversion impact the academic achievement of minority students?

2. What is the relationship between primary differences, voluntary minority children, and learning?

3. How can understanding minority students' primary cultural and language frames of reference aid educators?

4. What steps should be taken to facilitate the academic success of minority students with secondary cultural language differences?

5. How do minority communities influence students' educational perceptions and behaviors?

The Gender Issue

NEL NODDINGS

FOCUSING QUESTIONS

1. *How has the standard of the male experience influenced curriculum implementation?*
2. *What kinds of learning activities might diminish a bias towards males as the dominant culture?*
3. *In what ways can educators acknowledge the standards that are characteristic of women's culture?*
4. *What kind of curricular changes would be needed to incorporate standards common to women's and men's cultures?*
5. *How does imagery and symbolism influence perceptions of women's and men's cultures?*

The male experience is the standard not only in education but, more generally, in all of public policy. We must change the culture of schools— and the curriculum—to reflect both women's and men's perspectives.

Feminists often charge that the culture of schools, especially of secondary schools, is masculine (Grumet 1988). It's true that without realizing it, most of us look at gender issues in education with the masculine experience as the standard. What recommendations might emerge if we used the feminine perspective as our standard?

MEN'S CULTURE AS THE STANDARD

Because white men have long held most of the highly regarded positions in our society, we naturally use their experience when we think about gender, race, or ethnic equality. In an enlightened democracy, we want everyone to have access to the education and jobs formerly held by the fa-

vored group. Thus, some years ago, Congress passed legislation designed to provide more nearly equal resources for women's and men's sports in schools.

Considerable attention has also been given to attracting more women to mathematics and science. Indeed, observing a substantial lag between women's and men's participation in mathematics, researchers began to work on "the problem of women and mathematics." They did not ask what women were doing or how they had made their various choices. Rather, they assumed there was something wrong—with either women or schools—because women were not participating as men do in mathematics.

The male experience is the standard not only in education but, more generally, in all of public policy. It is supposed, for example, that women want access to the military and, even, to combat roles, and of course some women do want such access. Most professions monitor the number of women entering and see this number as an important social indicator. For the most part, this attention to equality is commendable, and few of us would suggest relaxing it.

Problems clearly arise, however, as a result of using the male experience as the standard. Law, for example, has long used a "reasonable man" standard to evaluate certain actions. In recent years, bowing to gender sensitivities, the standard has been renamed the "reasonable person" standard. The new title seems to cover men and women equally, but it was developed over many years almost entirely from male experience. Much controversy has arisen around its application to women. Consider one example.

If a man, in the heat of passion, kills his wife or her lover after discovering an adulterous alliance, he is often judged guilty of voluntary manslaughter instead of murder. If, however, the killing occurs after a "reasonable person" would have cooled off, a verdict of murder is more often found.

What happens when we try to apply this standard to women? When a woman kills an abusive husband, she rarely does it in the heat of the moment. Most women do not have the physical strength to prevail in such moments. More often the killing occurs in a quiet time—sometimes when the husband is sleeping. The woman reports acting out of fear. Often she has lived in terror for years, and a threat to her children has pushed her to kill her abuser. Many legal theorists now argue that the reasonable man standard (even if it is called a reasonable person standard) does not capture the experience of reasonable women (Taylor 1986).

Another area of concern to feminists is pregnancy and job leave. If women's lives had been used as the standard from the start, feminists argue, one can be sure that job leaves for pregnancy would have been standard procedure. But because men do not become pregnant and men have devised the standard, women must accept such leaves as a form of sick leave.

Many other examples could be given, but here I want to look at education and raise some questions rarely asked. For example, instead of asking why women lag behind men in mathematics, we might ask the following: Why do men lag behind women in elementary school teaching, early childhood education, nursing, full-time parenting, and like activities? Is there something wrong with men or with schools that this state of affairs persists?

WOMEN'S CULTURE AS THE STANDARD

Faced with the questions just asked, it is tempting to answer facilely that "these jobs just don't pay," and of course there is some truth in that. But elementary teaching often pays as well as high school teaching, and yet many more men enter high school teaching. In fact, neither teaching nor nursing pay as poorly as many occupations men enter in considerable numbers.

If we admit that pay is a significant factor, we still have to ask why work traditionally associated with women is so consistently ill paid. Why has so small a value been attached to work we all admit is important? It is hard to escape the conclusion that some men devalue work they have never done themselves and do not wish to do.

If women had set the standard when schools were founded and curriculums designed, what might our students be studying today? Perhaps schools would be giving far more attention to family and developmental studies. It also seems likely that these studies would not be regarded as soft, easy, or merely elective. A rigorous study of infancy, childhood, adolescence, adulthood, and old age would be coupled with a generous amount of supervised practice in care of the young and elderly. The maintenance of caring relationships might be a central topic.

An objection might be raised that these are all matters to be learned at home—not in school. But, given the dramatic changes in social conditions since the end of World War II, fewer children seem to be learning about these subjects adequately. It is questionable whether most ever learned them adequately at home. Family relationships—human relationships—are at the very heart of life, and yet they are considered peripheral to serious learning. With family life at the center of the curriculum, we could teach history, literature, and science more meaningfully than we do now.

A curriculum based on women's experience would occupy volumes, and I obviously cannot present a comprehensive description here. But several large areas of study might be significantly transformed if women's experience were the standard. Before we look at a few, one important caveat should be entered.

Women, like men, are all different. It is misleading to talk of a unitary "women's experience" or "women's culture." Nevertheless, strong central tendencies affect women's experience. Whether or not particular women became mothers or were involved in caregiving occupations, they all faced the expectation that a certain kind of work was appropriate for women. Women's culture has emerged out of these expectations, the work itself, and resistance to it. When I speak of women's culture, I will be referring to this common experience.

EDUCATION FOR CITIZENSHIP

Usually when someone mentions education for citizenship, we think of courses in civics or problems of American democracy. A "citizen," in one traditional view, is a person of recognized public rank—someone entitled to the "privileges of a freeman."

Learning to take up the duties of a "freeman" is certainly important, and schools have long been charged with promoting this learning.

But there is another side to citizenship. Citizens are also inhabitants of communities, and here their duties are more positive and voluntary than those prescribed by law. Neighborliness, helpfulness, and politeness are all characteristics of people we like to live near. These are all qualities parents, especially mothers, have long tried to inculcate in their children. Given the massive social changes of the last 40 years—among them the reduction in time many mothers have available to teach their children these qualities—it may be that schools need to pay more attention to them.

Another neglected aspect of citizenship is manners. I am certainly not talking about which fork to use for a particular course at dinner, but I do think that we should educate for social life as well as intellectual life. We are alarmed when high school graduates cannot compute simple bills and the change they should expect. We should also be alarmed when they do not know how to dress, speak, or comport themselves in various settings.

Much more can be said on this subject, of course, but my main point is to draw attention to what we see when we consciously use women's culture as the standard for our educational assessments. Looking at citizenship, we see our mutual dependence on neighborliness, the graciousness of good manners, the desirability of good taste. Even when we consider what good citizens must not do, we see that people often refrain from harmful acts because they do not want to hurt their neighbors and because they want their respect. It is not always regard for abstract law that produces acceptable behavior.

SOCIAL CONSCIOUSNESS

If women's culture were taken more seriously in educational planning, social studies and history might have a very different emphasis. Instead of moving from war to war, ruler to ruler, one political campaign to the next, we would give far more attention to social issues. Even before women could vote, many were crusaders against child labor, advocates for the mentally ill and retarded, teachers to immigrants, and, more generally, vigorous social reformers. (There are many sources of information on this topic; see, for example, Beard 1972, Brenzel 1983, Kinnear 1982, Smith 1970).

Many well-educated women in the 19th and early 20th century became involved in social issues because these were accepted as "women's work" and because they were unable to obtain positions commensurate with their educations (Rossiter 1982). Today we do not want to restrict women's activities to any particular sphere, but we should not devalue contributions women have made and are continuing to make to improve social conditions. Women's interest, as compared to men's interest, in social issues such as war, poverty, and childcare is revealed in a gender gap (about 20 percent) that still appears in both surveys and votes.

The point here is not so much the conventional one of insisting on the inclusion of women in history texts. More important, we must emphasize for all learners matters that have concerned women for centuries. Many contemporary feminists have this in mind when they suggest using women's culture as a standard for curricular decisions (Martin 1984, Tetreault 1986, Thompson 1986).

PEACE STUDIES

For centuries men have participated in warfare. The warrior has been as central to male culture as motherhood to female culture. It would be untrue, however, to say that men have promoted war and women have resisted it. Women, in fact, have often supported war (Elshtain 1987). But if we look at women's culture and the outstanding women admired within it, we find heroes steadfastly opposed to war. Jane Addams, much loved for her work at Hull House and in other social causes, firmly opposed U.S. participation in World War I. She lost a significant part of her political support as a result.

Women against war. Women tried very hard and very sensibly to stop World War I and to prevent World War II. The Women's International League for Peace and Freedom (WILPF) carried a peace proposal to 35 governments, and several male leaders acknowledged the good sense of the proposal—but the war went on. The group tried again at the 1919 Peace Conference to introduce measures designed to prevent a new war. After the second World War, Emily Greene Balch, the first Secretary General of the WILPF, was awarded the Nobel Peace Prize. Recounting this story, Brock-Utne quotes Gunnar Jahn, Director of the Nobel Institute:

I want to say so much that it would have been extremely wise if the proposal . . . had been accepted by the Conference. But few of the men listened to what the women had to say. . . . In our patriarchal world suggestions which come from women are seldom taken seriously. Sometimes it would be wise of the men to spare their condescending smiles (1985, p. 5).

And yet, if we consult an encyclopedia published in the late 1940s, we find half-page entries (with pictures) of Generals Pershing and Patton but no entry for Emily Balch.

In discussing citizenship and social consciousness, I've recommended not that we eliminate the male standard and substitute a female one but, rather, that we consider both traditions as we plan curriculum and instruction. On the issue of peace, however, many feminists think that more drastic revision is required. If our children and the world itself are to be preserved, the warrior model has to give way to a model that emphasizes caring relations and not relations of force and domination (Noddings 1989).

The ethics of care. Much is being written today about the ethics of care (Noddings 1984) and maternal thinking (Ruddick 1989). Motherhood has been an important feature of women's traditional culture, and experience in the direct care of children gives rise to interests in their preservation, growth, self-esteem, and acceptance in society. (Not all women have been mothers, of course, and not all mothers have been good mothers, but we select the best thinking and best examples as a standard for educational inclusion.) The logic of motherhood includes "preservative love" (Ruddick 1989), and this love should be in powerful opposition to war. Indeed, as Ruddick and others have described it, world protection—particularly protection from war—is a natural extension of maternal work.

We have to be careful not to oversimplify here. On the one hand, some men have also participated passionately in the quest for peace, but these men's voices have not reflected nor transformed the dominant male culture. On the other, women have often interpreted preservative love as a dedication to safeguarding not just the lives of their own children but a way of life. Preserving a way of life, paradoxically, has meant death for many children. But, despite the empirical fact of some women's support of war, the logic of maternal life is clearly anti-war, and the most eloquent voices of female culture have opposed war. Further, the arguments for peace advanced by women are frequently directly connected to the basic elements of life—love, birth, nurturing, growing, holding, creating. The distinctiveness of women's arguments and the representativeness of the voice for peace in women's culture suggest a far greater role for a female standard in education.

Women's call for peace is distinctive in another way. Many insist that peace must be studied for itself, not considered simply as the cessation of war. Peace, not war, must become central in our thinking. Further, we must not suppose that the world is "at peace" simply because major nations are not fighting. As long as substantial numbers of people live in daily fear of violence, the world is not "at peace."

Men's violence toward women. For feminists, eliminating the violence women suffer at the hands of men is part of the peace movement. Morgan has written forcefully on the cult of masculinity that maintains this violence—and war and terrorism as well:

> He glares out from the reviewing stands, where the passing troops salute him. He strides in skin-tight black leather across the stage, then sets his guitar on fire. He straps a hundred pounds of weaponry to his body, larger than life on the film screen. He peers down from huge glorious-leader posters, and confers with himself it summit meetings. He drives the fastest cars and wears the most opaque sunglasses. He lunges into the prize-fight ring to the sounds of cheers. Whatever he dons becomes a uniform. He is a living weapon. Whatever he does at first appalls, then becomes faddish. We are told that women lust to have him. We are told that men lust to be him (1989, pp. 24–25).

Both men and women suffer in a culture dominated by such images. A culture that ac-cepts—even admires—such models does not hate war; it only hates to lose wars. It does not abhor violence; it merely deplores the deglamorization of violence. Today such themes must be carefully examined in educational settings.

CONCLUSION

What, then, can we do to put some of these concepts into practice? To begin, citizenship education must be broadened to include decent, responsible behavior in personal and family relationships. Both men and women have much to learn in this area. Further, social consciousness should be a central theme in social studies, literature, and science. And the study of peace must be extended beyond an analysis of nations at war to a careful and continuing study of what it means to live without the fear of violence.

Schools must give more attention to issues and practices that have long been central in women's experience, especially to childrearing, intergenerational responsibility, and nonviolent resolution of conflict. Given current conditions of poverty, crime, and child neglect, our society may be ready to raise its evaluation of "women's work." Using standards that arise in women's culture can guide us in our educational planning toward a more caring community and a safer world.

REFERENCES

Beard, M. R. (1972). *Women as Force in History.* New York: Collier Books.

Brenzel, B. M. (1983). *Daughters of the State: A Social Portrait of the First Reform School for Girls in North America, 1856–1905.* Cambridge, Mass.: MIT Press.

Brock-Utne, B. (1985). *Educating for Peace: A Feminist Perspective.* New York and Oxford: Pergamon Press.

Elshtain, J. B. (1987). *Women and War.* New York: Basic Books.

Grummet, M. R. (1988). *Bitter Milk.* Amherst: University of Massachusetts Press.

Kinnear, M. (1982). *Daughters of Time: Women in the Western Tradition.* Ann Arbor: University of Michigan Press.

Martin, J. R. (1984). "Bringing Women into Educational Thought." *Educational Theory* 4, 34: 341–354.

Morgan, R. (1989). *The Demon Lover: On the Sexuality of Terrorism.* New York: W. W. Norton.

Noddings, N. (1984). *Caring: A Feminine Approach to Ethics and Moral Education.* Berkeley: University of California Press.

Noddings, N. (1989). *Women and Evil.* Berkeley and Los Angeles: University of California Press.

Rossiter, M. W. (1982). *Women Scientists in America: Struggles and Strategies to 1940.* Baltimore and London: Johns Hopkins University Press.

Ruddick. S. (1989). *Maternal Thinking: Towards a Politics of Peace.* Boston: Beacon Press.

Smith, P. (1970). *Daughters of the Promised Land.* Boston and Toronto: Little, Brown.

Taylor, L. (1986). "Provoked Reason in Men and Women: Heat-of-Passion Manslaughter and Imperfect Self-Defense." *UCLA Law Review* 33: 1679–1735.

Tetreault, M. K. (1986). "The Journey from Male-Defined to Gender-Balanced Education." *Theory Into Practice* 25: 227–234.

Thompson, P. J. (1986). Beyond Gender: Equity Issues in Home Economics Education." *Theory Into Practice* 25: 276–283.

DISCUSSION QUESTIONS

1. How should curricularists address gender issues?

2. In what way can attending to the context of learning environments facilitate a social consciousness?

3. What changes to textbooks and classroom materials should be considered in order to teach students about the standards characteristic of women's culture?

4. Should school-based curriculum reflect the male standard, the female standard, or both? Why? Why not?

5. How would integration of the male and female standards impact curriculum and instruction?

National Standards and Curriculum Reform

DIANE RAVITCH

FOCUSING QUESTIONS

1. *What is the purpose of establishing national standards?*
2. *Should the federal government be more involved in setting national goals and standards of achievement?*
3. *What role should states and local school districts play in creating national goals?*
4. *How will the adoption of national standards promote success for all students?*
5. *Will national goals promote educational excellence and equity? Why? Why not?*

In a school, standards tell students, teachers, and parents where their efforts are leading, and they make a clear case to community members when a principal calls upon them to support their school.

Principals well know the difficulty of demonstrating success when the goal itself is hazy. How can one succeed when there is no agreed-upon definition of success? Today's principal is expected to take on addiction, abuse, violence, AIDS, and family disintegration. A highly successful school, by some definitions, is a safe haven that manages to turn out more or less the same number of students it took in. Yet, professional educators know—and the public increasingly realizes—that no school is truly successful unless it provides students with the opportunity to learn challenging subject matter.

The movement to create national academic standards expresses a new determination that we must have high expectations for all students. For the past generation, we have lacked consensus about what students should know and be able to do. Textbooks have been progressively "dumbed down," and graduation requirements branded "elitist," while the scope of public demands on schools has expanded to encompass roles that parents and communities were once willing and expected to play. We have learned, I think, that schools cannot be all things to all people, and that they must focus their energy on developing the minds, talents, and abilities of students to the fullest.

GOALS, STANDARDS SET THE DIRECTION

Public support for the development of national standards was expressed in 1989, when President Bush and the 50 governors met in an historic education summit that led to the adoption of six National Education Goals, including the pledges that, by the year 2000 all American students will master challenging subject matter in history, English, geography, mathematics, and science (Goal 3); and American students will be first in the world in math and science (Goal 4).

In early 1992, the congressionally-established bipartisan National Council on Education Standards and Testing released its historic recommendations calling for the development of voluntary national standards and a voluntary national system of assessments. Both the Goals and the National Council's recommendations have been driving forces in the standards movement. National standards also have broad public and professional support. Eighty-one percent of the public and 65 percent of teachers believe that American education needs national standards.

The National Council of Teachers of Mathematics (NCTM) has led the way in demonstrating the power of national standards as a lever for education reform. Developed by teachers of mathematics during the past several years, the NCTM standards create a coherent plan for mathematics education from kindergarten through the twelfth grade. More than 40 states have made the NCTM standards the basis for changing mathematics education, with the result that instructional reliance on rote memorization and repetition is giving way to an emphasis on solving problems, applying mathematics to practical situations, and using hands-on approaches to learning. In response to the NCTM standards, math assessment is changing, textbooks are being rewritten, and teachers are being retrained.

Following the lead of the NCTM, the Department of Education is supporting the development of national standards by independent, nongovernmental organizations in other subject areas. In the fall of 1991, the Department funded the National Academy of Sciences to lead a consensus process of science educators to establish what all children should know and be able to do in science. In collaboration with the National Endowment for the Humanities (NEH), the Department is also supporting the development of national standards in American and world history. The National Center for History in the Schools at the University of California at Los Angeles will lead this effort.

In 1992, the Department of Education, with the NEH and the National Endowment for the Arts, is underwriting the development of voluntary national standards in the arts by a broad consortium of arts education groups representing music, dance, theater, and the visual arts. Similar efforts to develop voluntary standards by professional consensus are underway in the fields of geography, civics, and English.

More and more schools, districts, and states are recognizing that high expectations are a necessary ingredient for stimulating high student achievement. For example, the superintendent of the District of Columbia schools recently announced that, in the future, all district graduates will be expected to study algebra, as well as two years of foreign language.

New York City schools have also recently announced their intention to require all students to take algebra. And the College Board's Equity 2000 project, aimed at increasing the pool of minority students prepared for college, is encouraging more students to take more math in six school districts. The existence of national standards will promote this kind of activity in every major subject and probably every major school district.

National standards will not create a national curriculum. They are goals, and there are many ways to reach those goals. They are being developed by independent, nongovernmental organizations—and they will stand or fall according to their acceptance by teachers, schools, and the wider public. The Department's role in developing national standards is to help get these activities underway—and then to get out of the way. Once the grants are made to these groups, neither the Department of Education nor any other agency will exercise control over their standards-setting work.

EXCELLENCE, EQUITY IN EDUCATION

When standards are set in place, a successful school is one that provides both excellence and equity—a challenging education for every child. When a school adopts high standards for all, it is telling each of its students clearly, "We respect you and believe that you can learn." Standards for what all children should know and be able to do ensure that the principal, teachers, and students in a school are all working toward the same ends.

Standards are the guarantor of excellence and equity in education. Just as standards obviously drive student athletes' training and performance, standards can improve the quality of education and students' academic performance. Standards define what every child—not just a few—should have the opportunity to learn. When institutionalized throughout an education system, they guarantee poor parents that their children will have the same educational opportunity as the children of affluent parents—that their children will have access to the same challenging courses and will be expected to strive for the same standards.

Standards are the principal's best defense against public or parental complacency, and a sound basis for instructional leadership in a school. When curricula based upon high standards for all students are adopted, they provide coherence to a school's program. They make expectations of all members of a school community clear, and they guide the setting of a school's priorities.

National standards based on high expectations of all students provide a vision of what is possible in education. But the articulation of high standards will not instantaneously lift the quality of American education. The existence of high standards no more guarantees that children will achieve them than the existence of great literature, well-documented scientific discoveries, and compelling histories and biographies has guaranteed that students will be well educated in those fields.

If students are to achieve high standards, a state, community, or individual school must not only adopt high standards but also weave them into the whole fabric of the school or education system. High standards should be the basis for the improvement of instruction, classroom materials, teacher education, and assessments.

A FOUNDATION FOR REFORM

National standards will not provide a quick cure-all to the problems in American schools; but they nonetheless offer the foundation for systemwide educational reform. While schools may continue to need more resources or a redirection of their resources, and while their students will continue to face the social realities that schools alone cannot correct, standards will support schools in reclaiming their unique role of educating students.

In addition to promoting the establishment of national standards, the Department of Education is supporting systemwide reform in the states based on standards. We are funding the development by states of K–12 curriculum frameworks based upon high standards in mathematics and science, and we plan also to do so in history, English, geography, the arts, and foreign languages.

When adopted by a state, these curriculum frameworks—describing what every child in the state should know and be able to do in each subject—should become the basis for realigning assessments, teacher education, and textbooks to high standards. Once a state (or a community, or a school) decides what it wants children to learn, then it should take steps to ensure that teachers master what they are supposed to teach, and that the tests used are reliable indicators of the extent to which children are actually achieving high standards.

The Department of Education is seeking funding from Congress to help states and regions that are working to improve their assessments. We are also supporting research and development of new assessments, such as "performance assessments," that engage students in actually demonstrating what they know. (Our students are already familiar with performance assessments outside the academic realm. Consider what a Girl Scout or Boy Scout must do to earn a merit badge, or the skills a student must develop in order to pass a driver's test.)

The Department of Education does not support the development of a single national test. New kinds of assessments should be tied to high standards for what all young people should know and be able to do. They should, furthermore, be valid, reliable, and fair, as well as comparable measures of whether students are meeting high standards in core subjects.

What can principals do to enable their students to achieve to high standards?

- First, they must set clear goals—standards— for their students' achievement. If the state or district has not adopted standards, then the school itself should identify benchmarks of students' success.
- Every school should have ways to evaluate whether its students are meeting high standards. Some states are already putting good standards-based assessments in place. But many schools are also developing new ways to evaluate their students, through means such as performance assessments and portfolio assessments (which collect actual student work over time).
- Teachers should be closely involved in setting high standards and in rethinking the school's curriculum. For example, principals should involve the school's respected "lead" teachers in setting clear benchmarks for student learning, in selecting good texts and assessments, and in training new teachers. In addition, raising the level of instruction based on high standards will require ongoing collaboration among teachers in developing challenging courses and lesson plans. As Harold Stevenson and James Stigler describe in their new book, *The Learning Gap,* teacher collaboration is one of the keys to high achievement in Asian schools. Asian teachers' schedules are structured to allow them to work extensively together in designing engaging instruction for their classes.
- Successful schools are those that have created atmospheres in which learning and achievement are valued, and that respect students, parents, and teachers as partners in the educational enterprise.

Before you set out on a journey, you have to know where you are going. Likewise, before you can realistically expect to win support for any enterprise, you have to be able to communicate its mission to others. In a school, standards tell students, teachers, and parents where their efforts are leading; and they make a clear case to the community when a principal calls upon it to support its school.

CONCLUSION

Successful standards-based reform requires fundamental reconstruction of educational institutions and systems, so that high standards become the basis not only of curriculum but of textbooks and other instructional materials, of assessments, of graduation requirements, and of teacher education, certification, and training.

But standards will only have this effect when a school, community, or state embraces high standards but also takes the necessary steps to realign curriculum, textbooks, assessments, and teacher training and education to them—so that the whole school or education system is consciously directing its energies toward the same goal.

One of the great failures of our public education system has been that, in rooting out inequities, we have all too often crushed excellence as well. Too many educators have subscribed to the notion that anything excellent is "elitist" and must therefore be abandoned, diluted, or destroyed. In fact, we should aim to provide academically challenging education to all students. All students, regardless of who their parents are, need an excellent education that prepares them for a responsible, productive, thoughtful life.

International assessments during the last 25 years witness that American education is assuredly not excellent. In those half-dozen international assessments, our students have usually placed at or near the bottom. And studies of student transcripts and course taking show that American education is far from equitable. Where 47 percent of eighth graders from families with incomes above $50,000 took algebra in 1988, only 21 percent of eighth graders from families with income of less than $15,000 took algebra.

With standards and assessments, academic excellence becomes more than a vague matter of parental and public perceptions, or of students' self-opinion. Excellence becomes a matter of parents' and educators' high, concrete expectations and of students' hard work and actual achievement of high standards.

DISCUSSION QUESTIONS

1. How will the adoption of national standards affect curriculum delivery?
2. How will standards provide coherence to school-based curriculum?
3. Who should be involved in the process of developing rational standards?
4. What types of curriculum modifications will be needed?
5. What kind of assessments that correspond to national goals will be necessary?

35

Reform Versus Reality

HAROLD HODGKINSON

FOCUSING QUESTIONS

1. *What can schools do to assist children from atypical families?*
2. *What model of curriculum delivery should be employed in schools that have a majority of minorities?*
3. *How can day care agencies facilitate the success of disadvantaged students?*
4. *How can schools engage parents as partners in their children's education?*
5. *How do discrepancies in per pupil expenditures affect educational delivery?*
6. *What alternative conceptions of curriculum delivery should be considered for at-risk students?*

With regard to the problems of children in America, President Bush has said, "We have more will than wallet." Mr. Hodgkinson thinks the President has it backward.

To begin, think of the following analogy. American education is like a house. This house was beautiful and well maintained, one of the nicest houses in the world. But over time, the owners allowed the house to deteriorate. First, a leak in the roof developed, allowing water to enter the attic, then to trickle down to the second floor, and then to the main floor. Floors buckled, plaster fell from the walls, electric system rusted, windows began to fall out. The owners, returning after a long absence, hastily repaired the windows, the plaster, and the electric motors—but they neglected to fix the roof. The owners were surprised and angry when, after all their efforts, the house continued to deteriorate.

Basically, the publication of *A Nation at Risk* marked the return of the owners after a long absence to find education's house badly deterio-

rated. The first major sign of deterioration was declining scores on the Scholastic Aptitude Test (SAT), which Americans often hold to be *the* single barometer of educational quality. Since that time, a blizzard of education reform proposals has fallen, and states have raised the graduation standards for high schools, installed minimum standards for moving from one grade to the next, required new teachers to pass special examinations before being allowed to teach, instituted choice and magnet school programs, and so on.

But so far, there has been no change in high school graduation rates, in most test scores, or in other indicators of "quality." After nearly a decade, we have fixed the plaster in education's house, installed new windows, and repaired the electric motors. *But the roof still leaks.* Until we fix the roof, the house continues to deteriorate.

The leaky roof in our educational house is a metaphor for the spectacular changes that have occurred in the nature of the children who come to school. Until we pay attention to these changes, our tinkering with the rest of the house will continue to produce no important results. The fact is that at least one-third of the nation's children are at risk of school failure even before they enter kindergarten. The schools did not cause these deficits, and neither did the youngsters. A few examples may suffice:

▬ Since 1987, one-fourth of all preschool children in the U.S. have been in poverty.

▬ Every year, about 350,000 children are born to mothers who were addicted to cocaine during pregnancy. Those who survive birth become children with strikingly short attention spans, poor coordination, and much worse. Of course, the schools will have to teach these children, and getting such children ready for kindergarten costs around $40,000 each—about the same as for children with fetal alcohol syndrome.

▬ Today, 15 million children are being reared by single mothers, whose family income averages about $11,400 in 1988 dollars (within $1,000 of the poverty line). The average family income for a married couple with children is slightly over $34,000 a year.

▬ Twenty percent of America's preschool children have not been vaccinated against polio.

▬ The "Norman Rockwell" family—a working father, a housewife mother, and two children of school age—constitutes only 6% of U.S. households today.

▬ One-fourth of pregnant mothers receive no physical care of any sort during the crucial first trimester of pregnancy. About 20% of handicapped children would not be impaired had their mothers had one physical exam during the first trimester, which could have detected potential problems.

▬ At least two million school-age children have no adult supervision at all after school. Two million more are being reared by *neither* parent.

▬ On any given night, between 50,000 and 200,000 children have no home. (In 1988, 40% of shelter users were families with children.)

▬ In 1987, child protection agencies received 2.2 million reports of child abuse or neglect—triple the number received in 1976.

This is the nature of education's leaky roof: about one-third of preschool children are destined for school failure because of poverty, neglect, sickness, handicapping conditions, and lack of adult protection and nurturance. There is no point in trying to teach hungry or sick children. From this we can deduce one of the most important points in our attempts to deal with education: *educators can't fix the roof all by themselves.* It will require the efforts of many people and organizations—health and social welfare agencies, parents, business and political leaders—to even begin to repair this leaky roof. There is no time to waste in fixing blame; we need to act to fix the roof. And unless we start, the house will continue to deteriorate, and all Americans will pay the price.

Indeed, the first of the national goals for education outlined by the President and the nation's governors states that, "by the year 2000, all children in America will start school ready to learn." Three of the objectives attached to this goal read as follows:

▬ All disadvantaged and disabled children will have access to high-quality and developmentally appropriate preschool programs that help prepare children for school.

▬ Every parent in America will be a child's first teacher and devote time each day to helping his or her preschool child to learn; parents will have access to the training and support they need.

▬ Children will receive the nutrition and health care needed to arrive at school with healthy minds and bodies, and the number of low-birthweight babies will be significantly reduced through enhanced prenatal health systems.

While these are noble statements about the need to fix the roof, they are not at all informative on how this should be done. (It has been estimated that meeting just the first objective would cost $30 billion to implement.) We need to know more about *why* the roof is leaking—why so many of our children are at risk of failure in school and in life.

The fact is that more than one-third of American children have the deck stacked against them long before they enter school. Although America's best students are on a par with the world's best, ours is undoubtedly the worst "bottom third" of any of the industrialized democracies. We need to take a brief look at the kinds of changes that have brought about this concentration of children at risk.

CHANGES IN THE FAMILY

During the 1980s the American family continued to undergo major changes in its structure (see Table 35.1). Every kind of "atypical" family increased in number during the decade, while the "typical" family—married couple with children—actually declined in number. Today, almost 50% of America's young people will spend some years before they reach age 18 being raised by a single parent. In 1988, 4.3 million children were living with a mother who had never married (up 678% since 1970). Few have studied the consequences of being a child of an unmarried mother, but it's hard to think of this situation as an advantage. The 15 million children being raised by single mothers will have about one-third as much to spend on their needs as children being raised by two parents. (When both parents work, family income does not double; it *triples.*) For young children raised by a single mother, day care becomes a *vital educational issue,* as well as

a matter of family survival. The 2.5 million fathers raising children by themselves have also discovered the vital nature of day care.

Some things show up clearly in these numbers. First, only about a quarter of America's households have a child in the public schools, a fact that will make school bond elections more difficult to pull off as time goes by. Second, 25 million people live by themselves or with nonrelatives, which explains why America's fertility rates are so low! Third, the feminization of poverty is not just a slogan: 23 % of America's smallest children (birth to age 5) live in poverty, the highest rate of any industrialized nation. And many of them have a single parent, often a mother who works at a low-income service job. At present about six million workers in the U.S. earn the minimum wage, and more than five million others are within 50 cents of the minimum wage. Females over 25 with children to support—not teenage males saving for a car—account for the largest proportion of these low-wage workers. These women desperately need job skills to support their children, but they are not well represented in programs supported by the Job Training and Partnership Act or in other training programs.

We can begin to see how these areas interrelate when we think of a single mother with a low income who is raising a child. She must have a place to live; yet there are eight million qualified

TABLE 35.1 U.S. Households, 1980–90

	1980	1990	% CHANGE
All households	80,467,000	93,920,000	+16.7
Family households	59,190,000	66,652,000	+12.4
Married couples	48,990,000	52,837,000	+7.9
Married without children	24,210,000	28,315,000	+17.0
Married with children	24,780,000	24,522,000	−1.0
Single female head	8,205,000	11,130,000	+35.6
Single male head	1,995,000	2,575,000	+29.1
People living alone	18,202,000	22,879,000	+25.7
Living with nonrelatives	3,075,000	4,500,000	+46.3

low-income households trying to play musical chairs with only four million low-income housing units. (Literally no one is building new low-income housing units in the U.S.) She will pay a higher percentage—in some cases more than 50%—of her income for housing than any other category of worker. It is highly unlikely that her living unit will have a quiet place for a child to study.

In addition, this woman must get to work, often on public transportation if she can't afford a car. If her child is a preschooler, she will have to get the child to day care before she gets herself to work, an arrangement that may involve four or more bus trips at the end of each day. (For women in this situation, daycare centers, housing, and jobs are not usually located close to one another.) If the child gets ill, the logistics get even more complex. A missed bus or a conked-out car can mean that the rent cannot be paid. Then the salary check may be changed for a welfare check, a switch that is painful not only to her and her child, but also to the taxpayer who must pay for the switch! (It would be much cheaper for us to prevent her from going into poverty than to pay for the very expensive consequences, including her child being in poverty and the loss of her self-esteem.)

If the President and the nation's governors are serious about the first objective associated with the first national goal, we must deal with this single parent and her child. For this woman and her child (let's call him Carlos), education services, health services, day-care services, transportation services, housing services, and employment services must all function together to prevent Carlos from having a diminished future. Carlos *is* education's leaky roof!

There is no way that the education system alone can be responsible for the economic difficulties of this woman and her son, although educators will have to teach the person who is at the end of the service chain: Carlos. In order for the national goals to be achieved, our leaders will have to think of a way for Carlos and his mother to have an improved base of services so that Carlos will not become a liability to the taxpayer and the nation. This may seem difficult, but Carlos' problems are much easier to solve than those of the 350,000 cocaine-addicted babies born every year. The national goals are silent about such children, although they are already showing up in the schools.

CHANGES IN ETHNIC DISTRIBUTION

One of the good things about the 1990 Census is that we already know many of the most important numbers. For example, the American population grew by 10% between 1980 and 1990, reaching a new total of 249.8 million, an addition of 23 million people. The fastest growing groups are the eldest members of our population: 57,000 Americans are at least 100 years old, according to the 1990 Census, up from 32,000 in 1980. Minority populations also grew rapidly.

Ninety percent of the 23-million-person increase occurred in the South and West, although some eastern states, such as New York and New Jersey, have started growing again. Only *three* states account for almost half of the nation's growth: Texas, Florida, and California increased their populations by a total of 11.7 million. We can link this growth to some political changes if we look at the increased votes in the House of Representatives by the year 2000.

It is very clear that the states with the most population growth (and the most new political clout) are states with a great deal of ethnic diversity. Table 35.2 shows the increases in population for various ethnic groups between 1980 and 1990.

While the white population increased by 15 million, the nonwhite population increased by 14 million. Even though whites grew by 8%, their share of the total U.S. population declined from 86% to 84%.

The numbers get even more interesting when we project changes in the youth population from 1990 to 2010 (see Figure 35.1). During those two decades, the nation will gain in total population, but America's youth population will decline rapidly after 2000, because of the decline in women

TABLE 35.2   Population Increases (in Millions) by Ethnic Group, 1980–90

	1980 TOTAL	1990 TOTAL	% INCREASE
White	194.7	210.3	8
Black	26.7	31.0	16
Asian, other	5.2	8.6	65
Hispanic	14.6	21.0	44

entering the childbearing years. However, as the total youth cohort moves from 64 million to 65 million, then down to 62 million, the nonwhite component of the nation's youth cohort will increase dramatically, from 30% in 1990 to 38% in 2010. Note also that the white youth population declines during *both* decades. In fact, in 2010, 12 states and the District of Columbia will contain 30 million of our 62 million young people, with the percentages of minority youths as follows: Washington, D.C., 93.2%; Hawaii, 79.5%; New Mexico, 76.5%; Texas, 56.9%; California, 56.9%; Florida, 53.4%; New York, 52.8%; Louisiana, 50.3%; Mississippi, 49.9 %; New Jersey, 45.7%; Maryland, 42.7%; Illinois, 41.7%; South Carolina, 40.1%; U.S. total, 38.7%.

Many of these are large states, with a good deal of political and economic clout. But in all of them, a new question will arise: What do we call "minorities" when they constitute a majority? It behooves us all to make sure that *every* child in America has a good education and access to a good job. We cannot, as a nation, afford to throw *any* child away; we need them all to become successful adults if the economy, the community, the work force, the military—indeed, the nation—are to thrive. (And who else will generate the incomes that will pay for the Social Security benefits of the readers of this article?) Of the 20 million new workers who will be added to the American economy by 2000, only 18% of the net additions will be white males born in the U.S. The rest will be a combination of women, immigrants, or minorities.

By the 1980s the equity efforts of the 1960s had begun to pay off in terms of minority populations entering the middle class (defined by college education, suburban living options, and a white-collar or professional job). About 40% of the black population can be called middle class in 1990; Hispanics are not far behind, and Asians

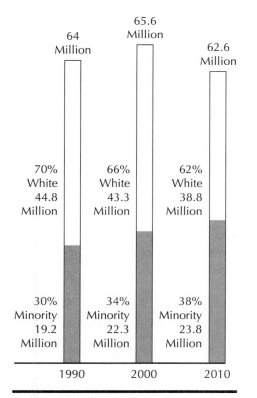

FIGURE 35.1   U.S. Youth (Birth–18) by Race, 1990–2010

Source: American Demographics, May 1989, p. 37.

are actually ahead. Different places in America have produced very different rates of black suburbanization, as the following list makes clear: Miami, 69%; Newark, 52.9%; Washington, D.C., 48.5%; Los Angeles, 46.5%; Atlanta, 46%; Oakland, 39.5%; St. Louis, 35.4%; Birmingham, 34.1%; Philadelphia, 27.7%; Cleveland, 27.2%; New Orleans, 24.6%; Baltimore, 23.5 %; Memphis, 15.4%; Dallas, 15.3%; Detroit, 14.9%; Houston, 14%; and Chicago, 9%.

As jobs follow people to the suburbs, the ability of a city to allow either suburbanization or the development of middle-income homes and jobs within the city limits (the latter, known as "gentrification," has been a major failure in America) will have a large effect on the ability of the metropolitan area—city plus suburbs—to be economically healthy.

With money, jobs, houses, and (to some extent) brains and aspirations having moved to the suburbs, serious questions must be raised about our most serious problem: America's inner-city schools, where the highest percentage of "at-risk"

students can be found; where classes are large (even though these children need the *most* individual attention); where health care, housing, transportation, personal security, and community stability are inadequate; where it is *very* hard to recruit and retain high-quality teachers and administrators; and where racial segregation still exists to an appalling degree, despite our best efforts. (It is pointless to desegregate schools if housing and jobs remain segregated.) The national education goals are conspicuous in their neglect of the special problems of inner-city schools in America.

It is particularly frustrating to realize that, if you equalize the environment in which a minority person lives (a home in the suburbs, parents who are college graduates and have managerial or professional jobs), you will tend to equalize his or her educational achievement as well. Indeed, for people of similar social and economic background, race *tends to go away as a predictor of educational achievement*. Figure 35.2 shows clearly that children of wealthy black families do

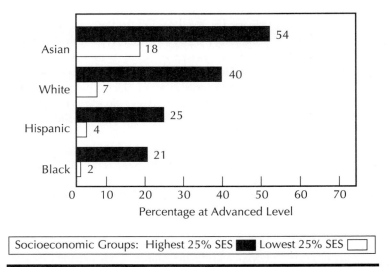

FIGURE 35.2 Percentage of Eighth-Graders in Low- and High-SES Groups Who Are Proficient in Advanced Mathematics, by Race

Source: National Center for Education Statistics, *Profile of the American Eighth-Grader* (Washington, D.C.: U.S. Department of Education, 1990).

better at math than do children of poor Asian families.

It is difficult to imagine a more exciting or optimistic conclusion. Nevertheless, millions of minority children and their parents are unable to enter the middle class, because they are locked into inner-city environments that offer no escape and scant possibility of improving conditions where they are. At the moment, there is no evidence of a truly permanent "underclass" in America, but give us two more generations of systematic neglect of inner-city youth, and there will be. By then, education's leaky roof will be beyond repair. Once again, schools cannot do the job in a social vacuum. Until job opportunities, health care, housing, transportation, and personal security improve in the inner cities, it is impossible to ask schools to get better. Trying to teach sick or hungry children is an exercise in futility.

INTERNATIONAL COMPARISONS

According to a study released by the Census Bureau in March 1990, American young people are at far greater risk for social, economic, and health problems than are children in the world's other developed nations. American children were the most vulnerable in most of the dimensions covered in the study, particularly in the following areas:

- number of children affected by divorce,
- youth homicide rate,
- number (and percentage) of youngsters living in poverty,
- infant mortality rate, and
- teenage pregnancy rate.

From a different source, in 1988 America ranked 22nd in infant mortality, with a rate of 10 deaths per 1,000 live births. Young males in the U.S. are five times as likely to be murdered as are their counterparts in other nations. Twenty-three percent of America's youths live in poverty, and the younger the children, the higher the poverty rate.

As I mentioned above, 15 million children in this country are being reared by single parents, mostly as a result of divorce. Finally, though it might seem unlikely that any other nation could compete with our figure of 4.3 million children being reared by a mother who never married and 371,000 children being reared by a never-married father, the facts are otherwise. Although 23% of America's children are born out of wedlock today, the rate for Sweden is 48% and for Denmark, 40%. However, in Sweden and Denmark, infant mortality is low, and child hunger and poverty are virtually nonexistent.

Children can be at risk on a variety of factors, some of which reflect a social or educational problem: single-parent home (22% of eighth-graders), low-income family (21% of eighth-graders' families below the 1988 figure of $15,000), held back one or more grades (19% of eighth-graders), home alone three or more hours a day (14%), parents with a low level of education (11%), and limited English proficiency (2%).

Some children are at risk because of medical factors: fetal alcohol syndrome, no medical care in the first trimester of a mother's pregnancy, a drug-addicted mother, poor maternal nutrition during pregnancy, a mother who smoked during pregnancy, exposure to lead during pregnancy or in infancy, premature birth, low birthweight, having a "teenage mother," and being a victim of child abuse or neglect.

Some children are at risk because of a problem that develops in adolescence: teen pregnancy, criminal conviction, suicide attempts, and alcohol and/or drug abuse.

Indeed, many children are at risk on more than one of these factors.

Like the Reagan Administration before it, the Bush Administration has made a major point of saying that Americans overspend on education. "Throwing money at problems will not make them go away" became the recurrent litany of these Presidents and their advisors. However, the data they cite to show that Americans spend more than other industrialized nations on education include figures for *higher education,* on which we spend a prodigious amount. (The U.S. has 5% of the world's elementary and secondary students and 25% of the world's higher education students.)

On the other hand, if we compare the percent of its gross domestic product that America spends on K-12 education with similar expenditures in other nations, the results are spectacularly different (see Figure 35.3). Even with the difficulties of establishing "levels of effort" for different nations, it is clear that many nations invest a larger share of their wealth in their children's education than we do. In addition, the discrepancies in per-pupil expenditures *within* the U.S. are unmatched by any nation with a centralized education system. In many states in the U.S., the amount spent on *some* children is three or four times the amount spent on other children in the same state. Recent court decisions in Kentucky and Texas indicate that this is an area of future concern.

This range of effort and expenditure devoted to children and youths is most characteristic of our nation. In terms of infant mortality and care, one can go from some of the best infant care in the world to some of the worst merely by taking the short drive from Scarsdale to Harlem.

These are a few of the reasons for my earlier assertion that America's "bottom third" of young people is more likely to fail than the "bottom third" of any nation with which we usually compare ourselves. If our goal is to ensure that every young person can graduate from high school with a high level of knowledge and skills, then we must concentrate a large measure of our fiscal and human resources on the children most likely to fail. At present, we concentrate our resources on those *least likely* to fail—children from relatively stable suburban families headed by parents who have high levels of education and income. The

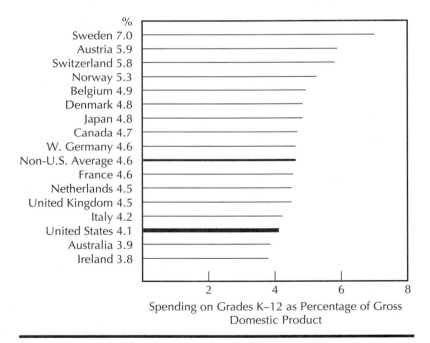

FIGURE 35.3 International Comparison of Education Expenditures, 1985

Source: M. Edith Rasell and Lawrence Mishel, *Shortchanging Education* (Washington, D.C.: Economic Policy Institute, 1990), p. 5.

national education goals give us not a single clue as to how this reallocation of resources should be brought about. Just how do we fix the roof?

EDUCATION—THE BEST WEAPON AGAINST POVERTY AND CRIME

Think for a moment about two young families with children. In one of the families, one or both of the parents has a high school diploma. In the other family, neither parent does. Which family is more likely to live below the poverty line? A good generalization is that increased levels of education will reduce the chances of living in poverty better than anything else. This is widely accepted.

But let's look at a different relationship. Let's look at the relationship between education and crime. Although it is not written about much, the relationship is quite strong. Today, more than 80% of America's one million prisoners are high school dropouts. Each prisoner costs taxpayers upwards of $20,000 a year. Moreover, the investment in prisoners is a bad one, in that 63% of released inmates are back in jail for serious crimes within three years. Taxpayers spend more by far on a prisoner than on *any other kind* of tax-supported individual. A college student is supported by about $3,300 of tax money—a very profitable investment indeed. Every dollar spent on a Head Start child will save taxpayers $7 in later services that the child will not need—a superb investment. Indeed, in Pennsylvania it is seven times more expensive for taxpayers to maintain someone in the *state pen* than it is to maintain someone at Penn State!

This correlation between being a high school dropout and becoming a prisoner is similar to the correlation between being a smoker and getting lung cancer. When you think about the public furor concerning the latter and the widespread ignorance concerning the former, you must wonder about America's youth policy. Table 35.3 shows the states with the highest and lowest high school dropout rates.[1] It is interesting to note that, with one exception, the states with the lowest dropout rates also have the lowest rates of prisoners per 100,000 people. With two exceptions, the states with the lowest graduation rates have the highest rates of prisoners per 100,000 people.

TABLE 35.3 High School Dropout Rates, 1987

STATE (LOWEST)	%	STATE (HIGHEST)	%
1. Minnesota	9.4	1. Florida	41.4
2. Wyoming	10.7	2. Louisiana	39.9
3. North Dakota	11.6	3. Michigan	37.6
4. Nebraska	13.3	4. Georgia	37.5
5. Montana	13.8	5. New York	37.1
6. Iowa	13.8	6. Arizona	35.6
7. Wisconsin	15.6	7. Mississippi	35.2
8. Ohio	17.2	8. Texas	34.9
9. Kansas	17.9	9. California	33.9
10. Utah	19.4	10. Alaska	33.3
11. Connecticut	19.5	11. South Carolina	33.1
12. South Dakota	20.3	12. Kentucky	32.6

Source: *State Education Performance Chart* (Washington, D.C.: Office of Planning, Budget, and Evaluation, U.S. Department of Education, May 1989).

JAIL CONSTRUCTION VERSUS CRIME REDUCTION

America's prison population *doubled* in less than a decade, reaching 1.1 million prisoners in 1990. (The U.S. incarceration rate in 1991 was the highest in the world, ahead of the Soviet Union and South Africa. In fact, in 1988 a black male in the U.S. was about five times as likely to be in prison as a black male in South Africa.) Given the increase in drug-related crime and the get-tough policies now in vogue, it is very likely that the number of inmates in U.S. prisons could reach two million before the decade is over. The cost of our prisons is increasing faster than that of *any other* social service, including education and health. Yet the return on the investment is extraordinarily low.

Many governors have discovered that, in order to show that they are "tough on crime," they can build a lot of jail cells and get reelected. Jails can also be built fairly quickly, which shows that the governor is a decisive leader. But there is one major problem with a campaign of building more jail cells: it doesn't reduce the crime rate. No sensible criminal is likely to stop committing crimes because more jail cells are available! (Criminals are not stupid.) There is, however, one thing that does reduce crime rates, and that is increased levels of education.

Let's return to our high school dropout family. With no high school diploma in the household, the best a family can usually manage is a minimun-wage job at $3.30 an hour. That adds up to about $9,000 a year for a full-time worker. Is that enough for our young family even to think about buying a house? Owning a car? Putting children through college? Clearly not. For young high school dropouts working minimum-wage jobs, there is little chance that the American Dream will become reality—unless, of course, they turn to crime. In 1989, four million Americans worked full-time but were still eligible for poverty benefits! Since Ben Franklin, America's deal with its citizens has been: if you work hard, you shouldn't be poor. Where is the reward for the work ethic for these four million people?

However, we know that as educational levels increase, so do earnings. And as earnings increase, the propensity for crime decreases. If you can make your way in the mainstream, a risky criminal "career" becomes less and less inviting. What we need to do is to work on America's crime rates, and the best policy for doing so is to make sure that *every* American child graduates from high school. Already, some school districts—e.g., Greeley, Colorado; and Springfield, Missouri—have developed strategic plans to achieve the goal of zero dropouts by 1995. To do so is to achieve a reduction in crime also, but that result won't show up for many years. Unfortunately, political pressures force elected officials to look for quick-fix solutions like jail construction rather than long-term solutions like ensuring that every young person graduates from high school.

CONCLUSION

I hope that readers take away from this chapter two main points. First, for the reasons I specified above, America's children are truly an "endangered species." And second, educators alone cannot "fix" the problems of education, because dealing with the root causes of poverty must involve health-care, housing, transportation, job-training, and social welfare bureaucracies.

We are left with two high-priority questions: What can educators do that they are not already doing to reduce the number of children "at risk" in America and to get them achieving well in school settings? And how can educators collaborate more closely with other service providers so that we all work together toward the urgent goal of providing services to the same client? These two questions must be answered by the nation before our schools will improve.

But we do *know* that it is possible to "fix education's leaky roof." With regard to the problems of children in America, President Bush has said, "We have more will than wallet." I think he has it backward. We have the resources to reduce the proportion of at-risk children to less than 5%. What we lack is the will to do it.

ENDNOTE

1. While dropout rates are notoriously unreliable as absolute numbers, *comparing* rates obtained from the same source—numbers with a "commonly held bias" is a valuable exercise. Something very different is happening in Minnesota, with its 9% dropout rate, than in Florida, with its 41% rate.

REFERENCES

Education and Human Services Consortium. *What It Takes: Structuring Interagency Partnerships to Connect Children and Families with Comprehensive Services.* Washington, D.C., 1991.

Hodgkinson, Harold. *All One System: Demographics of Education from Kindergarten Through Graduate School.* Washington, D.C.: Institute for Educational Leadership, 1985.

Hodgkinson, Harold. *The Same Client: Demographics of Education and Service Delivery Systems.* Washington, D.C.: Institute for Educational Leadership, September 1989.

House Select Committee on Children, Youth, and Families. *Children and Families.* Washington, D.C.: U.S. Government Printing Office, December 1988.

House Select Committee in Children, Youth, and Families. *U.S. Children and Their Families: Current Conditions and Recent Trends, 1989.* Washington, D.C.: U.S. Government Printing Office, 1989.

National Center for Education Statistics. *Profile of the American Eighth Grader.* Washington, D.C.: U.S. Department of Education, 1990.

National Health/Education Consortium. *Crossing the Boundaries Between Health and Education.* Washington, D.C., 1990.

Statistical Abstract of the United States, 1990. Washington, D.C.: U.S. Government Printing Office, 1989.

Waldrop, Judith, and Thomas Exter. "What the 1990 Census Will Show." *American Demographics,* January 1990.

DISCUSSION QUESTIONS

1. How have social and psychological ills of school-aged children impacted the work of educators?

2. Whar are the advantages and disadvantages of the national goals outlined by President Bush?

3. Why can't educators solve the problems of education alone?

4. How can educators work together with other service providers?

5. What changes might be necessary in early childhood, teacher, and administrative professional preparation programs and in the certification requirements to address the problems of at-risk students?

Educational Reform and the Ecology of Schooling

ELLIOT W. EISNER

FOCUSING QUESTIONS

1. *Why do teachers tend to resist reform efforts?*
2. *What procedures will be necessary to assist teachers with reform initiatives?*
3. *How can contextualized in-service programs benefit a teacher's professional development?*
4. *In what ways do parent and community views of education influence reform?*
5. *How does the ecology of the school affect reform?*
6. *In what ways will action research impact the relationship between universities and schools?*
7. *Should teachers be given the responsibility to establish local educational policy?*
8. *What alternative conceptions of curriculum programming might facilitate school reform?*

The aspiration to reform schools has been a recurrent theme in American education. This aspiration frequently is stimulated by changes outside the United States. For example, the successful launching of *Sputnik I* on October 4, 1957, was sufficiently traumatic to our sense of national security to motivate the Congress of the United States to provide funds for the development of curricula in science and mathematics in order to "catch up with the Russians." During the 1960s over $100,000,000 was spent in building new programs in these fields and in retraining teachers. Despite all the effort and all the money, there is little that now remains in American schools that reflects the aspirations of the curriculum reform movement of the 1960s: Few of the curricula are to be found. *Sputnik I* motivated many, but its educational residue is difficult to find.

Since *Sputnik I,* American schools have been subjected to numerous reform efforts. The latest was initiated at a presidentially sponsored education summit on April 18, 1991, a summit attended by the nation's governors, by the U.S. Secretary of Education, and by educators holding positions of high office, to announce Bush's new plans for educational reform. Yet only a few years earlier another president supported another effort at educational reform. *A Nation at Risk,* a document that enjoyed the highest level of visibility of any American educational policy paper published during this century, caught not only the attention but the enthusiasm of almost everyone.[1] Despite these reform efforts, the major features of schools remain largely as they were. What went wrong? Is there anything to learn from past efforts that might make current efforts more successful? This chapter first describes some of the conditions that make change in school difficult and then presents a potentially useful framework for developing a more effective agenda for school reform.

SCHOOLS AS ROBUST INSTITUTIONS

One thing is clear: It is much easier to change educational policy than to change the ways in which schools function. Schools are robust institutions whose very robustness provides a source of social stability.[2] But what is it about schools that makes them so stable? Consider the following nine factors.

INTERNALIZED IMAGES OF TEACHERS' ROLES

The images of what teachers do in classrooms, how they teach and organize children and tasks, are acquired very early in a child's life. In one sense, teaching is the only profession in which professional socialization begins at age five or six—when children begin school. In no other field do children have as much systematic opportunity to learn what a professional does in his or her work. Indeed, many children spend more time with their teachers than with their parents. This fact of early professional socialization should not be underestimated. Many young adults choose teaching because of their image of teachers and this image is not unrelated to what they believe being a teacher entails. Images of teaching and ways of being a teacher are internalized early in a child's life and bringing about significant changes in the ways in which teachers function requires replacing old images with new, more adequate ones. When a university teacher education program tries to promulgate a new image of teaching, but sends its young, would-be teachers back to schools that are essentially like the ones in which they were socialized, the prospects for replacing the old ideas in the all too familiar contexts in which new teachers work is dimmed:

The new wine is changed when it is poured into the old bottle.

ATTACHMENT TO FAMILIAR PEDAGOGICAL ROUTINE

Being a teacher, if it requires any set of skills and understandings, requires the ability to manage a group of children so that the class remains coherent and intact; nothing can be done if the class as such is in a state of disarray. But matters of management are only one part of the equation. The other is having something to teach. Teachers acquire a useful pedagogical repertoire by virtue of their experience in classrooms and that repertoire includes some degree of mastery of both the content they wish to teach and the methods and tactics through which to teach it.[3] This repertoire is extremely important to teachers, for it provides them with a source of security and enables them to cope with pedagogical demands efficiently. If a teacher does not know what to teach or is insecure about a subject, attention must be paid to matters of content. This can exacerbate both problems of management and problems of pedagogy. It is difficult to be pedagogically graceful when you are lost in unfamiliar territory. Teachers are often reluctant to relinquish teaching repertoires that provide an important source of security for them. New content areas might require new pedagogical routines. Given the overload that teachers typically experience in school—large numbers of students and many courses or subjects to teach—economy of effort is an important value.[4] Familiar teaching repertoires provide economy of effort; hence changes in schools that require new content and new repertoires are likely to be met with passive resistance by experienced teachers who have defined for themselves an array of routines they can efficiently employ. To make matters even less promising for school reform, few efforts at reform in the United States have provided time for teachers to develop mastery of new content or the skills required for new forms of teaching. Typically, new expectations for teachers are "add-ons" to already overloaded curricula and very demanding teaching schedules.

RIGID AND ENDURING STANDARDS FOR APPROPRIATE BEHAVIOR

A third source of school stability resides in the persistence of school norms. Every social occasion from the birthday party to the funeral service is pervaded by social norms that prescribe implicitly, if not always explicitly, ways to be in the world. Schools are no different. What teachers are supposed to be, how children are supposed to behave, what constitutes an appropriate and fair set of expectations for a subject, are defined by the norms of schooling. These norms have been described by Dreeben, Jackson, Lortie, Lightfoot, Powell, and Eisner, and decades earlier by Waller.[5] In the past two decades educational scholars on the political Left such as Apple and Giroux have also examined the ways in which the pervasive and sometimes covert norms of schooling shape attitudes, create inequities, and often reproduce the inequities of the society at large.[6] Undoubtedly, some of their observations are correct, but my point here is not so much to make a statement about what Bourdieu has called "cultural reproduction"[7] as to make it plain that if schools are to seriously address matters of intellectual development, the cultivation of sensibility, and the refinement of the imagination, changes must be made in educational priorities. Such changes will require institutional norms different from those now salient in schools.

Norms, after all, reflect values. They adumbrate what we care about. Trying to convert schools from academic institutions—institutions that attempt to transmit what is already known—into intellectual ones—institutions that prize inquiry for its own sake—will require a change in what schools prize. Most efforts at school reform fail to address this challenge. The tack taken in most educational policy papers is typically superficial and the language is technical. The problem is often thought to be solvable by curriculum "installation"; we are to "install" a new curriculum and then "align it" with other curricula. We typically employ a language of change that reveals a shallow and mechanistic conception of what real change requires. Policymakers cannot install new norms in schools any more than they can install new teaching methods. Both need careful cultivation and nurture. By persisting in using inappropriate mechanical metaphors for thinking about the process of school reform, we persist in misconceptualizing the problem and undermining genuine change.

TEACHER ISOLATION

A fourth factor that thwarts school reform is the fact that in the United States, we have structured schools and defined teaching roles in ways that make improved teaching performance difficult to achieve. Consider the ways in which teachers are insulated and isolated from their colleagues. Teaching, by and large, in both elementary and secondary schools is a lonely activity. It is not that teachers have no contact with people; after all, they are with students all day. The point is that they have very little contact with other adults in the context of their classrooms. Some school districts in the United States and some enlightened policies provide teachers with aides and with special assistance by certified professionals, but these human resources are relatively rare. Most teachers spend most of their time in their own classrooms, closed environments, with twenty-five to thirty-five children or adolescents. Of course, there are occasions—lunchtime and the occasional staff meeting, for example—where teachers see each other, but seldom in the context of teaching. Even teachers who have worked in the same school for twenty years are likely to have never seen their colleagues teach.

The result of professional isolation is the difficulty that teachers encounter in learning what they themselves do in their own classrooms when they teach. Classrooms, unlike the rooms in which ballerinas practice their craft, have no mirrors. The only mirrors available to teachers are those they find in their students' eyes, and these mirrors are too small. Hence the teacher, whether elementary or secondary, must learn on his or her own, usually by reflecting on how things went. Such personal reflection is subject to two forms of ignorance, one type remediable, the other not.

The two types of ignorance I speak of are primary and secondary ignorance. Primary ignorance about teaching, or about anything else for that matter, is when you do not know something but you *know* that you do not know it. In such a situation, you can do something about it. Secondary ignorance is when you do not know something but do *not know* you do not know it. In this case, you can do nothing about the problem. The professional isolation of teachers fosters secondary ignorance. How can a teacher learn that he or she is talking too much, not providing sufficient time for student reflection, raising low-order questions, or is simply boring students? Teachers unaware of such features of their own performance are in no position to change them. Educational reform efforts that depend on new and better approaches to teaching yet make it difficult for teachers to learn about their own teaching are destined to have a poor prognosis for success. Despite what seems obvious, we have designed schools both physically and organizationally to restrict the teacher's access to other professionals. Discretionary time for teachers is limited and although the school principal could make the time to provide teachers with useful feedback, he or she often does not have the inclination or the skills or is so preoccupied with other matters of lesser importance that attention to the improvement of teaching becomes marginalized. As a result, it is not unusual for teachers to feel that no one really cares about the quality of their work.[8]

INADEQUACIES OF IN-SERVICE EDUCATION

In-service education is the major means used in the United States to further the quality of teaching. But in-service education typically means that teachers will attend meetings or conferences to hear experts (often university professors who have had little contact with schools) provide advice on the newest developments in teaching mathematics, social studies, or the language arts. The assumption is that once teachers are exposed to such wisdom, they will implement the practices suggested in their own classrooms. The in-service seminar is one in which the advice-giver typically has never seen the teachers who comprise the audience. The advice-giver does not know the teachers' strengths or their weaknesses. The situation is much like a voice coach giving advice to a singer whom he or she has never heard sing. General recommendations go only so far.

Thus, we try to improve teaching by asking teachers to leave their classrooms so that they can travel to distant locations in order to get general advice from people who have never seen them teach. One does not need to be a specialist in learning theory to know that for complex forms of human action, general advice is of limited utility. Feedback needs to be specific and focused on the actor in context. What we do, however, is decontextualize in-service education and, as a result, weaken its potential usefulness.

My remarks should not be interpreted to mean that in-service programs for teachers cannot be useful, but that in-service education without some direct observation of teachers in the context of their own classrooms is not likely to be adequate. In this case, as in so many others, we have greatly underestimated what it will take to improve what teachers actually do in their own classrooms.

CONSERVATIVE EXPECTATIONS FOR THE FUNCTION OF SCHOOLS

Another factor that contributes to the robust quality of schools and their resistance to change is that the expectations of both students and parents regarding the function of schools and the forms of practice that are appropriate are usually conservative. What does a good teacher do? What kinds of questions are appropriate for students to ask?

How much freedom should teachers provide? What kinds of problems and projects should students be asked to engage in? How should students be evaluated? Should they have any role in their own assessment? Answers to each of the foregoing questions are related to expectations of what schools, classrooms, and teachers should be. The expectations of parents and students are often quite traditional on such matters.

The call for "back to basics"—a return to the educational practices of the past—is regarded by many as the way to save American schools from mediocrity or worse. Familiar practices are not threatening; the past almost always has a rosy glow. Practices that violate tradition are often regarded as subversive of high-quality education. School reform efforts that challenge tradition can be expected to encounter difficulties, especially from the segment of the population that has done well in socioeconomic terms and has the tendency to believe that the kind of schooling that facilitated their success is precisely the kind their own children should receive.

Expectations by students for practices with which they are familiar go beyond general forms of teaching practice; they include expectations for the way in which specific subjects should be taught. For example, students whose experience in art classes has not included learning about the history of art or writing about the qualities of particular works of art may regard such practices as distasteful; for many students reading and writing have no place in an art class. A program in social studies that requires group cooperation on project-centered work can be regarded as inappropriate by students whose concept of social studies is one that is devoted exclusively to individual tasks. Parents whose experience in learning mathematics emphasized drill and practice may regard an arithmetic program oriented toward the practical applications of arithmetic as less intellectual and less rigorous. The point here is that educational consumers can exercise a conservative function in the effort at educational reform. It is difficult for schools to exceed in aim, form, and content what the public is willing to accept.

DISTANCE BETWEEN EDUCATIONAL REFORMERS AND TEACHERS IMPLEMENTING CHANGE

Reform efforts in American education are almost always from the top down. For whatever reason, educational policymakers mandate change, often through national or state reports or through new educational legislation that sends the message of changed policies to those "on the front line." The tacit assumption is that once new policies are formulated, a stream of change will begin to flow with little further assistance. When assistance is provided it sometimes comes in the form of new policy papers, curriculum guides, and district conferences. Typically, the structural conditions of schools stay the same. Teachers remain on the receiving end of policy and have little hand in its formation.

The attraction of providing teachers with a hand in shaping educational policy is quite limited if one believes educational practice, at its best, will be uniform across school districts and geographic regions. If one's model of ideal educational practice is one of standardized practice, the way in which an efficient manufacturing plan might function, giving $2\frac{1}{2}$ million American teachers the opportunity to determine what is best for their own school or school district can appear chaotic or even nihilistic. Thus, there is a real tension in the process of school reform. At one end there is the desire to create a uniform and "equitable" program for children and adolescents, regardless of who they are or where they live. This requires centralized decision making. At the other end is the realization that unless teachers feel some commitment to change, they are unlikely to change. To feel such commitment it is important for teachers to have the opportunity to participate in shaping the change process.

Many veteran teachers, those who have seen educational reforms come and go, are skeptical about new reforms and respond with passive resistance: They simply ride out the new policies. This can be done without much difficulty for two reasons. First, educational reform policies come and go about every five or six years and are more visible in the media than in the classroom. Second, once the classroom door is closed, the ways in which teachers teach is essentially a private affair. Elementary school principals rarely monitor teaching practice closely, and, at the secondary level, they do not have the subject-matter expertise in a wide variety of fields to do so.

The growing desire to engage teachers in the change process has led to the notion of "teacher empowerment." In general, the idea is that, as important stakeholders in what schools do, teachers need to have authority to plan and monitor the quality of the educational process in their schools. The effort, in a sense, is to democratize educational reform by giving teachers a say-so in what happens. This say-so includes defining curricular goals and content, improving teaching practice, and developing ways to assess what children experience during the school day. In some cases, it includes decision making about budget allocations through a process called site-based management.

A practice related to this general thrust of teacher improvement is called *action research.* Action research is intended to encourage teachers to collaborate with other teachers and, at times, with university professors in order to undertake research in their own school or classroom.[9] The aim of the enterprise is to stimulate professional reflection by encouraging teachers to take a more reflective intellectual role in understanding and improving their own teaching practice.

It is not yet clear just how many teachers are interested in being "empowered." It is not yet clear how many teachers want to do educational research. It is not yet clear how many teachers are interested in assuming larger responsibilities such as the formulation of educational policy. Many teachers gain their deepest satisfaction in their own classroom. The classroom is their professional home and they are not particularly interested in collaboration or in doing educational research. As I indicated earlier, conceptions of the teacher's role are acquired early in development and teachers are often comfortable with these conceptions. If a bird has been in a cage for a decade and suddenly finds the door open, it

should not be too surprising if the bird does not wish to leave. The familiar is often more comfortable than the uncertainty of the unknown.

Empowering teachers is more complex than I have suggested. When innovative reform policies are formulated or new aims or programs presented, they are often prescribed *in addition* to what teachers are already doing; they are add-ons. Given that the teacher's day is already quite demanding, it should come as no surprise that taking on added responsibilities for the formulation of policy or for monitoring the school should be regarded by some as an extra burden. Put more bluntly, it is unrealistic to expect overworked teachers who have very little discretionary time in the school day to be more active in their school without some relief from some of their current responsibilities. To provide relief will require restructuring. Restructuring is likely to require money, something that is in scarce supply in many school districts. As a result, much of the activity in the context of school reform is more at the level of rhetoric than at the level of practice.

As educational reformers have become increasingly aware of the difficulty of bringing about significant change in the ways in which schools function, they have talked about the restructuring of schools.[10] For this term, which to me generates an image of fundamental rather than superficial change, there are almost as many meanings as there are writers. In my discussions with school principals and school superintendents, "restructuring" meant to them changing the ways in which funds were allocated rather than reconceptualizing the organization, content, and aims of schools. Conceptualized in terms of financial resource allocation, the power of the concept was neutralized.

Another complexity regarding teacher empowerment involves the question of authority and responsibility. If teachers are given the authority to change local educational policy in their schools, will they assume responsibility for the consequences of those policies? If so, how will those consequences be determined? What will be the responsibilities of the school district's superintendent and the district central office staff? Just what is the appropriate balance between authority and responsibility and who is responsible for what when responsibility and authority are localized?

These questions are not yet resolved. The recent interest in giving teachers a genuine role in the reform of schools is seen by many (including me) as salutary, but how lines of authority and responsibility are to be drawn is far from clear. Can genuine school improvement occur without commitment from teachers? It seems unlikely. Just how can such commitment be developed? These questions are on the current agenda of school reform in the United States.

ARTIFICIAL BARRIER BETWEEN DISCIPLINES AND BETWEEN TEACHERS

An eighth factor that impedes school reform pertains to the ways in which the school itself is organized. One of the most problematic features in the organization of schools is the fact that they are *structurally fragmented,* especially at the secondary level. By structurally fragmented I refer to the fact that curricula are divided and organized into distinct subject matters that make it difficult for students to make connections between the subjects they study.[11] In the United States, secondary school students will typically enroll in four to six subjects each semester. As a result, teachers must teach within narrow time blocks. They teach four to seven classes each day, see 130 to 180 students each day; students must move every fifty minutes to another teacher who teaches them another subject. There is no occupation in American society in which workers must change jobs every fifty minutes, move to another location, and work under the direction of another supervisor. Yet this is precisely what we ask of adolescents, hoping, at the same time, to provide them with a coherent educational program.

Structural fragmentation also pertains to the fact that the form of school organization that we have created isolates teachers. And as I have already indicated, isolation makes it difficult for teachers to receive critical and supportive feedback about their work. Teachers experience little colleagueship in the context of the classroom, and of course it is in the context of a classroom that the real business of education is played out. Unless there is significant change in the way in which teachers and students live and work together, any significant change in schools is illusory.

Because the forms of school organization are cultural rather than natural entities, they need not be regarded as being of necessity; that is, they can be other than the way they are. Moses did not receive instructions about school organization on Mount Sinai, at least as far as I know. Yet we persist in maintaining school structures that might not be in the best interests of either teachers or students. I can tell you that the organizational structure and the curricular requirements of the secondary school I attended forty years ago are quite like the organizational structure and curricular requirements secondary school students encounter today. How much structural and curricular overlap is there between the secondary school you attended and today's secondary schools?

FECKLESS PIECEMEAL EFFORTS AT REFORM

The last factor that impedes significant educational reform is the piecemeal and superficial way in which reformers think about educational reform. Minor efforts at change are eventually swamped by the factors in the school that do not change. Robust systems can withstand minor incursions. Thus the need, I believe, is to think about school reform ecologically, or at least systemically. Aspects of schooling that remain constant militate against those features of schooling that are being changed. For example, efforts to help teachers learn how to teach inductively are not likely to succeed if the evaluation system the school employs rewards other types of teaching. Efforts to encourage teachers to engage in reflective teaching are likely to be feckless if teachers have no time during the school day for reflection.

Efforts to create intellectual coherence in the student's understanding are likely to fail if the form that the curriculum takes makes coherence impossible. Improvement in teaching is unlikely as long as teachers get no useful feedback on the work they actually do in their own classrooms.

It is important in educational reform to think big even if one must start small. There needs, I believe, to be an overall conception of what schools are as forms of shared communal life as well as persuasive and attractive visions of what such shared living might become. The next section describes a means for securing a better understanding of what schools are as living organisms. The last section provides a model or framework that identifies important candidates for educational change.

Schools as Living Systems

The place to begin school reform is in the effort to understand the ways that schools actually function, what it is they teach both implicitly and explicitly, and how they reward the people who spend so much of their lives there. Unfortunately, the effects of efforts at school reform are based on the results of standardized achievement testing and the results of such testing say little about the processes that lead to them. We cannot know much about the educational quality of schools simply be examining test scores. We need a finer, more refined screen, one that focuses on the processes as well as the outcomes of schooling.

Much recent research in the United States has focused on the quality and process of schooling.[12] Some of these students have used ethnographic research methods or modifications of such methods.[13] Some studies have been rooted in critical approaches[14] and others in methods derived from the arts and humanities.[15] As a result of this work a number of salient features of schools, many of which are quite common across a variety of schools, have been identified: structural fragmentation, teacher isolation, didactic teaching, treaties between teachers and students, the particular ways in which effective teachers

and school administrators relate to students, the emphasis on extrinsic rewards, and the like. How salient are these features? Are there important differences? How can we know?

The only way I know to discover the salient and significant features of schools is to look. The implications of what is found will depend on what is found and on the educational values that give direction to the schools themselves.

To look at schools as I have suggested is not enough. Anyone can look. The trick is to see. Seeing requires an enlightened eye. It requires schemata through which different genres of teaching can be appreciated.[16] It is a mistake to assume that all good teaching has identical characteristics, that one size fits all. Thus, to see what happens in classrooms requires a willingness and a set of sensibilities and schemata that can pick up the distinctive features of particular types of teaching. These types of teaching are not simply generic. They emerge within the constraints and possibilities of particular subject matters—*what* one teaches counts. As Stodolsky says, "the subject matters."[17] Even more than this, any given subject matter—history, for example, or mathematics—can have a wide variety of aims and methods. Perceiving school processes requires an understanding of the types of teaching possible within the subject-matter field and an awareness of the varieties of quality that can be manifested within each.

This chapter is not the place to describe in detail the forms of perception and description of life in schools I have in mind. Readers interested in what I have called "educational connoisseurship" and "educational criticism" can find the approach described in a variety of articles and particularly in my latest book.[18] The point is that school reform should begin with a decent understanding of the schools themselves, not with old memories of schooling held by middle-aged men and women working in institutions far removed from schools. A major part of the current investment in school reform should be aimed, in my opinion, at trying to understand such processes as how teaching takes place in particular fields, what constitutes the implicit as well as the explicit norms of the school, the sense that students make of what they study, the aims that teachers say are important and the relationship of those aims to what they do in their classrooms. It should also deal with the intellectual quality of what is taught and the procedures that are used in the classroom to motivate and reward students and teachers. The aim of such inquiry is to secure an organic, cultural picture of schools as places to be. The basic questions direct attention to the value of what goes on in them. Such questions are easy to raise but difficult to answer, yet unless they are raised educational reform is likely to be predicated on very partial forms of understanding of what schools are like for teachers and students.

As I have indicated, the kind of study I am suggesting is one that is organic or cultural. To study schools in this way is likely to require an approach to educational research that is *qualitative* in character. It is an approach that pays attention to the processes of schooling and to the context in which those processes occur. I know of no way to find out what schools are like except by going to schools themselves to see, to describe, to interpret, and to evaluate what is occurring. Such an understanding can provide a foundation for reform that addresses what is genuinely important in education.

Five Major Dimensions of School Reform

In the final section of this article, I identify five dimensions of schooling that I believe must be considered in order to think comprehensively about the reform of schools. I call these dimensions the *intentional,* the *structural,* the *curricular,* the *pedagogical,* and the *evaluative.*

My thesis is that meaningful and educationally significant school reform will require attention to each of these dimensions. Attention to one direction without attention to the others is not likely to lead to change. Where change does occur, it is likely to be temporary and superficial.

The intentional refers to what it is that schools are intended to accomplish. What really counts in schools? Defining intentions pertains to both the general aims of schooling and the aims of the particular subject matters being taught. Consider, for example, intentions that are typically *not* given high priority in schools or in reform efforts: fostering a desire to continue learning what schools teach, the development of curiosity, stimulating the ability to think metaphorically, creating a caring attitude toward others, the development of productive idiosyncrasy, the ability to define one's own goals and the ability to pursue them, the ability to raise perceptive questions about what one has studied. An argument for each of these intentions could be made that is cogent and relevant to the world in which children live. If such intentions were taken seriously, their ramifications for educational practice would be considerable. My point here is not to advocate such intentions (although I do not reject them) but rather to illustrate the idea that the conventional intentions schools serve are not necessarily the most important ones. What is important will depend on an argued set of educational values and an understanding of the students and society schools serve.

Most efforts at school reform operate on the assumption that the important outcomes of schooling, indeed the primary indices of educational success, are high levels of academic achievement as measured by standardized achievement tests. Just what do scores on academic achievement tests predict? They predict scores on other academic achievement tests. But schools, I would argue, do not exist for the sake of high levels of performance in the context of schools, but in the context of life outside of the school. The significant dependent variables in education are located in the kinds of interests, voluntary activities, levels of thinking and problem solving, that students engage in when they are not in school. In other words, the real test of successful schooling is not what students do in school, but what they do outside of it.

If such intentions were genuinely central in our educational planning, we would probably make other arrangements for teaching, curriculum, and evaluation than those we now employ. Significant new intentions are likely to require new ways of leading educational lives.

The structural aspects of schooling pertain to the ways in which we have organized subjects, time, and roles. I have already alluded to the fact that we structure subjects by type. We use what Bernstein has called a collection-type curriculum.[19] Each subject is bounded and kept distinct from others. This boundedness is reinforced by how time is allocated, what is taught, and in some secondary schools, where on the school campus a subject matter department is located. In some schools there is a section of the school devoted exclusively to the sciences, another to the fine arts, another to business and computer studies. We emphasize separateness and reinforce that separateness through a departmentalized structure.

Departmentalization might be, in the long run, the most rational way to structure schools, but it is not the only way. My aim here is not to advocate a particular change, but to problematize the structures we have lived with for so long that we come to think about them as natural entities rather than as the results of decisions that could have been otherwise. Is a departmentalized structure the best way to organize schools? It depends on a set of educational values and an exploration of alternative modes of organization. In the United States very few efforts at school reform— open schooling being a vivid exception—have tried to restructure schools. The curriculum reform movement of the 1960s attempted to create curricula designed to fit into existing school structures. Can new messages change the school or will the school change the messages?

The structure of the school also influences the way in which roles are defined. In American schools there are basically two roles for adults: teacher and principal. The teacher spends his or her day with children or adolescents. The principal seldom is responsible for teaching functions and has far more discretionary time than do teachers. If a teacher wants to secure more professional life-space, he or she must leave teaching and become a school administrator. Once such a deci-

sion is made, for all practical purposes, there is no return to the classroom—as the caterpillar, once it becomes a butterfly, remains a butterfly until it dies.

Working as an educator in a school need not be limited to two roles, nor must these roles be conceived of as "permanent." Schools can be structured so that teachers who are interested can devote some years or parts of some years to curriculum development, to the design of better evaluation methods for their school, to serving as mentors to beginning teachers. Teachers could create liaisons with community agencies such as museums, hospitals, cultural centers, retirement homes, in order to secure services that could enhance and enrich school programs. Teachers could devote time to research in their own school and assist parents with children who are having difficulty in school. There is a host of possible roles that could make important generic contributions to a school's way of life, but for these contributions to be made, educators need to create school structures that permit them to be developed. American schools, with few exceptions, are structured to inhibit these roles rather than to encourage their formation. The paradigms we have internalized about the nature of schooling— the way time is allocated, the way subjects are defined, the way in which roles are specified— are so strong that efforts at reform are typically conceptualized to fit into the constraints of those structures, thus defining the parameters within which reform efforts are to occur.

The curricular is the third dimension that needs attention in any effort to create genuinely significant educational reform. Decisions about curriculum can be made about several of its features. Among the most important are those about the content that is to be provided, about the kind of activities that are to be used to help students experience that content, and the way in which the curriculum itself is to be organized. As I have indicated, most efforts at curriculum reform in the United States have left the organization of curriculum intact: Separate subjects separately taught has been the dominant mode of organization, although at the elementary level such organization is less prevalent than at the middle or secondary school levels. Yet in spite of frequent admonitions by educational scholars to reduce curriculum fragmentation,[20] the separation of subject matters persists and is supported by the infrastructure of professional education: testing programs, university admissions criteria, teacher training programs, specialization among subject-matter teachers. This collection-type form of curriculum organization[21] is not the only way in which curriculum can be organized. Whether it is the most appropriate form, given the potential costs of other forms of organization, depends upon our educational intentions. If integration of learning is desired, separation may indeed be problematic. Again, my point here is not to argue for a specific form of curriculum reorganization as much as to urge the careful rethinking of the organization that now prevails.

What is taught in the first place is of primary importance. One way to increase the probability that something *will not be learned* is to ensure that it *will not be taught,* that is, to make a subject matter a part of a *null curriculum.*[22] The fine arts are often relegated to this position. For many citizens the arts are someone else's pleasures. Large and important legacies of culture go unseen, unheard, unread, and as a result, unloved. Schools perpetuate this state of ignorance by withholding from the young important parts of their cultural legacy. The list could be expanded.

Regarding the activities that allow students to grasp or experience what is taught in schools, according to Goodlad, the lecture still dominates at the secondary school level.[23] Students typically have few opportunities to formulate their own questions and to pursue them. They are expected to do what the teacher requests; their role is in the application of means rather than the formulation of ends. They become, says Apple, deskilled, unable to formulate the aims and goals they seek to attain.[24]

The provision of opportunities for students to define at least some of their purposes is arguably an important educational aim and the ability to do so an important educational achievement. To what extent does it occur? Genuine reform of schools will require attention not only to intentions and school structure, but to the content, tasks, and forms of organization of the school curriculum. Which aspects of curricula should receive attention will depend on what is now occurring in schools; the only way to know that is to go to the schools to see.

The fourth dimension needing attention in genuine school reform is *the pedagogical* aspects of educational practice. If the curriculum is the systole of education, teaching is the diastole. No curriculum teaches itself and how it is mediated is crucial. In fact, I find it useful to distinguish between the *intended* curriculum and the *operational* curriculum.[25] What we plan to teach— materials, outlines, projected activities and goals—constitutes the intended curriculum. The operational curriculum is the curriculum that is played out in the context of classroom life. In this process pedagogy plays a crucial role. When programs call for new teaching skills that teachers do not possess—inductive teaching, for example— teachers understandably use the skills they possess and these may not be adequate to the task.

No intended curriculum can be followed by teachers as a script; the classroom is too uncertain a place for recipes. The professional teacher needs to use the curriculum as a resource, as an amplifier of his or her own ability. Different teachers need different amounts of guidance and specificity. Thus, the pedagogical is a central aspect of school reform. Unless classroom practices change, changes on paper, whether in policy or in curriculum, are not likely to be of much consequence for students.

How can students of education know about the ways in which teaching occurs? What are the strengths teachers possess and what are their weaknesses? Are there important educational consequences on both sides of the ledger? These questions are, of course, easy to pose but difficult to answer. At minimum, qualitative studies of classroom life must be undertaken. Such studies could provide the basis on which effective change strategies could be initiated and could provide a focus for efforts aimed at pedagogical issues.

Both curriculum and pedagogy need to be seen in context and both need attention for strengthening school reform.

Finally, the fifth dimension needing attention in school reform is *the evaluative*. It makes no sense whatsoever to write policy papers about educational reform and to prepare syllabi and curriculum guides for teachers that advocate a new direction for educational practice and continue to assess the outcomes of schooling on instruments that reflect older, more traditional views. Yet, this is what we often do. Consider the proposition that good schools increase individuality and cultivate productive idiosyncrasy. Consider the idea that good schools increase differences among students, not diminish them. If we truly embraced these views, how could we go about evaluating the educational effectiveness of schools? Would commensurability remain an important criterion? What kinds of opportunities could be provided to students to develop what they have learned? To what extent would we use closed-ended examinations?

High-stake assessment procedures symbolically and practically represent what "higher-ups" care about and performance on such procedures significantly affects both the options students have and the professional reputation of teachers. How outcomes are evaluated is a major agent influencing what teachers and school administrators pay attention to. Thus, the redesign of assessment instruments so that they provide information about what teachers and others care about most from an educational perspective is a fundamental aspect of school reform. Schools cannot move in one direction and assess teachers and students using procedures that represent values in quite another direction.

Evaluation, however, should not be conceived of exclusively in terms of outcome assessment. Evaluation, it seems to me, should be regarded as an educational medium. The processes of teaching and the quality of what is taught, as well their outcomes, are the proper subject matter of an adequate approach to educational evaluation. If the quality of the content being taught is poor, it does not matter much if the quality of teaching is good. Indeed, if the content being taught is pernicious, excellence in teaching is a vice.

Evaluation is an aspect of professional educational practice that should be regarded as one of the major means through which educators can secure information they can use to enhance the quality of their work. Evaluation ought to be an ongoing part of the process of education, one that contributes to its enhancement, not simply a means for scoring students and teachers.

CONCLUSION

These factors, the *intentional,* the *structural,* the *curricular,* the *pedagogical,* and the *evaluative,* are all important and interacting dimensions of schooling. Collectively they constitute a kind of ecology of schooling. To bring about reform in schools that is more than superficial and short-term requires attention to all of them.

To consider these dimensions not simply as an academic enterprise but as an activity leading to an agenda that can be acted on is the tough test of educational reform efforts. In some way that agenda has to be set. In setting this agenda teachers will need to be involved, as well as school administrators who themselves are not afraid of new forms of practice. The details of this agenda—the role, for example, that universities might play in school reform—cannot be addressed in this article. Yet unless the plan for school reform is comprehensive, it is likely to leave little residue in the long run. We sometimes say in the United States that educational reform is like a pendulum swing—we go back and forth. Pendulums are objects that move without going any place. Recognizing the ecological character of schools and facing up to the magnitude of the task of educational reform are important beginning efforts in dismounting from the pendulum.

ENDNOTES

1. USA Research. *A Nation at Risk: The Full Account* (Cambridge: USA Research, 1984).

2. Larry Cuban, "Reforming Again, Again, and Again," *Educational Researcher* 19, no. 1 (January–February 1990): 3–13.

3. David Berliner, "In Pursuit of the Expert Pedagogue," *Educational Researcher* 15, no. 7 (1986): 5–10.

4. D. Flinders, "What Teachers Learn from Teaching: Educational Outcomes of Instructional Adaptation" (Ph.D. diss., Stanford University, 1987).

5. Robert Dreeben, *On What Is Learned in School* (New York: Addison-Wesley, 1968); Philip W. Jackson, *Life in Classrooms* (New York: Holt, Rinehart & Winston, 1968); Dan C. Lortie, *School Teacher: A Psychological Study* (Chicago: University of Chicago Press, 1975); Sara Lawrence Lightfoot, *The Good High School: Portraits of Character and Culture* (New York: Basic Books, 1983); Arthur G. Powell, Eleanor Farrar, and David K. Cohen, *The Shopping Mall High School: Winners and Losers in the Educational Marketplace* (Boston: Houghton Mifflin, 1985); Elliot W. Eisner, *What High Schools Are Like: Views from the Inside* (Stanford: Stanford School of Education, 1985); and Willard W. Waller, *The Sociology of Teaching* (New York: John Wiley, 1932).

6. Michael Apple, *Education and Power* (Boston: Routledge & Kegan Paul, 1982); and Henry Giroux, *Critical Pedagogy, the State, and Cultural Struggle* (Albany: University of New York Press, 1989).

7. Pierre Bourdieu, *Reproduction in Education's Society and Culture* (London: Sage Publications, 1977).

8. Eisner, *What High Schools Are Like.*

9. J. M. Atkin, "Can Educational Research Keep Pace with Educational Reform?" *Kappan* 71, no. 3 (November 1989): 200–05.

10. *Restructuring California Education: A Design for Public Education in the Twenty-first Century, Recommendations to the California Business Round Table* (Berkeley: B. W. Associates, 1988).

11. Eisner, *What High Schools Are Like.*

12. John I. Goodlad, *A Place Called School: Prospects for the Future* (New York: McGraw-Hill, 1984); Theodore R. Sizer, *Horace's Compromise: The Dilemma of the American High School* (Boston: Houghton Mifflin, 1984); Powell, Farrar, and Cohen, *The Shopping Mall High School*; and Eisner, *What High Schools Are Like.*

13. H. Wolcott, *The Man in the Principal's Office* (Prospect Heights, Ill.: Waveland Press, 1984).

14. P. Willis, *Learning to Labor* (Lexington: D.C. Heath, 1977).

15. Lightfood, *The Good High School.*

16. Elliot W. Eisner, *The Enlightened Eye: Qualitative Inquiry and the Enhancement of Educational Practice* (New York: Macmillan, 1991).

17. S. S. Stodolsky, *The Subject Matters* (Chicago: University of Chicago Press, 1988).

18. Eisner, *The Enlightened Eye.*

19. Basil Bernstein, "On the Classification and Framing of Educational Knowledge," in *Knowledge and Control,* ed. M. Young (London: Collier-Macmillan, 1971), pp. 47–69.

20. Eisner, *What High Schools Are Like*; and Sizer, *Horace's Compromise.*

21. Bernstein, "On the Classification and Framing of Educational Knowledge."

22. Eisner, *What High Schools Are Like.*

23. Goodlad, *A Place Called School.*

24. Apple, *Education and Power.*

25. Eisner, *What High Schools Are Like.*

DISCUSSION QUESTIONS

1. If teachers were to assume the responsibility of creating local educational policy, should they be held accountable for the consequences of those policies? Why? Why not?

2. How does the organization of schools impede or support reform efforts?

3. How can qualitative forms of evaluation facilitate reform?

4. What role should universities play in local school reform?

5. What voice should students have in reform initiatives?

37

Getting Reform Right

MICHAEL G. FULLAN
MATTHEW B. MILES

FOCUSING QUESTIONS

1. *How does knowledge of the change process facilitate outcomes?*
2. *Why do reform efforts tend to result in failure?*
3. *How do individuals' personal agendas impact reforms?*
4. *In what way are reform and politics related?*
5. *What problems associated with reform efforts are reported to coincide with site-based management?*

After years of failed education reform, educators are more and more in the habit of saying that "knowledge of the change process" is crucial. But few people really know what that means. The phrase is used superficially, glibly, as if saying it over and over will lead to understanding and appropriate action.

We do believe that knowing about the change process is crucial. But there are as many myths as there are truths associated with change, and it is time to deepen the way we think about change. We need to assess our knowledge more critically and describe what we know. One needs a good deal of sophistication to grasp the fundamentals of the change process and to use that knowledge wisely.

We also believe that serious education reform will never be achieved until there is a significant increase in the number of people—leaders and other participants alike—who have come to internalize and habitually act on basic knowledge of how successful change takes place. Reformers talk of the need for deeper, second-order changes in the structures and cultures of schools, rather than superficial first-order changes.[1] But no change would be more funda-mental than a dramatic expansion of the capacity of individuals and organizations to understand and deal with change. This generic capacity is worth more than a hundred individual success stories of implementing specific innovations. As we shall see, even individual success stories don't last long without an appreciation of how to keep changes alive.

Rather than develop a new strategy for each new wave of reform, we must use basic knowledge about the do's and don'ts of bringing about *continuous improvement*. In this chapter we present this knowledge in the form of seven basic reasons why reform fails—and seven propositions that could lead to success.

WHY REFORM FAILS

Schools and districts are overloaded with problems—and, ironically, with solutions that don't work. Thus things get worse instead of better. Even our rare success stories appear as isolated pockets of excellence and are as likely to atrophy as to prosper over time. We get glimpses of the power of change, but we have little confidence that we know how to harness forces for continuous improvement. The problem is not really lack of innovation, but the enormous overload of fragmented, uncoordinated, and ephemeral attempts at change.

We begin with reasons why typical approaches do not work. In our view there are seven basic reasons why reforms fail. Though each one has its own form, these seven should be understood in combination, as a set.

1. Faulty Maps of Change

It's hard to get to a destination when your map doesn't accurately represent the territory you're to traverse. Everyone involved in school reform—teachers, administrators, parents, students, district staff members, consultants, board members, state department officials, legislators, materials developers, publishers, test-makers, teacher educators, researchers—has a personal map of how change proceeds. These constructs are often expressed in the form of a proposition or statement.

1. Resistance is inevitable, because people resist change.
2. Every school is unique.
3. *Plus ça change, plus c'est la même chose.*
4. Schools are essentially conservative institutions, harder to change than other organizations.
5. You just have to live reform one day at a time.
6. You need a mission, objectives, and series of tasks laid out well in advance.
7. You can never please everyone, so just push ahead with reforms.
8. Full participation of everyone involved in a change is essential.
9. Keep it simple, stupid: go for small, easy changes rather than big, demanding ones.
10. Mandate change, because people won't do it otherwise.

People act on their maps. But maps such as these don't provide reliable or valid guidance.

Some, like number 1, are simply self-sealing and tautological. Others, like number 2, are true in the abstract but totally unhelpful in providing guidance. Imagine if a Michelin guide book were to tell you that "each restaurant is unique," refuse to make ratings, and tell you that you're on your own.

Some, like number 3, have the seductive appearance of truth, though they are mostly false. It stretches the bounds of credulity to say that the schools we see today are no different from those of yesteryear or that all change efforts are self-defeating. Such maps are self-defeating. At their worst, they tell us that nothing really changes— and that nothing will work. On such self-exculpatory propositions as number 4, there's simply very little evidence, and what there is leads to the verdict of "not proven."[2]

Sometimes our maps are in conflict with themselves or with the maps of colleagues. For example, number 5 advocates the virtues of improvisation, while number 6 lauds rational planning. In fact, the literature on organizational change and a recent study of major change in urban high schools show that *neither* statement is valid as a guide to successful school reform.[3] The same appears to be true for propositions 7 and 8.

Still other mapping statements are directly contradicted by empirical evidence. For example, though number 9 looks obvious, studies of change have repeatedly found that substantial change efforts that address multiple problems are more likely to succeed and survive than small-scale, easily trivialized innovations.[4]

And number 10, as attractive as it may be politically, simply doesn't work. Indeed, it often makes matters worse. You can't mandate important changes, because they require skill, motivation, commitment, and discretionary judgment on the part of those who must change.[5]

Our aim here is not to debunk all our maps. Maps are crucial. But unless a map is a valid representation of the territory, we won't get where we want to go. Later in this article, we will outline a map that, we believe, corresponds well with the real territory of change.

2. Complex Problems

Another major reason for the failure of reform is that the solutions are not easy—or even known in many cases. A number of years ago Arthur Wise labeled this problem the "hyperrationalization" of reform:

> To create goals for education is to will that something occur. But goals, in the absence of a theory of how to achieve them, are mere wishful thinking. If there is no reason to believe a goal is attainable—perhaps evidenced by the fact that it has never been attained—then a rational planning model may not result in goal attainment.[6]

The reform agenda has broadened in fundamental ways in the last five years. One need only mention the comprehensive reform legislation adopted in virtually every state and the scores of restructuring efforts in order to realize that current change efforts are enormously complex—both in the substance of their goals and in the capacity of individuals and institutions to carry out and coordinate reforms.

Education *is* a complex system, and its reform is even more complex. Even if one considers only seemingly simple, first-order changes, the number of components and their interrelationships are staggering: curriculum and instruction, school organization, student services, community involvement, teacher inservice training, assessment, reporting, and evaluation. Deeper, second-order changes in school cultures, teacher/student relationships, and values and expectations of the system are all the more daunting.

Furthermore, higher-order educational goals for all students require knowledge and abilities that we have never demonstrated. In many cases, we simply don't know how to proceed; solutions have yet to be developed. This is no reason to stop trying, but we must remember that it is folly to act as if we know how to solve complex problems in short order. We must have an approach to reform that acknowledges that we don't necessarily know all the answers, that is conducive to developing solutions as we go along, and that sustains our commitment and persistence to stay with the problem until we get somewhere. In other words, we need a different map for solving complex rather than simple problems.

3. Symbols Over Substance

In the RAND-sponsored study of federal programs supporting educational change, Paul Berman and Milbrey McLaughlin found that some school districts adopted external innovations for opportunistic reasons rather than to solve a particular problem. These apparent reforms brought extra resources (which were not necessarily used for the intended purpose), symbolized that action was being taken (whether or not follow-up occurred), and furthered the careers of the innovators (whether or not the innovation succeeded). Thus the mere appearance of innovation is sometimes sufficient for achieving political success.

Education reform is as much a political as an educational process, and it has both negative and positive aspects. One need not question the motives of political decision makers to appreciate the negative. Political time lines are at variance with the time lines for education reform. This difference often results in vague goals, unrealistic schedules, a preoccupation with symbols of reform (new legislation, task forces, commissions, and the like), and shifting priorities as political pressures ebb and flow.

We acknowledge that symbols are essential for success. They serve to crystallize images and to attract and generate political power and financial resources. Symbols can also provide personal and collective meaning and give people faith and confidence when they are dealing with unclear goals and complex situations.[7] They are essential for galvanizing visions, acquiring resources, and carrying out concerted action. When symbols and substance are congruent, they form a powerful combination.

Nonetheless, reform often fails because politics favors symbols over substance. Substantial change in practice requires a lot of hard and clever work "on the ground," which is not the strong point of political players. After several experiences with the dominance of symbolic change over substantive change, people become cynical and take the next change that comes along much less seriously.

Symbolic change does not have to be without substance, however. Indeed, the best examples of effective symbols are grounded in rituals, ceremonies, and other events in the daily life of an organization. While we cannot have effective reform without symbols, we can easily have symbols without effective reform—the predominant experience of most educators and one that predisposes them to be skeptical about *all* reforms.

4. Impatient and Superficial Solutions

Reforms also fail because our attempts to solve problems are frequently superficial. Superficial solutions, introduced quickly in an atmosphere of crisis, normally make matters worse.[8] This problem is all the more serious now that we are tackling large-scale reforms, for the consequences of failure are much more serious.

Reforms in structure are especially susceptible to superficiality and unrealistic time lines, because they can be launched through political or administrative mandates. Two examples at opposite ends of the political spectrum provide cases in point. A recent study of the impact of statewide testing in two states found that, while new testing mandates caused action at the local level, they also narrowed the curriculum and created adverse conditions for reform:

> [C]oping with the pressure to attain satisfactory results in high-stakes tests caused educators to develop almost a "crisis mentality" in their approach, in that they jumped quickly into "solutions" to address a specific issue. They narrowed the range of instructional strategies from which they selected means to instruct their students; they narrowed the content of the material they chose to present to students; and they narrowed the range of course offerings available to students.[9]

Site-based management—opposite in many ways to the strategy of centralized testing—also shows problems associated with structural reforms. Daniel Levine and Eugene Eubanks, among others, have indicated how school-based models often result in changes in formal decision-making structures but rarely result in a focus on developing instructional skills or on changing the culture of schools.[10] There are numerous other examples of new legislation and policies—career ladders, reentering and induction policies, testing and competency requirements, and so on—being rushed into place with little forethought about possible negative consequences and side effects.

A related bane of reform is faddism. Schools, districts, and states are under tremendous pressure to reform. Innovation and reform are big business, politically and economically. The temptation is great to latch on to the quick fix, to go along with the trend, to react uncritically to endorsed innovations as they come and go. Local educators experience most school reforms as fads.

There are two underlying problems. One is that mistaken or superficial solutions are introduced; the other is that, even when the solution is on the right track, hasty implementation leads to failure. Structural solutions are relatively easy to initiate under the right political conditions, but they are no substitute for the hard work, skill, and commitment needed to blend different structural changes into a successful reform effort. In other words, changes in structure must go hand in hand with changes in culture and in the individual and collective capacity to work through new structures. Because education reform is so complex, we cannot know in advance exactly which new structures and behavioral patterns should go together or how they should mesh. But we do know that neglecting one or the other is a surefire recipe for failure.

5. Misunderstanding Resistance

Things hardly ever go easily during change efforts. Since change necessarily involves people, and people can commit willed actions, it seems natural to attribute progress that is slower than we might wish to their "resistance." Before a recent workshop, one of us asked a group of principals to list the problems they faced in a specific change project. More than half said "resistance"—variously known as intransigence, entrenchment, fearfulness, reluctance to buy in, complacency, unwillingness to alter behaviors, and failure to recognize the need for change. These traits were attributed to teachers and other staff members, though not to the principals themselves.

But it is usually unproductive to label an attitude or action "resistance." It diverts attention from real problems of implementation, such as diffuse objectives, lack of technical skill, or insufficient resources for change. In effect, the label also individualizes issues of change and converts everything into a matter of "attitude." Because such labeling places the blame (and the responsibility for the solution) on others, it immobilizes people and leads to "if only" thinking.

Change does involve individual attitudes and behaviors, but they need to be framed as natural responses to transition, not misunderstood as "resistance." During transitions from a familiar to a new state of affairs, individuals must normally confront the loss of the old and commit themselves to the new, unlearn old beliefs and behaviors and learn new ones, and move from anxiousness and uncertainty to stabilization and coherence. Any significant change involves a period of intense personal and organizational learning and problem solving. People need supports for such work, not displays of impatience.

Blaming "resistance" for the slow pace of reform also keeps us from understanding that individuals and groups faced with something new need to assess the change for its genuine possibilities and for how it bears on their self-interest. From computers across the curriculum, to mainstreaming, to portfolio assessments, to a radical change in the time schedule, significant changes normally require extra effort during the transitional stage. Moreover, there's little certainty about the kinds of outcomes that may ensue for students and teachers (and less assurance that

they will be any better than the status quo). These are legitimate issues that deserve careful attention.

Many reform initiatives are ill-conceived, and many others are fads. The most authentic response to such efforts is resistance. Nevertheless, when resistance is misunderstood, we are immediately set on a self-defeating path. Reframing the legitimate basis of most forms of resistance will allow us to get a more productive start and to isolate the real problems of improvement.

6. Attrition of Pockets of Success

There are many examples of successful reforms in individual schools—cases in which the strong efforts of teachers, principals, and district administrators have brought about significant chances in classroom and school practice.[11] We do not have much evidence about the durability of such successes, but we have reason to believe that they may not survive if the conditions under which they developed are changed.

Successful reforms have typically required enormous effort on the part of one or more individuals—effort that may not be sustainable over time. For example, staff collaboration takes much energy and time to develop, yet it can disappear overnight when a few key people leave. What happens outside the school—such as changes in district policies on the selection and transfer of teachers and principals—can easily undo gains that have been made.

Local innovators, even when they are successful in the short run, may burn themselves out or unwittingly seal themselves off from the surrounding environment. Thus schools can become hotbeds of innovation and reform in the absence of external support, but they cannot *stay* innovative without the continuing support of the district and other agencies. Innovative schools may enjoy external support from a critically important sponsor (e.g., the district superintendent) or from a given agency only to see that support disappear when the sponsor moves on or the agency changes policies. Of course, the failure to institutionalize an innovation and build it into the normal structures and practices of the organization underlies the disappearance of many reforms.[12]

We suspect that few things are more discouraging than working hard against long odds over a period of time to achieve a modicum of success—only to see it evaporate in short order as unrelated events take their toll. It is not enough to achieve isolated pockets of success. Reform fails unless we can demonstrate that pockets of success add up to new structures, procedures, and school cultures that press for continuous improvement. So far there is little such evidence.

7. Misuse of Knowledge About the Change Process

The final problem is related to a particular version of faulty maps: "knowledge" of the change process is often cited as the authority for taking certain actions. Statements such as "Ownership is the key to reform," "Lots of inservice training is required," "The school is the unit of change," "Vision and leadership are critical," and so on are all half-truths. Taken literally, they can be misused.

Reform is systemic, and actions based on knowledge of the change process must be systemic, too. To succeed we need to link a number of key aspects of knowledge and maintain the connections before and during the process of change. In the following section we offer seven such themes, which we believe warrant being called propositions for success.

PROPOSITIONS FOR SUCCESS

The seven basic themes or lessons derived from current knowledge of successful change form a set and must be contemplated in relation to one another. When it comes to reform, partial theories are not very useful. We can say flatly that reform will not be achieved until these seven orientations have been incorporated into the thinking and reflected in the actions of those involved in change efforts.

1. Change Is Learning—Loaded with Uncertainty

Change is a process of coming to grips with new personal meaning, and so it is a learning process. Peter Marris states the problem this way:

> When those who have the power to manipulate changes act as if they have only to explain, and when their explanations are not at once accepted, shrug off opposition as ignorance or prejudice, they express a profound contempt for the meaning of lives other than their own. For the reformers have already assimilated these changes to their purposes, and worked out a reformulation which makes sense to them, perhaps through months or years of analysis and debate. If they deny others the chance to do the same, they treat them as puppets dangling by the threads of their own conceptions.[13]

Even well-developed innovations represent new meaning and new learning for those who encounter them initially and require time to assimilate them. So many studies have documented this early period of difficulty that we have given it a label—"the implementation dip."[14] Even in cases where reform eventually succeeds, things will often go wrong before they go right. Michael Huberman and Matthew Miles found that the absence of early difficulty in a reform effort was usually a sign that not much was being attempted; superficial or trivial change was being substituted for substantial change.[15]

More complex reforms, such as restructuring, represent even greater uncertainty: first, because more is being attempted; second, because the solution is not known in advance. In short, anxiety, difficulties, and uncertainty are *intrinsic to all successful change.*

One can see why a climate that encourages risk-taking is so critical. People will not venture into uncertainty unless there is an appreciation that difficulties encountered are a natural part of the process. And if people do not venture into uncertainty, no significant change will occur.

Understanding successful change as learning also puts ownership in perspective. In our view, ownership of a reform cannot be achieved *in advance* of learning something new. A deep sense of ownership comes only through learning. In this sense, ownership is stronger in the middle of a successful change process than at the beginning and stronger still at the end. Ownership is both a process and a state.

The first proposition for success, then, is to understand that all change involves learning and that all learning involves coming to understand and to be good at something new. Thus conditions that support learning must be part and parcel of any change effort. Such conditions are also necessary for the valid rejection of particular changes, because many people reject complex innovations prematurely, that is, before they are in a sound position to make such a judgment.

2. Change Is a Journey, Not a Blueprint

If change involved implementing single, well-developed, proven innovations one at a time, perhaps we could make blueprints for change. But school districts and schools are in the business of implementing a bewildering array of innovations and policies simultaneously. Moreover, reforms that aim at restructuring are so multifaceted and complex that solutions for any particular setting cannot be known in advance. If one tries to account for the complexity of the situation with an equally complex implementation plan, the process will become unwieldy, cumbersome, and usually unsuccessful.

There can be no blueprints for change, because rational planning models for complex social change (such as education reform) do not work. Rather, what is needed is a guided journey. Karen Seashore Louis and Matthew Miles provide a clear analysis of this evolutionary planning process in their study of urban high schools involved in major change efforts:

> The evolutionary perspective rests on the assumption that the environment both inside and outside organizations is often chaotic. No specific plan can last for very long, because it will either become outmoded due to changing external pres-

sures, or because disagreement over priorities arises within the organization. Yet there is no reason to assume that the best response is to plan passively, relying on incremental decisions. Instead, the organization can cycle back and forth between efforts to gain normative consensus about what it may become, to plan strategies for getting there, and to carry out decentralized incremental experimentation that harnesses the creativity of all members to the change effort. . . . Strategy is viewed as a flexible tool, rather than a semi-permanent expansion of the mission.[16]

The message is not the traditional "Plan, then do," but "Do, then plan . . . and do and plan some more." Even the development of a shared vision that is central to reform is better thought of as a journey in which people's sense of purpose is identified, considered, and continuously shaped and reshaped.

3. Problems Are Our Friends

School improvement is a problem-rich process. Change threatens existing interests and routines, heightens uncertainty, and increases complexity. The typical principal in the study of urban schools conducted by Louis and Miles mentioned three or four major problems (and several minor ones) with reform efforts. They ranged from poor coordination to staff polarization and from lack of needed skills to heart attacks suffered by key figures. Problems arise naturally from the demands of the change process itself, from the people involved, and from the structure and procedures of schools and districts. Some are easily solved; others are almost intractable.

It seems perverse to say that problems are our friends, but we cannot develop effective responses to complex situations unless we actively seek and confront real problems that are difficult to solve. Problems are our friends because only through immersing ourselves in problems can we come up with creative solutions. Problems are the route to deeper change and deeper satisfaction. In this sense, effective organizations "embrace problems" rather than avoid them.

Too often, change-related problems are ignored, denied, or treated as an occasion for blame and defense. Success in school reform efforts is much more likely when problems are treated as natural, expected phenomena. Only by tracking problems can we understand what we need to do next to get what we want. Problems must be taken seriously, not attributed to "resistance" or to the ignorance and wrongheadedness of others.

What to do about problems? In their study of urban schools, Louis and Miles classified coping styles, ranging from relatively shallow ones (doing nothing at all, procrastinating, "doing it the usual way," easing off, or increasing pressure) to deeper ones (building personal capacity through training, enhancing system capacity, comprehensive restaffing, or system restructuring/redesign). They found that schools that were least successful at change *always* used shallow coping styles. Schools that were successful in changing could and did make structural changes in an effort to solve difficult problems. However, they were also willing to use Band-Aid solutions when a problem was judged to be minor. It's important to note that successful schools did *not* have fewer problems than other schools—they just coped with them better.

The enemies of good coping are passivity, denial, avoidance, conventionality, and fear of being "too radical." Good coping is active, assertive, inventive. It goes to the root of the problem when that is needed.

We cannot cope better through being exhorted to do so. "Deep coping"—the key to solving difficult problems of reform—appears to be more likely when schools are working on a clear, shared vision of where they are heading and when they create an active coping structure (e.g., a coordinating committee or a steering group) that steadily and actively tracks problems and monitors the results of coping efforts. Such a structure benefits from empowerment, brings more resources to bear on problems, and keeps the energy for change focused. In short, the assertive pursuit of problems in the service of continuous improve-ment is the kind of accountability that can make a difference.

4. Change Is Resource-hungry

Even a moderate-sized school may spend a million dollars a year on salaries, maintenance, and materials. And that's just for keeping schools as they are, not for changing them. Change demands additional resources for training, for substitutes, for new materials, for new space, and, above all, for time. Change is "resource-hungry" because of what it represents—developing solutions to complex problems, learning new skills, arriving at new insights, all carried out in a social setting already overloaded with demands. Such serious personal and collective development necessarily demands resources.

Every analysis of the problems of change efforts that we have seen in the last decade of research and practice has concluded that time is the salient issue. Most recently, the survey of urban high schools by Louis and Miles found that the average principal with a schoolwide reform project spent 70 days a year on change management. That's 32% of an administrator's year. The teachers most closely engaged with the change effort spent some 23 days a year, or 13% of their time on reform. Since we have to keep school while we change school, such overloads are to be expected.

But time is energy. And success is likely only when the extra energy requirements of change are met through the provision of released time or through a redesigned schedule that includes space for the extra work of change.

Time is also money. And Louis and Miles discovered that serious change in big-city high schools requires an annual investment of between $50,000 and $100,000. They also found some schools spending five times that much with little to show for it. The key seemed to be whether the money simply went for new jobs and expensive equipment or was spent for local capacity-building (acquiring external assistance, training trainers, leveraging other add-on funds, and so on). Nevertheless, some minimum level of funding is always needed.

Assistance itself can be a major resource for change. It may include training, consulting, coaching, coordination, and capacity-building. Many studies have suggested that good assistance to schools is strong, sustained over years, closely responsive to local needs, and focused on building local capacity. Louis and Miles found that at least 30 days a year of *external* assistance—with more than that provided internally—was essential for success.

We can also think of educational "content resources"—such big ideas as effective schools, teaching for understanding, empowerment, and school-based management—that guide and energize the work of change. In addition, there are psychosocial resources, such as support, commitment, influence, and power. They're supposedly intangible, but they are critical for success.

The work of change requires attention not just to resources, but to "resourcing." The actions required are those of scanning the school and its environment for resources and matching them to existing needs; acquiring resources (buying, negotiating, or just plain grabbing); reworking them for a better fit to the situation; creating time through schedule changes and other arrangements; and building local capacity through the development of such structures as steering groups, coordinating committees, and cadres of local trainers.

Good resourcing requires facing up to the need for funds and abjuring any false pride about self-sufficiency. Above all, it takes willingness to invent, to go outside the frame in garnering and reworking resources. (We are reminded of the principal who used money for the heating system to pay for desperately needed repainting and renovation, saying, "I knew that, if the boiler broke, they'd have to fix it anyway.") The stance is one of steady and tenacious searching for and judicious use of the extra resources that any change requires. Asking for assistance and seeking other resources are signs of strength, not weakness.

5. Change Requires the Power to Manage It

Change initiatives do not run themselves. They require that substantial effort be devoted to such tasks as monitoring implementation, keeping everyone informed of what's happening, linking multiple change projects (typical in most schools), locating unsolved problems, and taking clear coping action. In Louis and Miles' study, such efforts occurred literally 10 times more frequently in successfully changing schools than in unchanging ones.

There appear to be several essential ingredients in the successful management of change. First, the management of change goes best when it is carried out by a *cross-role group* (say, teachers, department heads, administrators, and—often—students and parents). In such a group different worlds collide, more learning occurs, and change is realistically managed. There is much evidence that steering a change effort in this way results in substantially increased teacher commitment.

Second, such a cross-role group needs *legitimacy*—i.e., a clear license to steer. It needs an explicit contract, widely understood in the school, as to what kinds of decisions it can make and what money it can spend. Such legitimacy is partly conferred at the front end and partly earned through the hard work of decision making and action. Most such groups do encounter staff polarization; they may be seen by others as an unfairly privileged elite; or they may be opposed on ideological grounds. Such polarization—often a sign that empowerment of a steering group is working—can be dealt with through open access to meetings, rotation of membership. and scrupulous reporting.

Third, even empowerment has its problems, and cooperation is required to solve them. Everyone has to learn to take the initiative instead of complaining, to trust colleagues, to live with ambiguity, to face the fact that shared decisions mean conflict. Principals have to rise above the fear of losing control, and they have to hone new skills: initiating actions firmly without being seen as "controlling," supporting others without taking over for them. All these stances and skills are learnable, but they take time. Kenneth Benne remarked 40 years ago that the skills of cooperative work should be "part of the general education of our people."[17] They haven't been, so far. But the technology for teaching these skills exists. It is up to steering groups to learn to work well together, using whatever assistance is required.

Fourth, the power to manage change does not stop at the schoolhouse door. Successful change efforts are most likely when the local district office is closely engaged with the changing school in a collaborative, supportive way and places few bureaucratic restrictions in the path of reform.

The bottom line is that the development of second-order changes in the culture of schools and in the capacity of teachers, principals, and communities to make a difference *requires* the power to manage the change at the local school level. We do not advocate handing over all decisions to the school. Schools and their environments must have an interactive and negotiated relationship. But complex problems cannot be solved from a distance; the steady growth of the power to manage change must be part of the solution.

6. Change Is Systemic

Political pressures combine with the segmented, uncoordinated nature of educational organizations to produce a "project mentality."[18] A steady stream of episodic innovations—cooperative learning, effective schools research, classroom management, assessment schemes, career ladders, peer coaching, etc., etc.—come and go. Not only do they fail to leave much of a trace, but they also leave teachers and the public with a growing cynicism that innovation is marginal and politically motivated.

What does it mean to work systemically? There are two aspects: 1) reform must focus on the development and interrelationships of all the main *components* of the system simultaneously—curriculum, teaching and teacher development, community, student support systems, and so on; and 2) reform must focus not just on structure, policy, and regulations but on deeper issues of the *culture* of the system. Fulfilling both requirements is a tall order. But it is possible.

This duality of reform (the need to deal with system components and system culture) must be attended to at both the state and district/school levels. It involves both restructuring and "reculturing."[19] Marshall Smith and Jennifer O'Day have mapped out a comprehensive plan for systemic reform at the state level that illustrates the kind of thinking and strategies involved.[20] At the school/district level, we see in the Toronto region's Learning Consortium a rather clear example of systemic reform in action.[21] Schools, supported by their districts, avoid ad hoc innovations and focus on a variety of coordinated short-term and mid- to long-term strategies. The short-term activities include inservice professional development on selected and interrelated themes; mid- to long-term strategies include vision building, initial teacher preparation, selection and induction, promotion procedures and criteria, school-based planning in a system context, curriculum reorganization, and the development of assessments. There is an explicit emphasis on new cultural norms for collaborative work and on the pursuit of continuous improvement.

Systemic reform is complex. Practically speaking, traditional approaches to innovation and reform in education have not been successful in bringing about lasting improvement. Systemic reform looks to be both more efficient and more effective, even though this proposition is less proven empirically than our other six. However, both conceptually and practically, it does seem to be on the right track.[22]

7. All Large-scale Change Is Implemented Locally

Change cannot be accomplished from afar. This cardinal rule crystallizes the previous six propositions. The ideas that change is learning, change is a journey, problems are our friends, change is resource-hungry, change requires the power to manage, and change is systemic all embody the fact that *local* implementation by everyday teachers, principals, parents, and students is the only way that change happens.

This observation has both an obvious and a less obvious meaning. The former reminds us all that any interest in system-wide reform must be accompanied by a preoccupation with how it plays itself out locally. The less obvious implication can be stated as a caution: we should not assume that only the local level counts and hand everything over to the individual school. A careful reading of the seven propositions together shows that extra-local agencies have critical—though decidedly not traditional—roles to play. Most fundamentally, their role is to help bring the seven propositions to life at the local level.

CONCLUSION

Modern societies are facing terrible problems, and education reform is seen as a major source of hope for solving them. But wishful thinking and legislation have deservedly poor track records as tools for social betterment. As educators increasingly acknowledge that the "change process is crucial," they ought to know what that means at the level at which change actually takes place. Whether we are on the receiving or initiating end of change (as all of us are at one time or another), we need to understand why education reform frequently fails, and we need to internalize and live out valid propositions for its success. Living out the seven propositions for successful change means not only making the change process more explicit within our own minds and actions, but also contributing to the knowledge of change on the part of those with whom we interact. Being knowledgeable about the change process may be both the best defense and the best offense we have in achieving substantial education reform.

ENDNOTES

1. Larry Cuban, "Reforming, Again, Again, and Again," *Educational Researcher,* April 1990, pp. 3–13; Richard F. Elmore, ed., *Restructuring Schools* (San Francisco: Jossey-Bass, 1990); and Michael Fullan, with Suzanne Steigelbauer, *The New Meaning of Educational Change* (New York: Teachers College Press, 1991).
2. Matthew B. Miles, "Mapping the Common Properties of Schools," in Rolf Lehming and Michael Kane, eds., *Improving Schools: Using What We Know* (Santa Monica, Calif.: Sage, 1981), pp. 42–114; and Matthew B. Miles and Karen Seashore Louis, "Research on Institutionalization: A Reflective Review," in Matthew B. Miles, Mats Ekholm, and Rolf Vandenberghe, eds., *Lasting School Improvement: Exploring the Process of Institutionalization* (Leuven, Belgium: Acco, 1987), pp. 24–44.
3. Karen Seashore Louis and Matthew B. Miles, *Improving the Urban High School: What Works and Why* (New York: Teachers College Press, 1990).
4. Paul Berman and Milbrey W. McLaughlin, *Federal Programs Supporting Educational Change, Vol. VIII: Implementing and Sustaining Innovations* (Santa Monica, Calif.: RAND Corporation, 1977); and Michael Huberman and Matthew B. Miles, *Innovation Up Close: How School Improvement Works* (New York: Plenum, 1984).
5. Milbrey W. McLaughlin, "The Rand Change Agent Study Revisited: Macro Perspectives and Micro Realities," *Educational Researcher,* December 1990, pp. 11–16.
6. Arthur Wise, "Why Educational Policies Often Fail: The Hyperrationalization Hypothesis," *Curriculum Studies,* vol. 1, 1977, p. 48.
7. Lee Bolman and Terrence Deal, *Reframing Organizations* (San Francisco: Jossey-Bass, 1990).

8. Samuel D. Sieber, *Fatal Solutions* (Norwood, N.J.: Ablex, 1982).

9. H. Dickson Corbett and Bruce Wilson, *Testing, Reform, and Rebellion* (Norwood, N.J.: Ablex, 1990), p. 207.

10. Daniel U. Levine and Eugene E. Eubanks, "Site-Based Management: Engine for Reform or Pipedream? Pitfalls and Prerequisites for Success in Site-Based Management," unpublished manuscript, University of Missouri, Kansas City.

11. Bruce Joyce et al., "School Renewal as Cultural Change," *Educational Leadership,* November 1989, pp. 70–77; Louis and Miles, op. cit.; and Richard Wallace, Paul LeMahieu, and William Bickel, "The Pittsburgh Experience: Achieving Commitment to Comprehensive Staff Development," in Bruce Joyce, ed., *Changing School Culture Through Staff Development* (Alexandria, Va.: Association for Supervision and Curriculum Development, 1990), pp. 185–202.

12. Miles and Louis, op. cit.; and Matthew B. Miles and Mats Ekholm, "Will New Structures *Stay* Restructured?," paper presented at the annual meeting of the American Educational Research Association, Chicago, 1991.

13. Peter Marris, *Loss and Change* (New York: Doubleday, 1975), p. 166.

14. Fullan, with Steigelbauer, op. cit.

15. Huberman and Miles, op. cit.

16. Louis and Miles, p. 193.

17. Kenneth D. Benne, "Theory of Cooperative Planning," *Teachers College Record,* vol. 53, 1952, pp. 429–35.

18. Marshall Smith and Jennifer O'Day, "Systemic School Reform," in Susan Fuhrman and Bruce Malen, eds., *The Politics of Curriculum and Testing* (Philadelphia: Falmer Press, 1990), pp. 233–67.

19. "Systemic reform" is both a more accurate and a more powerful label than "restructuring" because it explicitly encompasses both structure and culture. See Andy Hargreaves, "Restructuring Restructuring: Postmodernity and the Prospects for Educational Change," paper presented at the annual meeting of the American Educational Research Association, Chicago, 1991.

20. Smith and O'Day, op. cit.

21. Nancy Watson and Michael Fullan, "Beyond School District-University Partnerships," in Michael Fullan and Andy Hargreaves, eds., *Teacher Development and Change* (Toronto: Falmer Press, 1992), pp. 213–42.

22. See Peter Senge, *The Fifth Discipline* (New York: Doubleday, 1990); and Michael G. Fullan, *Productive Educational Change: Going Deeper* (London: Falmer Press, forthcoming).

DISCUSSION QUESTIONS

1. What problems do urban principals typically encounter during the change process?

2. Why must change agents respond vigorously to problems?

3. What is the relationship between schools that are successful at change and coping styles?

4. How does legitimization of the reform process influence outcomes?

5. In what way can cross-role group interactions impact change?

6. How are system components and system cultures related to reform efforts?

Three Nations' Curricula: Policy Implications for U.S. Curriculum Reform

GERALD UNKS

FOCUSING QUESTIONS

1. *What curriculum design models guide educational delivery in Germany, Japan, Great Britain, and the United States?*
2. *How much time should American students spend in classrooms?*
3. *Should the school day be lengthened? Why? Why not?*
4. *Should U.S. policy makers adopt a standard on how much time students spend doing homework?*
5. *What voice should curricular scholars have concerning homework policies, subject matter requirements, or lengthening the school year?*

We in the United States are disposed to superlative notions of ourselves and our institutions. Should evidence arise that calls these ideas into question, there is a national apprehension which—when the institution is dear, or the evidence is perceived as overwhelming—can translate into hysteria.

In 1957, the country was preoccupied with the idea that Ivan and Natasha might read better than Johnny and Mary. Beginning in the early '80s, an economic slide and foreign competition raised creeping doubt in some quarters about our youngsters' academic prowess relative to that of Taro, Hanako, Hans, and Petra.

A number of studies compared the achievement of students in the United States with that of the students of many nations (Finn, 1991; National Commission on Excellence in Education, 1983; Lapointe, Mead, and Phillips, 1989; Cheney, 1987; Ravitch and Finn, 1987). Most of these studies found American students to be

wanting, and the authors proposed a variety of solutions, some of which came from abroad.

What follows is a status study of the curricula of three nations. Germany and Japan were chosen because they are often cited as America's chief economic (and, by implication, educational) rivals. Great Britain was selected because it has established a national curriculum, something that some American educators have recently proposed. By studying these three nations' curricula, we can present a tentative answer to the question, "Do they contain policy implications for the curriculum in the United States?"

SIX PRECAUTIONARY NOTES

First, a description of the curriculum of an entire nation is inherently flawed. Meaning presents particular difficulty. For example, how many minutes constitute "a class period?" Similarly, what does "a subject" mean? Plane geometry may be clear, but literature, social studies, or (in Japan) "moral education" is rather murky.

The length of a school year is more easily measured; however, in some nations, teacher work days are not exempted from the total count. The length, in years, of the total schooling experience varies among nations. Thus, when a nation's curriculum guide specifies that "all children will study social studies for one period each day throughout their years in school," we have encountered a statement upon which the American grid of meaning cannot easily or reliably be imposed.

Second, generalization—with all its accompanying errors—is a necessity. Few are sufficiently naive as to believe that all students, teachers, administrators, or schools are identical. Simply because an external authority has mandated a course of study does not ensure that it will be followed to the letter (or at all) by a school or by a teacher. Nor is there any compelling evidence that teachers—even those who are bent on teaching a subject exactly as directed—can do so with equal levels of skill or obtain the same amount of success (Fishman and Martin, 1986).

Variability is the essence of humanity and all its institutions. When national curriculum patterns are presented as a generalized fact, one must acknowledge that much reality has been lost, and this loss increases in direct proportion to the level of autonomy given to local authorities and to individual schools and teachers.

Third, while the literature on international curriculum patterns is voluminous, most of it uses comparative data to measure the failure or success of American and foreign students. Most of these data report outcomes at the end of the secondary school experience, irrespective of how long the total schooling experience lasted or what it contained. A disproportionately large number of these studies focus only on achievement in science and math. It is difficult to obtain a year-by-year listing of what subjects the typical student studies in school, particularly in the early years. Finally, some of these comparative studies are selective in what they report, concentrating on

those data that support the authors' disposition for or against current educational practices in the United States rather than presenting the entire curricular picture of a nation. When seeking to describe a nation's total curriculum, researchers must rely upon old curriculum guides, dated national directives, and/or anecdotal information from administrators, teachers, and students.

Fourth, in this study, we will presume that a nation's curriculum is static. We know that this claim is essentially false, for although curriculum change is often viewed as glacial, in reality the curriculum is constantly being buffeted by the dynamics of a nation's political and social climate. The forces of liberalism and conservatism push and pull against the structure of the curriculum; each in turn, dominating and submitting, and waxing and waning in power and control.

In Germany, for example, the forces of elitism and egalitarianism maintain a constant tension in education policy, just as the Conservative, Liberal, and Labour parties in Great Britain each have distinctly different educational agendas. Readers must be cautioned, however, that—throughout the world—the terms "conservative" and "liberal" have one meaning when it comes to political and social policies and just the opposite when it comes to educational policies.

The political and social conservative fears concentrated political power, loathes governmental interference, champions things local, and celebrates individual decision making. The educational conservative is fond of centralized authority, favors top-down management, and often is possessed of a bottom-line distrust of teachers as ultimate decisionmakers.

On the other hand, the educational liberal finds little worth in the central office, disdains authority from above, and cherishes empowerment. In contrast, the political and social liberal finds little wrong with far-off, central governmental intervention, particularly when it is seen as besting the establishment's apparent exploitation of the powerless and less fortunate.

In Great Britain, when the Conservative government seeks greater control over local education authorities, it is acting in perfect educational character, just as educational conservatives in the United States are acting true to form when they demand a national curriculum and national achievement tests. We will report on national curricula in the present tense, neglecting the real truth: Curricula are in constant political and social flux.

Fifth, many curricularists define the curriculum as the total of all experiences that a student has in school. We accept this macro conception; however, in this study we are forced to adopt a micro definition of curriculum. This presentation is confined to a discussion of the subjects that are studied in schools. When an activity other than a subject seems particularly noteworthy or informative, it will be presented.

For example, Japanese students, rather than janitors, clean their own classrooms and school buildings. In England, there is an "act of worship" in every school every day. Nonetheless, these activities are exceptions; our rule is to present subjects as the complete curriculum. The "hidden curriculum," which some educators consider the most important element in schooling, will not be presented.

Finally, in so far as possible, an attempt will be made to eliminate value judgments. If one nation's students study math for 10 years, while another's study it for 6, the former will not be considered better or worse. Similarly, if a national curriculum mandates home economics while another completely omits it, no judgment will be made. This article rests on the presumption that readers can and will evaluate a national curriculum—drawing upon their own experiences, dispositions, and prejudices. With these six precautionary notes clearly in focus, the curricula of the three nations can be presented.

THE CURRICULUM OF JAPAN

To understand the Japanese curriculum, it is necessary to begin at the end, not at the beginning, and at the top, not at the bottom. The entire school apparatus appears to be driven by the Japanese University Entrance Examinations—a series of achievement tests that have been called a national obsession. The examinations consist of three stages, and the First Stage National Common test comprises Japanese, English, mathematics, two social science subjects, and two natural science subjects. The questions are primarily short answer and multiple choice—not essay. Since attaining high scores on these examinations is so important to the Japanese people, schools are expected to prepare students for them—almost to the exclusion of any other activity.

Were the exams not a sufficient force to produce a national curriculum, the educational governance system would be. In Japan, the curriculum is prescribed by the Ministry of Education. All Japanese public and private schools are required to follow it.

National achievement examinations and a national top-down system of governance have particular impact on what and how teachers test. It creates a big market for ready-made, as opposed to teacher-made, tests—created by publishers to accompany their textbooks. In a 1974 study, Nippon Kyoshokium Kumiai, the national teachers union, found that 89.9 percent of the schools used these tests—even at the elementary level. Their analysis of these tests found that they emphasized rote memory and tested fragmented knowledge.

Table 38.1 is a simplified representation of the subjects required of typical Japanese students. The Japanese curriculum is organized along the familiar "spiral" model, moving from the immediate and concrete to the remote and abstract. Understanding this concept is particularly important when analyzing this very basic chart as well as Tables 38.2 and 38.3. Geography in the second grade is "my neighborhood." "My world" does not begin until grade seven. Similarly, natural science in the third grade may consist of a classroom garden, an insect collection, or a class pet. Chemistry and physics also deserve special attention. Only one year of "pure chemistry" and "pure physics" is required at the secondary level.

TABLE E 38.1   Simplified Representation of the Subjects Required of Typical Japanese Students

	COMPULSORY SCHOOLING										ELECTIVE		
Approximate age	5	6	7	8	9	10	11	12	13	14	15	16	17
Year in School	1	2	3	4	5	6	7	8	9	10	11	12	13
Grade	K	1	2	3	4	5	6	7	8	9	10	11	12
	ELEMENTARY SCHOOL							LOWER SECONDARY			UPPER SECONDARY		
Japanese Language		X[1]	X[1]	X[1]	X[1]	X	X	X	X	X	X	X	X
Japanese Literature						X	X	X	X	X	X	X	X
Mathematics		X[2]	X[2]	X[5]	X[5]	X[5]	X[5]	X[6]	X	X	X[7]	X	X
Science				3									
Natural				X[4]	X	X	X	X	X	X			
Biology					X	X	X	X	X	X			
Physics					X	X	X	X	X	X			
Astronomy					X	X	X	X	X	X			
Chemistry					X	X	X	X	X	X			
History						X	X	X	X	X	X	X	X
Japanese Govt.						X	X	X	X	X	X	X	X
Social Science								X	X	X			
Geography				X[3]	X	X	X	X	X	X	X[8]	X[8]	X[8]
Music & singing		X[4]	X	X	X	X	X	X	X	X	X	X	X
Fine arts		X[4]	X	X	X	X	X	X	X	X	X	X	X
Physical education		X[4]	X	X	X	X	X	X	X	X	X	X	X
Foreign language								X	X	X	X	X	X
Mech. drawing											X[9]	X[9]	X[9]
Home economics								X[10]	X[10]	X[10]	X[10]	X[10]	X[10]
Industrial arts								X[11]	X[11]	X[11]	X[9]	X[9]	X[9]
Moral education					X	X	X	X	X	X	X	X	X
Martial arts											X[11]	X[11]	X[11]

Notes:

[1] primarily instruction in reading and writing
[2] primarily addition and subtraction
[3] not distinguished as a separate subject; integrated into reading and writing
[4] instruction begins at a simple, almost "play" level and progresses through the grades to ever higher skill levels
[5] primarily multiplication, division, fractions, and decimals
[6] algebra and some geometry are introduced
[7] higher mathematics are introduced
[8] elective course
[9] offered only in special, technical high schools
[10] only females are required to take this course
[11] only males are required to take this course
[12] only one year of this subject is required in the upper secondary school

☐ = Subjects are integrated with one another.

■ = Only one year is required during the Upper Secondary School experience.

Source: Lio, 1992; Yoshioka, 1992

TABLE E 38.2 Simplified Representation of the Subjects Required of Typical British Students

	COMPULSORY SCHOOLING												ELECTIVE
	PRIMARY SCHOOL							SECONDARY					
Approximate age	5	6	7	8	9	10	11	12	13	14	15	16	17	18
Year in School	R	1	2	3	4	5	6	7	8	9	10	11	12	13
CORE SUBJECT	KEY STAGE I			KEY STAGE II				KEY STAGE III			KEY STAGE IV		EXAM COURSES	
English		X	X	X	X	X	X	X	X	X	X	X		
Mathematics		X	X	X	X	X	X	X	X	X	X	X		
Science														
Natural		X	X	X	X	X	X	X	X	X	X	X		
Biology		X	X	X	X	X	X	X	X	X	X	X		
Physics		X	X	X	X	X	X	X	X	X	X	X		
Astronomy		X	X	X	X	X	X	X	X	X	X	X		
Chemistry		X	X	X	X	X	X	X	X	X	X	X		
FOUNDATION SUBJECTS														
Technology/design		X	X	X	X	X	X	X	X	X	X	X		
History		X	X	X	X	X	X	X	X	X	X	X		
Geography		X	X	X	X	X	X	X	X	X	X	X		
Art		X	X	X	X	X	X	X	X	X	X	X		
Physical education		X	X	X	X	X	X	X	X	X	X	X		
Foreign language								X	X	X	X	X		
Career education														
Guidance														
Health														
Personal/social ed.														
Gender issues														
Multicultural ed.														

(RECEPTION is indicated vertically in the first primary column; the right column reads: "Examination subjects are chosen by individual students on the basis of interest, aptitude, and ability.")

■ (shaded) = Subjects are integrated into a general course of study.

□ (white) = Subjects are taught as specialized entities.

■ (black) = Subjects are taught at appropriate stages and in some cases all stages.

Sources: Department of Education and Science, 1989; Lynch, 1992B.

TABLE E 38.3   Simplified Representation of the Subjects Required of Typical Students in The Federal Republic of Germany

		COMPULSORY SCHOOLING										ELECTIVE		
		PRIMARY SCHOOL				SECONDARY								
Approximate age	5	6	7	8	9	10	11	12	13	14	15	16	17	18
Year in School		1	2	3	4	5	6	7	8	9	10^4	11	12	13
Grade	K	1	2	3	4	5	6	7	8	9	10^4	11	12	13
SUBJECT German Language		X	X	X	X	X	X	X	X	X	X			
Sachunerricht (everyday life observations)		X	X	X	X									
Mathematics		X	X	X	X	X	X	X	X	X	X			
Physical education		X	X	X	X	X	X	X	X	X	X			
Music		X	X	X	X	X	X	X	X	X	X			
Art/textile work		X	X	X	X	X	X	X	X	X	X			
Religious instruct.		X	X	X	X	X	X	X	X	X	X			
Forderunterricht (remedial work for students to support and tutor them to catch up and to keep up)		X	X	X	X									
Social science						X	X	X	X	X	X			
Natural science						X^3	X^3	X^3	X^3	X^3	X^3			
Foreign language						X	X	X	X	X	X			
Required elective								X^2	X^2	X	X			
Orientation class						X	X							
Technicals, economics, home economics								X^1	X^1	X^1	X^1			

(Elective column note, set vertically: Gymnasium level courses. See text for description and discussion. Abitur (leaving examination) is usually taken at the end of year 13.)

Notes: [1] <u>Hauptschule</u> only
[2] <u>Hauptschule</u> and <u>Realschule</u>
[3] includes biology, geography, physics, and chemistry, depending upon the availability of teachers trained in the respective subjects
[4] some <u>Hauptschule</u> end at grade 9

Sources: Blasius, 1992; Fishman and Martin, 1986, p. 109, 147, 149; Fuhr, p. 233; Schweins, 1992.

Do not imagine Japanese sixth graders working at bunsen burners or on trajectory motion; they are more likely pouring vinegar on baking soda or looking at gears in a bicycle. Subjects tend to be integrated through the eighth grade, taking on their specialized quality only at the secondary level,

This movement from the simple to the complex makes curricular sense, but it also allows for errors in interpretation—particularly if a comparison between countries is sought. Japanese students appear to be studying about the same things at about the same time as the students of other industrialized nations—with a few exceptions presented below.

Virtually all Japanese children begin organized, state-financed preschool activities at age three, and this experience grows in complexity as the children approach entry into elementary school. Homework (about 30 minutes each day) begins with the first grade, and increases to seven hours a day by the end of primary school; by high school, the average student is doing eight hours of homework.

Beginning with fifth and sixth grade, 80 to 90 percent of the students enroll in *iuku* (private schools that prepare students for examinations and, occasionally, remediate), which they attend for about one and a half hours each day, four or five days a week. Educational time-on-task is greater in Japan than in the other nations presented in this study.

THE CURRICULUM OF GREAT BRITAIN

In 1988, Great Britain, which until then had left virtually every schooling decision in the hands of local head teachers and faculties, began to create a mandatory national curriculum. Until a few years ago, only two activities—an "act of worship each day" and religious education—were required of each school in Great Britain, and even this was variously interpreted. Parliament left schools to their own devices.

Today, a National Curriculum with extensive syllabi in each subject area has been written, and it is planned to be fully implemented by 1997. Coincidently (or not) the argument for a national curriculum in Great Britain was spearheaded by the threat of German and Japanese economic and productive superiority, much as it has been in the United States.

The National Curriculum for the typical British pupil is presented in Table 38.2. In contrast to the Japanese (Table 38.1), the British curriculum is extraordinarily comprehensive. Everything, it would seem, will be taught to everybody all the time. However, the reality is less all-encompassing. While the Department of Education and Science has mandated content, well-organized teachers' associations and schools have retained control over method. This suggests considerable variation.

Further, it is a British tradition to integrate across subject lines and to adhere to an experience-based, spiral-model curriculum, particularly at the elementary level; and tradition dies very hard in Britain. The Core Subjects and the Foundation Subjects (see Table 38.2) are similar to the offerings of other nations.

The organization of the British curriculum is sufficiently unique to require amplification and definition. The school year is divided into three terms, and children begin their schooling experience during the term closest to their fifth birthday, entering a teaching group (not a grade or a class) called Reception. The emphasis at this point is on social and psychological adjustment rather than on any particular set of subjects or academic skills.

There are four Key Stages in the National Curriculum, determined by the age of the pupil and defined in terms of the age of the majority of children in a teaching group. Key Stages, consequently, do not begin or end at an individual child's age.

The concept of the Key Stage is important for several reasons. First, it encompasses more time than the typical "grade" in Japan, Germany, or the United States. Second, it is hoped that a student will have the same teacher for an entire Key Stage, until he or she encounters specialized teachers and subjects at Key Stage III. Third, the concept embodies the traditional British disdain for absolutely linking age to year-in-school, consequently avoiding the problem of social promotion altogether. Finally, and possibly of greatest importance, National Assessment Tests are administered to all pupils at the end of each Key Stage.

These tests are possibly the most controversial part of the National Curriculum. Attainment Targets are differentiated but highly specific behavioral objectives that are the substance of the national tests. They are "the knowledge, skills, and understandings which pupils are expected to have at the end of each Key Stage, and there are 10 levels, arrayed in increasing difficulty over the four Key Stages."

In the subject of history, for example, pupils at the end of Key Stage I are expected to "distinguish between a fact and a point of view." At the end of Key Stage IV, they are expected to "show an understanding of the issues involved in trying to make history as objective as possible." Standard Assessment Tasks, taken at the end of each Key Stage, measure the extent to which the pupil has attained the target.

The National Curriculum is not without its critics, and since a similar proposal is being seriously advanced in the United States it is instructive for policymakers in this country to examine some of the British criticisms. Although the content of the National Curriculum is acknowledged as "familiar ground to teachers," and although it "will allow teachers considerable freedom in the way in which they teach, examples and materials used, selection of content and context, use of textbooks, etc." (Department of Education and Science, 1989, p. 12), it has been viewed with suspicion by many educators. Particularly bothersome is the idea of tests for primary pupils and the Attainment Targets that all students are expected to exhibit at the end of each Key Stage and on which they will be tested.

Critics point to the negative by-products that standard curricula and testing have produced in France, Germany, and the United States. There is also the natural apprehension that accompanies the gathering of new (and easily sensationalized) data about pupils and schools. Once these figures exist, the critics reason (not without justification), they will be used by someone, somewhere, at some time to rank, score, and judge pupils, teachers, and schools.

Further, skeptics note the irony in a capitalist, free-market-loving government's enacting such a curriculum. Highly standardized curricula, developed at the national level, are the ideal of authoritarian socialist states. Finally, some fear that the Attainment Targets will, over time, become a system of marks. British educators abhor rigid marking systems, and no marks are given on the primary level (Key Stages I and II). Few secondary schools (Key Stages III and IV) give marks, and if they do, they are not accorded in a rigid system.

When students begin to take courses in preparation for the General Certificate of Secondary Education Examination (taken at age 16+), some ability and subject grouping arises, but it is pupil-interest and pupil-ability driven, not school imposed.

The Japanese examinations might be described as "do or die"; however, the GCSE Examination carries no such weight. It is an achievement examination that covers the scope of a pupil's education to that point, concentrating on the particular subjects he or she has studied in preparation for the examination. While it is important to do well, it is not the maker or breaker of lives that the Japanese examinations appear to be. Further, while most of the questions on the Japanese examination are multiple-choice, the GCSE leans toward essays.

About 60 percent of British children have an extensive pre-school experience in either nursery schools or voluntary playgroups. Thus, a sizable proportion of English children are "behind" many of their Japanese and German counterparts, who begin a pre-school experience at age three. The British also have less homework than do the Japanese. It is almost non-existent in Key Stages I and II, increasing to an hour a night in Key Stage III. Two to three hours of homework each night are typical for Key Stage IV students.

THE CURRICULUM OF GERMANY

It is no accident that American readers will find some familiar elements in the curriculum of Germany. Horace Mann and other educational pioneers went, not to the mother country but rather to Germany, in search of models for an ideal American school. In addition, the federal organization of Germany into 16 states with expressed powers for enacting educational policies is similar to the 50 state's having the primary control over schools within their boundaries.

In a very real sense, Germany has 16 separate school systems, just as the United States has 50; they may be similar, but they are not identical. Unlike Japan and Britain, there is no central government dictating specific educational policies. Finally, as in most of the United States, the German states issue only broad guidelines, allowing local school districts considerable latitude in hiring personnel, choosing textbooks, and determining content.

Germany has a "leaving examination"—the *Abitur;* however, it is only required for a portion of the students. It is an achievement examination generally taken at the end of the thirteenth year in school by those who want the qualification for entrance into a university, whether they actually attend one or not. This examination is not the only way to obtain university entrance, but it does exercise at least an indirect national control over what is emphasized in the German curriculum.

Although Germany invented the kindergarten, pupils are not required to attend it. Most do, however. Further, kindergarten in Germany is defined as an institution for three to six-year-old children. Kindergarten tends to be provided under "youth welfare legislation" by parishes, rather than by the state. Further, as the number of women has grown in the work force, pressure to

add more kindergartens has increased, and staff is often unavailable or space is somewhat limited.

Table 38.3 is a simplified representation of the subject requirements of typical German students. In many respects, it is similar to those of Japan and England, particularly in the early years. One notable difference is that German students have no organized science until grade five. However, *Sachunterricht* often includes practical or applied science problems such as "how does a light bulb work?" or "why do leaves turn brown in fall?" As with Japan and Britain, the curriculum in Germany is organized on the spiral model.

However, what happens to German students at grade 5 differentiates them from their Japanese and British counterparts, for at this point they enter one of three types of secondary schools— the *Realschule,* the *Hauptschule,* or the *Gymnasium.* About one-third of the students go to each of the three types of schools.

The *Gymnasium,* which once stressed a classical education and was the jewel in the crown of German education, is in a state of transition. It is no longer the elite upper-middle-class school of former days, but its new role has not been fully re-defined. The *Realschule,* conceived in the nineteenth century as a "practical" alternative to the *Gymnasium,* is popular because of its curriculum, which stresses math, science, and modern languages as well as the numerous occupational opportunities it affords. The *Hauptschule,* once "the school of the people," has declined in number of enrolled pupils and status during the past three decades, and is regarded by some as the German "second class citizen" school.

This tripartite secondary school system does track students, but this does not make it necessarily evil or elitist. Not all students are qualified or would wish to be professors, intellectuals, physicians, or lawyers (the *Gymnasium* route). Many desire careers in business, industry, and the civil service (the *Realschule* route), while others are attracted to skilled trades (the *Hauptschule* route). One's secondary school selection is not irrevocably tied to one's life income or status, and there are many opportunities—at least in theory—to transfer from one school to another, particularly in grades 5 and 6, when "orientation" is part of all secondary schools' curricula.

In practice, the transfer can only be conveniently accomplished at the end of the sixth and tenth grades. Recently, a comprehensive school, the *Gesamtschule,* has been formed in some states, uniting the curricula of the three traditional schools. However, its popularity has waxed and waned with the fortunes of the Social Democratic Party, and, in 1980, only 3 percent of German students attended one.

An examination of Table 38.3 reveals that students in all three of the secondary school types take essentially the same subjects. Only the emphasis is different.

Each school adapts the various subjects to its particular mission: "pure" dominates the *Gymnasium,* "practical" is the substance of the *Realschule,* and "applied" is the way of the *Hauptschule.* The outside observer (and some Germans) can easily see this organization as a "pecking order," but it is essentially three roads to one end.

The system of homogeneous grouping within the comprehensive high schools of the United States also creates strong barriers against social and economic advancement. If there is a pecking order in Germany's trio of secondary schools, it is one of intellect and interest, not of wealth and privilege, and university education is totally financed by the government in Germany.

Two notable differences among the three school types are the *Gymnasium's* emphasis on foreign language study and its paucity of electives, and the *Hauptschule's* offering of technicals, economics, and home economics as well as supportive lessons (*Verstarkungsunterricht*). Further, some—but not all—*Hauptschule* end their programs at grade 9 rather than 10.

Years 11, 12, and 13 in Table 38.3 are all "*Gymnasium*-level" courses in which specialized, discrete subjects are studied at an advanced level—almost junior college level in the United States. Students can choose, virtually creating their own program. However, the student's program almost always consists of two "intensive" subjects (each studied for five to six hours per week), and at least five "less intensive" subjects (each studied for two to three hours per week). The examination at the end of the program concentrates on the two intensive subjects ("the major") and two of the less intensive subjects ("the minors").

This pupil discretion has virtually abolished weekly class schedules as they are known in Japanese, British, or American secondary schools. Irrespective of this freedom, students must "mix and balance" their majors and minors so as not to become too specialized; the goal is the well-rounded individual. German students do not "specialize" at the secondary level nearly as much as is often reported. Nevertheless, one must consider the three secondary school types and their emphases as a sort of specialization.

Homework is part of the student regimen beginning in first grade; however, it is only a matter of 10 minutes or so. The amount of homework increases gradually; fourth graders complete about an hour a night. In grades 5 through 10, students have up to two hours each evening. In the upper three grades, homework averages two to two and one-half hours a night.

POLICY IMPLICATIONS FOR THE UNITED STATES

There is a striking similarity in the apparent goals and objectives of each of the three nation's curricula as well as those in the United States. They are similarly lofty, noble, humanitarian, socially conscious, nationalistic, and vague. Regardless of what nation is considered, the gap between abstract national goals and concrete practices is wide indeed, and the similarity does not end at the national goal level. Except for the earliest years, "teacher-centered" is the state of the classroom, and (particularly in Japan) this condition increases as one moves up through the grades.

Further, while the school goals and the national goals are oriented toward process, it is apparent that product is the outcome that counts. Each nation's schools are driven by what is required in the schools at the next highest level. Most significantly, each nation's curriculum ends with a product-oriented achievement test. This is obviously a powerful curriculum builder, particularly at the secondary level.

At this point, the United States differs from the three nations because the SAT and the ACT are (or claim to be) aptitude tests. Evidence as to whether these tests affect the American high school curriculum is mixed. However, there is a movement to establish a national achievement test in the United States. Should it become a reality, it will probably affect the American curriculum; indeed, its proponents advocate just that.

A subject-centered curriculum, common to the three nations—and the United States—suggests that educational policymakers in all these nations embrace two rather dubious philosophical/psychological assumptions that have haunted education since the turn of the century and do little to achieve their national educational goals— faculty psychology and formal discipline.

Evidence is weak, suspicious, or non-existent that the study of any particular school subject (as it is usually conceived and taught) promotes outcomes such as critical thinking, creativity, citizenship, or many other desirable goals of an educational system. Transfer of training from studying mathematics to thinking critically is not an ensured fact, nor is the relationship between studying literature and creativity well established.

We have known since 1902 that diagramming sentences does nothing to improve writing ability. Studying national history does not ensure that good citizens will be graduated.

Examining the subjects that are taught in all of these nation's schools and comparing them to the stated goals of the nations' curricula suggests that much student and teacher time is being expended in pursuit of essentially unattainable ends.

If students of any of the nations are learning to think, to create, to be good citizens, etc., it may be in spite of what subjects they study rather than because of them. However, public—indeed, even teacher—rejection of faculty psychology and formal discipline, irrespective of how discredited, has been slow or non-existent. Nonetheless, the fact that it remains widely accepted does not diminish the truths about it nor its implications for the curriculum of any nation.

Many of the implications for U.S. practice can be placed into two categories—the essentially impossible and the remotely possible. It would be essentially impossible to create the highly academic atmosphere of the *Gymnasium* in the typical U.S. high school; American high schools simply are not primarily academic institutions, and there is little to suggest that they will become such. Nor is it realistic to expect that the child-centered, supportive, cooperative British method will be accepted by American elementary schools; the British conception of the open classroom was modified beyond recognition in the elementary schools of the United States. Finally, the regimen of the Japanese student may be admired in the abstract, but few American parents would actually want their children subjected to such demands.

There are, however, some implications that are remotely possible. This study centered on subjects, and even within this narrow conception of curriculum, there was little variation, with three exceptions: foreign language, music, and art. The number of years that Japanese, German, and now British pupils study a foreign language greatly exceeds that of American students. The issue of how much and when foreign language should be studied has appeared and disappeared as an issue in American curriculum building since Sputnik (Conant, 1959, 1967; Unks, 1983), and the debate will doubtless continue.

Japan and Germany, nonetheless, present a clear lesson; If the United States—as a national policy—wishes to graduate secondary school students, most of whom are capable of communicating effectively with the populations of the rest of the world, then it must require all students to study a foreign language, and that study must extend for no less than five years.

Each of the nations presented in this study requires that all students—bright and slow, irrespective of their postsecondary school plans—study music and art for the entire tenure of their primary and secondary schooling experience. This is similar to the physical education requirement in most U.S. curricula. If the United States truly wants its adult population to be as comfortable in the concert hall as it apparently is at the sports arena, then the Japanese, British, and German models are worthy of emulation.

Policymakers must also address the matter of the time spent in the schooling experience. This issue can be approached from several directions. First, how many years of formal schooling should be required? Germany requires 10 years, Britain requires 11 years, and Japan requires 12; the United States requires 10 years.

Second, how many days should there be in a school year? Japan has 220, Germany has approximately 200 (depending upon each state), Great Britain has 190, and the United States has approximately 180 (depending upon each state).

Third, at what age should the state-supported "educational experience" begin? Japan and Germany begin at age three, with pre-school and kindergarten. Early education has been shown to be associated with better social adjustment, increased readiness to learn, and later success in school. Japan, Germany, and (to a lesser extent) Britain recognize this truth and begin pre-school at age three. By postponing universal, government-financed programs that stimulate development through age and ability-appropriate activities until age five, the United States is losing two uniquely valuable years. Further, there is compelling evidence, extending over three decades, that those children most in need of such publicly-supported services are the least likely to receive them.

Ancillary to school subjects, but important when considering student time spent in learning, is homework. At every grade level, typical students in the United States spend less time at homework than do their counterparts in Japan, Germany, or Great Britain. While educational policymakers may not wish to adopt the Japanese

standard, they should seriously consider a substantial increase in this tax-free educational time-on-task experience.

The description and implementation of the National Curriculum in Great Britain contains a number of implications for American educational policymakers. Given the federal system of governance in the United States, enacting such a sweeping restructuring will be difficult. Convincing 50 sovereign states of the worthiness of any single curriculum is a daunting task compared to persuading one parliament. However, American policymakers—as their British counterparts did—can stress the commonalities that cut across individual school curricula, and they can make generous allowances for going beyond the essential studies, for example covering local history or geography.

The British model is also an example of liberal arts inclusiveness; physical education, art, and music are part of the curriculum at every level (as they are in Japan and Germany). The *AMERICA 2000* plan does not mention the words art or music, even once (*AMERICA 2000: An Education Strategy,* 1991). Exclusion does not create consensus.

This same British accommodation should also be extended to the coverage across a national curriculum of gender and multicultural issues. Proponents of a national curriculum in the United States have had a tendency to side (or, at least, be perceived as siding) with sexists and monoculturalists. The British policymakers placed the single concept of a national curriculum at the top of their priorities. Such a disposition is instructive for their U.S. counterparts. One characteristic that is—above all—notoriously American is the principle of compromise. When it comes to making a national curriculum, the British experience suggests that educational policymakers must possess this ability in abundance.

CONCLUSION

For a number of years, there has been a gnawing fear among many Americans that something was deeply wrong with their schools. During those same years, some citizens have looked to other countries for an answer. This study suggests that there is some foreign answer, but it is not a sufficient answer.

Japanese, Britons, and Germans apparently value the study of foreign languages, art, and music. They also seem to value long school years, state-supported preschool activities, and homework. Do similar values reside in the American culture? Examining other nations' curricula is a valuable exercise, not for the answers it gives us but for the questions it raises. In the final analysis, this exercise in examination does not so much tell us what it is we are to do as it forces us to ask of ourselves, "What is it we value?"

REFERENCES

AMERICA 2000: An Education Strategy. Washington, D.C.: U.S. Department of Education, 1991.

Cheney, L. V. *American Memory: A Report on the Humanities in the Nation's Public Schools.* Washington, D.C.: National Endowment for the Humanities, 1987.

Conant, J. B. *The American High School Today.* New York: McGraw-Hill, 1959.

————. *The Comprehensive High School: A Second Report to Interested Citizens.* New York: McGraw-Hill, 1967.

Department of Education and Science. *National Curriculum from Policy to Practice.* London: Crown copyright, 1989.

Finn, C. E., Jr. *We Must Take Charge: Our Schools and Our Future.* New York. The Free Press, 1991.

Fishman, S., and Martin, L. *Estranged Twins: Education and Society in the Two Germanies.* New York: Praeger, 1986.

Lapointe, A. E.; Mead, N. A.; and Phillips, G. W. *A World of Difference: An International Assessment of Mathematics and Science.* Princeton, N.J.: Educational Testing Service, January 1989.

National Commission on Excellence in Education. *A Nation at Risk: The Imperative for Educational Reform.* Washington, D.C.: U.S. Government Printing Office, 1983.

Ravitch, D., and Finn, C. E., Jr. *What Do Our 17-Year-Olds Know? A Report of the First National Assessment of History and Literature.* New York: Harper and Row, 1987.

Unks, G. "The Perils of a Single Language Policy." *Educational Leadership,* October 1983.

DISCUSSION QUESTIONS

1. Should music and art be required or elective subjects?

2. What implications does studying the curriculum of other nations have for establishing a national curriculum?

3. What procedures would need to be established to create a ministry of education in the United States?

4. What political, social, economic, and philosophical issues influence curriculum implementation within a nation?

5. Should the United States adopt a national curriculum? Why? Why not?

PRO-CON CHART 6

Should parent voice be a major consideration in determining where students attend school?

PRO	CON
1. The public school system is a monolithic structure that fosters middle class conformity.	1. School choice will promote a dual class educational system, schools for the rich and schools for the poor.
2. Public schooling perpetuates the existing power structure, including the subordination effects of class, caste, and gender.	2. Parental choice will breed intolerance for diversity and will further religious, racial, and socioeconomic isolation.
3. The reduced quality of public education necessitates that parents be given options in order to locate better learning environments.	3. Transporting students out of neighborhoods is costly for school districts and is time consuming for students.
4. Increasing choices means expanding educational opportunities for low income and minority students.	4. Choice may not increase equity. In fact, it may lead to further segregation of low-income and minority students.
5. Competitive schools should stimulate statewide efforts to implement school reform.	5. Choice is not a solution for securing adequate funding, upgrading teachers' pedagogical skills, or reforming education.

CASE STUDY 6

School Board Debates Use of In-School Vending Machines

Teacher union president Sarah Turner was poised for her presentation to the Victor School Board. The central issue that was certain to become a battleground was the teachers desire to maintain vending machines in the schools. The board president, Richard Rotberg, began the meeting by requesting that the gallery remain silent during the speaker presentations. He assured them that time would be allocated to address audience concerns and questions. Rotberg turned the meeting over to the evening's first speaker, President Turner. She advocated for the retention of the machines. Turner argued that vending machines allowed students and staff to purchase snacks as they desired, both efficiently and cost effectively. She informed the board that the school cafeteria closed at 1:00 p.m. daily and added that attempts to remove the machines would be upsetting to students and staff alike who considered snacks essential to their daily routines.

Board member Eva Ellman voiced her opposition. A registered nutritionist, Ellman cited medical research that highlighted the detrimental impact of potato and corn chips, which are high in fat content and the adverse effects of foods high in sugar and caffeine. Ellman stated that if school officials took actions that resulted in keeping vending machines on campus, in effect, they were endorsing poor dietary habits and potentially contributing to the number of physically unfit Americans. Ellman made a motion that the vending machines be removed from all Victor schools within the next sixty days. The motion was seconded. At once the gallery exploded with a cacophony of objection from student and faculty representatives and joy from parents and other concerned citizens. Rotberg pounded his gavel in an attempt to regain order. After nearly ten minutes of disruption, audience reactions quelled and order was restored. Scratching his forehead, Rotberg contemplated how he would proceed from this point.

Consider the following questions:

1. If you were Rotberg, what action would you take to resolve this matter?

2. How could needs assessment procedures be used to identify potential solutions?

3. What are some factors that need to be addressed before vending machines are installed on school campuses?

4. What are some alternatives to vending machines snacks?

5. Should the sale of vending machine snacks to students and staff be a school-based concern? Why? Why not?

Name Index

Subject Index

This page constitutes a continuation of the copyright page.

Chapter 1 Gail McCutcheon, "Curriculum Theory and Practice for the 1990s," *NASSP Bulletin,* Vol. 72, September 1988, pp. 33–42. Originally entitled "Curriculum Theory and Practice: Considerations for the 1990s and Beyond." Reprinted with permission of the *NASSP Bulletin,* Copyright © 1988 by the *NASSP Bulletin.* All rights reserved.

Chapter 2 Allan C. Ornstein, "Philosophy as a Basis for Curriculum Decisions," *The High School Journal,* Vol. 74, December-January 1991, pp. 102–109. Reprinted from *The High School Journal,* Vol. 74, No 2, December/January 1991. Copyright © 1991 by the University of North Carolina Press. Used by permission of *The High School Journal* and the University of North Carolina Press.

Chapter 3 Ronald S. Brandt and Ralph W. Tyler, "Goals and Objectives," in *Fundamental Curriculum Decisions,* ASCD Yearbook, 1983, pp. 40–51. Reprinted with permission of the Association for Supervision and Curriculum Development. Copyright © 1983 by the Association for Supervision and Curriculum Development. All rights reserved.

Chapter 4 M. Frances Klein, "Alternative Curriculum Conceptions and Designs," *Theory into Practice,* Vol. 21, Winter 1986, pp. 31–35. Reprinted with permission from *Theory into Practice,* Winter 1986, *21*(1) (theme issue on "Beyond the Measured Curriculum"). Copyright 1986 College of Education, The Ohio State University.

Chapter 5 Michael W. Apple, "Is There a Curriculum Voice to Reclaim?" *Phi Delta Kappan,* Vol. 71, March 1990, pp. 526–530. Reprinted with permission of *Phi Delta Kappan,* Copyright © 1990 by the *Phi Delta Kappan.* All rights reserved.

Chapter 6 Henry A. Giroux, "Teachers, Public Life and Curriculum Reform," *Peabody Journal of Education.* This chapter is adapted from an article which first appeared in the *Peabody Journal of Education,* Vol. 69, No. 3, Spring 1994. Reprinted with permission of the *Peabody Journal of Education.* Copyright © 1994 by the Peabody Journal of Education. All rights reserved.

Chapter 7 Herbert J. Walberg, "Productive Teachers: Assessing the Knowledge Base," *Phi Delta Kappan,* Vol. 71, February 1990, pp. 470–478. Reprinted with permission of *Phi Delta Kappan,* Copyright © 1990 by the *Phi Delta Kappan.* All rights reserved.

Chapter 8 Jere Brophy, "Probing the Subtleties of Subject-Matter Teaching," *Educational Leadership,* Vol. 49, April 1992, pp. 4–8. Reprinted with permission of the Association for Supervision and Curriculum Development. Copyright © 1992 by the Association for Supervision and Curriculum Development. All rights reserved.

Chapter 9 Allan C. Ornstein, "Research for Improving Teaching," This article is based on three of the author's works: "Teacher Effectiveness Research: Theoretical Considerations," in Hersholt C. Waxman and Herbert J. Walberg, eds., *Effective Teaching: Current Research,* pp. 63–80. Copyright 1991 by McCutchan Publishing Corporation, Berkeley, CA 94702. Permission granted by the publisher. "How to Recognize Good Teaching," *American School Board Journal,* 180 (1993), pp. 24–29. "The Human Dimension of Teaching," *Educational Forum,* in print (1995).

Chapter 10 Elliot Eisner, "The Art and Craft of Teaching," *Educational Leadership,* Vol.40, January 1983, pp. 4–13. Reprinted with permission of the Association for Supervision and Curriculum Development. Copyright © 1983 by the Association for Supervision and Curriculum Development. All rights reserved.

Chapter 11 Lee S. Shulman, "Knowledge and Teaching: Foundations of the New Reform," *Harvard Educational Review,* 57:1, pp. 1–22. Copyright © 1987 by the President and Fellows of Harvard College. All rights reserved.

Chapter 12 Katherine S. Cushing, Donna S. Sabers, and David C. Berliner, "Investigations of Expertise in Teaching," *educational HORIZONS,* Vol. 70, No. 3, Spring 1992, pp. 108–114. Reprinted with permission from *educational HORIZONS,* quarterly journal of Pi Lambda Theta, International Honor and Professional Association in Education, 4101 E. Third Street, Bloomington, IN 47407-6626.

Chapter 13 Carole A. Ames, "Motivation: What Teachers Need to Know." Reprinted by permission of the publisher from Tozer, Steven, Anderson, Thomas H., and Armbruster, Bonnie B., eds., Foundational Studies in Teacher Education: A Re-examination (New York: Teachers College Press, © 1990 by Teachers College, Columbia University. All rights reserved.), pp. 111–123.

Chapter 14 Matthew Lipman, "Critical Thinking—What Can It Be?" *Educational Leadership,* Vol. 46, September 1988, pp. 38–43. Reprinted with permission of the Association for Supervision and

Curriculum Development. Copyright © 1988 by the Association for Supervision and Curriculum Development. All rights reserved.

Chapter 15   Robert J. Sternberg and Todd I. Lubart, "Creating Creative Minds," *Phi Delta Kappan,* Vol. 21, April 1991, pp. 608–614. Reprinted with permission of *Phi Delta Kappan.* Copyright © 1991 by the *Phi Delta Kappan.* All rights reserved.

Chapter 16   Lawrence Kohlberg, "The Cognitive-Developmental Approach to Moral Education," *Phi Delta Kappan,* Vol. 56, June 1975, pp. 670–677. Reprinted with permission of *Phi Delta Kappan,* Copyright © 1975 by the *Phi Delta Kappan.* All rights reserved. Table 16.1 Definition of Moral Stages in "The Claim to Moral Adequacy of a Highest Stage of Moral Judgment," Reprinted with permission of the *Journal of Philosophy,* Vol. 70, October 1973, pp. 631–632. Copyright © by the *Journal of Philosophy.* All rights reserved.

Chapter 17   Robert E. Slavin, "Synthesis of Research on Cooperative Learning," *Educational Leadership,* Vol. 48, February 1991, pp. 71–82. Reprinted with permission of the Association for Supervision and Curriculum Development. Copyright © 1991 by the Association for Supervision and Curriculum Development. All rights reserved.

Chapter 18   Grant Wiggins, "Standards, Not Standardization: Evoking Quality Student Work," *Educational Leadership,* Vol. 48, February 1991, pp. 18–25. Reprinted with permission of the Association for Supervision and Curriculum Development. Copyright © 1991 by the Association for Supervision and Curriculum Development. All rights reserved.

Chapter 19   Allan C. Ornstein, "Academic Time Considerations for Curriculum Leaders," *NASSP Bulletin,* Vol. 73, September 1989, pp. 103–110. Reprinted with permission of the *NASSP Bulletin,* Copyright © 1989 by the *NASSP Bulletin.* All rights reserved.

Chapter 20   Benjamin S. Bloom, "The Search for Methods of Instruction," *Educational Researcher,* Vol. 13, June/July 1984, pp. 4–16. Originally entitled, "The 2 Sigma Problem: The Search for Methods of Group Instruction as Effective as One-to-One Tutoring." Reprinted with permission of Educational Researcher. Copyright © 1984 by the Educational Researcher. All rights reserved.

Chapter 21   Jeannie Oakes and Martin Lipton, "Detracking Schools: Early Lessons from the Field," *Phi Delta Kappan,* Vol. 74, February 1992, pp. 448–454. Reprinted with permission of *Phi Delta Kappan,* Copyright © 1992 by the *Phi Delta Kappan.* All rights reserved.

Chapter 22   Lorin W. Anderson and Leonard O. Pellicer, "Synthesis of Research on Compensatory and Remedial Education," *Educational Leadership,* Vol. 48, September 1990, pp. 10–16. Reprinted with permission of the Association for Supervision and Curriculum Development. Copyright © 1990 by the Association for Supervision and Curriculum Development. All rights reserved.

Chapter 23   Eliot Wigginton, "Home Culture—An Essential Curriculum," *Educational Leadership,* Vol. 49, December 1991–January 1992, pp. 60–64. Originally entitled, "Culture Begins at Home." Reprinted with permission of the Association for Supervision and Curriculum Development. Copyright © 1991 by the Association for Supervision and Curriculum Development. All rights reserved.

Chapter 24   Simon Hooper and Lloyd P. Rieber, "Teaching, Instruction, and Technology." Originally entitled "Teaching with Technology," in A. C. Ornstein, ed., *Teaching: Theory into Practice.* Boston: Allyn and Bacon, 1995.

Chapter 25   Allan C. Ornstein, "Curriculum Trends Revisited" *Peabody Journal of Education,* in press (1994). Reprinted with permission of the *Peabody Journal of Education.* Copyright © 1994 by the *Peabody Journal of Education.* All rights reserved.

Chapter 26   Allan C. Ornstein, "Curriculum, Instruction, and Supervision—Their Relationship and the Role of the Principal," *NASSP Bulletin,* Vol. 70, April 1986, pp. 74–81. Reprinted with permission of the *NASSP Bulletin.* Copyright © 1986 by the *NASSP Bulletin.* All rights reserved.

Chapter 27   Allan A. Glatthorn, "A New Concept of Supervision," *educational HORIZONS,* Vol. 65, Winter 1987, pp. 78–81. Reprinted with permission from *educational HORIZONS,* quarterly journal of Pi Lambda Theta, International Honor and Professional Association in Education, 4101 E. Third Street, Bloomington, IN 47407-6626.

Chapter 28   Dennis Sparks and Susan Loucks-Horsley, "Five Models of Staff Development for Teachers," *Journal of Staff Development,* Vol. 10, Fall 1989, pp. 40–57. Reprinted with permission of the *Journal of Staff Development.* Copyright © 1989 by the *Journal of Staff Development.* All rights reserved.

Chapter 29   Mary D. Phillips and Carl D. Glickman, "Peer Coaching: Developmental Approach to Enhancing Teacher Thinking," *Journal of Staff Development,* Vol. 12, Spring 1991, pp. 20–25.

Reprinted with permission of the *Journal of Staff Development*. Copyright © 1991 by the *Journal of Staff Development*. All rights reserved.

Chapter 30   Matthew B. Miles and Karen Seashore Louis, "Mustering the Will and Skill for Change," *Educational Leadership,* Vol. 47, May 1990, pp. 57–61. Reprinted with permission of Matthew B. Miles and Karen Seashore Louis. Copyright © 1990 by Matthew B. Miles and Karen Seashore Louis. All rights reserved.

Chapter 31   Thomas J. Sergiovanni, "Leadership and Excellence in Schooling," *Educational Leadership,* Vol. 41, February 1984, pp. 4–13. Reprinted with permission of the Association for Supervision and Curriculum Development. Copyright © 1984 by the Association for Supervision and Curriculum Development. All rights reserved.

Chapter 32   John U. Ogbu, "Understanding Cultural Diversity and Learning," *Educational Researcher,* Vol. 21, November 1992, pp. 5–14, 24. Reprinted with permission of *Educational Researcher.* Copyright © 1992 by the *Educational Researcher.* All rights reserved.

Chapter 33   Nel Noddings, "The Gender Issue," *Educational Leadership,* Vol. 49, December 1991–January 1992, pp. 65–70. Reprinted with permission of the Association for Supervision and Curriculum Development. Copyright © 1992 by the Association for Supervision and Curriculum Development. All rights reserved.

Chapter 34   Diane Ravitch, "National Standards and Curriculum Reform," *NASSP Bulletin,* Vol. 76, December 1992, pp. 24–29. Originally entitled "National Standards and Curriculum Reform: A. View from the Department of Education." Reprinted with the permission of the *NASSP Bulletin.* Copyright © 1992 by the *NASSP Bulletin.* All rights reserved.

Chapter 35   Harold Hodgkinson, "Reform versus Reality," *Phi Delta Kappan,* Vol. 73, September 1991, pp. 9–16. Reprinted with permission of *Phi Delta Kappan.* Copyright © 1991 by the *Phi Delta Kappan.* All rights reserved.

Chapter 36   Elliot W. Eisner, "Educational Reform and the Ecology of Schooling," *Teachers College Record,* Vol. 93, Summer 1992, pp. 610–627. Reprinted with permission of Teachers College Press. Copyright © 1992 by the Teachers College Press. All rights reserved.

Chapter 37   Michael G. Fullan and Matthew B. Miles, "Getting Reform Right," *Phi Delta Kappan,* Vol. 74, June 1992, pp. 745–752. Reprinted with permission of *Phi Delta Kappan.* Copyright © 1992 by the *Phi Delta Kappan.* All rights reserved.

Chapter 38   Gerald Unks, "Three Nation's Curricula: Policy Implications for U.S Curriculum Reform," *NASSP Bulletin,* Vol. 76 pp. 30–46. Originally entitled, "Three Nation's Curricula: What Can We Learn from Them?" Reprinted with permission of the *NASSP Bulletin.* Copyright © 1992 by the *NASSP Bulletin.* All rights reserved.